W9-DET-267

Wiley's Teach Yourself® C++

7th Edition

Al Stevens

WILEY

Wiley Publishing, Inc.

Wiley's Teach Yourself® C++, 7th Edition

Published by
Wiley Publishing, Inc.
909 Third Avenue
New York, NY 10022
www.wiley.com

Copyright © 2003 by Wiley Publishing, Inc., Indianapolis, Indiana

Library of Congress Control Number: 2003100999

ISBN: 0-7645-2644-8

Manufactured in the United States of America

10 9 8 7 6 5 4 3 2 1

7B/SQ/QT/QT/IN

Published by Wiley Publishing, Inc., Indianapolis, Indiana
Published simultaneously in Canada

No part of this publication may be reproduced, stored in a retrieval system or transmitted in any form or by any means, electronic, mechanical, photocopying, recording, scanning or otherwise, except as permitted under Sections 107 or 108 of the 1976 United States Copyright Act, without either the prior written permission of the Publisher, or authorization through payment of the appropriate per-copy fee to the Copyright Clearance Center, 222 Rosewood Drive, Danvers, MA 01923, (978) 750-8400, fax (978) 646-8700. Requests to the Publisher for permission should be addressed to the Legal Department, Wiley Publishing, Inc., 10475 Crosspoint Blvd., Indianapolis, IN 46256, (317) 572-3447, fax (317) 572-4447, E-Mail: permcoordinator@wiley.com.

LIMIT OF LIABILITY/DISCLAIMER OF WARRANTY: WHILE THE PUBLISHER AND AUTHOR HAVE USED THEIR BEST EFFORTS IN PREPARING THIS BOOK, THEY MAKE NO REPRESENTATIONS OR WARRANTIES WITH RESPECT TO THE ACCURACY OR COMPLETENESS OF THE CONTENTS OF THIS BOOK AND SPECIFICALLY DISCLAIM ANY IMPLIED WARRANTIES OF MERCHANTABILITY OR FITNESS FOR A PARTICULAR PURPOSE. NO WARRANTY MAY BE CREATED OR EXTENDED BY SALES REPRESENTATIVES OR WRITTEN SALES MATERIALS. THE ADVICE AND STRATEGIES CONTAINED HEREIN MAY NOT BE SUITABLE FOR YOUR SITUATION. YOU SHOULD CONSULT WITH A PROFESSIONAL WHERE APPROPRIATE. NEITHER THE PUBLISHER NOR AUTHOR SHALL BE LIABLE FOR ANY LOSS OF PROFIT OR ANY OTHER COMMERCIAL DAMAGES, INCLUDING BUT NOT LIMITED TO SPECIAL, INCIDENTAL, CONSEQUENTIAL, OR OTHER DAMAGES.

For general information on our other products and services or to obtain technical support, please contact our Customer Care Department within the U.S. at 800-762-2974, outside the U.S. at 317-572-3993 or fax 317-572-4002.

Wiley also publishes its books in a variety of electronic formats. Some content that appears in print may not be available in electronic books.

Trademarks: Wiley, the Wiley Publishing logo, Teach Yourself, and related trade dress are trademarks or registered trademarks of Wiley Publishing, Inc., in the United States and other countries, and may not be used without written permission. All other trademarks are the property of their respective owners. Wiley Publishing, Inc., is not associated with any product or vendor mentioned in this book.

WILEY is a trademark of Wiley Publishing, Inc.

Credits

Acquisitions Editor
Debra Williams Cauley

Project Editor
Kenyon Brown

Technical Editor
Al Williams

Copy Editor
Anne L. Owen

Editorial Manager
Mary Beth Wakefield

**Vice President and
Executive Group Publisher**
Richard Swadley

**Vice President and
Executive Publisher**
Bob Ipsen

Executive Editorial Director
Mary Bednarek

Project Coordinator
Dale White

Graphics and Production Specialists
Amanda Carter
Jennifer Click
Sean Decker

Quality Control Technician
Susan Moritz

Senior Permissions Editor
Carmen Krikorian

Proofreading
TECHBOOKS Production Services

Indexing
Al Stevens

About the Author

Al Stevens has written the "C Programming Column" in Dr. Dobb's Journal, the #1 programmer's magazine, since 1988. He is the author of more than a dozen best-selling titles for MIS:Press and M&T Books. A professional programmer since 1958, and an independent programming consultant and writer since 1978, Al maintains a loyal following of readers who appreciate his insight and clear writing style.

This book is dedicated to Spencer Alfred Long, a most perfect grandson who hadn't yet come along when I last wrote a book three years ago; consequently, he never had a book dedicated to him. Now he has. Maybe years from now when he reads this, he'll know why Granddad wasn't always there to play with him in the summer of '02. I didn't much like it either.

Preface

"Changes in attitude, changes in latitude,
Nothing remains quite the same."

Jimmy Buffet

Teach Yourself C++ is a tutorial approach to learning C++ by using the book in front of you while you run example programs on a PC.

This is the seventh edition of Teach Yourself C++. I published the first edition for MIS:Press in 1990. A lot has changed since then. Programming is not quite the same, the C++ language has grown substantially, the computer book business is different, and I've had my share of changes, too. We'll discuss all these changes soon, but first let's talk about who you are and how you might use this book.

Who Are You?

You are a programmer who wants to program in C++. I have to assume that you understand computer programming at some level. I expect you to know that a programming language is coded as text that a programmer writes with a text editor and that a compiler or interpreter processes into native machine program instructions. You should understand that the computer's operating system stores a program's machine code, usually on disk, and reads it into internal memory to execute it, thus running the program. You should know that the computer uses its internal memory to temporarily hold not only the program but the data, too, which are also permanently stored elsewhere, usually on a disk. It should be clear to you that the operating system, the compiler, the programmer's editor, and many other things, are themselves programs that someone else wrote to support computer users and programmers.

If you don't already understand these things, you should undertake to learn them before proceeding with studies of C++ or any other computer programming language.

Not a C Programmer?

That's okay, you don't need to already know C. This book stands alone as a tutorial in the C++ language, end to end. Many books on C++ assume that the reader already knows C. The first four editions of *Teach Yourself C++* made that assumption. By now, however, most C programmers have learned C++. Therefore, the principal audience for this book is the programmer who knows neither language and wants to learn C++, and starting with the fifth edition, I began teaching the complete language.

According to conventional wisdom, you should learn C first and then learn C++. That advice turns out not so wise after all. We have learned to avoid teaching the "C style" of programming so students won't learn unnecessary and unhealthy biases that then must be unlearned.

If you do not already know C, you should wade right into C++ according to more current conventional wisdom. I decided, therefore, to turn this work into a full treatment of C++ aimed at those who understand programming—but not necessarily any particular programming language.

Already a C Programmer?

It may seem to C programmers that much of Part I of this book is mostly about the C language component built into C++. A C programmer may be tempted to skim these chapters, but I recommend that you read them carefully. Chapter 2, for example, provides an introduction to the C++ console input/output iostream objects, which C++ programmers use instead of the getchar, putchar, gets, puts, printf, and scanf family of Standard C functions. Also watch for subtle differences in other parts of the C++ language scattered throughout these chapters. For example, the behavior of the C++ goto statement described in Chapter 4 is different from that of the C goto; a void pointer in C++ cannot be assigned to a pointer to a type without a typecast; the main function must be declared as returning int and cannot be called recursively in a C++ program; you must initialize a const object; variables cannot be declared implicitly as int; an enumerator is a type and not an int; and so on. I do not always point out these differences when they arise. Instead, I tend to treat C++ as a completely new subject. So do not depend on your C knowledge so much that you neglect the lessons that Part I teaches. Use Part I instead to review what you know, to discover small changes in what you are familiar with, and to reinforce your understanding of the similarities and differences between C and C++.

What Is This Book?

This book does not teach programming for a specific platform. It is not about Windows programming, or Unix programming, or Linux programming, or Macintosh programming, or programming for any other specific platform. This book is about Standard C++ programming. Standard C++ is a platform-independent language specification, and Standard C++ compilers exist for all the platforms I just mentioned and many others. The accompanying CD-ROM includes a compiler suite that runs on the Win32 platform. That is a matter of convenience for two reasons. First, it's the platform for which I develop software; second, it's the platform that most of you have. If you have a different development platform, you can move the example programs from the CD-ROM to that platform, and, if a Standard C++ compiler is available on that platform, you can run and test the example programs.

Changes in Yours Truly

Now I get to talk about me and how I've changed since writing the first edition of *Teach Yourself C++*. Why should you care? Many of you won't, but others have followed my work through the years and might be interested. If not, you have my permission to skip this discussion.

Besides growing older, I've learned a lot since 1990 about C++ from programming and writing projects. In addition to working on many C++ projects over the years, I've had to write one small publishable program almost every month for the C Programming Column in Dr. Dobb's Journal.

Publishing code is like programming without any pants on. You can't hide anything. You have to pay attention not only to how well the code solves the problem but also to how easily someone else can understand your code. You must learn and apply the coding conventions of the programming community; you must understand what caused those conventions to be defined and accepted; you must learn which practices are safe and which ones are inherently perilous. As conventions evolve, you change with the times. I try at all times to make those changes and make them always for the better.

I wasn't a total C++ convert when I wrote the first edition of this book a dozen years ago. I was still writing mostly C programs. That has changed. Programmers who are successfully writing working programs in other languages often see no compelling reason to switch. My compelling reasons were that C++ had a young and growing constituency and that, as a writer, I had a responsibility to supply what my readership wanted and needed. Only after fully taking the plunge did I discover the allure of C++ and the object-oriented programming paradigm.

During those years I observed as other similar languages gained acceptance. Java was the first to take hold after C++. Java targets a different development environment — web-based applications — and I have no current need to write programs for that target. C# is the latest to enter the field. I've read about both languages and find nothing in them to change my allegiance. So far, there's not much I want to do in a computer program that C++ cannot do, and do well.

These comments reflect a personal choice. Do not interpret them to be critical of Java and C#. Both languages have advantages and constituents. My comments also reflect a practical choice. C++ programmers are still very much in demand, much more so than programmers of other languages. I can't promise you that the demand will last. A dozen years ago I was saying the same thing about C.

Changes in Computer Books

The MIS:Press publishing imprint has changed, too. In 1990 MIS:Press was a small, upstart publisher in Portland, Oregon, run by a pioneer named Bob Williams, who was known to go out and sell computer books door to door. Bob virtually created the computer book business. He wrote and self-published a user's manual for a popular spreadsheet program, a manual that enabled people to make unauthorized copies of the software and run it without needing the official user's guide that you could get only by purchasing the program. The software company didn't like Bob's book very much. It sued him, and Bob won the lawsuit. As a result of Bob's trail-blazing efforts and the legal precedent that his case established, books about commercial PC applications began to spring up all over the place. After building a small publishing company named MIS:Press with a loyal stable of authors and a respectable list of titles, Bob sold the imprint to Henry Holt, who sold it to IDG Books, who sold it to Wiley, who owns it now. Throughout all those owners, the business of writing books for MIS:Press morphed to comply with the practices and preferences of each, sometimes for the better, sometimes not. During that time, demand for computer programming books changed, too, sometimes for the better, sometimes not.

Changes in C++

The C and C++ programming languages are, between them, older than many of the programmers who use them. C was developed in the early 1970s, and C++ saw first light in 1980. In the time since, C and C++ have evolved from a small tool built for personal use by a research laboratory programmer into the worldwide object-oriented language of choice for several generations of programmers. There are C++ compilers for virtually every computer and operating system, and C++ now enjoys the distinction of being the language with which most contemporary mini- and microcomputer applications are written.

In 1990 C++ was a small programming language that added object-oriented extensions to the venerable C language. The first edition of Teach Yourself C++ provided almost comprehensive coverage of the language in fewer than 300 pages. Ten years later the C++ language had grown substantially as the result of a process of international standardization. This seventh edition of Teach Yourself C++ is more than twice the size of the first.

C++ became an international standard programming language in 1998 with the approval and publication of a ponderous document titled impressively, "International Standard ISO/IEC 14882:1998(E), Programming Languages – C++." This document was the culmination of a nine-year effort by a team of volunteers comprising what was called "the X3J16 committee," or "X3J16," or, simply, "the committee," among other things. The volunteers consisted of C++ programmers representing industry, government, compiler vendors, virtually every kind of enterprise that develops programs and materials related to C++.

Traditionally, programming language standards committees try to define, in precise and unambiguous terms, the language as people are using it. They call it "codifying prior art," or something impressive like that. They restrict themselves to those language features that time and practice have proven to be useful, making changes only when compiler implementations collide with respect to some language characteristic. X3J16 did not restrict themselves in that manner. The committee members seized upon the opportunity to fix problems in the existing language and to add features.

Boy, did they ever add features! The phrase "programming language standardization" came to mean "programming language invention." Many new features that the committee added were untested and unproven, and the unconventional approach taken by X3J16 was nothing if not controversial. Standard C++ is so much bigger and so different from legacy C++, that now, fully four years after publication of the standard definition, Standard C++ still has features that have yet to be fully implemented in compilers.

Furthermore, Standard C++, when compared to its slimmer, trimmer ancestor, requires more hardware to use, takes longer to compile a program, and produces much larger executable binary files. It brings to mind that old cliché about a camel being a horse designed by a committee. Of course, computers are bigger and faster, nullifying some of the negative performance factors, and programmers have a much fuller selection of code idioms from which to select. And camels have a useful purpose, too.

Is this a good or a bad thing? I think it's mostly good. Of the many features that the committee invented that have been implemented and used, most stood the test of usage; people use features the way the committee intended them to be used, and the features seem to serve their intended purposes well. On the other hand, if you don't want, need, or care for a language feature, you don't have to use it, and, if the compiler is well designed, it usually doesn't cost you anything.

Changes in Programming

Finally, mainstream programming has changed substantially since 1990. At the time, C was the PC programming language of choice, and most mainstream applications were written for text-mode operating environments. C++ was available but not widely used. Another event in 1990 was instrumental in changing that circumstance. Microsoft introduced Windows 3, the graphical user interface operating environment destined to change how people used personal computers. PC users wanted applications that ran in the new, sexy graphical environment, and programmers set about to learn how to write programs for them.

Windows programming in C was and is a daunting task that requires coding a peculiar programming model, based on events and messages, and learning a substantial application programming interface (API) containing hundreds of message codes, functions and structures. Someone estimated that it takes a smart programmer at least a year of intensive study and experience to become a competent Windows C programmer.

A huge market wanted Windows programs, and programmers wanted to write Windows programs. But Windows programming was difficult. Compiler vendors, notably Microsoft and Borland, approached this problem by wrapping the Windows API in what they called "application frameworks." The Windows message-based, event-driven programming model was a natural for C++ classes, something you will learn about in this book. Framework libraries such as the Microsoft Foundation Classes (MFC) and Borland's Object Windows Library (OWL) were immediate hits among programmers. All they had to do was learn the C++ language. Most of them already knew C, so the learning slope was thought to be not too slippery and not too steep. Presumably, a programmer could become a productive Windows programmer faster by using C++. Maybe so, maybe not, but C++ gradually became the language of choice, primarily because of this convergence of coincidences.

Programmers of other platforms will disagree with — or, at least, resent — my conclusion that Windows programming is responsible for the success of C++ among mainstream programmers. Let them. The sheer number of programs being written for the Windows platform as compared to others and the sheer number of Windows users as compared to others make my case far better than I can.

About *Wiley's Teach Yourself C++*

Beginning in Chapter 1, this book leads you through the C++ learning process with a series of example programs. Each program includes C++ source code — in the book and on the CD-ROM — that you can compile and execute. To get the maximum benefit of these lessons, you should load, compile, and run the example programs as you go along.

The example programs guide you through the subjects in a sequence that introduces simpler concepts first, using them in successive programs as more complex subjects are developed. Each example program builds upon preceding ones. Therefore, you should follow the programs in the order in which they appear.

The example programs are small. They are not — nor are they intended to be — full-blown, useful programs that you take into the workplace. Each example demonstrates a particular feature of C++. The examples are complete programs in that they compile and link independently.

I try to use examples that programmers can relate to, that you can imagine coding yourself. Too often programming books use meaningless esoteric examples to explain language features, examples that no one would ever write programs for. They use class library examples that represent the genus of insects, the hierarchy of furniture, and an inventory of a person's wardrobe. You will find examples in some books that implement computer screen windows, strings and object containers, things that the language and operating system already provide. I have seen totally abstract examples with meaningless names like X and foo that do nothing other than demonstrate some language feature. Many books have no complete programs at all — only code fragments that you cannot compile, test and observe.

The success of such programming books notwithstanding, I do not care to use those teaching techniques when I can avoid it. My goal is to provide small, concise code examples that use real things that programmers will understand — dates, paychecks, and graphical shapes, for example — so you are not bogged down with trying to understand the problem domain when you ought to be learning about the language itself. You might never actually write code for a payroll system, but if you've ever had a paid job, you at least understand the problem. My good intentions notwithstanding, even this book has the occasional program with esoteric examples. Sometimes the lesson being taught needs a terse example, lest the student be sidetracked by what the example does and misses the point of how the example teaches the language.

Compiler Included

The CD-ROM in the back cover sleeve includes Quincy 2002, a Windows-hosted (Windows 95 or greater) C++ program development system that you can use to compile and run the example programs. Quincy leads you through the programs by having you select from a list that corresponds with the listing numbers and titles that appear in the book. Quincy is what is called an "integrated development environment" (IDE), which integrates a programmer's editor, compiler, and debugger in one package, in this case with a Windows interface. Appendix C is Quincy's quick start User's Guide, and it explains where to get upgrades to Quincy and the compiler system.

The Learning Loop

A complex subject such as a programming language often sends you into a learning loop. You cannot learn a lesson without knowing about a prerequisite lesson, which has some other prerequisite lesson, which in turn has the new lesson as a prerequisite. A case in point is the C++ `std::iostream` classes, which, among other things, define objects that read from and write to the standard input/output devices — typically the system console. To understand them thoroughly, you must understand C++ namespaces, classes, objects, and overloaded operators, all of which are advanced C++ topics. Yet, to progress to those advanced topics, you must run exercises that use the keyboard and screen console devices. The `std::iostream` classes support these devices. You have to use the system-defined `std::cin` and `std::cout` objects with an unquestioning faith that what they do and how they do it will eventually make sense.

Trust the book and be patient — if I've done my job properly, everything eventually becomes clear. There are forward references to chapters when topics are mentioned that you haven't yet learned. If a discussion is unclear, make a note to yourself and return to the discussion after you read more about the topic in the referenced chapter.

The Organization of This Book

Part I, Chapters 1 through 13, describes the basic elements of the C++ language, primarily those things that are most like the C language but with a few new things to learn.

Chapter 1 introduces you to programming in C++. It explains what you should know already and what you need in order to use the programs on the CD-ROM. This chapter includes a brief history of C++ and an overview of the C++ programming language with an introduction to the `main()` function, the entry point of every C++ program.

Chapter 2 is where you begin writing programs. I teach you more about the main() function, how to put comments in your code, how to include the header files of the standard libraries, and how to perform simple console output to view the results of your programs. You learn about C++ expressions and assignment statements. You also discover how to read data from the keyboard and display onscreen information. Chapter 2 also teaches you about C++ data types, including characters, integers, and floating-point numbers.

Chapter 3 focuses on functions. I show you how C++ programs declare, define, and call functions, while passing parameter arguments and getting return values. You learn how C++ functions are arranged into nested blocks of code. You also learn how to link C++ program modules with modules written in other languages, such as C.

Chapter 4 introduces program flow control. You learn the if...else, do, while, for, goto, switch, break, continue, and return statements.

Chapter 5 is about the organization of variables in a program. You learn about the scope of variables and the qualifiers that turn variables into constants and control where they are stored in the computer.

Chapter 6 is about structures, classes and unions, which comprise the C++ idiom that allows you to arrange data into data record formats in memory. Chapter 6 also introduces the class mechanism by expanding on what you can do with the struct. You learn about the data abstraction properties of intrinsic and user-defined types, data members and member functions, and access specifiers. This chapter is the first major departure from what a C programmer already understands.

Chapter 7 teaches several more things about C++ data. You learn about enumerated constants, how to define arrays, the program heap and stack, and C-style typecasts. Chapter 7 also introduces C++ typecasts, only touching upon the basics. Later, in Chapter 37, you learn this more advanced typecasting mechanism that supports casting between C++ classes and other things.

Chapter 8 covers the use of pointer variables and memory addresses in your programs.

Chapter 9 is about reference variables, a C++ feature that resembles but is not quite the same as pointers.

Chapter 10 teaches recursion, that feature in most contemporary programming languages that lets functions call themselves. You will learn how it works, why it is a useful feature, when you would use it, and why and how to avoid it in certain programming situations.

Chapter 11 focuses on the C++ preprocessor, which enables you to define macros and write compile-time conditional expressions that control how a program compiles.

Chapter 12 explains function templates, which enable you to create generalized functions that can work with different types of data. You learn about template parameters and arguments, and about more advanced template subjects, such as template overloading.

Chapter 13 teaches the organization of a program, its command line arguments, linking multiple compiled modules into an executable module, and how to have C and C++ source code files in one program.

Part II, Chapters 14 through 25, is about the C++ class mechanism, the language feature with which most of the Standard C++ Library is implemented, and the way that you extend C++ for you own purposes.

Chapter 14 discusses classes, explaining how to design a class with data members and member functions.

Chapter 15 explains class constructors and destructors, the special member functions that execute when a program that uses a class instantiates an object of that class and that execute when your program is finished with an object of the class.

Chapter 16 is about C++ type conversion wherein objects of one class can be automatically converted to objects of other classes through the use of conversion functions in your program.

Chapter 17 is about arrays of class objects and the special considerations you must make in class design to accommodate their requirements.

Chapter 18 provides details about class members, how they work and how they react to the way they are declared.

Chapter 19 is about a C++ feature called the "friend" that permits functions to access otherwise hidden members of a class.

Chapter 20 explains how classes use heap memory and how your program can modify that behavior.

Chapter 21 deals with overloaded operators — a feature that assigns behavior to class objects to mimic the behavior of intrinsic data types when used in expressions that include arithmetic, relational, and other operators.

Chapter 22 explains how to build and use class libraries. You will build two class libraries to use in subsequent chapters.

Chapter 23 introduces class inheritance, which enables you to build object-oriented class hierarchies consisting of base and derived classes. You learn about the object-oriented property called polymorphism.

Chapter 24 focuses on multiple inheritance, which is a C++ language feature that allows derived classes to inherit the properties of multiple-base classes.

Chapter 25 discusses class templates, a C++ feature that enables you to build generic parameterized classes.

Part III, Chapters 26 through 29, explains the various components of the Standard C++ Library including those parts that C++ inherits from Standard C.

Chapter 26 discusses some of the Standard C Library functions. You learn how to use header files for the standard functions that your programs call. You also learn about string functions, memory allocation functions, math functions, and others.

Chapter 27 introduces the Standard C++ Library. You extend your knowledge of the iostream input/output classes. This chapter also introduces you to the standard string and complex classes.

Chapter 28 describes managing and formatting string data in the iostream and stringstream classes.

Chapter 29 teaches using C++ streams to manipulate disk files including stream classes that read and write files. You learn, too, the difference between text and binary files.

Part IV, Chapters 30 through 34, describes what is known as the Standard Template Library (STL), a library of template classes that implement generic containers, algorithms, and iterators. You will learn about generic programming in Part IV.

Chapter 30 introduces you to the various types of classes defined in the STL, which include classes for objects such as sequences, associative containers, algorithms, and iterators. You will learn about the generic programming model that STL implements and supports.

Chapter 31 teaches you how to program with the STL sequence classes, which implement lists, queues, stacks, vectors, and more.

Chapter 32 explains how to use the associative container classes, which implement maps, sets, and bitsets.

Chapter 33 focuses on generic algorithms, which are a library of functions that enable your programs to process the data defined in STL objects. Such processing includes counting, sorting, and grouping.

Chapter 34 explains STL iterators, which are a special type of pointer that enables programs to move through the contents of a container in forward or reverse directions. You also learn how to use iterators to access the information stored in an element of a container.

Part V, Chapters 35 through 40, addresses advanced features that Standard C++ supports.

Chapter 35 is about exception handling, which allows a program to throw and catch exceptions in an orderly fashion.

Chapter 36 introduces namespaces and includes discussions on how to define a namespace. This chapter also explains namespace scope resolution, unnamed namespaces, and namespace aliases.

Chapter 37 describes the advanced C++ typecasting mechanism, including dynamic casts, static casts, and constant casts.

Chapter 38 describes C++'s Runtime Type Information (RTTI), a way that a program can determine information about an object at runtime.

Chapter 39 is about the C++ locale classes and how to use the classes to provide internationalization for your applications. You learn to set a locale and how to display information in the format required by that locale.

Chapter 40 describes the techniques used in object-oriented design and programming, including a discussion of such topics as abstraction, encapsulation, inheritance, and polymorphism.

Appendix A contains source code listings for class libraries that the book's example programs use.

Appendix B describes the CD-ROM included with this book.

Appendix C is a brief user's guide to the Quincy 2002 integrated development environment with which you can compile, debug, and run the exercise programs and with which you can write your own C++ programs for practice.

Appendix D describes the elements of the C++ language in easy-to-reference table form.

Appendix E is a bibliography of reference books that you may find useful.

The Glossary defines some common C++ programming terms. If I use a term in the book that you do not know, look in the Glossary to see if it's defined there. If not, send me a query at astevens@ddj.com.

Al Stevens
March, 2003

Acknowledgments

I've had a lot of help over the years with writing programs and writing about programming. Each previous edition of this work acknowledges compiler vendors who contributed their products, programmers who critiqued the manuscripts and code, others who downloaded and tested the Quincy IDE, and, always, my wife, best friend, alpha tester, and collaborator, Judy Stevens.

Rather than repeat the list, which grew quite long, I reference it here. Those who care may look for earlier editions at the library, in flea markets, on ebay, in the bargain trays in bookstores, and as doorstops in the offices of programmers around the globe.

Special mention, however, goes to two special people: Debra Williams Cauley, my patient and loving acquisitions editor, who pleaded and cajoled with me to return to the harried life of a computer book author just this one more time, and Al Williams, my friend and colleague, whose technical review of this work contributed immeasurably to its content.

Contents at a Glance

Contents

Part III: The Standard C++ Library   **393**

The C++ Language

Part I, Chapters 1 through 13, describes the basic elements of the C++ language, primarily those things that are most like the C language but with a few new things to learn. These are the chapters in Part I:

Chapter 1

An Introduction to Programming in C++

This chapter describes C++ at its most elementary level. It is an overview, so you might not fully understand the details this chapter presents, but don't worry; you will learn about all of these concepts and much more in the chapters that follow. As you proceed through the lessons beginning in Chapter 2, return from time to time to this introduction and watch everything fall into place.

A Brief History

In the early 1970s, Dennis Ritchie, a programmer at AT&T Bell Laboratories, adapted the minicomputer programming language BCPL into the first version of what he named C, a language that allows a programmer to access hardware with a programming language similar to assembly language but with the structured programming conveniences of high-level languages.

C ran on the Unix operating system, also an internal AT&T project. Eventually Ritchie rewrote the C compiler in C itself, and Ken Thompson rewrote Unix in C, a new concept, a compiler written in the language it compiles. By porting the C compiler to other computers, the developers made Unix into a portable operating system, a revolutionary idea at the time. These achievements distinguished C as a high-level language for writing systems programs, portable applications, and utility programs.

For years C and Unix remained internal AT&T software assets. Eventually AT&T offered Unix to universities, and a generation of students was exposed to Unix and C. As those students entered the programming world of business and industry, the Unix and C influence found its way into corporate America. The C language began to enjoy mainstream support in circles previously dominated by COBOL and FORTRAN at the top level and assembly language at the bottom.

In the late 1970s developers built C compilers for personal computers. Whereas BASIC had been the dominant microcomputer programming language, vendors began publishing C compilers, and programmers of home computers began making the switch. The IBM

PC, introduced in 1981, continued this trend. C became most programmers' favorite language for writing PC programs. At one time, more than a dozen C compilers were available for the PC. Most applications and systems software for the PC are written in C and C++.

C was defined in 1981 in *The C Programming Language* (Prentice Hall), by Brian Kernighan and Dennis Ritchie. Although not a formal language specification, the book, nicknamed "K&R" for the initials of its authors' last names and "the white book" for the cover design, described C the way Ritchie had implemented it at AT&T. The dialect of C that K&R describes is called K&R C. Compiler builders added features to K&R C, and as the industry accepted the best of those extensions, a de facto standard evolved.

In 1983, the American National Standards Institute (ANSI) and the International Standards Organization (ISO) formed a committee to standardize C. Their charter was to codify the language as it existed. They published a C Standard document in 1990. A second edition of the K&R book describes Standard C, also called "ANSI C," obscuring somewhat the identity of K&R C.

Bjarne Stroustrup, an AT&T Bell Labs researcher, designed and developed the C++ programming language circa 1980 to answer a need for a simulation language with the features of object-oriented programming, then a relatively new programming paradigm. Chapter 40 describes object-oriented programming. Dr. Stroustrup decided to build C++ upon the C language, writing a C++ compiler that emits C source language. The C source language could be compiled on any computer system that supported C. Stroustrup called his translator program cfront. Many implementations of C++ are ports of cfront and its successors, the source code of which is available under license from AT&T. The C++ language has been available outside AT&T since about 1985.

A joint ANSI/ISO committee formed in 1989 to define Standard C++. Their work was completed with the publication of the C++ international standard in 1998.

Introduction to C++

There are two parts to the C++ language. First is the core language itself, those elements that the compiler processes into native machine instructions. Second is the Standard C++ Library, a huge collection of functions and classes, written in the core language, which are heavily dependent on each other, and that implement common operations such as console and file input and output, string processing, object containers, algorithms, and internationalization. To understand the libraries, you must understand the core language.

C++ is an extensible language. Programmers extend the language by adding libraries of classes, functions, algorithms, and containers beyond those provided by the standard definition. The Standard Library supports a generic operating environment that includes text standard input and output and file input and output. Platform-dependent extensions, such as the MFC and OWL applications frameworks, implement specific features for a particular operating platform. Programmers further extend C++ by adding libraries to support their particular problem domains.

The Core C++ Language

C++ is a *procedural* programming language with object-oriented extensions. That means that you can design and code programs using traditional procedures. However, you can also group related procedures (and variables) into *classes*. Classes act like templates that allow you to create objects (or class instances). These objects usually model some real-world entity such as a file, an employee, or a URL. The key to describing your program's actions – with or without objects – is the function.

Functions

Here's what a C++ function looks like:

```
void donothing()
{
    return;
}
```

The function just shown is named `donothing` and, as its name suggests, it does nothing except return to its caller. The programmer selects the function's name. The function shown previously is a `void` function, which means that it returns no value. The braces following the function declaration define the function's statement body, which includes the coded statements that perform what the function does.

Note   Other programming languages would call the `donothing` function a "procedure" or "subroutine" because in mathematics and computer programming, functions traditionally return values, whereas in programming, procedures and subroutines perform some operation without returning anything. In C++, though, both kinds of code blocks are called "functions."

Some C++ functions do return values. Here's what one looks like:

```
int April()
{
    return 4;
}
```

The caller of such a function can place the function call on the right side of an assignment statement, assigning the returned value to a named data variable like this:

```
month = April();
```

Functions may declare parameters like this.

```
int daysinmonth(int month)
{
    int days[] = {31,28,31,30,31,30,31,31,30,31,30,31};
    return days[month];
}
```

The `daysinmonth` function has a month parameter and returns the number of days in the specified month without considering leap years and without validating the argument passed into its `month` parameter.

The function uses an initialized array named `days` and uses the `month` parameter to subscript into the array to retrieve a value to return. Chapter 7 explains arrays.

The caller of the function passes arguments that the function uses as the values for its parameters like this.

```
numberofdays = daysinmonth(10);
```

The constant value 10 is an argument that is copied to the function's `month` parameter when the function is called. An argument can be any C++ expression that returns a compatible type. A caller's argument types must match the types of the parameters declared for the function, or the compiler must know how to convert the argument's type to the parameter's type. For example, you can pass an integer argument to a function that is expecting a floating-point parameter, and the compiler knows how to make the conversion.

A function starts execution at its first (that is, topmost) statement and continues until the last, bottommost statement executes unless the function encounters a return statement before the end. Each function, upon completion, returns to its caller, and execution continues with the next statement in the calling function.

You can also use a function call as the argument that provides the parameter value to another function call, as an initializer to a local data variable, or as an element in an expression. Chapter 2 explains assignments, constants, variables, initializers, and expressions.

Chapter 3 explains functions in more detail.

Classes

Classes are aggregate definitions that consist of data members and member functions. A class encapsulates the implementation and interface of a user-defined data type and constitutes an abstract data type. A class represents an entity to the program, an aggregate of data variables and procedures that encapsulate something the program works with.

Here's what a C++ class looks like:

```
class newtype {
    // members
};
```

The class just shown is named `newtype`. Its name is assigned by the programmer. A class describes to the compiler some kind of data type or other abstraction that the programmer uses in the program. The class shown here has nothing inside its declaration except a comment, the line that begins with the characters `//`. Chapter 2 explains source code comments. Classes usually contain data members and member functions to define the class's behavior and interface for the program that uses it. A class can make certain members visible to other classes or it can make certain members private and only usable by the functions that comprise the class.

The class's *implementation* — its aggregate private members — usually is hidden from the class user (the programmer who instantiates objects of the class). The class's *public interface* usually is revealed to the class user in the form of methods: class member functions that operate on the data members of the class.

The class user instantiates objects of the class and invokes class methods against those objects by calling the class's member functions for the objects. A class is said to have *behavior*, which is another way of saying that an object of the class responds to its methods in ways that are understood by the class user at an abstract level without necessarily revealing the details of that behavior.

Chapter 6 introduces classes, and Part II explains classes in more detail.

The main Function

A C++ program begins execution in a function named main and terminates when the main function returns. Which brings us to the first of the exercise programs.

Program 1-1: **The minimum C++ program**

```
int main()
{
    return 0;
}
```

This is a good time to turn to Appendix C and learn how to use Quincy to run the tutorial listings. You can compile and run Program 1-1 if you want to, but it does nothing except return to the operating system.

Program 1-1 declares and defines the main function. That's all the program does. The program begins executing with the first statement in main and terminates when the main function returns.

The operating system calls main and returns its integer value to the operating system. The main function is the entry and departure point of your C++ program. No place in your program is allowed to call the main function.

The main function may call other, lower-level functions, which in turn may call even lower-level functions. Chapter 3 has further discussions of main.

Anatomy of a Function

The function in Program 1-1 illustrates several things about C++ functions in general. Unlike the donothing function, main returns a value. The first line provides the main function's return type and identifier. The main function returns an integer value (int) and always has the identifier main. The int keyword specifies the function's integer return type. You'll learn about integers and other data types in Chapter 2.

The parentheses after the function's name contain the function's parameter list. In this case, main has no parameters, so the parameter list is empty. An empty parameter list is represented by the () character sequence.

The function body follows the parameter list. The function body begins with a left brace character ({) and ends with a right brace character (}). In between are the function's statements — the lines of code that execute when the function is called. Program 1-1 has only one statement, the return statement that terminates the main function and, consequently, the program.

A group of statements surrounded by braces is called a *statement block*. Statement blocks may be nested. You'll see how this nesting contributes to program flow control in Chapter 4. Every function has at least one statement block (which could be empty); Program 1-1's main function has only one statement block.

A function finishes executing immediately after its last statement executes, or when the return statement executes. Program 1-1's main function terminates when its return statement returns the integer constant 0. A return statement can be positioned anywhere inside the function, assuming that statements following a return statement would be executed at other times based on conditional exception, which you learn about later.

A `void` function can return without using a `return` statement. We could have written `donothing` like this:

```
void donothing()
{
}
```

After a `void` function executes the last statement in its outermost statement block, the function returns to the function that called it.

Statements

Each function consists of one or more blocks of statements. The blocks within a function are nested (one enclosed within the other).

Statements fall into one of the following categories:

✦ **Declarations:** Declare variables and functions.

✦ **Definitions:** Define instances of variables and functions.

✦ **Procedural Statements:** Executable code statements that reside inside a function's definition.

Variables

Each statement block can declare local variables, which remain in scope (that is, valid) as long as statements in that block are executing. Here's an example:

```
void dosomething()
{
    int amount;
    // ...
}
```

The `dosomething` function has as its first statement the declaration of an integer variable named `amount`.

Observe the semicolon at the end of the statement. Every C++ statement is terminated with a semicolon.

A C++ program also can have variables declared outside any function. Those variables are said to have global scope, because the statements in all the functions in the same source file can reference them. Here's an example:

```
int external_amount;
void dosomething()
{
    // ...
}
```

The `external_amount` integer variable has global scope because it is declared outside any function definition.

Chapter 5 explains the scope of program elements in a C++ program.

A variable *declaration* specifies the variable's storage class, data type, type qualifier, level of indirection (if it is a pointer), name, and dimensions (if it is an array). Chapter 7 explains these things.

A function declaration (more frequently called its *prototype*) declares the function's return type, name, and the number and types of its arguments. Chapter 3 explains these concepts.

A variable *definition* includes the components of a declaration and may include an initializer if the variable has an initializing value. Chapter 2 explains initializers. A definition defines the instance of the variable and reserves memory for it. A function definition contains the function's executable code.

Usually, a variable's declaration and definition are the same statement. A function's prototype and definition are usually in different places, sometimes in different source code files. If the function's definition appears in the source code file ahead of all calls to the function, however, the function's definition may also serve as its prototype.

Identifiers and Keywords

You assign names to many different things in a C++ program. Those names are called *identifiers*, and they may consist of letters, digits, and underscore characters. An identifier may not, however, begin with a digit. You've already seen some identifiers in the program fragments in this chapter (for example, Month, external_amount, and dosomething). Some identifiers are reserved for the core language, and those identifiers are called *keywords*. This chapter has examples of some keywords, too. Chapter 2 explains identifiers in more detail and provides a list of reserved keywords, such as return. You'll learn the meaning and use of all the keywords as the lessons in later chapters proceed.

Procedural Statements

Procedural statements are assignments, expressions, or program flow control statements. Here's an example:

```
float compute_pay(float wage, int hours)
{
    float pay;
    pay = wage * hours;
    if (hours > 40)
        pay = pay + (hours - 40) * wage / 2;
    return pay;
}
```

The compute_pay function has two integer parameters, wage and hours, and returns a floating-point value. We can probably assume from the name of the function and the names of its parameters that the function returns the pay value for an employee based on the employee's wage and the number of hours the employee worked. Nothing in C++ requires you to assign meaningful names to things, but it's good practice to do so. For example, this equivalent function is much harder to understand:

```
float cp(float w, int h)
{
    float p;
    p = w * h;
    if (h > 40)
        p = p + (h - 40) * w / 2;
    return p;
}
```

As you've probably guessed, integer values do not include fractional parts, whereas floating-point values do. For this simple example, we can assume that C++ floating-point arithmetic is sufficient to manage dollars and cents. Chapter 2 has more information about float variables.

Let's look at the `compute_pay` function one statement at a time. The statements begin following the open brace character ({) that follows the function's declaration header.

The `compute_pay` function's first statement declares a floating-point variable named `pay`.

The second statement assigns to the `pay` integer the value returned by an expression that multiplies the `wage` parameter by the `hours` parameter. This statement is an assignment of the expression to a variable.

The third statement, which is on two lines of code, compares the `hours` parameter to the integer constant 40. That part of the statement is a conditional statement based on the boolean value returned by an expression. Chapter 4 explains conditional statements and boolean expressions.

If `hours` is greater than 40, the employee is paid time and a half for the extra hours worked. The `pay` variable already contains standard pay for all the hours, so, in the fourth statement, the function adds the overtime pay as one half the hourly rate times the hours over 40 that were worked.

An *expression* is a program statement that returns a value. In the `compute_pay` function, the expression `wage * hours` returns the product of `wage` and `hours`. An expression such as `hours > 40` returns a boolean `true` or `false` value. An expression such as

```
pay + (hours - 40) * wage / 2
```

is a combination of several expressions, which, in this case, compute the pay amount.

An expression can stand on its own or be on the right side of an assignment statement, as shown by this statement in the `compute_pay` function:

```
pay = pay + (hours - 40) * wage / 2;
```

Expressions consist of combinations of variables, constants, operators, and function calls. Chapter 2 contains more information about expressions.

Program Flow Control

C++ uses the control structures of structured programming, which include sequence (one statement executing after another), iteration (for and while loops), and selection (if-then-else and switch-case control structures). C++ also permits unstructured programming with the `goto` statement. Chapter 4 is all about controlling program flow with these language features.

Exception Handling

C++ supports exception handling with the `throw`/`try`/`catch` mechanism, which permits a program to make an orderly jump to a defined location higher in the program's executing hierarchy. Chapter 35 covers exception handling.

Templates

C++ supports the development of generic functions through its function template mechanism explained in Chapter 12. For example, you might write a template function that could compute the average of a list of numbers. You can use this template to generate an actual function that averages integers and another function that averages floating-point numbers.

C++ supports the design of generic parameterized types through its class template mechanism, a device that enables you to define and instantiate objects of generic data types. Chapter 25 explains class templates.

Namespaces

C++ addresses the issue of global namespace pollution with the namespace feature explained in Chapter 36. You can ensure that the global identifiers in your program do not conflict with those in third-party libraries you use by placing your code inside a unique namespace. The Standard C++ Library places all its global identifiers in the std namespace for just that reason.

Order of Declarations

You read a C++ program from the top to the bottom, but the functions do not have to be coded in that sequence. However, declarations of functions and variables must be coded in the program above any statements that reference them. That is, a function must be declared before it is called, and a variable must be declared before it is. You can declare a function by providing a function prototype that describes its name, return value, and parameters to the compiler. You must provide a function's prototype ahead of any calls to the function; you can put the function itself anywhere in the program. The function's declaration and all calls to it must match the prototype with respect to its return type and the types of its parameters. However, if the function itself is positioned in the source code ahead of any calls to it, the function can serve as its own prototype.

Let's look now at a program that uses some of what you just learned.

Program 1-2: **A simple C++ program**

```
float compute_pay(float wage, int hours)
{
    float pay;
    pay = wage * hours;
    if (hours > 40)
        pay = pay + (hours - 40) * wage / 2;
    return pay;
}

int main()
{
    float paycheck;
    paycheck = compute_pay(12.50, 43);
    return 0;
}
```

Program 1-2 computes the paycheck value, but it doesn't do anything with what it computes. You can step through the program with Quincy's debugger and watch the variables change, but a real program ought to have input and output. We'll remedy that situation in the next discussion.

The Standard C++ Library

The second part of the C++ language is the Standard C++ Library, which is a library of classes and functions written in C++ that support things common to most programming projects, including input and output.

Unlike languages such as COBOL, BASIC, and FORTRAN, C++ has no built-in input/output statements. Instead, input and output are implemented by C++ classes in the Standard C++ Library. Many features that are intrinsic parts of other languages are performed by classes in C++. Data conversions, string manipulations, and output formatting are three examples of operations that C++ supports with Standard C++ Library classes and functions rather than with intrinsic language features.

To demonstrate, we'll use the Standard C++ Library iostreams to add input/output functionality to the program we just wrote.

Program 1-3: A simple C++ program with console I/O

```
#include <iostream>

float compute_pay(float wage, int hours)
{
    float pay;
    pay = wage * hours;
    if (hours > 40)
        pay = pay + (hours - 40) * wage / 2;
    return pay;
}

int main()
{
    float paycheck;
    float wage;
    int hours;
    std::cout << "Enter wage and hours: ";
    std::cin >> wage;
    std::cin >> hours;
    paycheck = compute_pay(wage, hours);
    std::cout << "Pay = ";
    std::cout << paycheck;
    return 0;
}
```

Program 1-3 adds a lot to what you've seen so far. It includes a header file named <iostream> by using the #include preprocessor directive. #include is explained in Chapter 2. Preprocessor directives are explained in Chapter 11. <iostream> is introduced in Chapter 2 and discussed in more detail in Chapter 27. This include file contains declarations for system-defined functions and classes.

Program 1-3's main function declares variables and writes a prompt to the `std::cout` object, which represents the standard output device, which is usually the console monitor. Then it reads data into variables from the `std::cin` device, which represents the standard input device, which is usually the console keyboard. The program then calls the `compute_pay` function passing the input data as arguments. The `compute_pay` function computes and returns the pay amount, and the main function writes the returned amount to `std::cout` after which the `main` function returns zero to the operating system.

The `std::` prefix on the `cin` and `cout` object references tells the compiler that those identifiers are in the std namespace, which is reserved for the Standard C++ Library.

Source Code Files

A C++ source-code module is a text file (usually ASCII) that you can read and modify with any text editor, such as the Windows Notepad applet. The Quincy development system included on the CD-ROM that accompanies this book integrates a programmer's editor with a compiler and debugger.

Like most contemporary compiled programming languages, C++ programs typically consist of multiple source-code modules that are compiled into object-code modules, which are then linked with object-code modules from libraries into a single executable program module. Much of the object code in a typical C++ program comes from packaged libraries of previously compiled, reusable software components implemented as classes or functions. Chapter 13 discusses the organization of a program into source code modules.

Summary

This chapter got you started toward your goal of learning the C++ programming language. You gained an initial, if cursory, insight into the fundamental structure of the C++ language. It's a lot to absorb in only a few lessons; do not expect to start writing complex C++ programs after having read only this one chapter. The chapters that follow start at the beginning and lead you through these topics one at a time in a sequence designed to build each lesson on what you have learned in previous lessons. There are many more things to learn about, too. Overloaded operators, overloaded functions, namespaces, typecasts, locales, and so on are language features that you learn about in later chapters.

✦   ✦   ✦

Writing Simple C++ Programs

This chapter is the starting point, or, more precisely, the starting-over point. You saw three small programs in Chapter 1, but you didn't find out exactly what makes them tick. Now we'll start back at the beginning, learning every component of a C++ program one piece at a time in this and the following chapters.

Your First Program

As you learned in Chapter 1, C++ programs consist of variables and functions. A *function* consists of variable declarations and executable statements organized into nested statement blocks. As Program 1-1 demonstrates, a C++ program begins executing with a function named main. The best way to get started is with a real program. Program 2-1 is your first C++ program; one that has a main function and several other fundamental C++ language constructs.

Program 2-1: **Your first C++ program**

```cpp
#include <iostream>

int main()
{
    // write to the screen
    std::cout << "My first C++ program";
    return 0;
}
```

Program 2-1 is a tiny program that illustrates a lot of what makes up a C++ program. It has source-code comments, includes a standard library header file, and—from its main function—writes a message on the screen.

Program 2-1 displays a message onscreen and returns to the operating system. It does all that with only eight lines of code in a source-code file. The following sections examine Program 2-1 one line at a time.

The #include Directive

The first line of code in Program 2-1 looks like this:

```
#include <iostream>
```

This statement is a *preprocessing directive*. Historically, C compilers used a separate program to handle lines that started with the # character. This program would execute first, handle the special commands, and then send the results to the C compiler. Since the program ran before the compiler, it was known as the *preprocessor*. However, most modern compilers handle the preprocessing step internally, but the terms preprocessor and preprocessing continue to exist.

We discuss the preprocessor in more detail in Chapter 11.

The #include directive tells the compiler to include a different source-code file in the program. Program 2-1 includes the file named <iostream>, a standard library header file that describes classes, functions, and global values used for console input and output. The listing includes the header file so that the program can use the cout object. Most programs in this book include <iostream>. Don't worry about what else the header file contains just yet.

The file name in the #include directive is enclosed by angle brackets, another name for the combined use of the less-than and greater-than symbols. This usage identifies header files that the compiler system supplies. When you include your own header files, you surround those names with double quotes. Chapter 11 has more details about this usage.

White Space

The second line in Program 2-1 is a blank line. The C++ language is a free-form language, which means that white-space characters — newlines, spaces, tabs, and blank lines — are ignored. Except for the rare occasion when two keywords or identifiers are separated by a space (such as else if) or inside string constants (described later), a program needs no white space at all to compile. Without white space, however, most programs are hard to read. Here is what Program 2-1 looks like without much white space:

```
#include <iostream>
int main(){// write to the screen
std::cout << "My first C++ program";return 0;}
```

Programmers use white space to indent and separate code in various styles to make their programs legible. There are many styles for writing C++ code. We take no position with regard to style, although the exercises reflect my preferences. You will see other styles that use different conventions for indenting and the placement of brace characters, but there is no one right way. Choose a style that works for you, make it legible, and be consistent in its use. Some programmer's editors, Quincy, for example, include so-called *smart indenting* features that help you format your code. Some integrated development environments include a so-called *code beautification* tool that reformats code to match defined code styles. The Quincy IDE included with this book supports both features.

The main Function Declaration

Line 3 in Program 2-1 looks like this:

```
int main()
```

This line declares the `main` function as a function that returns an integer (`int`) value and that accepts no arguments. Chapter 3 discusses function declarations in more detail.

The main Function's Statement Block

Line 4 consists of a single left brace (`{`) character to define the start of `main`'s outermost statement block. The statement block continues until the matching right brace (`}`) character on line 8. This portion of the program, which comprises the `main` function's single program block, looks like this:

```
{
    // write to the screen
    std::cout << "My first C++ program";
    return 0;

}
```

Source-Code Comments

Line 5 contains a program comment in this format:

```
// write to the screen
```

Comments in a program's source code document the meaning of the code. They have no effect on the executable program itself. C++ comments begin with the characters `//` and continue to the end of the source-code line.

C++ also supports the traditional C comment format. C comments begin with the `/*` character sequence and continue through the `*/` character sequence like this:

```
/* write to the screen */
```

C comments may span several source-code lines and may not be nested. They may occupy lines of their own, or they may appear on lines that have other code. They can even appear in the middle of statements, although that usually doesn't lead to very legible code. For example, you might write:

```
SetColors(BLUE /* background */, YELLOW /* foreground */);
```

C++'s `//` comments do not span source-code lines, because there is no comment termination code like the C `*/` token. This book uses C++'s `//` comment format exclusively, except in the rare C source-code module that contributes to a C++ program.

Use comments throughout your programs. Make them meaningful with respect to what they convey to programmers who might be reading your code. Do not make the two common mistakes that many programmers make: assuming that you will be the only programmer who reads your code and assuming that you will always remember why you wrote a program a certain way. Comments document your intentions. Use them.

At the same time, don't depend only on comments to convey the code's meaning. Strive to write code that is itself clear and meaningful. With properly written code you can keep comments to a minimum, using them only to add to what the code already says to the reader.

Writing to the Console

Line 6 is the most complicated line in the program. That line looks like this:

```
std::cout << "My first C++ program";
```

This line's cryptic code tells the compiler to display a string constant on the screen. You'll learn more about displaying output later in this and subsequent chapters.

The return Statement

Line 7 is the statement that tells the `main` function to terminate processing and return a constant integer zero value to the operating system. Normally, `return` sends a result to the calling function. In this case, there is no calling function — the operating system is `main`'s caller. In most operating systems there is a way to determine what return code the program set. For example, in a DOS or Windows batch file, you can use the `IF ERRORLEVEL` statement. In Unix or Linux scripts the `$?` variable reflects the return code. Chapter 3 addresses the `return` statement in more detail. Constant expressions are discussed later in this chapter.

Terminating the Statement Block

Line 9, the last line in the program, contains the right brace (}) character that defines the end of the `main` function's statement block.

Identifiers

A C++ program consists of many elements — variables, functions, classes, and so on — all of which have names. The name of a function, variable, or class is called its *identifier*. As the programmer, you assign identifiers to the parts of your program. Other identifiers are assigned in the Standard C and C++ libraries. Following are the rules for identifiers in the C++ language.

✦ An identifier consists of letters, digits, and the underscore character.

✦ An identifier must begin with a letter. (Underscores are permitted in the first character, but leading underscores are reserved for identifiers that the compiler defines.)

✦ Identifiers are case-sensitive. For example, MyFunc and myfunc are different identifiers.

✦ An identifier may be any length, but only the first 32 characters are significant. Some early C implementations restricted the significance of external identifiers (ones with global scope) to six characters. This was because of limitations in the particular linker program and not because of any limitation in the C language.

✦ An identifier may not be one of the reserved C++ keywords, as listed in the following section.

Keywords

The C++ language reserves a number of keywords. You must not use these keywords as identifiers in your program. Table 2-1 lists the C++ keywords.

Table 2-1: Standard C++ Keywords

asm	do	inline	short	typeid
auto	double	int	signed	typename
bool	dynamic_cast	long	sizeof	union
break	else	mutable	static	unsigned
case	enum	namespace	static_cast	using
catch	explicit	new	struct	virtual
char	extern	operator	switch	void
class	false	private	template	volatile
const	float	protected	this	wchar_t
const_cast	for	public	throw	while
continue	friend	register	true	
default	goto	reinterpret_cast	try	
delete	if	return	typedef	

C++ includes other keywords that also cannot be used as identifiers. These keywords — alternatives to the cryptic three-letter codes (trigraphs) Standard C uses to replace special characters (such as ~) that might not appear on international keyboards — are designed for international keyboards that do not have the special characters used in English to express some operators. The Committee added these keywords so that international programs would be more readable. This book does not use any of these keywords, listed in Table 2-2, in any program.

Table 2-2: International C++ Keywords

and	bitor	or	xor_e
and_eq	compl	or_eq	not_eq
bitand	not	xor	

The Standard Output Stream

The std::cout variable, seen in Program 2-1, is the C++ standard output stream object, which writes to the console:

```
std::cout << "My first C++ program";
```

The string to be written is specified in the string constant, which is the character sequence between the double quotes. Just as a BASIC programmer knows that the PRINT statement writes data to the screen, a C++ programmer knows that the standard std::cout object does somewhat the same thing. The important difference is that PRINT is part of the BASIC language — an *intrinsic operator* whereas cout happens to be the name that a programmer many years ago gave to the standard output stream object, which usually displays data on the console monitor, and std:: is the namespace for objects that the compiler defines for the Standard C++ Library.

A *namespace* is a way to isolate identifiers from other parts of the program and to prevent name collisions when various library writers and the programmers themselves inadvertently use the same identifier for different external declarations. You learn all about namespaces in Chapter 36. For now, accept the fact that identifiers that the Standard C++ Library (Part III) defines are in the namespace named std and that to reference those identifiers, you must prefix the references with the std:: prefix. Thus, all references to the cout object are made like this: std::cout. You see the std:: prefix on many other identifiers throughout this book.

The << operator is, in this context, the output operator. It is called the *stream insertion operator*, because you use it to insert data objects into the output stream. The operator points symbolically from what is being sent to where it is going.

You can think of std::cout, std::cin, and std::cerr (std::cin and std::cerr are described later in this chapter) as devices. In C++ stream input/output, std::cout, std::cin, and std::cerr are identifiers that name objects (instances of classes). In the example just given, the string is being written to the std::cout object, which displays data on the standard output device, which is usually the console monitor. Later in this chapter, you'll learn how to display other data types.

This example is your first experience with C++ classes, the foundation of C++'s data abstraction and object-oriented programming support. A full understanding of the stream classes requires a thorough understanding of classes. For now, however, you need to understand only how a program uses objects of these classes so that you can manage console input/output. You will learn more about classes in Chapter 6 and in more detail beginning in Chapter 14.

Variables

You saw in Program 2-1 how a C++ program declares a function — in this case, the main function. Programs declare data variables, too. A variable is a storage location that contains a data value. Every variable has a type. The type defines the format and behavior of the variable. C++ supports boolean, character, integer, and floating-point data types. C++ has six intrinsic data types, also called built-in types. They are bool, char, wchar_t, int, float, and double. Here is how a program would instantiate an integer variable, for example:

```
int amount;
```

You can extend C++ and define your own types using the enum, class, struct, and union constructs. We'll talk more about these constructs in Chapters 6 and 7.

Each variable declaration in a program provides the variable's type and identifier. Variables can have other properties, as well. Integer type specifiers can include unsigned, long, or short to further define the type, like these examples:

```
long int bigamount;
unsigned int counter;
```

```
short int smallamount;
```

A double also can be a long double, increasing its precision.

You can use the static, extern, register, and auto storage classes to further define where a variable is stored and how it behaves in the program. There are const and volatile type qualifiers, too. You learn about these data properties in this and later chapters.

The size of a variable depends on its type. The size of each type depends on the C++ implementation and usually is expressed as the number of bytes an object of the type occupies in memory. The examples in this book use data types with sizes typical of 32-bit C++ compilers for the PC.

The bool Type

A bool variable is a two-state logical type that can contain one of two values: true or false. If you use a bool variable in an arithmetic expression, the bool variable contributes the integer value 0 or 1 to the expression depending on whether the variable is false or true, respectively. If you convert an integer to a bool, the bool variable becomes false if the integer is zero or becomes true if the integer is nonzero. Variables of type bool typically are used for runtime Boolean indicators and can be used in logical tests to alter program flow. Program 2-2 is an example of how the bool type is used.

Program 2-2: **Using a bool variable**

```cpp
#include <iostream>

int main
{
    bool senior;      // bool variable
    senior = true;    // set to true.
    // Test the senior variable.
    if (senior)
        std::cout << "Senior citizen rates apply";
    return 0;
}
```

Program 2-2 begins by declaring a bool variable named senior. The program introduces the assignment statement, which you study in more detail later in this chapter. An *assignment statement* assigns the value of an expression to a variable. The value can be any complex expression that returns a value of a compatible type. Until you learn more, however, the example programs use simple constants. In the case of Program 2-2, the constant is the reserved C++ keyword true, which, according to the rules of C++ semantics, can be assigned to a bool variable. The opposite of true is, of course, false.

Another new construct that you see in Program 2-2 is the C++ if statement, which tests whether the expression in parentheses is true or false. In this case, it is true, so the program executes the statement that follows, which displays a message on std::cout. You learn more about program flow control later in this chapter and in Chapter 4.

The char Type

A char variable contains one character from the computer's character set. Characters in PC implementations of the C++ language are contained in 8-bit bytes using the ASCII character set to represent character values. A program declares a character variable with the char type specification:

```
char ch;
```

This declaration declares a variable of type char with the identifier ch. Once you declare a variable in this manner, the program can reference it in expressions, which we discuss in the next section. Program 2-3 illustrates the use of a char variable.

Program 2-3: Using the char variable

```
#include <iostream>

int main
{
    char c;            // char variable
    c = 'b';           // assign 'b' to c
    std::cout << c;    // display 'b'
    c = 'y';           // assign 'y' to c
    std::cout << c;    // display 'y'
    c = 'e';           // assign 'e' to c
    std::cout << c;    // display 'e'
    return 0;
}
```

Program 2-3 employs std::cout three times to display three single characters on the screen:

```
bye
```

Program 2-3 also uses assignment statements to assign values to a char variable. The 'b', 'y,' and 'e' values are ASCII character constant expressions in the C++ language.

If you think that there must be a better way to display the "bye" message, you're right. At the very least, you can send a "bye" string constant to std::cout as in Program 2-1. Program 2-3, however, contrives to show you how to declare and use the char data type.

The char data type is, in fact, an integer 8-bit numerical type that you can use in numerical expressions just as you use any other integer type. As such, a char variable can be signed or unsigned. You declare an unsigned char variable this way:

```
unsigned char c;
```

Unless they are unsigned, char variables behave like 8-bit signed integers when you use them in arithmetic and comparison operations.

The wchar_t Type

C++ includes the wchar_t type to accommodate character sets that require more than 8 bits. Many foreign language character sets have more than 256 characters and cannot be represented by the char data type. An international standard character definition named Unicode is 16 bits wide. The wchar_t data type typically is 16 bits wide, but its actual width depends on the compiler implementation.

The Standard C++ iostream class library includes classes and objects to support wide characters. Program 2-4 repeats Program 2-3, but with the std::wout object—which is the wide-character version of the std::cout object.

Program 2-4: Using a wchar_t variable

```
#include <iostream>

int main
{
    wchar_t wc;              // wide char variable
    wc = 'b';               // assign 'b' to wc
    std::wout << wc;        // display 'b'
    wc = 'y';               // assign 'y' to wc
    std::wout << wc;        // display 'y'
    wc = 'e';               // assign 'e' to wc
    std::wout << wc;        // display 'e'
    return 0;
}
```

The GNU Compiler Collection (GCC) Standard C++ Library that Quincy 2002 uses does not yet implement wide-character library classes and stream objects. Consequently, Program 2-4 does not compile and run with the compiler. You can, however, compile and run it with many commercial Standard C++ compilers.

The int Type

Variables of integral types come in several varieties. The basic integer is a signed quantity that you declare with the int type specifier, like this:

```
int Counter;
```

An integer can be signed, unsigned, long, short, or a plain signed integer such as the one just shown. The following declarations display some of the different kinds of integers:

```
long int Amount;           // long integer
long Quantity;             // long integer
signed int Total;          // signed integer
signed Kellie;             // signed integer
unsigned int Offset;       // unsigned integer
unsigned Offset;           // unsigned integer
```

```
short SmallAmt;              // short integer
short int Tyler;             // short integer
unsigned short Landon;       // unsigned short integer
unsigned short int Woody;    // unsigned short integer
```

As the examples show, you can omit the `int` keyword when you specify `long`, `short`, `signed`, or `unsigned`. A long integer usually is 32 bits. A short integer usually is 16 bits. Quincy uses 16-bit short integers and 32-bit integers and long integers.

The `signed` qualifier is redundant, because the integral types are signed unless you specify the `unsigned` qualifier. C++ includes the `signed` keyword mainly to preserve symmetry in the language specification. Program 2-5 illustrates the use of the `int` data type.

Program 2-5: Using an int variable

```
#include <iostream>

int main
{
    int Amount;              // an int variable
    Amount = 123;            // assign a value
    std::cout << Amount;     // display the int
    return 0;
}
```

Program 2-5 declares an `int` variable named `Amount`. Next, it assigns an integer constant value to the variable. Then, it displays the variable on the console.

When a type has several properties, you can place the type keywords in any sequence. The following declarations are all the same:

```
// 8 ways to declare an unsigned long integer.
unsigned long Tyler1;
long unsigned Tyler2;
unsigned long int Tyler3;
unsigned int long Tyler4;
long unsigned int Tyler5;
long int unsigned Tyler6;
int unsigned long Tyler7;
int long unsigned Tyler8;
```

Floating-Point Numbers

C++ supports three kinds of floating-point numbers, which are distinguished by their precision. Following are declaration examples for all three:

```
float Amount;                  // single precision
double BigAmount;              // double precision
long double ReallyBigAmount;   // long double precision
```

Standard C++ does not specify the range of values that floating-point numbers can contain. These ranges depend on the particular implementation of the C++ language. The standard defines a header file, `<cfloat>`, with global symbols that identify the ranges.

Now that you know about the ranges of floating-point numbers, you can forget about them for a while. This book has very little math, using only what you need in Chapter 26 to demonstrate some standard math functions. If you are mathematically inclined, you already know about precision, mantissas, exponents, scientific notation, and so on. If not, you can write C++ programs for the rest of your life without ever having to know more about math than you do now. Program 2-6 illustrates the declaration and use of the `float` data type.

Program 2-6: **Using a float variable**

```
#include <iostream>

int main
{
    float realValue;       // a float variable
    realValue = 1.23;      // assign a value
    std::cout << realValue; // display the float
    return 0;
}
```

Program 2-6 declares a `float` variable named `realValue`. Next, it assigns a constant value to the variable. Then, it displays the value.

Constants

The next section explains C++ expressions, which consist of variables, operators, and constants. You already have learned about variables, and you have used some constants in the exercises. Now, let's discuss constants in a C++ program.

Constants, in this context, are what some languages call *literals* and others call *immediate values*. They are constant values that you use explicitly in expressions. A constant is distinguished from a variable in two ways. First, it has no apparent compiled place in memory except inside the statement in which it appears. Second, you cannot address the constant or change its value. Be aware that these constants are not the same as the `const` variable type qualifier discussed in Chapter 5.

Character Constants

Character constants specify values that a `char` variable can contain. Program 2-3 assigns character constants to a `char` variable. You can code a character constant with an ASCII expression – as shown in Program 2-3 or as an escape sequence surrounded by single quote characters (apostrophes). The following statements are assignments of character constants to char variables:

```
ch1 = 'A';    // ASCII char constant
ch3 = '\x2f'; // char constant expressed as hex value
ch3 = '\013'; // char constant expressed as octal value
```

Escape Sequences

The backslash in the second and third examples just shown begins an escape sequence. It tells the compiler that something special is coming. In this case, \x means that the characters that follow are hexadecimal digits, and \0 (backslash-zero) means that the characters that follow are octal digits. Other escape sequences — consisting of a backslash and other characters that represent ASCII values — do not have a displayable character (one that you can type and print) in the character set. These escape sequences apply to character constants and string constants, as described later. Table 2-3 shows all the escape sequences.

Table 2-3: Constant Escape Sequences

Escape Sequence	Description
\'	Single quote
\"	Double quote
\\	Backslash
\0	Null (zero) character
\0nnn	Octal number (nnn)
\a	Audible bell character
\b	Backspace
\f	Formfeed
\n	Newline
\r	Carriage return
\t	Horizontal tab
\v	Vertical tab
\x	Hexadecimal number (nn or nnnn)

The backslash-backslash (\\) escape sequence enables you to code the backslash character itself into the constant so that the compiler does not translate it as an escape sequence. The single quote (\') and double quote (\") escape sequences allow you to include those characters in character and string constants so that the compiler does not interpret them as the terminating character of the constant itself.

The newline (\n) escape sequence probably is the one you will use the most. When a screen output function finds a newline character in the output data, it resets the cursor to the leftmost column on the screen and moves the cursor down one line. The newline character acts like a carriage return on a typewriter.

Integer Constants

An integer constant specifies a long or short, signed or unsigned integer value.

Quincy supports signed short integer values of -32768 to +32767, and unsigned short integer values of 0 to 65535. These are the ranges that you can represent in a 16-bit integer.

The int and the long int are both 32 bits in Quincy. Quincy supports signed long integer values of -2147483648 to +2147483647 and unsigned long integer values of 0 to 4294967295. These are the ranges that you can represent in a 32-bit integer.

You can specify an integer constant as a decimal, hexadecimal, or octal value, as shown in these statements:

```
Amount = -129;       // decimal integer constant
HexAmt = 0x12fe;     // hexadecimal integer constant
OctalAmt = 0177;     // octal integer constant
```

The leading 0x specifies that the constant is a hexadecimal expression. It can contain the digits 0-9 and the letters A-F in mixed uppercase or lowercase. A leading zero alone specifies that the constant is octal and may contain the digits 0-7.

You can specify that a constant is long or unsigned by adding the L or U suffix to the constant:

```
LongAmount = 52388L;       // long integer constant
LongHexAmt = 0x4fea2L      // long hex constant
UnsignedAmt = 40000U;      // unsigned integer constant
```

The suffixes can be uppercase or lowercase. On compiler systems in which int and long are the same length (Quincy, for example), the L suffix is unnecessary; but you should use it if you expect your program to be portable across compiler platforms that support other int lengths. Many older MS-DOS compilers, for example, have 16-bit integers and 32-bit long integers.

Floating-Point Constants

A floating-point constant consists of integer and fractional parts separated by a decimal point. Some floating-point constants use scientific, or exponential, notation to represent numbers too big or too small to express with normal notation. Here are some examples:

```
Pi = 3.14159;            // regular decimal notation
SmallNumber = 1.234E-40; // 1.234 x 10 to the -40th power
BigNumber = 2.47E201     // 2.47 x 10 to the 201st power
```

Floating-point constants default to the double type unless you provide a suffix on the constant:

```
FloatNumber = 1.23E10F     // float constant
LongDoubleNumber = 3.45L   // long double constant
```

The suffixes can be uppercase or lowercase.

Address Constants

When you begin to use pointers in C++ programs, a subject covered in Chapter 8, you use address constants. Variables and functions have memory addresses, and C++ enables you to reference their addresses with address constants as shown here:

```
CounterPtr = &Counter;     // address of a variable
FunctPtr = &DoFunction;    // address of a function
```

Address expressions of array elements can be non-constant expressions, too. Chapter 7 discusses arrays.

String Constants

Program 2-1 passes `"My first C++ program"`, a string constant (also called a string literal), to the `std::cout` object. You code a string constant as a sequence of ASCII characters surrounded by double quote characters. Escape sequences inside the string constant work the same as they do in character constants. Here are some examples of string constants:

```
cp = "hello, dolly";
std::cout << "\nEnter selection: ";
std::cout << "\aError!";
```

The first statement apparently assigns a string constant to a variable, but it really assigns the address of the string constant to a pointer variable (refer to Chapter 8). The compiler finds a place in memory for the string constant and compiles its address into the statement.

The same thing happens in the second and third statements in the example. The compiler passes the addresses of the string constants to the `std::cout` object.

The string constants in the second and third statements include escape sequences. The second statement's escape sequence is \n, the newline character. The third statement's escape sequence is \a, the audible alarm character, which beeps the computer's speaker.

Adjacent string constants concatenate to form a single string constant. This feature allows you to code long string constants on multiple source-code lines, as shown in Program 2-7.

Program 2-7: **Concatenated string constants**

```
#include <iostream>

int main
{
    std::cout <<
            "This is the beginning of a very long message\n"
            "that spans several lines of code.\n"
            "This format allows a program to build long\n"
            "string constants without going past the\n"
            "program editor's right margin.\n";
    return 0;
}
```

Expressions

Statements in a function body consist of individual expressions terminated by the semicolon (;) character. All statements and declarations in C are terminated that way. The statement is not complete until the semicolon appears.

An *expression* is a combination of constants, variables, function calls, and operators that, when evaluated, returns a value. Following are some typical C++ expressions:

```
1+2;
Counter*3;
GrossPay-(FICA+GrossPay*WithHoldingRate);
```

By themselves, these expressions do nothing. They return values, but they have no effect because the program does nothing with the returned values. Expressions such as these take on meaning when placed on the right side of assignment statements (discussed next), or when used as arguments in a function call (discussed in Chapter 3).

The numerical value that an expression returns has a type. The implicit type of an expression depends on the types of variables and constants that contribute to the expression. Therefore, an expression might return an integer of any size, an address, or a floating-point number of any precision.

Each expression also has a logical property associated with its value. If the expression's value is nonzero, the expression is said to return a `true` value. If the value is zero, the expression returns a `false` value. These logical values can be used as conditions in program flow-control statements — the subject of Chapter 4.

Assignments

An *assignment statement* assigns to a variable the value returned by an expression. The variable's contents are the value of the expression after the assignment statement. Here are the preceding expressions used in assignment statements:

```
Amount = 1+2;
Total = Counter*3;
NetPay = GrossPay-(FICA+GrossPay*WithHoldingRate);
```

Now, the program does something meaningful with the expressions. Each of the assignment statements assigns an expression's returned value to a named variable. In this example, you can assume that the program declared the variables elsewhere.

A variable that receives an assigned value is called an *lvalue*, because its reference appears on the left side of the assignment. The expression that provides the assigned value is called an *rvalue*, because it is on the right side of the assignment. You will learn that this is an important distinction. Not all expressions can be used as lvalues. A constant, for example, is an rvalue but cannot be an lvalue. A variable can be an lvalue if it is not a `const` variable, which Chapter 5 discusses.

The next program illustrates how a program uses assignments such as those just shown. To do that, the program declares variables to receive the values returned by the expressions. Declarations of local variables are made in a statement block at the beginning of the block before any statements. You learn more about local and global variables in Chapter 5. Program 2-8 declares three integer variables, assigns to those integers the values returned by the expressions, and displays the new values of the integer variables on the screen.

Program 2-8: **Assignments and expressions**

```cpp
#include <iostream>

int main
{
    // Declare three integers.
    int HourlyRate;
    int HoursWorked;
    int GrossPay;
    // Assign values to the integers.
    HourlyRate = 15;
    HoursWorked = 40;
    GrossPay = HourlyRate * HoursWorked;
    // Display the variables on the screen.
    std::cout << HourlyRate;
    std::cout << ' ';
    std::cout << HoursWorked;
    std::cout << ' ';
    std::cout << GrossPay;
    return 0;
}
```

When you use Quincy's tutorial mode to run Program 2-8, observe that Quincy opens its Watch window at the bottom of the screen and displays the values of the three integer variables. As you step through the program, you can watch the values change when the assignment statements execute. Many of the programs use this automatic variable Watch feature in Quincy to assist you with the lesson.

When you run Program 2-8, it displays these three values on the screen:

```
15 40 600
```

The first value in the display, 15, reflects the contents of the HourlyRate variable. The second value, 40, is HoursWorked. The third, 600, is GrossPay.

If you are a mathematician, assignments may look to you like algebraic equations. In some respects, the two concepts are almost the same thing, but at other times they are not. Consider this assignment:

```
AmountDue = Dues + Penalty;
```

Before the assignment statement executes, the two sides can be different, so the assignment statement is not an equation. After the execution, the two sides are the same, so the assignment statement appears to be an equation. Now consider this assignment statement:

```
AmountDue = AmountDue + 37.43;
```

This assignment statement is never an equation. The two sides can never be equal at any given time.

Comma-Separated Declarations

C++ permits you to use a comma-separated list of identifiers to declare multiple variables that have the same type. The three declarations in Program 2-8 can be coded this way:

```
int HourlyRate, HoursWorked, GrossPay;
```

Some programmers use the comma-separated identifier notation but put each identifier on a separate line, like this:

```
int HourlyRate,       // hourly rate
    HoursWorked,      // number of hours worked
    GrossPay;         // gross weekly pay
```

This style provides visual separation of the identifiers and allows you to add comments about each variable. There is another advantage to this style: You can use it to group all related variables. Later, if the requirements of the program call for you to change the type of a number of related variables, you need only make the change on the first line of code in the declaration. The types of all the others then automatically are changed.

Operators in Expressions

An expression consists of function calls, variables, constants, and operators. The previous examples used some operators. Now, you learn what they mean. Operators can be arithmetic, logical, bitwise logical, bitwise shift, relational, increment, decrement, or assignment operators. Most operators are binary, which means that you code the operator between two expressions. The addition operator, for example, is binary. Other operators are unary, which means that the operator is associated with one expression only. Unary plus and minus operators are examples as shown here:

```
x = -123;
y = -value;
z = +32;
```

The minus unary operator returns a value that is the signed inverse of the expression whereas the plus unary operator does not.

Arithmetic Operators

The C++ language has two unary and five binary arithmetic operators, as shown in Table 2-4. The multiplication, division, and modulus operators have higher precedence than the binary addition and subtraction operators, and the unary plus and minus operators are higher than the others. See "Precedence and Associativity" later in this chapter.

Table 2-4: Arithmetic Operators

Symbol	Description
+	Unary plus
-	Unary minus

Continued

Table 2-4 *(continued)*

Symbol	Description
*	Multiplication
/	Division
%	Modulus
+	Addition
-	Subtraction

The following are examples of assignment statements, where the expressions on the right side of the assignments use some of the arithmetic operators from Table 2-4:

```
Celsius = 5 * (Fahrenheit - 32) / 9;
Height = Top - Bottom + 1;
Area = Height * Width;
```

Program 2-9 uses the first expression to calculate and display Celsius temperatures from Fahrenheit values that you type. This program is also your first use of the standard cin object, which reads keyboard data into program variables.

Program 2-9: **Assigning an expression**

```
#include <iostream>

int main
{
    int Celsius, Fahrenheit;
    // Prompt for Fahrenheit temperature
    std::cout << "\nEnter temperature as degrees Fahrenheit: ";
    // Read Fahrenheit temperature from keyboard
    std::cin >> Fahrenheit;
    // Compute Celsius
    Celsius = 5 * (Fahrenheit - 32) / 9;
    // Display the result
    std::cout << "Temperature is ";
    std::cout << Celsius;
    std::cout << " degrees Celsius";
    return 0;
}
```

Program 2-9 declares two integer variables and uses std::cout to prompt you to type in the temperature.

The std::cin object is the <iostream> input device. Observe that it uses the >> operator, which signifies that the data value flows from the device to the variable. The >> operator, in this context, is called the *stream extraction operator* because it extracts data values from the input stream.

When you run the program in Program 2-9, it displays the following messages. The value 75 in this example is what you type. The value 23 is the computed Celsius temperature. You can use other values to see their effects.

```
Enter temperature as degrees Fahrenheit: 75
Temperature is 23 degrees Celsius
```

The modulus operator (%) returns the remainder of a division when the first expression is divided by the second, as shown in the next example. The example uses a BitNumber variable, which contains a number from 0 to the highest bit in a bit array, to compute the ByteOffset and BitOffset variables:

```
ByteOffset = BitNumber / 8;   // offset to the byte
BitOffset = BitNumber % 8;    // bit offset within the byte
```

The unary minus operator returns the negative value of the numeric expression that follows it. If the value already was negative, the operator returns the positive value of the expression.

The unary plus operator is redundant and was added to Standard C++ for symmetry with unary minus. The unary plus operator doesn't change anything. For example, it does not make a negative expression positive.

Logical Operators

Logical operators use the true/false properties of expressions to return a true or false value. In C++, the true result of an expression is nonzero. When a nonzero value is subjected to a logical operation, the value is converted to 1. False values are always zero. Table 2-5 lists the logical operators.

Table 2-5: Logical Operators

Symbol	Description
&&	Logical AND
||	Logical OR
!	Unary NOT

Here are some expressions that use logical operators:

```
tf = flots && jets;  // 1 if flots and jets are nonzero
tf = flots || jets;  // 1 if flots or jets is nonzero
tf = !flots;         // 1 if flots is zero
```

Do not confuse the && and || operators with their bitwise & and | counterparts discussed in the next section.

The && and || logical operators can have more complex expressions on either side than are shown in these examples. These operators most often are used to form conditional expressions in the C++ language's if, for, and while program flow control statements, which Chapter 4 discusses.

Programs often use the unary NOT logical operator (!) to convert a variable's numeric value to its logical true/false property:

```
tf = !!blob; // 1 if blob is nonzero; 0 otherwise
```

This expression uses the unary NOT logical operator twice to compound the negation and return the desired 1 or zero, true or false value associated with the variable's numeric value. Chapter 4 includes examples that use logical operators within program flow control statements.

Bitwise Logical Operators

The *bitwise logical operators* perform bit setting, clearing, inversion, as well as complement operations on the expressions and return the results. Table 2-6 lists the bitwise logical operators.

Table 2-6: Bitwise Logical Operators

Symbol	Description
&	Bitwise AND
|	Bitwise OR
^	Bitwise exclusive OR (XOR)
~	One's complement

All except the last of the operators in Table 2-6 are binary operators. The one's complement operator is a unary operator. You can use these operators with integer expressions only. Bitwise logical operators typically are used to set, clear, invert, and test selected bits in an integer variable. Programmers often use bits as on/off switches in programs. Low-level hardware device driver programs often must manipulate bits in the input/output device registers.

The first three operators in Table 2-6 perform bit mask operations as shown in these examples:

```
result = InputCh & 0x80;  // clear all but most significant bit
newval = CtrlCh & ~0x80;  // clear the most significant bit
mask = KeyChar | 0x80;    // set the most significant bit
newch = oldch ^ 1;        // invert the least significant bit
```

The second example also uses the ~ one's complement operator to convert the 0x80 constant to its one's complement, which is 0x7f. This usage emphasizes the bit that is cleared rather than the bits that are not cleared.

Consider the following example, which shows a typical use for the bitwise AND operator–testing the setting of bits in a field:

```
if (Field & BITMASK)
    // at least one of the bits is set
```

The if statement tests the expression inside the parentheses that follow. If the expression returns a true value, the next statement or statement block executes. Otherwise, it is skipped. Chapter 4 covers the if statement in more detail, but for now the usage demonstrates logical AND in a conditional expression. In this example, the program uses the operator to test whether any of the bits in the BITMASK variable match the contents of the Field variable.

Bitwise Shift Operators

The bitwise shift operators in Table 2-7 shift integer values right and left a specified number of bits. You can use these operators with integer expressions only.

Table 2-7: Bitwise Shift Operators

Symbol	Description
<<	Left shift
>>	Right shift

The shift operators return a value that is equal to the leftmost expression shifted a number of bits equal to the value of the rightmost expression, as shown here:

```
NewFld = OldFld << 3;    // Shift OldFld 3 bits to the left
MyData = YourData >> 2;  // Shift YourData 2 bits to the right
```

In these statements, the field on the left of the assignment receives the shifted value. The variables on the right of the assignment are not shifted themselves. Instead, their values contribute to the expression, which returns a shifted value.

Shifting left inserts zero bits into the low-order bits of the result. Shifting right propagates the most significant bit. This behavior preserves the signed property of an integer.

Programmers often use the shift left operator to multiply integers and the shift right operator to divide integers when the multiplier or divisor is known to be a power of two.

Depending on the compiler (and the computer's math capabilities), replacing multiplies or divides with shifts may result in faster and more compact code. However, with many modern optimizing compilers, there won't be any difference since the compiler will notice the operation could be done more simply and make the appropriate substitution for you. For example, consider this statement:

```
x = y * 10;
```

Of course, 10 is not a power of two. However, you could rewrite this statement as:

```
x = y * 8 + y * 2;
```

Or, using shift operators:

```
x = y << 3 + y << 1;
```

This technique is most useful when you are desperate to make a program run as quickly as possible.

Relational Operators

Relational operators compare two expressions and return a true or false value depending on the relative values of the expressions and the operator. Table 2-8 shows the six relational operators.

Table 2-8: Relational Operators

Symbol	Description
>	Greater than
<	Less than
>=	Greater than or equal to
<=	Less than or equal to
==	Equal to
!=	Not equal to

Relational operators typically are used in conditional expressions for program control flow statements as shown here:

```
while (Counter > 0)  // test Counter for zero
{
    // ...
}
```

Why do you suppose that C++ uses == for equality and = for assignment? Other languages, such as BASIC, use the same = operator for both. The reason is that an assignment statement is an expression that returns a value. The following code is valid:

```
if (Amount = 123)
    // ...
```

The code looks like a test for equality between Amount and the constant value 123, but it is not, because it uses the assignment operator (=) rather than the equality operator (==). The assignment (Amount = 123) is an expression that returns the value 123. The if program flow control statement tests the true/false condition of the expression. This statement always returns a true value because 123, being nonzero, is always true. If the right side of the expression were a variable, then the true/false result of the test would depend on the value in the variable.

The syntax of the two operators and of conditional expressions invites coding errors. New C++ programmers often code the = operator when they mean to code the == operator. The previous statement is a valid statement, but because of the potential for confusion, most compilers issue a warning when they see such a statement. The warning says something like, "Possibly incorrect assignment."

To eliminate warnings and to clarify the code's intentions, most programmers who want to test the result of an assignment for a true/false condition use one of two ways. The first is shown here:

```
Amount = NewAmount;
if (Amount != 0)
    // ...
```

This combination of statements resembles the way you code the assignment and test in programming languages that do not treat assignments as conditional expressions. It is clear and unambiguous. No one misunderstands what the code is doing. Once you are experienced and comfortable with C++, however, you may opt for this format:

```
if ((Amount = NewAmount) != 0)
    // ...
```

This format is more concise than the first one, and many C++ programmers prefer it. The parentheses are important. As you soon learn, the != operator has higher precedence than the = operator. If you omit the parentheses, NewAmount != 0 is evaluated before the assignment, and Amount is assigned the true/false, one/zero result of that test. Without parentheses, the expression works like this one, which has parentheses added to emphasize the default precedence:

```
if (Amount = (NewAmount != 0))
    // ...
```

Chapter 4 includes examples that use relational operators within program control flow statements.

Increment and Decrement Operators

C++ includes several unique operators. Two of them, the ++ increment and -- decrement operators, increment or decrement a variable by the value of 1. Table 2-9 shows these operators.

Table 2-9: Increment and Decrement Operators

Symbol	Description
++	Increment operator
--	Decrement operator

The increment and decrement operators can be placed before (prefix) or after (postfix) the variable that they change, as shown in these examples:

```
--Counter;    // decrement Counter, prefix notation
Quantity--;   // decrement Quantity, postfix notation
++Amount;     // increment Amount, prefix notation
Offset++;     // increment Offset, postfix notation
```

As used here, the prefix and postfix forms of the operators have the same effect. But when they are used as part of a larger expression, the two forms have a different meaning. The prefix operators change the variable before it contributes to the expression, and the postfix operators change it afterward. Program 2-10 demonstrates that behavior.

Program 2-10: Increment and decrement operators

```
#include <iostream>

int main
{
    int Ctr, OldCtr, NewCtr;
    // Make the assignments
    OldCtr = 123;       // OldCtr is 123
    NewCtr = ++OldCtr; // NewCtr is 124, OldCtr is 124
    Ctr = NewCtr--;     // Ctr is 124, NewCtr is 123
    // Display the results
    std::cout << OldCtr;
    std::cout << ' ';
    std::cout << NewCtr;
    std::cout << ' ';
    std::cout << Ctr;
    return 0;
}
```

Program 2-10 declares three integer variables and assigns a value to one of them. Then, the program assigns the value of that variable to one of the other variables by using a prefix increment operator. The variable is incremented, and the incremented value is assigned to the receiving variable. The third assignment uses a postfix decrement operator. The variable on the right side is decremented—but not until after the assignment. The variable on the left side receives the value before the decrement. You can use Quincy's Watch window to observe these effects as they happen. Program 2-10 displays this output on the screen:

```
124 123 124
```

Assignment Operators

It might not be obvious, but the assignment statements you're learning about in this chapter are themselves expressions that return values. C++ has a number of assignment statement formats, all of which are shown in Table 2-10.

Table 2-10: Assignment Operators

Symbol	Description
=	Assignment
+=	Addition assignment

Symbol	Description
-=	Subtraction assignment
*=	Multiplication assignment
/=	Division assignment
%=	Modulus assignment
<<=	Shift left assignment
>>=	Shift right assignment
&=	Bitwise AND assignment
|=	Bitwise OR assignment
^	Bitwise exclusive OR (XOR) assignment

Consider first the garden-variety assignment operator that you have been using until now. Each assignment statement itself returns a value. The value that it returns is the value that is assigned to the variable on the left side of the assignment. That behavior makes possible a widely used C++ idiom that you do not see in other programming languages (except C, of course). This example shows that idiom:

```
FirstTotal = SecondTotal = 0;
```

The effect of this statement is to assign the value zero to both of the variables. Why is this? First, consider the order in which the assignment statements are evaluated. The assignment operator has right-to-left associativity, which means that the expressions are evaluated starting with the rightmost one. This means that SecondTotal = 0 is evaluated first. That expression returns the result of the assignment which, in this case, is zero. When the leftmost expression is evaluated, the zero return from the rightmost expression is assigned to the leftmost variable. It is as if you coded the expression this way:

```
FirstTotal = (SecondTotal = 0);
```

The parentheses are not needed to force the precedence of the rightmost expression over the leftmost expression, because the associativity of the operator takes care of that. Program 2-11 demonstrates this behavior.

Program 2-11: **Assigning assignments**

```
#include <iostream>

int main
{
    unsigned int This, That, Those;
    // Assign the same value to three variables
    This = That = Those = 62440;
    // Display three unsigned ints
    std::cout << This;
```

Continued

Program 2-11 *(continued)*

```
    std::cout << ' ';
    std::cout << That;
    std::cout << ' ';
    std::cout << Those;
    return 0;
}
```

The assignment statement in Program 2-11 assigns the same value to all three `unsigned int` variables and displays this output on the screen:

```
62440 62440 62440
```

Can you see why the following multiple assignment expression does not work?

```
(FirstTotal = SecondTotal) = 0;
```

C++ compilers report an error if you try to code an expression such as this one. The reason is that the leftmost expression, `(FirstTotal = SecondTotal)`, is not an *lvalue* and does not represent a variable that the program can modify. This expression is an *rvalue*—the value of an assignment—which would be whatever is in `SecondTotal` before the statement executes. You cannot assign a value to such an expression. An assignment expression is an *rvalue* and cannot appear on the left side of another assignment operator.

Compound Assignment Operators

The other assignment operators in Table 2-10 are unique to the C and C++ languages. Called compound assignment operators, they are a form of shorthand that provides a more concise way to modify a variable. Consider this simple assignment statement usage, which is common to most programming languages:

```
Total = Total + 3;
```

This statement assigns a value to a variable where the value is the result of an expression that includes the variable itself. C++ includes a set of compound assignment operators that do the same thing. The previous statement can be coded this way instead:

```
Total += 3;
```

Each of the other compound assignment operators in Table 2-10 has a similar effect on the variable. Program 2-12 demonstrates compound assignment.

Program 2-12: Compound assignments

```
#include <iostream>

int main
{
    long Total, SubTotal, Detail;
```

```
    // Initial values
    Total = 10000;
    SubTotal = 90;
    Detail = 5;
    SubTotal *= Detail;        // compute SubTotal
    Total += SubTotal;         // compute Total
    // Display all three
    std::cout << Total;
    std::cout << ' ';
    std::cout << SubTotal;
    std::cout << ' ';
    std::cout << Detail;
    return 0;
}
```

Program 2-12 displays this output on the screen:

```
10450 450 5
```

There is one significant difference between simple and compound assignment. In a simple assignment, such as A = A + 1, the A expression is evaluated twice; in a compound assignment, such as A += 1, the A expression is evaluated once. Usually, this difference has no effect on the operation of the program, but if the expression de-references an address returned from a function, the function is called twice. Most C++ programmers intuitively avoid those kinds of side effects. It may not make sense just yet, but put a bookmark in this place. After you learn about functions (Chapter 3) and pointers (Chapter 8), you may want to return here and reread this note.

The Conditional Operator

The conditional operator (?:) tests an expression and returns the result of one of two other expressions depending on the true/false value of the first. The operator takes this form:

```
<expression1> ? <expression2> : <expression3>
```

The evaluation tests the first expression. If that value is true, the resulting value is that of the second expression and otherwise, the resulting value is that of the third expression. Program 2-13 demonstrates the conditional operator with a simple algorithm that computes the penalty for overdue dues at 10 percent.

Program 2-13: **The conditional operator**

```
#include <iostream>

int main()
{
    float Dues;        // dues amount
    // Read the dues.
    std::cout << "Enter dues amount: ";
    std::cin >> Dues;
```

Continued

Program 2-13 *(continued)*

```
    // Are the dues paid on time?
    std::cout << "On time? (y/n) ";
    char yn;
    std::cin >> yn;
    bool Overdue;   // true if overdue, false if on time
    Overdue = yn != 'y';
    float AmountDue; // amount to be computed
    // Use conditional operator to compute.
    AmountDue = Overdue ? Dues * 1.10 : Dues;
    // Display the dues amount.
    std::cout << "Amount due: ";
    std::cout << AmountDue;
    return 0;
}
```

Observe the declaration of the char yn variable in Program 2-13. If you are a C programmer, you might think there is an error in this code. In C, all declarations in a brace-surrounded statement block must appear before all executable statements in the block—yet there are several executable statements ahead of the char yn declaration. In C++, a declaration can appear anywhere in the block as long as the item is declared before any other statements refer to it.

When you run Program 2-13, the program displays the following messages. The 35.50 is the amount you enter as dues. The n following the On time? (y/n) message is the response you type to the question. You can try the program with different dues amounts and different responses to the question.

```
Enter dues amount: 35.50
On time? (y/n) n
Amount due: 39.05
```

The conditional operator is a shorthand form of the traditional if-then-else program flow control operation. The preceding expression can be performed this way, as well:

```
if (OverDue)
    AmountDue = Dues * 1.10;
else
    AmountDue = Dues;
```

It also can be performed this way:

```
AmountDue = Dues;
if (OverDue)
    AmountDue *= 1.10;
```

And this way:

```
AmountDue = Dues;
if (OverDue)
    AmountDue += AmountDue * 0.10;
```

And so on. As you can see, C++ is not only the language of choice but also a language of choices.

Comma Operator

In C and C++, expressions can be separated by commas. Each comma-separated expression is evaluated, and the value returned from the group is the value of the rightmost expression. Program 2-14 is an example of this behavior.

Program 2-14: **Comma-separated expressions**

```
#include <iostream>

int main
{
    int Val, Amt, Tot, Cnt;
    Amt = 30;
    Tot = 12;
    Cnt = 46;
    // Compute Val = rightmost expression
    Val = (Amt++, --Tot, Cnt+3);
    // Display the result
    std::cout << Val;
    return 0;
}
```

Program 2-14 displays the value 49 on the screen, which is the value returned by the comma-separated expression.

Without the parentheses, Val is assigned the value in Amt before the increment. This is because the assignment operator has higher precedence than the comma operator. You learn just what that means in the next section.

Precedence and Associativity

Operators have two important properties: their *precedence* and their *associativity* (also called *order of evaluation*). These properties affect the results of an expression that contains more than one operator or that might produce side effects. They determine when and if each inner expression in an outer expression is evaluated. Table 2-11 shows the precedence and order of evaluation of the operators in the C++ language.

Table 2-11: Operator Precedence and Order of Evaluation

Precedence	Operators	Associativity
(Highest)	() []-> .	Left-right
	! ~ ++-- +- * & (type) sizeof	Right-left
	* / %	Left-right

Continued

Table 2-11 *(continued)*

Precedence	Operators	Associativity
	+ -	Left-right
	<< >>	Left-right
	< <= > >=	Left-right
	== !=	Left-right
	&	Left-right
	^	Left-right
	|	Left-right
	&&	Left-right
	||	Left-right
	?:	Right-left
	= += -= *= /= %= &= ^= |= <<= >>=	Right-left
(Lowest)	,	Left-right

The + and - operators in the second entry of Table 2-11 are the unary plus and minus operators. The ones in the fourth entry are the binary addition and subtraction operators.

The first two entries list some operators that you haven't learned yet. The first entry includes the parentheses operators for function calls—discussed in Chapter 3 and not to be confused with precedence-overriding parentheses—and array subscripts (Chapter 7) and structure members (Chapter 6). The second entry includes the * pointer operator, the & address-of operator, typecast notation, and the `sizeof` operator—all discussed in Chapters 7 and 8.

The operators in Table 2-11 are the ones that C++ shares with C. C++ adds several operators of its own: the `::` scope resolution operator, the `new` and `delete` memory allocation operators, and several typecasting operators. You learn about them in later chapters.

Associativity

Operators at the same level in Table 2-11 have equal precedence. The expressions affected by the operators are evaluated in the order specified in the associativity column of Table 2-11. For example, consider this expression:

```
Total = Price - Discount + SurCharge;
```

The binary minus (-) and plus (+) operators have equal precedence, and they have higher precedence than the assignment (=) operator. Therefore, the order of evaluation proceeds left to right starting with the + and - operators according to their associativity. The evaluation computes the value `Price - Discount`, adds `SurCharge` to that value, and assigns the value to `Total`, which sounds like a reasonable computation.

Suppose, however, that you want to subtract the sum of `Discount` and `SurCharge` from `Price`. The calculation just shown cannot work because of the associativity of the operators. You need to override the associativity and force the `Discount + SurCharge` expression to be evaluated first. You do this by putting parentheses around the expression:

```
Total = Price - (Discount + SurCharge);
```

Precedence

Similarly, there are times when the default precedence of operators does not produce the desired result. Consider this expression:

```
Total = Price - Discount * SalesTax;
```

The multiplication operator has higher precedence than the subtraction operator does. And, as a result, the expression evaluates `Discount * SalesTax` first and then evaluates the expression where the result from the multiplication is subtracted from `Price`. This is probably not what you want. Generally, you want to compute `Price - Discount` first and then multiply that result by the `SalesTax` rate. To do that, you override the expression's default precedence by using parentheses, just as you do to override associativity. Here is the same expression corrected to produce the desired result:

```
Total = (Price - Discount) * Tax;
```

When an Expression Is Not Evaluated

The `&&` and `||` operators evaluate the expressions starting with the leftmost one. As soon as the truth of the total expression is guaranteed, expression evaluation stops. This means that expressions with side effects might not be evaluated, and the side effects might not be realized. Consider this example:

```
if (MoreData() || MoreTime())
    // ...
```

If the `MoreData()` function call returns a true value, the full expression is assumed to be true, and it is not necessary to call the `MoreTime()` function. If the `MoreTime()` function takes some action that other parts of the program depend on, that action — also known as a "side effect" — does not get taken. Here's another example:

```
while (--aCounter && --bCounter)
    // ...
```

If the decrement of `aCounter` produces a zero result, the full expression is assumed to be false and the balance of the expression is not evaluated. This means that `bCounter` is not decremented.

The conditional operator (`?:`) behaves in a similar fashion, as shown in this example:

```
Amount = FirstTime ? InitialAmount++ : RunningAmount++;
```

Only one of the second two expressions is evaluated, depending on the `true`/`false` value of the first. This means that when `FirstTime` is `true`, only `InitialAmount` is incremented; and when `FirstTime` is `false`, only `RunningAmount` is incremented.

Initializers

Declaration of a variable does not put any data into the variable. The exercises so far have placed assignment statements after the declarations to provide initial data values. You can, however, initialize variables with data by providing an initializer as part of the declaration. Program 2-15 demonstrates three different variable initializers.

Program 2-15: Initializers

```
#include <iostream>

int main
{
    int Amount = 3;     // initialize an int
    char ch = 'A';      // initialize a char
    float Value = 1.23; // initialize a float
    // Display the initialized variables
    std::cout << Amount;
    std::cout << ' ';
    std::cout << ch;
    std::cout << ' ';
    std::cout << Value;
    return 0;
}
```

Usually, a variable is initialized each time the declaration is executed. Program 2-15 initializes the three variables immediately after the main function begins execution. Variables that are declared inside other functions and statement blocks are initialized every time the function or statement block begins execution. An exception is the static local variable, which is initialized the first time it is declared and never again. You learn more about functions and statement blocks in Chapter 3 and about static variables in Chapter 5.

Program 2-15 displays this message on the screen:

```
3 A 1.23
```

An initializer takes the form of an assignment statement, with the declaration on the left and an expression on the right. If the variable is global or static, the initializing expression must be a constant value. In other words, it cannot contain any function calls, references to other variables, or increment and decrement operators. It can contain multiple constants and operators, but that's all. Local variables — the kind you've been using until now — can contain any expression as their initializers.

There are two formats for coding initializers in C++. Program 2-15 demonstrates the format that C++ and C initializers use. The assignments in Program 2-15 can be coded with the alternative C++ initializer syntax as shown here:

```
int Amount(3);      // initialize an int
char ch('A');       // initialize a char
float Value(1.23);  // initialize a float
```

The alternative initializer syntax reflects the syntax with which a class object declaration calls a class constructor function with initializer values. You learn about class constructors in Chapter 15.

Type Conversion

The various numeric types — characters, integers, long integers, and floating-point numbers — have different ranges of values because of their sizes and their signed and unsigned properties. But, what happens when you use them interchangeably? What happens if you assign a long int variable to a char variable, for example? Or vice versa?

C++ applies certain rules of type conversion in these cases. Numeric types are interchangeable within certain limits. If you assign a variable of a smaller type to one of a larger type, the value is promoted to that larger type and no information is lost. If you assign a variable of a larger type to one of a smaller type, the value is demoted; and if the larger value is greater than the smaller type can contain, the demotion includes truncation of the excess data. Some compilers warn you when this can happen unless you use a typecast (Chapter 7) to tell the compiler that you know about it in advance. Program 2-16 illustrates several type conversions in action.

Program 2-16: **Type conversions**

```
#include <iostream>

int main
{
    // Three uninitialized variables, different types.
    char myChar;
    short int myInt;
    long myLong;
    // An initialized variable of yet another type.
    float myFloat = 7e4;
    // Assign and convert.
    myChar = myInt = myLong = myFloat;
    // Display the variables.
    std::cout << myChar;
    std::cout << ' ';
    std::cout << myInt;
    std::cout << ' ';
    std::cout << myLong;
    std::cout << ' ';
    std::cout << myFloat;
    return 0;
}
```

When you compile Program 2-16, the compiler issues this warning message, which alerts you that some data can be lost in the conversion in the assignment statement on source-code line 12:

```
pr02016.cpp:20: warning: assignment to 'long int' from 'float'
```

Program 2-16 displays this message on the screen:

```
p 4464 70000 70000
```

The myInt variable reflects the lost data when a long int variable with a value greater than can be held in 16 bits is assigned to a short int variable. The long int variable myLong loses no data when the float variable is assigned to it, because a long can hold the value represented by 7e4 — which is 7 times 10 raised to the 4th power, or 70000.

Console Input and Output

You have been using std::cin and std::cout in the exercises in this chapter. They usually read text from the keyboard and write text to the screen in Standard C++ programs, although they can be redirected from the command line to read and write files or to read the standard output from other programs and write to the standard input of other programs via pipes (Chapter 13). If you write a program that you intend to be portable, you probably should use std::cin and std::cout extensively, because they are the lowest common denominator for standard input/output across all implementations of the C++ language on all computers.

Many commercial C++ programs never use std::cin and std::cout. They use screen and keyboard libraries associated with the user interfaces of the system on which the program is to run: Windows, X-Windows, Macintosh, and so on. You might rarely use std::cin and std::cout again after finishing this book, although many small utility programs run from the command line and do not use exotic user interfaces.

This section introduces console input/output because you need to know how to read the keyboard and write the screen in order to use the exercises in this book that teach other parts of the C++ language.

The Standard Output Stream

Our use of std::cout has been primitive until now. We used one statement for every item that we wanted to display. But std::cout is more powerful than that, providing shortcuts that enable us to achieve the same effect with fewer lines of code. Look back at Program 2-15 and note how Program 2-17 gets the same result with less code.

Program 2-17: **Improved std::cout usage**

```
#include <iostream>

int main
{
    int Amount = 3;      // initialize an int
    char ch = 'A';       // initialize a char
```

```
    float Value = 1.23; // initialize a float
    // Display the initialized variables
    std::cout << Amount << ' ' << ch << ' ' << Value
              << std::endl;
    return 0;
}
```

Program 2-17 connects several data types with the << operator. The output is the same as that of Program 2-15. This behavior is a by-product of the C++ this pointer and the overloaded << operator for std::ostream objects. Both topics get full treatment later in the book. For now, don't worry about exactly how these things work; accept their behavior as this chapter describes it and forge ahead.

Observe that Program 2-17 sends an object named std::endl to the std::cout object at the end of the other transmissions. The std::endl object is the first of a set of *manipulators* that you learn about later in the book. The std::endl manipulator represents an *end-of-line* character. Sending it to an output stream usually is the same as sending a newline character, like this:

```
std::cout << '\n';
```

The difference between sending std::endl and the newline character is that the std::endl manipulator flushes the output stream after sending a newline character, whereas the newline character alone does not. This behavior makes a difference with some compilers and makes no difference with others. (Eventually, when all compilers comply with the standard, maybe their stream libraries all will work the same. Standard C++ leaves a lot of decisions to the compiler implementor.) This book uses std::endl in most of its example programs instead of the newline character to ensure that the message displays on the console when you expect it to irrespective of which compiler you use.

Formatted Output: Manipulators

Suppose you want to display the hexadecimal representation of an integer variable instead of its decimal value. The iostream class system associates a set of manipulators with the output stream. These manipulators change the displayed numerical base for integer arguments. You insert the manipulators into the stream to make the change. There are three such manipulators. Their symbolic values are std::dec, std::oct, and std::hex. Program 2-18 uses manipulators to display an integer in three numerical base representations.

Program 2-18: **Formatting numerical data**

```
#include <iostream>

int main
{
    int amount = 123;
    std::cout << std::dec << amount << ' '
              << std::oct << amount << ' '
              << std::hex << amount;
    return 0;
}
```

The exercise inserts the manipulators std::dec, std::oct, and std::hex into the stream to convert the value that follows — amount — into different numerical base representations. Program 2-18 displays the following result:

```
123 173 7b
```

Each of the values shown is the decimal value 123 in a different base representation.

The concept of sending so-called manipulators to a device might be alien to programmers who are more familiar with other languages. In BASIC, for example, all the data objects that you code after a PRINT statement get displayed. In C++, however, each console device is implemented as an object. The object reacts to the data you send it according to the data types. Manipulators are themselves data objects of a unique type defined within the iostream class system. When you send a manipulator to a stream object, the object uses the appearance of the manipulator to modify the console object's behavior for the next data object; in this case, the behavior to be modified is the format of the data to be displayed.

As you proceed through the exercises in later chapters, the programs use manipulators to control the display of their output. Whenever a new manipulator shows up, the discussion surrounding the exercise explains the manipulator.

The Standard Error Stream

The std::cerr object uses the same syntax as std::cout, except that std::cerr's output goes to the standard error device. This technique enables you to display error messages on the system console even when the program's user redirects the standard output device to a file or another program.

The Standard Input Stream

By using std::cout and std::cerr, you can display all types of data on the screen. You must also be able to read data into your programs. The iostream version of standard input is implemented with the std::cin object, which you learned about earlier in this chapter. Program 2-19 uses std::cin to read an integer from the keyboard.

Program 2-19: **The standard input stream**

```cpp
#include <iostream>

int main
{
    short int amount;
    std::cout << "Enter an amount...";
    std::cin >> amount;
    std::cout << "The amount you entered was " << amount;
    return 0;
}
```

Program 2-19 sends a string to `std::cout` to prompt you for input. The `std::cin` device writes the value into the `amount` integer variable. The program then displays the `amount` variable on `std::cout` to demonstrate that the `std::cin` operation worked. Program 2-19 displays the following messages. (The first three digits 123 are the value that you type into the program. It could be any digits that make up an integer value.)

```
Enter an amount...123
The amount you entered was 123
```

Suppose that you use this program in a system with a 16-bit short integer (Quincy, for example). If you enter the value 65535, the program displays -1. If you enter 65536, the program displays 0. These displays occur because the `amount` variable is a `signed` integer. Change the `amount` variable's type to an `unsigned` integer and retry the program. For another experiment, see what happens when you enter a value with a decimal point and digits to the right of the decimal point.

Try entering alphabetic characters instead of numbers. It doesn't work. The `std::cin` device is able to work with strings—character arrays, actually—as well as with numbers, but you must use the correct data type in the expression. To illustrate, Program 2-20 uses the `std::cin` device to read a string value from the keyboard into a character array.

Program 2-20: **Reading a string**

```cpp
#include <iostream>

int main
{
    char name[20];
    std::cout << "Enter a name...";
    std::cin >> name;
    std::cout << "The name you entered was " << name
              << std::endl;
    return 0;
}
```

Program 2-20 displays the following messages. (The name Tyler is used here for the name that you type into the program.)

```
Enter a name...Tyler
The name you entered was Tyler
```

Program 2-20 has a flaw: The character array is only 20 characters long. If you type too many characters, the program overwrites whatever follows the name array in the computer's memory, and peculiar things happen. An `iostream` function named `std::get()` solves this problem; you learn about `std::get()` in Part III. For now, the example programs assume that you do not type more characters than the declared character array can accept.

Some Things to Consider

The `std::cin`, `std::cout`, `std::cerr`, and `std::endl` objects are not themselves a part of the compiled C++ language. They are defined as part of Standard C++, but they are not intrinsic language components. Binary plus (+) and minus (-) are examples of intrinsic operators. C++ has no intrinsic input/output operators that coincide with BASIC's `PRINT` statement or COBOL's `WRITE` verb. The stream classes are not built-in data types, and the << and >> operators are not, in this context, built-in C++ operators. Input and output streams are implemented as C++ classes, and `std::cin` and `std::cout` are instances of those classes. This implementation exists outside the C++ language implementation. C++ allows you to define new data types and to associate custom operators with those data types, and that's what the designers of the `iostream` facility did to provide a standard console input/output system. This is a significant lesson. You learn how to do this for your own data types in later chapters.

Summary

In this chapter, you learned that a C++ program consists of functions and variables. You learned about including header files and putting comments in your program. You also learned the C++ data types, how to declare variables of those data types, and how to assign values to them. You learned about C++ constants, expressions, operators, and initializers. Finally, you discovered how to display data on the screen by using cout and how to read data from the keyboard into memory variables by using cin.

In the next chapter, you get a close look at functions and how you use them in your programs. You'll study such topics as arguments, prototypes, return types, identifier scope, inline functions, recursion, linkage specifications, and much more.

✦   ✦   ✦

Functions

This chapter describes C++ functions, the building blocks of a C++ program. Functions hold the executable code of a program. The entry and exit points of most C++ programs are in the main function except when a program terminates as a result of an unexpected, uncaught exception (Chapter 35) or explicitly calls a standard program terminating function such as std::exit (Chapter 26). The main function calls other functions, each of which returns to the main function. Those other functions may — and probably do — call lower-level functions. Calling a function executes the function immediately. The calling function suspends operation until the called one returns. Functions can accept arguments, as well as provide return values to their caller.

Programmers learn to think of lower-level functions as trustworthy *black-box* operations that do their jobs without the programmers having to know the details of how those jobs are done. All the standard library functions are in this category. Programmers also develop and acquire function libraries to serve in this capacity. When you study full-length programs, you seldom see the majority of the source code that contributes to the whole of the program since a great deal of it will likely be in library functions that are not written by the programmer.

The Function

A function has a function header and a statement body. The function header has three parts:

✦ A return type

✦ A name

✦ A parameter list

The return value is a C++ data type (one of the data types from Chapter 2), a pointer to one of the data types, a pointer to a structure, or a pointer to an array. You learn about pointers, structures, and arrays in Chapters 6, 7, and 8.

The function's name is unique within the program when qualified with its namespace, although for now your program function names will all be in the global namespace. Chapter 36 explains namespaces in detail. The function's name obeys the rules for identifier naming as discussed in Chapter 2. The parameter list consists of zero or more variables into which the caller's arguments are copied. The statement body holds the local variable declarations and executable code for the function. All the programs in Chapter 2 have `main` functions. None of them declare other functions, which is the subject of this chapter.

Remember the main

C++ programs usually require a `main` function. The Standard C++ definition says that programs developed for "standalone" platforms (embedded systems, for example) do not need a `main` function, and, for another example, programs developed for the Windows platform using the Win32 API use `WinMain` as their entry point, whereas programs developed with the Microsoft Foundation Classes library are entered at the `InitInstance` member function of the program's class derived from the library's `WinApp` class. These platforms have a `main` function, but it is hidden from the programmer and buried in the runtime library.

This book is mostly platform-independent, however, and we stick with `main` according to the convention for console applications.

The system declares `main`, and your program defines it. The `main` function returns an `int` data type and can accept two arguments.

The `main` function has two default parameters—an `int` and a pointer to an array of `char` pointers—yet the `main` functions in Chapter 2 have empty parameter lists. You learn about `main`'s default parameters in Chapter 13; but, for now, you should know that `main` is permitted to have a parameter list when arguments are, in fact, passed to it (these arguments usually reflect command-line arguments). Other functions are required to adhere to their declarations, but `main` is exempt from this rule.

Your program never calls the `main` function. Doing so is illegal, according to the ANSI /ISO C++ Standard. The system's startup procedure calls `main` to begin running the program. When `main` returns, the system shutdown procedures take over. You don't have to worry about the startup and shutdown procedures. The compiler provides them when you compile and link the program. However, by convention, when the program terminates successfully, it should return an integer with a zero value. Other values are implementation-dependent, although the value -1 usually represents unsuccessful completion of the program. Operating systems often use shell programs that execute applications programs from a batch command file and include batch operators to respond to the return values from applications programs. The MS-DOS command-line processor is one such shell program, and Unix has several.

To get you into the habit of returning values from `main`, all example programs in this book declare `main` with an `int` return value and return something, usually zero, as shown here:

```
int main
{
    // ...
    return 0;  // successful completion
}
```

You learn other ways to use the `return` statement later in this chapter.

Arguments Versus Parameters

The caller of a function passes expressions to the function as *arguments*. The apparently interchangeable terms *argument* and *parameter* appear frequently in discussions about the values passed. Here is the difference. A function has *parameters*, which are the variables into which the values passed are copied before the function begins executing. The function proto-type declares the parameter types in its parameter list. The caller of a function passes arguments, which are the values returned from expressions to be copied into the function's parameter variables. So when you call a function, you provide arguments. The function accesses these arguments using its parameters.

Declaring Functions by Using Prototypes

To call a function, you must declare the function first with respect to its return and parameter types. Standard C++ has strong type checking built into the language definition. Before you can call a function, you must tell the compiler the types of the function's parameters and return value. The declaration of a function is called its *prototype*. Here are examples of function prototypes:

```
unsigned int BuildRecord(char, int);
void GetRecord(char, int, int);
int isMonday(void);
void DoList(int, ...);
```

Unnamed Parameter Types

Observe that the parameter lists in the prototypes contain type specifications with no identifiers for the parameters. You can put parameter identifiers into prototypes, but the identifiers serve as documentation only. They need not correspond to the same identifiers in the function definition's parameter list. Some programmers prefer to omit the identifiers. Others prefer to assign meaningful parameter identifiers in the prototype to convey the meanings of the parameters to other programmers who read the prototype as shown here:

```
int GetStatus(int mode);
```

A Typical Prototype

Here is a typical prototype:

```
unsigned int BuildRecord(char, int);
```

This first prototype declares a function named BuildRecord with two parameters in its parameter list: a char argument and an int argument. The function returns an unsigned int value. You can see from this example why some programmers prefer to supply identifiers for prototype parameters. Nothing in the prototype just shown gives a clue as to the purpose of the parameters. A more descriptive (and less terse) prototype of the same function looks like this:

```
unsigned int BuildRecord(char RecordCode, int RecordNumber);
```

Functions Returning void

```
void GetRecord(char, int, int);
```

This prototype declares a function named GetRecord with three parameters of types char, int, and int. (This one is even more obscure than the previous one. Even if you remember the purposes of the parameters, you might easily forget which int comes first.) The void return type means that the function returns nothing. A void function cannot return a value, and you cannot call it in the context of an expression where it is expected to return a value. For example, you cannot call a `void` function from the right side of an assignment statement or as an argument in a function call. This statement would be illegal given the `GetRecord` prototype just shown because `GetRecord` returns `void`.

```
int rcd = GetRecord('a', 1, 2); // Error!
```

Functions with No Parameters

```
bool isMonday();
```

This prototype defines a function with no parameters. The empty parameter list identifies it as such. You cannot pass arguments to a function with an empty parameter list. You must assume that functions that accept no arguments get the data that they work on from external sources instead of from arguments passed by the caller. This function, for example, might return `true` or `false` if the current date (obtained from one of the Standard C++ Library date functions) falls on a Monday.

Functions with Variable Parameter Lists

```
void DoList(int, ...);
```

This prototype contains one integer parameter type and the ellipsis (. . .) token. The ellipsis identifies a function that accepts a variable number of arguments with unspecified types. The Standard C library `printf` and `scanf` functions are defined as accepting a variable number of arguments. That is how they can accept different numbers and types of arguments that match their formatting strings. Functions with variable argument lists require special handling, which Chapter 26 describes in the discussion about <cstdarg>.

Functions Returning Nothing and with No Parameters

```
void DoSomething();
```

What is the purpose of a function that takes no arguments and returns no value? In fact, many functions do just that. They apparently have no input and no output. They perform some task, perhaps using data taken from external sources or maintained internally, and post their results externally. All functions have some effect; otherwise, there is no reason to call them. The caller can invoke the function and not benefit directly from its execution, except when the caller uses an external data item that the called function modifies. An example is a `Beep` function that sounds an audible alarm to alert the user. It needs no parameters and has nothing meaningful to return that a caller can use. Its purpose is singular, and its effect is unaltered by external influences. There are many similar examples.

Standard Library Prototypes

The prototypes for all the standard library classes and functions are in their respective header files. That is why you need to include <iostream>, for example, before you can use `std::cin`, `std::cout`, `std::cerr`, or any of the other Standard Library classes, functions, and objects.

Functions Without Prototypes

You need not code a prototype when the function definition itself appears in the code ahead of any call to it — in which case the function definition serves as its own prototype. To preserve the top-down representation of a program's execution, many programmers do not take advantage of this feature. They put prototypes at the beginning of the program and always make the `main` function the first function defined in the program. Besides, using a separate prototype allows you to place the prototypes in a header file (just like the system-defined library does). That way, multiple files can use the exact same function prototypes and changes only require you to modify one file.

Defining and Calling Functions

You define a function when you write the code for its function header and statement body. All of the Programs so far have defined one function — the `main` function. When a function has a prototype, the function definition must match the prototype exactly with respect to the types of its return value and parameters. Program 3-1 defines and calls a function that displays a message on the screen.

Program 3-1: **Defining a function**

```
#include <iostream>

// Function prototype.
void ErrorMsg();

int main
{
    // Call the function.
    ErrorMsg();
    return 0;
}

void ErrorMsg()
{
    std::cout << "\aError!";
}
```

Program 3-1 declares a function named `ErrorMsg` in a function prototype. The `ErrorMsg` function returns nothing and accepts no arguments. The `main` function calls the `ErrorMsg` function. The `ErrorMsg` function uses `std::cout` to sound the audible alarm and display the message `"Error!"` on the screen. (The `\a` escape sequence sounds the alarm.)

Returning from Functions

A function stops executing in one of several ways. One way, as discussed in Chapter 26, is by calling the standard `std::exit` function, which terminates both the calling function and the program. A function can terminate by falling through the bottom of its definition, as the `ErrorMsg` function in Program 3-1 does. A function that terminates that way must be declared as returning `void`, because falling through the bottom returns no value. A function can execute the `return` statement from within its body. The `main` function in Program 3-1 executes `return` with a value. A `void`-returning function can use the `return` statement with no value. You can code the `ErrorMsg` function in Program 3-1 this way:

```cpp
void ErrorMsg()
{
    std::cout << "\aError!";
    return;   // return from the function
}
```

The `return` statement can appear anywhere in the function body, as illustrated by Program 3-2.

Program 3-2: **Returning with the return statement**

```cpp
#include <iostream>

void DecideWhen();  // Function prototype

int main
{
    DecideWhen();
    return 0;
}

void DecideWhen()
{
    int when;
    std::cout << "When to return (0 = now, 1 = later): ";
    std::cin >> when;
    if (when == 0)  {
        std::cout << "Returning now";
        return;    // return from inside the function
    }
    std::cout << "Returning later";
    return;         // traditional return at the bottom
}
```

Program 3-2 prompts you to enter 0 or 1. Depending on your entry, the program displays a message and returns. Observe that if you enter values other than 0 and 1, the program's behavior is unpredictable. This is a result of the way `std::cin` works. The program shows that you can return from anywhere in a function by using the `return` statement. Here are the messages that Program 3-2 returns when you enter 0 — and then run the program again and enter 1:

```
When to return (0 = now, 1 = later): 0
Returning now

When to return (0 = now, 1 = later): 1
Returning later
```

Some programming theorists contend that returning from anywhere except at the end of a function is one of several "improper" programming practices. C++ permits the usage, and many programmers, including myself, find it useful on occasion. There are, however, good reasons for this deprecation of what is a fairly common programming practice. If you always return from the last statement of a function, then you never need to search a function to see under what circumstances it returns. As with all choices in C++, use what works best for you.

Program 3-2 introduces a new construct: the nested, brace-enclosed statement block. The `if` statement's condition is followed by a left-brace character, which starts a statement block. The matching right-brace character three lines later closes the statement block. The block contains the statements that execute if the condition tested by the `if` statement is true. A program can return from inside a nested statement block, as the example demonstrates.

Returning Values from Functions

Functions that return values do so in their `return` statement. Both preceding examples in this chapter return a zero value `int` from their `main` functions. Functions that you define in your programs also can return values. The prototype declares the return value, as Program 3-3 shows.

Program 3-3: **Returning a value**

```cpp
#include <iostream>

int WidthInInches();  // prototype

int main
{
    // Call a function that returns a value.
    int wd = WidthInInches();
    // Display the returned value.
    std::cout << "Width in inches = " << wd;
    return 0;
}

int WidthInInches()
{
    int feet;
    std::cout << "Enter width in feet: ";
    std::cin >> feet;
    return feet * 12;
}
```

Program 3-3 displays this prompt and then the following message. The value displayed is the value returned from the `WidthInInches` function.

```
Enter width in feet: 37
Width in inches = 444
```

Ignoring Return Values

What happens when you call a value-returning function in a context in which no value is expected — in which you do not use the return value, do not assign it to anything, nor use it as an argument to another function? Nothing unusual happens. The function executes, and it dutifully returns its value. But the caller can choose to ignore it.

Passing and Using Arguments

The WidthInInches function in Program 3-3 functionally is not strong. It has multiple purposes. Sound program design principles call for the definition of functions, each of which has one specific task. The WidthInInches function performs two related, but independent, tasks. First, it reads the width in feet from the keyboard, and then it uses that value to compute the width in inches. A stronger design can break these tasks into separate functions. Then, other parts of the program independently can retrieve widths in feet and compute widths in inches without necessarily doing them both at the same time.

Strengthening Program 3-3 involves dividing the weak function into two stronger functions. One of the two functions illustrates how you pass arguments to functions, which is the point of this lesson. Program 3-4 is the program from Program 3-3, improved and strengthened.

Program 3-4: **Function arguments**

```cpp
#include <iostream>

// Prototypes
int WidthInFeet();
int WidthInInches(int feet);

int main
{
    // Initialize variables by calling functions.
    int feet = WidthInFeet();
    int wd = WidthInInches(feet);
    // Display results.
    std::cout << "Width in inches = " << wd;
    return 0;
}

int WidthInFeet()
{
    int feet;
    std::cout << "Enter width in feet: ";
    std::cin >> feet;
    return feet;
}
```

```
int WidthInInches(int feet)
{
    return feet * 12;
}
```

Ignore everything else that Program 3-4 does for the moment, except that it declares the WidthInInches function differently than Program 3-3 does. The prototype specifies in the parameter list that the function expects an int argument. The main function calls WidthInInches and passes an int variable argument named feet. The program defines WidthInInches to match the prototype with respect to the return type and parameter type, but the parameter list must assign an identifier to the parameter. This parameter, also named feet, is a local variable in the WidthInInches function. The function call copies the value of the argument into this variable. The return statement uses the feet variable in an expression to compute the return value. The declaration, call, and definition of functions that have parameters are the main lessons that Program 3-4 teaches. The program displays the same messages that Program 3-3 displays.

The Scope of Identifiers

Program 3-4 teaches other lessons in addition to the passing of arguments. First, observe that the main, WidthInFeet, and WidthInInches functions all have integer variables named feet. This is correct, because C++ supports variables with local scope. As long as an identifier is declared inside a statement block surrounded by curly braces, that identifier is visible only to the statements in that and lower blocks. Identical identifiers in other blocks outside the function are distinct from the local one. Identical identifiers in higher blocks in the hierarchy are effectively overridden by the lower declaration until the identifier goes out of scope. You learn more about the scope of identifiers in Chapter 5. The parameter variables declared in a function header are also local to the function, which is why the WidthInInches function can name its parameter feet.

Initializing with Function Calls

The declarations of the feet and wd variables in main have initializers obtained from calls to the WidthInFeet and WidthInInches functions. So far, you have seen initializers that contain constant expressions only. Initializers of automatic variables, such as these two variables, can contain any kind of expression that returns a value, including a call to a function. You learn about automatic variables in Chapter 5.

The Sequence of Initializer Execution

Another lesson in Program 3-4 is that the second initializer uses the first initialized variable as an argument to the function that the second initializer calls. This tells us that initializers are executed in the top-down order in which they occur in the program.

Passing Several Arguments

Some functions accept more than one argument. For example, a function that computes the volume of a brick-shaped object needs to know the height, width, and depth of the object. Program 3-5 is an example of a function with several parameters.

Program 3-5: **Functions with multiple parameters**

```
#include <iostream>

// Prototype
double Volume(double, double, long);

int main
{
    float ht, wd;
    long int dp;
    // Get the brick's dimensions
    std::cout <<
        "Enter height (x.xx), width (x.xx), depth (x): ";
    std::cin >> ht >> wd >> dp;
    // Compute and display the volume
    // calling a function with many arguments.
    std::cout << "Volume = " << Volume(ht, wd, dp);
    return 0;
}

double Volume(double height, double width, long depth)
{
    return height * width * depth;
}
```

Program 3-5 displays this message in response to your input:

```
Enter height (x.xx), width (x.xx), depth (x): 1.5 2.2 7
Volume = 23.1
```

Function Calls as Arguments

As with many example programs in this book, Program 3-5 teaches another lesson in addition to its principal one. This time, the call to the Volume function is coded as an argument to std::cout's << operator. It is perfectly acceptable to use a function call in the context of an expression that returns what the function returns. A more traditional programming language requires a temporary variable, an assignment, and the temporary variable passed as the argument. You can write C++ programs using that convention — as shown next — but most programmers prefer the more concise code used in Program 3-5.

```
double temp;    // temporary variable
temp = Volume(ht, wd, dp);
cout << "Volume = " << temp;
```

Note that this version of the code is a little easier to read than the previous version. C++ offers many coding tricks — such as using a function call as an argument — which can make program code extremely concise. However, this conciseness often comes at the expense of readability. As you develop your C++ coding style, you need to balance conciseness with readability.

Pass by Value

C++ programs pass their arguments to functions *by value* as opposed to *by reference*. This means that a function gets a copy of the argument in its matching parameter. Sometimes, as in the case of large structures, passing by value is inefficient, and you may prefer to pass a reference to the argument rather than a copy of it. Other times, the function's purpose is to modify the caller's copy of the argument. In both cases, you can build functions that accept the addresses of arguments instead of the arguments themselves. The function declares the parameter to be a pointer to the type of the argument, and the caller passes the address of the argument. You still pass by value, however, except that now you pass the value of the address of the argument. You learn about pointers and addresses in Chapter 8.

C++ also supports reference variables, which are aliases for real variables. You can use reference variables for pass-by-reference, too. Chapter 9 discusses reference variables.

Type Conversions in Arguments and Return Values

Although the return and parameter types of the prototype and function definition must match exactly, the caller of the function has a bit of leeway. The rules for type conversion, which Chapter 2 discusses, apply to function return values and arguments. Just as it does in assignments, the compiler appropriately promotes or demotes numeric values to accommodate the expressions that your program provides.

Unnamed Function Parameters

You can declare a C++ function with one or more parameters that the function does not use. This circumstance often occurs when several functions are called through a generic function pointer. Some of the functions do not use all the parameters named in the function pointer declaration. Following is an example of such a function:

```
int func(int x, int y)
{
    return x * 2;
}
```

Although this usage is correct and common, most C and C++ compilers complain that you fail to use the parameter named y. C++, however, allows you to declare functions with unnamed parameters to indicate to the compiler that the parameter exists and that the callers pass an argument for the parameter — but that the called function does not use it. Following is the C++ function coded with an unnamed second parameter.

```
int func(int x, int)
{
    return x * 2;
}
```

Why would you do this? Why would a program have a function with a parameter that it does not use? Why would someplace else in the program need to pass an argument that is not going to be used? The answer is found in an understanding of a C++ idiom known as the *callback* function. Typically your program passes the address of one of your functions to a library function that will call back your function. Typical uses of the callback function require all the parameters, but occasionally an argument is unneeded by your particular use of the callback function. The unnamed parameter feature allows you to provide a callback function that matches the prototype of the function that the library expects to call without getting compiler warnings about unused parameters.

Chapter 8 explains function pointers and addresses.

Default Function Arguments

A C++ function prototype can declare that one or more of the function's parameters have default argument values. When a call to the function omits the corresponding arguments, the compiler inserts the default values where it expects to see the arguments. You can declare default values for arguments in a C++ function prototype like this:

```
void myfunc(int = 5, double = 1.23);
```

The expressions declare default values for the arguments. The C++ compiler substitutes the default values if you omit the arguments when you call the function. You can call the function in any of the following ways:

```
myfunc(12, 3.45); // overrides both defaults
myfunc(3);        // effectively func(3, 1.23);
myfunc();         // effectively func(5, 1.23);
```

To omit the first argument in these examples, you must omit the second one; however, you can omit the second argument by itself. This rule applies to any number of arguments. You cannot omit an argument unless you omit the arguments to its right. Program 3-6 demonstrates the use of default arguments.

Program 3-6: **A function with default arguments**

```
#include <iostream>

// Prototype with default arguments
void show(int = 1, float = 2.3, long = 4);

int main
{
    show();             // all three arguments default
    show(5);            // provide 1st argument
    show(6, 7.8);       // provide 1st two
    show(9, 10.11, 12L); // provide all three arguments
    return 0;
}

void show(int first, float second, long third)
{
    std::cout << "  first = "  << first;
    std::cout << ", second = " << second;
    std::cout << ", third = "  << third << std::endl;
}
```

The first call to the show function in Program 3-6 allows the C++ compiler to provide the default values for the parameters just as the prototype specifies them. The second call provides the first parameter and allows the compiler to provide the other two. The third call provides the first two and allows the compiler to provide the last. The fourth call provides all three parameters, and none of the defaults are used.

inline Functions

You can tell the C++ compiler that a function is inline, which, in turn, suggests to the compiler that it compile a new copy of the function each time it is called. The inline function execution eliminates the function-call overhead of traditional functions. You should use inline functions only when the functions are small or when there are relatively few calls to them. Program 3-7 uses the inline keyword to make a small function into an inline function.

Program 3-7: **An inline function**

```
#include <iostream>
#include <cstdlib>

inline void error_message(char* s)
{
    std::cout << '\a' << s;
    std::exit(1);
}

int main
{
    error_message("You called?");
    return 0;
}
```

Observe that Program 3-7 declares the inline function ahead of the call to it. The C++ standard does not define where an inline function must be declared as such and under what conditions the compiler may choose to ignore the inline declaration, except to say that the compiler may do so. Because of this ambiguity in the language specification, compiler builders have leeway in how they interpret the requirements. You can declare an inline function (for performance reasons, perhaps), but the compiler may overrule you without saying so. To be safe, always declare inline functions ahead of all calls to them. If an inline function is to assume the appearance of an extern global function—if it is to be called by code in several source files, as Chapter 13 discusses—put its declaration in a header file.

Using inline supports two idioms. First, it offers an improved macro facility, which Chapter 11 discusses. Second, it permits you to break a large function with many nested levels of statement blocks into several smaller inline functions. This usage improves a program's readability without introducing unnecessary function-call overhead.

Chapter 11 compares inline functions to preprocessor #define macros.

Recursion

All C++ functions are recursive, which means that a function can call itself, either directly or indirectly, by a lower function that is executing as the result of a call made by the recursive function.

Functions can be recursive because each execution of a function has private copies of its arguments and local data objects, and those copies are distinct from the copies owned by other executions of the same function. Chapter 10 explains recursion in detail.

Overloaded Functions

C++ enables you to assign the same function name to multiple functions but with different parameter types. Then, all versions of the function are available at the same time. This feature is called function overloading.

Overloading for Different Operations

Sometimes you overload a function because it performs a generic task but there are different permutations of what it does. The Standard C std::strcpy and std::strncpy functions (Chapter 26) are examples. Both functions copy strings but in slightly different ways. The std::strcpy function copies a string from the source to the destination. The std::strncpy function copies a string, but stops copying when the source string terminates or after the function copies a specified number of characters. Program 3-8 provides two functions named string_copy() that copy strings two different ways.

Program 3-8: **Overloading functions, example 1**

```
#include <iostream>

void string_copy(char *dest, const char* src)
{
    while((*dest++ = *src++) != '\0')
        ;
}
void string_copy(char* dest, const char* src, int len)
{
    while (len && (*dest++ = *src++) != '\0')
        --len;
    while (len--)
        *dest++ = '\0';
}
int main
{
```

```
    char misspiggy[20], kermit[20];
    string_copy(misspiggy, "Miss Piggy");
    string_copy(kermit,
        "Kermit, the file transfer protocol", 6);
    std::cout << kermit << " and " << misspiggy;
    return 0;
}
```

There are two functions named `string_copy` in this program. What sets them apart is their different parameter lists. The first of the two `string_copy` functions has destination and source character pointers as parameters. The second function has the pointers, as well as an integer length. The C++ compiler recognizes that these are two distinct functions by virtue of these differences in their parameter lists. Overloaded functions can also have different return types, but that can't be the only difference.

Overloading for Different Formats

Program 3-8 shows how to overload a function to get a different algorithm on similar data. Another reason to overload a function is to get the same result from data values that can be represented in different formats. Standard C++ has various ways of representing the date and time. You can find other ways in Unix, and still others in MS-DOS. Program 3-9 shows how you can send two of the Standard C formats to the overloaded `display_time` functions.

Program 3-9: **Overloading functions, example 2**

```
#include <iostream>
#include <ctime>

void display_time(const struct std::tm* tim)
{
    std::cout << "1. It is now " << std::asctime(tim);
}
void display_time(time_t* tim)
{
    std::cout << "2. It is now " << std::ctime(tim);
}
int main
{
    std::time_t tim = std::time(0);
    struct std::tm* ltim = std::localtime(&tim);
    display_time(ltim);
    display_time(&tim);
    return 0;
}
```

Program 3-9 uses the Standard C data formats `std::time_t` and `struct std::tm`, loading them with the value of the current date and time using the Standard C `std::time` and `std::localtime` functions. (Chapter 26 describes these data formats and functions.) Then, the program calls its own overloaded `display_time` function for each of the formats. Program 3-9 displays the following results:

```
1. It is now Mon Jan 27 12:05:20 1997
2. It is now Mon Jan 27 12:05:20 1997
```

Dates and times are good ways to experiment with overloaded functions. There are many ways to represent them internally, many ways that different systems report them to a program, and many ways to display them. In addition to all these formats, there are many common date and time algorithms. A comprehensive date and time package is a solid addition to any programmer's tool collection.

Summary

In this chapter, you learned how to design and call functions. You learned that a function's prototype provides its declaration and that all uses of the function, as well as the function definition itself, must comply with the specification of the prototype. You also learned how to define a function by providing a return type, function name, parameter list, and statement body. You discovered some of the contexts in which function calls may be used: by themselves, in initializers of local variables, on the right side of expressions, and as arguments to other functions. Additionally, you learned that function calls pass their arguments by value. Finally, you learned about default function arguments and inline functions.

✦   ✦   ✦

Program Flow Control

This chapter is about C++ language statements that control the flow of a program's execution. C supports the sequence, selection, and iteration control structures of structured programming, as well as the goto operation of unstructured programming.

Statement Blocks

Every C++ function has at least one brace-surrounded statement block, the one at the outer level just under the function header. Program 3-2 in Chapter 3 includes a function with a statement block nested inside the outer statement block. A C++ function can have many nested levels of statement blocks. These nested blocks are important to C++'s ability to define groups of statements that execute under controlled conditions. They are also important to the management of local variable scope, as discussed in Chapter 5.

Nesting Depth

As you develop your programs, be wary of constructs that have a great many nested levels of statement blocks. If you indent your statements properly, your code shifts farther to the right of the page as the nested levels increase. Go too far, and the code becomes difficult to read and understand. Here's an example:

```
void func()
{
    if (whatever) {
        // ...
        while (fornow)   {
            // ...
            do   {
                // ...
                if (something) {
                    // and so on ...
                }
            } while (elsewhere);
        }
    }
}
```

It is better to reorganize the function and put the more deeply nested blocks into separate functions like this:

```
inline void SomeThings()
{
    if (something)  {
        // and so on ...
    }
{
inline void DoThings()
{
    do   {
        // ...
        SomeThings();
    } while (elsewhere);
{
inline void Whatever()
{
    while (fornow)   {
        // ...
        DoThings();
    }
}
void func()
{
    if (whatever)  {
        // ...
        Whatever();
    }
}
```

The `inline` specification (Chapter 3) eliminates unnecessary function calling overhead in the program. You split such code fragments into separate functions mainly to improve the program's readability.

Indentation Styles

There are several styles for indenting C++ code and for placing the braces that define statement blocks. C++, being a free-form programming language, mandates no particular style for braces, indenting, and white space. The style of the listings in this book reflects a personal preference. Here are examples of different styles for writing C++ code:

```
if (a == b)  { // then ... endif
    // ...
}

if (a == b)     // begin ... end
{
    // ...
}

if (a == b)     // do ... doend
    {
    // ...
    }
```

The comments in these style examples show how C++ programmers use brace punctuation to express blocks in ways that other languages use keywords. No one style is right, and no one style is wrong. You should strive for consistency, using the same style throughout a program. Eventually, you will find one that you like.

If you modify someone else's work, use the style that the program uses even if you don't like it. Consistency in code contributes to more readable and, therefore, more maintainable code.

If the other programmer's style is totally unreadable, ugly, or otherwise unacceptable to you, and if the project involves a substantial amount of code, and if the other programmer is out of the picture, you might want to consider using a code beautifier program to make the code more to your liking. Quincy 2002 includes such a program on its Tools menu. See Appendix C for details.

Selection: Tests

The power of the first digital computer was said to be in its ability to make decisions, and all its descendents inherited that ability. Programmers express decisions as tests of a *condition*, which is the true or false value of a bool expression. Almost every expression returns a value that the compiler can implicitly convert to a bool. Exceptions are calls to void functions (Chapter 3), which return no value, and calls to functions that return objects of struct (Chapter 6) or class (Part II) that have no conversions to types that can be tested for truth.

In the context of a condition, an expression is true if its value is not equal to zero; otherwise, it is false. As you learned in Chapter 2, an expression can consist of other expressions and operators and has a true/false value based on the result of the evaluation of the full expression, which can include arithmetic, logical, relational, and bitwise operations. Anytime an expression is used in a context in which the program is testing its true/false value, that use of the expression is said to be a condition.

The if Statement

C++ programs use the if...else program flow control statement to test conditions and execute one of two statements or statement blocks depending on the condition. Program 4-1 illustrates this usage.

Program 4-1: **Testing with if for zero**

```
#include <iostream>

int main()
{
    int selection;
    std::cout << "Enter 0 to compute: ";
    std::cin >> selection;
    if (selection == 0)
        std::cout << "You chose to compute";
    return 0;
}
```

The expression tested by an if statement is always enclosed in parentheses. It can be a complex expression and can include function calls, operators, variables, and constants.

Note   By now, you are accustomed to reading code and running programs — either with Quincy or your own C++ development system. Until now, this book has told you what to expect on the screen when you run the programs. You've reached the point where, in most cases, you can discern for yourself from the code what the programs display, and you certainly can see it on the screen when you run them. Unless it is either not obvious or is critical to some point being made, the book doesn't document example program output any further.

Program 4-1 an important lesson. The if statement tests to see whether the selection variable is equal to zero. This condition is true only if the variable is equal to zero. This might seem backwards. When the variable's value is zero, the expression is true. The explanation for this seeming anomaly is that the full expression includes a comparison with the constant 0. The condition returned by the expression depends on the value of the variable as compared with the constant 0 by the == equality operator; it does not depend on the value of the variable itself. Program 4-2 is the same program, except that it tests for anything but zero in the variable.

Program 4-2: **Testing with if for nonzero**

```
#include <iostream>

int main()
{
    std::cout << "Enter any number but 0 to compute: ";
    int selection;
    std::cin >> selection;
    if (selection)
        std::cout << "You chose to compute";
    return 0;
}
```

The if statement in Program 4-2 uses the variable name selection alone in the condition. A nonzero value in the variable satisfies the test. Many programmers prefer to code such tests explicitly:

```
if (selection != 0)
```

There is no difference between this usage and the usage in Program 4-2 except for personal preference.

Listings 4-1 and 4-2 execute one statement if the condition being tested is true. Program 4-3 shows that a test executes the statement block that follows immediately when the condition is true.

Program 4-3: **Conditionally executing a program block**

```cpp
#include <iostream>
#include <cmath>

int main()
{
    std::cout << "Enter a dimension to compute a cube: ";
    int dimension;
    std::cin >> dimension;
    if (dimension) {
        std::cout << dimension << " cubed = "
            << std::pow(dimension, 3);
        return 0;
    }
    std::cout << "You chose not to compute.";
    return 0;
}
```

Program 4-3 contains several new lessons. First, the program demonstrates that when the if statement finds a true condition—when you enter anything other than zero in response to the prompt—all statements in the following brace-surrounded statement block execute. The indentation of the code emphasizes that relationship, but has nothing to do with the effect. White space in a C++ program is for legibility and aesthetics only.

Also, observe that Program 4-3 includes the <cmath> header file and uses the Standard C std::pow function to compute the third power of the dimension variable. Compiler header files (ones expressed between angle brackets) with names that begin with "c," and that have no file extension, contain the declarations for the Standard C library functions. Standard C++ includes the complete Standard C library enclosed within the std namespace. Chapter 26 discusses the Standard C library in more detail. Chapter 36 discusses namespaces.

The std::pow function expects double types for its two parameters, yet Program 4-3 passes int arguments. This usage demonstrates a key point in Chapter 3 that function arguments are subject to the C++ language rules of type conversion. The compiler promotes the caller's arguments to the types expected by the std::pow function based on the function's prototype declaration in the <cmath> header.

Finally, the program calls upon a programming technique that, as you learned in Chapter 3, may be considered improper programming: The main function returns from a place other than the bottom of the function. This book takes no position about the propriety of such code, but the next lesson, which is really about else, shows how to remove the so-called improper code.

The if . . . else Statements

In addition to allowing statements that execute when a condition is true, a test can specify that different statements execute when the condition is false. C++ uses the else statement for that purpose. Program 4-4 modifies Program 4-3 to use the else statement.

Program 4-4: **Using else**

```cpp
#include <iostream>
#include <cmath>

int main()
{
    std::cout << "Enter a dimension to compute a cube: ";
    int dimension;
    std::cin >> dimension;
    if (dimension)
        std::cout << dimension << " cubed = "
            << std::pow(dimension, 3);
    else
        std::cout << "You chose not to compute.";
    return 0;
}
```

The else statement executes the statement or statement block that follows when the condition tested by the associated if statement is false. You can have an else statement only when it follows an if statement.

The else if Statements

Joining a sequence of if and else keywords produces the equivalent of the ELSEIF operator of other programming languages. It enables you to make a series of mutually exclusive tests. Program 4-5 demonstrates that usage by implementing a simple screen menu.

Program 4-5: **Using else if for a menu**

```cpp
#include <iostream>

// Prototypes
void DisplayMenu();
int GetSelection();

int main()
{
    // Display the menu.
    DisplayMenu();
    // Get the menu selection.
    int selection;
    selection = GetSelection();
    // Select the matching process.
    if (selection == 1)
        std::cout << "Processing Receivables" << std::endl;
    else if (selection == 2)
        std::cout << "Processing Payables" << std::endl;
    else if (selection == 3)
```

```
            std::cout << "Quitting" << std::endl;
    else
            std::cout << "\aInvalid selection" << std::endl;
    return 0;
}
void DisplayMenu()
{
    std::cout << "--- Menu ---" << std::endl;
    std::cout << "1=Receivables" << std::endl;
    std::cout << "2=Payables" << std::endl;
    std::cout << "3=Quit" << std::endl;
}
int GetSelection()
{
    int selection;
    std::cout << "Enter Selection: ";
    std::cin >> selection;

    return selection;
}
```

Program 4-5 displays a menu on the screen and reads the user's selection from the keyboard. Then the program uses the else if idiom to test the value of the selection and run an appropriate process, which in this case is simply a message to indicate which process the user selected.

The switch . . . case Statements

The switch...case statements provide a convenient notation for multiple else if tests when you test a single integral variable for multiple values. In Program 4-5, all of the if statements test the value of the integer variable selection. The program also can be written with a switch statement. Program 4-6 illustrates how to do that.

Program 4-6: **The switch . . . case statement**

```
int main()
{
    DisplayMenu();

    // Get the menu selection.
    int selection;
    selection = GetSelection();

    // Select the matching process
    switch (selection)
    {
        case 1:
            std::cout << "Processing Receivables" << std::endl;
            break;
```

Continued

Program 4-6 *(continued)*

```
        case 2:
            std::cout << "Processing Payables" << std::endl;
            break;
        case 3:
            std::cout << "Quitting" << std::endl;
            break;
        default:
            std::cout << "\aInvalid selection" << std::endl;
            break;
    }

    return 0;
}
```

For brevity, Listing 4-6 shows only the `main` function—the only change from Listing 4-5. The rest of the code is in the program nonetheless and in the program on the Quincy CD-ROM. Subsequent listings apply the same convention.

The condition tested by the `switch` statement must be an integral expression. This means that it can contain operators and function calls. The values tested by the `case` statements must be constant integral values. This means that they can have constant expressions and operators but cannot have variables, function calls, or side effects such as assignments and increment and decrement operators. When your tests use these things, or when the series of tests involves different variables, use the `else if` idiom.

No two `case` values may evaluate to the same constant value.

The `default` statement is followed by code that executes if none of the `case` values is equal to the `switch` expression. You may omit the `default` statement; but if you include it, there may be only one in a `switch`.

Braces always enclose the list of cases (including the default). The expression tested by the `switch` is always enclosed in parentheses.

A `break` statement follows the code in a `case` statement. If you omit the `break`, execution falls through to the code for the next `case` in the list. This is not always an error but often is exactly what you want. It allows you to assign the same statements to the same case, as shown here:

```
switch (keystroke)
{
    case 'a':
    case 'b':
    case 'c':
        doit("abc");  // executed for first three cases
        break;
    case 'd':
        // ...
    default:
        // ...
}
```

Declaration within an if Conditional Expression

You can declare a variable within the conditional expression of an if statement. The following code fragment is an example:

```
if (int selection = GetSelection())  {
    // selection is in scope ...
}
else  {
    // selection is in scope ...
}
// selection is not in scope ...
```

A variable declared in a conditional expression must be able to be converted to the bool type. The program can reference the selection variable in the preceding example anywhere in the statement block that executes if the condition returns a true value, and anywhere in the statement block that executes following an associated else statement. The program cannot reference the selection variable past those statement blocks. Chapter 5 explains the scope of variables in more detail.

The following syntax is not permitted, however:

```
if ((int selection = GetSelection()) == 1)
```

The declaration must appear first in the conditional expression with no parentheses.

Iterations: Looping

In addition to making decisions, a program must be able to *iterate*: repeat sequences of instructions against successive data values. These iterating processes are called *loops*, and C++ has three looping statements: while, do...while, and for.

Most programs loop. They operate on a set of data values from a database, the keyboard, a text file, or any of a number of data sources that contain multiple records of similar data. Loop iterations proceed from the first of these records through subsequent ones until there are no more records to process.

Other loops occur within a program's main loop. The program might iterate through arrays once for each input record. Loops can have inner loops, too, such as an array that has multiple dimensions, as discussed further in Chapter 7.

The while Statement

The while statement tests a condition and, if the condition is true, executes the statement or statement block immediately following. When each iteration of the loop is finished, the program returns to the controlling while statement and repeats its test. If the condition is false the first time, no iteration of the loop executes, and execution proceeds with the statement following the loop statements. If the test is true the first time, then something in the loop must, during the first or a subsequent iteration, cause the condition to become false. Otherwise, the loop never terminates.

In a typical mixed (or possibly confused) programming metaphor, a loop that never is terminated is said to be a *dead loop* or *infinite loop*. The program in Program 4-6 does not loop. It gets one menu selection from the user, processes it, and exits. More typically, programs process menu selections until the user chooses to exit. Program 4-7 uses the `while` statement to execute the program that way.

Program 4-7: **Iterating with while**

```cpp
int main()
{
    int selection = 0;
    while (selection != 3)  {
        // Display the menu.
        DisplayMenu();
        // Get menu selection.
        selection = GetSelection();
        // Select matching process
        switch (selection)  {
            case 1:
                std::cout << "Processing Receivables"
                          << std::endl;
                break;
            case 2:
                std::cout << "Processing Payables"
                          << std::endl;
                break;
            case 3:
                std::cout << "Quitting" << std::endl;
                break;
            default:
                std::cout << "\aInvalid selection"
                          << std::endl;
                break;
        }
    }
    return 0;
}
```

With one new line of code, Program 4-7 turns the earlier program into one that runs until the user says to stop. Note that because of the way the program is written, the first iteration of the loop always runs. The `selection` variable is initialized to 0, and the `while` statement tests it to be equal to 3. Often, a `while` statement does not execute its loop statements at all because the condition is `false` the first time it is tested.

The `selection` variable's initializer is necessary in Program 4-7, because there is no guarantee that local variables are initialized to anything in particular, and the random value that `selection` could have on startup might be a 3. Program 4-6 reads data into the variable before it tests it, so the initializer is not necessary.

Can you see the potential in Program 4-7 for a so-called dead loop? If the user never enters a 3, the `while` loop goes on forever. This arrangement is not a problem in an interactive situation such as this one. The user can be expected to understand from the menu display what is required. Eventually, he or she will enter that 3 to get out of the program and on with other things. Dead loops in a program usually are bugs, often occurring in loops that involve no interaction with the user. Here's a simple one:

```
int x = 0, y = 0;
while (x < 3)
    y++;
```

The loop increments y, but the `while` statement tests x, which never changes. You know when you are in such a dead loop. The program stops dead in its tracks. If you run the program in Quincy, you can break out of the loop by choosing the Stop command on the Project menu. If you run the program from the operating system's command line, you will have to use whatever measure the operating system provides for terminating programs that have locked out the user.

The do . . . while Statement

Sometimes a loop iteration must execute at least once, regardless of the condition of the variable being tested. The do...while statement allows you to write such a loop. Program 4-8 demonstrates this behavior.

Program 4-8: **Iterating with do . . . while**

```
#include <iostream>
#include <cstdlib>

int main()
{
    char ans;

    // Loop until user is done
    do  {
        // Choose a secret number
        int fav = std::rand() % 32;
        // Loop until user guesses secret number
        int num;
        do  {
            std::cout << "Guess my secret number (0 - 32) ";
            std::cin >> num;
            // Report the status of the guess
            std::cout << (num < fav ? "Too low"  :
                          num > fav ? "Too high" :
                                      "Right")
                      << std::endl;
        } while (num != fav);
        std::cout << "Go again? (y/n) ";
        std::cin >> ans;
    } while (ans == 'y');
    return 0;
}
```

Program 4-8 has two `do...while` constructs. Each `do` statement is followed by a statement block to be iterated, which is followed by the `while` test. Observe that the conditions following the `while` keywords are in parentheses and are terminated with semicolons.

The difference between `while` and `do...while` is that the test in a `while` happens before each iteration, and the test in a `do...while` happens after each iteration. This behavior is reflected in the way you code the two loops. You code the `while` statement ahead of the loop statements in a `while` test and after the loop statements for a `do...while` test.

The program in Program 4-8 computes a random number by calling the `<cstdlib>` Standard C `std::rand` function. This function returns a random integer between 0 and 32,768. The program reduces this number to a number between 0 and 32, by computing the remainder of the random number divided by 32. Then it goes into a `do...while` loop, letting you guess the number and telling you whether your guess is too high, too low, or right on the mark. When you guess the number, the loop terminates. An outer `do...while` loop allows you to exit or guess another number.

The ? : Compound Conditional Operator

Observe in Program 4-8 the message displayed on `std::cout` after you enter a guess. It uses a compound conditional operator (`?:`), explained in Chapter 2, to determine which message to display.

```
std::cout << (num < fav ? "Too low"  :
              num > fav ? "Too high" :
                          "Right") << std::endl;
```

As demonstrated here, the compound conditional operator is a shorthand alternative for an `if...else` test.

The first condition tested is `num < fav`. If that expression is true, the conditional operator passes the "Too low" message. If that expression is not true, the rightmost expression — which is evaluated and returned for the first conditional operator — is another conditional expression that tests `num > fav`. If that expression is true, the statement returns the "Too high" message. Otherwise, neither condition is true. This means that `num` is equal to `fav`, and the statement returns the "Right" message.

This example demonstrates how you can use a series of conditional operators to make a compound test that evaluates to a single `bool` expression.

Here is how you would code the same tests by using `if...else` style code:

```
if (num < fav)
    std::cout << "Too low";
else if (num > fav)
    std::cout << "Too high";
else
    std::cout << "Right";
std::cout << std::endl;
```

The for Statement

The C++ `for` statement is similar to BASIC's `FOR` operator in that it can control a loop, modifying an initialized variable in each loop iteration. C++'s `for` statement is more general than BASIC's, however. The statement consists of three expressions separated by semicolons.

The three expressions are surrounded by parentheses and followed by the statement or statement block that constitutes the iteration. The program evaluates the first expression once — when the `for` statement executes. Then, the program evaluates the second expression. If the second expression is true, the iteration executes, and the program evaluates the third expression. The loop continues with another test of the second expression, and so on until the second expression is false. This is the format of the `for` statement:

```
for ( <expr1>; <expr2>; <expr3> )
    <iteration>
```

Although the three expressions can be anything you want, including comma-separated expressions, the `for` statement is a convenient notation for a common programming idiom that you can write by using `while` notation this way:

```
<expr1>;
while ( <expr2> )  {
    <iteration>
    <expr3>;
}
```

Consequently, a typical use of the `for` statement is to assign a value to a variable, test that variable for a maximum value, use the variable in the loop iteration, and increment the variable at the end of the iteration. Program 4-9 illustrates that usage.

Program 4-9: **The for statement**

```
#include <iostream>
#include <cstdlib>

int main()
{
    int counter;
    for (counter = 0; counter < 10; counter++) {
        std::srand(counter+1);
        std::cout << "Random number " << counter+1 << ": "
                  << std::rand() << std::endl;
    }
    return 0;
}
```

In Program 4-9, the first expression in the `for` loop assigns a zero value to the `counter` variable. The second expression is a conditional expression that returns `true` if the `counter` variable is less than 10. The third expression increments the `counter` variable. This combination of expressions in a `for` statement iterates the loop 10 times, as long as nothing in the loop modifies the `counter` variable.

Each iteration uses the new value in the `counter` variable as an argument to the `<cstdlib>` Standard C function `std::srand`. The `std::srand` function seeds the standard random number generator. Then, the program displays the `counter` variable and the next computed random number.

If you do not provide a seed value, the std::rand function always starts with a seed of 1, and the random number sequence is predictable. Observe that the program in Program 4-8 always computes the same progression of secret numbers for you to guess. In Chapter 26, you learn to use values from the <ctime> functions to seed the random number generator in order to get less predictable results.

The for statement is convenient for iterating through the elements of arrays, which Chapter 7 discusses. Program 4-10 introduces this concept.

Program 4-10: **Iterating through an array**

```
#include <iostream>

int main()
{
    int items[5] = {9, 43, 6, 22, 70};
    for (int i = 0; i < 5; i++) {
        std::cout << "Item #" << i+1;
        std::cout << ": " << items[i] << std::endl;
    }
    return 0;
}
```

The items declaration is a C++ array. The value inside the square brackets specifies the dimension — the number of elements — in the array. The items variable is an array of int objects that contains five elements.

The for statement iterates the i integer variable from 0 through 4. The loop executes only when the second expression in the for statement is true; in this case, the expression is true only for the values 0 through 4. When the program increments the integer at the end of the loop to the value 5, the second expression, i < 5, becomes false and the loop is not executed again.

Array subscripts are relative to 0. Therefore, you can access the elements of a five-element array with subscripts 0 through 4. The argument in the std::cout statement, items[i], references the array element of items relative to the subscripted value in i. The expression items[0] returns the first element in the array, items[1] returns the second, and so on.

Declaration Within a for Conditional Expression

Observe that the first expression in the for statement declares the int i variable that the program uses to iterate the loop. This variable is in scope in the for statement and in the statement(s) in the iteration, which means that statements outside the statement block cannot reference the variable. You learn more about variable scope in Chapter 5.

Loop Control

Often, a `while`, `do...while`, or `for` loop needs to break out of the loop abruptly, regardless of the value of the conditional expression. Other times, you need to terminate the current iteration and return to the top of the loop. C++ provides the `break` and `continue` loop control statements for these purposes.

break

The `break` statement terminates a loop and jumps to the next statement following the iteration code. Be aware that this `break` statement is not the same as the one used in the `switch...case` selection statement. Program 4-11 illustrates the `break` statement from within a `while` loop.

Program 4-11: **The break statement**

```cpp
#include <iostream>
#include <cstdlib>

int main()
{
    char selection = '\0';
    while (selection != 'q') {
        std::cout << "S-how number, Q-uit: ";
        std::cin >> selection;
        if (selection != 's' && selection != 'q') {
            std::cout << '\a';
            break;   // Break out of the while loop.
        }
        if (selection == 's')
            std::cout << std::rand() << std::endl;
    }
    return 0;
}
```

Program 4-11 stays in a loop while the `selection` variable is not equal to the character constant 'q.' The user can type any character. As long as that character is 's,' the program displays a new random number. If the user presses 'q,' the loop terminates normally as the result of the `while` conditional expression. If the user presses any other key, the program sounds the audible alarm with the `std::cout << '\a'` statement and breaks out of the loop. Similarly, you can use the `break` statement to break out of `for` and `do...while` loops.

continue

Sometimes a program needs to return to the top of the loop iteration rather than break out of the loop. The program in Program 4-11 beeps and quits if the user enters an incorrect command code. A more hospitable program may give the user another chance. Program 4-12 uses the continue statement in place of break. This action terminates the current iteration and returns to the while statement to test for the next iteration.

Program 4-12: The continue statement

```cpp
#include <iostream>
#include <cstdlib>

int main()
{
    char selection = '\0';
    while (selection != 'q')    {
        std::cout << "S-how number, Q-uit: ";
        std::cin >> selection;
        if (selection != 's' && selection != 'q')   {
            std::cout << '\a';
            continue;
        }
        if (selection == 's')
            std::cout << std::rand() << std::endl;
    }
    return 0;
}
```

By using the continue statement instead of break, the program continues to display the menu until the user presses 'q.'

The continue statement works similarly with for and do...while loops. In a for loop, the continue statement jumps to evaluate the third expression in the for expression list and then to the evaluation of the second. This strategy continues the loop as you may expect. In a do...while loop, the continue statement jumps to the while test at the bottom of the loop.

Jumping: goto

The goto statement causes a program to jump immediately to an executable statement elsewhere in the function. The goto references an identifier that is declared as a *statement label* elsewhere in the same function. The label can be positioned ahead of any executable statement and is identified with a colon (:) suffix. You can jump in either direction, as well as into and out of loops. Program 4-13 shows how you can use goto to jump out of an inner loop when a simple break does not work.

Program 4-13: The goto statement

```
#include <iostream>

int main()
{
    for (int dept = 1; dept < 10; dept++)    {
        std::cout << "Department " << dept << std::endl;
        int empl;
        do   {
            std::cout << "Enter Empl # "
                            "(0 to quit, 99 for next dept) ";
            std::cin >> empl;
            if (empl == 0)
                goto done;
            if (empl != 99)
                std::cout << "Dept: " << dept << ", "
                            << "Empl: " << empl << std::endl;
        } while (empl != 99);
    }
done:
    std::cout << "Entry complete" << std::endl;
    return 0;
}
```

Invalid Uses of goto

You cannot use a goto statement to jump over statements that declare variables involving implicit or explicit initialization. C++ involves complicated initialization of class objects during construction, actions that must be undone when the object is destroyed. For example, class objects can allocate memory during initialization. If you were permitted to jump around the initialization of an object, its subsequent destruction — which the compiler automatically invokes, assuming that the object's initialization object occurred — can cause undesirable consequences. Furthermore, any use of such an uninitialized object also can be dangerous. Consider, for example, this code:

```
int main()
{
    std::cout << "Compute a random number? (y/n) ";
    char ans;
    std::cin >> ans;

    if (ans == 'n')
        goto done;

    int randomno = std::rand();
    std::cout << randomno;
done:
    return 0;
}
```

The program does not compile, because the goto statement jumps over the initialization of the randomno variable. A variable that needs initialization must be guaranteed to have undergone that initialization as long as the variable is in scope.

You cannot use goto to jump out of a function.

C++ goto versus C goto

The restriction I just described doesn't apply to the C language goto, which permits such jumps, assuming that the programmer takes responsibility for the integrity of all variables under such circumstances. But C variables do not involve the kinds of construction and destruction often found in C++ class objects. You learn about class object construction and destruction in Chapter 15.

Fixing an Invalid goto

There are two ways to fix the invalid goto in the previous example. The code in Program 4-14 is valid.

Program 4-14: The fixed goto program

```
#include <iostream>
#include <cstdlib>

int main()
{
    std::cout << "Compute a random number? (y/n) ";
    char ans;
    std::cin >> ans;
    if (ans == 'n')
        goto done;
    int ran;
    ran = std::rand();
    std::cout << ran;
one:
    return 0;
}
```

To fix the program wherein the goto jumps over an initialized variable, you can remove the initializer and replace it with an assignment. The compiler allows this usage because the jump does not bypass an initialization. The variable remains in scope and has no assigned value, but the compiler leaves that problem for you to solve. The code in Program 4-15 is valid, too.

Program 4-15: The fixed goto program -- again

```
#include <iostream>
#include <cstdlib>

int main()
{
    std::cout << "Compute a random number? (y/n) ";
    char ans;
    std::cin >> ans;
    if (ans == 'n')
        goto done;
    else    {
        int ran = std::rand();
        std::cout << ran;
    }
done:
    return 0;
}
```

By enclosing the `ran` declaration in a brace-surrounded statement block, you fix the program in a different way. The compiler accepts this usage, because the `goto` jumps over the entire scope wherein the program declares and initializes the `ran` variable.

Listings 4-14 and 4-15 are not particularly good examples of structured programming. Try to improve the programs by eliminating the `goto` statement and the label.

Should You Use goto?

Everyone who writes about programming deprecates the `goto` statement and cautions you not to use it. Structured programming purists forbid its use. Yet most structured programming languages include some variant of the `goto` statement. Pascal, originally designed to be a language for teaching structured programming to university students, supports `goto`. Writers who caution against using `goto` often suggest programming idioms where `goto` might result in clearer, more efficient programs.

Take another look at how Program 4-13 uses `goto`. The program represents the way most people who write and teach about structured programming demonstrate `goto` — as if such an example justifies the idiom's existence. Does it?

As the theory goes, without the `goto` statement, the program in Program 4-13 needs extra measures to force its way out of both loops when the user enters 0 into the employee number. In this particular program, such a measure would not be a terrible burden and would preserve structure and correctness in the code. But we once encountered a programming problem in which propriety wouldn't do.

The program in question was a time-critical, real-time simulation (a game, actually). It had several nested loops that repeated many times during the rendering of a complex animated graphical scene. As in Program 4-13, the innermost loop always found a reason to exit so that the program could proceed with the next sequence. Without the `goto`, the extra measures that the program took to exit gracefully from the loop levied too severe a performance burden on the program, and the screen refreshed its images too slowly. The result was jerky, flickering animation. By abandoning structure in this one case and applying the less graceful but more efficient `goto`, the program was able to achieve an acceptable refresh rate. Today, processors are faster, graphical hardware is more efficient, and compilers do a better job of optimizing runtime code. The `goto` might not be required now. Then, it was. Nowadays you are more likely to find it in small, real-time embedded system applications where efficiency preempts propriety.

All that notwithstanding, it has been proven conclusively that any algorithm can be designed with the three control structures of structured programming (sequence, selection, and iteration) and without the `goto` statement. Nonetheless, `goto` is a part of the C++ language, and you should know how it works and decide for yourself whether you need to use it.

Summary

In this chapter, you learned about C++ statements that manage program flow control. You learned about statement blocks and how they nest. You also learned how to use the `if`, `if...else`, `else if`, `switch...case`, `while`, `do...while`, and `for` flow-control statements. You learned about testing and looping and how to use break and continue to manage loops. You also learned how to jump with the goto statement.

✦   ✦   ✦

C++ Data Type Organization

This chapter adds to what you already know about C++'s intrinsic data types by explaining the ways that a C++ program stores, references, and retrieves data objects in memory.

Scope

Identifiers in C++ programs are said to be in *global*, *local*, or *file* scope. An identifier's *scope* determines which statements in the program may reference it — that is, its visibility to other parts of the program. Scope usually is implied by position in the program. The exception is file scope, which must be declared. Variables in different scopes sometimes have the same identifiers.

Global Scope

Some variables and functions have global scope, which means that they can be referenced from anywhere in the program. When a variable is declared outside any function, it is called an external variable and it has global scope by default. The declaration must occur before any references to the variable from within the same source-code file, but all functions past that point may reference it. Program 5-1 illustrates an external variable with global scope.

> Program 5-1: **Global scope**

```
#include <iostream>

// A variable with global scope.
int Counter;

void AddCounter(int);

int main()
{
    AddCounter(53);
    // Reference a global variable
```

Continued

Program 5-1 (continued)

```
    std::cout << "Counter = " << Counter;
    return 0;
}
void AddCounter(int incr)
{
    // Reference a global variable
    Counter += incr;
}
```

The `Counter` variable in Program 5-1 has global scope, because it is declared outside any function and is not `static` (which I explain later). Therefore, both the `main` and the `AddCounter` functions can reference `Counter`. All functions (except class member functions explained in Chapter 14) have global scope unless they are declared to be `static`.

A variable or function with global scope can be referenced from independently compiled source code files as long as each additional file that references the variable or function declares it to be external with the `extern` keyword. You learn about the `static` and `extern` storage classes later.

Chapter 13 discusses programs built from multiple source code files.

Local Scope

Most of the variables in the listings of earlier chapters have local scope. They are declared inside functions and are not accessible to the code in other functions. Function parameter variables also have local scope. They are in the scope of—and, therefore, are accessible to— all the statement blocks in the function.

Variables declared in a statement block are in the scope of that block, as well as all lower blocks in the declaring block. Program 5-2 illustrates variables with local scope.

Program 5-2: **Local scope**

```
#include <iostream>

int main()
{
    int i = 123;          // i is in scope from here down
    if (i > 0)         {
        int j = 456;      // j is in scope from here down
        if (j > 0)     {
            int k = 789; // k is in scope from here down
            // All 3 are in scope
            std::cout << i << ' ' << j << ' ' << k;
        }
    }
    return 0;
}
```

Variables in different scopes can have the same identifiers. If a variable in a lower scope in a function uses the same name as a previously declared variable, the new declaration hides the earlier one from the program until the newer one goes out of scope. A local variable goes out of scope when the statement block in which it is declared completes executing. Program 5-3 demonstrates this behavior.

Program 5-3: Variables hidden by scope

```
#include <iostream>

int var = 1; // global scope.

int main()
{
    std::cout << var << ' ';
    if (var > 0) {
        int var = 2;         // hides global var.
        std::cout << var << ' ';
        if (var > 1)  {
            int var = 3;    // hides prior local var
            std::cout << var << ' ';
        }
        std::cout << var << ' ';
    }
    std::cout << var << ' ';
    return 0;
}
```

Program 5-3 contains five std::cout statements, each one apparently displaying the value of the same variable. The first std::cout references the global var, because that is the only one that is in scope. The second std::cout references the local var that is initialized with the value 2 and that hides the global var. The third std::cout references the local var in an inner scope that is initialized with the value 3 and that hides both var objects in outer scopes.

When the innermost statement block completes executing, the next outer var comes back into scope. Similarly, when its statement block completes, the global var comes back into scope. Program 5-3 displays the following output on the screen:

```
1 2 3 2 1
```

Defining identical identifiers to different things is generally considered to be a bad practice since it can make the code confusing and hard to read. Nonetheless you must understand the behavior so you will recognize it when you see it.

The Global Scope Resolution Operator

As Program 5-3 shows, if a local variable and a global variable have the same name, all references to that name — while the local variable is in scope — refer to the local variable. To tell the compiler that you want to refer to a global variable rather than the local one with the same name, use the :: global scope resolution operator. The global scope resolution operator — which is coded as a prefix to the variable's name (for example, ::varname) — enables you explicitly to reference a global variable from a scope in which a local variable has the same name. Program 5-4 is an example of the global scope resolution operator.

Program 5-4: **Global scope resolution operator**

```
#include <iostream>

// A global variable.
int amount = 123;

int main()
{
    // local variable with same name as global variable
    int amount = 456;
    // display value of global variable
    std::cout << ::amount;
    std::cout << ' ';
    // display value of local variable
    std::cout << amount;
    return 0;
}
```

The listing has two variables named amount. The first is global and contains the value 123. The second is local to the main function. The first std::cout statement displays 123, the contents of the global amount variable, because that first reference to the variable name uses the :: global scope resolution operator. The second std::cout statement displays 456, the contents of the local amount variable, because that reference to the variable name has no global scope resolution operator and defaults to the local variable.

File Scope

File scope refers to external identifiers that are available only to functions declared in the same translation unit, which is the source-code file in which they are defined (including any source-code files specified by #include directives). The static storage class specifier declares identifiers with file scope. Program 5-5 illustrates the static storage class specifier.

Program 5-5: **File scope**

```
#include <iostream>

// A variable with file scope.
static int Counter;

// A prototype for a function with file scope.
static void AddCounter(int);
```

```
int main()
{
    // Reference a file-scope function.
    AddCounter(1940);
    // Reference a file-scope variable.
    std::cout << "Counter = " << Counter;
    return 0;
}
static void AddCounter(int incr)
{
    // Reference a file-scope variable.
    Counter += incr;
}
```

The Counter variable and the AddCounter function are declared with the static storage class specifier. This gives them file scope, which makes them available only to the functions in the translation unit in which they are defined. Program 5-5 consists of only one translation unit.

Most of the listings in this book have only one translation unit, because the programs are small examples. Larger C++ projects involve independent compilation of many source files, and the static storage class specifier hides the identifiers of functions and variables from other source-code files linked into the same program. However, as you learn in later chapters, C++ classes and namespaces virtually eliminate the need for any program to use the static storage class for functions and for variables declared outside a function.

Scope, Visibility, and Lifetime

The term *scope* describes which code in a program can reference an identifier during the *lifetime* of the object referenced by the identifier. Lifetime is the period of time from when the program creates an object to when the object is destroyed. This usage is correct, but it reflects some ambiguity in the way we talk about programming.

A variable declared within a function's statement block exists from the point of the declaration to the point that the program exits the statement block. Its lifetime seems to mirror its scope. As long as program execution stays within that statement block, or within a block nested inside the statement block, the variable is both alive and in scope. This period of time is its lifetime. If, while the variable is still alive, the program calls another function, then the variable goes temporarily out of scope until the function returns. The variable is no longer visible because the currently executing function cannot reference the variable. But the variable is still alive and well. Program 5-6 demonstrates this principle.

Program 5-6: **Scope versus lifetime**

```
#include <iostream>

void DisplayTitle();

int main()
```

Continued

> **Program 5-6** *(continued)*

```
{
    // auto storage-class specifier.
    auto int Amount = 500;
    DisplayTitle();
    std::cout << Amount;
    return 0;
}
void DisplayTitle()
{
    // main()'s Amount exists,
    // but is not visible here.
    std::cout << "Amt = ";
}
```

The best way to understand the lesson that Program 5-6 teaches is to step through the program with a debugger while watching the Amount variable in a watch window. When you run exercise programs with Quincy, the programming environment is set up for you. Before you step into the program, the watch window displays nothing for the Amount variable's value; this means that the debugger cannot fetch the value from memory because the program hasn't begun running. When you step into the main function, the display changes to a random integer value that displays whatever the variable's memory location contains before the program initializes the variable. This tells you that the Amount identifier is alive and in scope. After you step into the variable's initialized declaration, the value changes to 500, which is the initializer value. When you step into the DisplayTitle function, the watched display reverts to ??. The variable still exists, but it is invisible temporarily. You can see it in the main function by glancing up, but the DisplayTitle function cannot see it at all. When you step through the DisplayTitle return and back into the main function, the watched variable displays the value 500 again, telling you that the Amount variable is back in view.

Consequently, you sometimes hear that a variable is out of scope when the program calls out of the statement block in which the variable is declared. Other times you hear that an object is destroyed when it "goes out of scope." Try to understand that the seeming contradiction is simply a typical ambiguity in how we programmers say things.

Storage Classes

Variables can be declared with storage class specifiers that tell the compiler how variables are to be treated. The storage classes are auto, static, extern, and register. For convenience, C++ considers the typedef keyword to represent a storage class, but it serves a different purpose, as I explain later in this chapter.

The auto Storage Class

The auto storage class specifier identifies a local variable as *automatic*, which means that each invocation of the statement block in which the variable is defined gets a fresh copy with its own memory space and with reinitialization each time. Local variables implicitly are declared `auto` unless the program declares them otherwise. Use of the `auto` keyword, then, is optional. If you omit the `auto` keyword, and don't use any other storage class specifier on a local variable, that variable automatically is automatic, so to speak. The following code fragment illustrates the `auto` storage class specifier:

```
int main()
{
    // Auto storage class specifier.
    auto int Amount = 500;
    // ...
    return 0;
}
```

The code in this example works exactly the same whether or not you include the `auto` keyword in the declaration of the `Amount` variable. Function parameters are, by default, `auto` unless you declare them to be in the `register` storage class (discussed later).

The static Storage Class

You learned the meaning of the `static` storage class when you applied it to function declarations and external variables in Program 5-5. The `static` storage class has a different meaning with local variables: It is the opposite of `auto`. Although the scope of a static local variable begins inside the statement block in which the variable is declared and ends when the block terminates, the variable itself lives and retains its value between executions of the statement block. Initializers are effective only for the first execution of the statement block. Subsequent executions find that the variable has the value it had when the previous execution ended. Program 5-7 shows how static local variables work.

Program 5-7: **The static storage class**

```
#include <iostream>

int Gather();

int main()
{
    int gwool = 0;
    while (gwool < 60)        {
        gwool = Gather();
        std::cout << gwool << std::endl;
    }
      return 0;
}
int Gather()
{
    // A static local variable.
    static int wool = 50;
    return ++wool;
}
```

The `wool` variable in the `Gather` function is a static local variable with an initial value of 50. The function increments the variable and returns the incremented value. When you run the program, you can see from the output that the returned value is incremented each time, and the `wool` initializer does not have an effect after the first call of the function. If you were to remove the `static` storage class specifier from the declaration, the program would go into a dead loop, displaying the value 51 endlessly. This is because the `wool` variable would be `auto` rather than `static`, and its initializer would execute every time the function was called, resetting it to 50. The `while` test in the `main` function would never find a true condition, and the program would stay in the loop until you interrupted it manually.

The extern Storage Class

The `extern` storage class declares external variables that are not defined locally, but that the local source code needs to reference. Usually, an `extern` declaration refers to a variable defined in a different translation unit. Program 5-8 demonstrates a program that uses an `extern` variable. This program comprises two translation units: pr05008a.cpp and pr05008b.cpp.

Program 5-8a: The extern storage class, part 1

```
#include <iostream>

void AccumulateAmount(void);

int main()
{
    // A variable declared as external.
    extern float Amount;

    AccumulateAmount();
    std::cout << Amount;
    return 0;
}
```

Program 5-8b: The extern storage class, part 2

```
// Definition of the external variable.
float Amount;

void AccumulateAmount()
{
    Amount = 5.72;
}
```

The two translation units — source-code files — are compiled independently and are linked into a single executable module. Quincy refers to such a program as a *project* and includes a project file that lists the source-code files that comprise the project.

The Amount variable that the main function refers to actually is declared in a different translation unit, the pr05007b.cpp source-code file. Consequently, the compiler cannot compile an address for the variable when the compiler compiles pr05007a.cpp. The extern declaration tells the compiler to compile all references to Amount as an as-yet-unresolved reference, and to delay resolving those references until the compiled object-code modules are linked into an executable program module.

An extern variable declaration may be inside or outside the function that references the external variable. If the variable is outside, all functions in the translation unit following the declaration can reference the external variable. If the declaration is inside a function, only functions that contain the extern declaration of the variable can reference the variable.

A program can have several extern declarations of a variable but only one definition: a declaration without the extern storage class specifier. The definition must appear outside any functions. The declarations and definition may be scattered among many translation units, or all of them may be in the same unit. Only one definition or declaration may have an initializer. The initializer may be in the definition or in any of the extern declarations, but it may not be in a declaration that is inside a function. If an extern declaration has an initializer, the variable does not need a definition elsewhere in the program, although it may have one. If there is no initializer, then there must be at least one definition.

A declaration declares the format of a variable but does not reserve memory, and a definition defines the instance of a variable and reserves memory for it. Often, a variable's definition and declaration are the same C++ language statement.

Typically, a program declares all extern variables in project-specific header files that are included by all the translation units. Then, it defines each external variable in the C++ source-code module where the variable logically originates. This practice eliminates redundancy and ensures consistency in the declaration of extern variables.

The register Storage Class

A variable declared with the register storage class is the same as an auto variable, except that the program cannot take the variable's address. You learn about variable addresses later in this chapter. Program 5-9 demonstrates a register variable.

Program 5-9: **The register storage class**

```cpp
#include <iostream>

int main()
{
    // A register variable declaration.
    register unsigned int Counter;

    for (Counter = 100; Counter < 1000; Counter += 50)
        std::cout << "Counter: " << Counter << endl;
    return 0;
}
```

The register storage class is a relic whose purpose is to allow the programmer to specify conditions under which the program's performance can be improved if certain local, automatic variables are maintained in one of the computer's hardware registers. It states the programmer's intention to use the variable in ways that might work best if the variable resided in a hardware register rather than in the computer's main memory. The register storage class is only a suggestion to the compiler that the variable occupy a register. The compiler can ignore the suggestion.

You cannot take the address of register variables, because hardware registers on most computers do not have memory addresses (Chapter 8). The address restriction applies even when the compiler chooses to ignore the suggestion and puts the variable in addressable memory.

Effective application of the register storage class requires an assembly language programmer's understanding of the processor architecture with respect to the number and kinds of registers available to be used for variables and how the registers behave. That understanding does not apply necessarily to a different computer, so the register storage class does not contribute much to a portable program. In addition, contemporary optimizing compilers usually do a better job than the programmer of selecting which variables can be maintained in registers, although the register storage class conceivably can help an aggressive optimizer do its job.

Initial Default Values

Non-local and static local variables are guaranteed to be initialized with zeros if the program does not initialize them explicitly. Automatic variables are not guaranteed to have any particular initial value when they come into scope. You should either initialize them or assign an initial value to them before you use them. Parameters are always initialized with the values of the caller's arguments.

Type Qualifiers

C++ includes two type qualifiers, the keywords const and volatile, that further define the nature and behavior of variables.

The const Type Qualifier

A const variable is one that the program may not modify, except through initialization when the variable is declared. The phrase "const variable" seems to be an oxymoron. How can something be constant and variable at the same time? Nonetheless, the usage is common among programmers. Program 5-10 uses a const variable as the upper limit for a loop.

Program 5-10: **The const type qualifier**

```
#include <iostream>

int main()
```

```
{
    // A const variable declaration.
    const int MaxCtr = 300;

    for (int Ctr = 100; Ctr < MaxCtr; Ctr += 50)
        std::cout << "Ctr = " << Ctr << endl;
    return 0;
}
```

The const variable might or might not occupy memory, have an address, and be used in any context that does not modify the contents of the variable. Whether it has an address depends on how you use it and on the C++ compiler implementation. If you take the address of a const variable, the compiler must give it a memory location. Otherwise, the compiler is free to treat a reference to the expression as if it were coded as a constant in an expression. When a variable is qualified as const, the compiler prevents the program from modifying the variable's contents. The discussion on pointers in Chapter 8 contains more details about const.

The volatile Type Qualifier

A volatile variable is the opposite of a const variable. The volatile type qualifier tells the compiler that the program can change the variable in unseen ways. Those ways are implementation-dependent. One possibility is that a variable can be changed by an asynchronous interrupt service routine. The compiler must know about such a variable so that the compiler does not optimize its access in ways that defeat the external changes. Program 5-11 shows how you declare a volatile variable.

Program 5-11: **The volatile type qualifier**

```
#include <iostream>

// A volatile variable declaration.
volatile int Value = 300;

int main()
{
    int Counter;
    for (Counter = 100; Counter < Value; Counter += 50)
        std::cout << "Counter: " << Counter << endl;
    return 0;
}
```

Suppose that a program posts the address of a variable in an external pointer (Chapter 8) and that an interrupt service routine elsewhere in the program or in the system modifies the contents of the variable by dereferencing the pointer. If the compiler has optimized the function by using a register for the variable while the program uses its contents, the effects of the interrupt could be lost. The volatile type qualifier tells the compiler not to make such optimizations.

Program Memory Architecture

Programs load into, and execute from, the computer's core or semiconductor memory. This concept, the stored program, is the basis for all contemporary digital computers. The program's machine-language instructions and its data are stored in the same logical memory space. Moreover, the program is organized into four logical segments: executable code, statically allocated data, dynamically allocated data (the heap), and the stack.

✦ Executable code and statically allocated data are stored in fixed memory locations.

✦ Program-requested, dynamically allocated memory is drawn from a memory pool called *the heap*.

✦ Local data objects, function arguments, and the linkage from a calling function to a called function are maintained in a memory pool called *the stack*.

Depending on the operating platform and the compiler, the heap and stack can be operating system resources that are shared by all concurrently running programs, or they can be local resources owned exclusively by the programs that use them.

The actual location of these memory pools and their proximity to one another depends on how the operating platform and compiler organize programs. Standard C++ does not mandate any specific organization. But assume, for the purposes of this discussion, that Figure 5-1 is a typical memory organization for a program when it is executing.

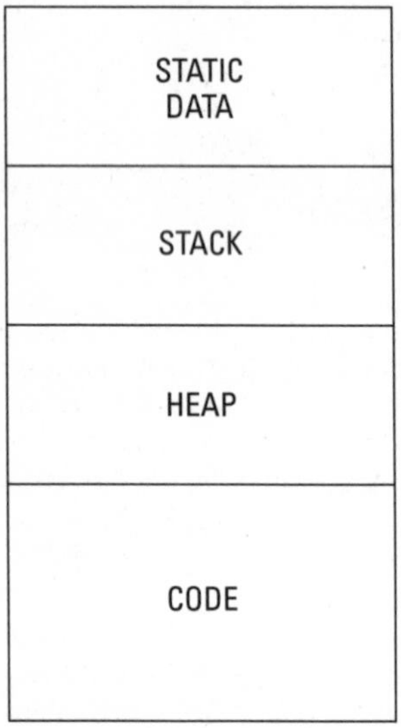

Figure 5-1: Typical C++ program memory organization

extern and static Variable Memory

External memory is a fixed memory pool allocated for the program before the program starts running. Variables declared as `extern` and `static` are maintained in external memory. Variables that have local scope and static storage class are also kept in external memory. All such variables are apparently constructed and initialized before `main` starts executing and destroyed after `main` returns to the operating system.

The Heap

A C++ program allocates and deallocates dynamic blocks of memory from a global store of memory sometimes called the *free store*, or more commonly called the *heap*. The heap is a resource that you control. Your program does the allocation by using the `new` operator, first discussed in Chapter 8. The heap is for *dynamic* memory allocation, which means that your program gets memory from the heap when it needs some and returns the memory to the heap when the program is finished with it. Heap memory allocation is usually done to allocate memory for a specific object — an array, a structure, a class. When the program gets that memory, the `new` operator returns the physical memory address assigned to the object. The program works with the object by dereferencing the object's address. When the program is finished with the object, the program returns the memory to the heap with the `delete` operator (Chapter 8) specifying the address of the object.

There are three problems associated with using the heap, and you must be aware of them and deal with them in your program. These problems are heap exhaustion, memory fragmentation, and memory leaks.

Heap Exhaustion

If your program tries to allocate more memory than the system has allocated for the heap, the heap is exhausted, and the system will throw an exception. There are ways to anticipate and deal with this situation, and Chapters 8 and 35 discuss them.

Memory Fragmentation

Since a program can allocate and deallocate variable length blocks of memory in a random order, it is possible to have a heap that has plenty of memory available, but no one contiguous block of memory large enough to fulfill a new allocation. This condition is called *memory fragmentation*, and its symptoms are identical to heap exhaustion. To avoid memory fragmentation, a programmer tries to balance allocations and deallocations to prevent it. Chapter 8 discusses this programming strategy.

Memory Leaks

A *memory leak* is a bug in the program. It happens when a program allocates memory and fails to deallocate it. Its symptoms can range from nothing to memory exhaustion. Many development environments include tests for memory leaks to help you find and fix them. Chapter 8 discusses programming techniques for avoiding memory leaks.

The Stack

The stack is another place where programs maintain copies of variables. Programs do not allocate memory explicitly on the stack as they do on the heap. The system allocates memory automatically when the program calls functions and declares local variables.

The stack, not to be confused with the Standard C++ Library std::stack container template class (Chapter 31), is fundamental to contemporary computer architecture and is usually supported in hardware.

Function parameters and automatic variables are maintained on the stack. Each running program in a computer has a stack. They might each have a private stack, they might all share one large stack with other running programs and the operating system, or there might be some combination of the two stack organizations. How it works depends on the operating system. You don't really have to know, but you should understand how the stack works. That understanding is fundamental to understanding automatic variables and recursion, which Chapter 10 explains.

A *stack* is a pushdown, pop-up data structure. It is a pool of memory with a pointer that points into it. This pointer is called the *stack pointer*. An application program does not have access to this pointer; the system maintains it. Initially the stack pointer points to the highest memory location available to the stack.

The runtime system pushes objects on the stack one at a time, after which the stack pointer moves down one entry. When the system pops an object from the stack, the most recently pushed object — the one just above the current stack pointer — is popped, and the stack pointer moves up one entry. When the pointer is at the top, the stack is empty. When the pointer is one past the bottommost entry, the stack is full.

The stack pointer exists in every C++ program. It is maintained not by the part of the program that you write, but rather by the runtime system. The runtime system maintenance actually is code that the compiler generates in the program. You do not see this code in your program, but it is there and you should understand what it does. This behavior and the pushdown, pop-up nature of a stack are what distinguish the stack from the heap.

Here is how the stack works. When one function (the caller) calls another function (the callee), the runtime system (the system) pushes all the caller's arguments and the caller's return address onto the stack. The stack pointer moves down as many places as necessary to accommodate these pushes. The last object pushed is the caller's return address.

When the callee starts executing, the system pushes the callee's automatic variables on the stack, moving the stack pointer down enough entries to make room for all the automatic variables that the callee declares.

The callee addresses its parameters on the stack as automatic variables created when the caller pushes its arguments. The callee addresses its own automatic variables on the stack, too. The stack pointer is, however, below all these local variables because of the pushes, but the callee uses negative and positive offsets from the stack pointer's original value when the callee started executing. You don't have to do this addressing in your program. The compiler generates code to do it when you reference the identifiers of parameters and local variables.

When a function references the address of a local variable (Chapter 8), the address returned is a memory address within the stack.

When the callee is about to return, the system pops the callee's automatic variables from the stack. The stack pointer now points to where it pointed when the callee first started and the automatic variables are destroyed. When the callee returns, the system pops the return address from the stack, and the caller resumes executing just past the call to the callee.

When the caller resumes executing, the system pops the caller's arguments from the stack, and the stack pointer now is positioned where it was before the caller called the callee.

Summary

In this chapter you learned about the scope of identifiers, storage classes, type qualifiers, and where in memory variables are maintained. Chapter 6 is about defining memory images of data aggregates by using the C++ `struct` and `union`.

✦　　✦　　✦

Structures and Unions

Dr. Stroustrup called early versions of C++ "C with classes." These early versions were his first attempts to extend the C language by using classes to implement an object-oriented programming model.

In traditional C, the only extensions you can add to the language are user-defined data types. You can also create global functions that perform functions. However, in C++ you can organize functions and variables into classes. A class represents a real-world entity like a file, a city, or an employee. If you had an employee class, you'd instantiate an object for each individual employee. That means C++ creates an object using the class as a template. Each object has its own data (name, salary, phone number, etc.) and a set of operations (WriteCheck, PrintW2, etc.).

C++ objects can also exist in hierarchies. So the hypothetical employee class might have related classes for full-time, part-time, and contract employees. This allows efficient code reuse as well as simplifies program design as you'll see in this chapter. Below you'll read about classes and data abstraction. First, you'll read about the underlying technology that supports C++ classes: C language structures and unions. C++ also supports these constructs, and classes are really C structures with some special extra features.

The struct

A C++ programmer can define collections of variables organized in a *structure*. A structure encapsulates related data into an aggregate. Programs can manipulate structures in ways similar to the manipulation of intrinsic data types. Another data aggregate, called a *union*, defines a single variable that can have multiple names and types. For example, you might create a union that can store either an integer or a floating-point number but not both at the same time.

Structures have much more power than you learn here. The C++ struct is a variant on the C++ class, discussed in Part II. This discussion concentrates on the struct as it is used in C language programs, but with a few C++ improvements.

You can declare instances of unions and structures, initialize those instances, assign them to one another, pass them to functions, and return them from functions. In the following sections, you learn to perform these programming tasks.

Declaring a struct

You declare a structure by using the struct keyword, giving the structure a name, and declaring the data types that are in the structure, as shown here:

```
// A structure named date.
struct Date
{
    short int month;   // Data members.
    short int day;
    short int year;
};
```

A structure declaration begins with the struct keyword followed by the name of the structure. The structure consists of variables, called the structure's *members*, whose declarations are surrounded by braces. You terminate a structure declaration with a semicolon.

The struct declaration does not reserve memory (that is, the previous code does not create any variables). It merely defines the format of the structure for later use by the program. The structure members can be any valid C++ type, including other structures.

Defining a struct Variable

You define a variable of the structure type by providing the struct keyword, the structure's name, and a name for the instance of the structure—the struct variable—as shown here:

```
// A Date structure named birthday.
struct Date birthday;
```

Because a structure declares a new data type, you can define a struct variable without including the struct keyword. This demonstrates one of the C++ improvements to the C structure:

```
// A Date structure named date_hired.
Date date_hired;
```

An exception to this improvement is when the struct name collides with another identifier in the same scope. In this case you must use the struct keyword to specify that, in this context, the name refers to the struct and not to the other thing with the same name.

```
// a struct named Person
struct Person {
    // ...
};
// a function named Person
void Person()
{
    // ...
}
```

Referencing struct Members

You reference the members of a structure by providing the name of the structure variable, the dot (.) operator, and the name of the member, as shown here:

```
// Assign a value to a structure member.
birthday.day = 24;
```

Program 6-1 declares and uses a `struct`.

Program 6-1: **The struct data type**

```cpp
#include <iostream>

// Declare a structure.
struct Date  {
    short int month, day, year;
};
int main()
{
    // A Date structure.
    Date dt;
    // Assign values to the structure members.
    dt.month = 6;
    dt.day = 24;
    dt.year = 1940;
    // Display the structure.
    std::cout << dt.month << '/' << dt.day << '/' << dt.year;
    return 0;
}
```

Initializing a Structure

Rather than assign values to each member of a structure variable, as Program 6-1 does, the program can initialize the variable when it is defined. Program 6-2 shows how to initialize a structure variable.

Program 6-2: **Initializing a structure variable**

```cpp
#include <iostream>

struct Date  {
    short int month, day, year;
};
int main()
```

Continued

```
{
    // An initialized Date variable.
    Date dt = {11, 17, 1941};
    // Display the structure.
    std::cout << dt.month << '/' << dt.day << '/' << dt.year;
    return 0;
}
```

The brace-surrounded, comma-separated list of expressions is the structure's initialization list. Each expression initializes a member of the structure. The types of the expressions must be compatible with the types of the members. You may have fewer expressions than the number of structure members — but not more. If you have fewer expressions, the compiler inserts zero values into the data members that are not initialized by your initialization list. An uninitialized automatic structure variable, however, is not filled with zeros. You need at least one initializing expression to pad the rest of the structure with zeros.

Structures Within Structures

A structure can have other structures as members. References to the members of the inner structure include the names of both structure variables, as shown in Program 6-3.

Program 6-3: **Structures within structures**

```
#include <iostream>

struct Date  {
    int month, day, year;
};
struct Employee      {
    int emplno;
    float salary;
    Date datehired;
};
int main()
{
    // An initialized Employee structure.
    Employee joe = {123, 35500, {5, 17, 82}};
    // Display the Employee information.
    std::cout << "Empl #: " << joe.emplno << std::endl
              << "Salary: " << joe.salary << std::endl
              << "Date hired: "
              << joe.datehired.month << '/'
              << joe.datehired.day   << '/'
              << joe.datehired.year << std::endl;
    return 0;
}
```

Program 6-3 declares two structures. The second one has an instance of the first one as a member. When the program initializes an instance of the outer structure, it includes initializers for the inner structure by enclosing them in their own pair of braces.

Referencing the members of the inner structure involves naming both structure variables, each one followed by the dot (.) operator and the member name as the rightmost identifier in the expression as in `joe.datehired.month` in the example.

Passing and Returning Structures to and from Functions

A function can accept a structure as a parameter, and a function can return a structure. For large structures, programmers usually pass structure pointers or reference variables (explained later) and let the calling and called functions share copies of the structures. This practice is more efficient, because it reduces the overhead of copying large memory segments. It is also somewhat safer. Arguments are passed on the stack, which can become exhausted if a program passes many large objects, particularly to recursive functions.

Nonetheless, sometimes you need to pass a private copy of a structure. Perhaps the called function changes the data and the calling function needs to preserve the original values of the data. Other times, a function returns a structure. Perhaps that function creates the structure as an automatic variable. The automatic structure goes out of scope when the function returns, so the program needs a copy that the function can return. Program 6-4 illustrates functions that pass and return structures.

Program 6-4: **Passing and returning structures**

```
#include <iostream>

struct Date   {
    int month, day, year;
};

Date GetToday(void);
void PrintDate(Date);

int main()
{
    Date dt = GetToday();
    PrintDate(dt);
    return 0;
}
Date GetToday(void)
{
    Date dt;
    std::cout << "Enter date (mm dd yy): ";
    std::cin >> dt.month >> dt.day >> dt.year;
    return dt;
}
void PrintDate(Date dt)
```

Continued

```
{
    std::cout << dt.month << '/';
    std::cout << dt.day << '/' << dt.year;
}
```

The union

A union looks just like a structure except that it has the union keyword instead of struct. The difference between unions and structures is that a structure defines an aggregate of adjacent data members, and a union defines a memory address shared by all of its data members. A union can contain only one value at a time, a value of the type of one of its members. All its members are positioned starting at the same memory location. The size of a union is the size of its widest member. Program 6-5 illustrates the behavior of a union.

Program 6-5: **The union data type**

```
#include <iostream>

union Holder {
    char holdchar;
    short int holdint;
    long int holdlong;
    float holdfloat;
};

void DisplayHolder(Holder, char*);

int main()
{
    Holder hld;
    // Assign to first member.
    hld.holdchar = 'X';
    DisplayHolder(hld, "char");
    // Assign to second member.
    hld.holdint = 12345;
    DisplayHolder(hld, "int");
    // Assign to third member.
    hld.holdlong = 7654321;
    DisplayHolder(hld, "long");
    // Assign to fourth member.
    hld.holdfloat = 1.23;
    DisplayHolder(hld, "float");
    return 0;
}
```

```
void DisplayHolder(Holder hld, char* tag)
{
    std::cout << "---Initialized " << tag << " ---"
              << std::endl;
    std::cout << "holdchar   " << hld.holdchar  << std::endl;
    std::cout << "holdint    " << hld.holdint    << std::endl;
    std::cout << "holdlong   " << hld.holdlong  << std::endl;
    std::cout << "holdfloat  " << hld.holdfloat << std::endl;
}
```

Running Program 6-5 demonstrates that changing one of a union's members changes the other members, too. When you assign a value to a particular member, the values of the other members only have coincidental meaning, because you overlay them with whatever bit configuration represents the assigned member's assigned value. You can observe this behavior by reading the output from the DisplayHolder function after each assignment, or by using Quincy's Watch window to watch each of the members. Exactly how a compiler overlays the members of a union is platform-specific. You will observe different behavior among platforms.

Initializing a Union

You can initialize only the first of a union's variables. Braces enclose the initializer, and there is only one data value, whose type must be compatible with the first member in the union, as shown here:

```
// Initialize a union variable.
Holder hld = {'X'};
```

If the first member of a union is a structure, the initialization may include the several expressions that initialize the structure. Program 6-6 demonstrates this usage.

Program 6-6: **Initializing a struct-containing union**

```
#include <iostream>

struct Date  {
    int mo, da, yr;
};
union Holder {
    Date hdt;
    int hint;
};
int main()
{
    Holder hld = {{6, 24, 1940}};
    std::cout << hld.hdt.mo << '/'
              << hld.hdt.da << '/'
              << hld.hdt.yr;
    return 0;
}
```

Anonymous Unions

A C++ program can declare unnamed unions. You might use this feature to save space or to intentionally redefine a variable. Program 6-7 illustrates the use of the anonymous union.

Program 6-7: **Anonymous unions**

```
#include <iostream>

int main()
{
    union    {
        int quantity_todate;
        int quantity_balance;
    };
    std::cout << "Enter quantity to date: ";
    std::cin >> quantity_todate;
    std::cout << "Enter quantity sold: ";
    int quantity_sold;
    std::cin >> quantity_sold;
    quantity_todate -= quantity_sold;
    std::cout << "Quantity balance = "
              << quantity_balance;
    return 0;
}
```

The program in Program 6-6 allows the two variables `quantity_todate` and `quantity_balance` to share the same space. After `quantity_sold` is subtracted from `quantity_todate`, `quantity_balance` contains the result shown by the program's output:

```
Enter quantity to date: 100
Enter quantity sold: 75
Quantity balance = 25
```

This feature eliminates many union-name prefixes in places where the only purpose for the union name is to support the union. You must declare a global anonymous union as static.

A Glimpse into Object-Oriented Programming

Object-oriented programming is often viewed as little more than extending the programming language by designing, implementing, and using data types beyond the intrinsic ones that the language provides. There's a lot more to it than that, and Chapter 40 contains a more complete discussion of the properties of object-oriented design and programming; but when you build C++ data aggregates that include their own behavior, you are on the edges of object-oriented technology. Let's take a brief look at those edges.

The Characteristics of Data Types

Before you can design your own custom data types, you must understand data types in general. Consider the intrinsic numeric C++ data types in Chapter 2. Each intrinsic data type has a *data representation* and exhibits predictable *behavior* when addressed in certain ways by the program. Each intrinsic data type has its own *implementation* (how the compiler implements the behavior) and its own *interface* (how a program invokes the behavior of an object of the data type). Let's use a universally known and intrinsically understood data type, the signed integer, as an example.

Data Representation

A signed integer typically contains 32 bits, although that is not a standard. The GNU C++ compiler used by Quincy supports a 32-bit signed integer, so we use that example in this discussion. A 32-bit signed integer can contain values ranging from - 2,147,483,648 to 2,147,483,647. That format is the signed integer data type's data representation.

Implementation

The internal twos-complement arithmetic of the `int` data type is the signed integer's implementation. The C++ compiler provides that implementation, usually based on the underlying architecture of the target computer's arithmetic registers.

Behavior

When you apply the increment (++) operator (refer to Chapter 2) to an object of type `signed int`, the object increments its value by 1. That reaction is a part of the `signed int` data type's behavior. Other behaviors are defined for other operators.

Interface

The source-code program's expression that applies the auto-increment operator to a `signed int` variable is part of the `signed int` data type's interface. You don't need to know how the compiler implements this behavior; you need know only how the interface provides the behavior. An `int` variable is an abstraction that the compiler provides.

Defining Data Types

The intrinsic numeric types suffice for most of a program's numerical needs, but there are times when you need to extend the language (for example, when your program requires user-defined data types, each with its own unique data representation, behavior, implementation, and interface).

Abstraction

In object-oriented programming, *abstraction* is the name given to the process by which you design a new data type that you and other programmers can view from a higher level of abstraction — concerning yourselves only with the interface and disregarding the details of the implementation.

A programmer must understand each data type's interface and behavior. Clearly, you need to know what happens when you add a constant value to an integer variable, for example. That understanding is the level of abstraction with which a programmer views an integer. You might understand (and often you must understand) the underlying data representation and implementation. However, the essence of object-oriented programming is that a programmer who uses objects of any data type views that type from a higher level of abstraction and pays little attention to the details of the data type's implementation.

What Are the Objects?

When do you need to use data abstraction in your design? How can you leverage what you already know about programming to help you understand this different view of a program, this so-called object-oriented view?

What kinds of data can't the compiler's intrinsic types represent? In procedural programming languages (for example, C, Pascal, COBOL, FORTRAN, PL/1, BASIC), you commonly group data elements into record formats to gather related data items into a logical aggregate with which the program can work. An employee record in a personnel system is one example. The department record is another. These aggregates may include among their members other data items that are themselves aggregates of data types (for example, date hired).

No matter what language you programmed with before you came to C++, you used data aggregates of one form or another. As a general rule, whenever you would have built a C structure, a BASIC TYPE, or a COBOL record definition, you now will use data abstraction to build the same thing as a user-defined data type described by a class or structure in C++. Let's examine that process in more detail.

Data Abstraction and Procedural Programming

To design a new data type with traditional procedural programming, you organized the basic types into a logical structure and wrote functions to process that structure. The functions were reusable throughout the program for other objects of the same structure, because you passed to the functions a reference to the affected object. Program 6-8 illustrates that principle.

Program 6-8: Data abstraction and procedural programming

```cpp
#include <iostream>
// Date Structure
struct Date  {
    int month, day, year;
};
void display(Date& dt)
{
    static char *mon[] = {
        "January","February","March","April","May","June",
        "July","August","September","October","November",
        "December"
    };
    std::cout << mon[dt.month-1] << ' '
            << dt.day << ", " << dt.year;
}
int main()
{
    Date birthday = {4, 6, 1961};
    std::cout << "Alan's date of birth is ";
    display(birthday);
    return 0;
}
```

Program 6-8 is a good example of procedural programming, and except for the use of the `std::cout` object and the reference parameter, it is what you expect to see in a C program that displays a date on the console. C is a procedural programming language.

The `Date` structure defines a data format. The format of the structure constitutes the data representation of the user-defined data type — in this case, a calendar date.

The `display()` function takes a reference to an object of the `Date` structure and displays the object's values on the console, constituting the behavior of the data type.

The `Date` data type's implementation of the display behavior sends to the `std::cout` object the three integers that represent the month, day, and year.

The type's interface is the `display()` function's identifier and parameter list.

Although Program 6-8 demonstrates data abstraction with procedural programming, it is a better example of why data abstraction with object-oriented programming is a superior programming model. The `display()` function is bound loosely to the `Date` structure because the function refers to the structure's members, dereferencing them through the address passed by the caller as an argument to the `dt` parameter. The `display()` function, and all calls to the function, must be declared in the same scope as the `Date` structure.

However, the `Date` structure's design is not perfect. The implementation and data representation are an open architecture. A program can easily instantiate an invalid `Date` object by initializing it with values that are out of the prescribed range of a calendar date. The program also can instantiate an uninitialized `Date` object with random invalid values in its data members. The program similarly can modify any of the data members of an existing `Date` object with invalid values. The design offers no protection from careless programming. Furthermore, the design permits unrelated functions that implement `Date`'s behavior to be scattered helter-skelter throughout the program.

The program distributes its dependency on the `Date` structure's implementation throughout all modules of the program's code that address `Date` objects. The details of the structure's data representation are public; the program depends on those details.

The `Date` structure and the `display()` function described earlier are bound loosely by the display function's use of a `Date` object reference. Anywhere the `Date` declaration is in scope, you can write such a function and alter the behavior of all `Date` objects for which the program calls that function. The `Date` data type's interface and behavior are distanced logically from its implementation and data representation.

The consequence of such a procedural design approach is that any modification to the `Date` structure's data representation levies a potential impact on widely distributed software modules, all of which are intimate with the details of the data type's implementation. This consequence is one of the principal reasons that complex procedural programs often are difficult to maintain.

Data Abstraction and Encapsulation

Although the `Date` structure and the `display()` function described earlier are bound loosely, they are not encapsulated. *Encapsulation* is an object-oriented design approach that closely binds the implementation of a class to its data representation, logically hides the details of the implementation from users of the data type, and provides a public interface to the data type's behavior.

Encapsulation is exactly what a compiler of any high-level programming language — object oriented or otherwise — does with intrinsic data types. An object-oriented programming language permits encapsulation of user-defined data types, too.

C++ uses features of the class mechanism to support encapsulation of user-defined data types. In the next section, we improve the procedural Date design by applying encapsulation. You can circumvent these improved design methods by using clever or careless C++ programming idioms, but C++'s support of encapsulation encourages you to write better programs.

Structures with Functions

A *structure*, as you learned earlier in this chapter, is an aggregate of data types forming a user-defined data type. The structure can contain characters, integers, enumerations, floats, doubles, arrays, pointers, typedefs, unions, and other structures. In other words, any valid data type can be a member of a structure. This convention is consistent with the traditional C definition of a structure.

C++ adds another type of member to the structure. *In C++, structures can include functions.*

Take a moment to consider the implications of what you just read. By adding functions to structures, you add the ability for a structure to include algorithms that are bound to, and work with, the other structure members. You closely associate the algorithms with the data they process; this association is how C++ supports encapsulation.

Adding Functions to Structures

Program 6-9 adds a function to the Date structure described earlier. The function's name is display(), and its purpose is to display the contents of an instance of the Date structure. This new function is a member of the structure and is called a *member function*. It eliminates the nonmember display function from the code fragment.

Program 6-9: **Structures with functions**

```
#include <iostream>

struct Date {
    int month, day, year;
    void display();  // A function to display the date.
};
void Date::display()
{
    static char *mon[] = {
        "January","February","March","April","May","June",
        "July","August","September","October","November",
        "December"
    };
    std::cout << mon[month-1] << ' ' << day << ", " << year;
}
int main()
{
    Date birthday = {4, 6, 1961};
    std::cout << "Alan's date of birth is ";
    birthday.display();
    return 0;
}
```

Program 6-9 codes the `display()` function's declaration outside the class declaration as `Date::display`. This notation tells the C++ compiler that the display member function exists to support instances of the `Date` structure. In fact, the only way to call this display function is as a member of a declared `Date`.

The `main()` function declares a `Date` named birthday and initializes it with a value. Then, the `main()` function calls the `Date::display()` function by identifying it as a member of the birthday structure with the following notation:

```
birthday.display();
```

The `Date::display()` function can reference members of the structure with which it is associated directly without naming an instance of the structure, because the function itself is a member of the structure.

The `Date::display()` function declares an array of pointers to character arrays initialized with literal strings. You haven't learned about such things yet. Chapter 8 explains pointers, and Chapter 7 explains arrays. For now, just take it on faith.

Multiple Instances of the Same Structure

You can declare more than one instance of the same structure; the member function associates itself with the data in the particular structure object for which you call the function. Program 6-10 adds two objects to the preceding listing to demonstrate this behavior.

Program 6-10: **Multiple instances of a structure**

```cpp
#include <iostream>

struct Date   {
    int month, day, year;
    void display();    // A function to display the date.
};

void Date::display()
{
    static char *mon[] = {
        "January","February","March","April","May","June",
        "July","August","September","October","November",
        "December"
    };
    std::cout << mon[month-1] << ' ' << day << ", " << year;
}

int main()
{
    Date alans_birthday = {4, 6, 1961};
    std::cout << "Alan's date of birth is ";
    alans_birthday.display();
    std::cout << std::endl;
```

Continued

Program 6-10 *(continued)*

```
    Date sharons_birthday = {10, 12, 1962};
    std::cout << "Sharon's date of birth is ";
    sharons_birthday.display();
    std::cout << std::endl;

    Date wendys_birthday = {4, 28, 1965};
    std::cout << "Wendy's date of birth is ";
    wendys_birthday.display();
    std::cout << std::endl;

    return 0;
}
```

The program in Program 6-10 declares three Date structures and uses the display() function to display the dates for all three.

Different Structures, Same Function Names

You can have different structures that use the same function name. Program 6-11 is an example of two different structures, each of which uses a function named display().

Program 6-11: **Two structures with the same function name**

```
#include <iostream>

struct Date {
    int month, day, year;
    void display();    // A function to display the date.
};

void Date::display()
{
    static char *mon[] = {
        "January","February","March","April","May","June",
        "July","August","September","October","November",
        "December"
    };
    std::cout << mon[month-1] << ' ' << day << ", " << year;
}

int main()
{
    Date alans_birthday = {4, 6, 1961};
    std::cout << "Alan's date of birth is ";
```

```
alans_birthday.display();
std::cout << std::endl;

Date sharons_birthday = {10, 12, 1962};
std::cout << "Sharon's date of birth is ";
sharons_birthday.display();
std::cout << std::endl;

Date wendys_birthday = {4, 28, 1965};
std::cout << "Wendy's date of birth is ";
wendys_birthday.display();
std::cout << std::endl;
return 0;}
```

The program in Program 6-11 has a Date structure and a Time structure. Both structures have functions named display(). The display() function associated with the Date structure displays the date; the display() function associated with the Time structure displays the time.

Observe the use of the call to the fill() function for the cout object. The fill() function is a member function of the std::ostream class, of which std::cout is an object. The function tells std::cout to fill any displayed items that are shorter than the space allotted for them (by the std::setw manipulator) with the argument character (in this example, a zero).

Observe also that the Standard C std::localtime() function returns a year value in the std::tm.tm_year data member. When added to the integer constant 1900, this value produces the correct year, even during and after the year 2000. Be ever mindful of the dreaded Year 2K issue and follow the example set by this book: *Do not write programs that have bugs built into them.*

Access Specifiers

By default, the members of a structure are visible to all the functions within the scope of the structure object. This visibility permits a program to modify the values of data members directly. Such access promotes weak programming idioms wherein unrelated parts of a program come to depend on the details of a data type's implementation. An objective of data abstraction is to hide those details from the user of the class, providing instead a public interface that translates the implementation for the user of the class.

You can limit this free access to a data type's data members by placing access specifiers in the structure's definition. You can modify the Date structure in Program 6-11 with the private and public access specifiers, as shown here:

```
struct Date  {
private:
    int month, day, year;
public:
    void display(void);
};
```

All members following the `private` access specifier are accessible only to the member functions within the structure definition. All members following the `public` access specifier are accessible to any function that is within the scope of the structure. If you omit the access specifiers, everything is public. You can use an access specifier more than once in the same structure definition.

A third access specifier, `protected`, is the same as the `private` access specifier unless the structure is a part of a class hierarchy—a subject that Part II addresses.

The preceding structure is unusable. Here's why. You cannot initialize an instance of that structure with a brace-separated list of integers, because the data members are private to the member functions and are not accessible to the rest of the program. The `Date` structure is useless, because it has no way for a program to put data values into the data members. You need to define and call a member function that initializes the data members before you use an object of this structure.

C++ structures and classes can have constructor and destructor member functions that are called automatically to handle initialization and destruction when objects of the classes enter and depart scope. You solve the problem of the unusable class in Part II, which, among many other things, explains constructors and destructors.

Should You Use Procedural Programming?

Nothing in C++ prevents you from using the procedural programming model of Program 6-8. Encapsulation of the `Date` structure's data representation and behavior occurs when member functions are declared as part of the structure declaration.

You can add to Programs 6-9, 6-10, and 6-11 a procedural `display()` nonmember function similar to the one in Program 6-8, and the program still works. However, by using access specifiers to make the data members private, you prevent functions that are not members of the structure from accessing the data members of an object of the structure. When you do that and when the class fully serves its purpose, data abstraction and encapsulation of that user-defined data type are complete.

The class

The class is the C++ mechanism by which a programmer expresses the design of custom data types. Classes are similar to the structure that you learn about in this chapter. In fact, they almost are identical. The structure described here is really the structure that C++ inherited from the C language. C++ adds substantially to the C structure and gives it a second identity with another name, which is *class*.

In its implementation of classes and structures, C++ significantly extends the support found in C of both elements. In C++, the class differs from the structure in the defaults that each assumes with respect to access specifiers, which we explain later in this chapter. Everything you learn about structures here applies to classes. Everything that you learn about classes in this chapter and subsequent chapters also applies to structures.

Let's use structures until you learn about access specifiers, whereupon we revisit the subject of the class versus the structure. Part II shifts focus to the C++ class.

The Class Versus the Structure

C++ defines structures and classes almost identically. To declare a class, you use the `class` keyword in place of the `struct` keyword. The only other differences are related to the default access specifiers. The members of a structure have public access by default. The members of a class have private access by default. There are similar differences when you declare classes and structures in hierarchies using class inheritance, a subject of Chapter 23.

The `Date` structure shown earlier is exactly the same as the `Date` class shown here:

```
class Date {
    int month, day, year;
public:
    void display(void);
};
```

So why have two different constructs when the differences are so small? The answer goes back to the early days of C++ when the class was evolving from the C structure. There is no technical reason that the C++ structure should include all the properties of the class. C++ cannot eliminate the structure altogether; it must, however, support the C structure to preserve compatibility between the languages, according to the original objectives of the C++ language. But without the explanation provided by Bjarne Stroustrup, the creator of C++, it is not clear why the structure needs member functions, access specifiers, and the ability to participate in class hierarchies. In *The Design and Evolution of C++* (Addison-Wesley, 1994), Dr. Stroustrup writes:

> "My intent was to have a single concept: a single set of layout rules, a single set of lookup rules, a single set of resolution rules, etc.... Only a single concept would support my ideas of a smooth and gradual transition from 'traditional C-style programming,' through data abstraction, to object-oriented programming."

So the reason is cultural rather than technical. Dr. Stroustrup goes on to explain that keeping the class and structure the same forestalls an otherwise unavoidable tendency on the part of language standardizers and specifiers to overwhelm the class specification with excess features while leaving the structure to implement only those features that involve low overhead and simplicity.

Given all that, when should you use a structure instead of a class? Many programmers adopt this rule: When the data structure's implementation is the same as its interface, use a structure; otherwise, use a class.

What are the implications of this rule? What does it mean when you say that the implementation is the interface? It means simply that you have a typical C structure with data members only (no member functions), all of which have public access so that the format of the data members is what the application program views. C++ programmers call such an aggregate "plain old data" and use the acronym POD.

Object-oriented purists contend that by following this rule, there is no valid application for the C++ structure. If you fall into that category, C++ supports your beliefs. Use classes exclusively. If you lean toward the pragmatic approach, C++ permits you to write code using either idiom. C++ has something for everyone.

Virtually none of the programs that follow in this book use structures. Part II shifts focus to the C++ class because you have now learned all you need to know about structures.

C++ Unions

C++ unions share some of the structure attributes that you learn in this chapter. A union can have function members, but it cannot be a part of a class hierarchy. You learn about class hierarchies in Chapter 23. A union can have constructor and destructor functions (Chapter 15), but it cannot have virtual functions (Chapter 23). Unions can have private and public members. You learn more about the private and public access specifiers in Chapter 14.

Summary

This chapter taught you about data abstraction and the C++ structure, its members, and its access specifiers. You had an introduction to the C++ class, a variation on the structure. In Part II, this book uses the class mechanism exclusively for declaring user-defined data types and building object-oriented class hierarchies.

✦   ✦   ✦

More About C++ Data

This chapter describes several C++ language features related to variables. You will learn about enumerated constants, arrays, the sizeof operator, the typecasting mechanism, and how dynamic variables are stored on the heap and automatic variables are maintained on the stack.

The enum Constant

An *enumerated* constant is one that associates identifiers with integer values within the context of an identified set of constants. For example, months are January, February, March, and so on; sexes are male and female; colors are red, green, blue, and so on; the states of a program being debugged are idle, running, breaking, and so on.

You define an enumerated constant by writing an enum declaration, which defines an enumerated constant data type. An enumerated constant consists of a group of related identifiers, each with an integer value. For example:

```
enum Colors {Red, Green, Blue};
enum month {jan, feb, mar, apr, may, jun,
            jul, aug, sep, oct, nov, dec};
```

In these enumerated constants, the first identifier in the brace-surrounded lists is equated with the numerical value zero, the second with 1, and so on. The names must be distinct, and they must not be keywords or any other identifiers in the current scope.

You can specify an initializer value for a particular enum identifier within the declaration. Values that follow immediately are incremented starting from that point. For example:

```
enum weekday {sun = 1, mon, tue, wed, thu, fri, sat};
```

In this example, sun equals 1, mon is 2, and so on.

You can declare variables of an enumerated type and use enumerated values wherever you use integers. You also can specify an enumerated type in a function's parameter list or anywhere else that you can use an integer constant.

Program 7-1 illustrates the use of an enumeration in a `switch` statement.

Program 7-1: **The enum data type**

```
#include <iostream>

enum colors {red = 1, green, blue};

int main()
{
    std::cout << "1=Red, 2=Green, 3=Blue. Select: ";
    int cl;
    std::cin >> cl;
    enum colors col = (enum colors) cl;
    switch (col) {
        case red:
            std::cout << "Red";
            break;
        case green:
            std::cout << "Green";
            break;
        case blue:
            std::cout << "Blue";
            break;
        default:
            std::cout << "??";
            break;
    }
    return 0;
}
```

Program 7-1 prompts you to enter a digit that represents one of the three colors. When you do, the program displays the name of the color by using the `col` variable, which is of type `color`, in a `switch` statement. Each `case` statement uses one of the `enum` values in its expression.

C programmers should observe that, unlike with C, the declaration of the `col` variable need not include the `enum` keyword. In C++, each `enum` type is a distinct new data type for the scope in which it is declared. That line of code could have been written like this.

```
colors col = (colors) cl;
```

Now, what is that part in parentheses? The program reads the selection into an integer variable because `std::cin` does not know how to read information into the `enum color` data type. Then, the program assigns the input value to a variable of type `color`. But because the compiler cannot implicitly convert an `int` to an `enum` (unlike C compilers, which can), the program must first cast the `int` to an `enum`, by using a `typecast`, discussed next.

Typecasts

As you saw in Program 7-1, sometimes you have to tell the compiler to treat a variable as if it is something other than what it really is. In Program 7-1, since the compiler cannot implicitly convert an `enum` variable to an integer, even though `enum`s are indeed integer values, you have to explicitly override the compiler's strong type-checking mechanism. The type-checking mechanism exists to catch unintentional type usage errors. The `typecast` mechanism exists to let you intentionally override type checking.

C Typecasts

When you need to coerce the compiler into thinking that a variable or constant is a different type from the one that you declared it to be or, as in the case of an expression, a different type from the one implied by its context, you can use a traditional C-style typecast, which has this format:

```
enum colors col = (enum colors) cl;
```

The `(enum colors)` prefix to the expression is a traditional C-style *typecast*, also called a cast. The cast tells the compiler to convert the value of the expression to the type in the cast.

Some casts are not permitted. You cannot cast a reference to a structure to something else. You can cast any numerical type to any other numerical type and any pointer to any other pointer. You also can cast numerical values to pointers and vice versa, although such practices generally are considered unsafe and unnecessary. Chapter 8 discusses pointers.

Casts can be used to suppress compiler warnings. Some compilers warn you when an implicit type conversion can result in the loss of information. For example:

```
long el = 123;
short i = (int) el;  // Compiler warning without the cast.
```

Many compilers alert you that the assignment of a `long` to a `short` can lose data. There are times when you know better, as in the example. The value 123 is well within the range of a short integer. Other times you don't care, such as when you need the integral part of a real number:

```
float rn = 34.56;
int i = (int) rn;    // i = 34
```

These are the best uses of the cast: to suppress compiler warnings about things that you do intentionally. Using the cast to override the compiler's type-checking facilities is a treacherous practice.

Casts usually are deprecated by the knowledgeable; but there are times when they are unavoidable, such as the cast from a `void` pointer to a specific pointer type as Chapter 8 explains.

C++ Typecasts

The C typecast mechanism is inherited from K&R C. C++ includes an improved typecasting mechanism to support those cases where casting is necessary. Chapter 37 is about the C++ typecasting mechanism.

Arrays

An array is an aggregate of objects of the same type that are contiguous in memory. Most programming languages support arrays. Arrays can have one or more dimensions.

All of C++'s intrinsic data types can be contained in arrays. The dimensions of an array are specified in its definition. The variables in an array are called its *elements*. You access the elements of an array by providing integer expression *subscripts*.

Declaring Arrays

You declare an array by providing its dimension or dimensions in bracketed expressions following its identifier. This lesson is about arrays with only one dimension. Here is an example of an array of integers:

```
int Offsets[10];
```

This code defines ten integer elements in an array named Offsets. The integers are adjacent in memory. The physical size of an array in bytes is the size of one of its elements multiplied by the number of elements in the array. The dimension expression within the brackets may have operators, but it must evaluate to a constant expression. The dimension is relative to 1. It specifies the number of elements in the array (which, as you will see shortly, doesn't correspond to the maximum legal array subscript).

Accessing Arrays with Subscripts

To access an element in an array, the program uses the array's identifier followed by a subscript expression in brackets:

```
Offsets[3] = 123;
```

The subscript expression is any expression that evaluates to an integer value. It does not have to be a constant expression. Subscripts are relative to zero, so the example just shown assigns 123 to the fourth element of the Offsets array of integers.

Initializing Arrays

You initialize an array by following its definition with a brace-enclosed initialization list. There may be as many initializers as there are elements in the array, as shown here:

```
// A 7-element array.
int Zones[5] = {43, 77, 22, 35, 89};
```

If you code more initializers than there are elements in the dimension, a compile error occurs. If you code fewer, the remaining elements are initialized with zero values. If you provide no initializers, the array is initialized according to its storage class as Chapter 5 explains in the discussion titled "Initial Default Values."

By using an empty dimension expression and initializers, you implicitly specify the array's dimension as being the number of initializers, as shown here:

```
// Five elements in this array
int Zones[] = {43, 77, 22, 35, 89};
```

Program 7-2 illustrates a simple array.

Program 7-2: **Array of integers**

```
#include <iostream>

int main()
{
    int Values[] = {1,2,3,5,8,13,21};
    for (int i = 0; i < 7; i++)
        std::cout << Values[i] << std::endl;
    return 0;
}
```

The program in Program 7-2 declares and initializes an array of seven integers. Then, it accesses the array in a for loop that iterates an integer variable from 0 through 6. The statement body of the for loop uses the iterating variable to subscript into the array, retrieve the values of the array's elements, and write them to the standard output device. Figure 7-1 shows the Values array in memory with a subscripted expression that dereferences the fifth element of the array.

Once again, subscripts are relative to 0 and dimensions are relative to 1.

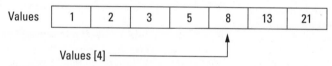

Figure 7-1: An integer array

Arrays of Structures

You can build an array of structure objects and reference the members of each of the array's structure elements by using subscripts. Initialization of the structure uses inner brace-enclosed structure initializers within the brace-enclosed array initializer. Program 7-3 demonstrates an array of structures.

Program 7-3: **Array of structures**

```
#include <iostream>

struct Employee
{
    int emplno;
    float wage;
};
```

Continued

Program 7-3 *(continued)*

```
Employee emps[] =
{
    { 1, 10.17 },
    { 2, 15.50 },
    { 3, 13.00 }
};
int main()
{
    int i;
    for (i = 0; i < 3; i++)
        std::cout << emps[i].emplno << ' '
                  << emps[i].wage << std::endl;
    return 0;
}
```

The `Employee` structure has two members. The `emps` array has three elements. The array initializer contains three inner initializers for the three structure elements in the array. The program iterates through the array with a `for` loop. Finally, the `std::cout` call dereferences the structure members with a bracketed subscript expression after the array identifier and before the structure member dot (.) operator.

Multidimensional Arrays

Sometimes an array has more than one dimension. For example, a grid of numbers reflecting a quarter's monthly revenues by cost center can be implemented as an array with two dimensions. You define a two-dimensional array by adding a second bracketed dimension expression to the definition, as shown here:

```
float Revenues[3][8];  // 3 months, 8 cost centers
```

This array is, in effect, three adjacent float arrays with eight elements each. It is organized in memory that way. The leftmost dimension's elements are adjacent. The first eight elements are followed by the second eight elements, which are followed by the third eight elements. Program 7-4 uses the preceding array to demonstrate how multidimensional arrays work.

Program 7-4: **Two-dimensional array**

```
#include <iostream>

// A two-dimensional array.
float Revenues[3][8] = {
    {45.33, 55.55, 78.00, 37.26, 98.35, 23.55, 45.65, 22.00},
    {35.43, 45.45, 79.00, 30.26, 47.55, 34.65, 52.79, 32.50},
    {55.37, 75.05, 68.10, 31.27, 62.36, 53.56, 43.68, 24.06}
};
```

```
int main()
{
    for (int mon = 0; mon < 3; mon++)    {
        std::cout << mon+1 << ':';
        for (int cc = 0; cc < 8; cc++)
            std::cout << ' ' << Revenues[mon][cc];
        std::cout << std::endl;
    }
    return 0;
}
```

Figure 7-2 shows how the two-dimensional array is organized in memory and how a sub-scripted reference accesses one of the array's elements.

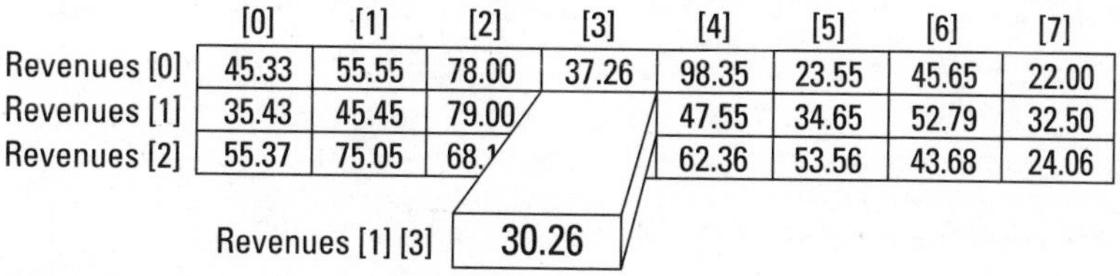

Figure 7-2: Two-dimensional array

If any of the inner initializer lists have fewer initializers than there are elements in their corresponding arrays, the remaining elements are initialized to zero.

You can eliminate all but the outermost pair of braces in an array initialization as long as you provide enough intializers for all the elements in the inner arrays. The array in Program 7-4 can be initialized like this:

```
float Revenues[3][8] = {
    45.33, 55.55, 78.00, 37.26, 98.35, 23.55, 45.65, 22.00,
    35.43, 45.45, 79.00, 30.26, 47.55, 34.65, 52.79, 32.50,
    55.37, 75.05, 68.10, 31.27, 62.36, 53.56, 43.68, 24.06
};
```

Arrays can have two, three, or more dimensions. Standard C++ imposes no limit on the number of dimensions an array can have, although working with a many-dimensioned array can be confusing.

Character Arrays: A Special Case

Character arrays get special treatment in C++. The C++ language has no intrinsic string data type like those of BASIC and other languages, although there is a standard `std::string` class that you learn about in Chapter 27. Instead, C++ supports arrays of `char` variables in special ways. You have seen what appear to be string data types in the string constants in the exercises in Chapter 2. These string constants actually are null-terminated arrays of characters. Consider the string constant in this example:

```
std::cout << "Hello";
```

The compiler builds an internal, unnamed character array. If you could see its declaration, the array would look like this:

```
char [] = {'H', 'e', 'l', 'l', 'o', '\0'};
```

The compiler passes the address of the internal array to the `std::cout` object, which can recognize a pointer to type `char`. (Pointers and addresses are discussed in detail in the Chapter 8.) No identifier is assigned to string literals, so the internal representation just shown has none. Observe the array's last character constant. It is initialized with the character constant `'\0'`, which is a zero value. This is the standard null terminator for a C++ string constant. Consequently, the `"Hello"` expression refers to an array of six char variables, the last of which has the implied initializer, `'\0'`.

You can initialize a character array with a string constant. Program 7-5 shows how this works.

Program 7-5: **Initializing a character array**

```
#include <iostream>

int main()
{
    char str[] = "Hello, Dolly";
    int i = 0;
    while (str[i] != '\0')
        std::cout << str[i++];
    return 0;
}
```

The sizeof Operator

Sometimes you need to compute the number of bytes that a type, variable, structure, or array uses in memory. This requirement often comes up when you want to write something to a disk record, for example, which is discussed in Chapter 29. Other times you might need to know how many elements are in an array when the array dimension is implied by the array's initializers.

You could determine something's size by applying what you know about it, adding it up, and putting its size in a constant expression. For example, you could count the bytes in a structure by adding the number of bytes in each of its members. There are three problems with doing that.

First, you could make a mistake and add it up wrong.

Second, if you change the size of the structure later during the program's development, you'll have to recompute its size. If you used an explicit constant size for the structure, you'll need to find all such references and change them.

The last problem is one of portability. If you compile the program with a different compiler or on a different computer, the sizes might be different, and the value you computed would be incorrect. The sizeof operator avoids all three of these problems.

The sizeof operator returns the size in characters of a variable or a type. The variable or type can be an array, structure, pointer, or one of the intrinsic types. When the operand is a type it must be surrounded by parentheses. When the operand is a variable identifier, the parentheses are optional. Here are examples:

```
// Some things to get the size of.
int w;
int* x;
int y[5];
struct z { int a,b,c; };
struct z zs;
struct z* zp;

// Some sizeof expressions.
sizeof w;           // The size of an int.
sizeof(int);        // The size of an int.
sizeof x;           // The size of a pointer.
sizeof &w;          // The size of an address constant.
sizeof *x;          // The size of an int.
sizeof y;           // The size of the array.
sizeof(struct z);   // The size of the structure.
sizeof zs;          // The size of the structure.
sizeof zp;          // The size of a pointer.
```

Programs use sizeof as a portable way to express structure sizes and the sizes of input/output buffers.

You also can use sizeof to compute at compile-time the number of elements in an array. Consider a program that has an array of structures such as the one in Program 7-3. That program is using a constant 3 to terminate the for loop's iteration through the array. But suppose that during maintenance of the program you sometimes change the number of elements in the array. You would have to find all places in the program where the number of elements was explicitly used. There is a better way.

By using sizeof to compute the number of elements, the program adjusts when you compile it to changes that you make. Program 7-6 shows how this works.

Program 7-6: **Using sizeof to compute array elements**

```
#include <iostream>

// An Employee structure.
struct Employee     {
    char name[20];
     int deptno;
};
```

Continued

Program 7-6 *(continued)*

```
// The employee roster
Employee employees[] = {
    { "Sam",    1 },
    { "Bill",   1 },
    { "Jim",    7 },
    { "Chick",  4 },
    { "Paul",   4 },
    { "Donald", 5 },
};

// dynamically computed number of employees
const int emplct = sizeof employees / sizeof(Employee);

int main()
{
    for (int i = 0; i < emplct; i++)        {
            std::cout << employees[i].deptno;
            std::cout << ' ';
            std::cout << employees[i].name;
            std::cout << std::endl;
    }
    std::cout << "Total: " << emplct;
    return 0;
}
```

Program 7-6 uses sizeof in two ways. The first usage computes the number of bytes used by the array of Employee structures named employees. This technique is what you would use, for example, to compute the number of bytes to write to a disk file if you were recording the array on disk. In this case, however, we want to know how many elements are in the array so we can iterate it. The second usage of sizeof returns the number of bytes in one Employee structure. By dividing this value into the size of the array, the program computes the number of elements in the array.

Here's another way the expression could have been written:

```
const int emplct = sizeof employees / sizeof employees[0];
```

In this usage the second half of the expression gets the size of one element in the array, which is the same thing as getting the size of the Employee struct, which is the type that that array contains. This usage also demonstrates that sizeof needs parentheses when you are getting the size of a type but does not need parentheses when you are getting the size of a variable.

typedef

The C++ typedef storage class specifier does not really specify a storage class. Instead, typedef is grouped with the static, extern, register, and auto storage classes (Chapter 5), because all five appear syntactically in the same place in a declaration and because they are mutually exclusive. Therefore, `typedef` is called a storage class specifier. However, `typedef` has a much different role: It enables you to assign your own names to types, pointers to types, and references to types. These names are aliases of existing things. Program 7-7 is an example of `typedef`.

Program 7-7: **The typedef storage class**

```
#include <iostream>

// Create an alias for the int data type.
typedef int RcdCounter;

int main()
{
    RcdCounter rc = 123;
    std::cout << rc << " records";
    return 0;
}
```

Program 7-7 uses `typedef` to declare an integer type for a record counter. If you decide later in the program's development that a record counter needs to be a different integral type— `long`, perhaps, or `unsigned`—you can change the `typedef` declaration, and the program adjusts all uses of the data type. Here are some of the ways that you can change the `typedef` in Program 7-7:

```
typedef long RcdCounter;
typedef unsigned RcdCounter;
typedef unsigned char RcdCounter;
```

The `typedef` storage class works with pointers and structures, too, and you can combine the `typedef` declaration with the `struct` declaration. Here is an example:

```
typedef struct graphic  {
    char *title;
    int x,y;
    int ht, wd;
} *Graphic;
```

(Chapter 8 explains pointers. Bookmark this discussion and return here when you complete Chapter 8.)

You can declare pointers to the `graphic` structure with the `Graphic` identifier like this.

```
Graphic pg;  // a pointer to struct graphic
```

Perhaps the structure and `typedef` declarations are in a header file, and the code that supports graphics is in a library. Programmers don't need to know that `Graphic` is a pointer or where that pointer points. The identifier might be treated as an abstract handle used to communicate between the applications program and the library software, as in this example:

```
#include "graphics.h"

void makepicture()
{
    Graphic handle = CreateShape("Blob", 3, 5, 10, 60);
    DisplayGraphic(handle);
    // etc...
}
```

The underlying structure of graphical elements in this example is unimportant to the programmer who uses the `Graphic` handle. This practice, called *information hiding*, is a basic concept in structured programming.

You can use one `typedef` statement to define multiple `typedefs` like this.

```
typedef struct graphic {
    // ...
} *PGraphic, &RGraphic, Graphic;
```

This statement defines three `typedefed` identifiers. `PGraphic` is a pointer to `struct graphic`, `RGraphic` is a reference to `struct graphic`, and `Graphic` is a `struct graphic`.

Chapter 8 explains pointers; Chapter 9 explains references.

Summary

This chapter taught you some of the different ways to work with variables in a C++ program. You learned how to define an enumerated constant, how to cast variables to other types, how to build and access arrays of variables, how to compute the size of things in memory, and how to define alias type names for other types.

Chapter 8 is about how you organize your source code files into a program and how to use the operating system's command line to control how your program executes.

✦   ✦   ✦

Pointers, Addresses, and Dynamic Memory Allocation

◆ ◆ ◆ ◆

In This Chapter

Pointer variables

Object addresses

Dynamic memory
allocation

◆ ◆ ◆ ◆

One of the most important topics in C and C++ programming is pointers. Pointers are the source of much confusion, as well as the cause of many programming errors. In this chapter, you learn the similarities between pointers, variables that contain addresses and addresses themselves, the values that pointers contain. You also learn to use pointers in your programs.

Pointers and Addresses

Pointers are variables that contain the addresses of other variables and functions. A C++ program can declare a pointer to any data type, including structures and unions. A program can use the address of any variable in an expression, except variables declared with the register storage class. A program can assign the address of a variable to a pointer variable. Furthermore, the program can pass the address of a variable as an argument to a function that has a pointer for a parameter. A program can use the address of a function in an assignment or in an initializer, or as a function argument. Additionally, a program can call a function through a pointer that contains the function's address.

Pointers are an important part of the C++ language. All arguments are passed to functions by value; this means that a copy of the argument is written into the called function's parameter variable. Programs may not, however, pass arrays by value. Pointers simulate passing by reference in that you can pass the address of an array, structure, or intrinsic data type to be copied into the function's pointer variable parameter. The function's reference to the caller's data is the address of the data in the pointer. Note that pointers are only one way to pass by reference. Reference variables, the subject of Chapter 9, are another way.

Pointers, addresses, and the notational relationship between pointers and arrays are the source of much confusion for new C and C++ programmers. As a learning aid, take the following code examples, hang them on the wall over your computer, and leave them there until pointers and addresses become second nature:

```
int i, j;   // int variables
int* ip;    // pointer to int variable
ip = &i;    // assign address of int variable to pointer to int
j = *ip;    // retrieve value that int pointer points to
int** ipp;  // pointer to int pointer
ipp = &ip   // assign address of pointer
j = **ipp;  // retrieve int through pointer to int pointer
```

Pointers to Intrinsic Types

You declare a pointer by specifying the type of data to which the pointer points, one or more asterisks, and the name of the pointer itself. The ip pointer variable definition in the preceding samples is an example.

C programmers typically declare pointers by putting the asterisk immediately to the left of the identifier:

```
int *ip;    // pointer to int variable
```

C++ programmers often prefer to use an idiom in which the asterisk is adjacent to the type:

```
int* ip;    // pointer to int variable
```

Either way works. The following ways also work, because the white space is optional:

```
int*ip;      // pointer to int variable
int * ip;    // pointer to int variable
```

Remember that pointers are variables themselves. They usually are of uniform size (which is platform-dependent) regardless of what they point to, and you can coerce any numeric value into one of them and dereference that value as if it were the address of a variable of the pointer's type. You must go out of your way, however, to get the C++ compiler to let you put into a pointer the address of data of a different type. Dereferencing such a pointer could cause your program to misbehave.

Program 8-1 demonstrates pointers to some of C++'s intrinsic types.

Program 8-1: **Pointers to intrinsic types**

```
#include <iostream>

int main()
{
    // Intrinsic type variables.
    char  c = 'A';
    int   i = 123;
    long  l = 54321;
    float f = 3.45;
    // Pointers.
    char* cp;      // to char
```

```
int*   ip;    // to int
long*  lp;    // to long
float* fp;    // to float
// Assign variable addresses to pointers.
cp = &c;
ip = &i;
lp = &l;
fp = &f;
// Reference the variables through the pointers.
std::cout << *cp << std::endl;
std::cout << *ip << std::endl;
std::cout << *lp << std::endl;
std::cout << *fp << std::endl;
return 0;
}
```

The address of operator (&) returns the address of the identifier that follows. Assigning the address of a variable to a pointer points that pointer to the variable. Referencing the pointer with the * pointer operator notation dereferences the pointer by returning the value of the variable to which the pointer points.

Pointer Arithmetic

Pointers are similar to integer variables. They contain numeric values that happen to be memory addresses, the formats of which depend on the hardware platform. You can add integer values to, as well as subtract them from, a pointer. The difference between a pointer and a normal integer is this: When you add or subtract an offset and a pointer, the compiler scales the offset by the size of the pointer's target data type. If you add 1 to or subtract 1 from a pointer, you really add or subtract the size of data to which the pointer points. When you add an integer value to, or subtract one from, a pointer, the expression returns the new address. You can subtract pointers of the same type from one another. This subtraction returns an integer that represents the number of instances of the type between the two addresses. Those arithmetic operations, along with their ++, --, += and -= operator counterparts, are the only ones you can perform on pointers. Program 8-2 is a simple example of pointer arithmetic.

Program 8-2: **Pointer arithmetic with the increment operator**

```
#include <iostream>

int CountDown[] = {10,9,8,7,6,5,4,3,2,1,0};

int main()
{
    // Initialize a pointer to the first array element.
    int* cdp = &CountDown[0];
    do      {
        // Display the array element.
        std::cout << *cdp << std::endl;
        // Increment the pointer.
```

Continued

```
        cdp++;
    } while (*cdp);
    std::cout << "blast-off";
    return 0;
}
```

The assignment in Program 8-2 assigns the address of the first element of the array to the `cdp` pointer. The next section explains a more convenient notation for taking the address of an array.

The statement that increments `cdp` does not add the integer value 1 to the address in the pointer. Because the pointer is declared with the `int` type, the increment adds the size of integer variables — which in the Quincy implementation of C++ is 4. For example, you can change the array and the pointer to a different integer type with a different size, and the program still works the same.

You can save some code in Program 8-2 by coding the `do` loop this way:

```
do
    std::cout << *cdp++ << std::endl;
while (*cdp);
```

The ++ auto-increment operator has a lower precedence than the * pointer operator, so the expression just shown retrieves what `cdp` points to and then increments `cdp`. To increment the pointer before you retrieve what it points to, code the statement this way:

```
std::cout << *++cdp;
```

Sometimes you may want to increment what the pointer points to rather than the pointer. For a postfix increment, you code the expression like this:

```
(*cdp)++
```

The parentheses override the default precedence and apply the increment operator to the variable to which the pointer points. The following notation applies the prefix increment operator to that:

```
++*cdp;
```

Parentheses are not needed in this case, because the increment operator applies to the `lvalue` that follows it, which is the variable to which the pointer points.

The preceding rules apply equally to the auto-decrement operator.

You can use expressions to add values to, and subtract values from, pointers. Once again, the notation must take into consideration the precedence of the pointer operator and the arithmetic operators. Here are examples using a pointer to type `int`:

```
int ia[] = { 97, 32, 128 };
int i;
int* ip = &ia[0];

i = *ip+1;          // ip -> 97, returns 98
i = *(ip+1);        // ip -> 97, returns 32
```

The first assignment to i gets the integer variable to which ip points, which is 97, and adds 1 to its value, returning 98.

The second assignment to i retrieves the integer array element one past where the pointer points. The variable in that position has the value 32, which the expression returns.

Observe that neither expression changes the values that are stored in the pointer or in the array. The expressions compute values and use those values to form the assignments. The difference between this kind of pointer notation and using auto-increment or auto-decrement operators is that the latter two actually change the value of the pointer or the value to which it points. Which notation you use depends on what the program is supposed to do. Program 8-3 uses a variable to iterate through an array with a pointer.

Program 8-3: **Pointer arithmetic with expressions**

```
#include <iostream>

float dues[] = {
    30.00,       // paid quarterly
    55.00,       // paid semiannually
    100.00       // paid annually
};
int main()
{
    float* dp = &dues[0];
    for (int i = 0; i < 3; i++)
        std::cout << *(dp+i) << std::endl;
    return 0;
}
```

Pointers and Arrays

Pointers and arrays have a special and often confusing relationship. The confusion begins when you learn that there are two ways to get the address of an array or one of its elements. The listings until now have used the address-of operator (&) and have taken the address of the first element in the array. An alternative notation uses just the name of the array. Using the name of an array in an expression is the same as taking the address of the array's first element (that is, element 0). The following example compares the notation in Program 8-3 with the alternative:

```
float* dp = &dues[0]; // Address of 1st element.
float* dp1 = dues;    // Address of array (same address).
```

Let's carry that notation further. If you use array address notation with the addition operator and an integer expression, it is the same as taking the address of the array's element subscripted by the expression. For example:

```
float* dp1 = &dues[2]; // Address of 3rd element.
float* dp2 = dues+2;   // Also address of 3rd element.
```

If the array has multiple dimensions, the same addressing notational conventions apply when you do not include subscripts for all the dimensions. Program 8-4 is an example.

Program 8-4: **Array address notation**

```
#include <iostream>

// A two-dimensional integer array.
int calendar[5][7] = {
    {  1, 2, 3, 4, 5, 6, 7 },
    {  8, 9,10,11,12,13,14 },
    { 15,16,17,18,19,20,21 },
    { 22,23,24,25,26,27,28 },
    { 29,30,31 }
};
int main()
{
    int* cp1 = &calendar[3][2]; // Address of 4th week,3rd day.
    int* cp2 = calendar[3]+2;   //  "     "   "     "    "   "
    int* cp3 = calendar[0];     // Address of array.
    int* cp4 = calendar[2];     // address of 3rd week,1st day.
    std::cout << *cp1 << ' '
              << *cp2 << ' '
              << *cp3 << ' '
              << *cp4;
    return 0;
}
```

To add to the confusion, you can dereference what a pointer points to by using array sub-script notation. The following usages of a pointer are equivalent:

```
int* ip;      // A pointer (with address of array assumed).
x = *(ip+3);  // Access 4th element of the array.
x = ip[3];    // Access 4th element with subscript notation.
```

As the example shows, even though ip is a pointer, you can use it with array element nota-tion when it points to an array.

And, as if that isn't enough, you can access an element of an array by using pointer notation, as shown here:

```
int ia[10];   // An array.
x = ia[3];    // Access 4th element of the array.
x = *(ia+3);  // Access 4th element with pointer notation.
```

No wonder arrays and pointers confuse new C and C++ programmers. You can reduce the level of confusion by sticking with a few basic usage conventions until you are comfortable with the interchangeable nature of pointers and arrays. Program 8-5 shows what you can do with pointers and arrays.

Program 8-5: **Pointers and arrays**

```cpp
#include <iostream>

char msg[] = "Now is the time\n";

int main()
{
    char* cp;      // A pointer to char.
    int i;         // An integer subscript
    // Pointer access, pointer notation.
    for (cp = msg; *cp; cp++)
        std::cout << *cp;
    // Subscript access, subscript notation.
    for (i = 0; msg[i]; i++)
        std::cout << msg[i];
    // Pointer access, subscript notation.
    for (cp = msg; cp[0]; cp++)
        std::cout << cp[0];
    // Subscript access, pointer notation.
    for (i = 0; *(msg+i); i++)
        std::cout << *(msg+i);
    // Pointer and subscript access, pointer notation.
    for (i = 0, cp = msg; *(cp+i); i++)
        std::cout << *(cp+i);
    // Pointer and subscript access, subscript notation.
    for (i = 0, cp = msg; cp[i]; i++)
        std::cout << cp[i];
    return 0;
}
```

Program 8-5 demonstrates six ways that you can use combinations of pointers, subscripts, and notations to achieve the same result. All six loops display the same message on the console.

Another variation on this theme occurs when you change the array itself to a pointer to an array. Change the msg declaration in Program 8-5 to a character pointer like this:

```cpp
char* msg = "Now is the time\n";
```

The program produces the same output that it does when msg is an array. As you can see, the notational conventions for pointers and arrays are virtually interchangeable, which introduces more confusion. Until you are used to it, you are never sure what you are looking at when you see an expression that uses pointer or subscript notation (or both). At first, it's best to use subscript notation with subscripts and pointer notation with pointers. The first two for loops in Program 8-5 reflect this convention.

The character pointer assignment just shown demonstrates that you can initialize a character pointer with a string constant. Recall that a string constant is a character array that the compiler builds internally; when you reference it, you are referencing its internal address. Therefore, assigning a string constant to a character pointer is really assigning the constant's address to the pointer.

Detractors of the C and C++ languages consider these pointer and array constructs to be convoluted. Its proponents — usually experienced C/C++ programmers — consider these constructs among the strengths of C and C++. But the opponents seem to be winning out. Neither Java nor C# support variable addresses or pointer variables.

Pointers to Structures

Pointers to structures work in the same way as other pointers. A structure pointer points to an instance of its structure type. Incrementing and decrementing the pointer changes its address in multiples of the structure's size, which, you recall, is the sum of the sizes of the structure's members plus any padding or alignment added by the compiler to the structure. You access members in the structure through pointers by using the member pointer (->) operator. Program 8-6 uses a structure pointer to iterate through an array of structures.

Program 8-6: **Pointers to structures**

```cpp
#include <iostream>

struct Employee
{
    int emplno;
    float wage;
};
Employee emps[] = {
    { 1, 10.17 },   // #1 initialized
    { 2, 15.50 },   // #2 initialized
    { 3, 13.00 },   // #3 initialized
    {-1, 0     }    // Terminal element
};
int main()
{
    // Initialize a pointer with the address of
    // the employee-records array.
    Employee* ep = emps;
    // Display the employee records.
    while (ep->emplno != -1) {
        std::cout << ep->emplno << ' '
                  << ep->wage << std::endl;
        ep++;
    }
    return 0;
}
```

Observe the two references to the structure members in the std::cout calls. Instead of the dot (.) structure member operator, they use the member pointer (->) operator. These operators differentiate direct member access to a named structure (.) from indirect member access made through a pointer to a structure (->).

I added the -1 terminal element to the array so that the `while` loop could determine when the ep pointer points to the end of the array. Here's another way to iterate the array and find the end without adding a terminal element to the array:

```
const int elements = sizeof emps + sizeof(Employee);
while (ep < emps+elements)  {
    // ...
    ep++;
}
```

This technique compares the ep pointer to the constant address returned by adding the number of elements in the array to the address of the first element in the array. When the ep pointer has iterated past the last element, its value will no longer be less than the address of one past the last element.

Pointers and Addresses as Function Arguments

When a function's prototype declares a pointer parameter, callers to the function are expected to pass an argument that is either a pointer variable or an address. There are two notational conventions for declaring a pointer parameter:

```
void ErrorMessage(char* msg);
void ErrorMessage(char msg[]);
```

The two prototypes are the same. You cannot pass an array as a function argument. The first notation implies that the parameter is a pointer to a character. The second notation implies that the parameter is a pointer to a character array. There is no difference except for the notation. They both work the same way.

If you declare a pointer parameter with array notation and a dimension, the compiler ignores the dimension. The following prototype is the same as the two preceding ones:

```
void ErrorMessage(char msg[25]);
```

All three prototypes tell the compiler that the parameter is a character pointer. Which form you use is up to you. Many programmers use the first usage, because it says exactly what the parameter is, a pointer to a character. Others prefer the second usage when the pointer is to a character array rather than just one character. Still others prefer the third usage because it documents the actual size of the array. Which usage you use is a matter of your preference.

What you pass as an argument can be either a pointer variable or the address of a variable of the pointer's type. Program 8-7 demonstrates calls to such functions.

Program 8-7: **Pointer arguments**

```
#include <iostream>

inline void ErrorMessage(char* msg)
{
    std::cout << "\aError: " << msg << std::endl;
}
int main()
{
    // A character array.
```

Continued

Program 8-7 *(continued)*

```
char* ep = "Invalid Input";
// Pass a pointer to the array.
ErrorMessage(ep);
// Another character array.
char msg[] = "Disk Failure";
// Pass an array address.
ErrorMessage(msg);
// Pass a constant address.
ErrorMessage("Timeout");
return 0;
}
```

Pointer parameters to multiple-dimension arrays must specify the outer dimensions if the function is going to be iterating through the array. The declaration tells the compiler the width of the outer arrays. Program 8-8 illustrates this usage.

Program 8-8: Pointer arguments to multiple-dimension arrays

```
#include <iostream>
#include <iomanip>

void DisplayCalendar(int cal[][7]);

int main()
{
    static int calendar[5][7] = {
        {  1, 2, 3, 4, 5, 6, 7 },
        {  8, 9,10,11,12,13,14 },
        { 15,16,17,18,19,20,21 },
        { 22,23,24,25,26,27,28 },
        { 29,30,31 }
    };
    DisplayCalendar(calendar);
    return 0;
}
void DisplayCalendar(int cal[][7])
{
    std::cout << "Sun Mon Tue Wed Thu Fri Sat" << std::endl;
    for (int week = 0; week < 5; week++)    {
        for (int day = 0; day < 7; day++)           {
            int date = cal[week][day];
            if (date)
                std::cout << std::setw(3) << date << ' ';
        }
        std::cout << std::endl;
    }
}
```

Chapter 2 explains that a program can modify how the `std::cout` object displays objects by sending `std::dec`, `std::hex`, and `std::oct` manipulators to the stream. Program 8-8 includes a header file named <iomanip>. This file contains the declarations for these and other stream manipulators. The listing uses one of them, the `std::setw` manipulator, to manage the format of the screen display. The `std::setw` manipulator includes an argument that specifies the minimum display width in character positions of the next object in the stream. By using `std::setw`, the program ensures that all the calendar's date displays line up properly:

```
Sun Mon Tue Wed Thu Fri Sat
  1   2   3   4   5   6   7
  8   9  10  11  12  13  14
 15  16  17  18  19  20  21
 22  23  24  25  26  27  28
 29  30  31
```

Returning Addresses from Functions

When a function is declared to return a pointer, it actually returns an address that the calling function can use in an expression for which a pointer or address is called. Program 8-9 is an example of a function that returns an address.

Program 8-9: **Returning an address**

```cpp
#include <iostream>

int* GetDate(int wk, int dy);

int main()
{
    int wk, dy;
    do      {
        std::cout << "Enter week (1-5) day (1-7) ";
        std::cin >> wk >> dy;
    } while (wk < 1 || wk > 6 || dy < 1 || dy > 7);
    std::cout << *GetDate(wk, dy);
    return 0;
}
int* GetDate(int wk, int dy)
{
    static int calendar[5][7] = {
        {  1, 2, 3, 4, 5, 6, 7 },
        {  8, 9,10,11,12,13,14 },
        { 15,16,17,18,19,20,21 },
        { 22,23,24,25,26,27,28 },
        { 29,30,31,-1 }
    };
    // Return the address of the date.
    return &calendar[wk-1][dy-1];
}
```

Observe that the second `std::cout` call in the `main` function calls `GetDate` with a pointer (*) operator. This notation dereferences the address that the function returns and passes to `std::cout` the integer to which the returned value points. You also can assign the return value to a pointer variable and then use it to iterate through the array. Program 8-10 illustrates that usage.

Program 8-10: Iterating with a returned pointer

```cpp
#include <iostream>

int* GetDate(int wk, int dy);

int main()
{
    int wk, dy;
    do      {
        std::cout << "Enter week (1-5) day (1-7) ";
        std::cin >> wk >> dy;
    } while (wk < 1 || wk > 6 || dy < 1 || dy > 7);
    int* date = GetDate(wk, dy);
    while (*date != -1)
        std::cout << *date++ << ' ';
    return 0;
}
int* GetDate(int wk, int dy)
{
    static int calendar[5][7] = {
        {  1, 2, 3, 4, 5, 6, 7 },
        {  8, 9,10,11,12,13,14 },
        { 15,16,17,18,19,20,21 },
        { 22,23,24,25,26,27,28 },
        { 29,30,31,-1 }
    };
    // Return the address of the date.
    return &calendar[wk-1][dy-1];
}
```

Program 8-10 contains a bug. If you enter a week and day that subscripts past the -1 terminal element in the array, the loop displays whatever it finds at the effective address until it coincidentally finds the value 31 somewhere in memory or until it reaches a memory location outside the program's space, which, in some operating systems, aborts the program. You would have to interrupt the running of the program to terminate the loop before that happens. Try to determine a way to prevent the program from going into such a loop.

Pointers to Functions

A pointer to a function contains the address of a function; you can call the function through the pointer. You declare a function pointer using this format:

```cpp
int (*fptr)();
```

The pointer's name is `fptr`. This particular pointer points to functions that return `int` and that accept no arguments. The pointer declaration must match those of the functions to which it points.

The parentheses around the pointer name and its pointer operator (*) override the default operator precedence. Without them, the pointer definition looks like a prototype of a function that returns a pointer to `int`.

To assign the address of a function to a function pointer, use one of these two formats:

```
fptr = &TheFunction;
fptr = TheFunction;
```

The & address-of operator is not required, because a function's identifier alone signifies its address rather than a call to the function, which would include an argument list in parentheses.

You call a function through its pointer using one of these formats:

```
x = (*fptr)();
x = fptr();
```

The second notation looks just like any other function call. Some programmers prefer to use the first notation, because it documents the fact that the function call is through a pointer rather than to a function of that name. Program 8-11 demonstrates how a function pointer works.

Program 8-11: **Function pointers**

```
#include <iostream>

void FileFunc(), EditFunc();

int main()
{
    // Declare a pointer to a function.
    void (*funcp)();
    // Put an address in the pointer
    funcp = FileFunc;
    // call the function through the pointer.
    (*funcp)();
    // Put another address in the pointer
    funcp = EditFunc;
    // call the function through the pointer.
    (*funcp)();
    return 0;
}
void FileFunc()
{
    std::cout << "File Function" << std::endl;
}
void EditFunc()
{
    std::cout << "Edit Function" << std::endl;
}
```

Program 8-11 demonstrates that a function pointer can have different function addresses at different times.

By using arrays of function pointers, you can build finite state machines in which the behavior of the program depends on the value of a state variable that determines which function executes next. One example of a finite state machine is a table-driven menu manager. Program 8-12 shows how you might write such a program. The four prototyped menu selection functions display messages just like the ones in Program 8-11. A production program has custom menu structures and functions to do the work of the menu selections.

Program 8-12: **A menu manager**

```cpp
#include <iostream>

struct Menu {
    char* name;
    void (*fn)();
};
// Menu selection function prototypes.
void FileFunc();
void EditFunc();
void ViewFunc();
void ExitFunc();
// The menu.
Menu menu[] = {
    { "File", FileFunc },
    { "Edit", EditFunc },
    { "View", ViewFunc },
    { "Exit", ExitFunc }
};
const int sels = sizeof menu / sizeof (Menu);
int main()
{
    unsigned sel = 0;
    while (sel != sels) {
        // Display menu choices.
        for (int i = 0; i < sels; i++)
            std::cout << i+1 << ": " << menu[i].name
                      << std::endl;
        std::cout << "Select: ";
        // Get the menu selection from the user.
        std::cin >> sel;
        // Call the requested function through
        // a function pointer.
        if (sel < sels+1 && sel > 0)
            (*menu[sel-1].fn)();
    }
}
```

```
void FileFunc()
{
    std::cout << "File Function" << std::endl;
}
void EditFunc()
{
    std::cout << "Edit Function" << std::endl;
}
void ViewFunc()
{
    std::cout << "View Function" << std::endl;
}
void ExitFunc()
{
    std::cout << "Exit Function" << std::endl;
}
```

Pointers to Pointers

Pointers to pointers can be tricky. You declare them with two asterisks like this:

```
char** cpp; // A pointer to a char pointer.
```

It follows that three asterisks declare a pointer to a pointer to a pointer, four asterisks declare a pointer to a pointer to a pointer to a pointer, and so on. You can deal with that level of complexity after you familiarize yourself with the simplest case. This book addresses pointers to pointers and goes no deeper than that.

You initialize a pointer to a pointer using the address of a pointer:

```
char c = 'A';         // A char variable.
char* cp = &c;        // A pointer to a char variable.
char** cpp = &cp;     // A pointer to a pointer.
```

You can use a pointer to a pointer to access either the pointer that it points to or the data item to which the pointed-to pointer points. Read that last sentence carefully. Here are examples using the pointers just defined:

```
char* cp1 = *cpp; // Retrieve the pointer pointed to.
char c1 = **cpp;  // Retrieve the char pointed to indirectly.
```

You may wonder how to use such constructs. You can use pointers to pointers to allow a called function to modify the calling function's local pointer and to manage arrays of pointers. The latter usage is addressed in the next discussion. Program 8-13 demonstrates the former usage.

Program 8-13: **Pointers to pointers**

```cpp
#include <iostream>

void FindCredit(float** fpp);

int main()
{
    float vals[] =
        {34.23, 67.33, 46.44, -99.22, 85.56, 0};
    float* fp = vals;
    FindCredit(&fp);
    std::cout << *fp;
    return 0;
}
void FindCredit(float** fpp)
{
    while (**fpp != 0)
        if (**fpp < 0)
            break;
        else
            (*fpp)++;
}
```

Program 8-13 initializes the `fp` pointer with the address of an array and passes the address of the pointer to the `FindCredit` function, which expects a pointer to a pointer as an argument to its only parameter. `FindCredit` dereferences the array values indirectly with the `**fpp` expression. To iterate through the array in search of a negative value, `FindCredit` increments the caller's pointer to the array rather than its own local pointer to the caller's pointer. The `(*fpp)++` statement says to increment what the pointer parameter points to, which in this case is a pointer in the caller's scope. The parentheses are necessary because the `*` operator takes precedence over the `++` operator. Without the parentheses, the `++` operator increments the pointer rather than what it points to, which, in this case, is also a pointer. When `FindCredit` returns, the `fp` pointer in `main` (the caller) points to the negative value in the table.

Pointers to Arrays of Pointers

Another use of pointers to pointers is to manage arrays of pointers. Some programmers prefer to use arrays of pointers rather than multidimensional arrays. One common use is to point to a table of strings, as shown in Program 8-14.

Program 8-14: **Pointers to arrays of pointers**

```cpp
#include <iostream>

char* Names[] = {
```

```
        "Bill",
        "Sam",
        "Jim",
        "Paul",
        "Charles",
        "Donald",
        0               // Null pointer to terminate array.
};
int main()
{
    // A pointer to a pointer.
    char** nm = Names;
    // Display the names.
    while (*nm != 0)
        std::cout << *nm++ << std::endl;
    return 0;
}
```

Program 8-14 initializes the nm pointer to the address of the Names array, which is an array of character pointers. Each std::cout call passes the character pointer that the nm pointer points to and then increments the pointer to the next element (pointer) in the array. Observe that the syntax for doing that is *nm++, which retrieves what the pointer points to and then increments the pointer itself.

Examine the zero initializer assigned to the last element of the array and tested for in the while loop. A zero value pointer frequently is used as a terminal symbol in arrays of pointers. Programmers call a pointer with a zero value a *null pointer*. By using a null pointer this way, you can add elements to, and remove elements from, the array without having to change the code that searches the array. The code adjusts to the new array because it iterates through the array until it finds the null pointer.

Pointers to const Variables

When you declare a pointer that points to a const variable, you are saying that the program cannot modify the variable through the pointer. The declaration looks like this:

```
const char* str;
```

Any reference to the character data that str points to must be read-only. This usage has a number of implications. First, you may not assign the address of a const variable to a pointer unless the pointer is declared as just shown. Furthermore, you may not pass the address of a const variable as an argument to a function in which the matching parameter is declared to be a pointer to a non-const variable. The following code illustrates this usage:

```
const char s1[] = "abcde"; // Const variable, cannot change.
char* cp1 = s1;            // Error, pointer is not to const.
const char* cp2 = s1;      // Ok, pointer is to const.
void foo(char* ps);
void bar(const char* ps);
foo(s1);                   // Error, parameter is not const.
bar(s1);                   // Ok, parameter is const.
```

Typical uses of a pointer to const are to qualify a function parameter so that the compiler prevents the function from trying to change the caller's copy of the variable and to allow callers to pass addresses of const variables. Program 8-15 demonstrates how this works.

Program 8-15: **const pointer arguments**

```
#include <iostream>
#include <cstring>
#include <cctype>

void cpytoupper(char* s1, const char* s2)
{
    char* s = s1;
    while ((*s1++ = std::toupper(*s2++)) != '\0')
        ;
}
int main()
{
    char rcv[25];
    const char snd[] = "Hello, Dolly";
    cpytoupper(rcv, snd);
    std::cout << rcv;
    return 0;
}
```

The call to cpytoupper works because the first parameter is non-const, the second parameter is const, and the arguments match. The function modifies what the first argument points to by reading the second argument. It uses the Standard C std::toupper function, declared in <cctype> and discussed in Chapter 26. The function also works if both arguments are non-const, but it is a compile-time error to pass a const argument for the first parameter. The non-const property of the parameter indicates that the function can modify what the pointer points to, so the compiler does not permit it to point to a const variable.

As a rule, declare pointer function parameters as pointing to const when the function needs read-only access to the argument. This arrangement permits you to call the function by passing the address of const variables.

const Pointer Variables

You can define pointers that cannot change their own contents after they have been initialized. This practice allows you to build a small amount of safety into your code. If a pointer should never be used to iterate—in other words, if it should always retain its original value—declare it as const in this way:

```
char* const ptr = buf;
```

This declaration builds a char pointer that is itself const. You also can have a const pointer as a function parameter. The function cannot modify the pointer itself. These measures enable the compiler to catch your errors. Program 8-16 demonstrates const pointers.

Program 8-16: **const pointers**

```cpp
#include <iostream>
#include <cctype>

void ShowAllUppers(char* const str);

int main()
{
    char hb[] = "happy birthday";
    ShowAllUppers(hb);
    return 0;
}
void ShowAllUppers(char* const str)
{
    int i = 0;
    while (*(str+i)) {
        *(str+i) = std::toupper(*(str+i));
        i++;
    }
    std::cout << str;
}
```

Program 8-16 calls a function that converts a string constant to uppercase and then displays the result. It uses the Standard C std::toupper function, declared in <cctype> and discussed in Chapter 26.

The function argument is a const pointer, which means that the function cannot change the value of the pointer. The reason, in this contrived example, is that the function needs the pointer's original value for the std::cout call after the conversion is done. The program works the same way if you remove the std::const qualification from the argument's declaration. If, however, you later modified the function to change the pointer, the compiler would not catch the error, and the std::cout call would use the wrong value.

You declare a pointer that itself is const and that points to a const variable by using this format:

```cpp
const char* const ptr = buf;
```

void Pointers

A void pointer can point to any kind of variable. It is declared like this:

```cpp
void* vptr;
```

You can assign any address to a void pointer. You cannot use a void pointer to dereference a variable unless you provide a typecast, described in Chapters 7 and 37. You cannot perform pointer arithmetic on a void pointer without a typecast. You use void pointers as parameters to functions that can operate on any kind of memory. You return void pointers from functions to assign to any of several different kinds of pointers. Program 8-17 shows how the void pointer mechanism works with a general-purpose function that displays a hex dump of a block of memory on standard output.

Program 8-17: **The void pointer**

```cpp
#include <iostream>
#include <iomanip>

struct Employee      {
    short int emplno;
    char name[20];
    float wage;
};
void HexDump(void* data, int length);
int main()
{
    Employee emp = {
            123,
            "Andy Jones",
            32.43
      };
     HexDump(&emp, sizeof emp);
     return 0;
}
void HexDump(void* data, int length)
{
     char* cp = (char*) data;
     for (int i = 0; i < length; i++)         {
            if ((i % 8) == 0)
                      std::cout << std::endl;
            unsigned int ch = *cp++ & 0xff;
            std::cout << std::setw(2)
                      << std::hex << ch << ' ';
     }
}
```

Program 8-17 calls its HexDump function to display a hex dump of the Employee structure on standard output. The HexDump function accepts a void pointer because it is unconcerned about what kind of object the pointer points to. It cares only about the memory address and number of bytes to display. It begins by assigning the void pointer variable to a char pointer variable to iterate through the memory block. A typecast is necessary for that assignment because whereas you can assign any kind of address to a void pointer you cannot do the reverse. The typecast, as you will recall from Chapter 7, tells the compiler to ignore what it knows about the type and assume instead what the typecast specifies.

C++ provides an improved typecasting mechanism as discussed in Chapter 37.

Dynamic Memory Allocation on the Heap

A C++ program allocates and deallocates dynamic blocks of memory from a global store of memory sometimes called the *free store*, or more commonly called the *heap*. You allocate memory from the heap with the new operator, and you return memory to the heap with the delete operator. You first learned about the heap in Chapter 5.

new and delete Operators

The new operator, when used with the name of a data type, class, structure, or array, allocates memory for the item and returns the address of that memory which the program can assign to the pointer.

The delete operator returns previously allocated memory to the heap. The operand must be the address of the previously allocated memory. The memory is then available to be reallocated with the new operator.

Program 8-18 demonstrates the new and delete operators.

Program 8-18: **The new and delete operators**

```
#include <iostream>

struct Date   {
    int month;
    int day;
    int year;
};
int main()
{
    // Allocate memory for a data structure.
    Date* birthday = new Date;
    // Assign values to the structure members.
    birthday->month = 6;
    birthday->day = 24;
    birthday->year = 1940;
    // Display the date structure.
    std::cout << "I was born on "
            << birthday->month << '/'
            << birthday->day   << '/'
            << birthday->year;
    // Return the allocated memory to the heap.
    delete birthday;
    return 0;
}
```

The Date structure in Program 8-18 defines a date. The program uses the new operator to allocate memory for an instance of the structure. Then, the program initializes the new Date instance with date values. After displaying the contents of the object, the program disposes of it by using the delete operator.

Allocating a Fixed-Dimension Array

Program 8-19 shows how to use new and delete to acquire and dispose of memory for an array.

Program 8-19: **Using the new and delete operators with an array**

```
#include <iostream>

int main()
{
    // Get memory for an array of integers.
    int* birthday = new int[3];
    // Assign values to the array elements.
    birthday[0] = 6;
    birthday[1] = 24;
    birthday[2] = 1940;
    // Display the values in the array.
    std::cout << "I was born on "
              << birthday[0] << '/'
              << birthday[1] << '/'
              << birthday[2];
    // Return the allocated memory to the heap.
    delete [] birthday;
    return 0;
}
```

Observe that a pair of brackets follows the delete operator in Program 8-19. This notation tells the compiler that the memory being deleted is an array. In this example, the notation probably has no effect—of course this depends on the compiler. By convention, programmers use the notation for all deletions of dynamically allocated arrays. The notation has consequences when the array contains objects of user-defined class types. You learn about classes and the heap in Part II.

Allocating Dynamic Arrays

Program 8-19 shows how the new operator accepts a data type with an array dimension. The dimension in the listing is a constant 3, representing the number of integers in the date. However, you can supply a variable dimension; the new operator allocates the correct amount of memory. Program 8-20 shows the use of a variably dimensioned array as allocated by the new operator.

Program 8-20: **The new operator and dynamic arrays**

```
#include <iostream>
#include <cstdlib>

int main()
{
    // Get the array size from the user.
    std::cout << "Enter the array size: ";
```

```
    int size;
    std::cin >> size;
    // Allocate memory for the array.
    int* array = new int[size];
    // Load the array with random numbers.
    for (int i = 0; i < size; i++)
        array[i] = std::rand();
    // Display the array contents.
    for (int i = 0; i < size; i++)
        std::cout << '\n' << array[i];
    // Return the allocated memory to the heap.
    delete [] array;
    return 0;
}
```

When running this program, you first type in the size for the array. The new operator uses the value you enter to establish the size of the memory buffer to be allocated. The new operator multiplies the size value by the size of the array type, which is int in this example, to determine how much memory to allocate from the heap. The program builds the array by using the new operator, fills it with random numbers, displays each of the elements in the array, and deletes the array by using the delete operator.

When the Heap Is Exhausted

So far, the example programs have not considered the question of what to do if the heap is out of memory when you use the new operator. Instead, they assume that the heap is never exhausted. Unless your program makes tremendous demands on the heap, it is unlikely that the program will ever exhaust the heap. So, should you plan for that happening? The C++ new operator throws a runtime exception if you request memory that the system cannot supply. Chapter 35 deals with C++ exception handling. There's not much a program can do if the system does not have enough memory to support it. If the program fails to catch the exception, however, the system aborts the program and the user has no idea why. What's more, if heap exhaustion is a consequence of a bug in your program, you will not know why the program is being aborted if you do not take measures to intercept the abort. You'll be in good company, though. You don't see many application programs that do anything about it. Bookmark this discussion for when you get to Chapter 35. Then consider putting try and catch blocks in the main function of your program to intercept the heap exhaustion exception and, at the very least, report something about it to the user.

Summary

This chapter taught you about pointers, memory addresses, and dynamic memory allocation. You will learn even more about these things in Part II when you learn about the implications of class objects being instantiated on the heap. The next chapter is about the C++ reference variable.

✦　　✦　　✦

Reference Variables

A *reference variable* is an alias, or synonym, for another variable. It is typically used for passing parameters and returning values by reference rather than by value. Like pointers, the reference enables you to pass and return large data structures without the overhead of copying them.

If you are a C programmer, you probably found pointers most troubling when you first learned C. You're not alone. Even veteran C programmers get bogged down trying to comprehend some of the complex operations allowed by C pointers, pointers to pointers, pointers to arrays, arrays of pointers, and so on, and a review of Chapter 8 reinforces that confusion. The C++ reference variable can give you the same kind of trouble until you understand it. Its syntax and usage, however, prevent many of the pointer pitfalls that trap C programmers.

References are much like pointers. As you will see later, anything you can do with a reference you can do with a pointer, but references offer certain advantages. For example, the reference lets you refer to a referenced object as if the reference were a real object, eliminating the pointer dereferencing (*) operator for simple objects and the pointer-to-member (- >) operator for members of referenced structures. A reference also can simplify notation when you dereference complex objects that are found inside arrays, structures, arrays of structures, arrays inside structures, structures inside structures, and so on.

Following is a list of attributes shared by references and pointers:

✦ You can pass and return references and pointers to and from functions.

✦ A call to a function that returns a reference or an address (a pointer) can appear on either side of an assignment.

Following is a list of attributes in which references are unlike pointers:

✦ A reference is a logical alias for an actual variable.

✦ You must initialize a reference to refer to a real object when the reference is declared.

✦ You may not change the value of a reference after it is initialized.

✦ There is no such thing as a null reference.

The Reference Is an Alias

A C++ reference is an alias for another variable. When you declare a reference variable, you give it a value that you cannot change for the life of the reference. The & operator identifies a reference variable, as in the following example:

```
int actualint;
int& otherint = actualint;
```

These statements declare an integer, named actualint, that has another name, otherint. Now all references to either name have the same effect. Program 9-1 demonstrates a simple reference variable.

Program 9-1: Reference variable

```
#include <iostream>

int main()
{
    int actualint = 123;
    int& otherint = actualint;
    std::cout << actualint << std::endl;
    std::cout << otherint  << std::endl;
    otherint++;
    std::cout << actualint << std::endl;
    std::cout << otherint  << std::endl;
    actualint++;
    std::cout << actualint << std::endl;
    std::cout << otherint  << std::endl;
    return 0;
}
```

Program 9-1 shows that all operations on the reference variable otherint act upon the actual variable actualint. The listing demonstrates that whatever you do to otherint, you do to actualint, and vice versa.

A reference is neither a copy of, nor a pointer to, the data object to which it refers. Instead, it behaves like another name that the compiler recognizes for the object to which it refers. The reference variable is not, however, implemented like a #define macro. Its internal implementation is more like that of a pointer but with restrictions, mainly involving initialization and modification of the reference variable. But in the programmer's view, the reference variable is more like an alias than a pointer.

Program 9-2 demonstrates the alias metaphor by displaying the values returned when you compare the address of an actual variable to the address of a reference to that variable.

> ## Program 9-2: **Addresses of references**

```
#include <iostream>

int main()
{
    int actualint = 123;
    int& otherint = actualint;
    std::cout << &actualint << ' ' << &otherint;
    return 0;
}
```

Program 9-2 displays something similar to the following message:

```
0x64fdac 0x64fdac
```

The format and values of these addresses depend on where your runtime system locates the variables and on the format of the hexadecimal address in your compiler. The point here is not what the two addresses are, but rather that they are the same.

Initializing a Reference

Unlike a pointer, the value of a reference variable cannot be changed. It is, as you know, an alias for something else — something real. It follows that you must initialize a reference (explicitly give the reference something to refer to) when you declare it unless one of the following statements is true:

✦ The reference variable is declared with `extern`, in which case it is initialized elsewhere.

✦ The reference variable is a member of a class, in which case the class's constructor function initializes the reference (see Chapter 18).

✦ The reference variable is a parameter in a function declaration, in which case the reference parameter variable is initialized by the caller's argument when the function is called.

As you work through the examples in this and later chapters, observe all uses of references to see that each one matches one of these criteria.

References to Reduce Complex Notation

You can use a reference to reduce the complex notation that some expressions use to dereference members of structures and elements of arrays. This idiom is useful when there are many such expressions after locating a particular element. Program 9-3 demonstrates this principle.

Program 9-3: **References to reduce complex notation**

```cpp
#include <iostream>

struct Date  {
    int month, day, year;
};
struct Employee      {
    int empno;
    char name[35];
    Date dates[3]; // hired, last review, terminated.
    float salary;
};
Employee staff[] = {
    { 1, "Bill", {{12,1,88},{2,24,92},{5,5,95}}, 35000 },
    { 1, "Paul", {{10,3,87},{5,17,94},{3,7,96}}, 25000 },
    { 1, "Jim",  {{ 9,5,80},{9,11,96},{0,0, 0}}, 42000 },
    { 0 }
};
int main()
{
    Employee* pEmpl = staff;
    while (pEmpl->empno != 0){
        for (int i = 0; i < 3; i++)  {
            Date& rd = pEmpl->dates[i];
            std::cout << rd.month << '/'
                      << rd.day   << '/'
                      << rd.year  << " ";
        }
        std::cout << std::endl;
        pEmpl++;
    }
    return 0;
}
```

Program 9-3 contains an array of employee records. Each record is an element in the array and consists of an object of a structure. This structure includes as one of its members an array of date structures, presumably to record an employee's date of hire, date of last review, and termination date. This example, although seemingly complex on the surface, is much less so than many typical data structures that C++ programmers deal with routinely.

The program assigns the address of the Employee array to a pointer and iterates through the array by incrementing the pointer until it points to the terminal entry. For each element in the array, the program iterates through the array of dates to display them on the console. By now, the members of the Date structure are pointed to by a pointer and subscripted by a subscript value. To simplify the dereferencing notation of these Date structure members, the program declares a reference to a Date object and initializes the reference to refer to the object to which it currently refers. Then the program displays the Date object's members by dereferencing the reference's members to send to the std::cout object.

Without the reference variable, the program has to use the following notation to address the members of the Date structure:

```
std::cout << staff[i].dates[1].month << '/'
          << staff[i].dates[1].day   << '/'
          << staff[i].dates[1].year  << std::endl;
```

References as Function Parameters

References often are used as function parameters. Except for the example of Program 9-2 wherein the reference provides shorthand notation for complex variable expressions, there is little need to build a reference that exists only in the scope of the variable to which the reference refers. You might as well use the original name of the variable. Programs 9-1 and 9-2 use references in that way, but the purpose of those examples is to demonstrate the behavior of references and not necessarily to show the best way to use them. But references serve a real purpose as function parameters. Following are some advantages of using references as function parameters rather than using copies of the caller's arguments:

✦ References eliminate the overhead associated with passing large data structures as parameters and with returning large data structures from functions.

✦ References eliminate pointer dereferencing notation used in functions to which you pass references as arguments.

✦ References permit the callee to act upon the caller's data as if the data is local to the callee.

Program 9-4 demonstrates these advantages.

Program 9-4: **References as function parameters**

```cpp
#include <iostream>

// A big structure.
struct bigone {
    int serno;
    char text[1000];
};
// Two functions with a structure parameters
void slowfunc(bigone p1);    // Call by value
void fastfunc(bigone& p1);   // Call by reference

int main()
{
    static bigone bo = {123, "This is a BIG structure"};
    // This call will take a while.
    slowfunc(bo);
    // This call will be faster than the previous one.
    fastfunc(bo);
    return 0;
}
```

Continued

Program 9-4 *(continued)*

```
// call by value
void slowfunc(bigone p1)
{
    std::cout << p1.serno << std::endl;
    std::cout << p1.text << std::endl;
}
// call by reference
void fastfunc(bigone& p1)
{
    std::cout << p1.serno << std::endl;
    std::cout << p1.text << std::endl;
}
```

Observe that the calls to both functions in Program 9-4 specify the name of the structure object. Observe also that both functions refer to the structure members by using the structure member dot (.) operator.

Unfortunately, nothing in the listing jumps out at you to demonstrate the advantage of using a reference parameter. The only apparent difference is the use of the reference (&) operator in the function's prototype and parameter declaration. But the differences are real, and you can see them if you use Quincy to step through the program. It takes a measurably longer time to call slowfunc than it does to call fastfunc. This difference is due to the overhead added by Quincy's debugger as it watches for the call statement to proceed, combined with the code that the compiler generates to copy the large structure. The difference is not as dramatic without the debugger overhead, but it is there. And the overhead compounds when the call occurs in a loop millions or billions of times as it may in a real program.

This example implies another performance consequence. You learn about the stack and recursion in Chapter 10. If a program recursively calls a function such as the slowfunc function, the stack pointer goes deeper and deeper with each recursive call. If the recursive descent goes deep enough, the program stack becomes exhausted, and the program probably crashes. This problem alone justifies the use of references as function parameters.

Call by Reference

When one function passes a reference as an argument to another function, the called function works on the caller's copy of the parameter and not on a local copy (as it does when you pass the variable itself). This behavior is known as *call by reference*. Passing the parameter's value to a private copy in the called function is known as *call by value*. Program 9-5 demonstrates call by reference.

Program 9-5: **Call by reference**

```cpp
#include <iostream>

struct Date  {
    int month, day, year;
};

void display(const Date&, const char*);
void swapper(Date&, Date&);

int main()
{
    // define two dates.
    static Date now  = {2,23,90};
    static Date then = {9,10,60};
    // Display the dates.
    display(now, "Now:  ");
    display(then, "Then: ");
    // Swap the dates and redisplay them.
    swapper(now, then);
    display(now, "Now:  ");
    display(then, "Then: ");
    return 0;
}
void swapper(Date& dt1, Date& dt2)
{
    Date save;
    save = dt1;
    dt1 = dt2;
    dt2 = save;
}
void display(const Date& dt, const char* ttl)
{
    std::cout << ttl;
    std::cout << dt.month << '/'
              << dt.day   << '/'
              << dt.year  << std::endl;
}
```

In Program 9-5, the first two dates are initialized with different values as local variables in the main function. The swapper function swaps those two dates. The function accepts two Date references and swaps them by using simple assignment statements. Because the parameters are references, the swapping occurs to the main function's copy of the structures.

const Reference Parameters

The swapper function in Program 9-5 is permitted to modify the caller's variables, because the parameters are references to those variables. But suppose that you want to prevent a function from being able to modify its caller's referenced variables. For example, the display function in Program 9-5 accepts two referenced arguments but does not modify them. By declaring those arguments as const, the program ensures the caller that the called function accesses but does not disturb the values in the referenced arguments.

Returning a Reference

You have seen how you can pass a reference to a function as a parameter. You also can return a reference from a function. When a function returns a reference, the function call can exist in any context in which a reference can exist, including on the receiving side of an assignment. Program 9-6 demonstrates this principle.

Program 9-6: **Returning references**

```
#include <iostream>

struct Date  {
    int month, day, year;
} birthdays[] = {
    {12, 17, 37},
    {10, 31, 38},
    { 6, 24, 40},
    {11, 23, 42},
    { 8,  5, 44},
};
const Date& getdate(int n)
{
    return birthdays[n-1];
}
int main()
{
    int dt = 99;
    while (dt != 0)  {
        std::cout << std::endl
                  << "Enter date # (1-5, 0 to quit): ";
        std::cin >> dt;
        if (dt > 0 && dt < 6){
            const Date& bd = getdate(dt);
            std::cout << bd.month << '/'
                      << bd.day   << '/'
                      << bd.year  << std::endl;
        }
    }
    return 0;
}
```

Program 9-6 displays a different date depending on your response to the prompt, which must be 1-5, or 0 to quit displaying. Observe that the program declares a `Date` reference named `bd` and initializes the reference with the reference returned by the `getdate` function. Taking that lesson one step further, you can eliminate the bd reference variable altogether and use the function call return value to directly access the referenced object.

```
std::cout << getdate(dt).month;
```

You would probably not use the function call this way when the same referenced object is needed several times as it is in Program 9-6.

const Return References

Observe that Program 9-6 declares the `getdate` function as returning a `const` reference. This usage prevents the caller from using the returned reference to modify the callee's returned variable. The bd reference, therefore, also must be `const`. If you remove the `const` qualifier from the bd declaration, the compiler issues an error message and refuses to compile the program.

For those times when you require a `const` reference to be non-`const`, you must cast away the "`const`ness" of the reference. Chapter 37 discusses the `const_cast` operator which permits you to do that.

Returning a Reference to an Automatic Variable

You must not return a reference to an automatic variable. The code in the following example is incorrect:

```
Date& getdate()
{
    Date dt = {6, 24, 40};
    return dt;   // Bad -- reference to auto variable.
}
```

The problem is that the `dt` variable goes out of scope when the function returns. Therefore, you are returning a reference to a variable that no longer exists, and the calling program is referring to a `Date` object that does not exist. Many C++ compilers (Quincy's GNU compiler, for example) issue a warning when they see code that returns references to automatic variables. If you ignore the warning, you get unpredictable results. Sometimes the program appears to work, because the stack location where the automatic variable existed is intact when the reference is used. A program that appears to work in some cases can fail in others because of device or multitasking interrupts that use the stack.

Pointers Versus References

When should you use a pointer and when should you use a reference? Following are some guidelines.

If the referenced variable might not exist, use a pointer. You can use a null address in a pointer parameter to indicate that the variable does not exist. There is no such thing as a null reference. If the variable must exist, use a reference.

If the program must iterate through an array of referenced objects, consider using a pointer. Pointer arithmetic is often more efficient than using subscript notation on a reference. The program needs to dereference two variables for the latter, the reference and the subscript, but only one, the pointer, for the former.

Anything you can do with a reference, you can do with a pointer. The reference variable is an improvement over the pointer in one respect. You cannot modify the reference variable or derive a new object address by applying pointer arithmetic, which eliminates much of the trouble that C programmers get into with pointers. Assuming that a reference is initialized properly to refer to an object of the referenced type, you cannot coerce the reference to refer elsewhere, perhaps where it should not refer. There are no guarantees, of course. Nothing in the language or in any C++ compiler prevents you from using this idiom or an equally troublesome variation:

```
Object* pObject = 0;         // null pointer
// ... later
Object& rObject = *pObject;  // refers to invalid object
```

Also, if the reference refers to an array, you can unintentionally use an invalid subscript and exceed the bounds of the array just as you can with the actual array.

Another advantage of the reference over the pointer is that the program can avoid using pointer dereferencing notation to refer to the referenced object. This advantage is one of perception and preference. Not all programmers agree on this issue.

Summary

This chapter covered the C++ reference variable. You learned how and when to use reference variables and what you can and cannot do with them. You learned about the similarities and differences between reference variables and pointers. The next chapter is about recursion, the ability for a function to directly or indirectly call itself.

✦   ✦   ✦

Recursion

Let's review what Chapter 3 says about recursion: Any C++ function can call itself, either directly or by a lower function that executes as the result of a call made by the recursive function. Recursion is a powerful mechanism that solves many programming problems.

Review also what Chapter 5 teaches about the stack. Recursion works because every function execution gets private copies of its parameters and local variables on the stack and because those copies are distinct from the copies owned by other executions of the same function.

Recursive Functions

The stack mechanism, which is the foundation of subroutine architecture in most contemporary programming languages, is what enables recursion. Suppose a caller function calls a callee function. Suppose then that the callee turns around and calls the caller. That call is a recursive execution of the caller, because it happens before the current execution of the caller has completed. It works, however, because the then-caller, now-callee function starts with a separate set of parameter arguments and automatic variables in a lower position on the stack. Its original parameters and variables are not disturbed during this recursive execution. The program executes what is called a *recursive descent* through its functions.

The programmer's responsibility is to ensure that a function to be used recursively does not change the values of static or global variables in ways that inappropriately could alter some other invocation of itself higher in the recursive descent through the program's functions. The programmer's responsibility also is to ensure that some condition enables a recursive descent to stop descending and find its way back to the top.

Program 10-1 demonstrates the behavior of a recursive function.

Program 10-1: **Recursion demonstrated**

```cpp
#include <iostream>

void rfunction(bool stop)
{
    std::cout << (stop ? "2: " : "1: ");
    std::cout << "stop is at: " << &stop << std::endl;
    if (!stop)
            rfunction(true);
}
int main()
{
    rfunction(false);
    return 0;
}
```

The `rfunction` function in Program 10-1 proves that each recursive execution gets its own copy of the local parameter variable, `stop`. It proves that by displaying the address of the variable on standard output. The `main` function calls `rfunction` passing a `false` argument to the `bool stop` parameter. The `rfunction` function displays "1:" if stop is false and "2: " if stop is true. Since `main` passed `false`, the first display is "1: ". The `rfunction` now displays the address of stop. Next, if `stop` is `false`, `rfunction` calls itself passing `true`. The second, recursive call to `rfunction` displays "2: " and the address of `stop`, which is a different address, farther down the stack, than that of the first call to `rfunction`. The second execution does not call `rfunction` because `stop` is now true.

A Simple Recursive Example

Program 10-1 demonstrates the behavior of recursion, but it does not provide a realistic example of why you would use this idiom.

Program 10-2 is a simple program that also uses a recursive function but to solve a problem we've contrived to demonstrate the usage. The contrived problem that the program solves is this: Give a list of names in a specific order and display the names in the reverse order in which they are listed.

Program 10-2: **Recursion**

```cpp
#include <iostream>

// Array of pointers to names.
char* Names[] =        {
    "Bill",
    "Sam",
    "Jim",
```

```
        "Paul",
        "Charles",
        "Donald",
        0              // null pointer to terminate array.
};
void DisplayNames(char** nm)
{
    if (*nm != 0)     {
        DisplayNames(nm + 1); // Recursive call
        std::cout << *nm << std::endl;
    }
}
int main()
{
    DisplayNames(Names);
    return 0;
}
```

The main function in Program 10-2 calls the program's DisplayNames function, passing the address of the first element of the array of pointers to name strings, which is terminated with a null pointer. The DisplayNames function examines its parameter to see whether it points to a null pointer. If it does not, DisplayNames calls itself and passes the address of the next element in the array. Those calls continue until DisplayNames finds that its parameter points to the null terminator pointer, whereupon the function returns.

Here's where it gets tricky. The first time the function returns, it returns to itself in its next-to-the-last execution, which has an argument that points to the last non-null pointer in the array. The function displays that name and returns to — guess where — the invocation of the function that points to the name immediately preceding the one that the function just displayed. And so on, until the function returns to the iteration of itself that points to the first element in the array. It displays that name and returns to the main function. Notice that the function does no real work until it's on its way back up from the recursive descent.

A Recursive Descent Calculator

Recursion is used in sorting and parsing algorithms. As a programmer, you use recursive-descent algorithms every time you compile source code. You don't write those algorithms, of course; the programmer who wrote the compiler wrote the algorithms. The algorithms parse the source code for correct syntax and to evaluate expressions. Perhaps you have wondered how that works.

Program 10-3 is a calculator program that evaluates numeric expressions similar to, but simpler than, those that you code with the C++ language. The small calculator implements only addition, subtraction, multiplication, division, and parentheses in an expression. You type the expression into the program with no white space. The program evaluates the expression and displays either the result or an error message if you type an invalid expression.

Why does a calculator program need recursion? For simple arithmetic expressions, it might not. But consider this expression:

3+2*5

Should the answer be 25 or should it be 13? The usual rules of precedence give the multiplication operator higher precedence than the addition, so an algorithm that parses the expression has to know how to multiply 2 times 5 and then add 3. Consider this expression:

```
5-2+1
```

Should the answer be 4 or should it be 2? The usual rules of associativity use left-to-right order of evaluation to the addition and subtraction operators, so the algorithm has to know to subtract 2 from 5 and then add 1.

Now consider these expressions:

```
(3+2)*5
5-(2+1)
```

These expressions have the same values and operators in the same order, but they override the usual rules of precedence and associativity by using parentheses. The algorithm must know how to do that override. The most common algorithm for parsing expressions such as these uses a *recursive descent*, which uses recursive functions. Program 10-3 demonstrates this kind of algorithm.

Program 10-3: **A recursive calculator**

```cpp
#include <iostream>
#include <cstdlib>
#include <cctype>

int addsubt();
int multdiv();
int number();
void error();

static char expr[81]; // calculator input buffer
static int pos;       // current position in buffer

int main()
{
    int ans;
    do      {
        // Initialize the input buffer subscript.
        pos = 0;
        // Read an expression.
        std::cout << "Enter expression (0 to quit):"
                << std::endl;
        std::cin >> expr;
        // Evaluate the expression.
        ans = addsubt();
        if (expr[pos] != '\0')
            error();
        if (ans != 0)
            std::cout << ans << std::endl;
```

```
    } while (ans != 0);
    return 0;
}
// Top of recursive descent: add/subtract.
int addsubt()
{
    int rtn = multdiv();
    while (expr[pos] == '+' || expr[pos] == '-')        {
        int op = expr[pos++];
        int opr2 = multdiv();
        if (op == '+')
            rtn += opr2;
        else
            rtn -= opr2;
    }
    return rtn;
}
// Highest precedence: multiply/divide.
int multdiv()
{
    int rtn = number();
    while (expr[pos] == '*' || expr[pos] == '/')        {
        int op = expr[pos++];
        int opr2 = number();
        if (op == '*')
            rtn *= opr2;
        else
            rtn /= opr2;
    }
    return rtn;
}
// Extract a number.
int number()
{
    int rtn;
    if (expr[pos] == '(')       {
        // Parenthetical expression.
        pos++;
        rtn = addsubt();        // Back to top.
        if (expr[pos++] != ')') // Must have ')'
            error();
        return rtn;
    }
    // Extract the number.
    if (!std::isdigit(expr[pos]))
        error();
    rtn = std::atoi(expr+pos);
    while (std::isdigit(expr[pos]))
        pos++;
    return rtn;
}
```

Continued

Program 10-3 *(continued)*

```
// Syntax error.
void error()
{
    std::cout << '\r';
    while (pos--)      // Position error pointer.
        std::cout << ' ';
    std::cout << "^ syntax error" << std::endl << '\a';
    std::exit(-1);
}
```

Program 10-3 scans the typed-in expression by subscripting through an array of characters that it reads with the standard std::cin object. When you type the expression, the program sets the pos subscript to zero and calls the addsubt function. Addition and subtraction have the same precedence and, in this calculator, the lowest precedence. First, the addsubt function calls the multdiv function. Multiplication and division have the same precedence as each other and the highest precedence of the operators.

Before doing anything else, the multdiv function calls the number function to extract the first operand from the expression. That function checks first for a left parenthesis. If the function doesn't find one, a number must be next. The program uses the Standard C std::atoi function, which converts a string of ASCII digits into an integer. The std::atoi function is declared in the <cstdlib> header file. The number function returns the integer to the multdiv function. But first the function uses the Standard C isdigit function, declared in the <cctype> header file, to bypass the digits in the number so that the scan proceeds with the next element in the expression.

<cstdlib> and <cctype> are discussed further in Chapter 26.

If the number function finds a left parenthesis instead of a number, precedence is overridden, and the function calls addsubt to evaluate the parenthetical expression. This is where recursion comes in. The addsubt function executes number indirectly, and yet the number function itself calls the addsubt function.

The recursive call to addsubt can initiate other recursive sequences depending on what is in the expression. Eventually they all return to number, which returns the value that addsubt returns.

The multdiv function stores the result from the number function. Then it looks for the multiplication and division operators. As long as it finds one, it calls the number function to get the second operand and computes its result by multiplying or dividing the two values returned by number. When it sees no more multiplication or division operators, the multdiv function returns its computed value. The addsubt function processes the values returned by multdiv in a similar way, but with the addition and subtraction operators.

When the first execution of addsubt returns to the main function, the expression evaluation is complete, and the value that it returns is the result of the evaluation.

The program continues to run, getting new expressions from the user until one of them evaluates to zero, telling the program to terminate.

If the evaluation scan finds an error, the program calls the `error` function, which displays an error message and terminates the program. It can't simply return, because the error might have occurred at any depth in the recursive descent. A return would cause the expression evaluation to continue from an illogical data position.

Observe that the `expr` character array and the `pos` subscript variable are declared outside any function. This positioning makes the variables accessible to all the functions in the program. Because of their static storage class, they are in file scope. You learn about storage classes and the scope of variables in Chapter 5.

One way to deal with such errors so that the program keeps running and gets another expression is to set a global error flag and have each function simply return if the flag is set. Eventually, the program gets back to the top of the algorithm. However, there are better ways to handle errors. You learn about them in Chapter 26 when you read about the Standard C `setjmp` and `std::longjmp` functions (`setjmp`, a macro, is not in the `std::` namespace) and in Chapter 35 when you read about C++ exception handling. We'll use these features to improve this program in those chapters.

The calculator program has a small bug. The `expr` array is only 81 characters long, and the program uses `std::cin` to read the string. If you type an expression of more than 80 characters, the input stream overruns the buffer, and the program behaves unpredictably. Also, because we use `std::cin`'s `>>` operator, you cannot type any white space into the expression.

There are other ways we can improve this program, and we will. We will encapsulate it into a class in Part II. We will permit the user to enter white space in the expression in Part III. We will use `std::vector` to collect the input in Part IV. We will add exception handling to the program in Part V, permitting the program to continue running after an error.

To Recurse or Not?

What are the penalties of recursion? What are the perils? One penalty involves performance. Every function call invokes some overhead as it uses space on the stack and takes the time to push arguments. One penalty is apparent if you build a recursive algorithm with an uncontrolled number of recursive calls: You'd exhaust the stack. In either of these situations you might look for a solution that does not involve recursion. For example, Program 10-2 could simply iterate the array in reverse order starting at the last element rather than the first like this:

```
int namect = sizeof Names / sizeof(char*) - 1;
while (namect > 0)
    std::cout << Names[--namect] << std::endl;
```

The calculator program can be written without recursion, too. One common technique for parsing expressions is to read each element in the expression—value, operator, parentheses—in left to right order and build a reverse Polish notation table to use in the evaluation. But that's another book.

Summary

This chapter explained how C++ functions are recursive and how you might use recursion to solve a programming problem. It also explained that recursion might not always be the best solution for a programming problem. Recursion is widely used in traversing tree structures. You can always convert recursion to a loop, but the resulting code can be less readable than the recursive version of the same algorithm. The next chapter is about the C++ preprocessor, a pass that the compiler makes to resolve #include, #define, and so on.

✦   ✦   ✦

The Preprocessor

T he term *preprocessor* defines a process that reads source code,
performs some preliminary translation of that code, and writes
new source code to be read by the compiler. The preprocessor processes source code before the compiler does.

The C and C++ languages have no built-in facilities for including other
source files during the compile, for defining macros, or for compile-
time directives that include some lines of code and exclude others
based on conditions. The preprocessor provides those capabilities.
Although it is integrated with most contemporary compilers, the preprocessor is regarded as a process independent of the compiler. The
preprocessor reads source code, looks for preprocessing directive
statements and macro invocations, and translates the source code
accordingly. It also eliminates program comments and excess white
space. This chapter describes how to use preprocessing directives in
a program.

Preprocessing Directives

Preprocessing directives are lines of code that begin with a pound sign
(#). The pound sign must be the first character on a line of code after
any optional white space. The directive keyword follows, with
optional white space between it and the pound sign. The entire line is
devoted to the directive, which affects the translation of the source
code to be passed to the compiler. Table 11-1 lists the preprocessing
directives.

Table 11-1: Preprocessing Directives

Directive	Description
#	Null directive, no action
#include	Include a source code file at the directive's position
#define	Define a macro
#undef	Remove the definition of a macro
#if	Compile code if the given condition is true
#ifdef	Compile code if macro is defined

Continued

Table 11-1 *(continued)*

Directive	Description
#ifndef	Compile code if macro is not defined
#elif	Compile code if previous #if... condition is not true and current condition is true
#endif	Terminate #if...#else conditional block
#error	Stop compiling and display an error message
#line	Change the file and line number the compiler reports for messages
#pragma	Platform-dependent directive

Preprocessing directives are effective beginning with their position in the translation unit and continuing until another directive changes their meaning.

Including Files

A *translation unit* is an independently compiled program module consisting of the C++ source-code file and any other source-code files that the program includes. By convention, C++ source-code files have a .cpp file name extension. They also include header source-code files, which — for standard libraries — have no file extension and which — for header files related to your program and from third-party libraries — have a file name extension of .h (and, infrequently, .hpp). All the function definitions are in the C++ source-code file. Header files contain declarations that are shared among translation units. Header files typically declare external variables, class, structure and union formats, macros, typedefs, and function prototypes. Header files do not contain any function or variable definitions. That is, they declare variables and functions that programs can use, but they don't actually provide the definition or implementation of these items.

The rules explained previously for what goes in a .cpp file and what goes in a header are conventions. The compiler does not prevent you from including any kind of source code file, including ones with function and variable definitions.

#include

The #include preprocessing directive includes the named file in the translation unit, replacing the directive. You can have multiple levels of includes; an included file can include other files. Standard C++ requires that a conforming compiler support nesting of at least eight levels of included header files.

There are two ways to include header files in a program:

```
#include <iostream>
#include "menus.h"
```

The first usage surrounds the file name with angle bracket symbols. This notation tells the preprocessor to search for the header file among the header files that came with the compiler or with an external library. The second usage surrounds the file name with double quotes.

This notation tells the preprocessor to search for the header file among the source code of the application being compiled; if the preprocessor does not find the header file there, the preprocessor searches the compiler's header files.

The theory is that a compiler, which is installed in a public subdirectory, compiles applications that are installed in their own private subdirectories. An application includes the compiler's public header files and the application's own private header files. The two notations allow the compiler to discern the one common set of header files from the many other sets.

Typically, compilers include command-line directives with which you specify additional paths in the file system where the compiler searches for system and public header files. Integrated development environments such as Quincy usually include dialog options with which you specify these paths.

Macros

A *macro* defines a meaning for an identifier. The preprocessor replaces macro invocations in the source code with values derived from the macro definition. The most common usage for macros defines a global symbol that represents a value. A second usage defines macros with parameters that, when invoked, resemble function calls but generate inline substitution of the invoking statement's arguments with the macro definition's parameters.

#define

The #define preprocessing directive defines a macro. In its simplest format, the directive declares an identifier and adds code that replaces the identifier wherever it appears in subsequent source code. Such macros isolate global value definitions, assigning mnemonic identifiers, as this example illustrates:

```
#define MAXNBRS 10
int narray[MAXNBRS];
for (int i = 0; i < MAXNBRS; i++)
    // ...
```

In this example, the MAXNBRS symbol has meaning to the programmer who reads the code. It is a mnemonic value associated with the maximum number of entries in that particular array. You might use the value many places in your program. By convention, some programmers use all uppercase letters to identify these macros. It tells them that they are looking at a macro invocation rather than a variable identifier when they see the identifier used in code.

If you decide later that the array needs to be a different size, you can change the macro and recompile the program. If the macro is used in more than one translation unit, you code the macro into a header file and include the header in all the source-code files that use the macro. Then, to change the value, you change the macro in the header file, recompile all the translation units, and relink the executable program. The idea is to isolate potential global changes in one source-code location and assign meaningful mnemonic symbols to what might otherwise be meaningless numerical values.

The substituted value can be a constant expression, and it can include identifiers that are declared in previous macros, as shown in this example:

```
#define SCREENHEIGHT 25
#define SCREENWIDTH 80
#define SCREENBUFFER (SCREENHEIGHT*SCREENWIDTH)
```

Observe the parentheses around the macro definition's expression. They are not necessary, but their use is prudent. Consider this example:

```
#define HEIGHT bottom-top+1
area=width*HEIGHT;
```

The preprocessor emits this code for the statement:

```
area=width*bottom-top+1;
```

Because of the rules of precedence, the result probably would be wrong. This is equivalent to:

```
area=(width*bottom)-top+1;
```

Here is how you should define the macro and how it expands:

```
#define HEIGHT (bottom-top+1)
area=width*HEIGHT;          // as coded
area=width*(bottom-top+1);  // as expanded
```

You can define a macro that expands to a string constant, as shown here:

```
#define VERSION "Version 4.1\nCopyright (c) 1994"
std::cout << VERSION;
```

#define with Arguments

Macros with parameters resemble functions that are expanded inline, but they do not work exactly like function calls. Consider this example:

```
#define Cube(x) ((x)*(x)*(x))
```

The parentheses are to prevent the kinds of macro side effects described shortly.

You can replace the x parameter with any numerical expression, including one with a function call. Observe again the parentheses. The complete expansion is enclosed in parentheses to preserve the integrity of its argument in the context of an enclosing expression. So are the macro parameters, for the same reason. Here is a typical, safe use of the Cube macro:

```
int height = 123;
int volume = Cube(height);
```

Here are some unsafe uses of Cube:

```
int volume = Cube(height++);
int randomvolume = Cube(std::rand());
```

If Cube were a function, these statements would be correct. However, because Cube is a macro, these usages have side effects. Their arguments are more than simple expressions; they do other things. The first usage auto-increments the argument and expands this way:

```
int volume = ((height++)*(height++)*(height++));
```

If height starts with a value of 123, the effective expression is this:

```
int volume = 123*124*125;
```

The second unsafe usage involves a function call. The preprocessor expands it to this code:

```
int randomvolume = ((std::rand())*(std::rand())*(std::rand()))
```

At best, this code is inefficient because it calls the `std::rand()` function three times. This example is a worse case, however, because the code produces the wrong result. The `std::rand()` function returns a different value for each call, and the result is not the volume of anything meaningful.

How do you use the `Cube` macro safely to produce the correct results? You could write it as an inline function (Chapter 3), which many C++ programmers prefer. However, if it must be a macro, you must remove the side effects by moving their actions outside the macro calls:

```
int volume = Cube(height);
height++;
int randomheight = std::rand();
int randomvolume = Cube(randomheight);
```

A macro's parameters can include expressions and references to previously defined macros, making for some exotic macro definitions. Consider Program 11-1, which follows.

Program 11-1: #define macros

```
#include <iostream>
#include <iomanip>

// Define a set of macros.
#define OVERTIME      1.5
#define TAXRATE       0.15
#define WKWEEK        40
#define REG(h)        ((h) < WKWEEK ? (h) : WKWEEK)
#define OTIME(h)      ((h) < WKWEEK ? 0 : h - WKWEEK)
#define OTIMEPAY(h,r) ((r) * OTIME(h) * OVERTIME)
#define REGPAY(h,r)   ((r) * REG(h))
#define GROSSPAY(h,r) (OTIMEPAY(h,r) + REGPAY(h,r))
#define WHOLDING(h,r) (GROSSPAY(h,r) * TAXRATE)
#define NETPAY(h,r)   (GROSSPAY(h,r) - WHOLDING(h,r))

void setformat();

int main()
{
    std::cout << "Enter hours (xx) rate (x.xx): ";
    int hours;
    float rate;
    std::cin >> hours >> rate;

    std::cout << "Regular:    ";
    setformat();
    std::cout << REGPAY(hours, rate)   << std::endl;

    std::cout << "Overtime:   ";
    setformat();
    std::cout << OTIMEPAY(hours, rate) << std::endl;
```

Continued

Program 11-1 *(continued)*

```
    std::cout << "Gross:        ";
    setformat();
    std::cout << GROSSPAY(hours, rate) << std::endl;

    std::cout << "Witholding: ";
    setformat();
    std::cout << WHOLDING(hours, rate) << std::endl;

    std::cout << "Net Pay:      ";
    setformat();
    std::cout << NETPAY(hours, rate)    << std::endl;
    return 0;
}
// Set the text output format.
void setformat()
{
    std::cout << std::setw(10)
              << std::setiosflags(std::ios::fixed)
              << std::setiosflags(std::ios::right)
              << std::setprecision(2);
}
```

The macros in Program 11-1 cooperate to compute values for a payroll. Read the macros carefully as you follow this explanation. The first three macros define constant global values, assigning identifiers to the values for the overtime rate (OVERTIME), tax withholding rate (TAXRATE), and the number of regular hours in a work week (WKWEEK).

The REG macro computes the number of regular (non-overtime) hours from the total number of hours worked that week. The expression returns the actual number of hours, if less than a workweek. Otherwise, it returns the number of hours in a workweek.

The OTIME macro computes the number of overtime hours from the total hours worked. If the number of hours worked is less than a workweek, the value returned is zero; otherwise, it is the difference between the number of hours worked and a workweek.

The OTIMEPAY macro computes the amount of overtime pay from the hours worked and the hourly wage. It multiplies the wage times the overtime hours times the overtime rate.

The REGPAY macro computes the amount of regular pay from the hours worked and the hourly wage. It multiplies the wage times the regular hours.

Observe that these macros call previously defined macros.

The GROSSPAY macro computes the sum of the overtime and regular pay from the hours worked and the hourly wage.

The WHOLDING macro computes the amount of taxes to withhold from the hours worked and the hourly wage. It multiplies the gross pay times the tax withholding rate.

The NETPAY macro computes the net pay from the hours worked and the hourly wage. It computes the difference between gross pay and withholding.

The program reads the number of hours worked and the hourly wage from standard input and displays the results on standard output. Following is a typical session:

```
Enter hours (xx) rate (x.xx): 45 18.50
Regular:        740.00
Overtime:       138.75
Gross:          878.75
Witholding:     131.81
Net Pay:        746.94
```

You can modify the algorithm by changing any of the first three constants and recompiling the program. In a real payroll program, tax rates are based on the employee's salary, number of dependents, and whatever tables the IRS has in effect for the current year.

All the macros with parameters can be functions. What is the advantage of using macros? First, a macro expands to inline code. No function call overhead is involved when you call a macro. Macros that are used often should not expand to a lot of code, because every call to them is an individual expansion.

You can code macros that have no parameters as `const` variables (refer to Chapter 5) with no loss of efficiency. C++'s `inline` function feature (Chapter 3) provides an improved facility for writing what were traditionally written as macros that have parameters.

Functions declared inline are similar to #define macros with these exceptions: An inline function is subject to the same C++ type checking as normal functions; inline functions are not subject to macro side effects. For example, consider this macro:

```
#define min(a,b) (a < b ? a : b)
```

As I discuss earlier in this chapter, the `min` macro has potential side effects. Suppose you call it this way:

```
int c = min(a++,b++);
```

The macro expansion, shown next, invokes undesirable side effects in that the lesser of the `a` and `b` variables is incremented twice.

```
int c = a++ < b++ ? a++ : b++;
```

Inline function calls, which the compiler treats as normal function calls, do not have such side effects.

Program 11-2 improves Program 11-1 by using preferred C++ idioms and avoiding the use of preprocessing directive macros.

Program 11-2: **No macros**

```
#include <iostream>
#include <iomanip>

const float overtime = 1.5;
const float taxrate = 0.15;
const int wkweek = 40;
```

Continued

Program 11-2 *(continued)*

```cpp
// inline functions.
inline int reg(int h)
{
    return h < wkweek ? h : wkweek;
}
inline int otime(int h)
{
    return h < wkweek ? 0 : h - wkweek;
}
inline float otimepay(int h,float r)
{
    return r * otime(h) * overtime;
}
inline float regpay(int h,float r)
{
    return r * reg(h);
}
inline float grosspay(int h,float r)
{
    return otimepay(h,r) + regpay(h,r);
}
inline float wholding(int h,float r)
{
    return grosspay(h,r) * taxrate;
}
inline float netpay(int h,float r)
{
    return grosspay(h,r) - wholding(h,r);
}
void setformat();

int main()
{
    std::cout << "Enter hours (xx) rate (x.xx): ";
    int hours;
    float rate;
    std::cin >> hours >> rate;

    std::cout << "Regular:    ";
    setformat();
    std::cout << regpay(hours, rate)   << std::endl;

    std::cout << "Overtime:   ";
    setformat();
    std::cout << otimepay(hours, rate) << std::endl;
```

```
    std::cout << "Gross:       ";
    setformat();
    std::cout << grosspay(hours, rate) << std::endl;

    std::cout << "Withholding: ";
    setformat();
    std::cout << wholding(hours, rate) << std::endl;

    std::cout << "Net Pay:     ";
    setformat();
    std::cout << netpay(hours, rate)   << std::endl;
    return 0;
}
void setformat()
{
    std::cout << std::setw(10)
              << std::setiosflags(std::ios::fixed)
              << std::setiosflags(std::ios::right)
              << std::setprecision(2);
}
```

Inline functions are not always as efficient as macros, because the compiled code includes the overhead of maintaining function parameters as variables on the stack. Also, the compiler may choose to not inline a function; it does not have that option with macros.

Notation and Justification

Chapter 5 introduces the <iomanip> header file, which declares stream manipulators that you send to a stream to control how the stream displays objects. You learn that the setw manipulator's argument specifies the minimum display width in character positions of the next object in the stream. Programs 11-1 and 11-2 use two additional manipulators. Before each display of one of the float objects, the programs call their setformat() function. That function uses std::setw to set the width of the numerical display. The two uses of std::setiosflags tell the stream to display the float value in fixed rather than scientific notation and to display the value right-justified. Chapter 28 discusses manipulators in more detail.

The # "Stringizing" Operator

The # operator within a macro definition converts into a string the argument for the parameter that follows. Consider an Error macro that displays the error code on standard output. Without the # operator, you can write the macro as shown here:

```
#define Error(n) std::cout << "Error " << n
```

You can get the same effect by using the # operator, sometimes called the stringizing operator. Program 11-3 demonstrates that usage.

Program 11-3: **The # stringizing operator**

```
#include <iostream>

#define Error(n) std::cout << "Error " #n

int main()
{
    Error(53);
    return 0;
}
```

The #n sequence in the macro definition tells the preprocessor to convert into a string whatever is passed as an argument. The macro call has 53 as the argument, so the macro expands this way:

```
std::cout << "Error " "53";
```

The adjacent strings are concatenated (pasted together) according to the syntax for string constants, and the effective statement is this:

```
std::cout << "Error 53";
```

The ## Operator

The ## operator concatenates arguments. The preprocessor takes the arguments that match the parameter references on either side of the ## operator and turns them into a single token. Program 11-4 is an example.

Program 11-4: **The ## token pasting operator**

```
#include <iostream>

#define BookChapterVerse(b,c,v) b ## c ## v

int main()
{
    unsigned bcv = BookChapterVerse(5,12,43);
    std::cout << bcv;
    return 0;
}
```

The program displays the value 51243, which is the constant long integer that results when you paste the three arguments 5, 12, and 43.

Understand that you don't get the same results by passing variables with those values to the macro. The macro is expanded by the preprocessor, which pastes the names of the variables rather than some future values that they might contain.

After the concatenation, the preprocessor rescans the resulting value, so you can use the facility to build some complex, if not bizarre, macros. Program 11-5 is a demonstration.

Program 11-5: **More ## pasting**

```
#include <iostream>

#define AbleBaker "alpha bravo"
#define cat(a,b)    a ## b

int main()
{
    std::cout << cat(Able, Baker);
    return 0;
}
```

The AbleBaker macro defines a string value. The cat macro is a general-purpose, two-argument concatenation macro. The std::cout call invokes the cat macro with the arguments Able and Baker. Those arguments concatenate to form the single identifier AbleBaker, which then expands into the string constant "alpha bravo" that gets passed to std::cout.

Note   Don't worry if all this confuses you. Few programmers understand ## until they need it or see it used meaningfully in a way that is relevant to a problem at hand. Most programmers never need it.

#undef

The #undef preprocessor directive removes the definition of a macro for the ensuing source-code lines in the translation unit. You use this directive when you want the meaning of the identifier to return to its default meaning or when you want to change the meaning. You cannot have multiple definitions of a macro in effect at the same time.

Compile-Time Conditional Directives

Compile-time conditional directives control which lines of code get compiled and which ones do not. You can control code compilation based on the value of an expression or on whether a particular macro is defined.

#if

The #if directive tests the constant expression that follows the directive keyword. If the expression evaluates to true, the ensuing source-code group — up to the next #else, #elif, or #endif — is passed to the compiler. Otherwise, it is not.

#endif

This directive is the terminator for all #if... preprocessing directives. Program 11-6 demonstrates #if and #endif.

Program 11-6: The #if and #endif preprocessing directives

```
#include <iostream>

#define DEBUG 1

int main()
{
#if DEBUG
    std::cout << "Debugging" << std::endl;
#endif
    std::cout << "Running" << std::endl;
    return 0;
}
```

The line of code between the #if and the #endif compiles only if the expression DEBUG evaluates to a true value. In this case it does, because DEBUG is defined as a global integer constant with a value of 1. Use the Quincy editor to change the definition to this:

```
#define DEBUG 0
```

Now when you compile and run the program, the line of code under the control of the #if, #endif pair does not compile. The same thing happens if you remove the #define statement.

#if defined

You can test to see whether a macro is defined rather than test its value, as shown in Program 11-7.

Program 11-7: #if defined preprocessing directive

```
#include <iostream>

#define DEBUG
```

```
int main()
{
#if defined DEBUG
    std::cout << "Debugging" << std::endl;
#endif
    std::cout << "Running" << std::endl;
    return 0;
}
```

To test that a macro is not defined, use this notation:

```
#if !defined DEBUG
```

#ifdef and #ifndef

The #ifdef and #ifndef directives are variations on #if defined and #if !defined, respectively. They work the same way.

#else

You can code the #else directive after the statement group that is controlled by one of the #if... directives. The statement group that follows the #else compiles if the condition tested by the #if... is not true. One #endif directive terminates the two groups, as shown in Program 11-8.

Program 11-8: **The #else preprocessing directive**

```
#include <iostream>

#define DEBUG

int main()
{
#if defined DEBUG
    std::cout << "Debugging" << std::endl;
#else
    std::cout << "Not debugging" << std::endl;
#endif
    std::cout << "Running" << std::endl;
    return 0;
}
```

#elif

The #elif preprocessing directive combines the effects of the #else and #if directives, as shown in Program 11-9.

Program 11-9: **The #elif preprocessing directive**

```
#include <iostream>

// Define the DEBUG symbol.
#define DEBUG

int main()
{
#if defined DEBUG
    std::cout << "Debugging" << std::endl;
#elif defined TESTING
    std::cout << "Testing" << std::endl;
#elif defined EXPERIMENTAL
    std::cout << "Experimental" << std::endl;
#else
    std::cout << "None of the above" << std::endl;
#endif
    std::cout << "Running" << std::endl;
    return 0;
}
```

#error

The #error directive causes the compiler to display an error message that includes whatever information you provide on the line to the right the directive keyword. It stops the compilation. It typically is used within the control of a compile-time conditional statement to alert the programmer that something is wrong in the way the compile is set up. You can construct complex compile-time conditions with nested and mutually exclusive tests. The #error directive enables you to assert a compile-time error if conditions are not correct. Program 11-10 is an example.

Program 11-10: **The #error preprocessing directive**

```
#include <iostream>

#define DEBUG    1
#define TESTING 1

#if DEBUG & TESTING
  #error DEBUG & TESTING both have values
#endif

int main()
{
#if DEBUG
    std::cout << "Debugging" << std::endl;
#elif TESTING
```

Function Templates

T his chapter is about C++ *templates*, a mechanism that supports a
programming idiom called *parameterized data types*. The
Standard C++ Library (Part III) depends heavily on templates, which
enable classes and functions to define (at compile time (the types of
data they manipulate and return. This chapter is about function templates; in Chapter 25, you learn about class templates.

Function Template Basics

A *function template* defines a parameterized nonmember function,
which enables a program to call the same function with different
types of arguments. The compiler determines which types are used
and generates the appropriate code from the template. For example,
the following lines define a function template:

```
template<class T>
T MyFunc(T num)
{
    return num*2;
}
```

This template defines a function named `MyFunc`, with an unspecified
data type as a return type and a parameter. Users of the template
specify the data types the function uses.

The first part of a function template definition is the template *specifier*.

```
template<class T>
```

The `T` identifier represents the parameterized data type throughout
the definition. The identifier can consist of any C++ data type, including intrinsic types and classes. The use of `T` for the primary template
parameter is a convention. You can use any valid C++ identifier.

The next line in the function template definition specifies the function's prototype, using the parameterized data type to indicate the
function's return type and parameters:

```
T MyFunc(T num)
```

Finally, you write the remainder of the function just as you do any
other function. For example, Program 12-1 defines and uses the template function.

Program 12-1: **A simple function template**

```
#include <iostream>

template<class T>
T MyFunc(T num)
{
    return num*2;
}
int main(int argc, char* argv[])
{
    int val1 = MyFunc(10);
    double val2 = MyFunc(25.25);
    std::cout << "val1 = " << val1 << std::endl;
    std::cout << "val2 = " << val2 << std::endl;
    return 0;
}
```

In `main`, the program calls `MyFunc` twice—once with an `int` argument and once with a `double` argument. The program's output looks like the following:

```
val1 = 20
val2 = 50.5
```

You can have as many parameters as you need, and you can name them whatever you like. However, you begin each with the `class` keyword (you may also use the `typename` keyword), and you must separate them with commas, like this:

```
template<class T1, class T2, class T3>
```

To see how templates become functions, we can analyze a less-contrived, working example, such as a `min3` function that can accept any type of arguments and find the smallest value of the three. Program 12-2 defines a `min3` function template. The program displays the smallest value of the three arguments sent to `min3`. This works because the compiler takes the template and creates functions for each of the data types compared in the program.

Program 12-2: **The min3() function template**

```
#include <iostream>

template<class T>
T min3(T arg1, T arg2, T arg3)
{
    T min;
    if ((arg1 < arg2) && (arg1 < arg3))
        min = arg1;
    else if ((arg2 < arg1) && (arg2 < arg3))
        min = arg2;
```

```
        else
            min = arg3;
        return min;
}
int main()
{
    std::cout << min3(10, 20, 30) << std::endl;
    std::cout << min3(100.60, 10.872, 5.897) << std::endl;
    std::cout << min3('C', 'A', 'Z') << std::endl;
    return 0;
}
```

The program's output looks like this:

```
10
5.897
A
```

Notice how the min3 template uses the parameterized data type T in three different places: its parameter list, its return type, and also in the body of the function. As you can see from this example, you use the parameter types just as you do any other type of data.

The min3 template will work only when T is a type that defines the < operator. The intrinsic C++ arithmetic types and pointers have that operator built in. But user-defined types, such as structures and classes, do not support the < operator unless the program overloads the operator to work with the structure or class (Chapter 21).

Function Template Specialization

Obviously, function templates are very powerful (so powerful, in fact, that you can get into hot water quickly. For example, when using the min3 function template, the data types given as parameters must be comparable. You cannot compare two classes, for example, unless the classes overload the < and > operators. If the compared classes fail to supply the correct operators, the program does not compile.

Another problem crops up when the template parameters perform comparisons differently than you may expect at first. For example, Program 12-3 tries to use the min3 function template to compare string literals.

Program 12-3: Comparing strings with the min3() function template

```
#include <iostream>

template<class T>
T min3(T arg1, T arg2, T arg3)
{
    T min;
```

Continued

Program 12-3 (continued)

```
    if ((arg1 < arg2) && (arg1 < arg3))
        min = arg1;
    else if ((arg2 < arg1) && (arg2 < arg3))
        min = arg2;
    else
        min = arg3;
    return min;
}

int main()
{
    std::cout << min3("Anderson", "Smith", "White")
              << std::endl;
    return 0;
}
```

You may assume that, in this case, min3 returns the string "Anderson." That may or may not be the result because the "Anderson," "Smith," and "White" string constants result in pointers to char. The program compiles fine, with the compiler creating a version of min3 that compares char pointers. Comparing pointers, however, is not the same as comparing strings. If "Smith" is stored lower in memory than "Anderson," for example, the char pointer is less than the pointer to "Anderson." The call to min3 then results in "Smith."

To correct this problem, you can write a specific replacement function for min3 that defines how to compare string constants. The compiler then uses that specialized function instead of one created from the template. Program 12-4 demonstrates function template specialization.

Program 12-4: Function template specialization

```
#include <iostream>
#include <cstring>

template<class T>
T min3(T arg1, T arg2, T arg3)
{
    T min;

    if ((arg1 < arg2) && (arg1 < arg3))
        min = arg1;
    else if ((arg2 < arg1) && (arg2 < arg3))
        min = arg2;
    else
```

```
        min = arg3;
    return min;
}
// specialized version of min3
const char* min3(const char* arg1, const char* arg2, const char* arg3)
{
    const char* min;

    int result1 = std::strcmp(arg1, arg2);
    int result2 = std::strcmp(arg1, arg3);
    int result3 = std::strcmp(arg2, arg1);
    int result4 = std::strcmp(arg2, arg3);

    if ((result1 < 0) && (result2 < 0))
        min = arg1;
    else if ((result3 < 0) && (result4 < 0))
        min = arg2;
    else
        min = arg2;
    return min;
}
int main()
{
    std::cout << min3(10, 20, 30) << std::endl;
    std::cout << min3(100.60, 10.872, 5.897) << std::endl;
    std::cout << min3('C', 'A', 'Z') << std::endl;
    std::cout << min3("Anderson", "Smith", "White")
              << std::endl;
    return 0;
}
```

The program's output looks like this:

```
10
5.897
A
Anderson
```

Sorting with a Template

The next example sorts arrays of parameterized types. The Standard C std::qsort function does this by having you provide a callback function that performs the comparisons of array elements. Using a template, however, is easier as long as the type supports comparisons by overloading relational operators. The following header file, named Quiksort.h, defines the quicksort function template.

Quiksort.h: **The quiksort.h function template header file**

```cpp
#ifndef QUIKSORT_H
#define QUIKSORT_H

template<class T>
inline void swap(T& t1, T& t2)
{
    T hold = t2;
    t2 = t1;
    t1 = hold;
}
template<class T>
void quicksort(T *array, int hi, int lo = 0)
{
    while (hi > lo)  {
        int i = lo;
        int j = hi;
        // Sort everything higher than median above it
        // and everything lower below it.
        do   {
            while (array[i] < array[lo] && i < j)
                i++;
            while (array[--j] > array[lo])
                ;
            if (i < j)
                swap(array[j], array[i]);
        }
        while (i < j);
        swap(array[lo], array[j]);
        // Sort the set with the fewer number of elements.
        if (j - lo > hi - (j+1))     {
            // Sort the bottom set.
            quicksort(array, j-1, lo);
            lo = j+1;
        }
        else {
            // Sort the top set.
            quicksort(array, hi, j+1);
            hi = j-1;
        }
    }
}
#endif
```

The template implements the *quicksort algorithm*, which sorts an array of types. Its parameters include the address of the array and the number of elements in the array.

The quicksort algorithm divides the array into two parts. First, it arbitrarily selects an element to represent the median value. (This implementation of the algorithm uses the first element in the array for the median value. As a guess, this approach is no better or worse selecting any other element in the array.) Then the algorithm places all elements greater than that value in the upper part and all the lower elements in the lower part. Next, it calls itself recursively, once for each of the two parts. When there is only one part left, the array is fully sorted. Program 12-5 uses the quicksort function template to sort integers.

Program 12-5: Using the quicksort function template

```cpp
#include <iostream>
#include <iomanip>
#include <cstdlib>
#include "quiksort.h"

int main()
{
    int dim;
    // Get the number of integers to sort.
    std::cout << "How many integers?" << std::endl;
    std::cin >> dim;
    // Build an array of random integers.
    int* arrs = new int[dim+1];
    int i;
    for (i = 0; i < dim; i++)
        arrs[i] = std::rand();
    // Display the random integers.
    std::cout << std::endl << "----- unsorted -----"
              << std::endl;
    for (i = 0; i < dim; i++)
        std::cout << std::setw(8) << arrs[i];
    // Sort the array.
    quicksort(arrs, dim);
    // Display the sorted integers.
    std::cout << std::endl << "----- sorted -----"
              << std::endl;
    for (i = 0; i < dim; i++)
        std::cout << std::setw(8) << arrs[i];
    delete arrs;
    return 0;
}
```

Program 12-5 builds an array of integers, reading the dimension for the array from standard input, the keyboard, usually. The program uses the Standard C std::rand function to fill the array with random numbers and displays the numbers in their random sequence. Then it calls the quicksort function template to sort the array. Finally, the program displays the array in its new sequence. Given that you enter 5 in response to the prompt, the program's output is as follows:

```
How many integers?
5

----- unsorted -----
     41    18467     6334    26500    19169
----- sorted -----
     41     6334    18467    19169    26500
```

Summary

Function templates enable the programmer to manipulate various types of data with a single function. In this chapter, you got some experience with function templates. Chapter 25 is about class templates. In the next chapter, you learn about how C++ programs are organized, command-line arguments, standard input/output redirection, linking source code modules into an executable binary, and how to print reports.

✦   ✦   ✦

Program Organization

This chapter explains several things about a program that don't fall neatly into one or another discussion of the C++ language and its library components. They have to do with the way programs are built from various sources, how you run programs from the command line, and, finally, something that is missing in Standard C++, how to print a report on the printer.

Many programmers will never use some of the lessons in this chapter. Command line arguments, input/output redirection, and writing to a printer are relics of an era when programs were run from a command line at the command-line prompt. Contemporary operating environments provide graphical user interfaces for almost everything. Static runtime arguments are taken from system managed script or registry files. Dynamic arguments are in pop-up dialogs and properties windows. Console input and output are managed by applications program interfaces that isolate the programmer from the keyboard, mouse, and screen. Printing is managed from a high-level, device-independent API in most operating systems.

The lessons of this chapter are, however, still relevant, because console input/output and the command line are the lowest common denominator across platforms. The only way to write truly platform-independent, portable programs is at that level, and all C++ programmers should understand it.

Program Components

To the user, a C++ program consists of its executable binary file and any data files that the program processes, including applications data and files that the program uses for its own purposes.

A C++ program to the programmer, however, consists of all those things plus everything it takes to build the executable binary file— source-code files and libraries.

Source Code Files

You've been working with source code files since Chapter 1. They are the text files that contain the code. There are two kinds of source code files. First are the files with executable C++ statements. The filename convention for these files in many development environments includes the file extension .cpp, so I'll call them CPP files in this discussion.

The CPP file that contains the `main` function is an example of a source-code file that contains executable C++ statements. There might be several CPP files associated with one executable file. You saw an example of this situation in Program 5-8 in Chapter 5. You'll see it again later in this chapter and even again later in the book.

The second kind of source -code file consists of the header files that the CPP files include with the `#include` preprocessing directive (Chapter 11). Header files can include other header files, too, and it is possible to have many nested levels of header files in a program. In fact, if you use the Standard C++ Library, that is exactly what happens, although it happens out of your view. When a program says `#include <iostream>`, for example, that program has just included numerous header files that the programmer rarely if ever sees.

Header and CPP files are ASCII text files. You prepare them with a programmer's editor program, as shown in Figure 13-1.

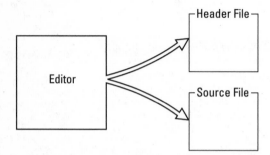

Figure 13-1: Source code files

You don't personally code all the header files that your source code files include. Some header files come with the compiler and are associated with the Standard C++ Library. Others might come from third-party class and function libraries that you use to support your program. But, irrespective of where they come from, virtually all header files originate in a text editor somewhere.

Note   If you are using an integrated development environment program that includes code generation features — such as the so-called "wizards" of Microsoft Visual Studio — these tools may automatically generate skeletal source-code files for you to modify. Even so, the templates from which those skeleton files are built originated somewhere in some programmer's text editor.

Translation Units

When you compile a single CPP source file, the combination of it and all the header files it directly or indirectly includes is called a *translation unit*. Figure 13-2 illustrates this relationship.

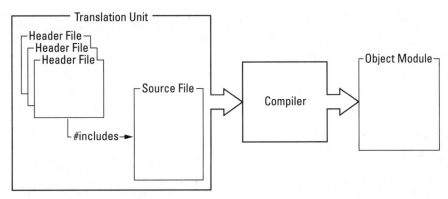

Figure 13-2: Compiling a translation unit

Although we think of compiling as one step in the process of building a program, it typically consists of three passes. The first pass, called the *preprocessor*, reads the source code, pulls in all the header files, resolves the macros and conditional directives, and produces raw C++ source code. You usually don't see these raw files since the compiler holds them in memory or temporary disk files. The second pass usually compiles the raw C++ source code into assembly language code, although not all compilers work this way. For the ones that do, the third pass assembles the assembly language code into relocatable object code.

Not all compiler systems use independent programs to implement these passes. Some compiler systems integrate them into a single executable compiler program.

Object Modules

Figure 13-3 illustrates compiling a translation unit and producing an *object module*. The object module contains the native machine code for the translation unit. But the object module may not be executable yet. It could contain declarations of and references to external symbols defined in other object modules. For example, if you use functions defined in the Standard C++ Library, you'll have to somehow merge the standard library with your object module to create a final executable. In some cases, this may involve making a copy of the library and your program into a single file. In other cases, the system will join your program with the necessary code to link to the library at runtime. In either case, when your program calls a library function, the system has to somehow provide the correct code to satisfy the request.

Object Libraries

Speaking of libraries, where do you suppose they come from? A *library* is a file that contains some number of related object modules, some of which your program might require. Libraries are built by a tool in the compiler suite called the *librarian*. This program collects object modules and puts them in one file. Object libraries maintain object modules that many programs need. If your application consists of many executable programs, and those programs share certain classes and functions, you probably will put the shared code into a library.

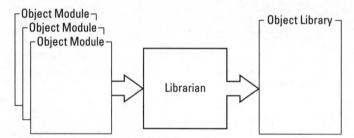

Figure 13-3: The object librarian

Later in the book, you will build some object libraries of your own.

Shared Object or Dynamic Link Libraries

There is another kind of library that the program might use. It is a library of functions that the program links to at runtime. These libraries are called *shared object libraries* under Unix and Linux; they are called *dynamic link libraries* (DLLs) under Windows. The operating system loads the library into memory the first time a program needs an object module in the library. A shared library remains in memory and is shared by all applications that need it until the last program that needs it terminates, whereupon the operating system removes it from memory. Obviously, the functions in a shared library must be *re-entrant*, which means that if the execution of one of the library functions is interrupted, the interrupting program can call the same function as if it were a clean copy.

Shared libraries are a platform-specific concept. Not all platforms implement them. Standard C++ does not address the subject of shared libraries.

Executable Files

You build an executable program file by linking your object modules together with other object modules including selected ones from object libraries. The linker program, shown in Figure 13-4, includes all your object modules in the program, but it selects from libraries only those object modules that define symbols that the program references, including references from other library object modules.

Integrated Development Environment

The collection of files that constitute a program is typically called a *project* and, in contemporary programming, is often managed by a program called an *Integrated Development Environment* (IDE). An IDE integrates a programmer's editor, compiler system, librarian, source-level debugger, a make utility, online help, file searching, and other programmer utilities. The IDE also supports the definition of a project as a collection of translation units and libraries.

You define a project within the IDE by specifying all the source code and library files that it takes to build the target executable program or library. You use the IDE's editor to write your code. When you tell the IDE to build the library or the executable program, it launches the compiler to compile the source-code modules that need to be compiled. By using a make utility, the IDE compiles only the translation units that changed since the most recent build. Then the IDE launches either the linker to link the object modules and libraries to build the program or the librarian to build the library. Finally, you use the IDE's debugger to debug your program.

Quincy 2002, which is included on the CD-ROM that accompanies this book, is such an IDE (Figure 13-5). You can read about Quincy in Appendix C.

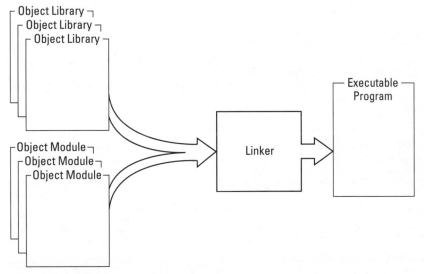

Figure 13-4: The linker

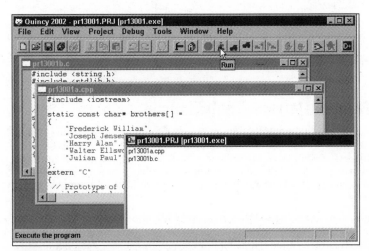

Figure 13-5: Integrated Development Environment

Type-Safe Linkages

Recall from Chapter 3 that you can overload functions, which means that several functions can have the same function identifier if they have different parameter lists.

Since you can give several functions the same name, what reconciles the apparent conflicts between similarly named functions that are declared in different translation units? It would seem that the linker could not know which like-named function to use to resolve a reference to one of them.

C++ solves this problem by applying a process called *name mangling* to the compiler's internal identifier of a function. The mangled name includes tokens that identify the function's return type and the types of its arguments. Calls to the function and the function definition itself are recorded in the relocatable object file as references to the mangled name — which is unique even though several functions can have the same unmangled name. (Name mangling is sometimes called *name decoration*.)

Consequently, a function with the prototype `int foobar(int, char*, struct tm&)` might really be internally named `f_int_foobar_int_charp_struct_tmr`, or something equally unreadable. Fortunately you rarely if ever have to read or understand such a name. You only need to know that mangled names exist and how they affect your programming environment.

Mangled names also transcend the use of prototypes to ensure that the functions match their calls. You cannot override the C++ type-checking system simply by using different prototypes for the same function. They would not resolve to the same mangled name.

Algorithms for name mangling vary among compilers, which should be of no concern to programmers, but it is. If you have an object library that was compiled with one compiler and want to link it with a program you are developing with a different compiler, you often cannot; the formats are incompatible if the two compilers use different name-mangling algorithms. A reference to a function in your program will not resolve to a function with the same name in the library. All you can do about this problem is get the source code for the library and rebuild it with the compiler system you prefer to use.

A programmer rarely sees mangled names. Source level debuggers are smart enough to translate mangled names into their original names before displaying them when you are debugging the program. But you must understand the underlying principle, because it creates a problem — one that C++ linkage specifications — discussed next — solves.

Linkage Specifications

Although C++ mangles function names, other languages do not (in particular, C compilers and assembly language assemblers). This presents a problem, because a C++ program might need to call functions that are compiled or assembled in other languages, and a C++ program might need to provide functions that are called from other languages. If the C++ compiler always mangled function names internally, references to external functions in other languages would not resolve properly.

The Standard C functions are compiled by the C compiler component of a C++ development system. Consequently, their names are not mangled internally. Your project might employ other function libraries, too. Without some method for telling the C++ compiler not to mangle references to those functions, you could never call them from a C++ program.

Standard C++ uses its *linkage specification* feature to access functions compiled by compilers of other languages. Unless you tell the C++ compiler otherwise, it assumes that external identifiers are subject to C++ name mangling. Therefore, you must tell the C++ compiler when a function has been (or must be) compiled with different linkage conventions.

The following code shows how a linkage specification tells the C++ compiler that a C compiler compiled the functions declared in a header file:

```
extern "C"                 // the linkage-specification
{
    #include "mychdr.h"    // tells C++ that functions in the
}                          // library were compiled with C.

int main()
{
    return foobar();  // call a C function
}
```

The `extern "C"` statement specifies that everything within the scope of the brace-surrounded block — in this case, everything in the "mychdr.h" header file — was compiled by a C compiler. Consequently, when the C++ program calls one of the functions declared in the header file, the compiler does not mangle the reference to the name.

Language environments that support both languages — which is to say, all Standard C++ language environments — manage the translation for you by hiding the linkage specification in the Standard C library header files for the C functions. The GCC compiler that Quincy launches uses the convention shown in the following code fragment:

```
/* --- typical Standard C Library header file --- */
#ifdef __cplusplus
extern "C" {
#endif
/* header file contents ... */
#ifdef __cplusplus
}
#endif
```

The compiler's front end defines with the `#define` preprocessing directive a global macro named `__cplusplus` when you compile a C++ source code file. Other compilers may use other macro names. The compiler's preprocessor uses the `#ifdef` and `#endif` directives in the header to include or exclude the linkage-specification statements depending on whether `__cplusplus` is defined. Chapter 11 explains the preprocessor and its directives.

So with respect to Standard C library functions, you can ignore the name convention differences between C functions and C++ functions. There are times, however, when you need to provide linkage specifications yourself. If you have a large library of custom C functions to include in your C++ system, and you do not want to or cannot port them to C++ (perhaps you do not have the source code or perhaps their source code is incompatible with the C++ language), then you must use linkage specifications. You can use the convention that the Standard C library uses, or you can code the linkage specifications directly into your C++ programs.

Program 13-1a is a C++ source-code file that calls a function compiled with a C compiler. The C++ program also has a function of its own that is called from the C program and, therefore, must be compiled with C linkages.

Program 13-1a: **The C++ source code**

```cpp
#include <iostream>

static const char* brothers[] =
{
    "Frederick William",
    "Joseph Jensen",
    "Harry Alan",
    "Walter Ellsworth",
    "Julian Paul"
};
extern "C"
{
 // Prototype of C function.
 void SortCharArray(const char**);
 // C++ function to be called from the C program
 int SizeArray()
 {
     return sizeof brothers / sizeof (char*);
 }
}
int main()
{
    // Sort the pointers by calling C function
    SortCharArray(brothers);
    // Display the brothers in sorted order.
    int size = SizeArray();
    for (int i = 0; i < size; i++)
        std::cout << brothers[i] << std::endl;
    return 0;
}
```

Program 13-1b is a C source code file that is unaware that it participates in building a program that includes C++ source code files. Program 13-1b provides a function named SortCharArray that other parts of the program call to sort an array. Program 13-1b expects somewhere else in the program to provide a function named SizeArray so that SortCharArray knows how many elements to sort. SizeArray and SortCharArray, which are external to Program 13-1b, are written in C++ in this example, but Program 13-1b does not know that. There is no way that it could. Standard C does not know about type-safe linkages, overloaded functions, and name mangling.

Program 13-1b: **The C source code**

```c
#include <string.h>
#include <stdlib.h>

int SizeArray(void); // prototype of C++ function
```

```
// -- local function to compare array elements
static int comp(const void *a, const void *b)
{
    return strcmp(*(char **)a, *(char **)b);
}
void SortCharArray(char **List)
{
    // call C function to get size
    int sz = SizeArray();
    // sort the array
    qsort(List, sz, sizeof(char *), &comp);
}
```

Here's how it works: Program 13-1, which is a Quincy project, consists of two source files: a C++ source-code module (Program 13-1a) and a C source-code module (Program 13-1b). The C module has a `SortCharArray` function that sorts an array of character pointers but does not know the length of the array. It calls a function named `SizeArray`, which is provided by the C++ caller to determine the length of the array. The C++ module declares two items within its `extern "C"` linkage specification: the `SortCharArray` C function that the C++ program calls, and its own `SizeArray` function that the C function calls.

The actual `SizeArray` function is defined within the `extern "C"` linkage specification. Without the linkage specifications, the C++ compiler would mangle the names of the C++ function and the C++ program's call to the C function. The linker would not be able to resolve the C++ program's call to the `SortCharArray` C function or the C function's call to the `SizeArray` C++ function.

In the real world, you would use other measures to give the length of the array to the C function. You can null-terminate the array, and the C function can determine the array length on its own. You can pass the length of the array as an argument to the C function. You can pass the address of a callback function in the C++ program, which wouldn't need to be compiled with C linkages. But maybe you can't do any of those things. Perhaps you are not in control of the C program, not having its source code, and you are stuck with whatever conventions the C programmer uses. Perhaps the C function is already used so widely that you cannot change it.

Linkage specifications can nest. For example, if you have C++ prototypes within a C linkage specification, you can code a nested C++ linkage specification.

Languages other than C and C++ can be supported by linkage specifications, in which case their string values are implementation-dependent. The C++ compiler must know how to encode the names for those languages. The other language must support C++-compatible conventions for passing arguments and return values. If you link with assembly language or some other language that employs no name mangling, you usually can use `extern "C"` as the linkage specification for those languages.

There are a few other things that Program 13-1 can show you, particularly with regard to the C source-code module in Program 13-1b. First, observe the #include directives. They specify `<string.h>` and `<stdlib.h>` whereas C++ source-code files specify `<cstring>` and `<cstdlib>`, as many of the listings in this book do. The C specifications name the actual Standard C library header files. The C++ specifications name Standard C++ header files that put the Standard C functions within the `std` namespace. Chapter 2 introduced the `std` namespace. Chapter 36 discusses the C++ namespace feature in detail.

Next, observe the prototype for the `SizeArray` function. C prototypes for functions with empty parameter lists must include the `void` keyword. C++ prototypes may include that keyword, but it is not necessary. The C requirement is to allow the compiler to distinguish prototypes from old-style K&R function declarations, which Standard C continues to support but which C++ does not support.

The C module uses C-style comments only. Many contemporary C compilers permit you to use the C++ double-slash (`//`) comment format in C source code. However, that usage is nonstandard, and you should avoid it in C-only source-code files if you are concerned about compliance and portability.

Finally, you might wonder why the C++ source-code file and the C source-code file have different names. Observe in the Quincy project that they are named pr13001a.cpp and pr13001b.c. Their unique .cpp and .c filename extensions ought to be enough to tell them apart. They could be named simply pr13001.cpp and pr13001.c. Yes they could, but the usual way of compiling things builds an object module with the same name as the source-code file. Consequently, both source-code files would compile an object module named pr13001.o (or perhaps pr13001.obj if you use a compiler system other than Quincy's). Whichever source-code file was compiled last would overwrite the output from the other source-code file's compile. You can get around this problem by controlling on the GCC command line the name of the object module for each source-code file, but Quincy does not have such controls built in. Consequently, the source-code files in a project must have unique names.

Command-Line Arguments: argc and argv

As you know, every C++ program has a `main` function. The `main` function has two parameters that you have not seen yet, because none of the programs have defined those parameters. All the programs so far have defined `main` with an empty parameter list. But `main` does indeed have two parameters. In fact, `main` is the only function that can get by without defining its parameters. The two parameters are an `int` and a pointer to an array of `char` pointers. The `int` parameter contains the number of command-line arguments that the user types on the command line to run the program. The `char*[]` argument points to an array of character pointers, which themselves point to the textual command-line arguments. Although you may name these two parameters anything you like, the convention is to name them `argc` and `argv` and to declare them in the `main` function header:

```
int main(int argc, char* argv[])
{
    // ...
}
```

The `argc` parameter always has a count of at least 1, and has a higher count if the user types arguments on the command line. There is always at least one `char` pointer in the array pointed to by `argv`, and it, `argv[0]`, points to the name of the program's executable file. If `argc` is greater than 1, the following `argv` parameters, `argv[1]`, `argv[2]`, and so on, point to the command-line arguments as they were entered on the command line. Arguments are separated by white space. If a command-line argument needs white space, the user surrounds the phrase with quote marks ("), assuming your operating environment supports such command-line expansion. For example, consider the following command line, which includes the program name that you type to run the program:

```
pr13002 foo bar "foo bar"
```

The parameters point to the following null-terminated strings as shown in Table 13-1.

Table 13-1: Example Command-Line Argument Values

Parameter	Null-Terminated String
argv[0]	pr13002
argv[1]	foo
argv[2]	bar
argv[3]	foo bar

Quincy is a Windows-hosted integrated development environment that acts as a front end to the GCC compiler and that provides integrated program editing, compiling, and debugging. Quincy is typical of the kind of development tools you will use in your programming work. You won't be debugging your C++ programs by running them from the command line. Instead, you will run them from within the integrated development environment. Quincy emulates command-line entries as do most IDEs that support console application development, and the next program takes advantage of this emulation. Before proceeding, refer to Appendix C to learn how to set command-line arguments in Quincy's operating environment. Program 13-2 shows how a program uses command-line arguments.

Program 13-2: **Command-line arguments**

```
#include <iostream>

int main(int argc, char* argv[])
{
    std::cout << "This program is " << argv[0] << std::endl;
    for (int arg = 1; arg < argc; arg++)
        std::cout << "Argument " << arg << ": "
                  << argv[arg] << std::endl;
    return 0;
}
```

Program 13-2 displays the command-line arguments on standard output by iterating the argv array through the element subscripted by the argc parameter. If you enter the command lines shown above and run the program from within Quincy, Program 13-2 displays these lines of text:

```
This program is C:\quincy2002\Programs\Chap13\pr13002.exe
Argument 1: foo
Argument 2: bar
Argument 3: foo bar
```

The program filename is fully qualified because that is how Quincy specifies a program's name when launching a program.

An application program interprets the meaning of command-line arguments and modifies how the program works accordingly. Command-line arguments can include program switch settings, modes, filename lists, path specifications, and so on.

Command-Line Wild Card Expansion

Some operating environments include console *shell* programs that expand user-entered wild card file specifications into file lists so the program sees unambiguous file specifications rather than asterisks and question marks in the arguments. Other environments do not expand wild cards but the compilers might include command-line expansion as a part of their startup code. For example, consider this command-line argument:

```
pr13002 *.c*
```

These are the lines of text that Program 13-2 displays:

```
This program is C:\quincy2002\Programs\Chap13\pr13002.exe
Argument 1: pr13001a.cpp
Argument 2: pr13001b.c
Argument 3: pr13002.cpp
Argument 4: pr13003.cpp
```

This output assumes, of course, that you are running the program from the subdirectory containing the example programs for Chapter 13, which is true if you run the program from within Quincy's integrated tutorial mode. It also assumes that you installed Quincy in c:\quincy2002.

Other operating and compiler environments do not expand command-line argument wild cards and display Program 13-2's output this way:

```
This program is C:\quincy2002\Programs\Chap13\pr13002.exe
Argument 1: *.cpp
```

Obviously you must know the platform's characteristics so you know whether the program must itself expand ambiguous file specifications. Some compiler systems include wild-card expansion functions that you can link with your program to effect the expansion shown here.

Command-Line Argument Conventions

You must learn how things work on your target platform and write your programs accordingly. Conventions for command-line argument formats have evolved over the years, but no universal standard exists. For example, some conventions prefix arguments with slashes, others use dashes, and some permit both. These are examples:

```
-x
/x
```

Some conventions use double dashes like this:

```
--n
```

Often an argument has a dashed or slashed prefix followed by a value like this:

```
-o filename.dat
```

Some such conventions do not permit the white space between the prefix and the value and must appear like this:

```
-ofilename.dat
```

You should learn the conventions your project uses and write programs that comply with them.

Standard Input/Output Redirection

C++ console applications read and write the standard input/output devices by using iostreams objects from the Standard C++ Library. Throughout this book, example programs have demonstrated this behavior by reading std::cin and writing std::cout. Usually these devices are the keyboard and video screen of the user's console. But the user can redirect standard devices to files, which means that a program that reads text from standard input can be told at runtime to read its input text from a file. Likewise a program that writes text to standard output can be told at runtime to write its output text to a file.

This process is called *standard input/output redirection* and, despite its name, is not a feature of Standard C++ but is instead a feature of the operating system or, more specifically, the operating system's command-line processor shell program. While not a part of Standard C++, the feature is common on platforms that support Standard C++ development, and you should understand how it works and how you might use it.

Standard input/output redirection was pioneered in Unix and adopted by other platforms. There are two ways to redirect standard input/output. One way redirects the devices to text files. The other way redirects the devices to other programs through a mechanism called a *pipe*.

Redirection to Files

You specify input/output redirection to files on the command line by using the less than symbol (<) to specify input redirection and the greater than symbol (>) to specify output redirection like this:

```
pr13003 < input.txt > output.txt
```

In this example, the program named pr13003 reads the file named input.txt instead of reading the console keyboard. It writes the file named output.txt instead of writing to the console video monitor. If input.txt does not exist, the program terminates without running. If outdata.txt already exists, it is truncated first.

Program 13-3 is a small program you can use to demonstrate this behavior.

Program 13-3: **Input/output redirection**

```cpp
#include <iostream>
#include <cctype>

int main()
{
    char ch;
    do {
        std::cin.get(ch);
        std::cout << (char)toupper(ch);
    } while (!std::cin.eof());
    return 0;
}
```

Program 13-3 reads a string of characters from standard input, converts them to uppercase, and writes them to standard output. The program uses the `get` member function of `std::cin` because the `>>` extraction operator skips white space in the input. Chapter 27 explains the `get` member function in more detail. The program uses the `std::toupper` function (Chapter 26) to convert the input character variable to uppercase. The `eof` function (Chapter 29) tests for end of file on an input stream. This program reads the text file until it reaches the end of the file. If you run the program without redirecting standard input, the program continues to read characters from the keyboard until you press Ctrl+Z (on Windows; Unix and Linux use Ctrl+D), which signals end of file on standard input from the keyboard.

When you run Program 13-3 from Quincy's integrated tutorial, it sets the command line to redirect standard input/output as shown in the previous command-line example. The tutorial files include a file named input.txt, which contains these lines of text:

```
this
is
test
data
```

After you run the program, use the Windows explorer to open the subdirectory named programs\chap13 under where you installed Quincy. Examine the file named output.txt, which the program just created. It will contain these lines of text.

```
THIS
IS
TEST
DATA
```

A variation on output redirection appends standard output to an existing file. Here is what that variation looks like on the command line:

```
pr13003 >> output.txt
```

Standard output from the program is appended to the text in output.txt. If output.txt does not exist, it is created.

Pipes and Filters

Operating environments that support C and C++ program development typically support a command-line feature called *pipes*, which is the ability for one program to read as its standard input the standard output of another program. Such programs are called *filters*, and the idiom was pioneered in Unix and adopted by other platforms. Many of the utility programs on Unix and Linux platforms are filters.

In Windows command-line mode, you specify the execution of filters on the command line by using the vertical bar character (|) as a pipe operator between program names like this:

```
program1 | program 2
```

You can pipe several programs together wherein each successive filter on the command line reads as standard input the standard output of the filter ahead of it on the command line. Programs using a pipe on one end can use file redirection on the other end like this:

```
program1 < indata.txt | program2 > outdata.txt
```

In this example, program1 reads standard input from a file named indata.txt and pipes its standard output to the standard input of program2, which writes its standard output to a file named outdata.txt. If outdata.txt already exists, it is truncated first.

Many command-line utilities work as filters because they use standard input and output to read and write data. Windows platforms include two command-line filters named *sort* and *find*. The sort filter reads standard input, sorts the text lines as they come in, and writes the sorted lines of text on standard output. The find filter reads standard input a line at a time and searches each text line for a match on an argument to the program, writing to standard output only those lines of text that match the search.

Suppose you have a text file consisting of names, address, and dates of birth. You want to extract from that file everyone who was born in August, sort the extracted records, and display the sorted records on the console. Here is how you would do that:

```
find < names.txt "August" | sort
```

The find filter reads lines of text from standard input that has been redirected to the file named names.txt. The string "August" is the argument for the find filter to find. Only those strings with the value "August" will be written to standard output, which is redirected through a pipe into the standard input of the sort filter. The sort filter reads the extracted lines of text, sorts them, and writes the sorted lines of text to standard output, which, since it has not been redirected, is displayed on the console monitor.

There are flaws in this procedure. If an entry in the text file abbreviates the month, the entry will not be selected. If a person's name or address includes the string "August," the entry will be extracted irrespective of the person's birthday. But, glitches notwithstanding, this example illustrates how filters and pipes work and how you might use them in your own system.

Many platforms include filters similar to the Windows find and sort filters, which are derived from the command-line tools of the older MS-DOS. Unix and Linux call the find filter "grep," a program with many advanced text selection features.

Quincy does not support running sequences of programs from its IDE, so there are no example filter programs to demonstrate pipes. By definition, filters are run from the command line. The concept is simple, though, and you can experiment with the filters that came with your operating system before writing your own filter programs.

Printing Reports

Readers of previous editions of this book often ask me, "Why don't you teach how to use the printer from a C++ program?" There is a good reason for that. Standard C++ does not define a way to write data to the printer. Programmers often wonder why, since printing reports is integral to many applications. But because printer command protocols and printing procedures are device- and platform-dependent, no standard definition exists for how to print on paper.

Operating systems and their applications programming interfaces (APIs) usually include high-level, device-independent interfaces to the printers attached to the computer. These APIs support text, vector graphics, bitmap graphics, fonts, print spooling, and an isolation layer from the low-level protocols that printers use. It is not reasonable to expect a programming language standard to define a standard API for these purposes. You might, however, expect a standard language to provide a standard way to write simple text reports. But although Standard C++ defines a standard output device compatible with text based display devices, it does not define a standard printer output device.

Generic printing is easy enough once you know how to direct text data to a printer device. You write text as if you were displaying it on the console's video screen. To eject to the next page, you send the '\f' form feed character. That's about all there is to it. But there is more to printing a complex report than that. A program must know how to select from the various printers that are attached to the computer. A program must know what to do if the printer is located elsewhere on a print server on a network. A program must know how to select the correct font for the report, changing fonts where necessary. A program must know how to render graphical images on a printer. A program must know how to deal with printer accessories such as paper feed trays and collators. A program must know what to do when the printer runs out of paper, has a paper jam, or goes off-line. These are things that the operating system typically manages, and no standard protocols exist for any of them.

Printing with Output Redirection

The easiest way to print generic text is to write the report on standard output and use the command line to redirect standard output to the printer using the operating system's conventions for addressing the printer device. This approach works, but because it appropriates the standard output device for the duration of the program, the program must use the standard error device (std::cerr) for console output. Program 13-4 demonstrates this technique for printing.

Program 13-4: **Printing with output redirection**

```
#include <iostream>

int main()
{
    std::cout << "this is a report\f" << std::flush;
    std::cerr << "finished reporting";
    return 0;
}
```

For this technique to work, the operating system has to support redirection to a printer device. Windows reserves the filename "prn" for the default printer. By redirecting standard output to that filename, text written to standard output is sent to the printer.

The program sends the `std::flush` manipulator (Chapter 27) to the printer because some printers need to be told to print and eject the last page of the report, and the `std::flush` manipulator usually does that.

Printing to a File

Another way to print a text report is to write the report data to a file and use the operating system's print commands to print the file. Chapter 29 explains file output in detail, but the next discussion and Program 13-5 provide an introduction to the topic.

Printing to the Printer Device

Some operating systems include printer device names that a program can open instead of a filename. The device name is either associated with the current default printer or it is the name of the serial or parallel port to which the printer is attached. You can print a text report by opening what looks to the program like a text file but with the name of the default printer (typically prn under Windows) or the device's port (com1:, com2:, lpt1:, and so on). Using the port name is somewhat inflexible. The program is permanently associated with the specific port unless the program gets the filename from a command-line argument. Program 13-5 prints a report by writing to the `prn` device, which, as you learned with the previous example program, is the filename reserved for the printer device.

Program 13-5: **Printing to prn**

```
#include <iostream>
#include <fstream>

int main()
{
    std::ofstream printer("prn");
    printer << "this is a report\f" << std::flush;
    std::cout << "finished reporting";
    return 0;
}
```

Program 13-5 instantiates an output stream file named "prn". The program must include `<fstream>` in order to declare an object of type `std::ofstream`, which is the type for output disk files (Chapter 29). Then the program writes text to the `printer` object just as it would write text to standard output, substituting the instantiated object's identifier (`printer`) for where you are accustomed to seeing `std::cout`. Note that `printer` is an arbitrary name chosen for this example program. You don't have to use that identifier. It can be any valid C++ identifier.

Summary

This chapter explained how programs are built from translation units, how to use translation units compiled from different programming languages in your program, and how functions retain their overloaded identity with respect to their differing parameter lists. You also learned about command-line arguments, input/output redirection, and printing. The latter two topics are part of virtually every C++ runtime environment but not part of Standard C++.

This chapter concludes Part I. You now have a fundamental understanding of the core C++ language at its most basic level. Part II introduces the C++ class, a mechanism that supports the development of object-oriented programs.

✦   ✦   ✦

Working with Classes

Part II is about the C++ class mechanism, the language feature with which most of the Standard C++ Library is implemented, and the way that you extend C++ for your own purposes. These are the chapters in Part II:

C++ Classes

C++ classes support data abstraction and object-oriented programming, both of which involve the design and implementation of data types. When you begin programming with classes, you should use them to extend the C++ language by designing and implementing custom data types: small types that the language lacks but that a typical application might need, such as dates, times, and currency. This approach enables you to learn the syntax and behavior of the class mechanism without worrying about new and exotic programming paradigms. Rather than trying to learn a complex and highly abstract concept such as object-oriented programming, you learn about the language features that support it. Later, you can apply this newfound knowledge of C++ classes to learning about object-oriented programming.

Consider the intrinsic numerical data types that C++ supports. These integer and floating-point types suffice for most of a programmer's numerical needs, but there are times when you need to extend the language to support more complex data types. In C, you organize the intrinsic types into a structure and write functions to manipulate that structure. With C++, you do the same thing, but you bind the data representations and their algorithms into a new data type by defining a class. A C++ class becomes a data type that you, the programmer, define. It is C++'s *data abstraction* mechanism. The class consists of data members, member functions, and custom operators.

Class Declaration

Let's begin by considering a simple class design, looking at an example of a class that describes the geometrical box form.

Before proceeding, ask yourself why you might want to build a class that describes a box. Perhaps you are writing a program that deals with three-dimensional containers of some kind, and the box is a basic unit with which the program must deal. Any data entity that your program might process is a candidate to be a class in C++, which begins to answer the question, "What are objects?" This is the first question asked by most functionally oriented programmers when they first encounter object-oriented programming.

Program 14-1 introduces classes by defining the Box class.

Program 14-1: **The Box class**

```cpp
#include <iostream>

class Box {
private:
    int height, width, depth;    // private data members.
public:
    Box(int, int, int); // constructor function.
    ~Box();             // destructor function.
    int volume();       // member function (compute volume).
};
// The constructor function.
Box::Box(int ht, int wd, int dp)
{
    height = ht;
    width = wd;
    depth = dp;
}
// The destructor function.
Box::~Box()
{
    // does nothing
}
// Member function to compute the Box's volume.
int Box::volume()
{
    return height * width * depth;
}
int main()
{
    // Construct a Box object.
    Box thisbox(7, 8, 9);
    // Compute and display the object's volume.
    int volume = thisbox.volume();
    std::cout << volume;
    return 0;
}
```

Many new C++ features are packed into Program 14-1. The program begins by declaring the Box class. The class has three private data members—the integers height, width, and depth—and three public functions: a constructor named Box, a destructor named ~Box, and a member function named volume. You learn about each of these types of functions and others as the lessons in this and later chapters progress.

Class Members

A class, as you learned in Chapter 6, is a souped-up C structure. As such, a class has members, just as a structure does. A class's declaration declares the class's members, which consist of data members, the constructor and destructor functions, overloaded operator functions, and other member functions.

Access Specifiers: Class Member Visibility

The private and public keywords in the Box class declaration are member *access specifiers*. They specify the visibility to the program of the members that follow the access specifiers. The access mode set by an access specifier continues until another access specifier occurs or the class declaration ends.

Private members can be accessed only by member functions of the same class. Public members can be accessed by member functions and by other functions in the program that declare an instance of the class. There are exceptions to these general rules. I address some of those exceptions in Chapter 19, which is about friend classes and functions. There are other rules, too, having to do with derived classes in an inheritance hierarchy of classes, as Chapter 23 explains.

The Box class in Program 14-1 uses the private keyword to specify that its three integer data members are visible only to the constructor and destructor functions and to the volume member function. All three member functions are visible to other functions in the program. You can use the private and public access specifiers as often as you want in a class declaration, but many programmers group private and public members separately.

All class declarations begin with private as the default access mode, so you can omit it in Program 14-1. The listing includes the private access mode for readability as well as to demonstrate its purpose. (In a struct, which is similar to a class, the default access mode is public.)

A third access specifier, the protected keyword, works the same as the private keyword except when you use class inheritance. Chapter 23 explains the protected keyword.

struct Versus class

Chapter 6 discusses C++ structures briefly, deferring the complicated aspects to this chapter. There are only a few small differences between the structure and the class as listed here:

✦ Structures begin with public access as the default.

✦ Classes begin with private access as the default.

✦ If a structure is derived (Chapter 23) from a base class, the base class is public by default.

✦ If a class is derived from a base class, the base class is private by default.

Chapter 23 discusses `public` and `private` base classes and class derivation (inheritance) in detail. Many programmers adopt a style in which they define a structure when its form complies with the C definition of a structure. Otherwise, they define a class.

C++ programmers refer to classes and structures that have `public` access for all members, no member functions, and do not participate in an inheritance hierarchy — in other words, C structures — as "plain old data," or "POD" for short. The rule of thumb is, for POD, use `struct`. For everything else, use `class`.

Data Members

Data members of the class are instances of data types. A data member can be of any valid C++ data type, including other classes, structures, pointers (Chapter 8), and references (Chapter 9). The `Box` class contains three data members: the integers `height`, `width`, and `depth`.

Initialization

The declaration of a class object can contain a list of initializers in parentheses, as shown in Program 14-1. The declaration of `thisbox` contains three integer values. These values are passed as arguments to the class's matching constructor function, which Chapter 15 describes. However, if the class has no private or protected members, has no virtual functions (discussed in Chapter 23), and is not derived from another class (also discussed in Chapter 23), you can initialize an object of the class with a brace-delimited, comma-separated list of initializers just as you initialize a C structure:

```
class Date
{
public:
    int mo, da, yr;
};

int main()
{
    Date dt = {1,29,92};
    // ...
    return 0;
}
```

The same restrictions apply to structures, by the way. You cannot use a brace-delimited initializer list if a structure has any of the attributes just mentioned.

Member Functions

Member functions are the functions that you declare within the class definition. You must provide the code for these functions just as you do for the functions in structures in Chapter 6.

There are several categories of member functions. The constructor and destructor, discussed in Chapter 15, are two of them. The others are regular member functions, which this chapter discusses, overloaded operator functions (Chapter 21), copy constructors (Chapter 15), friend functions (Chapter 19), conversion constructors and conversion member functions (Chapter 16), and virtual functions (Chapter 23). For now, observe that the Box class defines one member function, named volume.

Member functions, when defined outside the class declaration, are referenced with the class name followed by the :: operator followed by the function name. The name of the Box class's volume member function is, therefore, Box::volume. As you learned in Chapter 3, a function named simply volume is a global function and not a member function at all. In this case that is not what you would want.

The Box::volume function returns the product of the Box object's three dimensions. The program in Program 14-1 calls the volume function by using the period operator, as illustrated in the following example:

```
int vol = thisbox.volume();
```

Programs can also call member functions by using a pointer to an instance of the class type like this:

```
Box* boxptr = &thisbox;
int vol = boxptr->volume();
```

You can call the volume member function anywhere an object (or pointer or reference to an object) of type Box is in scope. Member functions of a class can call one another by using the function name without the object-name prefix. The compiler assumes that the call is being made for the same object for which the calling member function was called.

When a member function is private, only other member functions within the same class or friends of the class (Chapter 19) can call it.

Object-Oriented Class Design

Program 14-1 follows a convention that many C++ programmers consider to be sound C++ object-oriented design: When you design a class, make all the data members private. Make public only those member functions necessary to implement the public interface of the class.

As you learned in Chapter 6 and will learn more about in Chapter 40, a class design encapsulates the data members and algorithms into a user-defined abstract data type. The class hides the details of the type's implementation within the class's private members. The class's public interface, which is provided by public member functions, defines the using program's perception of the type. A class's hidden implementation can use private member functions, too, but these functions are not included in the public interface.

If you need to allow the class user to view or modify a private data value, do it with a public member function. Public member functions that provide access to data members are sometimes called *accessor* functions. Some programmers call them *getter* and *setter* functions. This convention is not a hard and fast rule, and there will be times when you find it necessary to do otherwise; but if you use the convention as a guideline, your programs will be more object-oriented and, consequently, of stronger design. Here's why. Suppose sometime later, after the class has been in use for a while, you decide it is easier to internally represent the box dimensions in millimeters instead of inches. You could still accept inches in the accessor functions and constructor but convert them to millimeters in the internal representation. If you had allowed other code to directly access the variables, this kind of change could result in a significant effort locating all code throughout the class user community that might look at the variables directly.

Is Box in Program 14-1 an object? No, Box is a *type*. The class declaration merely defines the class's format. It does not set aside any memory to hold an instance of the class. No instance of the class exists until a program declares one within the scope of the class declaration. A declared instance of a data type is an *object*. A class is a user-defined data type. Therefore, an instance of a class is an object. The thisbox variable in Program 14-1 is an object of type Box. These distinctions are important in object-oriented programming.

The Scope and Lifetime of a Class Object

Chapter 5 discusses the scope and lifetime of C++ objects. A class object is like any other instantiated data type with respect to scope. An automatic object comes into scope when the program defines it and goes out of scope when the program exits the block in which the class object is defined.

An extern class object is constructed when the program begins running and is destroyed when the program exits to the operating system. The object is in scope wherever a translation unit declares the object.

A static local class object is the same as that of an automatic object, but its lifetime is the same as that of an extern object. Understanding this behavior is important, because classes include special functions called constructor and destructor functions.

Every time an object is created, the constructor executes. If you don't provide a constructor, the compiler makes one for you (a default constructor). When an object is destroyed, its destructor executes, which is where the class cleans up any resources the object may be using.

Often, objects are created on the heap. In this case, construction occurs as part of the call to new and destruction occurs when you delete the object.

Inline Functions

A class can have inline member functions. You learned about regular inline functions in Chapter 3. The compiler may compile an inline copy of the function every time the program calls the function. The same guidelines apply when you decide whether a class member function should be inline. As a general rule, inline functions should be small. If they are too large or too complex, the compiler may elect not to inline them. There are two notations for defining inline functions for a class. In the first one, you code the body of the function directly into the class declaration rather than coding a prototype. Both the Box constructor function and the Box volume member function are small enough to be inline functions. Coding them as inline and removing the unnecessary destructor function significantly reduces the size of the program's source code.

Program 14-2 illustrates inline class member functions.

Program 14-2: **The Box class with inline functions**

```
#include <iostream>
class Box
{
    int height, width, depth;    // private data members
public:
```

```
        // Inline constructor function.
        Box(int ht, int wd, int dp)
        {
            height = ht;
            width = wd;
            depth = dp;
        }
        // Inline member function.
        int volume()
        {
            return height * width * depth;
        }
};
int main()
{
    // Construct a Box object.
    Box thisbox(7, 8, 9);
    // Compute and display the object's volume.
    int volume = thisbox.volume();
    std::cout << volume;
    return 0;
}
```

You often see inline class functions coded on a single line, a convention that reinforces the idea that inline functions should be small. If you cannot get the function's body on a single line, perhaps the function should not be inline.

The second notation for inline member functions uses the `inline` keyword in the function's definition outside the class. You can define the `volume` function, for example, as shown in the following class declaration and definition:

```
class Box
{
    int height, width, depth;      // private data members
public:
    // Inline constructor function.
    Box(int ht, int wd, int dp)
        { height = ht; width = wd; depth = dp; }

    // Member function.
    int volume();
};

inline int Box::volume()
{
    return height * width * depth;
}
```

When you code an inline member function this way, put it in the same source code file with the class declaration — usually a header file — so that the function is visible to all source-code modules that use the class.

Bear in mind that inline functions, which are coded as part of the class declaration, typically are in the class header file in their entirety. This means that if you change one of the inline functions, all the source-code files that include the header must be recompiled to reflect the changes. Functions that are likely candidates for change in a large project should probably not be inline so that you recompile only the source-code files that define the functions. This measure can save considerable build-time during the development of a large project.

Summary

This chapter introduced C++ classes. You learned how to define a class with data members and member functions. Building your own classes is how you add user-defined types to your programs and how you exploit the advantages of object-oriented programming (Chapter 40). Chapters 15 through 25 continue your exploration of C++ classes. Chapter 15 introduces class constructor and destructor functions, the mechanisms with which a class specifies how objects of the class are instantiated and initialized and how they are destroyed when the program no longer needs them.

✦   ✦   ✦

Constructors and Destructors

Constructors and destructors are special functions in classes and structures. As you might deduce from their names, you design constructors to build instances of the class and you design destructors to destroy those instances. The program does not explicitly call these functions; the compiler calls them when the program instantiates and destroys instances of classes, either automatically on the stack, dynamically on the heap, or statically when the program starts running and exits.

Constructors

A *constructor* is a function that executes when an object of a class is instantiated. It contains everything the class needs to initialize a new instance of the class. A class always has at least one constructor, even when the class does not define one. A class can have as many overloaded constructor functions as is required to build objects of the class.

How a Constructor Executes

When the program creates an instance of a class, a constructor function executes. The execution is automatic. Unlike some other object-oriented programming languages, C++ does not require you to explicitly call a constructor function. The compiler decides when to call a constructor function and which constructor function to call based on the context in which the program instantiates the object of the class.

A class can have one or more overloaded constructor functions. If you do not declare at least one constructor function, the compiler provides a hidden default constructor function for the class, which may or may not do anything. See the section on default constructors later in this chapter. You also get a default copy constructor if you do not declare one. See the section on copy constructors later in this chapter.

The Box class in Program 14-1 in the previous chapter has a constructor function named Box. Constructor functions always have the same name as the class, and they specify no return value, not even void. Here is the Box constructor function for you to review.

```
Box::Box(int ht, int wd, int dp)
{
    height = ht;
    width = wd;
    depth = dp;
}
```

A constructor function returns nothing. You do not declare it as void, but it is void by default. If a constructor function senses an error that it needs to report to the program, its only option is to throw an exception (Chapter 35). You may define multiple, overloaded constructor functions for a class. Each of them must have a distinct parameter list. You'll see how later in this chapter.

Memory for the Object

The runtime system allocates enough memory to contain the data members of a class when an object of the class is constructed. As you learned about objects of intrinsic types in Chapters 5 and 8, automatic objects of classes are instantiated on the stack and dynamic objects of classes are instantiated on the heap.

As with intrinsic types, stack memory returns to the system when an automatic class object is destroyed. For dynamically allocated class objects, you use the new and delete operators (Chapter 8) to allocate and free the memory. Chapter 20 discusses the heap as it applies to class objects.

Object Initialization

Like objects of intrinsic data types, the data members of external objects (objects declared with static and extern storage scope) are initialized to zeros. The runtime system does not initialize local objects. Their data members will contain random, unpredictable values unless the class's constructor function initializes them as the Box constructor function in Program 14-1 does.

The Box constructor function has three integer parameters and uses the arguments specified when the object is defined to assign values to data members. Once again, here is the statement in Program 14-1 that instantiates the object, supplies arguments for the constructor's parameters, and causes execution of the constructor function:

```
Box thisbox(7, 8, 9);
```

The declaration of thisbox follows the C syntax for declaring a variable. First comes the data type, which in this case is Box, and then the name of the object, thisbox. That's the same way you declare any variable, for example, an integer. The declaration of a class object contains an argument list in parentheses if the constructor has parameters. This list represents class object initializers and contains the arguments that are passed to the constructor function. The class declaration must contain a constructor function with a parameter list of data types that match those of the argument list in the class object declaration.

Now, compare the Box declaration with the declaration and initialization of intrinsic type variables as you learned in Chapter 2:

```
int Amount(3);      // initialize an int
char ch('A');       // initialize a char
float Value(1.23);  // initialize a float
```

The notation is the same — type, identifier, and parenthetical initializers. One difference is that intrinsic types have only one initializing expression, whereas class types can have one or more.

Instantiations of objects of intrinsic types can always use the traditional C initializer notation, as shown here:

```
int Amount = 3;     // initialize an int
char ch = 'A';      // initialize a char
float Value = 1.23; // initialize a float
```

Class types can use that notation only when there is a constructor with only one parameter and the constructor is not declared as being explicit. Constructors with one parameter are either copy constructors (described later in this chapter) when the parameter is of the same type as the class, or conversion constructors (Chapter 16) when the parameter is of a different type and the constructor is not explicit (also Chapter 16).

Constructors Without Parameters

If the constructor function has an empty parameter list, the declaration of the object does not require the parentheses, as shown here:

```
class foo {
public:
    foo();
    // ...
};
// ....
    foo fobj;   // no parens required
```

(Such a constructor is called a *default constructor*, described later in this chapter.)

Constructors with Default Arguments

You may want to initialize a Box object with dimensions as you did in Program 14-1, but at other times you may want a Box object with default dimensions.

Program 15-1 demonstrates a Box class that defaults to specified dimensions if you do not supply initializers.

Program 15-1: **Constructor with default parameters**

```
#include <iostream>

class Box {
    // Private data members.
    int height, width, depth;
public:
    // Constructor with default initializers.
    Box(int ht = 1, int wd = 2, int dp = 3)
    {
        height = ht;
        width = wd;
```

Continued

Program 15-1 *(continued)*

```
        depth = dp;
    }
    // Member function.
    int volume()
    {
        return height * width * depth;
    }
};
int main()
{
    // Construct two Box objects, one with
    // initializers and one without.
    Box thisbox(7, 8, 9);
    Box defaultbox;
    // Get and display the objects' volumes.
    int volume = thisbox.volume();
    std::cout << volume << std::endl;
    volume = defaultbox.volume();
    std::cout << volume;
    return 0;
}
```

The notation for default arguments in a constructor function is the same for default arguments in any function, as you learned in Chapter 3. The Box class constructor in Program 15-1 uses default arguments to permit you to instantiate Box objects by specifying zero, one, two, or three arguments. These would all be valid Box objects declarations:

```
    Box thisbox1;
    Box thisbox2(7);
    Box thisbox3(7, 8);
    Box thisbox4(7, 8, 9);
```

Using default arguments is better than writing multiple constructors to cover all possible ways to instantiate the object because one function is easier to maintain than several.

Default Constructors

A constructor with no parameters or a constructor with default arguments for all its parameters is called a *default constructor*. The constructor in Program 15-1 is a default constructor because you can instantiate an object without specifying initializing argument expressions.

If a class has no constructors whatsoever, the compiler provides a public default constructor, which usually does nothing. If, however, you provide at least one constructor of any kind, the compiler does not provide a default constructor. Therefore, if you provide one or more constructors with parameters, and you provide no default constructor, the class has no default constructor. Objects of that class cannot be instantiated without arguments. Default constructors are important. You will learn in Chapter 17 that you cannot instantiate arrays of objects of a class that has no default constructor.

Overloaded Constructors

A class can have more than one constructor function. Such constructor functions for a class, however, must have different parameter lists with respect to the number and types of parameters so that the compiler can tell the constructors apart. You code multiple constructors in cases in which the declarations of a class can occur with different initialization parameters. You may want to initialize a Box object with dimensions, as in Program 15-1, but at other times you simply may want an empty Box object with no initial dimensions—for example, to be on the receiving end of an assignment.

Program 15-2 shows the Box class with two constructor functions.

Program 15-2: **A class with two constructors**

```cpp
#include <iostream>

class Box {
    // Private data members.
    int height, width, depth;
public:
    // Overloaded constructors.
    Box()
     { /* does nothing */ }
    Box(int ht, int wd, int dp)
    {
        height = ht;
        width = wd;
        depth = dp;
    }
    // Member function.
    int volume()
    {
        return height * width * depth;
    }
};
int main()
{
    // Define two Box objects.
    Box thisbox(7, 8, 9);
    Box otherbox;
    // Assign to otherbox the value of thisbox.
    otherbox = thisbox;
    // Get and display the volume.
    int volume = otherbox.volume();
    std::cout << volume;
    return 0;
}
```

Program 15-2 uses the simplest of differences between constructors: One constructor has initializers, and the other does not. The differences between constructors can be much greater, depending on the types of the class's data members and the algorithms that associate with the constructor function. You will see more complex constructor functions in this and later chapters.

Program 15-2 is an example of a weak class design. It permits you to instantiate and then use an uninitialized Box object. There is no way to determine in advance what the volume member function returns if the program fails to assign the thisbox object to the otherbox object before calling volume. In a better design, the constructor with the empty parameter list assigns default values to the object:

```
class Box
{
    int height, width, depth;

public:
    Box()
        { height = 0; width = 0; depth = 0; }
    Box(int ht, int wd, int dp)
        { height = ht; width = wd; depth = dp; }
    int volume() { return height * width * depth; }
};
```

An even better design uses default arguments to eliminate altogether the constructor with the empty parameter list:

```
class Box
{
    int height, width, depth;

public:
    Box(int ht = 0, int wd = 0, int dp = 0)
        { height = ht; width = wd; depth = dp; }
    int volume() { return height * width * depth; }
};
```

This practice ensures that no Box object is ever instantiated without valid values in the data members.

Copy Constructors

A *copy constructor* is a constructor that executes in these cases: when you initialize a new object of the class with an existing object of the same class, when you pass a copy of an object of the class by value as an argument to a function, and when you return an object of the class by value. The copy constructor is similar to the conversion constructor function that you learned about earlier in this chapter. Conversion constructors convert the values in one class object to the format of an object of a different class. Copy constructors initialize the values from an existing object of a class to a new, instantiated object of that same class.

Chapter 21 explains how to overload the assignment operator (=) to manage the assignment of an object of a class to another object of the same class when the default assignment provided by the compiler causes problems. Similar problems occur when you initialize an object with the contents of another object, so you must have copy constructor functions.

How does initialization of an object with another object differ from assignment of one object to another?

✦ Assignment assigns the value of an existing object to another existing object.

✦ Initialization creates a new object and initializes it with the contents of the existing object.

The compiler can distinguish between the two by using an overloaded assignment operator for assignments and a copy constructor for initializations.

Initializing an object with the contents of another object of the same class requires the use of a copy constructor function, which is a constructor that can be called with a single argument of an object of the same class as the object being constructed. A copy constructor always is declared as taking a reference to the object from which it is copied. By convention, that parameter is const.

If you do not provide a copy constructor, the compiler always provides one by default. The default copy constructor performs a simple member-by-member copy of the class's data members. Program 15-3 demonstrates the copy constructor.

Program 15-3: **Copy constructor**

```
#include <iostream>
#include <cstring>

class Date {
    int mo, da, yr;
    char* month;
public:
    Date(int m = 0, int d = 0, int y = 0);
    // Copy constructor.
    Date(const Date&);
    ~Date();
    void display() const;
};
Date::Date(int m, int d, int y)
{
    static char* mos[] = {
        "January", "February", "March", "April", "May",
        "June", "July", "August", "September", "October",
        "November", "December"
    };
    mo = m;
    da = d;
    yr = y;
    if (m != 0) {
        month = new char[std::strlen(mos[m-1])+1];
        std::strcpy(month, mos[m-1]);
    } else
```

Continued

Program 15-3 *(continued)*

```
        month = 0;
}
Date::Date(const Date& dt)
{
    mo = dt.mo;
    da = dt.da;
    yr = dt.yr;
    if (dt.month != 0) {
        month = new char [std::strlen(dt.month)+1];
        std::strcpy(month, dt.month);
    } else
        month = 0;
}
Date::~Date()
{
    delete [] month;
}
void Date::display() const
{
    if (month != 0)
        std::cout << month << ' ' << da << ", "
                  << yr << std::endl;
}
int main()
{
    // First date.
    Date birthday(6,24,1940);
    birthday.display();
    // Second date.
    Date newday = birthday;
    newday.display();
    // Third date.
    Date lastday(birthday);
    lastday.display();
    return 0;
}
```

The copy constructor in this program resembles the overloaded assignment operator you will learn about in Chapter 21. The difference is that the copy constructor function executes when you declare a new `Date` object to be initialized with the contents of an existing `Date` object. Program 15-3 shows two ways to do this. One way uses the usual C++ variable initializer syntax:

```
Date newday = birthday;
```

The second way uses the constructor calling convention, in which the initializing object is an argument to the function's parameter:

```
Date lastday(birthday);
```

Constructor Parameter Initialization Lists

You must use the constructor's parameter initialization list to initialize any class object data member that does not have a default constructor. Otherwise, the compiler cannot know how to initialize the empty object awaiting assignment from within the constructor. Some programmers use the parameter initialization list to initialize all class object data members. Consider this code:

```
class Date
{
    int mo, da, yr;

public:
    Date(int m = 0, int d = 0, int y = 0);
};

class Employee
{
    int empno;
    Date datehired;

public:
    Employee(int en, Date& dh);
};
```

You can code the Employee constructor either of the following ways:

```
// Employee constructor, version 1.
Employee ::Employee(int en, Date& dh)
{
    empno = en;
    datehired = dh;
}

// Employee constructor, version 2.
Employee ::Employee(int en, Date& dh) : empno(en),datehired(dh)
{
}
```

The first version of the Employee constructor uses two logical steps to construct and initialize the datehired data member. The second version uses only a construction step specified in the member initialization list. Depending on the complexity of the Date object's default constructor, the difference between the two versions can be significant.

Destructors

When a class object goes out of scope, a special function called the *destructor* is called. You define the destructor when you define the class. The destructor function name is always that of the class with a tilde character (~) as a prefix. Program 14-1 in Chapter 14 demonstrated the syntax of the Box class's destructor function as repeated here:

```
class Box
{
    // ...
public:
    ~Box();              // destructor function.
    // ...
};
```

There is only one destructor function for a class. A destructor function takes no parameters and returns nothing. The destructor's purpose is to undo whatever the class object has done that needs to be undone, such as releasing allocated heap memory.

The destructor function for the Box class in Program 14-1 does nothing. The program includes the destructor to show its format. You can omit it and still get the same result. However, on other occasions, destructors are necessary. For example, some classes allocate memory from the heap in their constructor functions or elsewhere during the life of the class object and return the memory to the heap in the destructor function. Later programs in later chapters demonstrate this programming technique.

Using Destructors

Until now, the programs in this chapter have not included destructor functions, because the classes in them have not required anything in the way of custom destruction. To illustrate how destructors work, a new Date class includes a pointer to a string that contains the month spelled out. Program 15-4 shows the destructor function for the new Date class.

Program 15-4: **Destructors**

```
#include <iostream>
#include <cstring>

class Date {
    int mo, da, yr;
    char *month;
public:
    Date(int m = 0, int d = 0, int y = 0);
    ~Date();
    void display() const;
};
Date::Date(int m, int d, int y)
{
    static char *mos[] = {
        "January", "February", "March", "April", "May",
        "June", "July", "August", "September", "October",
        "November", "December"
    };
    mo = m;
    da = d;
    yr = y;
    if (m != 0) {
```

```
            month = new char[std::strlen(mos[m-1])+1];
            std::strcpy(month, mos[m-1]);
        } else
            month = 0;
    }
// The destructor definition.
Date::~Date()
{
    delete [] month;
}
// Display member function.
void Date::display() const
{
    if (month != 0)
        std::cout << month << ' ' << da << ", " << yr;
}
int main()
{
    Date birthday(6,24,1940);
    birthday.display();
    return 0;
}
```

The constructor function for the Date object uses the new operator to allocate dynamic memory for the string name of the month. Then, the constructor copies the name from its internal array into the Date object's month character pointer.

Note that the program does not check to ensure that the month argument is within the range 1 to 12. In a real program, you would make that check and perhaps throw an exception (Chapter 35) from the constructor when the month argument is out of range.

Note also that the constructor could have copied the pointer from the constructor's array into the class, but the point of the listing is to discuss destructors. If we copied the pointer, the object would have had nothing that needed destroying.

The destructor function deletes the month pointer, and this is where you can get into trouble. As programmed, the program has no problems; but as designed, the Date class can cause trouble when used in an assignment. Suppose you add the following code to the main function in Program 15-4:

```
Date newday;
newday = birthday;
```

You construct an empty Date variable named newday and then assign the contents of birthday to it. That looks reasonable, but when you consider what the destructor function does, you can see the problem.

If you do not tell the compiler otherwise, it assumes that class assignment is implemented as a member-by-member copy. In this example, the birthday variable has month, a character pointer initialized by the constructor's use of the new operator. The destructor uses the delete operator to release the memory when birthday goes out of scope. But when that happens, newday goes out of scope, too, and the destructor also executes for it. The month pointer in `newday` is a copy of the month pointer in `birthday`. The constructor deletes the same pointer twice, giving unpredictable results — a problem that you must deal with in class design.

Furthermore, suppose that `newday` is an external object and `birthday` is automatic. When `birthday` goes out of scope, it deletes the month pointer in the `newday` object.

Now, suppose that you have two initialized `Date` variables, and you assign one to the other, as in the following example:

```
Date birthday(6,24,40);
Date newday(7,29,41);
newday = birthday;
```

The problem compounds itself. When the two variables go out of scope, the `month` value originally assigned in `birthday` is in `newday` as a result of the assignment. The `month` value that the constructor's `new` operation puts into `newday` is overwritten by the assignment. Not only does the `month` value in `birthday` get deleted twice, but also the one that originally was in `newday` never gets deleted.

We'll solve that problem in Chapter 21.

Summary

This chapter introduced constructor and destructor class member functions. You learned how a constructor builds an object of a class and how a destructor destroys the object. Chapter 16 continues the constructor discussion by explaining how to use conversion constructors and conversion member functions.

✦   ✦   ✦

Conversion

Class Conversions

C++ intrinsic data types obey implicit type conversion rules. Suppose, for example, that an expression uses a `short int` variable in a context in which the compiler expects to see a `long int` variable. The compiler automatically invokes a type conversion rule to convert the short integer value to the long integer format. The compiler knows such implicit conversions for all pairs of data types that are compatible with respect to conversions. These implicit conversions occur in assignments, function arguments, return values, initializers, and expressions. You can provide equivalent conversion rules for your classes.

Conversion Functions

You build an implicit conversion rule into a class by building a *conversion function*, a member function to allow the compiler to convert between your types and either other user-defined types or intrinsic types. The conversion function's declaration tells the compiler to call the conversion function when the syntax of a statement implies that the conversion should take effect — that is, when the compiler expects an object of one type, but instead sees an object of the other data type.

There are two ways to write conversion functions. The first is to write a conversion constructor function; the second is to write a member conversion function. Which type of conversion function you write depends on whether you are converting to or from an object of the class.

Conversion Constructors

A constructor function with only one entry in its parameter list (or with additional entries that have default arguments) is a *conversion constructor* if the parameter is a different type than the class of the constructor. If the parameter is the same type, the constructor function is a copy constructor (Chapter 15).

A conversion constructor converts from an object of the type of the constructor's parameter to an object of the class. The conversion constructor works like any other constructor when you declare an object of the class type with a matching initializer argument. It is an implicit conversion constructor when you use an expression of the parameter type in a context in which the class type is expected.

Program 16-1 demonstrates a conversion constructor function that converts the time_t value returned by the Standard C std::time function (Chapter 26) to an object of the Date class.

Program 16-1: **Conversion constructor function**

```cpp
#include <iostream>
#include <ctime>
#include <stdio.h>

class Date {
    int mo, da, yr;
public:
    Date(time_t);     // conversion constructor function
    void display();
};
// Member function to display the date.
void Date::display()
{
    char year[5];
    if (yr < 10)
        std::sprintf(year, "0%d", yr);
    else
        std::sprintf(year, "%d", yr);
    std::cout << mo << '/' << da << '/' << year;
}
// Constructor conversion function.
Date::Date(time_t now)
{
    std::tm* tim = std::localtime(&now);
    da = tim->tm_mday;
    mo = tim->tm_mon + 1;
    yr = tim->tm_year;
    if (yr >= 100)
        yr -= 100;
}
int main()
{
    // Get today's date and time.
    std::time_t now = std::time(0);
    // Construct a Date object by invoking
    // the conversion constructor.
    Date dt(now);
    // Display the date.
    dt.display();
    return 0;
}
```

Chapter 26 explains the <ctime> header file and the Standard C time functions and data structures. Program 16-1 calls the std::time function to retrieve the current time expressed as a std::time_t object. Then, the program constructs a Date object by invoking the Date class's conversion constructor function, which accepts a std::time_t object. In this listing, the conversion constructor is the class's only constructor. That constructor function passes the std::time_t object to the Standard C std::localtime function, which returns a pointer to an object of type struct std::tm (declared in the Standard C <ctime> header file). The constructor then copies the structure members for day, month, and year to the Date object's data members, thus constructing a Date object from a std::time_t object.

Member Conversion Functions

A *member conversion function* converts an object of the class in which you define the function to an object of a different data type. A member conversion function uses the C++ operator keyword in its declaration. You declare a member conversion function in the class declaration:

```
operator long();
```

The long in this example is the type specifier of the converted data type. The type specifier can be any valid C++ type, including another class. You define the member conversion function with the following notation:

```
Classname::operator long()
```

The Classname identifier is the type specifier of the class in which the function is declared. The function converts objects of this class into, in this example, long objects. The function returns an object of the data type to which it is converting—in this case, a long.

The Date class that you have been using does not contain enough information to convert an object of that class back to the std::time_t variable, but you can convert one to, for example, a long integer containing the number of days since the beginning of the 20th century. Program 16-2 shows how you use a member function to make such a conversion.

Program 16-2: **Member conversion function**

```
#include <iostream>

class Date {
    int mo, da, yr;
public:
    Date(int m, int d, int y)
    {
        mo = m;
        da = d;
        yr = y;
    }
    operator long();    // member conversion function.
};
// The member conversion function.
Date::operator long()
```

Continued

Program 16-2 *(continued)*

```
{
    static int dys[]={31,28,31,30,31,30,31,31,30,31,30,31};
    long days = yr - 1900;
    days *= 365;
    days += yr / 4;
    for (int i = 0; i < mo-1; i++)
        days += dys[i];
    days += da;
    return days;
}
int main()
{
    Date xmas(12, 25, 2003);
    long since = xmas;
    std::cout << since << std::endl;
    return 0;
}
```

When the compiler sees the assignment of the xmas object to a long object, the compiler searches for valid ways to make that conversion. The compiler finds the Date::operator long function, which satisfies its requirements for specification of a conversion rule. Then the compiler generates a call to that function, which assigns at runtime the return value from that function to the long integer object.

Converting Class Objects

The conversion examples so far have converted class objects to and from intrinsic C++ data type objects. You also can define conversion functions that convert from one class object to another. Program 16-3 shows you how to convert class objects.

Program 16-3: Converting classes

```
#include <iostream>
class CustomDate {
public:
    int da, yr;
    CustomDate(int d = 0, int y = 0)
    {
        da = d;
        yr = y;
    }
    void display()
    {
        std::cout << std::endl
```

```
                    << yr << '-' << da;
        }
};
class Date {
    int mo, da, yr;
public:
    Date(int m = 0, int d = 0, int y = 0)
    {
        mo = m;
        da = d;
        yr = y;
    }
    // Constructor conversion function.
    Date(const CustomDate&);
    // Member conversion function.
    operator CustomDate();
    void display()
    {
        std::cout << std::endl
        << mo << '/' << da
        << '/' << yr;
    }
};
static int dys[] = {31,28,31,30,31,30,31,31,30,31,30,31};
// Constructor conversion function (Date <- CustomDate).
Date::Date(const CustomDate& jd)
{
    yr = jd.yr;
    da = jd.da;
    for (mo = 0; mo < 11; mo++)
        if (da > dys[mo])
            da -= dys[mo];
        else
            break;
    mo++;
}
// Member conversion function (CustomDate <- Date)
Date::operator CustomDate()
{
    CustomDate cd(0, yr);
    for (int i = 0; i < mo-1; i++)
        cd.da += dys[i];
    cd.da += da;
    return cd;
}
int main()
{
    Date dt(11,17,97);
    CustomDate cd;
    // Convert Date to CustomDate.
```

Continued

Program 16-3 *(continued)*

```
    cd = dt;
    cd.display();
    // Convert CustomDate to Date
    dt = cd;
    dt.display();
    return 0;
}
```

This listing has two classes: CustomDate and Date. A CustomDate object contains the year and the day of the year expressed as an integer value from 1 to 365 (366 in leap years). The conversion functions in Program 16-3 convert between the two date formats.

The date conversion algorithms in these listings do not consider things such as the millennium or leap years. These intentional omissions keep the listings simple. Always cover all such possibilities when you design a class, particularly one that others might use. After all, there is no way to tell how other programmers might use this class.

Both kinds of conversion functions are built into the Date class in Program 16-3. This approach works because you convert from the Date type to the CustomDate type with the operator CustomDate member conversion function, and from the CustomDate type to the Date type with the Date(const CustomDate&) conversion constructor.

You cannot have both a Date-to-CustomDate member conversion function in the Date class and a Date-to-CustomDate conversion constructor function in the CustomDate class. The compiler cannot know which function to call to perform the conversion and, consequently, generates an error message.

The conversion constructor that constructs a Date object from a CustomDate object has as its parameter a const reference to a CustomDate object. This usage passes a reference rather than a copy to the constructor, a technique that eliminates argument-passing overhead for large objects. The parameter is const to specify that the constructor function does not modify any of the data members of the CustomDate object.

Do not be concerned about the public data members in the CustomDate class. Chapter 19 deals with that issue when it explains *friends*.

Invoking Conversion Functions

There are three C++ forms that invoke a conversion function. The first is implicit conversion. For example, when the compiler expects to see a Date object and the program supplies a CustomDate object, the compiler calls the appropriate conversion function. The other two forms involve explicit conversions that you write into the code. The C++ cast is the first of these conversions. The second is an explicit call to the conversion constructor or member conversion function. Program 16-4 illustrates the three class-conversion forms.

Program 16-4: **Invoking conversions**

```cpp
#include <iostream>

class CustomDate {
public:
    int da, yr;
    CustomDate(int d = 0, int y = 0)
    {
        da = d;
        yr = y;
    }
    void display()
    {
        std::cout << std::endl << yr << '-' << da;
    }
};
class Date {
    int mo, da, yr;
public:
    Date(int m, int d, int y)
    {
        mo = m;
        da = d;
        yr = y;
    }
    operator CustomDate(); // conversion function
};
// Member conversion function (CustomDate <- Date).
Date::operator CustomDate()
{
    static int dys[] = {31,28,31,30,31,30,31,31,30,31,30,31};
    CustomDate cd(0, yr);
    for (int i = 0; i < mo-1; i++)
        cd.da += dys[i];
    cd.da += da;
    return cd;
}
int main()
{
    Date dt(11,17,89);
    CustomDate cd;
    // Convert Date to CustomDate via implicit conversion.
    cd = dt;
    cd.display();
```

Continued

Program 16-4 *(continued)*

```
// Convert Date to CustomDate via cast.
cd = (CustomDate) dt;
cd.display();
// Convert Date to CustomDate via constructor
cd = CustomDate(dt);
cd.display();
return 0;
}
```

The cast in Program 16-4 uses traditional C language casting notation, which works. C++ includes improved notations for casting. Chapter 37 discusses the C++ casting conventions.

The Contexts in Which Conversions Occur

So far, the example programs have invoked conversion functions through assignment. The assignment of one object to another object of a different type invokes the appropriate conversion function. The following list identifies other contexts that invoke conversion functions:

✦ Function arguments

✦ Initializers

✦ Return values

✦ Statement expressions

Program 16-5 illustrates some of the ways you can cause a conversion function to be called.

Program 16-5: **Contexts of conversions**

```
#include <iostream>

class CustomDate {
public:
    int da, yr;
    CustomDate()
    {}
    CustomDate(int d, int y)
    {
        da = d;
        yr = y;
    }
    void display()
    {
        std::cout << std::endl << yr << '-' << da;
    }
```

```
};
class Date {
    int mo, da, yr;
public:
    Date(int m, int d, int y)
    {
        mo = m;
        da = d;
        yr = y;
    }
    operator CustomDate(); // conversion function
};
// Member conversion function (CustomDate <- Date).
Date::operator CustomDate()
{
    static int dys[] = {31,28,31,30,31,30,31,31,30,31,30,31};
    CustomDate cd(0, yr);
    for (int i = 0; i < mo-1; i++)
        cd.da += dys[i];
    cd.da += da;
    return cd;
}
// A class that expects a CustomDate date as an initializer.
class Tester
{
    CustomDate cd;
public:
    explicit Tester(CustomDate c)
    {
        cd = c;
    }
    void display()
    {
        cd.display();
    }
};
// A function that expects a CustomDate date.
void dispdate(CustomDate cd)
{
    cd.display();
}
// A function that returns a CustomDate date.
CustomDate rtndate()
{
    Date dt(10,11,88);
    return dt;  // This will be converted to CustomDate.
}
int main()
{
    Date dt(11,17,89);
```

Continued

```
CustomDate cd;
// Convert Date to CustomDate via assignment.
cd = dt;
cd.display();
// Convert Date to CustomDate via function argument.
dispdate(dt);
// Convert Date to CustomDate via initializer.
Tester ts(dt);
ts.display();
// Convert Date to CustomDate via return value.
cd = rtndate();
cd.display();
return 0;
}
```

Explicit Constructors

Observe the `explicit` qualifier in the `Tester` class's constructor in Program 16-5. Without that keyword, the compiler treats the constructor as a conversion constructor to be invoked whenever the program uses an object of type `CustomDate` and the compiler expects to see an object of type `Tester`. Recall that conversion constructors have only one parameter (or, if there are multiple parameters, default values for the subsequent arguments) with a type that is other than the type of the constructor. There are times when you do not want a constructor with only one parameter to be used in conversions; instead you want the constructor to be used only for explicit construction of instantiated objects. In these cases, use the `explicit` qualifier in the constructor's declaration. The following line of code, when placed after the declaration of the `Tester` object in Program 16-5, produces a compiler error:

```
ts = cd; // error
```

This error tells you that even though the `Tester` class has a constructor that accepts a `Date` argument, the compiler does not treat it as a `Date`-to-`Tester` conversion constructor because the constructor is declared to be `explicit`.

Conversion Within an Expression

Conversion occurs in expressions in which one type is expected and another type is found. This process is apparent when the conversion is to a numeric type instead of to another class.

Program 16-6 uses the conversion of a `Date` object to a long integer to illustrate how the integral representation of a class can, through conversion, contribute directly to an expression.

Program 16-6: **Conversion in an expression**

```
#include <iostream>

class Date {
    int mo, da, yr;
public:
    Date(int m, int d, int y)
    {
        mo = m;
        da = d;
        yr = y;
    }
    operator long();    // member conversion function
};
// The member conversion function.
Date::operator long()
{
    static int dys[]={31,28,31,30,31,30,31,31,30,31,30,31};
    long days = yr;
    days *= 365;
    days += yr / 4;
    for (int i = 0; i < mo-1; i++)
        days += dys[i];
    days += da;
    return days;
}
int main()
{
    Date today(2, 12, 90);
    const long ott = 123;
    long sum = ott + today;    // today is converted to long.
    std::cout << ott << " + " << (long) today << " = " << sum;
    return 0;
}
```

The implicit conversion from within an expression occurs if the converted object can be converted to a numerical type or if the expression invokes an overloaded operator that works with the class. Chapter 21 discusses overloading operators.

If you define two conversion functions, one for converting from long and one for converting from int, for example, the compiler does not know which one to call if you use an object of the type in a context where either intrinsic type would work. You can view this behavior by inserting the following line of code into Program 16-6 and compiling the program:

```
operator int() { }
```

The compiler reports that it does not know which conversion function to call because either an `int` or a `long` can be used in the context where the program uses the `today` object. The GCC compiler calls this condition an *ambiguous overload*. It isn't that the two functions are ambiguous. Rather, the way the program uses the `today` object introduces an ambiguity. Given that there might be an occasion when a class needs both member conversion functions, you can remove the ambiguity by casting the object to the desired type like this:

```
long sum = ott + (long)today;
```

The same opportunity exists for ambiguity in your own conversion designs. If a class has conversion constructors for two class types and the two other classes can be used in the same context, the compiler does not know which conversion to invoke.

Summary

This chapter explained how to build classes that can convert between objects of themselves and objects of other intrinsic and class types. Class object conversion supports the C++ strong typing programming model by allowing conversion only between objects that are compatible. The programmer defines that compatibility with conversion functions in the classes. Chapter 17 is about arrays of class objects.

✦   ✦   ✦

Arrays of Class Objects

Class Objects in an Array

Class objects are like other C++ data types in that you can declare pointers to them and create arrays that contain them. The array notation is the same as that of an array of structures (Chapter 7). Program 17-1 demonstrates an array of Date structures.

Program 17-1: **Arrays of classes**

```
#include <iostream>

class Date {
    int mo, da, yr;
public:
    Date(int m = 0, int d = 0, int y = 0)
    {
        mo = m;
        da = d;
        yr = y;
    }
    void display() const
    {
        std::cout << mo << '/' << da
            << '/' <<yr << std::endl;
    }
};
int main()
{
    Date dates[2];
    Date temp(6,24,40);
    dates[0] = temp;
    dates[0].display();
    dates[1].display();
    return 0;
}
```

The constructor function in Program 17-1 uses default arguments to initialize the three data members to zero. This constructor serves as a default constructor, as well as one that constructs a Date object from three integer arguments (or two, or one, depending on how many arguments you provide). Observe, too, that since you can instantiate a Date object with only one integer argument, the constructor serves as a conversion constructor (Chapter 16) that coverts an int object to a Date object.

Class Object Arrays and the Default Constructor

Recall from Chapter 15 that a constructor with no parameters or a constructor with default arguments for all its parameters is a default constructor. If you provide no constructors for a class, the compiler provides one public default constructor that does nothing. If you provide at least one constructor of any kind, the compiler provides no default constructor.

You cannot instantiate an array of objects of a class that has no default constructor. The notation for instantiating an array of class objects does not permit an initializer list that conforms to the format of constructor function arguments.

The main function in Program 17-1 declares an array of two Date objects and a single date with initialized values. It assigns the initialized Date object to the first of the two Date objects in the array and then displays both dates. The first date in the array has a valid date value; the second has all zeros.

When you declare an array of objects of a class, the compiler calls the default constructor function once for each element in the array. It is important that you understand this relationship when you design constructor functions.

Program 17-2 is similar to Program 17-1, but it removes the default argument values and adds a default constructor with a display message to demonstrate that the default constructor gets called twice — once for each element in the array.

Program 17-2: **Constructors for arrays of classes**

```
#include <iostream>

class Date {
    int mo, da, yr;
public:
    Date();
    Date(int m, int d, int y)
    {
        mo = m;
        da = d;
        yr = y;
    }
    void display() const
    {
        std::cout << mo << '/' << da
        << '/' << yr << std::endl;
    }
};
```

```
// Constructor called for each element in a Date array.
Date::Date()
{
    std::cout << "Date constructor running for "
              << this << std::endl;
    mo = 0;
    da = 0;
    yr = 0;
}
int main()
{
    Date dates[2];
    Date temp(6,24,40);
    dates[0] = temp;
    dates[0].display();
    dates[1].display();
    return 0;
}
```

Program 17-2 displays the following messages:

```
Date constructor running for 0x22ff48
Date constructor running for 0x22ff54
6/24/40
0/0/0
```

As you can see, the default constructor function executes twice: once for each element in the array. The program displays no message for the constructor of the temp object, because that object calls the constructor function that accepts initializers, and that function has no message.

The hexadecimal addresses displayed in the messages indicate that the constructor runs for two adjacent objects. The difference between the two addresses is 12 bytes, which is the size of a Date object, which contains three integers, which are 32 bits each. This size and difference will vary from compiler to compiler depending on the size of an int. The size of a class object is not always the sum of the sizes of its data members. More complex classes contain hidden tables that support more complex language features such as virtual functions (Chapter 23). Some architectures involve byte alignment that adds padding bytes to structures. For now it is important only to understand that the two addresses shown (which might be different on your computer) are different and in close proximity to one another so that you can understand the behavior of the default constructor when the program declares an array of class objects.

Class Object Arrays and Destructors

When an array of objects of a class is destroyed, the compiler calls the destructor function once for each element of the array. Program 17-3 illustrates how destructors get called for class array elements.

Program 17-3: **Destructors for arrays of classes**

```cpp
#include <iostream>

class Date {
    int mo, da, yr;
public:
    Date(int m = 0, int d = 0, int y = 0)
    {
        mo = m;
        da = d;
        yr = y;
    }
    ~Date()
    {
        std::cout << "Date destructor running for "
                    << this << std::endl;
    }
    void display() const
    {
        std::cout << mo << '/' << da
            << '/' << yr << std::endl;
    }
};
int main()
{
    Date dates[2];
    Date* temp = new Date(6,24,40);
    dates[0] = *temp;
    dates[0].display();
    dates[1].display();
    delete temp;
    return 0;
}
```

Program 17-3 has a Date destructor function that does nothing except display a message on the console to prove that it runs more than once for an array of objects. The following display shows that the destructor runs three times — twice for the two elements in the dates array and once for the temp object:

```
6/24/40
0/0/0
Date destructor running for 0x3d3c50
Date destructor running for 0x22ff54
Date destructor running for 0x22ff48
```

Observe that the address of the first date destroyed is nowhere near the other two. That is because the unique date is instantiated on the heap, whereas the array is instantiated on the stack.

Summary

This chapter explained the special considerations for instantiating arrays of class objects. You learned that a class must have a default constructor if its objects are to be contained in an array. You also learned that the constructor and destructor execute multiple times — once for each object in the array. The array is a language construct that C++ inherits from C. The Standard Template Library offers much better ways of containing objects, however, and you learn about its container classes in Part III. Chapter 18 continues your study of C++ classes by discussing several issues related to class members.

✦   ✦   ✦

Class Members

Classes, as you have learned, have data members and member functions. You already know about instances of data types as data members, constructor and destructor member functions, and conversion functions. You know about the access specifiers that control the visibility of class members to the rest of the program. This chapter discusses some of the more advanced properties of class members and some common programming idioms that make a class design more robust.

The this Pointer

The this pointer is a special local pointer that exists while a non-static member function is executing. The this pointer is a pointer to an object of the type of the class, and it points to the object for which the member function currently is executing.

The this pointer always is named this and is a hidden argument passed to every member function as if the member functions were declared, as shown in this example:

```
void Date::myFunction(Date* this); // really void
Date::myFunction();
```

The function declaration really does not contain the parameter when you write the code. I show it here to help you understand the underlying mechanism that supports the this pointer.

When your program calls a member function for an object, the compiler inserts the address of the object into the argument list for the function as if the function were declared as just shown and as if the function call looked like this example:

```
dt.myFunction(&dt); // really dt.myFunction();
```

Once again, you do not include the object's address as an argument when you write code that calls a member function. The compiler puts the address of dt in the hidden this pointer argument and then calls the function. This example shows what the compiler generates as the hidden argument for the member function's hidden this pointer parameter.

The this pointer does not exist in static member functions. (See the discussion on static members later in this chapter.)

When you call a member function for an object, the compiler assigns the address of the object to the `this` pointer and then calls the function. Therefore, every reference to any member from within a member function implicitly uses the `this` pointer. Both output statements in the following example are the same.

The second statement explicitly uses the pointer notation that the first statement uses implicitly:

```
void Date::month_display()
{
    // These two statements do the same thing.
    std::cout << mo;
    std::cout << this->mo;
}
```

You can include the `this` pointer, as the second statement does in the preceding function. To do so, however, is redundant, because the compiler provides the `this` pointer reference by default.

Using this to Link Objects

The `this` pointer is convenient in applications in which a data structure uses self-referential members. An example is the simple linked list. Program 18-1 builds a simple singly linked list of objects of a class named `Family`. Each Family object includes a pointer that refers to the object's immediate ancestor.

Program 18-1: **The this pointer and a linked list**

```
#include <iostream>
#include <string>
#include <cstring>

class Family* last;

class Family {
    Family* ancestor;
    std::string name;
public:
    Family(const std::string& nm)
    {
        ancestor = last;
        last = this;  // self-reference
        name = nm;
    }
    void display() const
    {
        std::cout << name << std::endl;
    }
    Family* Ancestor() const
    {
        return ancestor;
    }
};
```

```
int main()
{
    while (1) {
        std::cout << std::endl
        << "Enter a name ('end' when done): ";
        char name[25];
        std::cin >> name;
        if (std::strncmp(name, "end", 3) == 0)
            break;
        // Make a list entry of the name.
        Family* list = new Family(std::string(name));
    }
    // Display the names in reverse order.
    while (last != 0) {
        last->display();
        Family* hold = last;
        last = last->Ancestor();
        delete hold;
    }
    return 0;
}
```

Program 18-1 prompts you to enter a series of names. When you're finished, you enter the word "end." The program then displays the names in the reverse order in which you entered them.

The Family class in Program 18-1 contains a string value and a pointer to the previous entry in the list. The constructor function puts into the newly instantiated object's ancestor pointer the most recently instantiated Family object's address from the global last pointer. It then puts its own object address as contained in the this pointer into the global last pointer, which at any time points to the last object instantiated.

A member function named Ancestor returns the ancestor pointer to the object's ancestor. The display member function displays the object on standard output.

The main function prompts you to enter names of family members. All main has to do is instantiate a new Family object on the heap. The Family constructor adds the object being constructed to the list. After the last name, you enter the word "end." Then, main navigates the list and displays the entries beginning with the object pointed to by last and using the ancestor data member to find each previous entry in the list. Because each prev pointer points to the previous entry, the names display in the opposite order in which you enter them.

Program 18-1 implements a simple singly linked list to demonstrate how the this pointer is used by an object to refer to itself. If what you need is a linked list in a real program, you should use the Standard C++ Library's std::list template container (Chapter 31). A class library with more complex interobject relationships would use something similar to what Program 18-1 uses. For example, a family tree application might require an object representing a family member to refer to two parental family member objects.

Chapter 21 explains how to use the this pointer when you overload the assignment operator in a class.

Manipulating Private Data Members

All the data members in the `CustomDate` class in Programs 16-3, 16-4, and 16-5 in Chapter 16 are public. This approach allows the conversion functions in the `Date` class to read and write the data members of the `CustomDate` object. Making the members public is one way to permit this access, but when you do, you also make the members public to all other functions in your program. You might not want to do that. Remember the object-oriented convention for keeping data members private and interface member functions public. To get their point across, those programs violated that convention. You should consider alternative ways to get the same results without violating convention.

Suppose, for example, you decided to change the class to store dates in a different internal format. Many programmers had to do this during the Y2K non-crisis. The way things are now, you'd have to find every piece of code that refers to the public members and change the associated programs. In this case, that isn't a big deal, but if this were a reusable library used by many parts of your code it would be more difficult. If the code were in a library that you distributed widely (perhaps on the Internet), it might not be possible at all. Next we will consider other ways you could write this class to take better advantage of C++ object oriented features.

Observe how Program 18-1 just shown includes a member function named `Ancestor` to return the `ancestor` pointer data member. This technique is called a *getter function* (also called an *accessor* function), and it is a common C++ idiom as described next.

Getter and Setter Member Functions

To repeat our object-oriented convention: As a general rule, make all data members private. How, then, does a user of the class access an object's data values? The class design includes a public interface that contains public member functions to read and write data values. Some programmers call these functions *getter* and *setter functions*.

The values returned from getter functions and passed to setter functions are not necessarily one-for-one matches to the types of all the data members. Instead, you should provide getter and setter functions that represent the public interface, permitting the class user to extract data values from the class object and provide data values that modify the content and behavior of the class object.

Usually, you will not have a getter and setter function for every data member. Moreover, if the public interface consists only of simple getter and setter functions for every data member, you might just as well use a C structure instead of a class (unless you think you'll need to make the getter and setter functions more complicated in the future).

Program 18-2 shows how the `Date` class can have member functions that provide controlled access to the data members.

Program 18-2: **Manipulating data members through member functions**

```
#include <iostream>

class Date {
    int mo, da, yr;
```

```
public:
    Date(int m, int d, int y)
    {
        mo = m;
        da = d;
        yr = y;
    }
    // A member function to return the year.
    int getyear() const
    {
        return yr;
    }
    // A member function to set the year.
    void setyear(int y)
    {
        yr = y;
    }
};
int main()
{
    // Set up a Date.
    Date dt(4, 1, 89);
    // Use a member function to read the year value.
    std::cout << "The year is: " << dt.getyear() << std::endl;
    // Use a member function to change the year.
    dt.setyear(97);
    std::cout << "The new year is: " << dt.getyear();
    return 0;
}
```

By consistently using this approach, you ensure that member functions that are bound to the class manage accesses and changes to the data of a class. This binding strengthens a software design and makes it easier to maintain. Suppose, for example, that you change the internal data representation of the Date class. You also then modify the getyear and setyear functions to deal with that other data representation. However, users of the class do not have to change their code. They can recompile their programs, and, if both you and they do everything right, their programs continue to work the same way they did before you modified the class.

const Member Functions

Observe that the getyear function in Program 18-2 is declared as const. You can guarantee that a member function never modifies the object for which it is called by declaring it with the const qualifier. No change to the Date::getyear() function is permitted that modifies the data members in the object. This approach ensures that the member function accesses data values from the object, only to retrieve the data for the user, display the data, or perform some other nonmutating operation.

Furthermore, if the program declares a Date object as const, the program cannot call any non-const member functions for the object whether or not those functions actually change the object's data values. By declaring all functions that do not change values as const, you permit users of const objects to call those functions.

An Improved Member Conversion Function

Program 18-3 improves the CustomDate and Date classes. The new class design eliminates public data members in the CustomDate class with getter and setter member functions. The design improves the Date classes member conversion function that converts a Date object to a CustomDate object. The improvement uses CustomDate's setter function to modify the day field.

Program 18-3: Conversions with proper data hiding

```
#include <iostream>

class CustomDate {
    int da, yr;
public:
    CustomDate()
    {}
    CustomDate(int d, int y)
    {
        da = d;
        yr = y;
    }
    void display() const
    {
        std::cout << std::endl << yr << '-' << da;
    }
    // Member functions to read and write a day.
    int getday() const
    {
        return da;
    }
    void setday(int d)
    {
        da = d;
    }
};
class Date {
    int mo, da, yr;
public:
    Date(int m, int d, int y)
    {
        mo = m;
        da = d;
        yr = y;
    }
    operator CustomDate() const; // conversion function
};
```

```
// Member conversion function (CustomDate <- Date).
Date::operator CustomDate() const
{
    static int dys[] = {31,28,31,30,31,30,31,31,30,31,30,31};
    CustomDate cd(0, yr);
    int day = da;
    for (int i = 0; i < mo-1; i++)
        day += dys[i];
    cd.setday(day);
    return cd;
}
int main()
{
    Date dt(11,17,89);
    CustomDate cd;
    // Convert Date to CustomDate via assignment.
    cd = dt;
    cd.display();
    return 0;
}
```

Observe that the program declares the Date::operator CustomDate function in Program 18-3 as const. This is valid usage, because the function does not modify the data values of the Date object for which it is running. Instead, it modifies the data values of the temporary CustomDate object that it constructs to return to its caller.

static Members

You can declare a member of a class as static, in which case only one instance of the member exists. The member is accessible to all the member functions. No instance of the class needs to be declared for the static members to exist, although the rest of the program cannot access a static member that is not public. However, the declaration of a static member in a class does not define the variable or function automatically. You must define it outside the class definition to create the member.

static Data Members

You use a static data member to maintain a global value that applies to all instances of the class. Member functions can access and modify this value. If the static member is public, all code in the scope of the class declaration — inside and outside of the class — can access the member. As an example, consider the linked list used in Program 18-1. Its last pointer is global and not a part of the class it supports. Program 18-4 improves the Program 18-1 by making the last pointer a public static data member.

Program 18-4: **Static members and the linked list**

```cpp
#include <iostream>
#include <string>
#include <cstring>

class Family {
    Family* ancestor;
    std::string name;
public:
    static Family* last;
    Family(const std::string& nm)
    {
        ancestor = last;
        last = this;  // self-reference
        name = nm;
    }
    void display() const
    {
        std::cout << name << std::endl;
    }
    Family* Ancestor() const
    {
        return ancestor;
    }
};

Family* Family::last;

int main()
{
    while (1) {
        std::cout << std::endl
            << "Enter a name ('end' when done): ";
        char name[25];
        std::cin >> name;
        if (std::strncmp(name, "end", 3) == 0)
            break;
        // Make a list entry of the name.
        Family* list = new Family(std::string(name));
    }
    // Display the names in reverse order.
    while (Family::last != 0) {
        Family::last->display();
        Family* hold = Family::last;
        Family::last = Family::last->Ancestor();
        delete hold;
    }
    return 0;
}
```

Program 18-4 implements an improved Family class. By using a static data member to keep a record of the end of the list, the class assumes all the responsibility for list integrity.

For the main function in Program 18-4 to retrieve the Family::last pointer value to begin iterating the list, Family::last is a public data member, a practice that violates our object-oriented guidelines for keeping data members private. Let's deal with that situation next.

static Member Functions

Member functions can be static. You can use static member functions to perform tasks in the name of the class or an object when the function does not need access to the members of any particular instance of the class. Usually, you use a static member function when you need to access only static data members (or no data members) of the class. The code might be something that affects all instances of the class or something that performs a service without respect to the class instances themselves. For one contrived example, a personal diary class might display the time of day on the screen, a process that exists only to support the diary. It could be implemented as a member function uses no data in any instance of the diary.

static member functions have no this pointer. Because they typically have no access to nonstatic members, they cannot use the this pointer to implicitly point to anything. A static member function might, however, get the address of an instance of the class from somewhere else, in which case the static member function can indeed access the members of that instance.

Program 18-5 adds a Last static member function to the Family class to retrieve the address of the last entry added to the list as stored in the last data member, which now is declared as private, as it should be.

Program 18-5: **Static member functions**

```
#include <iostream>
#include <string>
#include <cstring>

class Family* last;

class Family {
    Family* ancestor;
    static Family* last;
    std::string name;
public:
    Family(const std::string& nm)
    {
        ancestor = last;
        last = this;  // self-reference
        name = nm;
    }
    void display() const
```

Continued

Program 18-5 *(continued)*

```
    {
        std::cout << name << std::endl;
    }
    Family* Ancestor() const
    {
        return ancestor;
    }
    static Family*& Last()
    {
        return last;
    }
};

Family* Family::last;

int main()
{
    while (1) {
        std::cout << std::endl
            << "Enter a name ('end' when done): ";
        char name[25];
        std::cin >> name;
        if (std::strncmp(name, "end", 3) == 0)
            break;
        // Make a list entry of the name.
        Family* list = new Family(std::string(name));
    }
    // Display the names in reverse order.
    while (Family::Last() != 0) {
        Family::Last()->display();
        Family* hold = Family::Last();
        Family::Last() = Family::Last()->Ancestor();
        delete hold;
    }
    return 0;
}
```

A Reference to a Pointer

Observe the declaration in Program 18-5 of the `Family::Last` member function as repeated here:

```
static Family*& Last();
```

This declaration is a function that returns a reference to a pointer as indicated by the *& token pair. The function returns a reference to the last pointer. Because the reference is not const, the program can use the returned reference to assign a new value to the last pointer, which the program does in this line of code:

```
Family::Last() = Family::Last()->Ancestor();
```

Public static Members

If a static member is public, like the one in Program 18-5, it is accessible to the entire program. You can call a public static member function from anywhere without associating it with a particular instance of the class. A public static member function is not quite global. It exists only within the scope of the class in which it is defined. However, you can call it from anywhere within that scope by prefixing it with the class name and using the :: scope resolution operator.

A Brief Essay on const

If you declare an object as const, you cannot call any of the class's member functions (except the constructor and destructor, which are called implicitly by the compiler) that are not const also. Consider this code fragment:

```
class Date
{
    int month, day, year;

public:
    Date(int m, d, y) : month(m), day(d), year(y)
        { }
    void display()
        { std::cout << month << '/' << day << '/' << year; }
};

int main()
{
    const Date dt(6, 24, 1940);
    dt.display();        // --- error!
}
```

The call to the display member function generates a compiler error message because you are calling a non-const function for a const object. Even though the function does not change the data members of the object, the compiler has no way of knowing that, and it generates the error.

Why, you might ask, does the compiler not look at the code in the body of the display function and figure out for itself that the function makes no changes? The answer is that the compiler is looking only at the function's declaration and not at its implementation. The implementation, in fact, can be elsewhere in the program — in another source-code file perhaps — and out of view of the compiler. The following example shows three separate source-code files:

```
///////////////////////////////
// date.h
class Date
{
    int month, day, year;

public:
    Date(int m, d, y);
    void display();
};

///////////////////////////////
// date.cpp
#include <iostream>
#include "date.h"

Date::Date(int m, d, y) : month(m), day(d), year(y)
{
}

void Date::display()
{
    std::cout << month << '/' << day << '/' << year;
}

///////////////////////////////
// program.cpp
#include <iostream>
#include "date.h"

int main()
{
    const Date dt(6, 24, 1940);
    dt.display();       // --- error!
}
```

The solution, as you learned earlier, is to make the display function const:

```
// In date.h
    void display() const;
```

```
// In date.cpp
void Date::display() const
{
    std::cout << month << '/' << day << '/' << year;
}
```

Another solution is to omit the const qualifier from the declaration of the Date object:

```
    Date dt(6, 24, 1940);
```

This solution, however, has a cost. There are times when you want to declare a const object to ensure that your program does not change its value after it is constructed and initialized.

Sure, you can promise yourself that you never intentionally will mess with the object, but these features are built into the C++ language to provide a measure of protection against mistakes. You might as well take advantage of them.

Here's another scenario:

```
void foobar(const Date& dt)
{
    // ...
    dt.display(); // Error if Date::display is not const
}
```

The `foobar` function declares a `const` reference to a `Date` object, meaning that the function has no intentions of ever modifying the caller's copy of the argument. If the `Date::display` function is not `const`, the `foobar` function cannot call it because the compiler senses the potential for `Date::display()` to modify an object that `foobar` promises not to modify.

Some compilers issue warning messages in these cases and compile the program nonetheless. Others issue error messages and refuse to compile the program until you correct the error.

Now, let's consider the situation in which a class object must modify a data member in all cases, whether or not the objects are `const`. The ANSI/ISO committee considered this situation and invented the `mutable` keyword.

mutable Data Members

Suppose that you want to keep a count of every time an object is reported, irrespective of its "constness." The class includes an integer data member to record that count. A `const` member function may modify a data member only if the data member is declared with the `mutable` qualifier. Program 18-6 is an example of that idiom.

Program 18-6: **Using mutable data members**

```
#include <iostream>

class AValue {
    int val;
    // Number of times the object is reported.
    mutable int rptct;
public:
    AValue(int v) : val(v), rptct(0)
    { }
    ~AValue()
    {
        std::cout << "Avalue: " << val << " was reported "
        << rptct << " times.";
    }
    void report() const;
};
```

Continued

```cpp
void AValue::report() const
{
    // Modify data member even though const.
    rptct++;
    std::cout << val << std::endl;
}
int main()
{
    const AValue aval(123);
    aval.report();
    aval.report();
    aval.report();
    return 0;
}
```

Reference Data Members

Chapter 9 explained references. Everything you know about using references with the Standard C++ data types and structures applies equally to objects of classes. Using references to class objects as function parameters and return values adds a measure of efficiency that would not exist if you had to pass every object by value, an important consideration with classes since instances of them can be much larger than instances of intrinsic types.

You also can declare references as class data members, but there are a few things to consider. First, remember that a reference must be initialized. You usually do not initialize a class object with a brace-surrounded initialization list as you do with a structure; instead, you initialize it with a constructor. Therefore, the class constructor must initialize class member references. Remember, too, that references are aliases. References in classes behave just as if they were data members of the class with the same notational syntax, but operations on member references actually operate on the objects that are used to initialize them. Program 18-7 shows the use of a class that has reference data members.

Program 18-7: **A class with a reference**

```cpp
#include <iostream>

class Date {
    int da, mo, yr;
public:
    Date(int d,int m,int y)
    {
        da = d;
        mo = m;
        yr = y;
    }
```

```
        void Display() const
        {
            std::cout << da << '/' << mo << '/' << yr;
        }
};

class Time {
    int hr, min, sec;
public:
    Time(int h, int m, int s)
    {
        hr = h;
        min = m;
        sec = s;
    }
    void Display() const
    {
        std::cout << hr << ':' << min << ':' << sec;
    }
};

class DateTime {
    // References to Date and Time.
    const Date& dt;
    const Time& tm;
public:
    // Constructor with reference initializers.
    DateTime(const Date& d, const Time& t) : dt(d), tm(t)
    { /* empty */  }
    void Display() const
    {
        dt.Display();
        std::cout << ' ';
        tm.Display();
    }
};
int main()
{
    Date today(25,3,93);
    Time now(4,15,0);
    DateTime dtm(today, now);
    dtm.Display();
    return 0;
}
```

Observe the `DateTime` constructor specification. The colon operator specifies that a list of initializers — the parameter initialization list — follows. You must initialize reference data members in this manner. You cannot wait and do it in the body of the constructor. If the constructor is not inline, as this one is, you put the colon and initializer list in the constructor's definition rather than in its prototype in the class declaration like this:

```
class DateTime
{
    // References to Date and Time.
    const Date& dt;
    const Time& tm;

public:
    DateTime(const Date& d, const Time& t);
};

DateTime::DateTime(const Date& d, const Time& t) : dt(d), tm(t)
{
    // ... empty
}
```

You can use the constructor's parameter initialization list to initialize any data member. You should use it to initialize any const data members; as with references, you cannot assign values to const data members from within the constructor's statement body.

You cannot write a complete overloaded assignment operator function for a class that has reference data members, because you cannot modify the value of a reference once it is instantiated and initialized.

Summary

This chapter added to what you know about class members as they are used in simple class design. You will learn much more about class members in Chapter 21, which addresses overloaded operators, and Chapter 23, which addresses class inheritance. First, however, Chapter 19 teaches about an unusual C++ feature, the *friend*, and Chapter 20 teaches about how class objects work with heap dynamic storage allocation.

✦   ✦   ✦

Friends

Having learned in Chapters 14 and 18 that hidden access to data members is best, you must now consider exceptions to that rule. There are times when a class declaration must allow specific outside functions to read and write the class's private data members directly.

The `friend` keyword in a class specifies that a particular function or all the member functions of another class can read and write the original class's private data members. This technique enables a class to maintain a private implementation while granting specific classes and functions controlled access to that implementation.

Friend Classes

The first kind of friend is the *class friend*. A class can specify that all the member functions of another class can read and write the first class's private data members by identifying the other class as a friend. Program 19-1 illustrates the use of the friend class.

Program 19-1: **Friend classes**

```
#include <iostream>

// A forward reference.
class Date;

class CustomDate {
    int da, yr;
public:
    CustomDate(int d = 0, int y = 0)
    {
        da = d;
        yr = y;
    }
    void display() const
    {
        std::cout << std::endl << yr << '-' << da;
    }
    // Allow Date member functions to
    // see CustomDate private members.
    friend Date;
```

Continued

```
};

class Date {
    int mo, da, yr;
public:
    Date(int m, int d, int y)
    {
        mo = m;
        da = d;
        yr = y;
    }
    operator CustomDate();
};
// Member conversion function (CustomDate <- Date).
Date::operator CustomDate()
{
    static int dys[] = {31,28,31,30,31,30,31,31,30,31,30,31};
    CustomDate cd(0, yr);
    for (int i = 0; i < mo-1; i++)
        cd.da += dys[i];
    cd.da += da;
    return cd;
}
int main()
{
    Date dt(11,17,89);
    CustomDate cd(dt);
    cd.display();
    return 0;
}
```

Observe this new construct in the CustomDate class of Program 19-1 in the following
example:

```
friend Date;
```

This statement tells the compiler that all member functions of the Date class have access to
the private members of the CustomDate class. The conversion functions of the Date class
need to see the individual data components of the CustomDate class, so the entire Date class
is named as a friend of the CustomDate class.

Implied Construction

Observe the call to the CustomDate constructor in Program 19-1. It seems that the
CustomDate class would need a conversion constructor such as this one:

```
CustomDate(Date& dt);
```

Yet, the only constructor is this one:

```
CustomDate(int d = 0, int y = 0);
```

Here's what happens. The compiler sees a need to construct a `CustomDate` object from a `Date` object. There is no such conversion constructor defined for the `CustomDate` class. There is, however, a member conversion function defined for the `Date` class that converts `Date` objects to `CustomDate` objects.

The compiler now looks to see whether the `CustomDate` class includes a copy constructor (Chapter 15) that constructs a `CustomDate` object from an existing `CustomDate` object. There is no `CustomDate` copy constructor, so the compiler provides a default one that simply copies each of the members from the existing `CustomDate` object to the new `CustomDate` object.

Now, given that the compiler can convert a `Date` object to a `CustomDate` object and can construct a `CustomDate` object from a `CustomDate` object, the compiler compiles a call to the conversion function to construct a hidden, temporary, anonymous `CustomDate` object from the `Date` object. The compiler uses this temporary object as the argument to a call to its default copy constructor; thus, the new `CustomDate` object is constructed.

Forward References

Program 19-1 uses another interesting C++ feature. The beginning of the program contains the following statement:

```
class Date;
```

This statement is a *forward reference*. It tells the compiler that a class named `Date` is defined later. The compiler needs to know that information because the `CustomDate` class refers to the `Date` class, and the `Date` class refers to the `CustomDate` class. You must declare one of them first, so the statement serves to resolve the forward reference to `Date` that occurs in the `CustomDate` class.

By using forward references, you can declare friends for, and pointers and references to, as yet undefined classes. You cannot include any statements that require the compiler to know the details of the definition of the forward-referenced class. For example, you cannot declare an instance of the class or refer to any members of the class.

Explicit Friend Forward Reference

You can eliminate the need for the forward reference outside the class by including the `class` keyword in the `friend` declaration inside the class. Program 19-2 modifies the Program 19-1 program by using the `class` keyword. The listing that follows shows only the `CustomDate` class to demonstrate the usage. The example program on the CD-ROM is complete.

> ## Program 19-2: **Friend classes, forward reference**

```
class CustomDate {
    int da, yr;
public:
    CustomDate(int d = 0, int y = 0)
```

Continued

```
    {
        da = d;
        yr = y;
    }
    void display() const
    {
        std::cout << std::endl << yr << '-' << da;
    }
    // Allows Date member functions to
    // see CustomDate private members.
    friend class Date;
};
```

Friend Functions

Sometimes, you do not want an entire class to be a friend of another class. Unless it is necessary to access data in such a broad way, you should not do so. What you need is a way to specify that only selected member functions of another class may read and write the data members of the current class. In these cases, you may specify that a particular function, rather than an entire class, is a friend of a class. This type of function is called a *friend function*.

Program 19-3 restricts the access to the data members of the CustomDate class only to the member function of the Date class that needs it. Once again, the listing shows only the part of the program that changed.

Program 19-3: **Friend functions in a class**

```
class CustomDate;

class Date {
    int mo, da, yr;
public:
    Date(const CustomDate&);  // conversion constructor.
    void display() const
    {
        std::cout << std::endl << mo
             << '/' << da << '/' << yr;
    }
};

class CustomDate {
    int da, yr;
public:
    CustomDate(int d = 0, int y = 0)
    {
        da = d;
```

```
        yr = y;
    }
    // Friend conversion function.
    friend Date::Date(const CustomDate&);
};
```

For this technique to work, the Date class must be declared first because the CustomDate class needs to know about the Date class's constructor. Since Date's conversion constructor refers to CustomDate, there must be a forward reference to CustomDate ahead of the Date class declaration.

Nonmember Friend Functions

Sometimes the function that is to be a friend is not a member of another class at all. Such a function has the special privilege of reading and writing a class object's private data members, yet the function is not a member of any class. This feature is particularly useful when you're overloading operators (the subject of Chapter 21).

A common use of nonmember friend functions is to bridge classes. A function that is a friend to two classes can have access to the private members of both classes. Suppose you have a Time class and a Date class and you want a function that displays both. Program 19-4 shows how a friend function that has access to the private data members of both classes can bridge the two.

Program 19-4: **Bridging classes with a friend function**

```cpp
#include <iostream>

class Time;

class Date {
    int mo, da, yr;
public:
    Date(int m, int d, int y)
    {
        mo = m;
        da = d;
        yr = y;
    }
    // Bridge function.
    friend void display(const Date&, const Time&);
};
class Time {
    int hr, min, sec;
public:
    Time(int h, int m, int s)
    {
        hr = h;
        min = m;
```

Continued

Program 19-4 *(continued)*

```
        sec = s;
    }
    // Bridge function.
    friend void display(const Date&, const Time&);
};
// A bridge friend function.
void display(const Date& dt, const Time& tm)
{
    std::cout << dt.mo << '/' << dt.da << '/' << dt.yr;
    std::cout << ' ';
    std::cout << tm.hr << ':' << tm.min << ':' << tm.sec;
}
int main()
{
    Date dt(2,16,97);
    Time tm(10,55,0);
    display(dt, tm);
    return 0;
}
```

The display function is not a member of any class. Yet it can access the private data members of the Date and Time classes because both classes declare the display function to be their friend. A consequence of this idiom is that the display identifier is declared in the global namespace. It is possible for that identifier to collide with some other global identifier elsewhere in the program, perhaps in a third-party library over which you have no control. The C++ namespace (Chapter 36) feature addresses this problem. Another way to avoid it is to declare a class within your application with the sole purpose of containing such bridge functions as member functions. Program 19-5 shows how that might work.

Program 19-5: Bridging classes with a friend function

```
#include <iostream>

class Time;
class Date;

class Bridges {
public:
    static void Bridges::display(const Date& dt,
                                 const Time& tm);
};

class Date {
    int mo, da, yr;
public:
    Date(int m, int d, int y)
    {
        mo = m;
```

```
            da = d;
            yr = y;
        }
        // Bridge function.
        friend void Bridges::display(const Date&, const Time&);
};
class Time {
    int hr, min, sec;
public:
    Time(int h, int m, int s)
    {
        hr = h;
        min = m;
        sec = s;
    }
    // Bridge function.
    friend void Bridges::display(const Date&, const Time&);
};

// A bridge friend function.
void Bridges::display(const Date& dt, const Time& tm)
{
    std::cout << dt.mo << '/' << dt.da << '/' << dt.yr;
    std::cout << ' ';
    std::cout << tm.hr << ':' << tm.min << ':' << tm.sec;
}

int main()
{
    Date dt(2,16,2003);
    Time tm(10,55,0);
    Bridges::display(dt, tm);
    return 0;
}
```

Summary

This chapter taught the use of the C++ friend mechanism to selectively expose the private members of a class to member functions of other classes and to nonmember functions. Chapter 20 explains dynamic allocation class objects on the heap.

✦   ✦   ✦

Classes and the Heap

In Chapter 8, you learned about the C++ heap, as well as the new and delete memory management operators. This section discusses those operators and their special relationship to classes and class objects.

Constructors and new; Destructors and delete

You used new and delete in a few earlier programs to get and release memory for class objects. When you use new to get memory for a class object, the compiler executes the new operator function first to allocate the memory and then calls the class's constructor function. When you use delete to return the memory, the compiler calls the class's destructor function and then calls the delete operator function. The compiler provides default new and delete operator functions, which you typically use. However, you can provide custom versions for specific purposes on a per-class or global basis. The default versions are the same ones the compiler uses to allocate intrinsic types.

Program 20-1 demonstrates the relationships involving new and constructor functions and delete and destructor function.

Program 20-1: **The new and delete operators with constructors and destructors**

```
#include <iostream>

class Date {
    int mo, da, yr;
public:
    Date()
    {
        std::cout << "Date constructor" << std::endl;
    }
    ~Date()
    {
```

Continued

Program 20-1 *(continued)*

```
        std::cout << "Date destructor" << std::endl;
    }
};
int main()
{
    Date* dt = new Date;
    std::cout << "Process the date" << std::endl;
    delete dt;
    return 0;
}
```

Program 20-1 defines a Date class with a constructor and a destructor. These functions display messages when they run. When the new operator initializes the dt pointer, the constructor function executes. When the delete operator deletes the memory pointed to by the pointer, the operation calls the destructor function.

Program 20-1 displays messages to demonstrate the order in which the constructor and destructor functions are executed. The output looks like this:

```
Date constructor
Process the date
Date destructor
```

The Heap and Class Arrays

You learned earlier that constructor and destructor functions are called once for every element in an array of class objects. The following code fragment illustrates the wrong way to delete an array of class objects instantiated on the heap:

```
Date* dt = new Date[5];
// Doesn't delete all objects in the array!
delete dt;
```

The dt pointer points to an array of five dates. The Date constructor function executes five times from the new operator, because that is what the array notation tells the compiler to do. You learned about that behavior in Chapter 17. But the compiler has no indication from the call to delete that the pointer points to more than one Date object, so it builds only one call to the destructor function.

To solve this problem, C++ enables you to tell the delete operator that the pointer being deleted points to an array. You do so by adding the [] subscript operator to the delete operator like this:

```
delete [] pointername;
```

Program 20-2 illustrates the correct use of the delete operator where an array is involved.

> **Program 20-2: Deleting arrays of new classes**

```cpp
#include <iostream>

class Date {
    int mo, da, yr;
public:
    Date()
    {
        std::cout << "Date constructor" << std::endl;
    }
    ~Date()
    {
        std::cout << "Date destructor" << std::endl;
    }
};
int main()
{
    Date* dt = new Date[5];
    std::cout << "Process the dates" << std::endl;
    // Deletes all five array elements.
    delete [] dt;
    return 0;
}
```

Program 20-2 displays the following messages to demonstrate that the destructor is called once for each element in the array:

```
Date constructor
Date constructor
Date constructor
Date constructor
Date constructor
Process the dates
Date destructor
Date destructor
Date destructor
Date destructor
Date destructor
```

If you use the [] notation when deleting an object that has no destructors, the compiler ignores the notation. However, by convention you should include the [] notation whenever you delete memory that was allocated for an array — even when the objects being deleted are not class objects or do not have destructors. The programs in this chapter do just that.

Overloaded Class new and delete Operators

Chapter 8 taught you how to manage dynamic memory by using the new and delete operator functions. Those examples used the global new and delete operators. You can overload global new and delete; but unless you are involved in low-level systems or embedded programming or writing a debugging tool, it usually is not a good idea. As always, there are exceptions to any guideline. This book neither teaches nor encourages overloading global new and delete.

However, quite justifiably, you can overload the new and delete operators from within the scope of a class declaration. This feature allows a class to have its own custom new and delete operators. You typically use this feature to gain a performance benefit from class-specific knowledge about the memory requirements of a class that can avoid the general-purpose overhead of the global new and delete operators. Global heap operations often rely on operating system functions to allocate and free memory. These operations can be inefficient, particularly in a program that frequently allocates and frees many small blocks of memory in tight iterations.

Suppose you know that there are never more than a certain small number of instances of a class at any one time. You can allocate the necessary memory for all instances of that class and use class-specific new and delete operators to manage the memory. Another important use for class-specific new and delete operators is allocating fixed size objects from a pool. If you know, for example, that each class object is 100 bytes, you can allocate 1000 bytes once and dynamically allocate memory from it with your class-specific new and delete operators.

Program 20-3 illustrates a class with overloaded new and delete operators that are specific to the class.

Program 20-3: **Class-specific new and delete operators**

```
#include <iostream>
#include <cstring>
#include <cstddef>
#include <new>

const int maxnames = 5;

class Names {
    char name[25];
    static char Names::pool[];
    static bool Names::inuse[maxnames];
public:
    Names(char* s)
    {
        std::strncpy(name, s, sizeof(name));
    }
    void* operator new(size_t) throw(std::bad_alloc);
    void operator delete(void*) throw();
    void display() const
    {
        std::cout << name << std::endl;
    }
};

// Simple memory pool to handle fixed number of Names.
char Names::pool[maxnames * sizeof(Names)];
bool Names::inuse[maxnames];

// Overloaded new operator for the Names class.
```

```
void* Names::operator new(size_t) throw(std::bad_alloc)
{
    for (int p = 0; p < maxnames; p++) {
        if (!inuse[p]) {
            inuse[p] = true;
            return pool+p*sizeof(Names);
        }
    }
    throw std::bad_alloc();
}
// Overloaded delete operator for the Names class.
void Names::operator delete(void* p) throw()
{
    if (p != 0)
        inuse[((char*)p - pool) / sizeof(Names)] = false;
}
int main()
{
    Names* nm[maxnames];
    int i;
    for (i = 0; i < maxnames; i++) {
        std::cout << std::endl << "Enter name # "
            << i+1 << ": ";
        char name[25];
        std::cin >> name;
        nm[i] = new Names(name);
    }
    for (i = 0; i < maxnames; i++) {
        nm[i]->display();
        delete nm[i];
    }
    return 0;
}
```

Program 20-3 prompts you for five names and then displays them. The program defines a class named Names, for which the constructor initializes the name value of an object of the class by using the std::strncpy function (Chapter 26). This class defines its own new and delete operators. Because the program is guaranteed never to exceed maxnames names at one time, the programmer decides to improve execution speed by overriding the default new and delete operators.

The simple memory pool that supports Names is a pool character array with enough space to hold all the concurrent names the program expects. The associated inuse bool array contains a true/false value for each name to indicate whether an entry in the pool is in use.

The overloaded new operator finds an unused entry in the pool and returns its address. The overloaded delete operator marks the specified entry as unused.

Overloaded new and delete functions within a class definition always are static and have no this pointer associated with the object being created or deleted. This is because the compiler calls the new function before it calls the class's constructor function, and it calls the delete function after it calls the destructor.

The new function executes before the class's constructor function. The new function cannot access any of the class's members, because no memory exists for them until new allocates it and because the constructor function has not performed any other class-specific initializations yet. The delete operator executes after the destructor function. Consequently, the delete operator cannot have access to the class members.

Testing for Exceptions

The design in Program 20-3 lacks the bulletproofing that you want to include in a real program. For example, the overloaded delete operator function does not test its parameter argument to ensure that it falls within the boundaries of the memory pool. If you are absolutely positive that your program never passes a bad pointer value to the delete operator, you can omit such validations in the interest of efficiency, particularly when efficiency is the motive for overloading the operators in the first place. You should consider, however, installing such tests for a debug version of your software, using the preprocessor's compile-time conditional statements (described in Chapter 11) to remove the tests from the production version of the program. The Standard C++ assert macro (Chapter 26) is a good way to control such tests.

Overloaded new and delete Exceptions

Both overloaded operator functions in Program 20-3 use exception handling, a C++ feature that you have not learned yet. The throw expressions in the function declarations and headers and the throw statement at the bottom of the overloaded new operator function implement the standard exception-handling mechanism for memory allocation. Do not worry about how it works just now. You will learn about exception handling in Chapter 35. For now, accept the fact that these operations are required. If you change Program 20-3 so that the program tries to allocate more Names buffers than the memory pool contains, the overloaded new operator function throws the exception and the program terminates. Chapter 35 explains how you can catch and process such exceptions.

Overloaded Class new[] and delete[]

When a class design includes overloaded new and delete operators such as those in Program 20-3, the overloaded operator functions are not called for allocations of arrays of objects of the class. Suppose that the program in Program 20-3 included these statements:

```
Names *nms = new Names[10];
// ...
delete [] nms;
```

These statements would call the global new and delete operators rather than the overloaded ones. To overload the new and delete operators for array allocations, you must overload the new[] and delete[] operator functions, as Program 20-4 demonstrates.

> Program 20-4: **Class-specific new[] and delete[] operators**

```
#include <iostream>
#include <cstring>
#include <cstddef>
```

```
#include <new>

const int maxnames = 5;
class Names {
    char name[25];
    static char pool[];
    static short int inuse[maxnames];
public:
    Names(char* s = 0)
    {
        if (s)
            strncpy(name, s, sizeof(name));
    }
    void* operator new[](size_t) throw(std::bad_alloc);
    void operator delete[](void*) throw();
    void display() const
    {
        std::cout << name << std::endl;
    }
};

// Simple memory pool to handle fixed number of Names.
char Names::pool[maxnames * sizeof(Names)];
short int Names::inuse[maxnames];

// Overloaded new[] operator for the Names class.
void* Names::operator new[](size_t size) throw(std::bad_alloc)
{
    int elements = size / sizeof(Names);
    // Find the first empty element (if any).
    int p = -1;
    int i = 0;
    while (i < maxnames) {
        if (inuse[i] == 0)    {
            p = i;
            break;
        }
        ++i;
    }
    // Not enough room.
    if ((p == -1) || ((maxnames - p) < elements))
        throw std::bad_alloc();
    // Mark the elements as used.
    inuse[p] = elements;  // number of elements this allocation
    for (int x=1; x<elements; ++x)
        inuse[p+x] = -1;  // set the others to non-zero
    // Return pointer to memory.
    return pool+p*sizeof(Names);
}
// Overloaded delete[] operator for the Names class.
void Names::operator delete[](void* b) throw()
{
```

Continued

Program 20-4 *(continued)*

```
    if (b != 0) {
        int p = ((char*)b - pool) / sizeof(Names);
        if (p >= 0 && p < maxnames)  {
            if (inuse[p] > 0){
                int elements = inuse[p];
                for (int i = 0; i < elements; i++)
                    inuse[p + i] = 0;
            }
        }
    }
}
int main()
{
    Names* np = new Names[maxnames];
    int i;
    for (i = 0; i < maxnames; i++) {
        std::cout << std::endl << "Enter name # "
            << i+1 << ": ";
        char name[25];
        std::cin >> name;
        *(np + i) = name;
    }
    for (i = 0; i < maxnames; i++)
        (np + i)->display();
    delete [] np;
    return 0;
}
```

When you overload new[] and delete[], you have more things to worry about than you do for overloaded new and delete. Inasmuch as the new[] operator is allocating memory for an array, it needs a way to remember the size of the array so that the overloaded delete[] operator can return the proper number of buffers to the pool. In this simple example, we replace the bool array that flagged buffers in use, substituting an array of integers. When Names::operator new[] allocates a block of memory, it puts the number of buffers allocated into the first inuse element allocated and -1 into the other elements allocated for the array. Then, when the delete[] operator function returns buffers to the pool, the function uses the value in the element of the array pointed to by the argument to determine how many buffers to return. This technique is extremely simple and serves to support the small example program in Program 20-4. A more complex buffer requirement might demand a more complex solution.

Summary

This chapter explained how to design classes so their objects can be instantiated on the heap both as single objects and in arrays. It also explained how to overload the new and delete operators so a class can manage its own memory allocation. Chapter 21 is overloading operators in C++ so that objects of a class can exhibit arithmetic and relational behavior similar to the behavior of instrinsic types.

✦   ✦   ✦

Overloading Operators

This chapter covers extending the C++ language by adding operators to user-defined data types — classes. You learned in Chapters 6 and 14 how to add dates and other such types by binding data structures and functions. Now you will add to those classes the behavior of C++ operators.

C++ enables you to build custom operators that implement unary and binary operations that take objects as arguments. For example, you might specify how to add a date and an integer (to produce a new date). You might define an array index operator to allow programs to index into a phone book using a string.

This C++ feature is called *operator overloading*, and with it you can add member functions to the class to implement the overloaded operators.

To Overload or Not to Overload

A wise man once observed that C++ programmers first learn to overload operators, and then they learn not to overload them. A wiser interpretation says that first you learn how to overload operators, and then you learn when to do it and how to do it appropriately.

Here are some guidelines to follow:

- ✦ Overload the assignment operator to assign objects of your types to one another.

- ✦ Overload the arithmetic operators for numerical types to give them arithmetic properties.

- ✦ Overload relational operators when objects of your class can be compared logically.

- ✦ When you overload arithmetic and logical operators, bear in mind the commutative properties of arithmetic and logical operations. If, in your operator overloading scheme, A + B = C, then include overloaded operators so that B + A = C, C - B = A, and so on. Likewise, if B < A, then A > B, A != B, and so on. You learn more about this as we continue in this chapter.

- ✦ Overload the subscript bracket operators [ ] to retrieve elements from container classes.

✦ Overload the << insertion and >> extraction operators to enable you to read and write objects of your class from and to I/O streams (Chapters 27 and 28).

✦ Overload the pointer-to-member -> operator to implement so-called *smart pointers*.

✦ On rare occasions, overload the new and delete operators, as discussed in Chapter 20.

✦ Don't overload any other operators.

Any operator overloading outside these guidelines might seem natural and intuitive to you when you devise it. But it probably will seem abstruse to others when they first see it and likely will seem alien and, perhaps, contrived to you when you take another look at it later. We strongly counsel you to view operator overloading with much skepticism and distrust. Anything that you can do with an overloaded operator you can do just as well with a member function. C++ is an extensible language, but don't extend it beyond recognition.

You implement overloaded operators by writing special functions that the compiler calls when it sees matching operators associated with objects of types for which the operators are overloaded. You learn about these functions in this chapter. But be warned: Nothing says that an overloaded binary addition operator function, for example, must perform addition. In one notable exception, the Standard C++ std::string class (see Chapter 27) overloads the addition (+) operator to concatenate strings the way that BASIC does, and that has nothing to do with addition. Everyone accepts that usage, because tradition has accustomed us to the idiom. But an overloaded operator function, being nothing more than a function, does whatever its code tells it to do. The compiler generates a call to the overloaded operator function when the program applies the operator in a context that fits the function's parameter types. You may have guessed by now that you can overload the addition operator to perform subtraction. Yes, you can, but it is not a wise thing to do.

A Case for Overloaded Operators

Consider a class that implements a numerical type. Let's articulate some requirements for the class:

✦ The program computes the sum of a column of objects of the type.

✦ The program increments, decrements, adds, and subtracts other numerical types to and from objects of the class.

✦ The program compares two of the objects to see whether they are equal or one is greater.

You can build class member functions to perform these operations and call them the way you call, for example, the Standard C function std::strcmp. Or you can overload the arithmetic and relational operators to achieve the same effect.

In Chapter 20, you overloaded the new and delete operators to build custom memory management. You already have used overloaded operators extensively in most of the example programs. Every time you display a value on the std::cout object, you use the << bitwise shift left operator, which is overloaded by the ostream class. Of course, the ostream class doesn't use << for shifting; it completely redefines the meaning of this operator. This redefinition represents a convention that Standard C++ establishes that disobeys the rules for how to overload operators intuitively, which is why the rules given above include one that lets you overload << and >> similarly.

Overloading an operator means that you write a function to execute when your program uses the operator in prescribed ways with an object of your class. For example, you can perform these operations with a `Date` class:

```
Date dt1(1,2,83);
Date dt2(2,4,93);
dt1 += 100;                     // add 100 days
int dif = dt2-dt1;              // compute the delta
if (dt2 < dt1)                  // compare two dates
    dt1 = dt2;                  // assign dates
std::cout << dt1 << ' ' << dt2; // display the dates
```

Look at the last of the examples just shown. Chapter 22 shows you how to overload the << and >> operators.

The Rules of Operator Overloading

Overloaded operators must obey the rules listed here:

1. The overloaded operator must comply with the syntax of the language. For example, as you cannot do the following in C++:

   ```
   int a;
   / a;    // error: / is not a unary operator
   ```

   You, therefore, cannot overload the / operator to do the following:

   ```
   Date dt(1,2,83);
   / dt;    // error: / is not a unary operator
   ```

2. If you can put an operator between two identifiers, you can overload it for custom use with your classes even if the operator would not be acceptable to the compiler otherwise. Consider the following statement:

   ```
   std::cout << "Hello";
   ```

   Without an overloaded << operator, that expression seems to shift `std::cout` a number of bits equal to the value of the pointer to the string, none of which would have passed the compiler's syntax check. But the statement is correct grammar — it is legitimate in some cases to have two expressions separated by the << operator — so you can write an overloaded operator function that executes when this construct appears. The compiler sees the overloaded operator in the context of the two data types and associates the statement with the overloaded operator function.

3. You cannot overload the way an operator works with the intrinsic C++ data types. For example, you cannot overload the binary integer addition operator. You can, however, overload the way an operator works with an instrinsic data type and a class data type.

4. You cannot invent new operators that do not exist in the C++ language. For example, the dollar sign ($) is not a C++ operator, so you cannot use it as an overloaded operator.

5. You cannot overload these operators:

   .   Class member operator

   .*   Pointer-to-member operator

:: Scope resolution operator

?: Conditional expression operator

6. You cannot change the precedence of operator evaluation. So, given the expression X+Y*Z, the compiler will always evaluate the * operator before the + operator no matter what their overloaded operator functions actually do.

Overloaded Assignment Operator

You can assign an object of a class to another object of the same class without taking any measures. That's becasue the compiler generates a default assignment operator if you don't provide an explicit overloaded assignment operator function.. Consequently, the following usage is always valid:

```
class Text  {
    // ...
};
Text t1;
Text t2;
t2 = t1;
```

(Recall that you learned in Chapter 15 the difference between assignment, which assigns an existing object of a class to another existing object the class, and a copy constructor, which initializes an object being built with an existing object of the class.)

Given that the compiler generates a default assignment operator function for every class, why would you need to write your own? It is because the compiler's default assignment operator function does not always work properly. Just as a default copy constructor (Chapter 15) performs a member-by-member copy of the class objects during initialization, a default assignment operator performs a member-by-member copy of the class objects during assignment. This behavior presents a problem that you solve by overloading the assignment operator. However, before getting into the problem and how to solve it, we'll look at a simple overloaded assignment operator.

Declaring an Overloaded operator=

Assuming a class named Text, you declare an overloaded assignment function by using the following notation within the class definition:

```
class Text  {
    // ...
public:
    Text& operator=(const Text&);
    // ...
};
```

The overloaded assignment operator function is named operator=. It returns a reference to an object of the class being assigned to. You'll learn why later. The equal sign (=) after the operator keyword identifies to the compiler that in this case the operator being overloaded is the assignment operator. To overload other operators, you use the appropriate operator character where this example uses the equal sign, as you will learn later in this chapter. The assignment operator is, in C++, a binary operator, so the compiler recognizes that this notation declares a function to be called when the program assigns an object of the class to another object of the same class like this:

```
Text t1;  // a Text object
Text t2;  // another one
t2 = t1;  // assign one to the other
```

When the compiler sees the assignment statement, it calls the `operator=` member function for the object on the left side of the assignment, passing as an argument a reference to the object on the right side of the assignment. It is up to you to put the proper code in the `operator=` member function to effect the assignment.

Defining an Overloaded operator=

The following code fragment is a skeleton of what most overloaded assignment functions will look like:

```
Text& Text::operator=(const Text& t)
{
    if (&t != this)  {
        // details of the assignment
        // of t to this object
    }
    return *this;
}
```

The `operator=` function first tests to see if the program is trying to assign an object to itself. If so, the function has nothing to do in the way of assignment. Although assigning an object to itself is something you wouldn't think any program would do, sometimes it happens as a coincidence when the program iterates containers or refers to objects through references or pointers. The function returns a reference to the object on the receiving end (left side) of the assignment. The following discussion explains why.

Returning *this

You learned about the `this` pointer in Chapter 18. To review, whenever a non-static member function is running, a pointer variable named `this` is in scope. The `this` pointer is declared by the compiler as a pointer to an object of the class type of the object. The `this` pointer always contains the address of the object for which the member function is being run.

One common use of the `this` pointer is for a member function to return the invoking object (or its address or a reference to it) to the caller. The overloaded assignment operator function shown earlier is an example of that usage, which allows the program to string assignments together in the C++ format as follows:

```
a = b = c;
```

Let's review some of what you learned in Chapter 2, in particular the discussion associated with Program 2-11. A compound assignment expression such as the one just shown works in C++ because every expression returns something—unless, of course, the expression is a call to a function returning `void`. You can express the assignment in the following way:

```
b = c;
a = b;
```

Because the first statement is an expression that returns the value assigned, you can combine the two expressions as follows:

```
a = (b = c);
```

Because the rightmost assignment operator has higher precedence than the leftmost one, the parentheses are not required, and the preceding example is expressed in the following way:

a = b = c;

To make your overloaded class assignments work in the same way that conventional, nonoverloaded assignments do, you must make the assignment function return the result of the assignment, which happens to be the destination object. This also happens to be what the this pointer points to while the overloaded assignment function is executing. Consequently the return *this; statement in the overloaded assignment operator function achieves this purpose.

A Simple Overloaded Assignment Operator Function

Let's put what you've learned so far into a working program, as shown in Program 21-1.

Program 21-1: **Overloaded class object assignment**

```
#include <iostream>
#include <cstring>

const int len = 100;
class Text {
    char text[len];
public:
    Text(const char* txt = 0)
    {
        std::strncpy(text, txt ? txt : "", len);
    }
    Text& operator=(const Text&);
    void display()
    {
        std::cout << (*text ? text : "(null)") << std::endl;
    }
};
Text& Text::operator=(const Text& t)
{
    if (&t != this)
        std::strncpy(text, t.text, len);
    return *this;
}
int main()
{
    Text t1("Spencer");
    t1.display();
    Text t2;
    t2.display();
    t2 = t1;
    t2.display();
    return 0;
}
```

Program 21-1 declares a Text class that contains and displays an array of up to 100 characters of text. Its constructor builds the object by copying no more than 100 characters of the argument into the text data member by using the Standard C std::strncpy function (Chapter 26). If the constructor argument is a null pointer, the constructor copies a zero length string of characters to the text data member. The class's overloaded assignment operator function simply copies the text array from the argument object.

The overloaded assignment operator in Program 21-1 does what the default assignment operator function would do, so the function isn't necessary. Next we'll discuss the circumstances under which such a function is necessary.

The Reason for Overloading Assignment

The discussion in Chapter 15 titled "Using Destructors" identifies a problem with assigning objects of classes that have data member pointers to dynamically allocated blocks of memory. To review, consider this fragment of a class:

```
class Text {
    char *text;
public:
    Text(int size);
    {
        text = new char[size];
    }
    ~Date();
    {
        delete [] text;
    }
};
```

The constructor function uses the new operator to dynamically allocate a block of memory. The destructor function uses the delete operator to return the allocated block of memory to the heap. So far, so good. But consider this usage of the class:

```
Text t1(10);
Text t2(20);
// ...
t1 = t2;
```

The compiler implements the class object assignment as a member-by-member copy of the object on the right side of the assignment expression to the object on the left side. This situation creates a problem when the two objects are destroyed. After the assignment, both objects contain a pointer data member that points to the same heap memory block. Both data member pointers contain the same address, which is an address on the heap.

When one of the objects is destroyed, its destructor returns the memory to the heap. At this time, the undestroyed object is unstable because its data member pointer points to a memory block that the object no longer owns. The heap owns the memory block because the earlier class destructor gave it back. Even if the program does not use the as-yet undestroyed object, its destructor is going to try to return to the heap a memory block that the object no longer owns. The outcome cannot be predicted.

Recall from Chapter 15 that Program 15-3 implemented a copy constructor, which does not have this problem. Instead of copying the pointer data member from the argument object into the object being constructed, the copy constructor allocates a duplicate block of memory for the new object and copies the data from the argument object into the object being constructed. When each object is destroyed, the object deletes its own copy of the heap memory block, and no problem exists.

You deal with the same problem in assignments by overloading the default assignment operator function. Your overloaded assignment function uses the new operator to get a different pointer from the heap. Then it takes the value pointed to in the assigning object and copies it into the area pointed to in the assigned object.

Program 21-2 demonstrates a situation under which a class needs an overloaded assignment operator function.

Program 21-2: **Necessary overloaded assignment operator**

```cpp
#include <iostream>
#include <cstring>

class Date {
    int mo, da, yr;
    char *month;
public:
    Date(int m = 0, int d = 0, int y = 0);
    ~Date();
    // Overloaded assignment operator.
    Date& operator=(const Date&);
    void display() const;
};
Date::Date(int m, int d, int y)
{
    static char *mos[] =
    {
        "January", "February", "March", "April", "May",
        "June", "July", "August", "September", "October",
        "November", "December"
    };
    mo = m;
    da = d;
    yr = y;
    if (m != 0) {
        month = new char[std::strlen(mos[m-1])+1];
        std::strcpy(month, mos[m-1]);
    } else
        month = 0;
}
// The destructor definition.
Date::~Date()
{
    delete [] month;
}
// Display member function.
void Date::display() const
{
    if (month != 0)
```

```
        std::cout << month << ' ' << da
        << ", " << yr << std::endl;
}
// Overloaded Date assignment.
Date& Date::operator=(const Date& dt)
{
    if (this != &dt) {
        mo = dt.mo;
        da = dt.da;
        yr = dt.yr;
        delete [] month;
        if (dt.month != 0) {
            month = new char [std::strlen(dt.month)+1];
            std::strcpy(month, dt.month);
        } else
            month = 0;
    }
    return *this;
}
int main()
{
    // Original date.
    Date birthday(6,24,40);
    Date oldday, newday;
    // Assign first to second to third.
    oldday = newday = birthday;
    birthday.display();
    oldday.display();
    newday.display();
    return 0;
}
```

The Date class in Program 21-2 is just like the one in Program 15-4 in Chapter 15, with the addition of the overloaded assignment operator function.

The overloaded assignment function makes all necessary data member assignments and then uses the delete operator to return to the heap the string memory pointed to by the month pointer of the receiver.

Then, if the sending object's month pointer is initialized, the function uses new to allocate memory for the receiving object and copies the sending object's month string to the receiver. (If the sending object's month pointer is not initialized, it means that the sender was not initialized when it was constructed.)

The first statement in the overloaded Date assignment operator compares the address of the sending object to the this pointer as you learned earlier. This operation protects against the occasion when a program assigns an object to itself, which would not have been a problem in Program 21-1 but which would definitely be a problem here. Without the test, the overloaded assignment operator function would delete the memory owned by the destination object and try to use the memory owned by the source object. But since both objects are the same, the source object's memory would have just been deleted, and the results would be unpredictable.

This use of the `this` pointer is difficult to grasp sometimes because it applies several C++ constructs that are unfamiliar to programmers of other languages, including C. Picture what is happening when you make the following assignment:

```
newday = birthday;
```

The assignment executes the overloaded assignment operator function for the `Date` class. That function has two parameters. The first parameter is implied. It is the address of the object for which the function is being called. In this case, the function is being called for the object on the left side of the assignment: the `newday` object. The second parameter is supplied as an argument and is the object on the right side of the assignment — in this case, the `birthday` object. In the function, the `birthday` argument becomes the `dt` parameter. The first assignment statement in the function is as follows:

```
mo = dt.mo;
```

The preceding statement also can be read the following way:

```
this->mo = dt.mo;
```

The statement assigns the value in the `mo` data member of the `birthday` object to the `mo` data member of the `newday` object. The other assignments work the same way. When the function is finished, it returns a reference to what `this` points to: the `newday` object. Consequently, the overloaded assignment operator function, in addition to performing the assignment, returns a reference to the object that receives the assignment, making possible the following statement:

```
oldday = newday = birthday;
```

By understanding this mechanism and, of course, operator overloading, you can see how the chained `std::cout` statements used in previous listings work. In many of the listings, you use statements similar to the following example:

```
cout << a << b << c;
```

Binary Arithmetic Operators

Consider a `Date` class such as the ones used by examples in this and earlier chapters. Suppose you want to compute a new `Date` object by adding an integer number of days to an existing `Date` object. You can write a member function and call it, as shown here:

```
newdate.AddToDate(100);
```

Rather than call a function to make the addition, you might prefer to use this more intuitive syntax:

```
newdate = newdate + 100;
```

Let's assume that `newdate` is an object of type `Date` with a valid data value already assigned to it, and assume that you have overloaded the binary addition operator (+) in this context correctly. The result would be the `newdate` object of type `Date` with the effective month, day, and year incremented by 100 days.

Class Member Operator Functions

To perform addition on objects of a class, write a class member function that overloads the binary addition (+) operator when it appears between a `Date` object and an integer. Here is how that function is declared in the class definition:

```
Date operator+(int) const;   // Overloaded + operator
```

The function declaration says that the function returns an object of type Date, that the function's name is operator+, that it has one parameter of type int, and that the function is const. As you learned with the overloaded assignment operator, whenever the compiler sees a function named operator suffixed by a real operator, the compiler treats that function as an overloaded operator function to be called when — in the case of binary operators such as the + operator — an expression has an object of the class type on the left side of the operator and an object of the parameter on the right. Consequently, the function just declared would be called in the following case:

```
Date dt(2,3,99);   // Declare a date object
dt = dt + 100;     // Invoke the overloaded operator
```

Unlike the assignment operator, the compiler generates no class default overloaded operator functions for other operators.

Incidentally, rather than have the compiler infer the overloaded operator function call from the context of an expression, you can call the overloaded operator function explicitly as shown here:

```
dt.operator+(100);
```

However, few programmers use this notation.

Program 21-3 overloads the binary addition operator to compute the sum of an integer and an object of the Date class, returning an object of the Date class.

Program 21-3: **Overloading the + operator**

```
#include <iostream>

class Date {
    int mo, da, yr;
    static int dys[];
public:
    Date(int m=0, int d=0, int y=0)
    {
        mo = m;
        da = d;
        yr = y;
    }
    void display() const
    {
        std::cout << mo << '/' << da << '/' << yr;
    }
    // Overloaded + operator.
    Date operator+(int) const;
};

int Date::dys[]={31,28,31,30,31,30,31,31,30,31,30,31};

// Overloaded + operator definition.
```

Continued

Program 21-3 *(continued)*

```
Date Date::operator+(int n) const
{
    Date dt = *this;
    n += dt.da;
    while (n > dys[dt.mo-1]) {
        n -= dys[dt.mo-1];
        if (++dt.mo == 13) {
            dt.mo = 1;
            dt.yr++;
        }
    }
    dt.da = n;
    return dt;
}
int main()
{
    Date olddate(2,20,1997);
    Date newdate;
    newdate = olddate + 21;     // three weeks hence
    newdate.display();
    return 0;
}
```

Here is how the overloaded `operator+` function works. When the compiler sees the expression `olddate + 21`, it recognizes that `olddate` is an object of type `Date` and that the `Date` class includes an overloaded binary addition operator function. The compiler substitutes a call to the overloaded operator function with the integer value as the argument. You can code the substituted call yourself this way:

```
newdate = olddate.operator+(21);
```

The `operator+` part of the statement is the name of the member function. The 21 is the integer argument. Although you can call an overloaded operator function this way, these functions are meant for use in the context of an expression that uses the operator, as in this statement:

```
newdate = olddate + 21;
```

Here's what happens with an expression such as this one. The compiler sees the expression on the right side of the assignment expression. The compiler calls `Date::operator+` for the `olddate` object passing the integer argument 21. The `Date::operator+` function computes and returns to the assignment expression a temporary `Date` object. The compiler then calls the class's assignment operator function to assign the temporary object to the object on the left side of the assignment expression.

Remember the discussion on the overloaded assignment operator earlier in this chapter. If the `Date` class had an overloaded assignment operator function, the statement just shown would call it after calling the overloaded binary addition operator function to assign the result to `newdate`. Program 21-3 has no overloaded assignment operator, so the compiler creates a default one to make a copy of the original.

Observe that the overloaded binary addition operator function in Program 21-3 does not modify the Date object on the right side of the expression; therefore, the function can be declared const. The olddate object declared in the main function retains its value. This behavior mimics that of similar expressions with intrinsic numerical types. This is a valuable lesson. Strive to overload operators in intuitive ways.

Nonmember Operator Functions

Recall the guideline to overload operators to preserve the commutative properties of arithmetic operations. Program 21-3 provides for an expression permitting a Date object on the left side of the operator and an integer on the right. But suppose you also wanted to support the following expression:

```
Date newdate = 100 + olddate;
```

There is no way to design a class member overloaded operator function to support such an expression. Class member overloaded operator functions for binary operators always assume that the object for which the function is executing is on the left of the operator in the expression. However, you can write a nonmember function to overload the operator with a different type on the left and a Date object on the right. Here is how you declare and define such a function outside any class definition:

```
Date operator+(int n, Date& dt)
{
    // ...
}
```

The declaration tells the compiler to call this function when it sees an expression involving an integer object to the left of the + operator and a Date object to the right. Program 21-4 adds such a nonmember function to the program in Program 21-3 to overload the binary addition (+) operator.

Program 21-4: Overloading + with a nonmember function

```cpp
#include <iostream>

class Date {
    int mo, da, yr;
    static int dys[];
public:
    Date(int m=0, int d=0, int y=0)
    {
        mo = m;
        da = d;
        yr = y;
    }
    void display() const
    {
        std::cout << mo << '/' << da << '/' << yr;
    }
    // Overloaded + operator.
```

Continued

Program 21-4 *(continued)*

```
    Date operator+(int) const;
};

int Date::dys[]={31,28,31,30,31,30,31,31,30,31,30,31};

// Overloaded + operator: Date + int.
Date Date::operator+(int n) const
{
    Date dt = *this;
    n += dt.da;
    while (n > dys[dt.mo-1]) {
        n -= dys[dt.mo-1];
        if (++dt.mo == 13) {
            dt.mo = 1;
            dt.yr++;
        }
    }
    dt.da = n;
    return dt;
}
// Overloaded operator: int + Date.
Date operator+(int n, const Date& dt)
{
    return dt + n;
}
// The main() function.
int main()
{
    Date olddate(2,20,1997);
    Date newdate;
    newdate = 11 + olddate + 10;  // three weeks hence
    newdate.display();
    return 0;
}
```

The overloaded nonmember `operator+` function in Program 21-4 uses the class's overloaded `operator+` member function to perform the addition. If a given class does not have such a function (although it should), the overloaded nonmember operator function needs to access the class's private data members to compute the addition. The class needs to declare the overloaded nonmember `operator+` function to be a friend, as shown here:

```
class Date
{
    friend Date operator+(int n, Date& );
    // ...
};
```

Overloaded operator functions, such as the one in Program 21-4, have both parameters declared. The function is not a member of a class. Because it does not execute as a class member function, there is no implied object.

You also can write the first overloaded binary addition function as a friend function. Some programmers overload all their class operators as friend functions by convention. You would declare it like this:

```
Date operator+(Date& dt1, const Date& dt)
{
    // ...
}
```

Observe that the expression in Program 21-4 uses two integer constants to compute the result. The effective expression is `(11+olddate)+10`. The first part uses the overloaded non-member function, and the second part uses the overloaded member function. Using these two overloaded functions, you can write an expression that consists of a `Date` object and any number of integer expressions to compute the effective new `Date` object. You cannot add two dates, because there is no overloaded operator function that permits that usage. The result would not be meaningful anyway.

Here are some things to ponder. As you have seen, adding a `Date` object to an integer returns a `Date` object that reflects the sum of the two arguments, irrespective of which argument type is on which side of the expression. Subtracting an integer from a `Date` object should likewise return a `Date` object reflecting the difference when the integer is subtracted from the `Date` object.

```
Date operator-(Date& dt1, int n)
{
    // ...
}
```

Subtracting a `Date` object from an integer does not make sense. But subtracting a `Date` object from another `Date` object does, and such an overloaded operator function should return an integer, reflecting the number of days between the two dates.

```
int operator-(Date& dt1, const Date& dt)
{
    // ...
}
```

The examples just given deal with addition and subtraction. You can use the same approaches to develop overloaded multiplication, division, relational, modulus, Boolean, and shifting operator functions. Once again, nothing requires you to make those functions perform intuitively, and some C++ programs have wildly overloaded operators that only their creators can understand. If you must overload arithmetic and relational operators, always try to overload them so that they perform operations that resemble their use with intrinsic data types in the C++ language.

Relational Operators

Suppose you want to compare dates. Perhaps you need to use an expression such as the following:

```
if (newdate < olddate)
// ....
```

You can overload relational operators in the same way that you overload the addition operator. Program 21-5 shows the `Date` class with overloaded operators that compare dates.

Program 21-5: **Overloading relational operators**

```cpp
#include <iostream>
class Date
{
    int mo, da, yr;
public:
    Date(int m=0, int d=0, int y=0)
    {
        mo = m;
        da = d;
        yr = y;
    }
    void display() const
    {
        std::cout << mo << '/' << da << '/' << yr;
    }
    // Overloaded operators.
    bool operator==(Date& dt) const;
    bool operator<(Date&) const;
};
// Overloaded equality operator definition.
bool Date::operator==(Date& dt) const
{
    return (this->mo == dt.mo &&
            this->da == dt.da &&
            this->yr == dt.yr);
}
// Overloaded less-than operator definition.
bool Date::operator<(Date& dt) const
{
    if (this->yr == dt.yr)    {
        if (this->mo == dt.mo)
            return this->da < dt.da;
        return this->mo < dt.mo;
    }
    return this->yr < dt.yr;
}
int main()
{
    Date date1(12,7,1941),
    date2(2,22,1990),
    date3(12,7,1941);
    if (date1 < date2) {
        date1.display();
        std::cout << " is less than ";
        date2.display();
    }
    std::cout << '\n';
    if (date1 == date3) {
        date1.display();
        std::cout << " is equal to ";
```

```
            date3.display();
        }
    return 0;
}
```

The Date class in Program 21-5 has two overloaded relational operators: the equal to (==) and the less than (<) operators. The main function declares three dates, compares them, and displays the following messages:

```
12/7/41 is less than 2/22/90
12/7/41 is equal to 12/7/41
```

You can overload other relational operators as variations on the two in Program 21-5. For example, you can code the != (not equal) operator in the following way:

```
bool Date::operator!=(Date& dt) const
{
    return !(*this == dt);
}
```

Similarly you can code the > (greater than) operator like this:

```
bool Date::operator>(Date& dt) const
{
    return !(*this == dt || *this < dt);
}
```

More Assignment Operators

You learned how to overload the assignment operator (=) in the discussion on class assignment earlier in this chapter. C++ has other assignment operators (+=, -=, <<=, >>=, |=, &=, ^=) in which the assignment includes an arithmetic, Boolean, or shift operation applied to the receiving field. You can overload these operators to work with your classes. Program 21-6 adds the overloaded += operator to the Date class by using the overloaded + operator that the class already has.

Program 21-6: **Overloading the += operator**

```
#include <iostream>

class Date {
    int mo, da, yr;
    static int dys[];
public:
    Date(int m=0, int d=0, int y=0)
    {
        mo = m;
        da = d;
        yr = y;
    }
```

Continued

Program 21-6 *(continued)*

```
    void display() const
    {
        std::cout << mo << '/' << da << '/' << yr;
    }
    // Overloaded + operator.
    Date operator+(int) const;
    // Overloaded += operator.
    Date operator+=(int n)
    {
        *this = *this + n;
        return *this;
    }
};

int Date::dys[]={31,28,31,30,31,30,31,31,30,31,30,31};

// Overloaded + operator definition.
Date Date::operator+(int n) const
{
    Date dt = *this;
    n += dt.da;
    while (n > dys[dt.mo-1]) {
        n -= dys[dt.mo-1];
        if (++dt.mo == 13) {
            dt.mo = 1;
            dt.yr++;
        }
    }
    dt.da = n;
    return dt;
}
int main()
{
    Date olddate(2,20,1997);
    olddate += 21;          // three weeks hence
    olddate.display();
    return 0;
}
```

Observe that the overloaded `operator+=` function in Program 21-6 is not `const`. It cannot be, because it modifies its own object.

Auto-Increment and Auto-Decrement

You can overload the auto-increment (++) and the auto-decrement (--) operators and specify whether these operators are prefix or postfix:

```
Date dt;
++dt;    // calls the overloaded prefix ++ operator
dt++;    // calls the overloaded postfix ++ operator
```

Program 21-7 adds the overloaded auto-increment (++) prefix and postfix operators to the Date class by using the overloaded binary addition operator that the class already has.

Program 21-7: Overloading the ++ operator

```
#include <iostream>

class Date {
    int mo, da, yr;
    static int dys[];
public:
    Date(int m=0, int d=0, int y=0)
    {
        mo = m;
        da = d;
        yr = y;
    }
    void display() const
    {
        std::cout << '\n' << mo << '/' << da << '/' << yr;
    }
    // Overloaded + operator.
    Date operator+(int) const;
    // Overloaded prefix ++ operator.
    Date operator++()
    {
        *this = *this + 1;
        return *this;
    }
    // Overloaded postfix ++ operator.
    Date operator++(int)
    {
        Date dt=*this;
        *this=*this+1;
        return dt;
    }
};
int Date::dys[]={31,28,31,30,31,30,31,31,30,31,30,31};
// Overloaded + operator definition.
Date Date::operator+(int n) const
{
    Date dt = *this;
    n += dt.da;
    while (n > dys[dt.mo-1]) {
        n -= dys[dt.mo-1];
        if (++dt.mo == 13) {
```

Continued

Program 21-7 *(continued)*

```
            dt.mo = 1;
            dt.yr++;
        }
    }
    dt.da = n;
    return dt;
}
int main()
{
    Date olddate(2,20,1997);
    olddate++;
    olddate.display();
    ++olddate;
    olddate.display();
    return 0;
}
```

As the program shows, you specify that the auto-increment and auto-decrement operators are prefix or postfix, as shown here:

```
Date operator++();     // prefix ++ operator
Date operator++(int);  // postfix ++ operator
```

The compiler calls the overloaded prefix operator function when it sees the prefix notation. The unnamed int parameter in the overloaded postfix operator function declaration tells the compiler to call this function for the postfix operator. Note that the compiler makes no further distinction except to call the correct function. The code in the functions is responsible for supporting prefix or postfix operations. In Program 21-7, the overloaded operator++ function increments the object and returns it. The overloaded operator++(int) function saves the value of the object before incrementing it and then returns the saved object.

Unary Plus and Minus Operators

You can overload the unary plus and minus operators to work with a class. You declare the overloaded function with no parameters, telling the compiler to use the function when the plus or minus operator is used as a unary operator. The function declaration looks like this:

```
int operator-() const;
```

Suppose you have a class that describes an inventory quantity and you need to express that quantity with the plus and minus unary operators. Program 21-8 is an example of how overloading the unary minus operator might work.

Program 21-8: Overloaded unary minus

```
#include <iostream>
#include <cstring>
```

```
class ItemQty {
    int onhand;
    char desc[25];
public:
    ItemQty(int oh, char *d)
    {
        onhand = oh;
        std::strcpy(desc, d);
    }
    void display() const
    {
        std::cout << '\n' << desc << ": " << onhand;
    }
    // Overloaded unary - operator.
    int operator-() const
    {
        return -onhand;
    }
};
int main()
{
    ItemQty item1(100, "crankshaft");
    ItemQty item2(-50, "driveshaft");
    item1.display();
    std::cout << '\n' << -item1;    // invoke the overloaded -
    item2.display();
    std::cout << '\n' << -item2;    // invoke the overloaded -
    return 0;
}
```

The program declares two ItemQty objects: one with a positive onhand value and one with a negative. It calls the display function to display the record contents and then uses the overloaded unary minus operator to display the quantity with the unary minus operator applied, as shown in the following display:

```
crankshaft: 100
-100
driveshaft: -50
50
```

Subscript Operator

Overloading the subscript ([]) operator can be useful. You can use it to provide access to elements of list data structures. For example, a Text class that stores a string value can overload the subscript operator to provide subscripted access to the character positions of the string value. Program 21-9 overloads the [] operator in a small string class.

Program 21-9: **Overloaded [] subscript operator**

```cpp
#include <iostream>
#include <cstring>

class Text {
    char* sptr;
public:
    Text(char* s = 0);
    ~Text() { delete [] sptr; }
    void display()
        { std::cout << sptr << std::endl; }
    // Overloaded [] operators.
    char& operator[](int n)
        { return *(sptr + n); }
    const char& operator[](int n) const
        { return *(sptr + n); }
};
Text::Text(char* s)
{
    if (s) {
        sptr = new char[std::strlen(s)+1];
        std::strcpy(sptr, s);
    } else
        sptr = 0;
}
int main()
{
    Text text1("The Ides of March");
    text1.display();
    // Change some text characters.
    text1[4] = '1';
    text1[5] = '5';
    text1[6] = 't';
    text1[7] = 'h';
    text1.display();
    // Change a part of text1.
    strncpy(&text1[4], "21st", 4);
    text1.display();
    // const text, cannot be modified.
    const Text text2("Et tu, Brute?");
    for (int i = 0; i < 13; i++)
        std::cout << text2[i];
    return 0;
}
```

The program declares and displays a Text object with a value. Then the program uses the Text class's first overloaded [] operator function to change individual character values in the Text object. Because the [] operator function returns a non-const reference to the character being subscripted, the program can use the expression on the left side of an assignment. With that notation, the program inserts the string value "15th" one character at a time into the string. Then, by using the address of the returned character reference, the program uses std::strncpy (Chapter 26) to insert the string value "21st" into the string.

You can use the same overloaded operator[] function to retrieve characters only if all Text objects are not const. To support const Text objects, the class adds a second overloaded operator[] function. The function returns a const reference to the subscripted character, and the function itself is declared const, so the program can use that function to retrieve characters from a const Text object.

Overloaded [] subscript operator functions must be nonstatic member functions. Furthermore, you cannot implement them as friend functions as you can with other operators.

Pointer-to-Member Operator

The -> operator, when overloaded, is always a postfix unary operator with the class object (or reference to same) on its left. The overloaded operator function returns the address of an object of some class.

Although the overloaded -> operator is postfix unary, its use requires the name of a class member on the right side of the expression. That member must be a member of the class for which the overloaded operator returns an address.

You can overload the -> operator to ensure that a pointer to a class object always has a value — in other words, to create a smart pointer to an object. The pointer always guarantees that it points to something meaningful — or throws an exception (Chapter 35) when it does not — and you avoid problems associated with dereferencing null and garbage pointers.

To understand where you might need a smart pointer, consider the following program, which uses the Date class from earlier programs and, at the beginning of the program, a pointer to an object of the Date class:

```
int main()
{
    Date *dp;          // date pointer with garbage in it
    Date dt(3,17,90);  // Date
    dp = &dt;          // put address of date in pointer
    dp->display();     // display date through the pointer
    return 0;
}
```

The program declares a Date object, puts its address in the pointer, and calls the display member function through the pointer. Nothing is wrong with that. However, if the programmer neglects to assign a valid address of a Date object to the pointer, the program misbehaves because the pointer points nowhere meaningful. Whatever gets executed by that function call is not likely to be a valid function. Program 21-10 overloads the -> operator to add a so-called smart pointer to the program.

Program 21-10: **Overloaded operator->**

```cpp
#include <iostream>

class Date {
    int mo, da, yr;
public:
    Date(int m=0, int d=0, int y=0)
    {
        mo = m;
        da = d;
        yr = y;
    }
    void display()
    {
        std::cout << '\n' << mo << '/' << da << '/' << yr;
    }
};
// Smart Date pointer.
class DatePtr {
    Date* dp;
public:
    DatePtr(Date* d = 0)
        { dp = d; }
    Date* operator->();
};
// overloaded pointer-to-member operator
Date* DatePtr::operator->()
{
    static Date nulldate(0,0,0);
    if (dp == 0)            // if the pointer is null
        return &nulldate;   // return the dummy address
    return dp;              // otherwise return the pointer
}
int main()
{
    // uninitialized Date pointer
    DatePtr dp;
    // Use it to call display function.
    dp->display();
    Date dt(3,17,90);
    // Put address of date in pointer.
    dp = &dt;
    // Display date through the pointer.
    dp->display();
    return 0;
}
```

An object of the `DatePtr` class is a pointer that knows whether a value has been assigned to it. If the program tries to use the pointer without first assigning the address of a `Date` object to it, the pointer contains the address of a null `Date` instead of garbage. The `DatePtr` object always returns the address of a `Date` object or the address of the null `Date`, because the `DatePtr` conversion constructor function accepts no value that is not the address of a `Date` and substitutes zero if a `DatePtr` is constructed without a parameter. When the overloaded `->` operator function sees that the `dp` pointer is 0, it returns the address of the null `Date` object rather than the value in the pointer.

Note that the overloaded `->` pointer operator must be a nonstatic member function. You cannot implement it as a friend function in the manner of other operators.

The smart pointer in Program 21-10 is by no means complete. It should include overloaded +, -, ++, --, +=, and -= operators so that objects of the class can react to addition and subtraction just as real pointers do. It should include overloaded relational operators, too.

Summary

This chapter showed you how to overload C++ operators to work with your classes. You can overload other operators that this chapter did not address. The function call operator (`operator()`) and the address-of operator (`operator&`) are two examples. The notation for overloading these operators is the same as for others. We do not include examples of them for two reasons. First, we do not think it is a good idea to overload these operators except in the most extreme circumstances. Second, we cannot contrive believable examples of circumstances under which a programmer would want to overload these operators. There is one notable exception: The Standard Template Library (Part IV) overloads the function call operator to implement container callback function objects called predicates.

✦   ✦   ✦

Class Libraries

Chapter 13 discussed object libraries and the relationship between header files, source code files, and translation units. This chapter explains how to build object and template libraries that are used by example programs in later chapters. You might be able to use these libraries in your own programs. You certainly will need to understand how to build and use libraries of your own. Chapter 13 also explains the difference between static object libraries, also known as archives, and dynamic link libraries (DLLs), also known as shared object libraries. This chapter is about building static object libraries.

Libraries are a platform-specific feature not defined by Standard C++. Yet every C++ implementation includes some kind of library mechanism if only to support the Standard C++ Library. This chapter discusses the architecture implemented by the GCC compiler suite hosted by Quincy, which is the IDE included with the companion CD-ROM. The GCC library architecture is typical.

The chapters that follow in this book use a few common classes to teach their lessons. Until now, source code files in examples have contained class declarations and definitions in the example programs that use them. Examples in later chapters continue to do that, but some of them also use common classes stored in libraries.

If you are using Quincy to compile and run the example programs, you must build the libraries that this chapter describes before proceeding to subsequent chapters. The programs in those chapters depend on the libraries being in place and available. If you neglect to build a library that an example needs, Quincy's integrated tutorial reminds you to return here and build the libraries.

Appendix A contains listings of the source code for the class libraries that this chapter discusses. Some of the libraries use C++ language features with which you are already familiar. Some use features that later chapters explain. You can study the source code now if you wish, but you should probably put it off until you get to the chapters that use the libraries. This chapter is more about the class library mechanism itself rather than the contents of the libraries the chapter discusses.

Objects versus Objects

C++ suffers from a semantic ambiguity based on its heritage derived from multiple disciplines. The term "object" has two different meanings. First, C++ source code compiles to relocatable *object code*. This usage goes back to the 1960s when assemblers and compilers emitted object code. Second, C++ supports the *object-oriented* programming model, which Chapter 40 explains, and which originated in programming languages such as Simula in the 1960s and Smalltalk in the 1980s. The object-oriented model defines an *object* as the instantiation of a type. Consequently, in C++ we have object modules that define instantiated objects. But the so-called objects defined are only part of the so-called object code. Usually, this collision of terms is not a problem; the context within which we use them makes our meaning clear. But, in writing this chapter, I found myself tripping over the dual usage. Consequently, I decided to refer to instantiated objects as *variables* in this chapter only to avoid confusion.

Organizing and Building an Object Library

Object libraries store object modules that contain functions and global variables that can be referenced by many programs. You link libraries to your program's object modules when you build the executable program. Libraries support problem domains, user interfaces, common data processing subroutines, and so on. The Standard C and C++ Libraries (Part III) are implemented as object libraries.

Header and Object Module Files

Recall from Chapter 13 that a program's source code includes header files and that the combination of one source code module and the header files it includes is a *translation unit*. Header files typically declare classes, external variables, and functions.

Example programs in previous chapters have used variations of a `Date` class, declaring the class in the source code that uses the class. But if many programmers want to use a generic `Date` class in many source code files, reproducing its code in every source code file would be redundant, time consuming, and error prone. Instead, you would declare the class in a header file, perhaps named date.h, which might look something like this:

```
#ifndef DATE_H
#define DATE_H

class Date {
    int month, day, year;
public:
    Date(int mo, int da, int yr);
    // ...
};
```

Such a header file is located with your other source code if the class is specific to one application. Your application programs' source code files would include it with this statement:

```
#include "date.h"
```

If the class is useful across many applications, locate the header file in a subdirectory accessible to all the projects being developed, add that subdirectory to the paths the compiler uses to find system header files (either with an IDE option or on the command line when you run the compiler), and include the header in your application source code files like this:

```
#include <date.h>
```

By including the date.h header file, an application program's source code has the class decla-ration and can instantiate objects of the class. But the definitions of the member functions are not included. You could add the member functions to the header file, but there is a good reason not to do that. If several translation units in the program need to instantiate Date objects, each translation unit would include the header file, and the member functions would be defined more than once. This condition results in an error when you link the translation units into an executable module. There can be only one copy of a given function in a transla-tion unit. The only member functions you should include in the header file are inline member functions.

Instead of defining the member functions in the header file, you should define them in their own source code file, which includes the header file, and which, along with whatever else it includes, is its own translation unit. Such a source code file might be named date.cpp and might look something like this:

```
#include "date.h"
Date::Date (int mo, int da, int yr)
{
    month = mo;
    day = da;
    year = yr;
}
```

You can compile date.cpp into an object module, which you then link with the application program's object modules. Or, if there are multiple source code modules that declare member functions for multiple classes, you can add date.cpp's object module to an object library.

If the object library is useful only to one project, you can keep it in the directory where you have the source code. If, however, the object library contains class definitions that many pro-jects can use, put it in a subdirectory available to all projects and add the subdirectory to the paths the linker uses to find libraries either with an IDE option or on the command line when you run the linker.

Library Filenames

Object libraries are files of object modules. The filenames are dependent on the compiler sys-tem that you use to build the libraries. The GCC system that Quincy hosts uses a convention wherein object library filenames always have the prefix "lib" and the filename extension ".a". For example, the Standard C++ Library is named libstdc++.a. This convention reflects the GNU convention, which is adopted from the Unix way of doing things. The filename identifies the file as a library (lib) maintained in an archive (.a). Quincy hosts a Win32 port of the Gnu Compiler Collection (GCC). Other Win32 compiler systems use a filename convention wherein the filename is anything you want it to be and the extension is always ".lib".

Library Compatibility

A library built with one compiler is not necessarily compatible with the linkers and function calling protocols of other compilers. The GCC compiler cannot process the ".lib" files of other compilers and vice versa, for example. Furthermore, C++ libraries include functions with man-gled names (Chapter 13), and name mangling algorithms are not the same in all compilers. Consequently, C++ libraries built with one compiler might not be compatible with those built with another, even when the platform and the library file format are the same.

For this reason, most Win32 dynamic link libraries targeted for general use are either written in C, which has no name mangling, or written with the `extern "C"` linkage specification (Chapter 13) surrounding all global identifiers.

Class and Function Libraries

Programmers often speak of class libraries and function libraries as if they are two different things. Conceptually they are different, but technically they are identical. Both kinds of libraries contain external variable and function definitions, and both kinds of libraries are usually associated with header files that declare what the library defines.

But here's the difference: Function libraries define global objects and functions not associated with classes, whereas class libraries define static data members and member functions associated with classes. Function libraries are the only kind of libraries that the C language supports. C++ supports both kinds of libraries, but C++ programmers learn to encapsulate most if not all of their global variables and functions within classes.

Template Libraries

Template libraries are a special kind of library in that no object module is involved. Templates are patterns that the compiler uses to generate customized versions of classes (Chapter 25) and functions (Chapter 12). These patterns are typically declared in header files. The compiler uses the parameterized instantiation of a template class or function to define specialized member and nonmember functions based on the template's parameters and the instantiation's type arguments.

The Standard Template Library (Part III) consists of a library of header files that your program includes. STL includes function templates that implement generic algorithms and class templates that implement generic containers. You already built and used function templates in Chapter 12; you will build and use class templates in Chapter 25.

Linking with an Object Library

Almost every time you build a program from C++ source code, you link the object modules from your source code with libraries that support the platform system for which you are developing. For example, most of the programs in this book link with the Standard C++ Library when you build them.

Object modules are *relocatable*. That is, the variables and functions that an object module addresses have one of two formats: If they are defined in the object module that addresses them, the referenced addresses are relative to the beginning of the object module. If they are defined in another object module to be linked with the current one, the referenced addresses are identified as unresolved external addresses, and the object module includes the name of the thing to which the address must refer.

The linker builds an executable program by concatenating object modules. The linker relocates and resolves all addresses relative to the beginning of the executable module. If the program references something not found among the object modules, the linker reports an unresolved reference error and fails to build the executable program file.

The executable program file has addresses that need yet one more relocation process. When the operating system loads the program into memory to execute, the operating system positions the program in memory wherever there is room for it. At this time, the executable program is configured by the operating system's program loader such that all the program's referenced addresses refer to an actual memory location based on where the program is loaded.

Relocation can be, and often is, more complex than this explanation provides — the details are platform dependent — but this discussion should give you a general understanding of the mechanism.

An object library typically contains many object modules, and not every program uses them all. When your code references an external variable or function defined in an object library, the linker searches the libraries you have told it to include in the link. The linker is looking for the specific object module that defines the variable or function. The linker extracts only the modules from the library that the program needs. If library modules themselves reference things defined in other library object modules, the linker extracts those other object modules from the library. The advantages to this procedure are you don't have to explicitly declare everything the linker needs to find, and your program is linked only with those object modules it needs, thus keeping the program's size to a minimum.

When deciding which functions and variables to put into one object module to store in a library, you should strive to group those functions and variables that are likely to be referenced by the same programs. When you reference any variable or function that is defined in one of a library's object modules, the linker includes the complete object module, including the parts you don't need. Consequently, you should not build huge object modules unless most programs that need any of it are likely to need most of the things the module defines.

The Kinds of Object Libraries

Object libraries serve many purposes ranging from general purpose classes to support programming in general to very specific classes to support a problem domain or operating environment. The discussions that follow address one of each of these kinds of object libraries.

General Purpose Libraries

A general purpose library supports things that most programs need, irrespective of the target platform or the problem domain. The best example of this kind of library is the combined Standard C and C++ Libraries, which Part III of this book addresses, and which is included with every contemporary Standard C++ compiler system.

General purpose libraries are not usually dependent on the platform on which you build or run the program. They are not specific to the problem domain or any particular kind of applications programming. They support programming in general, and, wherever possible, they are source-code portable to other platforms that support C++ development.

General Data Type Libraries

General data type libraries extend the C++ suite of functions and classes by adding support for data types not anticipated by the framers of Standard C++. The standard specifies an international language. Consequently, it does not address things that are specific to one locale, irrespective of how pervasive the conventions of the locale might be. Standard C++ does not mandate formats for date, time, and currency representation, for example, because these are things that are different from locale to locale. Standard C++ does provide a *locale* mechanism for writing portable programs that can adjust to the difference in locale conventions. Chapter 39 addresses locales.

General data type libraries are not usually dependent on the platform on which you build or run the program. They are not specific to the problem domain, support applications programming in general, and, wherever possible, are source-code portable to other platforms that support C++ development.

The Date Class

To illustrate how a general data type library works, we take the Date class from previous chapters and combine its variations into one Date class that subsequent programs will use.

Quincy is configured to find all these things automatically when you install it from the companion CD-ROM. If you use a different development environment to work with the example programs, you must manage their locations and dependencies yourself.

For the exercises in subsequent chapters, we'll modify the function named Display that we used to display objects on the console. That mechanism was convenient for learning about member functions, but it bound the classes to the std::cout object. What if you want to display the object on std::cerr? What if you want to print it (Chapter 13)? What if you want to record the object in a stream file (Chapter 29)? The Display functions so far do not do any of that. A more practical approach is to give the Display function a parameter with which the caller specifies where to display the information. The new Date::Display function is declared like this:

```
void Display(std::ostream& os);
```

The new Display function writes Date objects to an object of type std::ostream, which is a Standard C++ Library class declared when you include <iostream> in your program. The std::cout, std::cerr and std::clog devices are objects of type ostream.

Programs that use the Display member function to display a Date object on standard output follow this convention:

```
Date dt;
// ...
dt.Display(std::cout);
```

The new Date class has an alternative for its Display member function. The class also overloads operator<< to write its objects to an object of type std::ostream. This procedure is almost identical to what the Display function does. The Display function, however, also displays the name of the class for which a date is being displayed. So far, the only such class you know about is the Date class. There will be more discussed in Chapter 23.

The std::ostream class overloads operator<< for all the intrinsic C++ types. The corresponding std::istream class, of which std::cin is an object, similarly overloads operator>>. These two sets of overloaded operators allow the input and output operations, such as the following, that many of the exercises use:

```
int n;
std::cin >> n;    // read a value into n from the console
std::cout << n;    // display the value from n on the console
```

From this point on, we will overload << and >> for any classes that need to display themselves. The Date class in the DataTypes class library adds this behavior with these functions:

```
std::ostream& operator<<(std::ostream& os, const Date& dt);
std::istream& operator>>(std::istream& is, Date& dt);
```

Actually, these overloaded operator functions are not part of the Date class; they must be non-member functions because they are called with objects of type std::ostream and std::istream on the left side of the expression. The Date class conveniently provides member functions to get and set the day, month, and year values; so overloaded << and >> operator functions do not need access to the private data members of the class for which they are working. Therefore, the overloaded operator functions do not need to be friends of the Date class.

The following code fragment shows how examples in subsequent chapters might display date values:

```
#include <Date.h>

Date dt;
// ...
std::cout << dt << std::endl;
```

The exercises use the specialized Display member functions, which themselves use the overloaded operator functions, to demonstrate the behavior of member functions in base and derived classes (Chapter 23).

SSN and Money: Two More Data Abstractions

Because some of the examples also use money, the Datatypes library includes a simple Money class to support dollars and cents and the SSN class to encapsulate a Social Security Number. Following are the public interfaces for these classes:

```
class Money
{
public:
    Money(double val = 0);
    operator double() const;
    friend std::ostream& operator<<(std::ostream&,
        const Money&);
};
```

The Money class uses a double variable to implement dollars and cents. The Money class has enough intelligence built in to ensure that its data representation is always two decimal places and that it displays itself properly. A more comprehensive money class would overload all the arithmetic and relational operators. To keep everything simple, disregard that part of the design for these exercises.

The nonmember overloaded operator<< function is a friend of the Money class so that it can read the data members. The function displays the money in the familiar dollars and cents format:

```
class SSN {
public:
    explicit SSN(long unsigned int sn = 0);
    friend std::ostream& operator<<(std::ostream& os,
        const SSN& ssn);
};
```

The SSN constructor ensures that no Social Security Number has more than nine decimal digits. A more comprehensive class would use the Social Security Administration's rules for forming Social Security numbers to validate the constructor's argument properly.

The nonmember overloaded operator<< function is a friend of the SSN class so that it can read the data member. The purpose of the function is to display the Social Security number in the familiar nnn-nn-nnnn format.

The source code for date.h, date.cpp, money.h, and money.cpp are listed in Appendix A.

If you are following along with the examples by using Quincy, you should now build Program 1 for Chapter 22, which is this chapter. The DataTypes library's header files are called date.h, money.h, and ssn.h and are located in the Include subdirectory along with other headers for other libraries. DataTypes' source code files, date.cpp, money.cpp, and ssn.cpp, are located in the DataTypes subdirectory, which is where the object library is built.

Problem Domain Libraries

Problem domain libraries typically define classes that support the application. The classes are not likely to be used by other applications. Whereas a Social Security Number might be used by personnel, payroll, and banking applications, and date and currency classes can be used in accounting, personnel, inventory, sales, project management, and so on, other classes are more specific to a particular problem domain.

Problem domain libraries are not usually dependent on the platform on which you build or run the program. They should be specific to the problem domain itself and, wherever possible, portable to other platforms that support C++ development.

To illustrate how a problem domain library works, we build a Personnel Class Library to be used later in the book. This library includes classes that define a hierarchy of personnel types. Those classes are `Person`, `Employee`, `WagedEmployee`, `SalariedEmployee`, and `Contractor`. These classes are more complex than the simple `Date`, `Money`, and `SSN` classes in the Datatypes library. See Appendix A to view their public interfaces.

If you are following along with the examples by using Quincy, you should now build Program 2 for Chapter 22, which is this chapter. The Personnel library's header files are called person.h, employee.h, contractor.h, salariedemployee.h, and wagedemployee.h and are located in the Include subdirectory along with other headers for other libraries. There are corresponding .cpp source code files in the Personnel subdirectory, which is where the object library is built.

The source code for the files associated with the Personnel class library are listed in Appendix A.

Application Frameworks

Applications frameworks support development of programs with a specific user interface usually on a specific development and target platform. They include classes that define what an application looks like and how the user operates it. Graphical windows, dialogs, menus, forms, messages, controls, and so on are typically encapsulated in an application framework class library.

The typical framework class library depends on the operating system for which it is being developed. Some framework libraries are cross-platform compatible. By designing to the lowest common denominator, or by using compile-time conditional preprocessing directives, a program can be compiled from the same source code to operate on multiple platforms. The most popular frameworks are, however, highly platform dependent. A prominent example is the Microsoft Framework Classes (MFC) library with which C++ programmers build Windows applications.

Library Headers

The library source code files in Appendix A include the headers that declare the classes. Those #include preprocessing directives use angle bracket notation, whereas previous includes of header files associated with example programs used double-quote characters around the filename. The angle bracket notation means that the compiler should not look for the header file in the same subdirectory where it finds the .cpp file but should search the paths specified to the compiler for system headers.

Class Template Libraries

Some libraries are not implemented as object libraries. Examples are function templates (Chapter 12) and class templates (Chapter 25), which, in most contemporary C++ development systems, you include in your program in header files. The Standard Template Library (Part IV), which is part of the Standard C++ Library, is, as its name implies, implemented as templates.

Summary

This chapter explained how to design, build, and use class libraries. Most software projects of consequence use system libraries, third-party libraries and libraries specific to the application with object modules to be shared among programs in the project. Knowing how to build and use libraries is an essential skill for C++ programmers. The libraries built in this chapter are to be used in later chapters, including Chapter 23, which teaches class inheritance.

✦　✦　✦

Class Inheritance

CHAPTER

23

*C*lass inheritance is a programming technique you use to construct specialized classes from existing ones and to design and implement object-oriented class hierarchies. This chapter describes these processes by using classes and class hierarchies to demonstrate how inheritance works and how to use it.

Please take note of the following seeming departure from convention in this book's presentation of source code beginning with this chapter. Previous chapters contain example programs with file names that reflect the chapter number and the program listing number within the chapter. Program 21-1 is represented by a file named pr21001.cpp, for example. This convention works because most programs until now were self-contained. Beginning with this chapter, you will have multiple listings per program because the programs include specialized header files and involve multiple translation units. Whichever source code file contains the main function preserves the program number convention of previous chapters. Other source code files contributing to a particular program have unique file names and are listed with listing numbers rather than program numbers. Consequently, this chapter contains Programs 23-1 through 23-7 and Listings 23-1 through 23-5. To add to the confusion, class library listings from Chapter 22 are in Appendix A. This chapter refers to those listings as Listings A-1, A-2, and so on. This new convention persists in some of the chapters that follow.

Class Inheritance

Inheritance is one of the four identifying characteristics of an object-oriented design. The other three are abstraction, encapsulation, and polymorphism. Chapter 40 provides an overview of object-oriented design and programming. You learn about abstraction in Chapter 6. This chapter focuses on how the C++ language supports inheritance and polymorphism.

With *inheritance*, you derive a new class from an existing class. The class from which you derive is called the *base class*, sometimes called the *super class*, and the class that you derive is called the *derived class*, sometimes called the *subclass*. The act of designing a derived class sometimes is called subclassing. Figure 23-1 shows the relationship between a base class and a derived class.

In This Chapter

Specialization of data abstractions

Base and derived classes

Object-oriented problem domain class hierarchies

Abstract base classes

Virtual functions and polymorphism

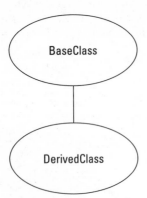

Figure 23-1: Base and derived classes

Figure 23-1 shows the architecture of a simple, two-class design. In more complex designs, a base class has multiple derived classes, each of which itself can be the base of other derived classes, all of which forms a class hierarchy. With multiple inheritance, discussed in Chapter 24, a derived class can have more than one base class, each of which can have one or more base classes of its own. For now let's keep it simple.

Following is the C++ syntax for coding base and derived classes:

```
// The base class.
class Base
{
    // ...
};

// The derived class.
class Derived : public Base
{
    // ...
};
```

As you can see, a derived class names its base class in the class declaration header. The colon tells the compiler that a base class specification is next. The `public` keyword specifies which of the base class's members the derived class may access. More about that later.

A derived class inherits the characteristics of its base class, which accounts for the term inheritance. The derived class automatically acquires the data members and member functions of the base class. This means that a program can instantiate an object of the derived class and access the public members of the base class. The derived class can add its own data members and member functions, as well as override the member functions of the base. By adding and overriding members, you specialize the behavior of a base class to form a derived class.

This is a powerful idea. If you have a class that is almost what you need, you can reuse as much of it as you can and only provide the new or different parts. This is sometimes called *design by difference*. For example, suppose you have a class that represents a person in a database. Employees are people, but unlike ordinary people, they have an hourly wage and a length of service associated with them. Customers are also people, but they may require additional data such as credit card information and an account number.

Of course, a derived class can also be a base class. The employee class, for example, might serve as a base class for a manager class. Managers don't have an hourly wage, but a monthly salary, perhaps.

Figure 23-2 illustrates this concept.

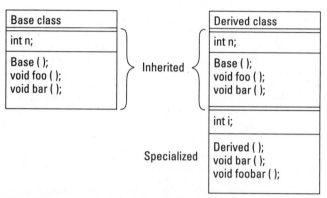

Figure 23-2: Inheritance between base and derived classes

The base class in Figure 23-2, which is named Base for this discussion, has one data member and three member functions. Those are the characteristics of the class, and a program can instantiate an object of type Base and call the foo and bar member functions. The derived class in Figure 23-2 is named Derived. It inherits all the members of the Base class, adds its own data member, adds a member function named foobar, and provides a specialization of the base class's bar function. As you soon learn, both bar functions are available to the program that uses this class. Following is an example of how you might declare these two classes:

```
// The base class.
class Base
{
    int n:
public:
    Base();
    void foo();
    void bar();
};

// The derived class.
class Derived : public Base
{
    int i:
public:
    Derived();
    void bar();
    void foobar();
};
```

You have been dealing with potential base classes since Chapter 6. Any C++ structure or class that has public (or protected) constructors and destructors can have derived classes. The base class does not define its participation in an inheritance; the derived class does. The base class has nothing in it that tells it which classes, if any, inherit from it.

Do not be confused by the use of the names `Derived` and `Base` in these examples. They are not keywords or anything else tied to the C++ language. They merely are identifiers arbitrarily chosen as the names of the two classes for the examples.

A derived class specifies the base class from which it inherits data members and behavior. The `public Base` notation following the semicolon in the `Derived` class declaration specifies that `Derived` is deriving itself from `Base`. (This association somewhat violates the inheritance metaphor. Outside object-oriented programming, heirs usually do not associate themselves with the estates of their benefactors.) But even though the derived class has the responsibility of declaring derivation, a class can include constructs that make it work better as a base class. Furthermore, some classes are designed to serve as base classes only.

Why Inherit?

Why use inheritance to create a custom class based on an existing class? Why not just change the existing class, making it do what you want it to do? There are several reasons:

✦ The base class might be used by other parts of your program and by other programs, and you want its original behavior to remain intact for those objects that already use it. By deriving a class from the base, you define a new data type that inherits all the characteristics of the base class without changing the base class's operation in the rest of the program and in other programs.

✦ The source code for the base class might not be available to you. To use a class, all you need are its class declaration in a header file and the object code for its member functions in a relocatable object file. If you use class libraries from other sources, you might not have the source code for the member functions, and thus cannot change it.

✦ This is the most common reason — the base class might define a component in a class library that supports a wide community of users. Consequently, you must not modify the base class even if you can. One prominent example is the application framework class library, which this chapter addresses.

✦ The base class might be an abstract base class, which is a class designed to be a base class only. A class hierarchy can contain general-purpose classes that do nothing on their own. Their purpose is to define the behavior of a generic data structure to which derived classes add implementation details.

✦ You might be building a class hierarchy to derive the benefits of the object-oriented approach. One of these benefits is the availability of general-purpose class methods that modify their own behavior based on the characteristics of the subclasses that use them. The class hierarchy approach supports this ability through the virtual function mechanism. You learn about this technique later in the chapter.

There are two reasons to derive a class. One reason is that you want to specialize the behavior of an existing class. *Specialization* is the act of creating a new data type by leveraging the effort that went into the development of an earlier data type.

The other reason for derivation is that you are building a well-organized, object-oriented class hierarchy in which custom data types that model the application's problem domain descend from a common base class. These two reasons are design approaches; but the class inheritance behavior of C++ that supports them is the same, with the same rules and boundaries. In this chapter, we look at both reasons to use inheritance.

Specialized Data Abstraction Class Design

Let's consider a realistic example of class specialization. Suppose your project uses a Date class similar to the ones that we used in the exercises of Chapters 14 and 21. This Date class has it all: the ability to display itself, a copy constructor, and overloaded operators to support assignment, arithmetic, and comparisons. But suppose that you need a Date class that displays itself in a different way. The boring old Date class that everyone else on the project uses displays itself in the boring old American mm/dd/yyyy format. You want a date class that has all the features of the project's Date class but that displays itself in the snazzy "Month dd, yyyy" format. You also want to be able to determine whether a date object has a null value as opposed to a valid date value—a feature that the current Date class does not support.

You can design a completely new class to support your new requirements, or you can use inheritance to take advantage of the fact that the existing Date class already does much of what you need. You can design a derived class that inherits the characteristics of the Date class and adds some specialized behavior of its own. Figure 23-3 illustrates the relationships between the Date base class and the SpecialDate specialized derived class.

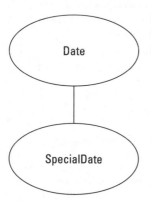

Figure 23-3: The Date base class and the derived SpecialDate class

We use the vertical proximity of the two balloon symbols to represent the base and derived classes. The higher symbol is the base class. You cannot always do this in a complex class hierarchy design, particularly when you need to depict other relationships between classes that do not involve inheritance. Class designers often use arrowhead notations to show the direction of inheritance and use other symbols to represent other relationships.

The Base Class

Let's start by defining the Date class that, in our make-believe scenario, the entire programming staff uses. This design combines many of the components of the Date classes used in previous exercises.

Listing A-1 in Appendix A is the source-code header file, Date.h, which declares the Date class.

The declaration of the Date class defined in Date.h includes constructs that support using the class as a base. The protected access specifier for both data members and the virtual qualifier on the destructor and Display member functions are all measures that class designers use to support subsequent derivation from a class. The designer of the Date class was not compelled to include these things merely to make Date objects work. The designer, instead, was looking ahead to the possibility that this class could someday become a base class. You learn about protected members and virtual functions later in this chapter.

Observe the two IsLeapYear member functions in Listing A-1. One is a member function that determines whether the date object falls within a leap year. The other IsLeapYear function takes an integer year argument. There are occasions when member functions of the class (and, later, of derived classes) need to test to see whether a year's value is a leap year before the Date object is fully formed, such as during construction of the object.

Designing for Efficiency

The Date class's data representation uses a long integer value to store the number of days inclusive since January 1, AD 1, for the Date object. This implementation is designed for efficiency in a system in which programs perform a lot of date arithmetic and comparison. Observe that the overloaded operator functions are all inline and that they are relatively small. It is a trivial matter to add and subtract dates and integers when the date representation is itself a single integer datum.

This approach represents a conscious design decision. If you were to use the Date class instead in an application that mostly initialized and displayed the month, day, and year data values, you probably would design the class with separate integer data members for the three date components. That Date class would look more like those we used in earlier chapters.

The potential of this decision teaches an important lesson. If you decide to use the earlier Date class data representation — even if you decide to change it after many programs use the current design — the public interface to the class is the same. The calling conventions for such a Date class's member functions are no different from those of Listing A-1, Date.h. The differences, of course, are seen in private and protected data members and in member function code — the so-called hidden details of implementation.

Incidentally, the overloaded assignment operator function and the copy constructor function are unnecessary in the class as it is currently designed. The compiler-supplied default functions do exactly the same thing. They are included here to remind you that such functions might be necessary if someday you modify the data representation to include pointers to allocated memory resources. Inasmuch as they are implemented as inline functions, there is no performance penalty if you define them yourself.

Listing A-2 in Appendix A is Date.cpp, the source-code file that implements the Date class's member functions that are not inline.

As you can see from Listing A-2, the majority of the class's processing occurs when you construct a Date object from month, day, and year integers and when you extract those data values from the integer data representation of the Date class.

Single Inheritance

The class hierarchy that we use in this discussion represents a design that employs *single inheritance*, which means that all derived classes have no more than one base class. We address multiple inheritance in Chapter 24. For now, let's consider our derived class, the one that specializes the behavior of the base Date class.

The Derived Class

Listing 23-1 is SpecialDate.h, the header source-code file that declares the specialized SpecialDate class, which is derived from the Date class. There are several lessons you can learn from this derivation.

Listing 23-1: **SpecialDate.h**

```
#ifndef SPECIALDATE_H
#define SPECIALDATE_H

#include <iostream>
#include <Date.h>

class SpecialDate : public Date {
    static char* mos[];
public:
    SpecialDate(int da, int mo, int yr) : Date(mo, da, yr)
        { }
    bool IsNullDate() const
        { return ndays == 0; }
    friend std::ostream& operator<<(std::ostream& os,
                                    SpecialDate& dt);
    void Display(std::ostream& os)
        { os << "SpecialDate: " << *this; }
};
#endif
```

Protected Members

Observe the `protected` access specifier that appears ahead of the `ndays` data member in Date.h, Listing A-1. Protected members are private to users of the class. If the program instantiates an object of type `Date`, the program cannot access the protected `ndays` data member. In this respect, protected members are the same as private members.

If a base class has private members, those members are not accessible to the derived class. Protected members, however, are public to derived classes — but, as I just explained, private to the rest of the program. Use of the `protected` keyword is one acknowledgment by the `Date` class in Date.h that it might be used as a base class.

When you design a class, consider whether the class might someday be used as a base class — even if you have no such intentions at the start. Specify the `protected` keyword for members that could be accessible to derived classes.

Derived and Specialized Members

The `SpecialDate` class has one static data member of its own: the `mos` array of pointers. The class inherits two other data members from the `Date` class: the protected static `dys` array of integers and a long integer named `ndays`. If the `dys` array member were private to the `Date` class, the member functions of the `SpecialDate` class would not be able to read or write the array except through public member functions of the `Date` class. Since there are no such accessing public member functions, the `dys` array would be a hidden implementation detail of the `Date` class, hidden even from derived classes. The `dys` array is protected, however, so that later exercises in derivation can use it. It also is `const` so that the program cannot change the values in the array after the array is initialized.

The `Date` class's `ndays` data member is also protected, so member functions of the derived `SpecialDate` class can read and write that data member.

Public and Private Base Classes

The `SpecialDate` class declares that it is derived publicly from the `Date` class. A derived class can specify that a base class is public or private by using the `public` or `private` access specifier in the definition of the derived class:

```
class SpecialDate : public Date  { /* ... */ };
class OtherDate : private Date { /* ... */ };
```

The `public` access specifier in this context means that the protected members of the base class are protected members of the derived class and that the public members of the base class are public members of the derived class. The `private` access specifier in this context means that the protected and public members of the base class are private members of the derived class. This distinction is important if you ever extend the class hierarchy with classes derived from the current derived class.

If you do not provide an access specifier, the compiler assumes that the access is private unless the base class is a structure, in which case the compiler assumes that the access is public.

Constructors in the Base and Derived Classes

When you declare an object of a derived class, the compiler executes the constructor function of the base class followed by the constructor function of the derived class. The parameter list for the derived class's constructor function can differ from that of the base class's constructor function. Therefore, the constructor function for the derived class must tell the compiler which values to use as arguments to the constructor function for the base class.

The derived class's constructor function specifies the arguments to the base class's constructor function in SpecialDate.h by using a parameter initialization list for the base class:

```
SpecialDate(int da, int mo, int yr) : Date(mo, da, yr)
    { }
```

The colon (:) operator after the derived constructor's parameter list specifies that a parameter initialization list follows. You learned to use parameter initialization lists to initialize `const` and reference data members in Chapter 15. You use the same syntax here to specify the arguments for a base class's constructor. The argument list is in parentheses and follows the name of the base class.

Unless the base class has a default constructor (one that expects no arguments or has all default arguments for its parameters), you must provide a base class parameter initialization list. It follows then that if the base class does not have a default constructor, the derived class must have a constructor if only to provide arguments for the base class constructor. Note that the derived constructor, however, may itself be a default constructor and pass preset arguments to the base class.

The arguments to the base class constructor function are expressions that may use constants, global variables, and the arguments from the parameter list of the derived class's constructor function. The base class arguments can be any valid C++ expressions that match the types of the base constructor's parameters. In the `SpecialDate` example, the constructor passes its own arguments to the `Date` constructor, changing their order according to the following requirements. The designer of the `SpecialDate` class decides that date class users prefer to express date values in the day, month, year order rather than the month, day, year order that the `Date` class mandates. Consequently, the `SpecialDate` constructor function declares those parameters in a different order from those of the `Date` class and reorders them in the parameter initialization list for the `Date` class constructor.

When a base class has more than one constructor function, the compiler decides which one to call based on the types of the arguments in the derived class constructor's parameter initialization list for the base constructor.

Specializing with New Member Functions

Class specialization through inheritance often includes the addition of member functions to the derived class that the base class does not have. The SpecialDate class in this example includes a member function named IsNullDate. The Date class has no such member function. If you instantiate an object of type Date, you cannot call the IsNullDate function for that object, because the class has no such member function. However, if you instantiate an object of type SpecialDate, you can call the IsNullDate function for that object.

The IsNullDate function takes advantage of the fact that the base Date class specifies the ndays data member as protected and tests that data member for a zero value. If the SpecialDate class could not access ndays, then the IsNullDate function would have to call one of the Date class's member functions — GetDay, GetMonth, or GetYear — and test the return value for zero. The overhead required to extract a date component from the long integer data representation makes it more efficient to use the actual long integer data value.

Specializing by Overriding Base Class Member Functions

When a base class and a derived class have member functions with the same name, parameter list types, and const specification, the function in the derived class overrides that in the base class when the function is called as a member of the derived class object. This technique allows the derived class to provide specialized behavior for a particular method.

Both the base Date class and the derived SpecialDate class in our example have functions named Display. A program that declares an object of type Date can call the Display function for that object, and the Date class's version of that member function executes. A program that declares an object of type SpecialDate can call the Display function for that object, and the SpecialDate's version of that member function executes. You see an example of that behavior soon.

Listing 23-2 is SpecialDate.cpp, the source-code file that implements the static data member and non-inline member function of the SpecialDate class.

Listing 23-2: **SpecialDate.cpp**

```cpp
#include "SpecialDate.h"

char* SpecialDate::mos[] =
{
    "January", "February", "March", "April",
    "May", "June", "July", "August",
    "September", "October", "November", "December"
};

std::ostream& operator<<(std::ostream& os, SpecialDate& dt)
{
    if (!dt.IsNullDate())
```

Continued

Listing 23-2 *(continued)*

```
        os << dt.mos[dt.GetMonth()-1] << ' '
            << dt.GetDay() << ", " << dt.GetYear();
    return os;
}
```

Building the Program

Until now, the exercises in this book have been independent, stand-alone programs. That approach works well for simple example programs, but you seldom will find yourself working in such a small environment. To learn about inheritance, you declare classes in header files, put member functions in separate, class-specific source files, and link the object code compiled from those multiple source files to make running programs. In other words, you view these examples from an environment that is more like those in which you do real programming.

A program that uses the SpecialDate class must include the SpecialDate.h header file and link the program's compiled object file with the object files that the compiler generates when you compile SpecialDate.cpp. You don't need to include Date.h, because SpecialDate.h does that for you. The program must also link with the DataTypes object library (Chapter 22), because the SpecialDate class is derived from the Date class that is implemented in that library.

Most C++ development systems permit you to compile and link with multiple object files. Most systems also support libraries of object files. If you use Quincy to run the exercises, the tutorial includes special project files for the programs that are built from more than one object file and/or that include object libraries.

Program 23-1 instantiates an object of a derived class and uses that class's specialized behavior.

Program 23-1: **Class specialization**

```
#include <iostream>
#include "SpecialDate.h"

int main()
{
    for (;;) {
        std::cout << "Enter dd mm yyyy (0 0 0 to quit): ";
        int da, mo, yr;
        std::cin >> da >> mo >> yr;
        if (da == 0)
            break;
        SpecialDate dt(da, mo, yr);
        if (dt.IsNullDate())
            std::cout << "Try again";
        else
            dt.Display();
```

```
        std::cout << std::endl;
    }
    return 0;
}
```

The real lesson of Program 23-1 is found not in the application program but in the source-code files SpecialDate.h and SpecialDate.cpp, which demonstrate how an abstract data type is specialized through inheritance.

Scope Resolution Operator with Base and Derived Classes

Often in a program, you want to call the base class's version of a function that has been overridden in a derived class. A program can use the scope resolution operator (::) to bypass the override of a base class member and call the base class's function instead. You express the call to the base class function by coding the base class name and the double colons ahead of the member name to bypass the overridden member:

```
SpecialDate dt(29, 6, 1990);
dt.Date::Display();
```

Program 23-2 demonstrates this usage with the Date class's Display function.

Program 23-2: **Class scope resolution**

```
#include <iostream>
#include "SpecialDate.h"

int main()
{
    SpecialDate dt(29, 6, 2003);
    dt.Display(std::cout);
    std::cout << std::endl;
    dt.Date::Display(std::cout);
    std::cout << std::endl;
    return 0;
}
```

The program in Program 23-2 instantiates an object of the derived type SpecialDate and uses the SpecialDate class's Display member function to display the date. Then, the program uses the scope resolution operator to display the same date object by using the base Date class's Display member function.

Using the scope resolution operator without specifying a type on its left from within a member function compiles a call to a global, nonmember function with the same name and parameter list.

More Than One Derived Class

A program can derive more than one class from a single base class. Recall the CustomDate class from the programs in Chapters 16, 18, and 19. A CustomDate date is one that is expressed as the year and a day value representing the 1-based number of days since January 1. Inasmuch as the Date class in this chapter records the date information in an integer data member, we can implement the CustomDate class by deriving from Date, forming a simple object-oriented class hierarchy. Figure 23-4 shows that relationship.

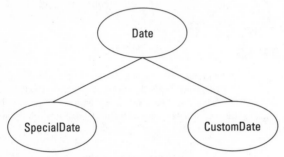

Figure 23-4: Multiple derived classes

A Second Derived Class

Listings 23-3 and 23-4 are CustomDate.h and CustomDate.cpp, which implement a second class derived from the base Date class.

Listing 23-3: **CustomDate.h**

```cpp
#ifndef CUSTOMDATE_H
#define CUSTOMDATE_H

#include "Date.h"

class CustomDate : public Date {
public:
    CustomDate(int yr, int da);
    int GetDay() const;
    friend std::ostream& operator<<(std::ostream& os,
                                    const CustomDate& dt);
    void Display(std::ostream& os)
        { os << "CustomDate: " << *this; }
};
#endif
```

Listing 23-4: CustomDate.cpp

```cpp
#include <iostream>
#include "CustomDate.h"

CustomDate::CustomDate(int yr, int da)
{
    if (yr < 1 || da < 1 ||
            da > (IsLeapYear(yr) ? 366 : 365))
        return;
    int mo;
    for (mo = 1; mo < 13; mo++) {
        int dy = dys[mo-1];
        if (mo == 2 && IsLeapYear(yr))
            dy++;
        if (da <= dy)
            break;
        da -= dy;
    }
    SetDate(mo, da, yr);
}
int CustomDate::GetDay() const
{
    int mo, da, yr;
    GetDate(mo, da, yr);
    int day = 0;
    for (int m = 1; m < mo; m++) {
        day += dys[m-1];
        if (m == 2 && IsLeapYear(yr))
            day++;
    }
    return day + da;
}

std::ostream& operator<<(std::ostream& os,
                         const CustomDate& dt)
{
    os << dt.GetDay() << '-' << dt.GetYear();
      return os;
}
```

The CustomDate constructor in Listing 23-4 has no parameter initialization list for the base Date class. It cannot provide all three arguments, because it has no month argument and because its day argument is a different data representation from the day argument of the Date constructor. You can omit a base class parameter initialization list when the base class has a default constructor. Look at Date.h in Appendix A. The Date class constructor has default argument values for all its parameters. This means that the constructor function serves two purposes. It is an initializing constructor, and it is the default constructor. The CustomDate constructor builds the three date values that initialize a Date object and then calls the base Date class's SetDate member function, passing those three date values as arguments.

The CustomDate class's GetDay member function overrides the base Date class's GetDay member function to compute and return the custom version of the day rather than the traditional day of the month value. The Date class's GetYear member function works without being overridden, because you compute the year value the same way for both kinds of dates. A program may also call the GetMonth member function for a CustomDate object; the Date class's GetMonth member function would execute and return the proper month. You can prevent this usage by overriding GetMonth in the CustomDate class to return a zero.

Using the Base Class and Both Derived Classes

Program 23-3 uses all three of the date variations to display several birth dates.

> ### Program 23-3: **Multiple derived classes**

```
#include <iostream>
#include "SpecialDate.h"
#include "CustomDate.h"

int main()
{
    // Process a Date.
    Date dt(6,29,1990);
    std::cout << std::endl << "Tyler: ";
    dt.Display(std::cout);
    // Process a CustomDate.
    CustomDate cdt(1962, 285);
    std::cout << std::endl << "Sharon: ";
    cdt.Display(std::cout);
    std::cout << " (";
    cdt.Date::Display(std::cout);
    std::cout << ')';
    // Process a SpecialDate.
    SpecialDate sdt(20, 1, 1992);
    std::cout << std::endl << "Kellie: ";
    sdt.Display(std::cout);
    return 0;
}
```

Program 23-3 instantiates and displays three dates by using three date classes. Two of those classes are derived from the third.

The Lack of a Relationship Between Derived Classes

The only thing in common between the SpecialDate and CustomDate classes is that they have the same base class. The two classes have no knowledge of, or relationship with, each other. You cannot call the specialized member functions of one class for an object of the other class. You cannot cast an object of one type to the other type. You cannot initialize or copy between objects of these two classes. You cannot do these things because the classes do not have the necessary conversion and copy constructor member functions. You must provide these functions explicitly, as you learned to do in Chapter 16. It is important to understand that no implied relationships exist between classes derived from a common base class.

Classes Derived from Derived Base Classes

You can derive a class from a base class that was derived itself from another base class. Suppose that the CustomDate class is not exactly what you want every time. Perhaps you need a specialized custom date class, called SpecialCustomDate, which displays its objects in the same way that the SpecialDate class does. Assuming that you do not want to modify an existing class, you have these three design choices:

✦ Derive a class from SpecialDate and add the CustomDate construction behavior.

✦ Derive a class from CustomDate and add the SpecialDate display behavior.

✦ Use multiple inheritance and derive a class from both SpecialDate and CustomDate.

Figure 23-5 illustrates all three of these design choices.

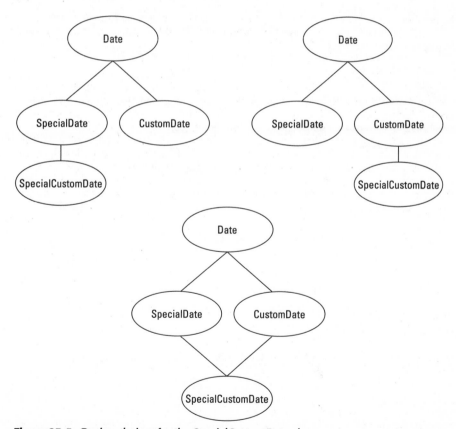

Figure 23-5: Design choices for the SpecialCustomDate class

The third choice (at the bottom of Figure 23-5), which uses multiple inheritance, is not a viable one at this time. First, it has some inherent design problems that typically are encountered with multiple inheritance. Also, you don't learn about multiple inheritance until you get to Chapter 24.

Either of the first two choices (at the top of Figure 23-5 from left to right) involves some amount of duplication. The second choice involves duplicating the array of pointers that the SpecialDate class uses for the names of the months. That class provides no apparent easy way for a nonderived class to get to that array. Remember that in our contrived situation, you may not modify the SpecialDate class, so you cannot declare this new class to be a friend. A possible solution to that problem is to declare a class derived from SpecialDate with the sole purpose of returning a pointer to the static array. Let's explore that possibility. Consider this class:

```
class MonthArray : public SpecialDate {
public:
    static const char* GetMonth() const
        { return mos; }    // Error. Why?
};
```

Remember that SpecialCustomDate, in this discussion, is derived from CustomDate. The SpecialCustomDate class's Display function gets the address of SpecialDate's static array of month names this way:

```
const char* months = MonthArray::GetMonth();
```

Can you see why this does not work? The designer of the SpecialDate class did not make the static array a protected data member. Whatever the reason, the MonthArray class cannot access that member and the compiler issues an error when the MonthArray::GetMonth() function is declared. That eliminates this solution. If you still want to derive SpecialCustomDate from CustomDate, you must provide a second, identical array for the new class. There is something unappealing about solutions that duplicate design features and that duplicate what is stored in memory, so most programmers look for other ways. Fortunately, one is close at hand. The first choice in Figure 23-5 derives SpecialCustomDate from SpecialDate, and that solution works if you add some creative design components. Figure 23-6 shows the effective class hierarchy for the SpecialCustomDate class.

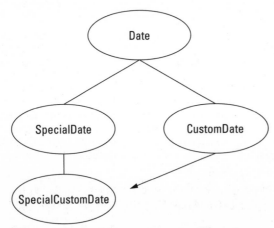

Figure 23-6: SpecialCustomDate class hierarchy

Figure 23-6 illustrates the relationship that now exists between the classes. SpecialCustomDate is directly derived from SpecialDate and indirectly derived from Date through SpecialDate's derivation. SpecialCustomDate, therefore, inherits the properties of both classes. SpecialCustomDate also uses the services of CustomDate, as Figure 23-6 shows. Figure 23-6 uses a bold arrow symbol to differentiate this interclass relationship from that of inheritance.

Even though SpecialCustomDate inherits from both classes, this relationship is not what is called multiple inheritance. SpecialCustomDate is indirectly derived from Date only because SpecialCustomDate's direct base class, SpecialDate, itself is derived directly from Date. You learn about multiple inheritance in Chapter 24.

Listing 23-5 is SpecialCustomDate.h, the header file that implements the SpecialCustomDate class.

Listing 23-5: **SpecialCustomDate.h**

```
#ifndef SPECIALCUSTOMDATE_H
#define SPECIALCUSTOMDATE_H

#include "SpecialDate.h"
#include "CustomDate.h"

class SpecialCustomDate : public SpecialDate  {
public:
    SpecialCustomDate(int yr, int da) : SpecialDate(0,0,0)
    {
        CustomDate cd(yr, da);
        SetDate(cd.GetMonth(),cd.Date::GetDay(),
                                    cd.GetYear());
    }
    void Display(std::ostream& os)
        { os << "SpecialCustomDate: " << *this; }
};
#endif
```

The SpecialCustomDate class needs only a constructor and a Display member function. Both are inline, so no .cpp file is needed. The constructor must build the object from the constructor arguments usually provided for a CustomDate object. You can copy the CustomDate class constructor code here, but there is a better way. The SpecialCustomDate constructor function instantiates a CustomDate object from the year and month constructor arguments. (This instantiation represents the relationship mentioned earlier wherein the SpecialCustomDate class uses the services of the CustomDate class.) Then the constructor calls the indirect base Date class' SetDate function, passing the values returned from the CustomDate object's GetMonth, GetDay, and GetYear functions, except that the call to the GetDay function uses the scope resolution operator to call the Date class's GetDay function rather than the CustomDate class's GetDay function.

The SpecialCustomDate constructor must provide a parameter initialization list for the SpecialDate constructor — in this case, all zero arguments — because the SpecialDate class has no default constructor.

Program 23-4 instantiates an object of the SpecialCustomDate class.

Program 23-4: A class derived from a derived class

```
#include <iostream>
#include "SpecialCustomDate.h"

int main()
{
    // Process a SpecialCustomDate.
    SpecialCustomDate scdt(1941, 321);
    std::cout << std::endl << "Judy:    ";
    scdt.Display();
}
```

Problem Domain Class Hierarchy Design

Now you are ready for some object-oriented design. Any program supports what programmers call the *problem domain* (Chapter 22). The idea is to model the data components of a problem domain in an object-oriented class hierarchy. Figure 23-7 is a small example of such a class hierarchy.

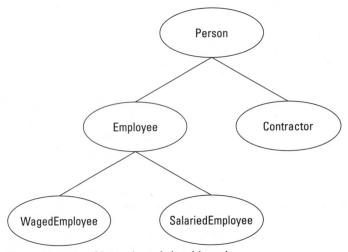

Figure 23-7: An object-oriented class hierarchy

Each balloon in Figure 23-7 represents a class. Derived classes are below their base classes on the chart and are connected to their base classes by a single line. These base and derived classes represent the major components of the problem domain — in this case, a personnel accounting system such as one you might see in payroll and labor distribution applications. We will build these classes in this chapter and use them as examples for learning the behavior of C++ and object-oriented class hierarchies.

The Person class is the root base class. Everything in this hierarchy is related to people, so the Person class encapsulates the data and behavior related to personnel accounting that all people have in common.

Two classes are derived from Person. The Employee class specializes the Person class with data and behavior specific to employees. The Contractor class does the same thing for workers that the organization hires on a temporary basis from temp agencies and job shops, as well as workers hired as private consultants. Employees are specialized further by the WagedEmployee and SalariedEmployee classes.

So far, we haven't considered what the common and specialized behaviors are or how they affect our application. For now, we are looking at the overall design.

The hierarchy in Figure 23-7 — and any class hierarchy — is not the same as a hierarchical database. When you instantiate an object of type Contractor, for example, only one object exists, and it contains all the members of both classes. A database hierarchy, on the other hand, represents the relationships between different objects, such as department objects, project objects, and employee objects. The significant difference is that a WagedEmployee is an Employee (which is a Person), whereas a department contains employees who work on projects (which are in the province of departments).

C++ Versus Pure Object-Oriented Design

Pure object-oriented design, a subject of much debate, employs one class hierarchy; everything descends from a common root class. The data types, the data structures, and even the program itself are all classes in the hierarchy, and they all descend from the common root. Figure 23-8 is an example of that concept.

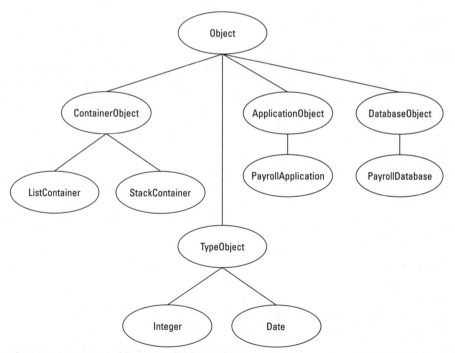

Figure 23-8: A pure object-oriented hierarchy

A pure object-oriented application begins running when its application object is created, usually as the result of the object's declaration somewhere in the program. This arrangement is analogous to the declaration of the single main function somewhere in a C++ program. The pure object-oriented program's application object communicates with other objects by instantiating them and sending them messages. This approach is analogous to a C++ program declaring objects of classes and calling the member functions of those classes through the objects.

C++ programs usually do not reflect pure object-oriented programming. Depending on the application's requirements, they typically have several unrelated class hierarchies: one or more for the problem domain, another for the application framework, perhaps a few data abstractions, and some data structure and container classes.

C++ programs tend to reflect a combination of object-oriented and functional (also called procedural) programming models. (Object-oriented purists might argue, then, that C++ programs are not object-oriented at all.) A C++ program launches from its main function rather than from the instantiation of an application object. Some application framework class libraries start with an application object; but even when using such an application framework, a C++ program instantiates the application object in or below its main function.

Do not worry, therefore, when you see C++ class hierarchies that do not descend from a common, all-encompassing root object. That multiple-hierarchy idiom is the norm rather than the exception in C++ programs. It makes code reuse more likely, because it is more difficult to extract parts from one huge monolithic hierarchy.

More Data Abstractions

As you might expect, it takes more classes than Figure 23-8 shows to implement a personnel application. You do not always depict every class in a design diagram. It is not necessary to show the relationship between problem domain classes and classes from the Standard C++ Library, for example. Other data abstraction classes may or may not be on the diagram. A personnel application certainly needs to represent dates for different reasons. We developed a Date class early in this book, and then in Chapter 22 we put it in a class library to make it more appropriate for general-purpose use. We built two other data abstractions to encapsulate the data and behavior of money and Social Security numbers, neither of which we have used so far. We'll be using them in the next few exercises.

Listings A-3 and A-4 in Appendix A are money.h and money.cpp, the source code files that implement the Money class. Listings A-5 and A-6 are ssn.h and ssn.cpp, the source code files that implement the SSN class.

Figure 23-9 expands the personnel application's problem domain class hierarchy to include these three data abstraction classes.

Observe the bold lines that have small circles at the end. This notation represents a relationship in which the class at the circle end of the line has, as a data member, one or more instances of the class at the other end of the line.

As you can see, such a diagram can become complex. That is why you often stop diagramming at the level of detail that Figure 23-7 shows and allow the source code of your class hierarchy design to document relationships such as those added by Figure 23-9.

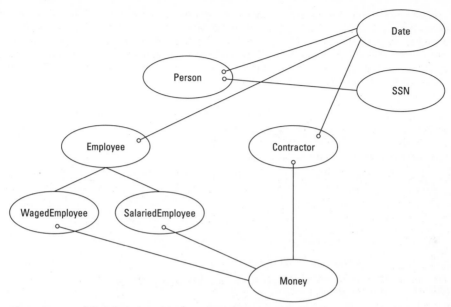

Figure 23-9: Class hierarchy with data abstraction classes

The Standard C++ String Class

Standard C++ defines a standard string class named, of course, `std::string`. You can concatenate, compare, assign, display, and make substrings of C++ string objects. I discuss the standard string class in more detail in Chapter 27. Until then, we'll use the basic properties of the `std::string` class to make the classes in this chapter easier to design and understand.

Person: The Base Class

The top of the class hierarchy in Figure 23-7 is the `Person` class, the class from which all the other classes in the hierarchy descend. The `Person` class encapsulates those data and behavioral traits that are common to all people and of interest to this problem domain. Listings A-7 and A-8 in Appendix A are Person.h and Person.cpp, the source-code files that implement the Person class.

Enumerations in a Class

The `Person` class declares two enumerated data types — `Sex` and `MaritalStatus` — as public. Here is a fragment of the `Person` class showing these declarations:

```
class Person {
public:
    enum Sex {unknown, male, female};
    enum MaritalStatus {single, married, divorced, widowed};
    // ...
};
```

The enumerated types are public so that programs that use the `Person` class can refer to the enumerated constant values. They are declared within the class declaration so that their identifiers are not in the global scope. This practice avoids any potential for name collisions with other parts of the program. Member functions of the class can refer to the enumerated values without qualification, but a program that uses them from outside the class must use the scope resolution operator to specify the values like this:

```
empl.SetSex(Person::male);
```

Virtual Functions in a Base Class

Two of the functions in the `Person` class are declared with the `virtual` qualifier. A virtual function indicates that the class designer expects the function to be overridden in a derived class by a function with the same function name and parameter types. We will revisit this subject and examine the effects of virtual and nonvirtual function overrides in the discussion of the class hierarchy's derived classes. The `Person` class's destructor function is one of the two virtual functions, a significant characteristic that you soon learn about. Note that virtual functions are not as efficient as non-virtual functions, but there are times when they are necessary.

Abstract Base Class: The Pure Virtual Function

The Person class's `FormattedDisplay` member function is the other virtual member function. Here is its declaration:

```
virtual void FormattedDisplay(std::ostream& os) = 0;
```

Notice the equal sign followed by a zero (= 0). This notation specifies that the member function is a *pure virtual function*. This means that the base class is an *abstract base class*, and the class designer intends the class to be used only as a base class. The base class may or may not provide a function body for the pure virtual function. In either case, a program that uses this class may not declare any objects of an abstract base class directly. If the program declares an object of a class directly or indirectly derived from the abstract base class, then the pure virtual function must be overridden—either in the class of the object being declared or in a class above the object's class and below the abstract base class in the hierarchy. In other words, when you derive from an abstract base class, you must provide definitions for all the pure virtual functions unless you intend to derive another abstract base class. You can only instantiate classes that derive from the abstract base class and provide definitions for (at least) the pure virtual functions.

Two Ways to Display

The `Person` class includes two display techniques. The `FormattedDisplay` member function displays the `Person` data in a format conducive to query responses and report fields. I use it here to demonstrate the behavior of `virtual` functions. The overloaded `operator<<` non-member function displays raw data.

Derived Classes

The class hierarchy in Figure 23-7 includes several derived classes, discussed next.

The Employee Class

Listings A-9 and A-10 in Appendix A are Employee.h and Employee.cpp, the source-code files that implement the Employee class, which is derived directly from the Person class as shown here:

```
class Employee : public Person   {
protected:
    Date datehired;
    // ...
};
```

The Employee class, like its base Person class, is an abstract base class through its pure virtual FormattedDisplay member function; to use the Employee class, you must derive a class from it. The Employee class specializes the Person class by adding a datehired data member. All employees are hired, but not all persons are hired. Contrast this specialization with that of the Contractor class discussed later.

Overriding a Function Override

The Employee::FormattedDisplay member function in Employee.cpp begins by calling the Person::FormattedDisplay member function by using the Person class name and the scope resolution operator as shown here:

```
void Employee::FormattedDisplay(std::ostream& os)
{
    Person::FormattedDisplay(os);
    // ...
}
```

This technique allows the derived class to use the base class's overridden behavior. Recall that the SpecialDate class (earlier in this chapter) totally overrode its base Date class's Display function to provide custom specialization for the derived class. SpecialDate objects display differently from Date objects. The Employee class, on the other hand, needs only to add to the base class's behavior by displaying the specialized datehired data member.

The overloaded operator<< function similarly calls the overloaded operator<< function for the Person class by casting the Employee reference argument to a reference to type Person as shown here:

```
std::ostream& operator<<(std::ostream& os, Employee& empl)
{
    os << ((Person&)empl) << '\n';
    // ...
}
```

In this case, you cannot use the scope resolution operator to call an overridden member function because the overloaded operator<< functions are not members of any class. Instead, they are functions to be called when the compiler sees an std::ostream object on the left of the << operator and a Person or Employee object on the right. The cast coerces the compiler into treating the Employee reference as if it referred to its base Person class. The cast also calls the overloaded operator<< function that deals with Person objects. That function works correctly because the Employee object, derived from the Person class, includes all the data members and member functions of the Person class.

The WagedEmployee Class

Listings A-11 and A-12 in Appendix A are WagedEmployee.h and WagedEmployee.cpp, the source-code files that implement the `WagedEmployee` class, which is derived directly from the Employee class as shown here:

```
class WagedEmployee : public Employee {
    Money hourlywage;
    // ...
};
```

The `WagedEmployee` class is what is called a *concrete data type*, which is a data type defined by a class for which you can instantiate an object. The `WagedEmployee` class specializes the `Employee` class by adding the `hourlywage` data member. Not all employees work for an hourly wage, so you must represent this behavior with a specialized derived class. Contrast this behavior with that of the `SalariedEmployee` class, discussed in the next section.

By deriving from the `Employee` class, the `WagedEmployee` class directly inherits all the data and behavior of the `Employee` class and, because `Employee` is derived from `Person`, indirectly inherits all the data and behavior of the `Person` class. A `WagedEmployee`, therefore, is a specialized `Employee` that is a specialized `Person`.

The SalariedEmployee Class

Listings A-13 and A-14 in Appendix A are SalariedEmployee.h and SalariedEmployee.cpp, the source-code files that implement the `SalariedEmployee` class, also directly derived from the Employee class as shown here:

```
class SalariedEmployee : public Employee {
    Money salary;
    // ...
};
```

The `SalariedEmployee` class is also a concrete data type. It specializes the `Employee` class by adding the `salary` data member. Not all employees work for an annual salary, so you must represent this behavior with a specialized derived class. Contrast this behavior with that of the `WagedEmployee` class, discussed in the previous section.

By deriving from the `Employee` class, the `SalariedEmployee` class directly inherits all the data and behavior of the `Employee` class and, because `Employee` is derived from `Person`, indirectly inherits all the data and behavior of the `Person` class. A `SalariedEmployee`, therefore, is a specialized `Employee` that is a specialized `Person`.

We now have two specialized `Employee` derivations having individual behavior and behavior in common that they inherit from their common base class.

The Contractor Class

Listings A-15 and A-16 are Contractor.h and Contractor.cpp, the source-code files that implement the `Contractor` class, which is directly derived from the `Person` class as shown here:

```
class Contractor : public Person {
    Date startdate;
    Date enddate;
```

```
    Money hourlyrate;
    // ...
};
```

The Contractor class is a concrete data type derived from the Person class. A contractor is not an employee and, therefore, does not have a date hired, an hourly wage, or a salary. A contractor has start and end dates for the contracted period and, in this example, an hourly rate. The difference between a contractor's hourly rate and a waged employee's hourly wage might seem inconsequential in this small example, but a more comprehensive personnel accounting system surely would include other differences that would distinguish the two classes more dramatically.

Building Object Libraries

Let's review what you learned in Chapter 22 about libraries. A typical software development project compiles its problem domain classes separately and stores them in object libraries. An object library is a file that contains compiled object files that usually are related. A program can link with an object library. Then, the linker includes in the executable program only those object files from the library that define functions and variables to which the program refers.

Applications programs include the header files that declare the classes and that link with the compiled object libraries to use the non-inline member functions in the class declaration. This is the same way that you link programs to the Standard C++ library classes and functions. The difference is that your project-specific libraries and header files are maintained in private subdirectories rather than in the public ones that contain the Standard C++ files.

If you look at the subdirectory structure for the example programs, you see that it has several subdirectories. The Include subdirectory contains all the header files for the libraries, which are to be included in the applications programs in this and later chapters. The other subdirectories contain source code, object libraries, and Quincy project files that you use to build the object libraries from the source code. The DataTypes subdirectory contains date.cpp, money.cpp, ssn.cpp, datatypes.prj, and, after you build the library, DataTypes.a. These files represent generic user-defined data types that any application might use. The Personnel subdirectory contains personnel.prj, personnel.a, and the .cpp files for the Person class and its derived classes.

The project files (.prj) in these subdirectories are configured to search the Include subdirectory for header files and to build their associated object libraries (.a).

The project files for the applications programs are configured to search the Include subdirectory for header files to include and to search the other subdirectories for object library files to link. They also are configured to link with the particular object file libraries that contain class methods for the classes that the programs use.

Using the Problem Domain Class Hierarchy

We now have a problem domain class hierarchy to support a personnel system. That hierarchy uses other general-purpose data abstraction classes, which we have built. Now we need an application to use the classes. Let's begin with a straightforward application program, as shown in Program 23-5.

Program 23-5: A personnel application program

```cpp
#include <WagedEmployee.h>
#include <SalariedEmployee.h>
#include <Contractor.h>

std::string ReadString(const std::string& prompt)
{
    std::string str;
    std::cout << prompt << ": ";
    std::getline(std::cin, str);
    return str;
}
Date ReadDate(const std::string& prompt)
{
    Date dt;
    std::cout << prompt << " (mm dd yyyy): ";
    std::cin >> dt;
    return dt;
}
Money ReadMoney(const std::string& prompt)
{
    double mn;
    std::cout << prompt << ": ";
    std::cin >> mn;
    return mn;
}
void PersonInput(Person* pPerson)
{
    static std::string str;
    std::getline(std::cin, str); // flush the input buffer
    pPerson->SetName(ReadString("Name"));
    pPerson->SetAddress(ReadString("Address"));
    pPerson->SetPhone(ReadString("Phone"));
    pPerson->SetDob(ReadDate("Date of birth"));
    long int ssn;
    std::cout << "SSN: ";
    std::cin >> ssn;
    pPerson->SetSSN(SSN(ssn));
    char sx;
    do {
        std::cout << "Sex (m/f) ";
        std::cin >> sx;
    } while (sx != 'm' && sx != 'f');
    pPerson->SetSex(sx == 'm' ?
                    Person::male : Person::female);
}
void EmployeeInput(Employee* pEmployee)
{
    pEmployee->SetDateHired(ReadDate("Date hired"));
}
void WagedEmployeeInput(WagedEmployee* pWagedEmployee)
```

```
{
    pWagedEmployee->SetHourlyWage(ReadMoney("Hourly wage"));
}
void SalariedEmployeeInput(SalariedEmployee*
                                        pSalariedEmployee)
{
    pSalariedEmployee->SetSalary(ReadMoney("Salary"));
}
void ContractorInput(Contractor* pContractor)
{
    pContractor->SetStartDate(ReadDate("Start date"));
    pContractor->SetEndDate(ReadDate("End date"));
    pContractor->SetHourlyRate(ReadMoney("Hourly rate"));
}
int main()
{
    Person* pPerson = 0;
    std::cout << "1 = Salaried employee" << std::endl
             << "2 = Waged employee"    << std::endl
             << "3 = Contractor"        << std::endl
             << "Enter selection: ";
    int sel;
    std::cin >> sel;
    switch (sel) {
        case 1:
            pPerson = new SalariedEmployee;
            PersonInput(pPerson);
            EmployeeInput((Employee*)pPerson);
            SalariedEmployeeInput((SalariedEmployee*)pPerson);
            break;
        case 2:
            pPerson = new WagedEmployee;
            PersonInput(pPerson);
            EmployeeInput((Employee*)pPerson);
            WagedEmployeeInput((WagedEmployee*)pPerson);
            break;
        case 3:
            pPerson = new Contractor;
            PersonInput(pPerson);
            ContractorInput((Contractor*)pPerson);
            break;
        default:
            std::cout << "\aIncorrect entry";
            break;
    }
    if (pPerson != 0) {
        pPerson->FormattedDisplay(std::cout);
        delete pPerson;
    }
    return 0;
}
```

The program in Program 23-5 is a motley assortment of object-oriented and functional programming. The object-oriented part uses the personnel system's class hierarchy to instantiate and display objects of type `SalariedEmployee`, `WagedEmployee`, and `Contractor`. The functional part uses nonmember functions for the user interface.

The first three functions in the program are generic user-input functions to prompt for, and read data values into, objects of the `std::string`, `Date`, and `Money` classes. The next five functions — which call the first three — prompt for, and read data values into, objects of the `Person`, `Contractor`, `Employee`, `WagedEmployee`, and `SalariedEmployee` classes. Because `Person` and `Employee` are abstract base classes, these functions are not called for objects of those classes, but instead are called for objects of classes derived from those abstract base classes.

The `main` function displays a menu, reads the user input, and uses `case` statements to process the user's selection. Each `case` instantiates an object of the type selected by the user. The instantiation allocates memory from the heap by using the `new` operator and assigns that memory to a pointer of type `Person`, which is the root base class of the hierarchy. Then, each `case` calls a set of the class-input functions, passing the pointer. The function calls to those functions that expect pointers to type `Contractor`, `Employee`, and `WagedEmployee` use casts to cast the `Person` pointer to a pointer of the correct type. C++ does not convert a pointer to a base class into a pointer to one of its derived classes automatically, although the opposite conversion is acceptable. You could pass the address of an object of a derived class to a function that expects the address of an object of one of the class's base classes.

Virtual Functions

Virtual functions are functions in a base class that can be overridden by functions with same name and parameter types in a derived class. They differ from nonvirtual functions in that the program can call the function through a pointer or reference to the base class, and the compiler will call the corresponding member function for the derived class of which the class instance is a type.

Calling Virtual Functions by Reference

When you call a method through a normal instance variable (as opposed to a pointer or reference) it is clear what method you want to call. However, when you make a call through a pointer or a base class, the compiler may have to do extra work to figure out your intent.

For example, suppose you have a pointer to a Person. The actual object that this pointer refers to might be a SalariedEmployee (or it might be a WagedEmployee). When you call the FormattedDisplay method, you want the specific version of FormattedDisplay that pertains to the object's type – not the generic FormattedDisplay method in the Person class. For example, here is a fragment from Program 23-5:

```
Person* pPerson = new SalariedEmployee;  // instantiate object
pPerson->FormattedDisplay(std::cout);    // call object's func
```

The problem is there is no way for the compiler to figure out the proper behavior at compile time. Instead, runtime code must examine the object that pPerson points to and then transfer control to the proper function. This requires some overhead in each object and also exacts a small execution time penalty.

If `Person::FormattedDisplay` were a nonvirtual member function, Program 23-5 always would call the `FormattedDisplay` member function in the `Person` class irrespective of the type of the object to which that `pPerson` pointed.

If the derived class has no function to override the base class's virtual function, the base class's function executes regardless of the pointer or reference type.

Overriding the Virtual Function Override

If you want a base class's virtual function to execute even when the calling object is of a derived class that has an overriding function, use the base class name and scope resolution operator to specify that the base class function is to execute:

```
pPerson->Person::FormattedDisplay(std::cout);
```

The overriding function call does not have to specify the topmost base class with the scope resolution operator; it can name any class up the hierarchy. If the named class does not override the virtual function, the compiler searches up the hierarchy until it finds a class that does; that is the function that is executed. If, for example, the Employee class does not have a FormattedDisplay member function (it does, but pretend for this discussion that it does not) the following code executes the Person::FormattedDisplay function:

```
Person* pPerson = new WagedEmployee;
//...

pPerson->Employee::FormattedDisplay(std::cout);
```

Virtual Destructors

Usually, when an object of a derived class is destroyed, the destructor for the derived class executes and then the destructor for the base class executes. But suppose that an object is declared with the new operator and that the pointer type is that of a base class with a nonvirtual destructor. For example, suppose that the address of a WagedEmployee instance is in pPerson and the program deletes pPerson with the delete operator. In this case, the base class destructor executes instead of the derived destructor because the program is being told to destroy an object of the base type. Program 23-6, which departs from the personnel class hierarchy to make its point, demonstrates this behavior.

Program 23-6: **Nonvirtual base class destructor**

```
#include <iostream>

class Shape {
public:
    Shape()
        { }
    ~Shape()
      { std::cout << "Executing Shape dtor" << std::endl; }
};
class Circle : public Shape {
public:
    Circle()
        { }
    ~Circle()
```

Continued

Program 23-6 *(continued)*

```
        { std::cout << "Executing Circle dtor" << std::endl; }
};
int main()
{
    Shape* pShape = new Circle;
    // ...
    delete pShape;
    return 0;
}
```

When you run Program 23-6, observe that only the Shape destructor message displays on standard output. Even though the object is a Circle, the delete operator does not know at runtime the type of the object pointed to by pShape. Usually, this is not what you want. You must assume that derived classes can require custom destruction and that their destructors must be called when their objects are destroyed.

When a base class destructor is virtual, the compiler calls the correct destructor function irrespective of the type of the pointer, as shown in Program 23-7.

Program 23-7: Virtual base class destructor

```
#include <iostream>

class Shape {
public:
    Shape()
    {}
    virtual ~Shape()
      { std::cout << "Executing Shape dtor" << std::endl; }
};
class Circle : public Shape {
public:
    Circle()
    {}
    ~Circle()
      { std::cout << "Executing Circle dtor" << std::endl; }
};
int main()
{
    Shape* pShape = new Circle;
    // ...
    delete pShape;
    return 0;
}
```

Declaring the Shape destructor as virtual solves the problem. The delete operator now knows to execute the Circle destructor. When you run the program, observe that it displays first the message from the Circle destructor and then the message from the Shape destructor. A derived class destructor calls its base class destructor after the derived class destructor does everything else.

If the base class needs no custom destruction, you still must provide a virtual destructor (with an empty statement block) to permit the proper destructor calls for dynamically allocated objects. All the classes in the personnel class hierarchy have virtual destructors.

Although destructor functions can be virtual, constructor functions cannot be virtual. If there is any chance your class might be used as a base class in a polymorphic hierarchy, make the destructor virtual.

Which Member Functions Should Be Virtual?

Using virtual functions in your class design does not come without cost. When a class has at least one virtual function, the most compilers build a table of virtual function pointers for that class. This table, commonly called the vtbl (pronounced "vee-table"), contains an entry for each virtual function in the class. Programmers usually do not have to worry about the vtbl except to know that its presence is a consequence of having virtual functions. Each object of the class in memory includes a hidden pointer variable called the vptr (pronounced "vee-pointer"), which points to the class's common vtbl. Therefore, don't make every function in your class a virtual function just to cover the possibility that someone someday will derive another class from your class.

Each instance of a class with virtual functions has a single vptr no matter how many virtual functions it contains. But such a class has only one vtbl no matter how many instances there are. A class with one hundred virtual functions would have one large vtbl shared by all instances and each instance would have a single secret vptr that points to this vtbl. Adding a virtual function to the class doesn't make the instances occupy more memory, but it does increase the size of the single vtbl.

Standard C++ does not specify that a compiler must implement virtual functions with the vtbl and vptr mechanism. But virtually all contemporary C++ compilers use this technique.

When you design a class hierarchy, consider each member function with respect to whether it should be virtual. Ask first whether the class is likely ever to be a base class. If it is, make sure that you provide a virtual destructor even if it does nothing. Then ask whether any derived class might have overriding functions (the same name and parameter list as your potential base class's functions). Next, ask whether calls to those functions will be in the name of the actual object always or whether they might be through a pointer or reference to your base class. Answering all that, you can determine whether such calls need the services of the function that is a member of the base class or whether they need a virtual function that finds its way to the member function of the actual class of which the object is a type. These are the kinds of decisions that face the designer of an object-oriented class hierarchy.

Polymorphism

You just learned how virtual member functions work in C++. They are a C++ language idiom. Now here is an explanation of *polymorphism*, the object-oriented concept that they support.

Polymorphism is the ability of different objects in a class hierarchy to exhibit unique behavior in response to the same message. It is the name given to the behavior of the FormattedDisplay member functions in the personnel class library just discussed. Polymorphism is from the Greek *poly*, meaning "many," and *morph*, which means "shape." An object referred to from the perspective of its base class can assume one of many shapes depending on the nature of the base class's derived classes and depending on which of these classes from which the object is instantiated.

As you just learned, Employee and Contractor classes derived from the base Person class exhibit different behavior when a member function is called for one of their objects through a pointer or reference to the base Person class. It's one thing to understand the behavior of a polymorphic class. It's quite another matter to imagine a realistic scenario wherein the concept might apply. The Contractor class in our example class hierarchy assumes the existence of only one kind of contractor. In reality, a company can employ several kinds of contractor personnel: subcontractors, independent contractors, contractors from temporary agencies, contractors from job shops, and so on. The company's accounting requirements could vary for each of these kinds of contractors. You might need to derive more classes from the concrete Contractor class, as Figure 23-10 shows, to support these various requirements.

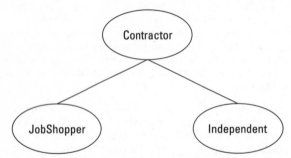

Figure 23-10: Deriving from a concrete data type class

You will not implement these classes in example programs. Instead, I discuss them briefly. Now it would be good experience for you to use what you have learned and try to implement one or more classes derived from Contractor. You might need to add virtual functions to the Contractor class. Consider this application function:

```
void ReportCompensationForAll(const Contractor *ctrs[])
{
    while (*ctrs)
        *(ctrs++)->ReportCompensation();
}
```

This function iterates through a list of Contractor objects and calls a function to report contractor compensation. This function does not exist in the Contractor class that we implemented earlier in this chapter. You would have to add the function and then provide overriding functions in your derived classes.

The ReportCompensationForAll function assumes that all the pointers in the argument array point to Contractor objects; in fact, some of them might point to Contractor objects, others to JobShopper objects, and the rest to Independent objects. Depending on the type of the object, the effects of the member function call can vary. The object itself provides the polymorphic behavior through its overriding ReportCompensation member function. The calling ReportCompensationForAll function does not care about the details of the report, only that it gets done. In some cases, the effect could be that no action is taken. To override the behavior of a base class virtual function to do nothing at all, you can provide an overriding function with an empty statement list. For example, there might be no requirement to report compensation to a JobShopper object. Some other part of your accounting system — accounts payable, perhaps — receives an invoice and pays the bill to the job shop.

Summary

This chapter taught you how to use inheritance for data abstraction, for designing an object-oriented class hierarchy, and for integrating your application into an application framework class library. Chapter 24 carries these concepts a step further by addressing multiple inheritance, a language feature that permits a class to be derived directly from more than one base class.

✦　　✦　　✦

Multiple Inheritance

This chapter discusses *multiple inheritance* (MI), an object-oriented design technique that's the subject of much debate and disagreement. Many object-oriented programmers believe that you should avoid using MI at all times because of inherent problems associated with the design model. This belief finds its way into new language design; Java and C#, for example, do not support MI for class design. Other programmers view MI as a tool to be used when appropriate. C++ supports MI, so we explain it in this chapter. We leave it to you to choose which side of the debate you prefer to join.

Multiple Base Classes

In multiple inheritance, a derived class has more than one base class. This technique enables you to define a new class that inherits the characteristics of several unrelated base classes. Figure 24-1 illustrates this principle with a simple property accounting system.

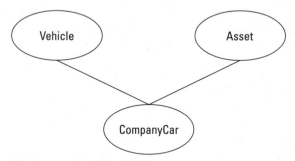

Figure 24-1: Multiple inheritance

Figure 24-1 illustrates the design model under which you apply MI. This example suggests a class design that supports an organization's vehicles and assets. The Vehicle class encapsulates the data and behavior that describe vehicles. Date acquired, useful life, and maintenance schedules might be included in the Vehicle class. Classes that support specific kinds of vehicles — trucks, airplanes, and cars — are derived from the Vehicle class. The Asset class encapsulates the data and behavior of the organization's assets, including date acquired and depreciation schedule data for accounting purposes. A class that derives from both base classes represents a company car — both a vehicle and an asset.

You might wonder why the design does not simply put the vehicle and asset data and behavior into the `CompanyCar` class. The reason is twofold. First, not all vehicles are assets. The company might use lease cars, for example, which are expensed rather than depreciated for tax purposes. Those vehicles are not assets in the accounting sense of the word. Second, not all assets are vehicles. The company has other depreciable assets — office furniture, copiers, computers, and so on.

For this discussion, assume that the `Vehicle` and `Asset` classes are defined as shown here:

```
class Vehicle {
public:
    Vehicle(int vehno);
    // ...
};

class Asset {
public:
    Asset(int assetno);
    // ...
};
```

You specify more than one base class when you define a derived class with multiple inheritance. The following code shows how you define the `CompanyCar` class given that the `Vehicle` and `Asset` class definitions are in scope:

```
class CompanyCar : public Vehicle, public Asset {
    // ...
};
```

As with single inheritance (Chapter 23), the colon operator after the class identifier specifies that base class specifications follow. The comma operator separates the base classes.

The constructor function declaration in a class derived from multiple bases specifies the arguments for the constructors of all the base classes, as shown here:

```
CompanyCar::CompanyCar(int vehicleno, int assetno)
                : Vehicle(vehicleno), Asset(assetno)
{
    // ...
}
```

Constructor Execution with Multiple Inheritance

When the program declares an object of a class that is derived from multiple bases, the constructors for the base classes are called first. The order of execution is the order in which the base classes are declared as bases to the derived class. In the case of the `CompanyCar` class, the constructor for the `Vehicle` class executes first, followed by the constructor for the `Asset` class. The constructor for the `CompanyCar` class executes last.

If the class definition includes an object of another class as a data member, that class's constructor executes after the constructors for the base classes and before the constructor for the class being defined. Consider the following example:

```
class CompanyCar : public Vehicle, public Asset
```

```
{
    Date NextOilChange;
    // ...
};
```

The order of constructor execution is `Vehicle`, `Asset`, `NextOilChange`, `Date` and `CompanyCar`.

Destructor Execution with Multiple Inheritance

When an object of a class is destroyed, the destructors execute in the reverse order of the constructors. So, for a CompanyCar object, the order of destructor execution is `CompanyCar`, `Date`, `NextOilChange`, `Asset`, and `Vehicle`.

Refining the Property System Design

We won't implement these classes in an exercise until you understand more about the requirements from a practical point of view. The relationships just discussed are an oversimplification of the real problem domain.

To follow these examples, it helps to know that an organization's physical property is divided into two categories for accounting purposes: depreciable assets and expensed items. To deduct from taxes the cost of a depreciable asset, which the organization owns, you distribute the asset's cost over several years. This distribution is called *depreciating the asset*. The number of years and the amount you write off each year are written into tax law and are a function of the kind of asset you depreciate. Computers, vehicles, and office buildings, for example, are depreciated according to distinct formulas. Expenses, on the other hand, are not depreciated; you write off the total cost of each expense in the year that you incur the expense. Expensed items include office supplies, leased items, and other tangible property that is not depreciated; these items are accounted for along with intangible expenses such as labor, professional fees, insurance, and rent. The IRS provides guidelines as to which kinds of property to expense and which kinds to depreciate. The accounting procedures for depreciable assets and expenses differ, so an automated accounting system must provide different behavior for objects of the two categories.

With that in mind, let's take a different view of the problem. Depreciable assets and expensed items, as property, have some things in common. Each category of property has a control number, name, date acquired, and cost. You can represent these shared attributes with a `Property` base class. Figure 24-2 shows these relationships in a single-inheritance class hierarchy.

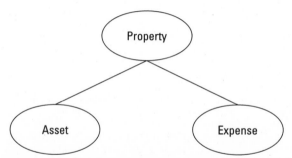

Figure 24-2: Asset and Expense derived from Property

Vehicles have common characteristics unrelated to whether they are assets or expenses, so the `Vehicle` class is not derived from anything; rather it serves as a base class for the various kinds of vehicle classes, which then must be further specialized according to their property category.

Given that we must account for vehicle and non-vehicle assets and expenses, the class hierarchy for our property system might look like Figure 24-3.

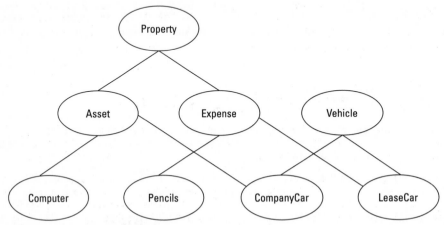

Figure 24-3: An MI class hierarchy

The design shown in Figure 24-3 uses MI in two places. The `CompanyCar` class derives from `Vehicle` and `Asset`, and the `LeaseCar` class derives from `Vehicle` and `Expense`. These models reflect the design objective that derived classes are specializations of their base classes.

Overriding Members with Multiple Inheritance

Suppose that the `Property`, `Vehicle`, and `LeaseCar` classes all have functions with the same name and argument list and that some of the base classes have data members with the same name, as shown here:

```
class Property {
public:
    int ctlno;
    virtual void Display();
    // ...
};

class Expense : public Property {
    // ...
};

class Vehicle {
public:
    int ctlno;
    virtual void Display();
    // ...
```

```
};

class LeaseCar : public Expense, public Vehicle {
public:
    virtual void Display();
    // ...
};
```

The `LeaseCar::Display` function overrides both base class `Display` functions just as it does in a single-inheritance hierarchy. The `LeaseCar::Display` function can call the two base class `Display` functions by using the scope resolution operator, as shown here:

```
void LeaseCar::Display()
{
    Expense::Display();
    Vehicle::Display();
    // ...
}
```

Notice that the `LeaseCar::Display` function calls `Expense::Display` even though the `Expense` class has no `Display` member function. The compiler searches up the hierarchy until it finds a matching member function. In this case, the compiler finds the `Display` member function in the `Property` class.

Ambiguities with Multiple Inheritance

The class hierarchy that Figure 24-3 represents appears to be solid with no ambiguities. One potential data member ambiguity exists in the code, however, so we will contrive another ambiguity, a member function, to demonstrate how to deal with and resolve ambiguities. The problems represented by the ambiguous behavior discussed next are among the reasons that many programmers disapprove of using MI in class design.

Ambiguous Member Functions

Suppose that the `LeaseCar` class had no `Display` function to override the virtual `Display` functions of the two base classes:

```
class LeaseCar : public Expense, public Vehicle {
public:
    // ...
};
```

This omission introduces a potential ambiguity into the design: A call to `LeaseCar::Display` does not work, because the compiler does not know which of the base class `Display` functions to call. The ambiguity is not a problem if you do not attempt to call the `Display` function directly through an object of type `LeaseCar` or a pointer or reference to one. But suppose that you want to call one of the `Display` functions. You can resolve the ambiguity by using the scope resolution operator to specify which class's `Display` function to call:

```
LeaseCar myChevy;
myChevy.Vehicle::Display();
myChevy.Expense::Display();
```

Ambiguous Data Members

The class design has another potential ambiguity not related to ambiguous member functions. Both base classes have a public integer data member named ctlno, and the derived class has no such data member. In this case, the member functions of the derived class must use the scope resolution operator to resolve which base class's data member to use:

```
void LeaseCar::Display() {
    std::cout << Vehicle::ctlno;
    // ...
}
```

In this example, the ambiguous members are public. The program that instantiates an object of the class cannot access such an ambiguous member directly through the object. The program must use the scope resolution operator and the base class name:

```
LeaseCar myChevy;
myChevy.Vehicle::ctlno = 123;
myChevy.Vehicle::Display();
```

Resolving Ambiguities in the Design

Generally, you try to resolve ambiguities in the class design. In this case, you would put member functions into the LeaseCar class that provide the necessary access to the base classes. The first version of LeaseCar in this discussion does just that for the Display member function. Because data members typically are private and are accessed through member functions, the class design probably would look like this:

```
class Property {
protected:
    int ctlno;

public:
    virtual void Display();
    // ...
};

class Expense : public Property {
    // ...
};

class Vehicle {
protected:
    int ctlno;
public:
    virtual void Display();
    // ...
};

class LeaseCar : public Expense, public Vehicle
{
public:
    virtual void Display();
    void SetVehicleCtlNo(int cno)
        { Vehicle::ctlno = cno; }
```

```
    void SetExpenseCtlNo(int cno)
        { Expense::ctlno = cno; }
    int GetVehicleCtlno() const
        { return Vehicle::ctlno; }
    int GetExpenseCtlno() const
        { return Expense::ctlno; }
    // ...
};
```

The ambiguous `ctlno` data members are protected, and that means that only member functions of the classes can access them. The `LeaseCar` public interface includes getter and setter member functions that resolve the ambiguity by providing specific access to the base class data members.

Unavoidable Ambiguities

Would you intentionally introduce such ambiguities into a class design? Would you design `Property` and `Vehicle` classes with member names that collide? Probably not, but suppose that you derive the `LeaseCar` class from two existing classes that other programs and other applications use extensively. Maybe you extend the application's design to support leased cars because the organization recently decided to lease cars. Maybe the `Vehicle` class comes from a completely different application, such as a maintenance management system. All these factors can contribute to circumstances under which class designs involve ambiguities beyond your control. You must be prepared to understand and deal with them.

Virtual Base Classes

With multiple inheritance, the potential exists for a derived class to have too many instances of one of the bases. Suppose that the property system class hierarchy is designed in a pure object-oriented environment and all classes derive directly or indirectly from a common base class. For this example, let's use a class called `DisplayObject`. Its purpose — contrived for this example — is to store and report on demand the date and time the object was created, perhaps as a debugging aid. Figure 24-4 updates the class hierarchy diagram accordingly.

The `DisplayObject` class is an abstract base class from which the `Property` and `Vehicle` classes derive. Because all the other classes in the hierarchy descend from one of these two, all the classes inherit the characteristics of the `DisplayObject` class.

This MI design has a built-in problem. `LeaseCar` and `CompanyCar` are derived multiply from classes that are derived themselves from `DisplayObject`. Consequently, `LeaseCar` and `CompanyCar` inherit `DisplayObject`'s data members twice. You do not want that to happen. Objects of those derived classes do not need two copies of `DisplayObject`'s data members. Furthermore, any attempt to address a `DisplayObject` data member for a `LeaseCar` or `CompanyCar` object results in a compile-time ambiguity that the program can resolve only by applying the scope resolution operator to associate the member with one of the intermediate base classes. The two copies of `DisplayObject`'s data members, no doubt, represent compromised integrity of the design when they are modified and accessed from different places in the hierarchy.

The problem just revealed is another of the reasons that many programmers disapprove of using MI in a design. C++ addresses the problem with the virtual base class. C++ enables you to specify in the definition of a derived class that a base class is virtual.

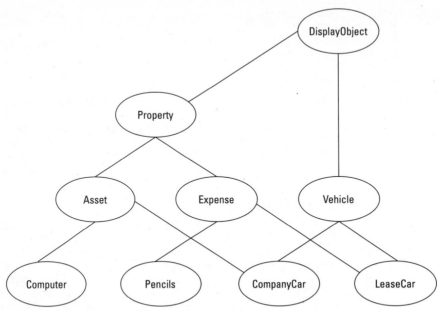

Figure 24-4: An object-oriented MI class hierarchy

All virtual occurrences of the base class throughout the class hierarchy share one actual occurrence of it when an object of a derived class is instantiated. That is, if a class has two or more virtual base classes that are the same, the compiler combines them so that the object only has one base class of that type. So, if as in Figure 24-4, Vehicle derives directly from DisplayObject and Property derives indirectly from DisplayObject, then CompanyCar and LeaseCar, each of which derives from both, each has two sets of all the instance data for DisplayObject. If you make the DisplayObject base class virtual, then CompanyCar and LeaseCar objects will each have only one set of members that belong to DisplayObject.

To specify a virtual base class in the derived class definition, use the following notation:

```
class Vehicle : public virtual DisplayObject {
    // ...
};
```

There are rules, however, about how a virtual base class can be specified itself. A class whose constructor has parameters cannot be a virtual base class. If this restriction did not exist, the compiler would not know which constructor argument list from which derived class to use. Another restriction: A pointer to a virtual base class cannot be cast to a class that is derived from it either directly or further down the class hierarchy. So you couldn't take a DisplayObject pointer and cast it to a CompanyCar in the above example (although casting from a CompanyCar to a DisplayObject would be allowed).

Implementing the Design

To demonstrate that all these theories work, let's implement and use the class hierarchy that we just designed. The classes are small, and we use header files and inline member functions to keep the example as simple as possible.

The DisplayObject Class

We begin with the class definition of the root base class, DisplayObject, shown in Listing 24-1 as the source-code file DisplayObject.h.

Listing 24-1: **DisplayObject.h**

```
#ifndef DISPLAYOBJECT_H
#define DISPLAYOBJECT_H
#include <iostream>
#include <ctime>
class DisplayObject
{
    std::time_t tm;
protected:
    DisplayObject()
        { tm = std::time(0); }
    virtual ~DisplayObject()
        { }
public:
    void ReportTime()
    {
        std::cout << "Obj constructed: "<< std::ctime(&tm);
    }
};
#endif
```

The DisplayObject class constructor uses the Standard C std::time function (Chapter 26) to record in a std::time_t data member the time the object was constructed. The constructor is protected, and that makes the class an abstract base class.

The Vehicle Class

Listing 24-2, Vehicle.h, implements the Vehicle class.

Listing 24-2: **Vehicle.h**

```
#ifndef VEHICLE_H
#define VEHICLE_H

#include <string>
#include "DisplayObject.h"

class Vehicle : public virtual DisplayObject {
    int year;
    std::string model;
public:
```

Continued

Listing 24-2 *(continued)*

```
    Vehicle(int yr, const std::string& md) :
            year(yr), model (md)
    { }
    virtual ~Vehicle()
    { }
    void MaintenanceSchedule()
    {
        std::cout << "Maintenance Schedule" << std::endl;
        std::cout << year << " " << model << std::endl;
    }
};
#endif
```

The Vehicle class derives from the virtual base DisplayObject class. Vehicle includes data members to store the vehicle model year and name. This class is typical of one that represents cars. In a real system, you probably would have a Vehicle base class with derived classes named Car, Truck, Forklift, Airplane, Tugboat, and so on.

The Property Class

Listing 24-3, Property.h, implements the Property class.

Listing 24-3: **Property.h**

```
#ifndef PROPERTY_H
#define PROPERTY_H

#include <string>
#include <Date.h>
#include <Money.h>
#include "DisplayObject.h"

class Property : public virtual DisplayObject {
    int idnbr;          // id number
    std::string name;   // property name
    Date dateacquired;  // date acquired
    Money cost;         // cost
protected:
    Property(int id) : idnbr(id)
    { }
    virtual ~Property()
    { }
public:
    int GetNbr() const
        { return idnbr; }
    void SetName(const std::string& nm)
        { name = nm; }
```

```
        const std::string& GetName()
            { return name; }
        void SetDate(Date dt)
            { dateacquired = dt; }
        const Date& GetDate() const
            { return dateacquired; }
        void SetCost(Money cst)
            { cost = cst; }
        Money GetCost() const
            { return cost; }
};
#endif
```

The `Property` class derives from the virtual base `DisplayObject` class. It includes data members that store the property's identification number, the name of the property item, the date it was acquired, and its cost. Its public interface includes getter and setter functions that provide access to the data members. The constructor and destructor are protected, so `Property` is an abstract base class.

The Asset and Expense Classes

Listing 24-4, Asset.h, implements the `Asset` class, and Listing 24-5, Expense.h, implements the `Expense` class.

Listing 24-4: **Asset.h**

```
#ifndef ASSET_H
#define ASSET_H

#include "Property.h"

class Asset : public Property {
public:
    enum type { straight, sliding };
private:
    int type;
public:
    Asset(int id, int ty) : Property(id), type(ty)
        { }
    virtual ~Asset()
        { }
    virtual void Schedule()
    {
        std::cout << "Schedule for "
        << GetName() << std::endl;
    }
};
#endif
```

Listing 24-5: Expense.h

```
#ifndef EXPENSE_H
#define EXPENSE_H

#include "Property.h"

class Expense : public Property  {
public:
    Expense(int id) : Property(id)
        { }
    virtual ~Expense()
        { }
};
#endif
```

The Asset and Expense classes are derived from the Property class. The principal difference is that the Asset class includes an asset type initializer and data member that presumably would be used in computing its depreciation schedule—a process that is simulated in this example by the Schedule member function. The Expense class has no type or Schedule members.

The Computer and Pencils Classes

We don't implement the Computer and Pencils classes as a part of this exercise even though they are included in the class hierarchy diagram in Figure 24-4. Their behavior is trivial in this context, and they do not employ MI, so they have nothing to add to this lesson that you did not learn in Chapter 23.

The CompanyCar and LeaseCar Classes

Now, we get to the part of the example that involves MI. Listing 24-6, Cars.h, implements the CompanyCar and LeaseCar classes.

Listing 24-6: Cars.h

```
#ifndef CARS_H
#define CARS_H

#include "Vehicle.h"
#include "Asset.h"
#include "Expense.h"

class CompanyCar : public Vehicle, public Asset {
public:
    CompanyCar(int id, int year, const std::string& model) :
            Vehicle(year, model), Asset(id, Asset::straight)
        { }
```

```
};

class LeaseCar : public Vehicle, public Expense {
public:
    LeaseCar(int id, int year, const std::string& model) :
                    Vehicle(year, model), Expense(id)
        {  }
};

#endif
```

The CompanyCar class is derived multiply from Vehicle and Asset. The LeaseCar class
is derived multiply from Vehicle and Expense. Remember that Asset and Expense
each are derived from Property and that Property and Vehicle each are derived from
DisplayObject. That is why DisplayObject must be a virtual base class in this hierarchy.

The Application

Program 24-1 represents the application that uses the class hierarchy we just formed.

Program 24-1: **Using multiple inheritance**

```
#include "cars.h"

int main()
{
    CompanyCar car1(1, 2002, "Chevy");
    LeaseCar   car2(2, 2003, "Ford");
    car1.MaintenanceSchedule();
    car1.ReportTime();
    car2.MaintenanceSchedule();
    car2.ReportTime();
    return 0;
}
```

Program 24-1 does not use all the features of the class hierarchy. It does not add costs,
names, or dates acquired, and it does not report all the data values. It calls the
Vehicle::MaintenanceSchedule function for both objects to identify the object. Then, it
calls the ReportTime member function of the root base class DisplayObject to demonstrate
the behavior of the virtual base class.

Some Practice

Please take a moment now to turn back to Chapter 23 and review Figure 23-5, where we discussed design choices for the SpecialCustomDate class. We chose a design approach that
did not involve MI, because you had not learned about MI yet. Given what you have learned in
this chapter, redesign the SpecialCustomDate class with MI, as diagrammed in Figure 24-5.

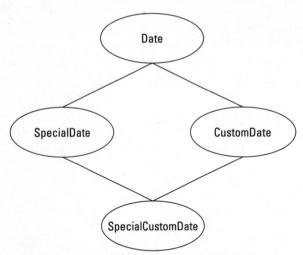

Figure 24-5: Revising the SpecialCustomDate class

Summary

Now that you understand the behavior of MI in a class hierarchy, you can decide for yourself whether the model suits your programming style. When base classes are not virtual, the potential ambiguities and duplicate data members can make for designs that are complex and difficult to comprehend. Like a chain saw, MI is a tool that can serve you well when you use it properly but can be troublesome if you misuse it.

✦   ✦   ✦

Class Templates

The C++ class template is a mechanism that enables you to describe a generic data type or process. Class templates typically are used to build general-purpose container classes, such as stacks, lists, and queues, in which the maintenance of the container is generic but the item in the container is specific. For example, you might want to construct a list of integers, another of strings, and another of Date class objects. These lists all behave in the same way except for the data they store within the lists. The Standard C++ library (Part III of this book) includes many such template container classes. In this chapter, you learn the programming techniques that make such classes possible. You also learn how the class template mechanism provides a higher level of abstraction that you cannot achieve by using normal C++ classes.

Class Template Basics

Suppose that your application needs a way to contain some objects. Perhaps your application might need to contain integers in some places and objects of a Date class in others. You could build two container classes, one for integers and another for dates. Later, if you needed to contain objects of other types, you could build additional container classes for those types. Or you could build a generic container class by using the C++ template mechanism. Then, to contain objects of any type, you simply instantiate an object of the template class using the type of the object you want to contain as an argument. It sounds complicated, but bear with us, and we'll take it one step at a time.

Why would a program need to contain objects? Perhaps you are writing a teacher's assistant. In some places, the program needs to work with lists of grades (integers). There are other portions of the program that work with test and holiday dates. Later, you might need to manage lists of names (strings). Instead of inventing new classes for each type of list, it would be better to write one list class that the compiler can adapt for each data type automatically. That's the idea behind templates. But don't worry too much for the moment about why a program might need to contain objects. The container requirement is contrived to demonstrate the template mechanism.

A class template can define a generic container class with an unspecified data type to appear in the list. Later, the program associates specific classes with the template.

The following example shows the format of such a class template specification:

```
template<class T>
class Container
{
    T item;
public:
    Container() { }
    void Store(const T& i);
};
```

The template specifies objects of type Container (this is just an identifier for the class; there is nothing special about the word "Container") with the unspecified data type T as a parameter. Users of the template specify the data type that the container holds. The first part of a class template definition and its member function definitions is the template specifier:

```
template<class T>
```

The T identifier represents the parameterized data type throughout the definition. The identifier can consist of any C++ data type, including intrinsic types and classes. The use of T for the primary template parameter is a convention. You can use any valid C++ identifier.

As with normal classes, you must provide the member functions for a class template. The Container example might have a Store member function. You define the function as shown here:

```
template<class T>
void Container<T>::Store(T& i)
{
    item = i;
}
```

These function definitions belong in the header file that contains the class definition. They must be visible to the program that declares objects of the class template. By themselves they do not generate any executable code. The compiler generates code for the member functions when the program instantiates objects of the class template.

You declare an object of a class template by specifying the name of the class and its parameterized data type:

```
Container<int> mycontainer;
```

This statement declares an object from the Container template with the int data type as the parameter.

Think of C++ templates as sophisticated macros. The compiler uses the object declaration to build the class definition and functions. Also, the compiler substitutes the template argument, which is int in the preceding example, for the template parameter, which is T in the Container template example.

Declaring Multiple Objects of a Class Template

You can declare more than one object of a class template in the same program. For example, given the preceding Container template, a program can declare two different linked lists:

```
Container<char*> strs;
Container<Date> dates;
```

These statements declare two `Container` objects. The first one is a list of character pointers. The second one is a list of `Date` objects. These two statements cause the compiler to generate two copies of the data members and member functions in the template. Each copy is customized to work with the type specified in the declaration.

This example has a copy of the code for character pointers and a second one for the `Date` class. Wherever the template definition uses `T`, the compiler substitutes `char*` for the first object and `Date` for the second. This means that the code in the template's member functions must work in the context of those types.

If you instantiate two `Container` objects with the same type parameter as shown here, the compiler builds two memory objects with the data members but only one copy of the member functions: This is the same way it works with objects of regular (nontemplate) classes.

```
Container<int> month;
Container<int> year;
```

Calling Class Template Member Functions

The using program calls a class template's member functions just as it calls member functions of other classes. For example, you can put things in the `Container` objects with these calls:

```
Date dt(6,24,93);      // A date
dates.Store(dt);       // Add the date to DateList
char* name = "Dolly";  // Pointer to char array
strs.Store(name);      // Add the pointer to str
int n = 123;           // An int
mycontainer.Store(n);  // Add the int to IntList
```

Declaring Multiple Parameters

A template can contain more than one data-type parameter, making it possible to build parameterized data types of considerable complexity. The parameters can consist of classes, which are identified by the `class` keyword. Other parameters can be specific data types, as shown here:

```
template <class T, class S, int b>
```

At least one parameter should be a class. When you declare an object of the class template, you must use actual types where they are called for. In the preceding example, you can use any type for the first two parameters, but the third type must be an `int`. Program 25-1 illustrates how a class template works.

Program 25-1: **A simple class template**

```
#include <iostream>

template<class T1, class T2>
class TwoThings {
```

Continued

```
        T1 thing1;
        T2 thing2;
public:
        TwoThings(T1 t1, T2 t2) : thing1(t1), thing2(t2)
            {  }
        template<class T3, class T4>
        friend std::ostream& operator<<(std::ostream& os,
                                const TwoThings<T3, T4>&);
};
template<class T1, class T2>
std::ostream& operator<<(std::ostream& os,
                    const TwoThings<T1, T2>& tt)
{
        std::cout << tt.thing1 << ' ' << tt.thing2;
        return os;
}
int main()
{
        int a = 123;
        double b = 456.789;
        TwoThings<int, double> my_twothings(a, b);
        std::cout << my_twothings << std::endl;
        return 0;
}
```

The template in Program 25-1 builds a parameterized type from two parameters. The class template stores and displays values. Meanwhile, the main function declares an object of the type with int and double as the parameters. Then it tells the object to display itself. Program 25-1 displays this output:

```
123 456.789
```

Program 25-1 calls attention to something you should consider when using a template. The template writes its parameterized types to a std::ostream object by overloading the << insertion operator. Therefore, any type you use with the template must be compatible with that operation—this means that if the type is another class, there must be an overloaded operator<< function that accepts std::ostream objects on the left and objects of the parameterized type on the right. Program 25-1 works because the std::ostream class can accept integers and doubles with the << operator. If a class template uses relational operators to compare objects of the parameterized type, the type must be able to use those operators, too. C++ intrinsic types work with such a template, but user-defined types do not work if their classes don't overload the relational operators.

Overloaded Operator Template Functions

Program 25-1 illustrates also how to overload operators in class templates when the overloaded operator function is a nonmember function and must be a friend of the class function. The overloaded operator<< function is a function template because its second parameter is of a template type. Consequently, its friend declaration in the `TwoThings` class template must be preceded by its declaration as a function template like this:

```
template<class T3, class T4>
friend std::ostream& operator<<(std::ostream& os,
                         const TwoThings<T3, T4>&);
```

Similarly, the definition of the overloaded function is declared as a function template like this:

```
template<class T1, class T2>
std::ostream& operator<<(std::ostream& os,
                     const TwoThings<T1, T2>& tt)
{
    // ...
}
```

Default Argument Values

When you specify a specific type for a class template parameter, you also can specify a default value for that argument. For example, Program 25-2 modifies the template in Program 25-1 to accept a third parameter that is an integer with a default value of zero. The template adds the value of the third parameter to the values of the first and second parameters. The `main` function in Program 25-2 creates two objects from the class template—one that supplies a value for the third parameter and one that accepts the default value.

Program 25-2: Default values for parameters of a specific type

```
#include <iostream>

// template with a default argument
template<class T1, class T2, int num = 0>
class TwoThings {
     T1 thing1;
     T2 thing2;
public:
     TwoThings(T1 t1, T2 t2)
     {
            thing1 = t1+num;
            thing2 = t2+num;
     }
     template<class T3, class T4, int n>
     friend std::ostream& operator<<(std::ostream& os,
                           const TwoThings<T3, T4, n>&);
};

template<class T1, class T2, int num>
std::ostream& operator<<(std::ostream& os,
                     const TwoThings<T1, T2, num>& tt)
{
     std::cout << tt.thing1 << ' ' << tt.thing2;
```

Continued

> **Program 25-2** *(continued)*

```
        return os;
}

int main()
{
        int a = 123;
        double b = 456.789;
        // instantiate with the default argument
        TwoThings<int, double> myfirst2things(a, b);
        // instantiate and override the default argument
        TwoThings<int, double, 100> mysecond2things(a, b);
        std::cout << myfirst2things << std::endl;
        std::cout << mysecond2things << std::endl;
        return 0;
}
```

Program 25-2 produces the following output:

```
123 456.789
223 556.789
```

A Bounded Array Class Template

C and C++ programmers often build bugs into their programs because the language does not test whether an array subscript is within the bounds of the array. The following code passes the compiler's error tests and executes with no runtime bounds-checking:

```
int main()
{
    int array[10];
    for (int i = 0; i <= 10; i++)
        array[i] = 123;

    return 0;
}
```

The problem with this code is that the subscript is allowed to go beyond the end of the array. The array has 10 elements. The subscript can go as high as 10, which references the 11th (nonexistent) element. However, the program writes an integer into the next integer position in memory beyond the array. The result depends on the program and the compiler. If you are lucky, the program aborts early in testing and you find the problem. If you are not so lucky, the 11th array element is in a harmless position and you do not encounter the bug until much later when it is more difficult to isolate.

Other languages have bounded arrays. The runtime systems of those languages do not enable you to address an array with a subscript that is beyond the array's boundaries. The cost is in runtime efficiency. C++'s Standard Template Library (Part IV) has an improved array mechanism called std::vector<> (Chapter 31), which is implemented as a class template. Rather than ask you to immerse yourself in the murky mire of STL source code, which is different depending on which STL implementation your compiler uses, we'll implement a simpler bounded array class template so you can learn how class templates are used.

The technique in the next example program depends on your understanding not only of templates but also of the Standard C assert macro (Chapter 26). Listing 25-1, named barray.h, is the class template for the bounded array.

Listing 25-1: **Class template header**

```
#ifndef BARRAY_H
#define BARRAY_H

#include <cassert>

template <class T, int b = 100>
class Array {
    T elem [b];
public:
    Array() { /* ... */ }
    T& operator[] (int sub)
    {
        assert(sub >= 0 && sub < b);
        return elem[sub];
    }
};

#endif
```

This simple template has one purpose: to check all subscripted references to array elements and to abort the program if a subscript is out of bounds. The template specifier has two parameter types, and the second parameter type must be an integer and have a default argument, as shown here:

```
template <class T, int b = 100>
```

The overloaded operator[] function in the Array class template grants read/write subscripted access to elements of the array. The assert macro validates the subscript's value. If the value is less than zero or greater than the array's dimension minus 1, the assert macro displays an error message on the stderr device and aborts the program. Program 25-3 demonstrates the use of the bounded-array template.

Program 25-3: **Using a bounded array template**

```
#include <iostream>

#include <Date.h>
#include "Barray.h"

int main()
```

Continued

Program 25-3 *(continued)*

```
{
    const int size = 5;
    // A bounded array of dates.
    Array<Date, size> dateArray;
    // Some dates.
    Date dt1(12,17,37);
    Date dt2(11,30,38);
    Date dt3(6,24,40);
    Date dt4(10,31,42);
    Date dt5(8,5,44);
    // Put the dates in the array.
    dateArray[0] = dt1;
    dateArray[1] = dt2;
    dateArray[2] = dt3;
    dateArray[3] = dt4;
    dateArray[4] = dt5;
    // Display the dates.
    for (int i = 0; i < size; i++)
        std::cout << dateArray[i] << std::endl;
    Date dt6(1,29,92);
    // Try to put another date in the array,
    // which may be outside the range of the array dimension
    dateArray[size] = dt6; // if so assertion aborts
    std::cout << dateArray[size] << std::endl;
    return 0;
}
```

Program 25-3 declares an `Array` object of `Date` objects with a subscript limit of 5. Then it declares five `Date` objects, which it puts into the array. After displaying all five objects, the program tries to put another `Date` object into the array's sixth position, which does not exist. The assert macro's test is false, and the program aborts. Program 25-3 displays this output:

```
12/17/37
11/30/38
6/24/40
10/31/42
8/5/44
```

```
Assertion failed: sub >= 0 && sub < b, file Barray.h, line 13
```

The format of the error message depends on the compiler's implementation of the Standard C `assert` macro, but the information displayed is the same.

You can see how the `Array` class's default argument works by changing the `dateArray` object's declaration so that it does not override the default like this:

```
Array<Date> dateArray;
```

With this modification, the program does not abort. The default argument of 100 array elements is more than enough for the program's requirements.

After your program is tested fully, you can remove the assertion code by inserting the following line before the include of <cassert>:

```
#define NDEBUG
```

When to Use Class Templates

Templates surround other types with generic management. The types that you provide as parameters have their own behavior. Class templates provide a way to contain objects of those classes in general-purpose containers. The details of their containment are unrelated to their purposes. A Date class has its own behavior, as does a string class. A class that encapsulates a person's name, address, and phone number also has its own behavior. Their participation in a queue, list, bag, linked list, balanced tree, or any other kind of container is unrelated to their purpose. It is natural and proper to use the features of a programming language to separate these two unrelated behaviors.

Before C++ supported templates, programmers used inheritance to associate data types with container classes. In other cases, they built cumbersome classes that used void pointers and casts to manage the containment of unrelated types in various containers. These approaches worked well enough, but were not always the best ones. As a rule, you should use inheritance when the derived class modifies the functional behavior of the base. When the relationship manages objects of the class without changing the class's behavior, use templates.

There are, however, other considerations. If the management algorithm entails a lot of code in the class definition and its member functions — and if you plan to instantiate many different parameterized versions of the template — think twice before you build the entire algorithm as a template. Remember that each distinct use of the template generates a new copy of the code. If the template manages a significant number of different types, the executable program can be big. Programmers often separate the common code that is not influenced by the parameterized type into a base class from which they derive the class template. The base class code is instantiated only once, irrespective of the number of discrete type instantiations in the derived class template.

Template Specialization

You can generate a specialized version of a complete class template or of selected member functions of a class template. Specialized templates and functions enable the programmer to define specific behavior related to a particular type. Using the specialized type, the specialized class or function overrides the class template or template member function when a template object is instantiated.

Class Template Specialization

Program 25-4 illustrates the specialization of a class template. It defines a class template named Set, which has a constructor and a member function named display. The display function sends to the standard cout object the data value of the type being parameterized. Not all types, however, overload the << operator in this way. The Date class, as an example, does not. Program 25-4, therefore, provides a specialized class for instantiation of the Set template when the type being parameterized type is a Date.

Program 25-4: Class template specialization

```
#include <iostream>
#include <date.h>

// generic Holder template
template <class T>
class Holder {
    T t;
public:
    Holder(T st) : t(st)
    { }
    void Report(std::ostream& os);
};
// Report member function for generic Holder
template <class T>
void Holder<T>::Report(std::ostream& os)
{
    os << "Reporting item: "<< t << std::endl;
}
// specialized Holder<Date> template
class Holder<Date>
{
    Date t;
public:
    Holder(Date st) : t(st)
    { }
    void Report(std::ostream& os);
};
// Specialized class template member function.
void Holder<Date>::Report(std::ostream& os)
{
    os << "Reporting Date: " << t << std::endl;
}
int main()
{
    Holder<int> intholder(123);
    intholder.Report(std::cout);
    Holder<Date> dateholder = Date(1,2,2003);
    dateholder.Report(std::cout);
    return 0;
}
```

Program 25-4 displays these values:

```
Reporting item: 123
Reporting Date: 1/2/2003
```

Template Member Function Specialization

The program in Program 25-4 specializes the complete Holder class template even though only the Report member function changes in the specialization. An alternative approach is to specialize only the member functions that change. Program 25-5 modifies the program to eliminate the specialized class template and to substitute only a specialization of the display member function.

> **Program 25-5: Template member function specialization**

```
#include <iostream>
#include <Date.h>

template <class T>
class Holder {
    T t;
public:
    Holder(T st) : t(st)
    { }
    void Report(std::ostream& os);
};

template <class T>
void Holder<T>::Report(std::ostream& os)
{
    os << "Reporting item: "<< t << std::endl;
}

// Specialized class template member function.
void Holder<Date>::Report(std::ostream& os)
{
    os << "Reporting Date: " << t << std::endl;
}

int main()
{
    Holder<int> intholder(123);
    Holder<Date> dt = Date(1,2,2003);
    intholder.Report(std::cout);
    dt.Report(std::cout);
    return 0;
}
```

The specialized member function cannot be inline in the original template. It must be defined outside the template definition.

Partial Template Specialization

You also can create a *partial specialization* of a class template, which is a class template that uses the same name as a primary template but whose parameters represent a special case. For example, suppose you have a class template that accepts two objects as parameters and reports those objects. Now suppose that you want the template to handle a special case in which the second parameter is a char value to be added as an integer to the object in the first parameter. Program 25-6 is a program that demonstrates how you can solve this problem by using class template partial specialization.

Program 25-6: **Template partial specialization**

```cpp
#include <iostream>

// generic class
template <class T1, class T2>
class TwoThings {
    T1 obj1;
    T2 obj2;
public:
    TwoThings(T1 o1, T2 o2) : obj1(o1), obj2(o2)
    {}
    void Report(std::ostream& os);
};

template <class T1, class T2>
void TwoThings<T1, T2>::Report(std::ostream& os)
{
    os << "TwoThings Report\n";
    os << "----------------\n";
    os << "Thing 1: " << obj1 << std::endl;
    os << "Thing 2: " << obj2 << std::endl;
    os << std::endl;
}

// partially specialized class
template <class T>
class TwoThings<T, unsigned int> {
    T obj1, obj2;
public:
    TwoThings(T o1, unsigned int c) : obj1(o1), obj2(o1)
    {
        obj2 += c;
    }
    void Report(std::ostream& os);
};

template <class T>
void TwoThings<T, unsigned int>::Report(std::ostream& os)
{
    os << "Partially Specialized TwoThings Report\n";
    os << "-------------------------------------\n";
    os << "Thing 1: " << obj1 << std::endl;
    os << "Thing 2: " << obj2 << std::endl;
    os << std::endl;
}
int main()
{
    TwoThings<int, int> mt1(10, 20);
    mt1.Report(std::cout);
    TwoThings<long int, unsigned int> mt2(72000, 456);
    mt2.Report(std::cout);
}
```

Program 25-6 produces the following output:

```
TwoThings Report
----------------
Thing 1: 10
Thing 2: 20

Partially Specialized TwoThings Report
--------------------------------------
Thing 1: 72000
Thing 2: 72456
```

Default Type Parameters

Just as you can supply default values for class template parameters of a specific type, you also can supply default types for a parameter. For example, the following line from a class template declaration declares a template that accepts two parameters, the second of which has a default type of int:

```
template<class T1, class T2 = int>
```

To create an object from this class template, you can write something like this:

```
TwoThings<int, double> myfirst2things(a, b);
```

In this case, the template's default type is ignored and the second parameter has a type of double. However, you also can create an object from the template like this:

```
TwoThings<int> mysecond2things(a, 365);
```

Notice that, in this case, the declaration supplies only the first of the two template parameter types as arguments. For that reason, the second value supplied for the object mt2 is treated as an integer, which is the default type for the second template parameter. Program 25-7 shows how class template default parameters work.

Program 25-7: **Default template parameters**

```
#include <iostream>

// template with a default type parameter
template<class T1, class T2 = int>
class TwoThings {
    T1 thing1;
    T2 thing2;
public:
    TwoThings(T1 t1, T2 t2)
        { thing1 = t1; thing2 = t2;}
    void display()
    {
        std::cout << thing1 << ' ' << thing2 << std::endl;
```

Continued

Program 25-7 *(continued)*

```
    }
};

int main()
{
    int a = 123;
    double b = 456.789;
     // instantiate specifying both type parameters
    TwoThings<int, double> myfirst2things(a, b);
     // instantiate with the default type parameter
    TwoThings<int> mysecond2things(a, 365);
    myfirst2things.display();
    mysecond2things.display();
    return 0;
}
```

Program 25-7 produces the following output:

```
123 456.789
123 365
```

The typename Keyword

Standard C++ added the typename keyword to the language to solve some semantic ambiguities introduced by the class template mechanism and to make template declarations more intuitive to the human reader.

typename to Remove Template Ambiguities

To understand the ambiguities that typename addresses, we first review two other topics discussed earlier, the typedef mechanism and public class members.

You recall that a program can define a new type name by using the typedef statement (Chapter 7) like this:

```
typedef int* pint;
```

Given this statement, the compiler treats the pint identifier as a type defined to be the same as pointer to int. The program can now declare and use variables of type pint like this:

```
pint ptr;
ptr = &num;
(*ptr)++;
```

You can declare a typedef within a class definition like this:

```
class Placecard {
public:
```

```
    typedef Placecard* iter;
    // ...
};
```

The `iter` `typedef` declaration, which is in this case a pointer to type `Placecard`, is not in global or file scope. It is declared as a public member of the `Placecard` class. The program declares objects of type `iter` by qualifying the type reference with the name of the class that declares it and the scope resolution operator like this:

```
Placecard::iter pi;
```

The `pi` variable just as it would a pointer to type `Placecard`. The compiler knows how to translate the `typedef` name `Placecard::iter` into a type that is, in this example, a pointer to `Placecard`.

Suppose you are building a class template that expects its parameterized class to declare a type named `iter` as `Placecard` does. That class template might look something like this:

```
template <class T>
class Table {
// ...
    void position()
    {
        T::iter * y;
        // ...
    }
};
```

The ambiguity is in the code just shown. It might not be immediately obvious, but the compiler does not know what to do with this statement:

```
        T::iter * y;
```

First, the compiler does not know what `T` is at this time because it has to parse the class template code without having seen an instantiation of the class template with a parameterized type. That is a normal circumstance with which the compiler routinely deals. Not knowing what `T` is, the compiler does not know what `T::iter` is, either. Because the compiler does not know that, it cannot tell whether the statement declares a pointer to type `T::iter` named `y` or is an expression that multiplies whatever `T::iter` is times whatever `y` turns out to be. If `y` is not defined in the current scope, the compiler reports an unidentified `y`. In either case, the compiler does not know what to do with the statement, which it assumes is an expression.

To eliminate this ambiguity, Standard C++ adds the `typename` keyword. The class template and its member functions qualify all references to types defined in the parameterized type with the `typename` keyword as shown here:

```
typename T::iter * y;
```

When the compiler sees the `typename` keyword, it knows that what follows is a type and parses the code assuming a type name will be filled in by the instantiation. The Standard requires the `typename` qualifier for all types referenced in a template that are defined in the templatized class even when no ambiguity would result from omitting it. Program 25-8 demonstrates the use of `typename` in this manner.

Program 25-8: **Using typename to disambiguate**

```cpp
#include <iostream>

static int y;

template <class T>
class Table {
    typename T::iter t;
public:
    explicit Table(const typename T::iter& ti) : t(ti)
    {  }
    void position()
    {
        typename T::iter * y;
        y = &t;
        std::cout << (*y)->p;
    }
};
class Placecard {
public:
    typedef Placecard* iter;
    int p;
    Placecard(int pos) : p(pos)
    {  }
}
;
int main()
{
    Placecard pc(3);
    Table<Placecard> settable(&pc);
    settable.position();
    return 0;
}
```

There are other kinds of expressions in class template member functions that would result in ambiguities that the `typename` keyword disambiguates. C++ syntax permits parentheses where you rarely see them, as shown here:

```cpp
int (num);
```

This statement declares an `int` variable named `num`. The parentheses are superfluous, but they are permitted. Suppose, however, that a class template member function contains this statement:

```cpp
T::iter(num);
```

The compiler does not know whether this statement declares a variable named `num` of type `T::iter`, or calls a function named `T::iter` passing an argument named `num`, quite possible if there is a nonlocal variable of that name in the current scope when the class template is instantiated. The `typename` keyword corrects this ambiguity the same way it does the earlier example:

```cpp
typename T::iter(num);
```

By requiring the `typename` qualifier for all references to types declared in the parameterized class, the Standard ensures that such ambiguities cannot occur.

typename versus class

Given the introduction of the `typename` keyword into Standard C++ by the committee, the members of the committee decided to use it in templates where `class` was used to declare the parameterized types. Previous implementations of templates prior to the publication of the Standard C++ specification use the `class` keyword just as this chapter and Chapter 12 used it in their template declarations like this:

```
template<class T1, class T2>
```

This syntax can be misleading because the actual parameterized types in an instantiation of a template can be classes, intrinsic types, pointers and references to things, and `typedefs`, many of which are not classes at all. Consequently, the Standard allows the `typename` keyword instead of `class` in template declaration statements like this:

```
template<typename T1, typename T2>
```

The Standard could not simply replace `class` with `typename` in this context because too much existing code would have been broken. The template mechanism was in place in many implementations long before `typename` became part of the Standard. Whether you use `class` or `typename` in this context is a matter of preference.

Program 25-9 demonstrates `typename` instead of `class` in the template declaration statements for function templates and class templates.

Program 25-9: **typename versus class**

```cpp
#include <iostream>

template<typename T>
T DoubleValue(T value)
{
    return value * 2;
}

template<typename T1, typename T2>
class TwoThings {
    T1 thing1;
    T2 thing2;
    T1 thing3;
public:
    TwoThings(T1 tt1, T2 tt2)
    {
        thing1 = tt1;
        thing2 = tt2;
        thing3 = DoubleValue<T1>(tt1);
    }
    void display()
    {
        std::cout << thing1 << ' ' << thing2 << ' '
            << thing3 << std::endl;
    }
};
```

Continued

Program 25-9 *(continued)*

```
int main()
{
    int a = 123;
    double b = 456.789;
    TwoThings<int, double> my2things(a, b);
    my2things.display();
    return 0;
}
```

Class Templates and Abstraction

This chapter shows how to use class templates to build generic container classes. Chances are you will never have to build a container class, because the Standard Template Library (Part IV) provides virtually all the containers a programmer should need. Class templates are, however, often used as a mechanism for abstraction rather than only for containers. For example, the Standard C++ Library's input/output classes use class templates to implement a common library that works with virtually all the world's character sets. The library classes and functions do not only contain the characters; they also specialize their behavior depending on the character sets themselves.

Rather than burden this book with abstruse examples of abstractions built with templates, I refer you to the software that you use to run all the other example programs. Quincy 2002 is an integrated development environment that integrates into its environment a programmer's editor. The editor includes two features common to contemporary text editors. One feature is the undo/redo capability. The other feature is the ability to select a marked block of text, display the selection, and so on, for clipboard and text move/copy/replace/delete operations. Both undo/redo and data selection are implemented in Quincy 2002 by using class templates. These templates are parameterized based on the document being processed.

I used those same templates to implement similar features in other applications that required undo/redo and data selection. One such application was a musical notation program. I was able to use the class templates without modifying them. The processes of undo/redo and data selection have much in common across applications even though the kinds of data that are edited are quite different. Class templates allow such processes to be built as abstractions that fit themselves to the programming problem based on the kinds of data provided as arguments to template parameters.

The source code for Quincy 2002 is on the CD-ROM that accompanies this book. You can study how I used these abstract template classes by first examining selection.h and undo.h, and then reading the source code that implements and instantiates objects of the class templates.

Summary

Templates provide support for generic objects and functions to C++. As you learned in Chapter 12, function templates add a great deal of flexibility to the C++ language. Class templates extend this flexibility to C++ classes. This chapter closes Part II. You now should understand the C++ language at an advanced level. Part III is about the Standard C++ Library, those functions and classes that extend the C++ language with support for strings, input/output, and other extensions.

✦   ✦   ✦

The Standard C++ Library

Part III explains the various components of the Standard C++ Library, including those parts that C++ inherits from Standard C. These are the chapters in Part III:

Standard C Library Functions

Standard C includes a full library of portable, general-purpose functions. Inasmuch as Standard C is included in Standard C++, the complete Standard C library is a part of Standard C++. You use a few of the Standard C functions in various listings of earlier chapters. However, this book does not attempt to teach the complete Standard C library. Instead, it discusses selected library functions that are the most useful to C++ programmers and that best teach the language and its software development environment. Some Standard C functions support features that Standard C++ supports in improved ways. Others are not supported by Standard C++ except through the inclusion in Standard C++ of the Standard C library.

This chapter is organized alphabetically by the header files where library functions are declared. To use a function from the standard library, you must include its header file in your program ahead of any references to the function. Some of the standard header files define global values, macros, functions, and data structures that support the library and your use of it. (A macro may look like a function; in some cases, a macro assigns an identifier to a value. You learned how to build your own macros by using the #define preprocessor directive discussed in Chapter 11.)

This chapter describes many of the functions and macros without including detailed examples. You already have used some of the functions, and many of them are similar enough that you need nothing more than a description. However, where examples provide better explanations, this chapter includes listings. You learn about the functions in the following header files:

- ✦ <cassert>
- ✦ <cctype>
- ✦ <cerrno>
- ✦ <cmath>
- ✦ <csetjmp>
- ✦ <cstdarg>
- ✦ <cstdio>
- ✦ <cstdlib>
- ✦ <cstring>
- ✦ <ctime>

In This Chapter

Assertions, character functions, and error values

Math functions

setjmp and std::longjmp

Variable argument lists

The printf family of functions

Numerical, memory allocation, system, and random-number functions

String functions

Time functions

The C++ Standard specifies that when you include these headers, all external identifiers that the headers declare and that are not macros shall be in the std namespace; you must qualify all references to those identifiers accordingly. (Chapter 36 discusses namespaces in detail.) If you include the traditional Standard C headers (<assert.h>, <ctype.h>, and so on), the identifiers shall be in both the std and the global namespaces, and no qualification is required.

Use of the Standard C headers (<*.h>) instead of the Standard C++ headers (<c*>) is deprecated by the C++ standard when used in C++ programs, which means the old headers are supported in the current version of the standard but may be eliminated in future versions.

<cassert>

The <cassert> header is used for debugging. It defines the assert macro, which enables you to add debugging code to your programs.

When you write programs, you often come across data objects or conditions that the program expects to be in a certain state. For example, a function might assume that a passed parameter is a valid, non-null pointer. To ensure that the program is in the required state, you could add a lot of extra code that checks data objects or conditions for the expected state. However, you don't want to have all that extra code in the final, shipped program. After all, once the program is written and tested, the status checks are no longer necessary.

By using the assert macro, you can have your validation code during testing and remove it for the production program without much fuss. The assert macro asserts that a condition is true. If it is not, the macro displays the condition, indicates where in the program the test failed, and aborts the program. The assert macro compiles to null code (code that is not executed and that uses no program memory space) when you compile with the NDEBUG macro defined.

When the program is completely checked out and none of the assertions fail, you disable the assert macro by defining the NDEBUG macro and doing a final compile. The NDEBUG macro changes all assert macro calls to null expressions. Program 26-1 demonstrates the use of the assert macro.

Program 26-1: **The assert macro**

```
// #define NDEBUG    // uncomment to disable the assert

#include <iostream>
#include <cassert>

void DisplayMsg(char* msg);

int main()
{
    char* cp = 0;
    DisplayMsg(cp);
    return 0;
}

void DisplayMsg(char *msg)
```

```
{
    assert(msg != 0);
    std::cout << msg;
}
```

Program 26-1 contains a bug, which the assert macro catches. The main function calls the DisplayMsg function with a null (zero-value) pointer argument. When you run this program, the assert macro displays something like the following message and aborts the program:

```
Assertion failed: msg != 0, file pr26001.cpp, line 17
```

The message tells you that the assert call on line 29 of the translation unit pr26001.cpp failed. It even displays the false condition that caused the abort.

When you use the assert macro, you assert that a condition must be true. It is a good practice to use assert in places where your program makes assumptions about values and other conditions.

You can correct the program by passing a valid pointer to DisplayMsg like this:

```
char* cp = "Hello";
```

Then, you can insert this line ahead of the #include statement that includes <cassert>:

```
#define NDEBUG
```

It is better to use this technique than to take out all the assert calls. Leave them in. They are there to help you debug the program when you make modifications to it later.

<cctype>

The functions in <cctype> convert char variables and test them for defined ranges. For example, you use the std::toupper function, which converts characters to uppercase, in Chapter 8. Note that in some C++ implementations the <cctype> functions are macros. Table 26-1 summarizes the <cctype> functions.

Table 26-1: <cctype> Functions and Macros

Function/Macro	Returns
int isdigit(int c);	true if c is a digit (0-9)
int isupper(int c);	true if c is an uppercase letter (A-Z)
int islower(int c);	true if c is a lowercase letter (a-z)
int isalpha(int c);	true if c is an alphabetic character (A-Z, a-z)
int isalnum(int c);	true if isalpha(c) or isdigit(c) is true
int isprint(int c);	true if c is a displayable ASCII character
int isspace(int c);	true if c is a white space character
int toupper(int c);	the uppercase equivalent of c
int tolower(int c);	the lowercase equivalent of c

Do not use expressions that could have side effects when you call macros in <cctype>. Depending on how the macro is implemented, the side effects can produce incorrect results. This statement, for example, has potential side effects:

```
a = std::toupper(*cp++);
```

A *side effect* is an action that changes the value of a variable in an argument or an argument that uses a function call in its expression. The auto-increment operator changes the variable argument. The expansion of the macro may cause the argument expression to be evaluated more than once. Then the variable would be incremented more than once, which is a hidden side effect of the macro. You learned about macro side effects in Chapter 11.

<cerrno>

The <cerrno> header defines a global modifiable variable named errno and global symbols named EDOM and ERANGE. The errno variable is implemented with a macro and, consequently, is not in the std:: namespace.

Some library functions set errno to indicate that an error occurred in a function call. The Standard C defines only two error values, EDOM, which means that an error occurred in an argument to a math function, and ERANGE, which means that a floating-point number is too big.

The value of errno is zero when the program starts. If a library function sets it to some value, it retains that value until something changes it. Therefore, if you want errno to reflect the status of a particular function call, set errno to zero before making the call. Otherwise, you might erroneously detect an error from an earlier to call to another function. Program 26-2 demonstrates the use of errno.

Program 26-2: **Using errno**

```
#include <iostream>
#include <cmath>
#include <cerrno>

int main()
{
    double f;
    do {
        errno = 0;
        std::cout << "Enter positive float (0 to quit) ";
        std::cin >> f;
        if (f != 0) {
            double sq = std::sqrt(f);
            if (errno == 0)
                std::cout << "Square root of " << f
                << " is " << sq << std::endl;
            else
                std::cout << "Invalid entry" << std::endl;
        }
    } while (f != 0);
    return 0;
}
```

Program 26-2 uses the `sqrt` function from <cmath>, discussed next, to compute the square root of a number entered by the user. If, for example, you enter a negative number or a number that's too big to be held in a double, the function sets `errno` to a nonzero value. The program displays the square root only if there is no error indicated by `errno`.

<cmath>

The <cmath> header declares the standard math functions. You just used one of them, `sqrt`, in Program 26-2. Table 26-2 lists the math functions.

Table 26-2: <cmath> Functions

Function	Returns
double acos(double x);	Arc cosine of x
double asin(double x);	Arc sine of x
double atan(double x);	Arc tangent of x
double atan2(double y,double x);	Arc tangent of y/x
double ceil(double x);	Smallest integer not < x
double cos(double x);	Cosine of x
double cosh(double x);	Hyperbolic cosine of x
double exp(double x);	Exponential value of x
double fabs(double x);	Absolute value of x
double floor(double x);	Largest integer not > x
double log(double x);	Natural logarithm of x
double log10(double x);	Base-10 logarithm of x
double pow(double x,double y);	x raised to the power of y
double sin(double x);	Sin of x
double sinh(double x);	Hyperbolic sine of x
double sqrt(double x);	Square root of x
double tan(double x);	Tangent of x
double tanh(double x);	Hyperbolic tangent of x

<csetjmp>

The <csetjmp> header defines a macro, `setjmp`, a function, `std::longjmp`, and a data type, the `std::jmp_buf` structure. You use the functions in <csetjmp> to jump from somewhere in the depths of the called functions to a defined place higher in the program. Why would you want to do that? One example is a program that validates records in an input stream. The program might detect an error in a function that is deep inside the function-calling stack. This is particularly true if the program uses recursive-descent parsing logic. The program needs to reject the data in question and return to the top of the program to read the next record.

One approach is to set an error variable and return. Every function tests the error variable upon return from every lower function call and returns to its caller rather than proceeding with the current input record. This approach is error-prone and uses additional code to manage and test the error variable.

Standard C provides setjmp and std::longjmp to serve this purpose. The setjmp macro records the program's operating state in a std::jmp_buf structure. A std::longjmp call from a lower function can reference the std::jmp_buf structure and cause an immediate jump to the place where the matching setjmp occurs.

Refer to the calculator program in Chapter 10. When it found an input error, it aborted the program. Program 26-3 modifies that program to use setjmp and std::longjmp to keep the program running after an error is found. The listings shown here include the modified main and error functions, the #include <csetjmp> statement, and the definition of the std::jmp_buf variable. The rest of the program is the same as Program 10-3.

Program 26-3: Using setjmp() and longjmp()

```cpp
#include <csetjmp>

// Error jmp_buf buffer
static std::jmp_buf errjb;

int main()
{
    int ans;
    do {
        // Mark the top of the parsing descent.
        if (setjmp(errjb) == 0) {
            // Initialize string subscript.
            pos = 0;
            // Read an expression.
            std::cout << "Enter expression (0 to quit):"
                << std::endl;
            std::cin >> expr;
            // Evaluate the expression.
            ans = addsubt();
            if (expr[pos] != '\0')
                error();
            if (ans != 0)
                std::cout << ans << std::endl;
        } else {
            // An error occurred.
            std::cout << "Try again" << std::endl;
            ans = 1;
        }
    } while (ans != 0);
```

```
        return 0;
}

// Syntax error.
void error()
{
    std::cout << '\r';
    // Position the error indicator.
    while (pos--)
        std::cout << ' ';
    std::cout << "^ syntax error" << std::endl << '\a';
    // Return to the top of the program.
    std::longjmp(errjb, 1);
}
```

The setjmp macro marks the program's position and context and stores that information in its std::jmp_buf argument. Then, setjmp returns zero. The std::longjmp function restores the program's context from its std::jmp_buf argument and jumps to the associated setjmp expression, causing the setjmp call to return the value of the std::longjmp call's second argument. If the program finds an error in the user's expression entry, it jumps to the main function at the point of the setjmp call, returning the value 1. The error function invocation that reports the error could be several levels down in the recursive-descent parsing algorithm, but the std::longjmp call restores the program's function depth context to the top of the program.

The setjmp macro and std::longjmp function are C idioms. They work well in the calculator program because the program declares no C++ class objects that require destruction between the top of the program and the detection of any error. Standard C++ offers a much-improved mechanism, C++ exception handling, which you learn about in Chapter 35. You should never use setjmp and std::longjmp in a new C++ program.

<cstdarg>

Recall from Chapter 3 that functions with variable parameter lists are declared with ellipses such as this:

```
void DoList(int, ...);
```

Several of the functions declared in <cstdio>, discussed next, use ellipses. It is the mechanism by which calls to the Standard C std::printf function, for example, can pass any kind and number of arguments after a formatting string. The ellipses tell the compiler not to check parameter types against the arguments or the number of arguments in calls to the function. In this example, the compiler ensures that the first argument is an integer; it ignores the rest of the arguments.

You write a function with a variable argument list by including <cstdarg> and using a typedef as well as the three macros defined there. The typedef defines the std::va_list type. The macros are va_start, va_arg and va_end. Program 26-4 shows how to use these macros.

Program 26-4: **Variable argument lists**

```cpp
#include <iostream>
#include <cstdarg>

// A function with a variable argument list.
void Presidents(int n, ...)
{
    std::va_list ap;
    va_start(ap, n);
    while (n--) {
        char* nm = va_arg(ap, char*);    // char* argument.
        int year = va_arg(ap, int);      // int argument.
        std::cout << year << ' ' << nm << std::endl;
    }
    va_end(ap);
}

int main()
{
    Presidents(6, "Carter", 1976, "Reagan",  1980,
                  "Bush",   1988, "Clinton", 1992,
                  "Bush",   2000, "??", 2004);
    return 0;
}
```

A function with a variable argument list usually needs at least one fixed argument that it can use to determine the number and types of the other arguments. Program 26-4 takes an integer first argument as a count of the pairs of arguments that follow. Then, it assumes that the list has that many argument pairs of one character pointer and one integer.

The macros use the std::va_list variable as a point of reference. Scanning of the variable argument list starts with the va_start macro call, which takes the names of the std::va_list variable and of the function's fixed argument as macro arguments. The va_start macro establishes the starting point for the variable argument list scan and stores that information in the std::va_list variable. If the function has more than one fixed argument, the va_start macro uses the identifier of the last one immediately before the ellipsis.

The function uses the va_arg macro to extract arguments from the variable argument list. The va_arg macro's arguments are the va_list variable and the type of the next expected argument. Observe that the two va_arg macro calls have int and char* as their second argument. The function knows what types of arguments to expect. It also knows the number of arguments, thanks to the value stored in the first, fixed argument.

The va_end macro takes the std::va_list variable as an argument. In many C++ language implementations this macro does nothing. You should always include it, though, so that your programs are portable to other compilers and other computers.

Because the compiler does no type checking of arguments represented by the ellipsis in function declarations, you can pass anything at all to a variable argument list function. Naturally, if you pass something other than what the function expects, you get unpredictable results.

<cstdio>

Most of what is in <cstdio> is of little use to a C++ programmer who is writing a C++ program from scratch. Virtually everything defined in this header is superceded by improved Standard C++ Library classes, which Chapter 27 addresses. You should, however, understand <cstdio> to a certain degree, because you are likely to run into it when you maintain legacy programs or read documentation aimed at C programmers.

The <cstdio> header declares functions and global symbols that support standard input and output for programs written in the C language. These functions and symbols are also available to C++ programs. The functions in <cstdio> support C programming idioms for console and file input/output. C++ provides improved techniques implemented in the <iostream> class library, which Chapter 27 discusses. But because C++ programmers often encounter C idioms in legacy programs, this chapter briefly explains the C conventions for processing standard input and output.

Global Symbols

<cstdio> declares several global symbols with `typedef` statements and `#define` macros. Most of these symbols have to do with Standard C functions for working with disk files. Curiously, <cstdio> also defines `NULL`, a global symbol that represents a null pointer. `NULL` has nothing to do with standard input/output except that some of the functions return a null pointer. <cstdio> defines it by tradition. C++ programmers by tradition do not use the `NULL` global symbol, preferring to address zero pointer values with the constant integer value, 0.

Console Functions

C programmers typically use the `std::scanf` and `std::printf` functions to process the standard input output devices. They also use functions such as `std::sprintf`, `std::fprintf`, `std::sscanf`, and `std::fscanf` to format strings and disk file records. Those functions use formatting conventions exactly like `std::scanf` and `std::printf`, which we will discuss here. Programmers often call these functions the "`printf` and `scanf` family of functions."

To use the `printf` and `scanf` family of functions you must include <cstdio>. This header provides the function prototypes.

Formatting Strings and Tokens

The `std::printf` function and its family accept a formatting string and a variable number of arguments. The formatting string is written to the output after the function replaces certain formatting tokens with the contents of the arguments. The function depends on you to specify formatting tokens that match the types of the arguments exactly. The tokens appear in the string in the order that their corresponding arguments appear in the `std::printf` call's argument list.

Every std::printf formatting token begins with a percent sign and ends with a character that specifies the type of the argument. There can be other parts of the token that qualify the display of the argument. Here is what can follow the % and precede the type specification character.

First, you can have zero or more of the flags shown in Table 26-3 in any sequence.

Table 26-3: Flags in *printf* Formatting Token

Flag	Meaning
-	Left-justify the converted argument.
+	Precede signed numeric argument with + or -. (If you omit this flag, - precedes a negative argument, but a positive argument displays unsigned.)
space	Prefix a space to an unsigned numeric argument.
#	Alternate form (see Table 26-4).
0	Display numeric types with leading zeros.

The # alternate form flag in Table 26-3 affects the conversion of the argument depending on its type. Table 26-4 summarizes those effects and lists the type specifier characters.

Table 26-4: Alternate Forms in *printf* Formatting Token

Type Specifier	Alternate Forms
o	1st digit will be 0
x,X	add 0x or 0X prefix
e,E,f	add decimal point
g,G	add decimal point, do not remove trailing zeros

Following the flags (if there are any) and following the % (if there are no flags) can be a minimum width specifier encoded as a number or as an asterisk (*) flag. If the * flag is in the formatting token, it represents an argument in the argument list that is the next argument's minimum width. The target argument displays in at least as many characters, padded by spaces on the left or right, depending on whether the - flag in Table 26-3 has been applied.

Next you can specify the *precision*, which is a period followed by a number which specifies one of the following:

✦ The minimum number of digits that display for the d, i, o, u, x, and X type specifiers

✦ The number of digits to the right of the decimal point for e, E, and f type specifiers

✦ The maximum number of significant digits for the g and G type specifiers

✦ The maximum characters to be displayed from a string

The precision can also be a period followed by an asterisk (*) flag, which corresponds to an argument in the argument list. Using the asterisk flags for the width and precision allows you to dynamically control the display of numbers by using width and precision variables in the argument list.

Next you may have one of the characters shown in Table 26-5.

Table 26-5: Format Qualifiers

Format Qualifier	Meaning
h	integer is short
l	integer is long
L	double is long

Finally, in a std::printf format token, you have the type specification character as shown in Table 26-6.

Table 26-6: Type Specifier Characters

Type Specifier	Meaning
d,i	Signed *int*
o,u,x,X	*unsigned* octal, decimal, hexadecimal *int*
f	*double* as -ddd.ddd
e,E	*double* as -d.ddde-dd
g,G	*double* as -ddd.ddd with trailing zeros removed
c	*int* is converted to *unsigned char*
s	String
p	Pointer to *void*
n	Pointer to *int* to receive the number of characters written
%	The % is displayed

The std::printf Function

What you have just learned is a lot to assimilate in one lesson. Don't try to memorize it. Use it as a reference when you want to know how use std::printf, std::sprintf, or std::fprintf to format output. Program 26-5 illustrates a std::printf call with several formatting tokens in the string.

Program 26-5: std::printf

```
#include <cstdio>

int main()
{
    int cnt = 123;
    long amt = 67300;
    unsigned int qty = 40500;
    float tot = 1.765;
    std::printf("\ncnt: %+05d"  // zero-filled, 5-wide int
                "\namt: %ld"    // long int
                "\nqty: %5u"    // 5-wide unsigned int
                "\ntot: %.4f",  // double with 4 decimals
                cnt, amt, qty, tot);
    return 0;
}
```

Program 26-5 displays these messages on the screen.

```
cnt: +0123
amt: 67300
qty: 40500
tot: 1.7650
```

The std::scanf Function

The std::scanf function also uses a formatting string. As with std::printf, the string specifies with formatting tokens the types of the input data values. The matching arguments are *addresses* of the variables that receive the data.

The % may be followed by a decimal maximum field width. Then there may be h, l, or L, with the same meanings as in Table 26-5 above. Next comes the type specifier character, which is taken from Table 26-6. You can put as much white space as you want between format tokens.

Program 26-6 demonstrates the std::scanf function.

Program 26-6: std::scanf

```
#include <cstdio>

int main()
{
    int a;
    char b;
    unsigned c;
    std::printf("Enter int char unsigned: ");
```

```
    std::scanf("%d %c %u", &a, &b, &c);
    std::printf("%d %c %u", a, b, c);
    return 0;
}
```

Program 26.6 displays the three values that you enter in response to the prompt. Enter the values with spaces between them and with no other punctuation as shown in this example:

```
Enter int char unsigned: 123 X 40000
```

The std::sprintf and std::sscanf Functions

These functions work just like `std::printf` and `std::scanf` except that they write into and read from memory instead of from devices. For example, here is how you would format a string into an array by using `std::printf`:

```
char msg[50];
int num = 123;
std::sprintf(msg, "The number is %d", num);
```

The first argument to std::sprintf is the address of the memory location into which the formatted string is to be written. Following these statements, the character array named `msg` would contain the string value, `"The number is 123"`.

The std::fprintf and std::fscanf Functions

These functions are the file input/output equivalents of `std::printf` and `std::scanf`. Their first argument is a pointer to a `FILE` structure. The `FILE` structure is defined in <cstdio>. Standard C file input/output uses the structure. This book does not teach Standard C file input/output. Nonetheless, when you see `std::fprintf` and `std::fscanf` in a program, you will know from this brief mention what they are.

The std::getchar and std::putchar Functions

The `std::getchar` and `std::putchar` functions read and write single characters from and to the standard input and output devices Program 26-7 uses `std::getchar` and `std::putchar` to copy the input to the output, changing all uppercase characters to lowercase.

Program 26-7: **std::getchar and std::putchar**

```
#include <cstdio>
#include <cctype>

int main()
{
    int c;
    while ((c = std::getchar()) != EOF)
        std::putchar(std::tolower(c));
    return 0;
}
```

The `while` statement in Program 26-7 tests to see if the incoming character was the `EOF` value, an identifier defined in <cstdio> that represents the end-of-file character. When you run the program it waits for you to type characters. Even though the program is written to display each character when it is read, the buffered nature of standard input causes the program to wait until you press the Enter key before the program actually reads any keys. You enter EOF and terminate the program by typing Ctrl+Z with DOS and Windows and Ctrl+D with Linux and Unix.

<cstdlib>

<cstdlib> declares a number of standard library functions and macros in four categories: numerical functions, memory allocation functions, system functions, and random number generation.

Numerical Functions

Table 26-7 lists the <cstdlib> numerical functions and describes what each one returns.

Table 26-7: <cstdlib> Numerical Functions

Function	Returns
`int abs(int i);`	The absolute value of i
`int atoi(const char *s);`	The integer value of the string
`long atol(const char *s);`	The long integer value of the string
`float atof(const char *s);`	The float value of the string

Memory Allocation Functions

C and C++ programs have a store of memory available for dynamic allocations. That store is called the heap. A program can allocate memory from the heap and return the memory to the heap when the program is finished using it. Dynamic memory allocation allows a program to use memory buffers only when they are needed. In that way, a program can operate in a system with an amount of available memory smaller than the program's total requirement. Table 26-8 lists the Standard C memory allocation functions.

Table 26-8: <cstdlib> Memory Allocation Functions

Function	Returns
`void *calloc(int sz, int n);`	Address of buffer or 0
`void *malloc(int sz);`	Address of buffer or 0
`void free(void *buf);`	Nothing

The std::malloc function allocates a block of memory from the heap. The parameter specifies the size of the block as a character count. The std::free function returns a previously allocated memory block to the heap. The std::calloc function is similar to std::malloc with these exceptions: First, instead of specifying a character count for the memory allocation, you specify an item size and the number of items. Second, std::calloc initializes the allocated memory to zeros, whereas std::malloc does not.

If there is not enough memory available for either std::malloc or std::calloc, they return a zero-value null pointer. Programs should always check for a zero return and handle the error when that happens. Ignoring a zero return could crash the system when the program tries to assign values through a zero-value pointer.

C++ programmers seldom use the C memory allocation functions. C++ employs a much improved memory allocation mechanism implemented with the new and delete operators, which Chapter 8 explains. The only time you might want to use the C functions is when you overload operators new and delete for some reason. Chapter 20 explained overloading new and delete for classes.

System Functions

<cstdlib> declares the following functions related to the operation of the program:

```
void abort();
void exit(int n);
int system(const char *cmd);
```

The std::abort and std::exit functions terminate the program. You use the std::abort function for an abnormal termination. Standard C does not define a value for std::abort to return, except to specify that it returns an implementation-dependent, unsuccessful termination value. The std::exit function is for normal termination. It closes all open stream files and returns to the operating system whatever value you pass as an argument. It does not, however, unwind the stack or destroy any automatic class instances that are still in scope.

The std::system function executes an operating system command. In MS-DOS or Windows, the commands executed are the same as commands you type on the DOS command line. The following code shows the std::system function executing the DOS dir command to view a list of document files:

```
#include <cstdlib>
int main()
{
    std::system("dir *.doc");
    return 0;
}
```

Random Number Generation Functions

Programs 4-8, 4-9, 4-11, and 4-12 from Chapter 4 use the std::rand and std::srand functions, whose prototypes are shown here:

```
int rand();
void srand(unsigned int seed);
```

Recall that Program 4-8 is a guessing game. The program computes a random number, and you guess what it is. The problem with that program is that the random number generator is predictable. It always starts with the same number and progresses through an identical sequence of numbers—a process that isn't random at all. Program 26-8 adds one line of code to the program to make the first random number less predictable. The new line calls std::srand to seed the generator with a value based on the current date and time. The std::time function, described later in this chapter, returns an integer value based on the system clock. That value is the seed used by the program in Program 26-8.

Program 26-8: Seeding the random number generator

```
#include <iostream>
#include <cstdlib>
#include <ctime>

int main()
{
    std::srand(time(0));
    char ans;
    // Loop until the user is done.
    do {
        // Choose a secret number.
        int fav = std::rand() % 32;
        // Loop until the user guesses the secret number.
        int num;
        do {
            std::cout << "Guess my secret number (0 - 32) ";
            std::cin >> num;
            // Report the status of the guess.
            std::cout << (num < fav ? "Too low"  :
                          num > fav ? "Too high" :
                          "Right") << std::endl;
        } while (num != fav);
        std::cout << "Go again? (y/n) ";
        std::cin >> ans;
    } while (ans == 'y');
    return 0;
}
```

<cstring>

The <cstring> header declares functions that work with null-terminated character arrays. There are two comparison functions, two copy functions, two concatenation functions, one function to return the length of a string, and one function to fill an area of memory with a specified character value. Here are the function prototypes:

```
int strcmp(const char *s1, const char *s2);
int strncmp(const char *s1, const char *s2, int n);
char *strcpy(char *s1, const char *s2);
char *strncpy(char *s1, const char *s2, int n);
int strlen(const char *s);
```

```
char *strcat(char *s1, const char *s2);
char *strncat(char *s1, const char *s2, int n);
char *memset(void *s, int c, int n)
```

Program 26-9 demonstrates the std::strcmp, std::strcpy, and std::strlen functions.

Program 26-9: **std::strcmp, std::strcpy, and std::strlen**

```cpp
#include <iostream>
#include <cstring>

int main()
{
    int len;
    char msg[] = "Wrong.";
    std::cout << "Password? ";
    char pwd[40];
    std::cin >> pwd;
    // Find the string length.
    len = std::strlen(pwd);
    // Compare the string with a string constant.
    if (std::strcmp(pwd, "boobah") == 0)
        // Copy constant to message.
        std::strcpy(msg, "OK.");
    std::cout << msg << " You typed " << len << " characters";
    return 0;
}
```

When you run the program in Program 26-9, enter a password in response to the prompt. Do not enter more than 39 characters or you will overwrite the 40-character pwd array. The program passes the address of the password to std::strlen to get the length of the input string, which counts all the characters except the null terminator. The std::strcmp function compares two strings; it returns zero if the two strings are equal, less than zero if the first string is less than the second string, and greater than zero if the first string is greater than the second string. Comparisons proceed from the first character in both strings and iterate forward until null terminators are found or different character values are found in the strings. If one string is shorter than the other and if all the character values are equal up to the end of the shorter string, the longer string compares greater than the shorter one.

If the password you type is equal to the constant password, the program calls std::strcpy to copy the string literal "OK." to the msg string. This operation overwrites the msg string's initialized value of "Wrong." The msg array has six elements based on the default dimension declared by its initializer. The std::strcpy function copies only four characters: 'O', 'K', '.', and a null terminator. The resulting msg array looks like this in memory:

'O', 'K', '.', '\0', 'g', '.', '\0'

If the second string argument to std::strcpy is longer than five characters plus a null terminator, the results are unpredictable. Usually, the program fails immediately—or soon afterward—because it overwrites whatever coincidentally follows the receiving array in memory.

The std::strcat function appends the string value of its second argument to the string in its first argument. There must be enough space past the significant characters (up to the null terminator) of the first argument for the second argument and its null terminator. For example:

```
char s[13] = "Hello";  // must be at least 13 chars
std::strcat(s, ", Dolly");  // s1 = "Hello, Dolly"
```

The std::strncmp, std::strncpy, and std::strncat functions are similar to the preceding three functions except that each has a third integer parameter that specifies the maximum number of characters to compare, copy, or concatenate. If the second argument to std::strncpy has fewer characters to copy than the integer argument specifies, the function pads the remaining characters in the first argument with zeros.

Finally, the std::memset function is not just a string function. It fills a block of memory with a specified character. The function's first argument is a void pointer to the block of memory. By using a void pointer in its declaration, the function allows you to use it to initialize any buffer. The second argument specifies the fill character value. The third argument specifies the length of the memory area to be filled. The std::memset function is used most often to zero-fill uninitialized memory for data aggregates such as structures and arrays.

<ctime>

<ctime> declares several functions, a structure, and a data type related to time and date. The structure is shown here:

```
struct tm
{
    int    tm_sec;    // seconds (0-61)
    int    tm_min;    // minutes (0-59)
    int    tm_hour;   // hours   (0-23)
    int    tm_mday;   // day of the month (1-31)
    int    tm_mon;    // months since January (0-11)
    int    tm_year;   // years since 1900
    int    tm_wday;   // days since Sunday (0-6)
    int    tm_yday;   // days since January 1 (0-365)
    int    tm_isdst;  // Daylight Saving Time flag
};
```

The data type is typedef long time_t, which is an integer value that represents the date and time (as the number of clock ticks) since a defined time in the past. Applications programs do not deal with the actual integral representation of the time. Instead, they accept and pass std::time_t values between functions declared in <ctime>. Here are the prototypes for the <ctime> functions:

```
char *asctime(const struct tm *tim);
char *ctime(const time_t *t);
double difftime(time_t t1, time_t t2);
struct tm *gmtime(const time_t *t);
struct tm *localtime(const time_t *t);
time_t mktime(struct tm *tim);
time_t time(time_t *t);
```

The std::asctime function converts the std::tm structure pointed to by its argument into a null-terminated string suitable for displaying. The string appears in this format:

"Mon Apr 25 14:41:22 1994\n"

The std::ctime function converts the std::time_t variable pointed to by its argument into a string in the same format as the string produced by std::asctime.

The std::difftime function returns a double value representing the difference in seconds between its two std::time_t arguments by subtracting the second argument from the first.

The std::gmtime function converts the std::time_t variable pointed to by its argument into a struct tm variable representing Coordinated Universal Time, also called Greenwich mean time. The std::gmtime function returns a pointer to the structure that it builds.

The std::localtime function converts the std::time_t variable pointed to by its argument into a std::tm variable representing local time. It returns a pointer to the structure that it builds.

The std::mktime function converts the std::tm variable pointed to by its argument into a std::time_t variable, which std::mktime returns.

The std::time function returns the current time as a std::time_t variable. If its argument is not NULL, the function also copies the std::time_t variable into the variable pointed to by the argument.

Program 26-10 uses some of the functions described here to display the current Greenwich mean time.

Program 26-10: **<ctime> functions**

```
#include <iostream>
#include <ctime>

int main()
{
    std::time_t now = std::time(0);
    std::cout << std::asctime(std::gmtime(&now));
    return 0;
}
```

Summary

This chapter discussed some of the Standard C library functions. When you begin using other compiler systems, you may find that they offer not only the Standard C library, but also many other compiler-dependent function libraries. You also can use third-party libraries that support various functional applications and operating environments. There are libraries for graphics, user interfaces, database management, communications, mathematics, direct access to DOS functions, and many more. Chapter 27 is an introduction to the Standard C++ Library, which supports standard, general-purpose classes and functions for string and input/output processing.

✦   ✦   ✦

Introduction to the Standard C++ Library

This chapter is an introduction to the Standard C++ Library. You learned about the Standard C Library in Chapter 26; the C++ Library consists of classes that implement strings, character streams, data files, containers, and so on. This chapter addresses string, IOStream, and complex number classes.

String and IOStream Templates

In the Standard C++ Library, string and IOStream classes are implemented as template classes that can be specialized for different character types. Standard C++ includes two sets of specialized classes for the two standard character types — `char` and `wchar_t` — but the mechanism provides for the specialization of any character set of any character width.

To prevent these discussions from being overly complex, this book deals with the string and IOStream classes as they are specialized for the `char` data type. We do not try to use the complex parameterized template notation to identify class and member names. This method of presentation is intentional; it presents the concept of character-based classes from the perspective of a programmer who uses them for typical input/output operations in routine work. Once you are familiar with them from this perspective, you might want to study in more detail how the classes are implemented and how you can specialize them. Appendix E, the Bibliography at the back of this book, lists works that you can study to learn more about C++.

The std::string Class

The Standard C++ `std::string` class implements character string processing. To use it, you include the `<string>` header. You used the `std::string` class in the example programs of previous chapters, but those programs mostly instantiate, initialize, display, and read data into string objects. The `std::string` class does much more than that.

Constructing Strings

Using the std::string class, you construct std::string objects in several ways. You can construct an empty std::string object by instantiating an object of type std::string with no initializers like this:

```
std::string s1;
```

You can construct a std::string object from a null-terminated character array like this:

```
std::string s2("this is a string");
```

You can construct a std::string object from another string object like this:

```
std::string s3(s2);
```

Assigning Strings

Once you construct std::string objects, you can assign the value of one std::string object to another std::string object. You also can assign a null-terminated character array or a single character variable to a std::string object. The following demonstrates how you can assign a single character to a std::string object:

```
s1 = s3;
s2 = "a different string";
s3 = 'X';
```

Concatenating Strings

You can build new strings by *concatenating* existing strings with other strings, null-terminated character arrays, and single characters. The concatenation operators, shown here, are + and +=:

```
std::string s4("hello ");   // "hello "
std::string s5("dolly");    // "dolly"
std::string s6 = s4 + s5;   // "hello dolly"
s4 += s2;                   // "hello dolly"
s4 += '!';                  // "hello dolly!"
```

Subscripting Strings

You can use the overloaded subscript operator[] function or the at(int) member function to retrieve a single character from a string and to change a character in a string:

```
char ch1 = s4[1];     // ch1 = 'e'
char ch2 = s4.at(2);  // ch2 = 'l'
s4[5] = ',';          // "hello,dolly!"
s4.at(0) = 'J';       // "Jello,dolly!"
```

Comparing Strings

The std::string class supports all the relational operators. You can compare strings with one another and with null-terminated character arrays:

```
std::string s7("hello ");
if ("goodbye" < s7)
    // ...
if (s7 == "hello")
    // ...
```

Substrings

The `std::string::substr` function extracts a substring from a string and returns the extracted substring. The first argument is the zero-based position in the original string of the substring. The second argument is the number of characters in the substring:

```
std::string s8("my goodbye");
std::cout << s8.substr(3, 4);   // displays "good"
```

The `std::string` class has no right and left member functions similar to the string data types of other languages. You can simulate the left operation by using the `substr` function with a zero value position argument:

```
std::string s9("hello dolly");
std::string s10(s6.substr(0, 5));   // s7 = "hello"
```

You can use the `std::string` class's `length` function, which returns the length of the string, to simulate the right operation:

```
std::string s11(s6.substr(s6.length()-5,5)); // s11 = "dolly"
```

Searching Strings

The `std::string` class includes several overloaded `find` and `rfind` functions. The `find` functions search forward, starting at the beginning of the `std::string` object. The `rfind` functions search in reverse, starting at the end of the `std::string` object. You can search for a matching substring, a single character, and a null-terminated character array. The functions return a zero-based index into the string, or -1 if the search argument is not found. Following are some examples. The comments on each line specify the value returned by the function.

```
std::string s12("hello dolly");
int ndx;
ndx = s12.find("dolly");   // 6
ndx = s12.find("ll");      // 2
ndx = s12.rfind("ll");     // 8
ndx = s12.find('o');       // 4
ndx = s12.rfind('o');      // 7
ndx = s12.find("bye");     // -1
```

String Operations

Table 27-1 lists a few of the more commonly used `std::string` member functions.

Table 27-1: std::string Member Functions

Member function	Purpose
void clear()	Clears the string object to a zero-length value
bool empty()	Returns a bool that indicates whether the string is empty (true) or has string data (false)
size_t length()	Returns the number of characters in the string object
const char* c_str()	Returns a const pointer to the string data buffer character array

Program 27-1 demonstrates several of the properties of the std::string class.

Program 27-1: std::string

```
#include <iostream>
#include <string>

int main()
{
    // string construction
    std::string s1;                       // empty string
    std::string s2("this is a string");   // from char*
    std::string s3(s2);                   // from a string

    // string assignments
    s1 = s3;
    s2 = "a different string";
    s3 = 'X';

    std::string s4("hello ");  // "hello "
    std::string s5("dolly");   // "dolly"

    // concatenation
    std::string s6 = s4 + s5;  // "hello dolly"
    s4 += s2;                  // "hello dolly"
    s4 += '!';                 // "hello dolly!"

    // subscript operator
    char ch1 = s4[1];      // ch1 = 'e'
    char ch2 = s4.at(2);   // ch2 = 'l'
    s4[5] = ',';           // "hello,dolly!"
    s4.at(0) = 'J';        // "Jello,dolly!"

    // string comparison
    std::string s7("hello ");
    if ("goodbye" < s7)
```

```
    ;// ...
if (s7 == "hello")
    ;// ...

// substrings
std::string s8("my goodbye");
std::cout << s8.substr(3, 4);    // displays "good"

std::string s9("hello dolly");
std::string s10(s6.substr(0, 5));              // "hello"
std::string s11(s6.substr(s6.length()-5,5)); // "dolly"

// string searching
std::string s12("hello dolly");
int ndx;
ndx = s12.find("dolly");   // 6
ndx = s12.find("ll");      // 2
ndx = s12.rfind("ll");     // 8
ndx = s12.find('o');       // 4
ndx = s12.rfind('o');      // 7
ndx = s12.find("bye");     // -1

return 0;
}
```

Program 27-1 has no output. You can add to the program to display the string objects on standard output as they are constructed and modified. Write a string object on standard output like this:

```
std::string str("farewell");
std::cout << str;
```

IOStream Classes

The example programs in this book use the C++ IOStream class library to read input from standard input and display the results on standard output. But the IOStream class library has capabilities beyond those that read and write the system console and many more features than this chapter describes. See Chapters 28 and 29 for more details.

C++ doesn't have input/output operators as intrinsic or integral parts of the language. Just as C relies on function libraries to extend the language with input/output functions, C++ depends on class libraries for its input and output. C++ manages file, printer and console input/output as streams of characters. C++ programs manage data values as data types, such as integers, structures, classes, and so on. The std::IOStream library provides the interface between the data types a program views and the character streams of the input/output system.

Disk file input/ouput is supported by *file* IOStreams. File IOStream classes derive from the IOStream classes and inherit all their characteristics. But disk files have requirements of their own that character devices such as standard input and output do not. Files have file names and locations in the file system. A program can append data to an existing file. A program can seek to a specified position in a file and read from that position or write over existing data. Chapter 29 discusses file input/output streams.

The Standard C++ Library supports *string* IOStream classes, too, wherein memory buffers behave as if they were IOStream device objects. Chapter 28 discusses string IOStreams.

The std::ios Class

C++ streams are implemented as class templates. The `std::cout` and `std::cin` objects are global instances of those classes, which are derived from a base class named `std::ios`. The objects are declared by the system. There is not much to know about `std::ios`, although later you will use constant values and functions that `std::ios` defines — including `std::ios::beg` and `std::ios::setprecision(int)`. A program deals mostly with objects of types derived from the `std::ios` class, such as `std::istream` and `std::ostream`. Many of the member functions that you use for objects of these classes are defined in the `ios` class and inherited by the lower classes in the hierarchy.

The std::ostream Class

A class named `std::ostream`, which derives from `std::ios`, manages stream output. You learned to display a message onscreen with a statement such as the following one:

```
std::cout << "Hello, Dolly";
```

The `std::cout` object is an external object of the `ostream` class. The library declares the `cout` object, and an `extern` declaration of `cout` appears in `<iostream>` so that it is available to any program that includes `<iostream>`.

Besides `std::cout`, `<iostream>` declares other objects as instances of the `std::ostream` class. The `std::cerr` object writes to the standard error device and uses unbuffered output. The `std::clog` object also writes to the standard error device, but it uses buffered output.

A program writes to an `std::ostream` object by using the overloaded << insertion operator. The examples in this book use this feature extensively. The `std::ostream` class provides sufficient overloaded << insertion operators to support writing most standard C++ data types to the output stream. You learned how to overload the << insertion operator to write your own classes to a `std::ostream` object in Chapter 22.

The std::istream Class

The `std::istream` class manages stream input in the same way that the `std::ostream` class manages output. The `std::istream` class is declared in `<iostream>`. The `std::cin` object reads data values from the standard input device.

The `std::istream` class uses the overloaded >> extraction operator to read input. There are sufficient overloaded extraction >> operators to support reading the standard C++ data types; a user-defined class can overload the >> extraction operator to read data from a `std::istream` object. You learned how to do that in Chapter 22.

Buffered Output

The data characters written to an std::ostream object usually are buffered. For example, the std::ostream class collects output bytes into a buffer and does not write them to the actual device associated with the object until one of the following events occurs:

✦ The buffer is filled

✦ The program tells the object to flush its buffer

✦ The program terminates

✦ The program reads data from the std::cin object when the output object is std::cout

The std::cout and std::clog objects use buffered output. The std::cerr object does not.

Sometimes you need to tell the program to flush a stream's buffer. A program tells an std::ostream object to flush itself by sending it the std::flush manipulator, as the following code fragment demonstrates:

```
std::cout << "Please wait..." << std::flush;
```

Output Member Functions

The std::ostream class includes two member functions that write characters and memory blocks to output stream objects as alternatives to the overloaded << insertion operator. The put member function writes a single character to the output stream. The following two statements are the same:

```
std::cout.put('A');
std::cout << 'A';
```

Program 27-2 demonstrates using the put member function with the std::cout object, as compared with using the insertion operator.

Program 27-2: **The std::ostream::put member function**

```
#include <iostream>

int main()
{
    std::cout.put('H');
    std::cout.put('i');
    std::cout.put('!');
    std::cout << std::endl;
    std::cout << 'H';
    std::cout << 'i';
    std::cout << '!';
    return 0;
}
```

Program 27-2 displays the following output:

```
Hi!
Hi!
```

The `std::ostream::write` member function writes any block of memory to the stream in binary format. Because `write` does not terminate when it sees a null terminator character, it is useful for writing the binary representations of data structures to stream files (Chapter 29). Here's an example of using the `write` function:

```
std::cout.write(data, sizeof data);
```

Program 27-3 illustrates the `write` function with the `std::cout` object.

Program 27-3: **The std::ostream::write function**

```
#include <iostream>

int main()
{
    static struct {
        char msg[23];
        int alarm;
        int eol;
    }
    data = { "It's Howdy Doody time!", '\a', '\n' };
    std::cout.write(reinterpret_cast<char*>(&data),
                    sizeof data);
    return 0;
}
```

In Program 27-3, the program writes the message, sounds the alarm, and advances to the next line.

Note the cast to `char*` before the address of the structure object. The `write` function accepts `char` pointers and `unsigned char` pointers only. The address of the structure must be cast to one of these. Chapter 37 explains the C++ typecasting mechanism. The statement in Program 27-3 could have been written this way using the C-style typecasting mechanism (Chapter 7):

```
std::cout.write((char*)&data, sizeof data);
```

Input Member Functions

The `>>` extraction operator has a limitation that programs sometimes need to overcome: it bypasses white space. If you type characters on a line that the extraction operator reads, only the nonspace characters come into the receiving character variable. The spaces are skipped. Similarly, if the program uses the extraction operator to read a string of words, the input stops when it finds a space character. The next word is read into the next use of the extraction operation on the `std::istream` object, and all spaces between the words are lost.

You cannot override this behavior by resetting the `std::ios::skipws` flag. That flag does not affect the `>>` extraction operator. You must use the `std::istream` class's `get` and `getline` member functions to read input characters that include white space.

The `get` member function works just like the `>>` extraction operator, except that white space characters are included in the input.

Program 27-4 demonstrates the difference between using the `get` member function and using the extraction operator to acquire input from a stream.

Program 27-4: **The std::istream::get member function**

```
#include <iostream>

int main()
{
    char line[25], ch = 0, *cp;
    std::cout << " Type a line terminated by 'x'"
              << std::endl << '>';
    cp = line;
    while (ch != 'x') {
        std::cin >> ch;
        *cp++ = ch;
    }
    *cp = '\0';
    std::cout << ' ' << line;
    std::cout << "\n Type another one" << std::endl << '>';
    cp = line;
    ch = 0;
    while (ch != 'x') {
        std::cin.get(ch);
        *cp++ = ch;
    }
    *cp = '\0';
    std::cout << ' ' << line;
    return 0;
}
```

Program 27-4 reads two strings from the keyboard one character at a time. The first input uses the extraction operator, and the second one uses the `get` member function. If you type `now is the timex` for both entries, the screen looks like the following display:

```
Type a line terminated by 'x'
now is the timex            (entered by you)
nowisthetimex               (echoed by the program)
Type another one
now is the timex            (entered by you)
now is the timex            (echoed by the program)
```

The extraction operator skips over the white space, and the get function does not. The program needs the "x" terminator because it needs to know when to stop reading. Because the std::cin object reads buffered input text, the program does not start to see characters until you type the Enter key.

A variation of the get function enables a program to specify a buffer address and the maximum number of characters to read. Program 27-5 shows how the get function can specify a buffer address and length, instead of a character variable, to receive the input.

Program 27-5: **Using std::istream::get with a buffer address and length**

```
#include <iostream>

int main()
{
    char line[25];
    std::cout << " Type a line terminated by carriage return"
              << std::endl << '>';
    std::cin.get(line, 25);
    std::cout << ' ' << line;
    return 0;
}
```

Program 27-5 reads into the structure whatever you type and echoes it to standard output.

The length value minus 1 is the maximum number of characters the program reads into the buffer. You can type more than that number, but the excess characters are discarded.

The getline function works similarly, retrieving a line of text from the stream, as shown here:

```
std::cin.getline(line, 25, 'q');
```

This function call allows a third argument that specifies the terminating character for input. If you do not include that argument, its default value is the newline character.

Program 27-6 uses the getline function with a third argument to specify a terminating character for the input stream.

Program 27-6: **The std::istream::getline member function**

```
#include <iostream>

int main()
{
    char line[25];
    std::cout << " Type a line terminated by 'q'"
              << std::endl << '>';
    std::cin.getline(line, 25, 'q');
    std::cout << ' ' << line;
    return 0;
}
```

If you type "after this I quit," the console displays the following:

```
Type a line terminated by 'q'
after this I quit          (entered by you)
after this I              (echoed by the program)
```

The `std::istream` class's `read` member function is the input equivalent of the `write` function. It reads the binary representation of the input data into the buffer without bypassing white space. It usually is used with file input/output. An example follows:

```
std::cin.read(&data, sizeof data);
```

Program 27-7 shows an example of using the `read` function to read a string of characters from standard input into a structure.

Program 27-7: **The std::istream::read function**

```
#include <iostream>

int main()
{
    struct {
        char msg[23];
    } data;
    std::cin.read(reinterpret_cast<char*>(&data),
        sizeof(data));
    std::cout << data.msg;
    return 0;
}
```

Program 27-7 reads into the structure whatever you type and echoes it to standard output.

The std::complex Class

The `std::complex` class is a template class that the library specializes for three intrinsic types: `float`, `double`, and `long double`. The class overloads the arithmetic and relational operators, the insertion and extraction operators, and the assignment operator. The overloaded arithmetic and relational operator functions can accept a single argument of any parameterized complex type or any combination of two arguments of the parameterized type and a parameterized complex type. The overloaded arithmetic operator functions can accept a complex argument and either another complex argument or a scalar variable of the type upon which the complex number is parameterized.

The `std::complex` class includes functions to extract values from a complex object, as shown in Table 27-2.

Table 27-2: Complex Class Value Functions

Function	Description
abs(x)	Returns the magnitude of x
arg(x)	Returns the phase angle of x
conj(x)	Returns the complex conjugate of x
imag	Returns the imaginary part
norm(x)	Returns the squared magnitude of x
polar(rho, theta)	Returns the complex value corresponding to a complex number whose magnitude is rho and whose phase angle is theta
real	Returns the real part

Program 27-8 is an example of using the complex class.

Program 27-8: The std::complex class

```
#include <iostream>
#include <complex>

int main()
{
    std::complex<float> cn(5, 3);
    cn += std::complex<float>(1, 2);
    std::cout << cn;
    return 0;
}
```

Summary

The Standard C++ Library brings together a host of useful classes that enable C++ programmers to spend more time programming and less time reinventing the wheel. The library includes string-handling classes, stream classes, container classes, exception classes, and more. Chapter 28 is about C++ IOStream and string IOStream formatting; Chapter 29 is about C++ file handling using file IOStreams.

✦   ✦   ✦

Formatting IOStreams and the stringstream Classes

IOStream

This chapter explains how a program sends formatted output to IOStream class objects. Most of the example programs in this book display unformatted data. The C++ IOStream class library includes techniques for managing the format of displayed data. This chapter also explains the std::stringstream classes, which are a specialization of IOStreams that use memory buffers that emulate stream devices and files.

Formatted Output

Chapter 2 discusses the std::dec, std::oct, and std::hex manipulators. These manipulators set the default format for input and output. If you insert the std::hex manipulator into the output stream, for example, the object translates the internal data representation of the object into the correct display. Program 2-18 in Chapter 2 demonstrates this behavior. Several other manipulators and functions control the format of stream output.

You may need to display numbers in various formats. The C++ IOStream libraries support such formatting with the library's manipulators, flags, and member functions. To start, take a look at Program 28-1 — a simple program that displays an unformatted column of floating-point numbers.

Program 28-1: **Displaying columns of numbers**

```
#include <iostream>

int main()
{
    static double values[] =
        { 1.23, 35.36, 653.7, 4358.224 };
    for (int i = 0; i < 4; i++)
        std::cout << values[i] << std::endl;
    return 0;
}
```

Program 28-1 displays the following output:

```
1.23
35.36
653.7
4358.22
```

If you need to display a simple list of numbers, the `std::cout` object works just fine. However, programming is not often that simple. Next, let's use the formatting features of the Standard C++ IOStream system to modify output in various ways.

Manipulators, Flags, and Member Functions

The IOStream library supports several different ways to manage string displays. This discussion explains the manipulators, flags, and member functions that enable a program to display data in almost any way. These manipulators and member functions set flags within the output object. The `std::ios` class keeps the current settings of the flags and values in data members. You can change many of the flags and values with either a manipulator or a member function. Following is a discussion of the more commonly used manipulators and member functions

The ios::width Function

By default, objects of type `std::ostream` write data without padding. The programs in this book typically insert the space character between data values in the output stream to separate them. However, you may want displays lined up in columns, which means that the program must write the display of each element with a fixed width.

A program can specify a default width for all of the following display elements by calling the `std::ostream::width` member function. The `width` member function takes a width parameter. The width value remains in effect for the `std::ostream` object until you change it. An example of a call to the `width` member function follows:

```
std::cout.width(10);
```

Program 28-2 demonstrates how the width member function manages output width. By calling the width function with an argument of 10, the program specifies that the displays are to appear in a column at least ten characters wide.

Program 28-2: The width member function

```
#include <iostream>

int main()
{
    static double values[] = { 1.23, 35.36, 653.7, 4358.224 };
    std::cout.setf(std::ios::fixed, std::ios::scientific);
    for (int i = 0; i < 4; i++) {
        std::cout.width(10);
        std::cout << values[i] << std::endl;
    }
    return 0;
}
```

Program 28-2 displays the following output:

```
      1.23
     35.36
     653.7
   4358.22
```

The std::setw Manipulator

Sometimes, a report needs to use different widths for different data elements. It is more convenient to insert width commands into the stream than to interrupt the output to call formatting functions. The std::setw manipulator provides this capability. An example of using the std::setw manipulator follows:

```
std::cout << std::setw(6)  << names[i]
          << std::setw(10) << values[i]
          << std::endl;
```

Suppose you have data that you need to display in table form. Program 28-3 demonstrates the use of the std::setw manipulator to display columns that have data elements with different width requirements.

Program 28-3: The std::setw manipulator

```
#include <iostream>
#include <iomanip>
```

Continued

Program 28-3 *(continued)*

```
int main()
{
    static double values[] =
        { 1.23, 35.36, 653.7, 4358.224 };
    static char *names[] =
        {"Zoot", "Jimmy", "Al", "Stan"};

    std::cout.setf(std::ios::fixed, std::ios::scientific);
    for (int i = 0; i < 4; i++)
        std::cout << std::setw(6)  << names[i]
                  << std::setw(10) << values[i]
                  << std::endl;
    return 0;
}
```

You must include `<iomanip>` to use the `std::setw` manipulator.

Program 28-3 displays the following output:

```
  Zoot      1.23
 Jimmy     35.36
    Al     653.7
  Stan   4358.22
```

Note that using `std::setw` or `width` does not cause truncation. If the displayed data value is wider than the current width value, then the entire data value is displayed and does affect the format of the displays that follow on the same line. You should be aware of this behavior when you design well-formatted displays that use the `std::setw` manipulator or the `width` member function. Note also that the default width you specify applies only to the object for which you specify it — in this case, the `std::cout` object — and not for other objects of the class.

To return the object to the default width, call the `width` member function or use the `std::setw` manipulator with zero arguments.

The std::ios::fill Function

You can use the `fill` member function to set the value of the padding character for output that has a width other than the default width. An example follows:

```
std::cout.width(10);
std::cout.fill('*');
std::cout << values[i] << std::endl;
```

You might need to pad a data display with a specific character. Checks, for example, are often printed with asterisks preceding the dollar value, filling all space to the left of the number. Program 28-4 demonstrates this usage by padding a column of numbers with asterisks.

Program 28-4: **The fill() member function**

```
#include <iostream>

int main()
{
    static double values[] =
        { 1.23, 35.36, 653.7, 4358.224 };

    for (int i = 0; i < 4; i++) {
        std::cout.width(10);
        std::cout.fill('*');
        std::cout << values[i] << std::endl;
    }
    return 0;
}
```

Program 28-4 displays the following output:

```
******1.23
*****35.36
*****653.7
***4358.22
```

Output Justification

Often, you may want values to be right-justified rather than left-justified. An example is numbers that represent money. You can set justification using the std::setiosflags and std::resetiosflags manipulators, as shown here:

```
std::cout << std::setiosflags(std::ios::left)
          << std::setw(6) << names[i]
          << std::resetiosflags(std::ios::left)
          << std::setiosflags(std::ios::right)
          << std::setw(10) << values[i]
          << std::endl;
```

Suppose that you want the names displayed in Program 28-3 to be left-justified and the number to remain right-justified. You can use the std::setiosflags manipulator to specify left- or right-justified output. Program 28-5 demonstrates std::setiosflags by modifying the display from Program 28-3 so that the names are left-justified.

Program 28-5: **The setiosflags and resetiosflags manipulators**

```
#include <iostream>
#include <iomanip>
```

Continued

Program 28-5 *(continued)*

```
int main()
{
    static double values[] =
        { 1.23, 35.36, 653.7, 4358.224 };
    static char* names[] =
        {"Zoot", "Jimmy", "Al", "Stan"};
    for (int i = 0; i < 4; i++)
        std::cout << std::setiosflags(std::ios::left)
                  << std::setw(6)  << names[i]
                  << std::resetiosflags(std::ios::left)
                  << std::setiosflags(std::ios::right)
                  << std::setw(10) << values[i]
                  << std::resetiosflags(std::ios::right)
                  << std::endl;
    return 0;
}
```

Program 28-5 displays the following output:

```
Zoot       1.23
Jimmy     35.36
Al        653.7
Stan    4358.22
```

The program sets the left-justification flag by using the `std::setiosflags` manipulator with an argument of `std::ios::left`. This argument is a constant value defined in the `ios` class, so its reference must include the `std::ios::` prefix. The `std::resetiosflags` manipulator turns off the left-justification flag so the program can return to the default right-justification mode. Similarly, the `std::resetiosflags` manipulator turns off right justification so the program can return to left justification. If you do not reset a justification, you cannot set the opposite justification.

The setprecision Manipulator

The `std::setprecision` manipulator tells the object to use a specified number of digits of precision. An example follows:

```
std::cout << std::setiosflags(std::ios::left)
          << std::setw(6)
          << names[i]
          << std::resetiosflags(std::ios::left)
          << std::setiosflags(std::ios::right)
          << std::setw(10)
          << std::setprecision(1)
          << values[i]
          << std::endl;
```

Suppose that you want the floating-point numbers in Program 28-5 to display with only one decimal place. The `std::setprecision` manipulator tells the object to use a specified number of digits of precision. Program 28-6 adds the `std::setprecision` manipulator to the program.

> Program 28-6: **The setprecision manipulator**

```
#include <iostream>
#include <iomanip>

main()
{
    static double values[] = { 1.23, 35.36, 653.7, 4358.224 };
    static char* names[] = {"Zoot", "Jimmy", "Al", "Stan"};

    for (int i = 0; i < 4; i++)
        std::cout << std::setiosflags(std::ios::left)
                  << std::setw(6)
                  << names[i]
                  << std::resetiosflags(std::ios::left)
                  << std::setiosflags(std::ios::right)
                  << std::setw(10)
                  << std::setprecision(1)
                  << values[i]
                  << std::resetiosflags(std::ios::right)
                  << std::endl;
    return 0;
}
```

Program 28-6 displays the following output:

```
Zoot         1
Jimmy     4e+001
Al        7e+002
Stan      4e+003
```

Scientific and Fixed Notation

Floating-point numbers are displayed in either *fixed-point* or *scientific (exponential)* notation. Observe that Program 28-5 uses fixed-point notation and Program 28-6 employs scientific notation. The std::setprecision manipulator overrides the default fixed-point notation mode, as shown in the following example:

```
std::cout << std::setiosflags(std::ios::left)
          << std::setw(6)
          << names[i]
          << std::resetiosflags(std::ios::left)
          << std::setiosflags(std::ios::fixed)
          << std::setiosflags(std::ios::right)
          << std::setw(10)
          << std::setprecision(1)
          << values[i]
          << std::endl;
```

Scientific notation may not be what the program needs to display. The two flags
std::ios::fixed and std::ios::scientific control the notation with which floating-point numbers display. A program can set and clear these flags with the std::setiosflags
and std::resetiosflags manipulators. Program 28-7 uses the std::setiosflags manipulator to set the std::ios::fixed flag so that the program does not display results in scientific notation.

Program 28-7: Setting the ios::fixed flag

```
#include <iostream>
#include <iomanip>

int main()
{
    static double values[] = { 1.23, 35.36, 653.7, 4358.224 };
    static char* names[] = {"Zoot", "Jimmy", "Al", "Stan"};
    for (int i = 0; i < 4; i++)
        std::cout << std::setiosflags(std::ios::left)
                  << std::setw(6)
                  << names[i]
                  << std::resetiosflags(std::ios::left)
                  << std::setiosflags(std::ios::fixed)
                  << std::setiosflags(std::ios::right)
                  << std::setw(10)
                  << std::setprecision(1)
                  << values[i]
                  << std::resetiosflags(std::ios::right)
                  << std::endl;
    return 0;
}
```

Program 28-7 displays the following output:

```
Zoot       1.2
Jimmy     35.4
Al       653.7
Stan    4358.2
```

The default notation in some C++ implementations is std::ios::scientific. In others, the
default is std::ios::fixed. Until all compilers comply with the standard specification, it's
wise to be specific if you expect portability of your programs among compilers and operating
platforms.

The std::ios::setf and std::ios::unsetf Functions

Program 28-7 inserts the std::setiosflags manipulator into the stream to control justification and notation. The std::ios class, from which std::ostream is derived, also includes
unsetf and setf member functions that clear and set flags to control the output format.

The following example uses `unsetf` to clear the `std::ios::scientific` flag and `setf` to set the `std::ios::fixed` flag:

```
std::cout.unsetf(std::ios::scientific);
std::cout.setf(std::ios::fixed);
```

The following `setf` call differs from the previous one. This variation on the call has two parameters: the flag to set and a mask that defines the flags to clear:

```
std::cout.setf(std::ios::fixed, std::ios::scientific);
```

Formatting Flags

Table 28-1 lists the formatting flags that the `std::ios` class defines. These flags have mutually exclusive bit values that you can OR together to form a single bit mask. The `std::setiosflags` and `std::resetiosflags` manipulators and the `setf` and `unsetf` member functions accept OR'd masks of these flags as arguments.

Table 28-1: ios Formatting Flags

Flag	Description
std::ios::boolalpha	Inserts and extracts `bool` type in alphabetic format. Default setting: off
std::ios::hex	Displays integers in base 16. Default setting: off
std::ios::internal	Fills between sign and value. Default setting: off
std::ios::left	Left-aligns fields. Default setting: on
std::ios::oct	Displays integers in base 8. Default setting: off
std::ios::right	Right-aligns fields. Default setting: off
std::ios::scientific	Displays floating-point numbers in exponential notation. Default setting: off
std::ios::showbase	Displays an integer's numeric base. Default setting: off
std::ios::showpoint	Displays decimal point and trailing zeroes. Default setting: off
std::ios::showpos	Displays + for positive numeric values. Default setting: off
std::ios::skipws	Bypasses white space. Default setting: off
std::ios::stdio	Stays in sync with `<cstdio>` functions. Default setting: off
std::ios::unitbuf	Flushes the stream after each insertion. Default setting: off
std::ios::uppercase	Displays A-F for hex values and E for scientific notation. Default setting: off
std::ios:dec	Displays integers in base 10. Default setting: on
std::ios:fixed	Displays floating-point numbers in fixed notation. Default setting: off

Formatting Manipulators

Table 28-2 lists the manipulators that <iomanip> defines. Each of these manipulators compiles to an expression that returns an internal type (std::smanip) that the std::ios object (std::cout, for example) uses to manage the format of the data stream. You insert manipulators into output streams with the << insertion operator.

Table 28-2: <iomanip> Manipulators

Manipulator	Description
std::resetiosflags(int m)	Resets (turns off) flags in OR'd mask m expression
std::setbase(int b)	Sets numeric base to b (8, 10, or 16)
std::setfill(int c)	Sets padding fill character to c
std::setiosflags(int m)	Sets (turns on) flags in OR'd mask m expression
std::setprecision(int p)	Sets floating-point precision to p
std::setw(int w)	Sets field width to w

Table 28-3 lists the manipulators that <iostream> defines to control streams. You insert the first six manipulators in Table 28-3 into output streams using the << insertion operator. You insert the last manipulator (std::ws) into input streams with the >> extraction operator.

Table 28-3: <iostream> Manipulators

Manipulator	Description
std::endl	Inserts a newline character ('\n'); flushes the stream
std::ends	Inserts a null character ('\0')
std::dec	Displays integers in base 10
std::flush	Flushes the stream
std::hex	Displays integers in base 16
std::oct	Displays integers in base 8
std::ws	Skips white space in the input stream

Formatting Functions

The std::ios class includes several functions that control the format of a stream. You call these functions through an object of the class (cout, for example). Table 28-4 lists the ios formatting functions.

Table 28-4: ios Formatting Functions

Function	Description
`int std::ios::fill`	Returns current padding fill character
`int std::ios::fill(int c)`	Sets padding fill character to c; returns previous character
`int std::ios::precision`	Returns current floating-point precision
`int std::ios::precision(int p)`	Sets precision to p; returns previous precision
`int std::ios::setf(int m)`	Turns on flags in OR'd mask m; returns previous flags
`int std::ios::setf (int m1, int m2)`	Turns on flags in OR'd m1; Turns off flags in OR'd m2; returns previous flags
`void std::ios::unsetf(int m)`	Turns off flags in OR'd m
`int std::ios::width`	Returns current width
`int std::ios::width(int w)`	Sets width to w; returns previous width

The std::stringstream Classes

The `std::stringstream` classes allow the program to treat memory strings as if they were input/output devices. You can read data from a `std::istringstream` object by using the same operators and functions that you use with a `std::istream` object. You can write data to a `std::ostringstream` object the same way you write to a `std::ostream` object. The difference is, of course, that objects of types `std::istream` and `std::ostream` are usually devices or files, whereas objects of types `std::istringstream` and `std::ostringstream` are strings in memory. Because of this, `stringstream` classes have many of the same properties as file streams (Chapter 29). You can do the equivalent of input and output seek operations, for example, to position the extraction and insertion points of `stringstream` objects.

The std::istringstream Class

Program 28-8 demonstrates the use of the `std::istringstream` class.

Program 28-8: **The std::istringstream class**

```
#include <iostream>
#include <sstream>
#include <cstdlib>
#include <string>

int main()
```

Continued

Program 28-8 *(continued)*

```
{
    char instr[100];
    std::cout << "Enter an integer, a float, and a string: ";
    std::cin.getline(instr, 100);
    std::istringstream istr(instr);
    int n;
    float f;
    std::string s;
    istr >> n >> f >> s;
    std::cout << "Extracted from istringstream: "
         << n << ' ' << f << ' ' << s << std::endl;
    return 0;
}
```

Program 28-8 reads three data values from standard input into a character array by using std::cin's getline member function. Then it instantiates an object of type std::istringstream named istr with the character array and length as initializers. These steps prepare the std::istringstream object so you can see how it works. The program then uses the >> extraction operator to extract the three data values from the std::istringstream object, which is the point of this exercise. Data values are extracted into the three variables just as if you had used std::cin instead of the istr object.

The std::ostringstream class

Program 28-9 demonstrates the use of the std:ostringstream class.

Program 28-9: **The std::ostringstream class**

```
#include <iostream>
#include <sstream>

int main()
{
    std::ostringstream ostr;
    ostr << "This is only a test" << std::ends;
    const std::string& sp = ostr.str();
    // display the ostringstream object.
    std::cout << sp;
    return 0;
}
```

Program 28-9 instantiates an object of type std::ostringstream named ostr. Then the program writes a string value to the ostr object just as you would to std::cout.

The std::ends object appends the data written with a null terminator. To demonstrate the ostr object's contents, the program uses the std::ostringstream::str member function to extract from the ostr object its std::string component, which the program displays on standard output.

The std::stringstream class

The std::stringstream class supports read/write strings that resemble read/write file stream objects (Chapter 29). Program 28-10 demonstrates the behavior of the std::stringstream class.

Program 28-10: **The std::stringstream class**

```
#include <iostream>
#include <sstream>
#include <string>

int main()
{
    std::stringstream sstr;
    sstr << "Number ";
    sstr << 666;

    sstr.seekg(6);

    int n;
    sstr >> n;
    std::cout << "Extracted int: " << n << std::endl;

    sstr.clear();
    sstr.seekg(0);
    std::string s;
    sstr >> s;
    std::cout << "Extracted string: " << s;
    return 0;
}
```

Program 28-10 instantiates an object of type std::stringstream named sstr. The program writes data to the object just as it would to std::cout. Then the program calls the seekg member function to position the current stream input pointer at the sixth character in the stream. The seekg member function usually supports random access file access (Chapter 29). Because a stringstream object behaves like a file, you can seek to a position within it prior to reading and writing.

The program uses the >> extraction operator to extract the int value in the sstr object, which, at the position following the seekg call, is 666. The program displays the extracted value on standard output to demonstrate that the extraction works.

The program now calls the `clear` member function. This call resets the `sstr` object's state following the `seekg` and data extraction. Those two operations put the object's current extraction pointer at the end of its buffer, and further input operations, including seeking, will not work until the end-of-file state is reset. Streams have several states, and Chapter 29 explains them in more detail.

Next the program seeks to the beginning of the `sstr` object and extracts a string, which it displays on standard output.

The `wchar_t` versions of `std::istringstream`, `std::ostringstream`, and `std::stringstream` are named `std::wistringstream`, `std::wostringstream`, and `std::wstringstream`.

Summary

In this chapter, you learned the various ways you can use streams to manipulate and format data in your programs. The next chapter demonstrates how to use IOstreams to manage stream data in disk files.

✦   ✦   ✦

File I/O Streams

The Standard C++ Library includes I/O classes for managing disk files. Those classes are part of the IOStream class hierarchy. An IOStream is a series of bytes heading between somewhere, typically a of device and somewhere else, typically memory. In the case of file streams, the two entities connected by the stream are the computer's memory and a file on a disk drive. This chapter explains the `std::ofstream`, `std::ifstream`, and `std::fstream` classes and how you use them to manage disk I/O. A program that uses the file IOStream classes must include the `<fstream>` header file.

File Stream Objects

To perform file operations, a program instantiates an object of one of the three file stream classes, `std::ofstream`, `std::ifstream`, and `std::fstream`. These objects support file input, output, and combined input/output, respectively. The program specifies what the file name is, where the file is located, and how the program intends to use the file. The program does so by including arguments to the stream class constructors or by instantiating an uninitialized file stream object and using the `open` member function for the file stream object at a later time. The `open` member function and its corresponding `close` member function are addressed later in this chapter. For now, we will discuss instantiating file stream objects and initializing those objects by providing arguments to their constructors. All the argument values are the same when applied to the `open` member function.

The first argument the program must provide is the file specification, as shown here:

```
std::fstream iofile("filespec");
```

The `"filespec"` argument represents a file specification, which is the path and name of the file to be processed. This argument is of type `const char*`. The file specification argument conforms to the operating system's conventions for naming and locating files. It can be a fully qualified, unambiguous file specification, or it can be relative to the currently logged-on subdirectory. The format for the path and file name specification depends on the target platform.

The std::ios:: Prefix

Throughout this chapter are flag values and other things with an std::ios:: prefix on their names. Chapter 27 briefly introduced std::ios as a base class in which many things are defined that IOStream objects use. By now you might be getting curious enough to pore over the standard header files that come with your compiler. What you find is that std::ios is not itself a class. Instead, std::ios is a typedef of class std::basic_ios<char>, a specialization of template class std::basic_ios<T>, which is derived from std::ios_base, which is at the top of the IOStream class hierarchy and which defines formatting, state, mode, and other flags for all the classes in the hierarchy. This book's use of std::ios:: instead of std::ios_base:: keeps the book's code shorter and works in the book's examples because they assume IOStreams parameterized by the char character type. If you are writing programs that use the wchar_t type, use std::wios:: where these examples use std::ios::. If you are writing programs for one character size that might someday be converted to the other character size, use std::ios_base:: where these examples use std::ios::.

Open Modes

A program specifies how a file is to be opened by providing an *openmode* argument, as shown here:

```
std::fstream iofile("filespec", std::ios::trunc);
```

There are six openmode values. To specify more than one openmode value for a file stream object, the program combines them with the bitwise OR operator (|) like this:

```
std::fstream iofile("filespec",
        std::ios::trunc | std::ios::binary);
```

Table 29-1 lists the openmode values and their meanings.

Table 29-1: Openmode Values

Flag	Description
std::ios::app	Seek to end-of-file before each write
std::ios::ate	Open and seek to end
std::ios::binary	Open the file in binary, rather than text, mode
std::ios::in	Open the file for input
std::ios::out	Open the file for output
std::ios::trunc	Delete (truncate) the file's current contents upon open

Given these six values and three types of objects, std::fstream, std::ofstream, and std::ifstream, there are many possible open statements.

Default Openmodes

Depending on the class of the file stream object, there are default openmode values. If the program does not specify an openmode argument, the compiler provides the default. If the program specifies an openmode argument, the compiler ORs the specified argument with the default openmode. Table 29-2 shows the defaults.

Table 29-2: Default Openmode Values

`std::ofstream`	`std::ios::out | std::ios::trunc`
`std::ifstream`	`std::ios::in`
`std::fstream`	(none)

When opening a file with the `std::fstream` class, the program must provide all the openmode arguments.

Valid Openmode Combinations

Not all combinations of openmodes are permitted. Table 29-3 and the discussion that follows show the valid combinations and their meanings. (Openmode values are shown in the table without the `std::ios::` qualification.)

Table 29-3: Valid Openmode Combinations

Openmode Value	Effect	File Exists	File Does Not Exist
`in`	Open for reading		Error
`out` `out | trunc`	Open for writing	Truncated	Created
`out | app`	Open for writing at end of file		Created
`in | out`	Open for input/output		Created
`in | out | trunc`	Open for input/output	Truncated	Created

Any of these combinations can be combined with the `std::ios::binary` openmode, which is explained later. Any of these combinations can be combined with the `std::ios::ate` openmode, which opens the file with the file pointer pointed at the end of the file.

Any other combination of openmodes results in an error condition, and the file is not opened.

Combining `std::ios::trunc` and `std::ios::out` by themselves is redundant. The latter implies the former except when `std::ios::in` is also specified. Combining `std::ios::trunc` and `std::ios::ate` are redundant. A truncated file is at the end of file by default. Combining `std::ios::app` and `std::ios::ate` is also redundant. The latter is implied by the former, but not vice versa.

The error condition returned when using std::ios::in on a nonexistent file and other error conditions and exceptions are explained later in this chapter.

For each openmode combination, the file might or might not exist. Table 29-3 shows what effect that condition has on the program and the file.

Common Open Circumstances

Following are some common ways that you can open files based on what you want to do. In these examples, "filespec" represents the file specification including its name and path. The identifiers ofile, ifile, and iofile represent the names of the file stream objects the program instantiates. The example programs that follow in this chapter demonstrate each of these operations.

```
std::ofstream ofile("filespec");
```

The statement just shown opens a file for output. If the file does not exist, the statement creates the file. If the file exists, it removes the file's former contents.

```
std::ofstream ofile("filespec", std::ios::out | std::ios::ate);
std::ofstream ofile("filespec", std::ios::out | std::ios::app);
```

The statements just shown open an existing file for output, retaining its previous contents. Both forms open an existing file or create a new file if one does not exist. Both position the file output pointer at the end of the file, which is the zero position if the file did not already exist or was empty. The std::ios::ate ("at end") variation permits the program to seek and write to somewhere other than the end of the file once the file is open. The std::ios::app ("append") variation always seeks to the end of the file immediately before each write to the file.

```
std::ifstream ifile("filespec");
```

The statement just shown opens a file for input. If the file does not exist, an error condition exists, which the program can test.

```
std::fstream iofile("filespec", std::ios::in | std::ios::out);
```

The statement just shown opens a file for input and output. This is an update mode. The program can read records, seek records, rewrite existing records, and add records to the end of the file. The file is opened with input and output pointers at the beginning of the file. If the file does not exist, an error condition exists, which the program can test.

```
std::fstream iofile("filespec",
         std::ios::in | std::ios::out | std::ios::trunc);
```

The statement just shown also opens a file for input and output. If the file does not exist, it is created. If the file exists, its contents are truncated. You should write data before reading.

Suppose, however, you want to open a file for input and output. If the file exists, its current contents are preserved. If the file does not exist, it is created. No way exists to open such a file with a single statement. You have to use a combination of opens and tests, which Program 29-11 demonstrates later in this chapter.

Binary and Text File Streams

The `std::ios::binary` openmode argument specifies that the file is to be opened as a binary file rather than a text file. On some operating platforms — Unix, for example — there is no difference between binary files and text files, and the `std::ios::binary` openmode argument has no effect. Other platforms — Windows, for example — require the argument in some cases. Those platforms that differentiate between text files and binary files do so in these ways:

✦ When the program writes a newline character (`'\n'`) to a binary file, the file system writes the single newline character. On most platforms, this newline character is the same as the linefeed (`0x0a`) character.

✦ When the program writes a newline character to a text file, the file system writes two characters: a carriage return character (`0x0d`) followed by a linefeed character (`0x0a`).

✦ When the program reads a newline character from a binary file, the file system reads the single newline character into memory.

✦ When the program reads a carriage return/linefeed character pair from a text file, the file system translates the pair into a single newline character in memory.

✦ When the program reads a single newline character — a linefeed that is not preceded by a carriage return character — from a text file, the file system inserts the newline character into memory.

This approach has significant implications that involve not only the translation of newline character representations but also file position operations — *seeking* and *telling*. (Seeking is finding a given position within a file, whereas telling is retrieving the current file position.) A text file's data representation in memory has a different length than its data representation on disk because of the bidirectional translations between single newline memory characters and carriage return/linefeed character pairs on disk. Consequently, seeking and telling are unreliable operations when applied to text files on those platforms that differentiate between text and binary files. If such a program needs to seek within the file and/or tell the current file position, the program should open the file with the `std::ios::binary` openmode. If the program reads such a file, the program should expect `"\r\n"` character sequences in the file to be read into memory with no conversion. If the program writes such a file and expects the file to behave as a text file, the program should write the carriage return/line feed sequence `"\r\n"` instead of just the newline character `'\n'` or `std::endl`.

The std::ofstream Class

The `std::ofstream class` is for writing stream data to disk files. You can create a new file and write data to an existing file. You can append data to or replace data in an existing file.

In the most elementary use of `std::ofstream`, the program declares an object of type `std::ofstream` and passes a file name argument to the constructor. Then the program writes to the file through the object. When the object is destroyed, the file closes. Here's a brief example:

```
std::ofstream ofile("test.txt");
ofile << "These are test data";
```

You also can append to a file, as shown here:

```
std::ofstream ofile("test.txt", std::ios::app);
ofile << ", and these are more";
```

Here is an example of calling the `write` function to write to a binary file stream:

```
std::ofstream ofile("date.dat", std::ios::binary);
ofile.write(&dt, sizeof dt);
```

Creating a File

To create a disk file and write data to it, instantiate an object of the `std::ofstream` class. Program 29-1 uses an `std::ofstream` object in its simplest form.

Program 29-1: **File output**

```
#include <iostream>
#include <fstream>

int main()
{
    std::cout << "Opening output file..." << std::endl;
    std::ofstream ofile("test.txt");
    if (!ofile.fail()) {
        std::cout << "Writing to file..." << std::endl;
        ofile << "These are test data";
    }
    else
        std::cout << "cannot open";
    return 0;
}
```

The program creates a file named test.txt and, if the open was successful, writes a string of character data to the file. The program uses the `fail` member function to determine whether the open is successful. The open would fail if the disk is full or is a read only medium, such as a CD-ROM or write-protected diskette, if the file is locked by another process, or if the user does not have write permissions to the file or its directory. To view the test.txt file and verify that the program works on the Windows platform, double-click the file's icon to open the file in the Windows Notepad applet.

Appending to an Existing File

You also can use the `std::ofstream` class to append to an existing file. Program 29-2 appends a string to the file that Program 29-1 created.

> Program 29-2: **Appending to an output file**

```
#include <iostream>
#include <fstream>

int main()
{
    std::cout << "Opening file..." << std::endl;
    std::ofstream ofile("test.txt", std::ios::app);
    if (!ofile.fail()) {
        std::cout << "Appending to file..." << std::endl;
        ofile << ", and these are more";
    }
    else
        std::cout << "cannot open";
    return 0;
}
```

Notice the use of the `std::ios::app` flag:

```
std::ofstream ofile("test.txt", std::ios::app);
```

This mode flag tells the `ofile` object that it should open the file for appending. This mode leaves the existing data intact in the file and positions the write file pointer at the end of the file prior to every output operation.

File Stream Member Functions

The `std::ofstream` and `std::ifstream` classes have many member functions for managing disk files. Some of these member functions are defined in the class itself, whereas the class inherits others from base classes such as `std::ostream`. Table 29-4 lists the most commonly used member functions of the stream classes.

Table 29-4: File Stream Member Functions

Function	Description
attach	Associates an open file with the stream
close	Closes the file after flushing any unsaved data
flush	Flushes the stream
open	Opens a file and associates it with the stream
put	Writes a byte to the stream
rdbuf	Returns the `filebuf` object associated with the stream

Continued

Table 29-4 *(continued)*

Function	Description
seekp	Sets the position of the stream's file pointer
setmode	Sets the stream to binary or text mode
tellp	Gets the position of the stream's file pointer
write	Writes a set of bytes to the stream

The write Member Function

Rather using the overloaded insertion operator<< to send data to a file, which typically writes formatted text output, you can call the stream object's write member function to write a binary image of an object. Program 29-3 shows how the write function records the binary representation of a class object into a data file.

Program 29-3: The write member function

```
#include <iostream>
#include <fstream>
#include <Date.h>

int main()
{
    Date dat(6, 24, 1940);
    struct date {
        int mo, da, yr;
    } dt;
    dat.GetDate(dt.mo, dt.da, dt.yr);
    std::cout << "Opening file..." << std::endl;
    std::ofstream ofile("date.dat", std::ios::binary);
    if (!ofile.fail())  {
        std::cout << "Writing to file..." << std::endl;
        ofile.write(reinterpret_cast<char*>(&dt), sizeof dt);
    }
    return 0;
}
```

The program instantiates a Date object, using the Date class used in earlier chapters. Then the program declares a generic date structure and uses Date::GetDate to load the Date object's month, day, and year values into the date structure's data member. The program creates the file and writes the binary value of the struct date object into it. The write function does not stop writing when it reaches a null character, so the complete class structure is written regardless of its content.

Program 29-3 teaches another valuable lesson. You may wonder why the program uses an interim, contrived data structure instead of simply writing the Date object like this:

```
ofile.write(static_cast<char*>(&dat), sizeof dat);
```

First, the Date class is an externally designed, abstract data type. You may not know how the class implements its data representation. (Sure, you can always look at the Date.h header file, but read on.)

Second, if you depend on the details of that format — and if the Date class designer changes the implementation — you must recompile all programs and convert all data files that depended on the previous data representation.

Third, and most important, the Date class can have one or more virtual functions. (It does.) A class that has virtual functions includes among its data members a hidden private pointer (vptr) to the class's virtual table (vtbl). If the class is derived from other classes, there are vptr data members for all the base classes. Those pointers' values are physical memory addresses based on where in memory the compiler put the class's vtbl for this particular program. The address-of operator (&) returns the memory address of the complete object, and the sizeof operator includes all vptr data members. There is no standard that specifies where in an object's memory the compiler must put vptr data members, so you cannot bypass it in any portable way. You also cannot reference the vptr data member — not even from within a member function — so consequently, you cannot save and restore its value. Not only is the vptr data value meaningless to the storage of a date's value, but if you were to read it from the file into a Date object in another program, you probably would trash the other program's pointer with a value that points to nowhere in particular. Later, when the program accessed the vptr to execute a virtual function or resolve a use of the typeid or dynamic_cast operator, the program would crash.

Given all those issues, why use the write member function at all? Looking at the Date class in Date.h (Appendix A), we see that it overloads operator<< to write its data to an ostream object. Why not simply write the date data to the file like this?

```
ofile << dat;
```

Program 29-3 does not use the overloaded insertion operator<< because Program 29-3, in this example, is writing a binary file that is expecting a fixed length data in a binary, three-integer, month, day, year format. In a larger program, such date information might be part of a record in a database, and its format could not rely on the formatted textual output that the overloaded insertion operator produces.

Other Member Functions: open, put, tellp, close

Program 29-4 puts several of the std::ofstream class's member functions to work. The open member function associates an uninitialized std::ifstream, std::ofstream, or std::fstream object with a file specification, opening the file and applying the implied and specified openmode arguments. Instead of naming the file when declaring the object, the program names the file in an open function call. The put member function works the same with file streams as it does with other IOStream objects, as you learned in Chapter 27. The tellp function returns the current output position of an std::ofstream object. The close member function disassociates a file stream object from the file with which it is associated.

Program 29-4: open, put, tellp, and close member functions

```cpp
#include <iostream>
#include <fstream>
#include <string>

int main()
{
    std::string str("This is a test");
    // Create an output stream object.
    std::ofstream ofile;
    // Associate a file with the stream.
    ofile.open("testfile.txt", std::ios::binary);
    if (!ofile.fail())  {
        // Write a string one character at a time.
        for (int x = 0; x < str.size(); x++) {
            std::cout << "File pointer: " << ofile.tellp();
            ofile.put(str[x]);
            std::cout << "   " << str[x] << std::endl;
        }
    }
    // Close the file.
    ofile.close();
    return 0;
}
```

Program 29-4's output looks like this:

```
File pointer: 0   T
File pointer: 1   h
File pointer: 2   i
File pointer: 3   s
File pointer: 4
File pointer: 5   i
File pointer: 6   s
File pointer: 7
File pointer: 8   a
File pointer: 9
File pointer: 10  t
File pointer: 11  e
File pointer: 12  s
File pointer: 13  t
```

The std::ifstream Class

The std::ifstream class objects are input files. A program can declare an input file stream object and read it. Also, a program can use the extraction operator>>, the get function, or the getline function as if the stream were the console device rather than a file. A program also can use the read member function to read binary blocks into memory. Here's an example:

```
std::ifstream ifile("date.dat");
ifile.read(&dt, sizeof dt);
```

The read Member Function

The `std::ifstream` class reads input from a disk file. To read data from a file, a program instantiates an object of the `std::ifstream` class. Program 29-5 reads the `Date` object from the file that Program 29-3 writes.

Program 29-5: **The read member function**

```
#include <fstream>
#include <Date.h>

int main()
{
    struct date {
        int mo, da, yr;
    } dt;
    std::ifstream ifile("date.dat", std::ios::binary);
    if (!ifile.fail())   {
        ifile.read(reinterpret_cast<char*>(&dt), sizeof dt);
        Date dat(dt.mo, dt.da, dt.yr);
        std::cout << dat;
    }
    return 0;
}
```

Program 29-5 displays the date 6/24/1940 onscreen. Observe that the program uses the same technique that Program 29-4 uses to isolate the details of the `Date` class implementation from the details of the file implementation. It reads the file data into the structure object. Then it instantiates a `Date` object from the data members of the structure. The program uses the `Date` class's overloaded insertion `operator<<` to display the date on standard output.

Reading Until End-of-File

Often, when reading data from a file, your program needs to know when it reaches the end of the file. The `std::ifstream` class provides the `eof` member function for this task. (Actually, the `eof` member function is defined in a class higher in the IOStream hierarchy, but it is most often used to test for end-of-file in a file stream object.) The `eof` member function returns a `true` value when an input stream object reaches the end of its character stream. A program typically uses this test to determine whether a program has reached the end of a file and should try no more reads of the data, as shown here:

```
std::ifstream ifile("test.txt");
while (!ifile.eof())
    // read and process data ...
```

Program 29-6 opens the text file that Program 29-1 created and Program 29-2 modified, and reads the file data one character at a time. The program writes each character to std::cout as the character is read and then stops at end-of-file.

Program 29-6: **Testing end-of-file**

```
#include <iostream>
#include <fstream>

int main()
{
    std::ifstream ifile("test.txt");
    if (!ifile.fail()) {
        while (!ifile.eof()) {
            char ch;
            ifile.get(ch);
            if (!ifile.eof())
                std::cout << ch;
        }
    }
    return 0;
}
```

Assuming you ran Programs 29-1 and 29-2, Program 29-6 displays this message:

```
These are test data, and these are more
```

Seeking Within a File

File IOStreams support random access of binary files. A program can modify the current position of a file stream using one of the member functions seekg or seekp. The seekg function changes the position of the next input operation on a file opened for input, as shown here:

```
ifile.seekg(6);
```

The seekp function changes the position of the next output operation on a file opened for output, as shown here:

```
ofile.seekp(16);
```

You can determine the current position for input with the tellg member function and the current position for output with the tellp member function. Here are examples:

```
std::streampos inpos = ifile.tellg();
std::streampos outpos = ofile.tellp();
```

Program 29-7 opens a file, changes the input position by using the seekg function and then reads to end-of-file.

> Program 29-7: **The seekg member function**

```
#include <iostream>
#include <fstream>

int main()
{
    std::ifstream ifile("test.txt", std::ios::binary);
    if (!ifile.fail()) {
        ifile.seekg(6);          // Seek six characters in
        while (!ifile.eof()) {
            char ch;
            ifile.get(ch);
            if (!ifile.eof())
                std::cout << ch;
        }
    }
    return 0;
}
```

Program 29-7 displays this message:

```
are test data, and these are more
```

By adding an argument to the member function call, a program can specify that a seekg or seekp operation occurs relative to the beginning of the file, the end of the file, or the current position. Following are examples of the function calls:

```
ifile.seekg(5, std::ios::beg);
ifile.seekg(10, std::ios::cur);
ifile.seekg(-15, std::ios::end);
```

If you do not provide the second argument, the seek occurs from the beginning of the file.

You can determine the current position for input with the tellg member function and the current position for output with the tellp member function. You saw the tellp function being used in Program 29-4. Program 29-8 illustrates the tellg function.

> Program 29-8: **The tellg member function**

```
#include <iostream>
#include <fstream>

int main()
{
    std::ifstream ifile("test.txt", std::ios::binary);
    if (!ifile.fail()) {
        while (!ifile.eof()) {
```

Continued

Program 29-8 *(continued)*

```
            char ch;
            std::streampos sp = ifile.tellg();
            ifile.get(ch);
            if (ch == ' ')
                std::cout << "\nPosition "
                          << sp << " is a space";
        }
    }
    return 0;
}
```

Program 29-8 displays these messages:

```
Position 5 is a space
Position 9 is a space
Position 14 is a space
Position 20 is a space
Position 24 is a space
Position 30 is a space
Position 34 is a space
```

The program reads the file built by the earlier programs and displays messages showing the character positions where it finds spaces. The `tellg` function returns an integral value of type `std::streampos` — a `typedef` defined in one of the compiler's internal header files related to IOStreams.

The std::fstream Class: Reading and Writing a Stream File

Often, you may want to open a file for read/write access. To do this use the `std::fstream` class with both `std::ios::in` and `std::ios::out` openmode arguments. Program 29-9 reads the text file from the earlier programs into a character array and writes an uppercase-only copy of the bytes at the end of the file.

Program 29-9: Reading and writing a stream file

```
#include <iostream>
#include <fstream>

int main()
{
    // open fstream object for both input and output.
    std::fstream iofile("test.txt",
            std::ios::in | std::ios::out | std::ios::binary);
```

```
    if (iofile)          {
        iofile.seekp(0, std::ios::end);
        iofile << "\r\nMore test data";
        iofile.seekg(0);
        int i = 0;
        char tdata[100];
        while (!iofile.eof() && i < sizeof tdata)
            iofile.get(tdata[i++]);
        std::cout << tdata;
    }
    return 0;
}
```

The program modifies the file so that it contains these contents:

```
These are test data, and these are more
More test data
```

Observe that Program 29-9 uses the seekp function to change the output insertion location for the output component of the file.

Observe also that the program sends the string "\r\n" to the file, rather than the std::endl manipulator or the newline character, as a line separator. The program uses this procedure because the file is opened with the std::ios::binary openmode, and the listings (as distributed) compile and run under Windows. See the "Binary and Text Files" section in this chapter for a discussion of the differences between binary and text files.

Associating and Disassociating Files with Streams

It is possible to use a single stream object to represent different files at different times. To do this, you construct a stream object without supplying the name of the associated file. You then call the stream object's open member function to associate the stream with a file and call the close member function to disassociate the file. Program 29-10 demonstrates how to do this.

> Program 29-10: **The open and close member functions**

```
#include <iostream>
#include <fstream>

int main()
{
    // An ofstream object without a file.
    std::ofstream ofile;
    std::cout << "Creating the test1.txt file..."
              << std::endl;
    ofile.open("test1.txt");
```

Continued

```
    if (!ofile.fail()) {
        ofile << "This is TEST1";
        ofile.close();
        std::cout << "Creating the test2.txt file..."
                << std::endl;
        ofile.open("test2.txt");
        if (!ofile.fail()) {
            ofile << "This is TEST2";
            ofile.close();
        }
    }
    return 0;
}
```

A Variation on Input/Output

Earlier in this chapter we mentioned the requirement to open a file for input and output. If the file exists, its current contents are preserved. If the file does not exist, it is created. As you learned, no way exists to open such a file with a single statement. You have to use a combination of opens and tests, which Program 29-11 demonstrates here.

Program 29-11: **A variation on input/output**

```
#include <iostream>
#include <fstream>

int main()
{
    const char* fn = "test.txt";
    std::fstream iofile;
    // test to see if the file exists
    iofile.open(fn, std::ios::in);
    if (iofile.fail()) {
        // file does not exist, create it for input/output
        iofile.clear(); // clear the failbit
        iofile.open(fn,
            std::ios::in | std::ios::out | std::ios::trunc);
    }
    else    {
        // file exists, close and reopen for input/output
        iofile.close();
        iofile.open(fn,
            std::ios::in | std::ios::out | std::ios::ate);
    }
```

```
    if (!iofile.fail()) {
        // now have a file open for input/output
        // and ready to write at the end
        iofile << "\nTest data at the end of the file";
        iofile.seekg(0);
        while (!iofile.eof()) {
            char ch;
            iofile.get(ch);
            if (!iofile.eof())
                std::cout << ch;
        }
    }
    return 0;
}
```

Program 29-11 tests to see if the file exists by opening it with the std::ios::in openmode. If the file does not exist, the open operation fails. At this point the program calls the clear member function to clear the failbit flag set by the open operation. (See "Testing Errors" later in this chapter.) Then the program opens the file for input and output and includes the std::ios::trunc openmode so that the file will be created. Without that openmode, this second open would fail, too.

If the file exists when the program first tests for it, the program closes the file and reopens it for input and output, including the std::ios::ate openmode so the first output operation is at the end of the file.

Whether the file existed or not, the program now has an open file ready for input and output — unless, of course, some other error condition, such as a read-only medium or an access privilege violation prevented the file from being opened at all. With the file open, the program writes a string of text at the end of the file — which is also the beginning of the file if the file did not exist or was empty. Then the program seeks to the beginning of the file, reads its contents a character at a time, and displays them on standard output.

You can test the operation of this program by using the test.txt test data file built by earlier programs in this chapter. Then you can test the program's operation when the file does not exist by deleting the file and rerunning the program.

Testing Errors

There are several ways to test for exceptional conditions in a file stream object. The programs in this chapter up to this point use the fail member function to determine whether a file opens properly. There is more to testing for the condition of a file stream object, however. For example, you can test to see if an object is properly associated with an open file as the next discussion demonstrates.

File stream classes define and maintain state flag bits that reflect a file stream object's current state. Table 29-5 lists these flag bits and the conditions that set them.

Table 29-5: Stream State Flag Bits

Flag Bits	Condition Indicated When Flag is Set
std::ios::goodbit	No error or exceptional conditions
std::ios::eofbit	Input operation tried to read past the end of the file
std::ios::failbit	File failed to open or input or output failed
std::ios::badbit	Stream integrity has been compromised

There are various program conditions that set these bits. The eofbit flag is set when a character read tries to read a character and the input file pointer points one past the last character of the file. The eofbit is not set when that last character was read. On the other hand, when a program extracts variable values from the stream, the extraction of the last integer string, for example, sets the eofbit because the stream keeps reading digits until it reads past the end of file.

Once a file stream has passed the end of file, no further input or seek operations can be performed until the eofbit is cleared. The clear member function clears the eofbit flag so the program can seek back into the stream. If a file stream object has failed for an operation and the program uses the object for further input/output, the program uses the clear member function to clear the failbit flag. Chapter 28's Program 28-10 and Program 29-11 in this chapter used the clear member function in these ways.

The failbit flag is set when the program tries to open a file that it cannot open for one reason or another or when input or output fails. A program cannot open a file for input if the file does not exist or if the program's user does not have access privileges to the file. A program cannot open a file for output if the file is marked as read only, the file path specification specifies a read only medium such as a CD-ROM, or the path specifies a location where the program's user does not have write access privileges. A program input operation sets the failbit flag when the program tries to read a specified kind of variable and the stream object has no such variable available to be read.

The badbit flag is set in extreme cases. Running out of memory for the buffer is one such case. Others are usually platform-specific.

A program tests the state of a stream by calling member functions for the file stream object. Table 29-6 shows the member functions that report a file stream's state.

Table 29-6: State Checking Member Functions

Member Function	Reports a File Stream State
bool good()	true if no flag bit is set
bool eof()	true if eofbit is set
bool fail()	true if failbit or badbit is set
bool bad()	true if badbit is set

The file stream classes overload `operator!()` and `operator void*()` to return `true` and `false` values if you use the object name in a conditional expression. Suppose that you declare a file stream object without an initializing name and do not associate a name with that object. The following code shows how you can test for that condition:

```
std::fstream file;   // No file name given
if (!file)         // This test returns true
    // ...
```

The preceding test is the same as this one that you have already seen:

```
if (!file.fail())
    // ...
```

The overloaded `operator void*()` function returns a null pointer value if `failbit` or `badbit` are set. Consequently, you can use it to test the success of input/output operations like this:

```
if (ofile << "hello")
    // successful output
```

which is the same as saying:

```
ofile << "hello";
if (ofile.good())
    // successful output
```

File Stream Exceptions

You can direct a file stream to throw a C++ exception when one of the error conditions discussed here occurs. Chapter 35 explains file stream exceptions.

Deleting Files

To delete a file from the file system, call the Standard C `remove` function like this:

```
#include <cstdio>
// ...
std::remove("test.txt");
```

Program 29-12 removes from the hard drive all the test data files that this chapter built.

Program 29-12: **Deleting files with std::remove**

```
#include <cstdio>

int main()
{
    std::remove("test.txt");
    std::remove("test1.txt");
```

Continued

> **Program 29-12** *(continued)*
>
> ```
>     std::remove("test2.txt");
>     std::remove("testfile.txt");
>     std::remove("date.dat");
>     return 0;
> }
> ```

The remove function returns an int value zero if it succeeds and nonzero if it fails.

Summary

Using the Standard C++ Library's stream classes, you easily can handle any type of file input or output task. The three main file classes — `std::ofstream`, `std::ifstream`, and `std::fstream` — provide all the functionality you need to manage everything from a text file to a random-access file. In the next chapter, you start learning about C++'s Standard Template Library (STL), which enables you to create and manipulate various types of standard containers, such as stacks and queues.

IV

The Standard Template Library

Part IV describes what is known as the Standard Template Library (STL), a library of template classes that implement generic containers, algorithms, and iterators. You will learn about "generic programming" in Part IV, which consists of these chapters:

Introduction to STL

The *Standard Template Library (STL)* is a library of container class templates and algorithms. Using STL, a programmer can implement many standard types of containers — such as stacks, lists, and queues — as well as manipulate the contents of these containers in various ways.

Why STL?

You can find the rationale for STL in the following observation. Given one set of data types, another set of container types, and a third set of common algorithms to support the containers, the amount of software developed with traditional C++ methods is a product of the number of elements in the three sets. Suppose you have integer, Date, and Personnel objects to contain in lists, queues, and stacks. If you need insert, extract, and sort algorithms for each class, there are 27 (3x3x3) traditional C++ algorithms to develop. With templates, you can define the containers as generic classes and reduce the number to nine algorithms — three algorithms for each of the three containers.

However, suppose you design the algorithms themselves as templates that perform generic operations on parameterized containers. There are only three algorithms in this case, which is the underlying basis of STL.

That explanation is a simplification of the STL rationale, but it hints at larger advantages that you cannot ignore. If class template containers are sufficiently generic, they can support any user-defined data type that meets their requirements with respect to operator overloading and behavior. You can contain any data type within any kind of supported container without having to develop custom container code. Furthermore, if the algorithms are sufficiently generic, you can use them to process containers of objects of user-defined data types.

You can add containers of your own design by conforming to the rules of STL; all the existing algorithms automatically work with the new containers.

Finally, as you add conforming algorithms, you find that they work with all containers and all contained data types — those of the present and those not yet designed.

To summarize, if you stick to the rules, you can add to any of the three components that make up STL — the containers, the algorithms, and the contained data types — and all existing components automatically accept the new addition and work seamlessly with it.

♦   ♦   ♦   ♦

In This Chapter

Introducing the Standard Template Library

Sequences, adapters, and containers

Iterators, algorithms, predicates, and allocators

♦   ♦   ♦   ♦

The STL Programming Model

STL supports several container types categorized as *sequences* and *associative containers*. A hierarchy of iterator objects, which resemble C++ pointers, manages access to containers. Iterators point to objects in the containers and permit the program to iterate through the containers in various ways.

All the containers have common management member functions defined in their template definitions: `insert`, `erase`, `begin`, `end`, `size`, `capacity`, and so on. Individual containers have member functions that support their unique requirements.

A standard suite of algorithms provides for searching, copying, reordering, transforming, and performing numeric operations on the objects in the containers. The same algorithm performs a particular operation for all containers of all object types.

As I explain the container types, remember that they are implemented as templates; the template arguments given when the program instantiates the containers determines the types of objects they contain.

Sequences

A *sequence* is a container that stores a finite set of objects of the same type in a linear organization. An array of names is a sequence. You use one of the three sequence types — vector, list, or deque (double-ended queue) — for a particular application depending on its retrieval requirements. Following is an overview of the three sequence types. You learn more about sequences in Chapter 31.

A *vector* is a sequence that you can access at random. You append entries to, and remove entries from, the end of the vector without undue overhead. Insertion and deletion at the beginning or in the middle of the vector take more time because they involve shifting the remaining entries to make room or to close the deleted object space. A vector is an array of contiguous objects with an instance counter or pointer that indicates the end of the container. Random access is a matter of using a subscript operation.

A *list* is a sequence that you access bidirectionally; it enables you to perform insertions and deletions anywhere without undue performance penalties. Random access is simulated by forward or backward iteration to the target object, which might not be very efficient depending on the size of the list. A list consists of noncontiguous objects linked with forward and backward pointers.

A *deque* is like a vector, except that a deque allows fast insertions and deletions at the beginning as well as at the end of the container. Random insertions and deletions take more time.

Container Adapters

A *container adapter* uses existing container classes and implements a unique interface. You select the existing container based on the requirements of the problem. You instantiate a container adapter class by naming the existing container in the declaration:

```
std::stack< std::list<int> > stackedlist;
```

The preceding example instantiates a stack container — one of the three container adapters supported by STL — using the list container as the underlying data structure.

A container adaptor hides the public interface of the underlying container and implements its own. A stack data structure, for example, resembles a list but has its own requirements for its user interface.

STL includes three container adapters: `std::stack`, `std::queue`, and `std::priority_queue`, which are summarized in the following paragraphs. You learn more about container adaptors in Chapter 31.

A *stack* is a data structure that exhibits pushdown, pop-up behavior. The most recently inserted (pushed) element is the only one that can be extracted. Extraction of the logically topmost element pops that element from the stack — removes it so that the element inserted immediately before the popped element is now the next available element. The `stack` template class implements two accessor functions, `push` and `pop`, to insert and extract elements in the data structure.

A *queue* is a data structure wherein you insert elements at the end and extract elements from the beginning. The `queue` template class implements two accessor functions, `push` and `pop`, to insert and extract elements in the data structure.

A *priority queue* is a data structure wherein you insert elements at the end and extract the element that has the highest priority. The `priority_queue` template class implements two accessor functions, `push` and `pop`, to insert and extract elements in the data structure.

Associative Containers

Associative containers provide for fast, keyed access to the objects in the container. They are constructed from key objects and a compare function that the container uses to compare objects. Associative containers consist of `std::set`, `std::multiset`, `std::map`, and `std::multimap` containers. You use associative containers for large dynamic tables that you can search sequentially or at random. Associative containers use tree structures — rather than contiguous arrays or linked lists — to organize the objects. These structures support fast random retrievals and updates. Following is an overview of the STL associative containers. You learn more about associative containers in Chapter 32.

✦ The *set* container holds objects that are key values. The set container does not permit duplicate keys.

✦ The *multiset* container holds objects that are key values. The multiset container permits duplicate keys.

✦ The *map* container holds objects that are key values and associates each key object with another parameterized type object. The map container does not permit duplicate keys.

✦ The *multimap* container holds objects that are key values and associates each key object with another parameterized type object. The multimap container permits duplicate keys.

Iterators

Iterators provide a common method of access into containers. They resemble and have the semantics of C++ pointers. In fact, when the parameterized type is a built-in C++ type (int, double, and so on), the associated iterators are C++ pointers.

Each container type supports one category of iterator depending on the container's requirements. The categories are input, output, forward, bidirectional, and random access. STL defines a hierarchy of iterators, as shown in Figure 30-1.

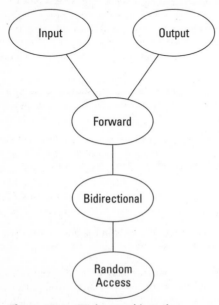

Figure 30-1: STL iterator hierarchy

Each iterator category has all the properties of those above it in the hierarchy. Those properties specify the behavior that the iterator must exhibit in order to support the container. Iterators are so-called smart pointers. They are permitted to have values that represent one of a set of defined states. Table 30-1 lists and explains these states.

Table 30-1: STL Iterator States

Iterator State	Description
Singular	The iterator's value does not dereference any object in any container. (You can uninitialize the iterator or set it to a logical null value.)
Dereferenceable	The iterator points to a valid object in the container.
Past-the-end	The iterator points to the object position past the last object in the container.

Iterators can be initialized, incremented, and decremented, and their bounds can be limited by the current extent of the containers. If you cause an iterator to be equal to another iterator by incrementing the first one, the second iterator is reachable from the first, which means that a subsequent series of increments from the first one is guaranteed to eventually result in an iterator value equal to the second one. The two iterators also are known to refer to the same container. Therefore, the two iterators can define a range of objects in the container.

Iterators can be set as the result of a search of the container or by subscripted reference into the container. Containers include member functions that return iterators pointing to the first object and the past-the-end object position. Iterators are the objects with which STL algorithms work. You learn more about iterators in the following chapters and especially in Chapter 34.

Algorithms

Algorithms, the backbone of STL, perform operations on containers by dereferencing iterators. Each algorithm is a function template parameterized on one or more iterator types. The standard algorithms are grouped into four categories: nonmutating sequence operations, mutating sequence operations, sorting operations, and numeric operations. You learn more about these different categories of algorithms in Chapter 33.

Algorithms accept iterators as arguments. The iterators tell the algorithm which object, or range of objects, to operate on in a container. Every container has a fixed set of iterator values the program can use by calling member functions that return the iterator values. For example, the `begin` function returns the value that represents the first logical element in a sequence container; the `end` function returns a value that represents the container position one past the last element.

Predicates

Algorithms also accept *predicates*, which are function object arguments. A *function object* is an object of a class that overloads `operator` and that you pass to an algorithm as a callback function argument. The algorithm calls the predicate for each object it processes from the container. In some cases, the predicate is a `bool` function that returns `TRUE` or `FALSE` to tell the algorithm whether to select the object. In other cases, the predicate processes the objects that the algorithm finds and returns an object of the type in the container. STL provides a set of standard arithmetic, comparison, and logical function objects that you can use as predicates.

The associative containers require a predicate as an argument to the template instantiation. The predicate argument specifies how elements are stored and retrieved with respect to one another. You learn more about using predicates in the following chapters.

Allocators

Every STL container class defines an allocator class that manages the allocation of memory for the container. STL provides a default allocator object for each container, so you should not need to deal directly with the allocator class. For this reason, we do not cover allocators in detail in this book. Applications that need to allocate container memory from memory pools other than the heap would use specialized allocators. One example would be embedded systems that do not have conventional memory.

Summary

STL consists of generic containers with iterators, along with algorithms that operate on those containers through their iterators. STL is almost a different programming model — another paradigm, if you will. It flies in the face of pure object-oriented theory by apparently separating the data from the functions. Algorithms are not bound to classes. They are not methods. They are function templates. Their binding to the data occurs as a function of their parameterized argument types.

This overview of STL is by no means an exhaustive study. It should serve, however, as an introduction to the underlying concepts of the Library. The remaining chapters in this part of the book explain the STL library in greater detail, beginning with sequences in Chapter 31.

✦   ✦   ✦

STL Sequence Containers

STL *sequence containers* are template classes that contain in memory objects of the type for which the container is parameterized. There are three container classes. There are also three container adaptor classes that specialize one of the three container classes by using templates.

The behavior of these classes is similar but their performance differs. You choose which container class to use based on how you are going to store and retrieve the objects. Each container class's performance is optimized for a particular kind of use. Chapter 30 discusses the way to put each container class to best use. This chapter explains the details of using sequence containers.

Although this chapter uses containers of intrinsic data types as examples, STL sequence containers can contain objects of classes as well.

Sequence Containers

STL implements its sequence containers with the following class templates and adaptors:

  ✦ std::vector: A type of random-access array that provides fast random access to array elements, as well as fast insertion and deletion at the end of the sequence. A std::vector object can change its size as needed.

  ✦ std::deque: A type of random-access array that provides for fast insertion and deletion at both the beginning and end of the sequence. A std::deque object can change its size as needed.

  ✦ std::list: A type of array that does not support random access. That is, because STL implements a std::list object as a doubly linked list, accessing an element in the list requires that you follow pointers from one end of the list. However, insertion or deletion is a constant-time operation, meaning that the time needed to insert or remove an element from the std::list object is the same regardless of where in the list the element is placed.

- ✦ std::queue: A type of adapter container that creates a *first in, first out (FIFO)* container from a std::deque or std::list object.

- ✦ std::priority_queue: A type of adapter container that creates a sorted sequence from a std::vector or std::deque object.

- ✦ std::stack: A type of adapter container that creates a *first in, last out (FILO)* container from a std::vector, std::deque, or std::list object.

In the following sections, you explore the various types of sequences and how to use them in your programs.

The vector Class Template

An std::vector object is similar to an array in that it provides random access to elements placed into the sequence. However, unlike a traditional array, an std::vector object (at run-time) can resize itself dynamically in order to hold any number of elements. A std::vector object can insert or remove new elements at the end of its sequence quickly, but insertion or removal from anywhere else in the sequence is not as efficient. This is because the std::vector object must shift the position of elements to accommodate the new element or to close up the space left by a removed element.

You construct an std::vector object in one of several ways, as shown here:

```
std::vector<type> name;
std::vector<type> name(size);
std::vector<type> name(size, value);
std::vector<type> name(myvector);
std::vector<type> name(first, last);
```

The first example creates an empty std::vector object named *name* that can hold data of the type *type*. For example, to create an empty std::vector object for integers, you can write:

```
std::vector<int> intVector;
```

The second example creates an std::vector object with an initial size of *size*, whereas the third example creates an std::vector object with an initial size of *size* — each element of which is initialized to *value*. The fourth example uses the copy constructor, which makes an std::vector object from an existing vector, *myvector*. Finally, the fifth example creates a vector from a range of elements that are specified by the iterators *first* and *last*.

Program 31-1 shows how to create and display the contents of an std::vector object:

Program 31-1: **Creating a simple vector**

```
#include <iostream>
#include <vector>

int main()
{
    std::vector<int> intVector(10, 1);
```

```
    int x = 0;
    std::vector<int>::iterator iter;
    for (iter = intVector.begin(); iter != intVector.end(); iter++)
        std::cout << "Element #" << x++ << ": " << *iter << std::endl;
    return 0;
}
```

Program 31-1 displays the following output:

```
Element #0: 1
Element #1: 1
Element #2: 1
Element #3: 1
Element #4: 1
Element #5: 1
Element #6: 1
Element #7: 1
Element #8: 1
Element #9: 1
```

The first thing to notice about Program 31-1 is the `#include <vector>` line, which includes the appropriate header file for the `std::vector` class template. The program creates a ten-element `std::vector` object, of which all the elements are initialized to 1. Notice how the program accesses elements of the `std::vector` object by using the `iter` iterator object. You can think of an iterator as a pointer to an element stored in the container. The call to the vector's `begin` member function returns an iterator that points to the first data element in the vector, whereas the call to `end` returns an iterator that points to the data element at the end of the vector. The `for` loop uses the `++` operator to increment the iterator object so that it points to the next element in the vector.

Inserting and Accessing Vector Elements

To insert new elements to the end of the sequence stored in an `std::vector` object, use the `push_back` or `insert` member function. Program 31-2 creates an empty `std::vector` object, populates the sequence with the characters "A" through "J," and displays the contents of the `std::vector` object.

Program 31-2: **Adding elements to a vector**

```
#include <iostream>
#include <vector>

int main()
{
    std::vector<char> charVector;
    int x = 0;
    for (int i=0; i<10; ++i)
```

Continued

Program 31-2 *(continued)*

```
        charVector.push_back(65 + i);
    std::vector<char>::iterator iter;
    for (iter = charVector.begin(); iter != charVector.end(); iter++)
        std::cout << "Element #" << x++ << ": " << *iter << std::endl;
    return 0;
}
```

Program 31-2 displays the following output:

```
Element #0: A
Element #1: B
Element #2: C
Element #3: D
Element #4: E
Element #5: F
Element #6: G
Element #7: H
Element #8: I
Element #9: J
```

You can specify exactly where to insert new elements by calling the std::vector object's insert member function, which takes as arguments the position at which to start the insertion, the number of elements to insert, and the value to insert. To insert a single element, simply supply an iterator for the position and the value to insert. Program 31-3 creates an empty std::vector object and populates the sequence with the characters "A" through "J." Then the program removes characters from the start of the sequence one at a time, displaying the results as it goes.

Program 31-3: Inserting elements anywhere within a vector

```
#include <iostream>
#include <vector>

int main()
{
    // Create and populate the vector.
    std::vector<char> charVector;
    for (int i=0; i<10; ++i)
        charVector.push_back(65 + i);
    // Display the starting vector.
    std::cout << "Original vector: ";
    std::vector<char>::iterator iter;
    for (iter = charVector.begin(); iter != charVector.end(); iter++)
        std::cout << *iter;
    std::cout << std::endl;
    // Insert five Xs into the vector.
    std::vector<char>::iterator start = charVector.begin();
    charVector.insert(start, 5, 'X');
    // Display the result.
```

```
    std::cout << "Resultant vector: ";
    for (iter = charVector.begin(); iter != charVector.end(); iter++)
        std::cout << *iter;
    return 0;
}
```

Program 31-3 displays the following output:

```
Original vector: ABCDEFGHIJ
Resultant vector: XXXXXABCDEFGHIJ
```

Removing Vector Elements

To delete elements from the end of the sequence stored in an `std::vector` object, use the `pop_back` or `erase` member function. Program 31-4 creates an empty `std::vector` object and populates the sequence with the characters "A" through "J." Then the program removes characters from the sequence one at a time, displaying the results as it goes.

Program 31-4: **Removing elements from a vector**

```
#include <iostream>
#include <vector>

int main()
{
    std::vector<char> charVector;
    for (int i=0; i<10; ++i)
        charVector.push_back(65 + i);
    int size = charVector.size();
    for (int i=0; i<size; ++i) {
        charVector.pop_back();
        std::vector<char>::iterator iter;
        for (iter = charVector.begin(); iter != charVector.end(); iter++)
            std::cout << *iter;
        std::cout << std::endl;
    }
    return 0;
}
```

Program 31-4 displays the following output:

```
ABCDEFGHI
ABCDEFGH
ABCDEFG
ABCDEF
ABCDE
ABCD
ABC
AB
A
```

You can specify the elements to delete by calling the `std::vector` object's `erase` member function, which takes as arguments the position at which to start the deletion and the position of the element at which the deletion should stop (that is, this last element is not deleted). The second argument is not required. To delete a single element, simply supply an iterator for the element as the `erase` member function's single argument. Program 31-5 creates an empty `std::vector` object and populates the sequence with the characters "A" through "J." Then the program removes characters from the start of the sequence one at a time, displaying the results as it goes.

Program 31-5: **Removing elements anywhere within a vector**

```
#include <iostream>
#include <vector>

int main()
{
    std::vector<char> charVector;
    for (int x=0; x<10; ++x)
        charVector.push_back(65 + x);
    int size = charVector.size();
    for (int x=0; x<size; ++x) {
        std::vector<char>::iterator start =
            charVector.begin();
        charVector.erase(start);
        std::vector<char>::iterator iter;
        for (iter = charVector.begin(); iter != charVector.end(); iter++)
            std::cout << *iter;
        std::cout << std::endl;
    }
    return 0;
}
```

Program 31-5 displays the following output:

```
BCDEFGHIJ
CDEFGHIJ
DEFGHIJ
EFGHIJ
FGHIJ
GHIJ
HIJ
IJ
J
```

Comparing Vectors

The `std::vector` class template defines a full set of operators. Among these operators are ones needed to perform comparisons between `std::vector` objects. A program can determine which vectors are equal to each other, or which vector is less than or greater than another. Two `std::vector` objects are equal when they have the same number of elements and all elements in the vector have the same value. Program 31-6 demonstrates how to compare vectors.

Program 31-6: **Comparing vectors**

```
#include <iostream>
#include <vector>

int main()
{
    // Create two vector objects.
    std::vector<char> charVector1;
    for (int x=0; x<10; ++x)
        charVector1.push_back(65 + x);
    std::vector<char> charVector2;
    for (int x=0; x<10; ++x)
        charVector2.push_back(66 + x);
    // Display the vectors.
    std::cout << "Vector 1: ";
    std::vector<char>::iterator iter;
    for (iter = charVector1.begin(); iter != charVector1.end(); iter++)
        std::cout << *iter;
    std::cout << std::endl;
    std::cout << "Vector 2: ";
    for (iter = charVector2.begin(); iter != charVector2.end(); iter++)
        std::cout << *iter;
    std::cout << std::endl;
    // Compare the vectors.
    if (charVector1 == charVector2)
        std::cout << "vector1 == vector2";
    else if (charVector1 < charVector2)
        std::cout << "vector1 < vector2";
    else if (charVector1 > charVector2)
        std::cout << "vector1 > vector2";
    return 0;
}
```

Program 31-6 produces the following output:

```
Vector 1: ABCDEFGHIJ
Vector 2: BCDEFGHIJK
vector1 < vector2
```

Vector Member Functions

The preceding examples show you how to perform the most needed operations with an `std::vector` object. The `std::vector` class template, however, defines more functions than I have shown you so far. Table 31-1 lists some more `std::vector` member functions, along with their descriptions.

Table 31-1: Vector Member Functions

Function	Description
assign(first, last)	Replaces the vector elements with the elements specified by the iterators first and last
assign(num, val)	Replaces the vector elements with num copies of val
at(n)	Returns the value of the element located at position n in the vector
back	Returns a reference to the element at the end of the vector
begin	Returns an iterator that points to the first element in the vector
capacity	Returns the current maximum number of elements that can fit into the vector
clear	Erases all elements of a vector
empty	Returns a true value if the vector is empty
end	Returns an iterator that points to the last element in the vector
erase(start, end)	Erases a range of vector elements specified by the iterators start and end
erase(i)	Erases the vector element pointed to by the iterator i
front	Returns a reference to the element at the start of the vector
insert(i, x)	Inserts value x into the vector at the position specified by iterator i
insert(i, start, end)	Inserts the range of values specified by the iterators start and end into a vector at the position specified by the iterator i
insert(i, n, x)	Inserts n copies of x into a vector at the position specified by the iterator i
max_size	Returns the maximum size (the greatest number of elements that can fit) of the vector
pop_back	Removes the vector's last element
push_back(x)	Places the value x at the end of the vector
rbegin	Returns a reverse iterator that points beyond the last element in the vector
rend	Returns a reverse iterator that points to the first element of the vector
reverse	Reverses the order of the elements
resize(n, x)	Resizes the vector by n elements, initializing the new elements with the value x
size	Returns the size (the number of elements) of the vector
swap(vector)	Swaps the contents of two vectors

The deque Class Template

An std::deque object is similar to a vector. However, a deque object is efficient at placing elements in, or removing elements from, both the start and the end of the sequence. A vector is efficient only when performing such operations at the end of the sequence. Like a vector, a std::deque object provides random access to its elements and can resize itself dynamically as needed, but insertion or removal from anywhere else in the sequence is not as efficient.

You can construct an std::deque object in several ways, as shown here:

```
std::deque<type> name;
std::deque<type> name(size);
std::deque<type> name(size, value);
std::deque<type> name(mydeque);
std::deque<type> name(first, last);
```

The first example creates an empty std::deque object named *name* that can hold data of the type *type*. For example, to create an empty std::deque object for integers, you can write:

```
deque<int> intDeque;
```

The second example creates an std::deque object with an initial size of *size*, whereas the third example creates an std::deque object with an initial size of *size*, each element of which is initialized to *value*. The fourth example uses the copy constructor, which makes a std::deque object from an existing deque, *mydeque*. Finally, the fifth example creates a deque from a range of elements that the iterators *first* and *last* specify.

Program 31-7 shows how to create and display the contents of an std::deque object.

Program 31-7: **Creating a simple deque**

```cpp
#include <iostream>
#include <deque>

int main()
{
    std::deque<int> intDeque(10, 1);
    int x = 0;
    std::deque<int>::iterator iter;
    for (iter = intDeque.begin(); iter != intDeque.end(); iter++)
        std::cout << "Element #" << x++ << ": " << *iter << std::endl;
    return 0;
}
```

Program 31-7 displays the following output:

```
Element #0: 1
Element #1: 1
Element #2: 1
Element #3: 1
```

```
Element #4: 1
Element #5: 1
Element #6: 1
Element #7: 1
Element #8: 1
Element #9: 1
```

The first thing to notice about Program 31-7 is the #include <deque> line, which includes the appropriate header file for the std::deque class template. The program creates a ten-element std::deque object, of which all the elements are initialized to 1.

Inserting and Accessing Deque Elements

To insert new elements into the sequence stored in a std::deque object, you can use either the push_front or push_back member function. (Note that the std::vector template class does not define a push_front member function because inserting new elements into the beginning of a vector is not an efficient operation.) Program 31-8 creates an empty std::deque object, populates the sequence with the characters "J" through "A," and displays the contents of the std::deque object.

Program 31-8: **Adding elements to a deque**

```
#include <iostream>
#include <deque>

int main()
{
    std::deque<char> charDeque;
    int x = 0;
    for (int i=0; i<10; ++i)
        charDeque.push_front(65 + i);
    std::deque<char>::iterator iter;
    for (iter = charDeque.begin(); iter != charDeque.end(); iter++)
        std::cout << "Element #" << x++ << ": " << *iter << std::endl;
    return 0;
}
```

Program 31-8 displays the following output:

```
Element #0: J
Element #1: I
Element #2: H
Element #3: G
Element #4: F
Element #5: E
Element #6: D
Element #7: C
Element #8: B
Element #9: A
```

You can specify exactly where to insert new elements by calling the std::deque object's insert member function, which takes as arguments the position at which to start the insertion, the number of elements to insert, and the value to insert. To insert a single element, simply supply an iterator for the position and the value to insert. Program 31-9 creates an empty std::deque object and populates the sequence with the characters "J" through "A." Then the program removes characters from the start of the sequence one at a time, displaying the results as it goes.

> **Program 31-9: Inserting elements anywhere within a deque**

```
#include <iostream>
#include <deque>

int main()
{
    // Create and populate the deque.
    std::deque<char> charDeque;
    for (int x=0; x<10; ++x)
        charDeque.push_front(65 + x);
    // Display the starting deque.
    std::cout << "Original deque: ";
    std::deque<char>::iterator iter;
    for (iter = charDeque.begin(); iter != charDeque.end(); iter++)
        std::cout << *iter;
    std::cout << std::endl;
    // Insert five Xs into the deque.
    std::deque<char>::iterator start =
        charDeque.begin();
    charDeque.insert(start, 5, 'X');
    // Display the result.
    std::cout << "Resultant deque: ";
    for (iter = charDeque.begin(); iter != charDeque.end(); iter++)
        std::cout << *iter;
    return 0;
}
```

Program 31-9 displays the following output:

```
Original deque: JIHGFEDCBA
Resultant deque: XXXXXJIHGFEDCBA
```

Removing Deque Elements

To delete elements from the sequence stored in an std::deque object, you can use the pop_front or pop_back member function. Program 31-10 creates an empty std::deque object and populates the sequence with the characters "J" through "A." Then the program removes characters from the sequence one at a time, displaying the results as it goes.

Program 31-10: **Removing elements from a deque**

```
#include <iostream>
#include <deque>

int main()
{
    std::deque<char> charDeque;
    for (int x=0; x<10; ++x)
        charDeque.push_front(65 + x);
    int size = charDeque.size();
    for (int x=0; x<size; ++x) {
        charDeque.pop_back();
        std::deque<char>::iterator iter;
        for (iter = charDeque.begin(); iter != charDeque.end(); iter++)
            std::cout << *iter;
        std::cout << std::endl;
    }
    return 0;
}
```

Program 31-10 displays the following output:

```
JIHGFEDCB
JIHGFEDC
JIHGFED
JIHGFE
JIHGF
JIHG
JIH
JI
J
```

You can specify the elements to delete by calling the std::deque object's erase member function, which takes as arguments the position at which to start the deletion and the position of the element at which the deletion should stop (that is, this last element is not deleted). The second argument is not required. To delete a single element, simply supply an iterator for the element as the erase member function's single argument. Program 31-11 creates an empty std::deque object and populates the sequence with the characters "J" through "A." Then the program removes characters from the start of the sequence one at a time, displaying the results as it goes.

Program 31-11: **Removing elements anywhere within a deque**

```
#include <iostream>
#include <deque>

int main()
```

```
{
    std::deque<char> charDeque;
    for (int x=0; x<10; ++x)
        charDeque.push_front(65 + x);
    int size = charDeque.size();
    for (int x=0; x<size; ++x) {
        std::deque<char>::iterator start =
            charDeque.begin();
        charDeque.erase(start);
        std::deque<char>::iterator iter;
        for (iter = charDeque.begin(); iter != charDeque.end(); iter++)
            std::cout << *iter;
        std::cout << std::endl;
    }
    return 0;
}
```

Program 31-11 displays the following output:

```
IHGFEDCBA
HGFEDCBA
GFEDCBA
FEDCBA
EDCBA
DCBA
CBA
BA
A
```

Comparing Deques

Like the `vector` class template, `std::deque` defines a full set of operators. A program easily can determine which deques are equal to each other, or which deque is less than or greater than another. Two `std::deque` objects are equal when they have the same number of elements and all elements in the deque have the same value. Program 31-12 demonstrates how to compare deques.

Program 31-12: **Comparing deques**

```
#include <iostream>
#include <deque>

int main()
{
    // Create two deque objects.
    std::deque<char> charDeque1;
    for (int x=0; x<10; ++x)
```

Continued

Program 31-12 *(continued)*

```
        charDeque1.push_front(65 + x);
    std::deque<char> charDeque2;
    for (int x=0; x<10; ++x)
        charDeque2.push_front(66 + x);
    // Display the deques.
    std::cout << "Deque 1: ";
    std::deque<char>::iterator iter;
    for (iter = charDeque1.begin(); iter != charDeque1.end(); iter++)
        std::cout << *iter;
    std::cout << std::endl;
    std::cout << "Deque 2: ";
    for (iter = charDeque2.begin(); iter != charDeque2.end(); iter++)
        std::cout << *iter;
    std::cout << std::endl;
    // Compare the deques.
    if (charDeque1 == charDeque2)
        std::cout << "deque1 == deque2";
    else if (charDeque1 < charDeque2)
        std::cout << "deque1 < deque2";
    else if (charDeque1 > charDeque2)
        std::cout << "deque1 > deque2";
    return 0;
}
```

Program 31-12 produces the following output:

```
Deque 1: JIHGFEDCBA
Deque 2: KJIHGFEDCB
deque1 < deque2
```

Deque Member Functions

The preceding examples show you how to perform the most needed operations with an std::deque object. The std::deque class template, however, defines more functions than I have shown you so far. Table 31-2 lists the std::deque member functions, along with their descriptions.

Table 31-2: Deque Member Functions

Function	Description
assign(first, last)	Replaces the deque elements with the elements specified by the iterators first and last
assign(num, val)	Replaces the deque elements with num copies of val
at(n)	Returns the value of the element located at position n in the deque

Function	Description
back	Returns a reference to the element at the end of the deque
begin	Returns an iterator that points to the first element in the deque
clear	Erases all elements of a deque
empty	Returns a true value if the deque is empty
end	Returns an iterator that points to the last element in the deque
erase(start, end)	Erases a range of deque elements specified by the iterators start and end
erase(i)	Erases the deque element pointed to by the iterator i
front	Returns a reference to the element at the start of the deque
insert(i, x)	Inserts value x into the deque at the position specified by iterator i
insert(i, start, end)	Inserts the range of values specified by the iterators start and end into a deque at the position specified by the iterator i
insert(i, n, x)	Inserts n copies of x into a deque at the position specified by the iterator I
max_size	Returns the maximum size (the greatest number of elements that can fit) of the deque
pop_back	Removes the deque's last element
pop_front	Removes the deque's first element
push_back(x)	Places the value x at the end of the deque
push_front(x)	Places the value x at the start of the deque
rbegin	Returns a reverse iterator that points beyond the last element in the deque
rend	Returns a reverse iterator that points to the first element of the deque
resize(n, x)	Resizes the deque by n elements, initializing the new elements with the value x
size	Returns the size (the number of elements) of the deque
swap(deque)	Swaps the contents of two deques

The list Class Template

An std::list object is similar to a vector or a deque, except that a list object provides no random access. However, an std::list object is efficient at placing elements in, or removing elements from, anywhere in the sequence. Also, like a vector or a deque, an std::list object can resize itself dynamically as needed. You can construct an std::list object in several ways, as shown here:

```
std::list<type> name;
std::list<type> name(size);
std::list<type> name(size, value);
std::list<type> name(mylist);
std::list<type> name(first, last);
```

The first example creates an empty `std::list` object named *name* that can hold data of the type *type*. For example, to create an empty `std::list` object for integers, you can write:

```
list<int> intList;
```

The second example creates a `std::list` object with an initial size of *size*, whereas the third example creates a `std::list` object with an initial size of *size*, of which each element is initialized to *value*. The fourth example uses the copy constructor, which makes a list object from an existing list, *mylist*. Finally, the fifth example creates a list from a range of elements that are specified by the iterators *first* and *last*.

Program 31-13 shows how to create and display the contents of a list object.

Program 31-13: **Creating a simple list**

```
#include <iostream>
#include <list>

int main()
{
    std::list<int> intList(10, 1);
    int x = 0;
    std::list<int>::iterator iter;
    for (iter = intList.begin(); iter != intList.end(); iter++)
        std::cout << "Element #" << x++ << ": " << *iter << std::endl;
    return 0;
}
```

Program 31-13 displays the following output:

```
Element #0: 1
Element #1: 1
Element #2: 1
Element #3: 1
Element #4: 1
Element #5: 1
Element #6: 1
Element #7: 1
Element #8: 1
Element #9: 1
```

The first thing to notice about Program 31-13 is the #include <list> line, which includes the appropriate header file for the list class template. The program creates a ten-element std::list object, of which all the elements are initialized to 1.

Inserting List Elements

To insert new elements into the sequence stored in an std::list object, you can use the push_front, push_back, or insert member functions. All such insertion operations are efficient. Program 31-14 creates an empty std::list object, populates the sequence with the characters "J" through "A," and displays the contents of the std::list object.

Program 31-14: **Adding elements to a list**

```cpp
#include <iostream>
#include <list>

int main()
{
    std::list<char> charList;
    int x = 0;
    for (int i=0; i<10; ++i)
        charList.push_front(65 + i);
    std::list<char>::iterator iter;
    for (iter = charList.begin(); iter != charList.end(); iter++)
        std::cout << "Element #" << x++ << ": " << *iter << std::endl;
    return 0;
}
```

Program 31-14 displays the following output:

```
Element #0: J
Element #1: I
Element #2: H
Element #3: G
Element #4: F
Element #5: E
Element #6: D
Element #7: C
Element #8: Б
Element #9: A
```

You can specify exactly where to insert new elements by calling the std::list object's insert member function, which takes as arguments the position at which to start the insertion, the number of elements to insert, and the value to insert. To insert a single element, simply supply an iterator for the position and the value to insert. Program 31-15 creates an empty std::list object and populates the sequence with the characters "J" through "A." Then it inserts five Xs into the list's second position.

Program 31-15: **Inserting elements anywhere within a list**

```
#include <iostream>
#include <list>

int main()
{
    // Create and populate the list.
    std::list<char> charList;
    for (int x=0; x<10; ++x)
        charList.push_front(65 + x);
    // Display contents of list.
    std::cout << "Original list: ";
    std::list<char>::iterator iter;
    for (iter = charList.begin(); iter != charList.end(); iter++)
        std::cout << *iter;
    std::cout << std::endl;
    // Insert five Xs into the list.
    std::list<char>::iterator start = charList.begin();
    charList.insert(++start, 5, 'X');
    // Display the result.
    std::cout << "Resultant list: ";
    for (iter = charList.begin(); iter != charList.end(); iter++)
        std::cout << *iter;
    return 0;
}
```

Program 31-15 displays the following output:

```
Original list: JIHGFEDCBA
Resultant list: JXXXXXIHGFEDCBA
```

Removing List Elements

To delete elements from the sequence stored in an `std::list` object, you can use the `pop_front`, `pop_back`, `erase`, or `remove` member functions. Program 31-16 creates an empty `std::list` object and populates the sequence with the characters "A" through "E." Then the program removes the "E" character from the sequence and displays the results.

Program 31-16: **Removing elements from a list**

```
#include <iostream>
#include <list>

int main()
{
    std::list<char> charList;
```

```
    for (int x=0; x<10; ++x)
        charList.push_back(65 + x);
    // Display contents of list.
    std::cout << "Original list: ";
    std::list<char>::iterator iter;
    for (iter = charList.begin(); iter != charList.end(); iter++)
        std::cout << *iter;
    std::cout << std::endl;
    charList.remove('E');
    // Display contents of list again.
    std::cout << "Resultant list: ";
    for (iter = charList.begin(); iter != charList.end(); iter++)
        std::cout << *iter;
    std::cout << std::endl;
    return 0;
}
```

Program 31-16 displays the following output:

```
Original list: ABCDEFGHIJ
Resultant list: ABCDFGHIJ
```

You can specify the elements to delete by calling the `std::list` object's `erase` member function, which takes as arguments the position at which to start the deletion and the position of the element at which the deletion should stop (that is, this last element is not deleted). The second argument is not required. To delete a single element, simply supply an iterator for the element as the `erase` member function's single argument. Program 31-17 creates an empty `std::list` object and populates the sequence with the characters "A" through "J." Then the program erases the character from the sequence's second position, displaying the results.

Program 31-17: **Removing elements anywhere within a list**

```
#include <iostream>
#include <list>

int main()
{
    std::list<char> charList;
    for (int x=0; x<10; ++x)
        charList.push_front(65 + x);
    std::list<char>::iterator start =
        charList.begin();
    charList.erase(++start);
    std::list<char>::iterator iter;
    for (iter = charList.begin(); iter != charList.end(); iter++)
        std::cout << *iter;
    return 0;
}
```

Program 31-17 produces the following output:

```
JHGFEDCBA
```

Comparing Lists

A program easily can determine which lists are equal to each other or which list is less than or greater than another. Two std::list objects are equal when they have the same number of elements and all elements in the list have the same value. Program 31-18 demonstrates how to compare lists.

Program 31-18: **Comparing lists**

```cpp
#include <iostream>
#include <list>

int main()
{
    // Create two list objects.
    std::list<char> charList1;
    for (int x=0; x<10; ++x)
        charList1.push_front(65 + x);
    std::list<char> charList2;
    for (int x=0; x<10; ++x)
        charList2.push_front(66 + x);
    // Display the lists.
    std::cout << "list 1: ";
    std::list<char>::iterator iter;
    for (iter = charList1.begin(); iter != charList1.end(); iter++)
        std::cout << *iter;
    std::cout << std::endl;
    std::cout << "list 2: ";
    for (iter = charList2.begin(); iter != charList2.end(); iter++)
        std::cout << *iter;
    std::cout << std::endl;
    // Compare the lists.
    if (charList1 == charList2)
        std::cout << "list1 == list2";
    else if (charList1 < charList2)
        std::cout << "list1 < list2";
    else if (charList1 > charList2)
        std::cout << "list1 > list2";
    return 0;
}
```

Program 31-18 produces the following output:

```
list 1: JIHGFEDCBA
list 2: KJIHGFEDCB
list1 < list2
```

List Member Functions

The preceding examples show you how to perform the most needed operations with an std::list object. The std::list class template, however, defines more functions than I have shown you so far. Table 31-3 lists the std::list member functions, along with their descriptions.

Table 31-3: List Member Functions

Function	Description
assign(first, last)	Replaces the contents of the list with the elements pointed to by the first and last iterators
assign(num, val)	Replaces the contents of the list with num elements of the value val
back	Returns a reference to the element at the end of the list
begin	Returns an iterator that points to the first element in the list
clear	Erases all elements of a list
empty	Returns a true value if the list is empty
end	Returns an iterator that points to the last element in the list
erase(start, end)	Erases a range of list elements specified by the iterators start and end
erase(i)	Erases the list element pointed to by the iterator i
front	Returns a reference to the element at the start of the list
insert(i, x)	Inserts value x into the list at the position specified by iterator i
insert(i, start, end)	Inserts the range of values specified by the iterators start and end into a list at the position specified by the iterator i
insert(i, n, x)	Inserts n copies of x into a list at the position specified by the iterator I
max_size	Returns the maximum size (the greatest number of elements that can fit) of the list
merge(listref)	Inserts all the elements in the list referenced by listref into the list
pop_back	Removes the list's last element
pop_front	Removes the list's first element
push_back(x)	Places the value x at the end of the list
push_front(x)	Places the value x at the start of the list
rbegin	Returns a reverse iterator that points beyond the last element in the list

Continued

Table 31-3 *(continued)*

Function	Description
remove(val)	Removes all occurrences of val from the list
remove_if(pred)	Removes all occurrences of elements for which the predicate pred is true
rend	Returns a reverse iterator that points to the first element of the list
resize(n, x)	Resizes the list by n elements, initializing the new elements with the value x
reverse	Reverses the order of the elements in the list
size	Returns the size (the number of elements) of the list
sort	Sorts the list based on the default predicate
sort(pred)	Sorts the list based on the specified predicate
swap(listref)	Swaps the contents of two lists
unique	Removes all the elements necessary to create a list of unique elements — that is, a list that contains no duplicate elements
unique(pred)	Removes all the elements necessary to create a list of unique elements based on the specified predicate

The std::stack Container Adaptor

If you've been programming for long, you know that a stack is a sequence that implements first-in, last-out operations on its elements. Because stacks are such a common data structure, STL implements them. However, stacks are implemented in STL not by a new container class template as you might expect, but rather by a container adaptor named, appropriately enough, std::stack. You can use the std::stack container adaptor to create a stack from an std::vector, std::deque, or std::list object.

Construct a std::stack object, as shown here:

```
std::stack<type, container> name;
```

The type parameter is the type of data the stack manipulates, and the container parameter is the type of container used in the stack implementation — either std::vector, std::deque, or std::list. For example, to create a std::stack object for integers based on a std::list object, you can write:

```
std::stack<int, std::list<int> > intStack;
```

Program 31-19 shows how to create and manipulate an std::stack object.

Program 31-19: **Managing a stack**

```cpp
#include <iostream>
#include <list>
#include <stack>

int main()
{
    std::stack<int, std::list<int> > intStack;
    std::cout << "Values pushed onto stack:" << std::endl;
    for (int x=1; x<11; ++x) {
        intStack.push(x*100);
        std::cout << x*100 << std::endl;
    }
    std::cout << "Values popped from stack:" << std::endl;
    int size = intStack.size();
    for (int x=0; x<size; ++x) {
        std::cout << intStack.top() << std::endl;
        intStack.pop();
    }
    return 0;
}
```

Program 31-19 produces the following output:

```
Values pushed onto stack:
100
200
300
400
500
600
700
800
900
1000

Values popped from stack:
1000
900
800
700
600
500
400
300
200
100
```

Because stacks are such simple data structures, they require only basic operations. For this reason, the std::stack container adaptor defines only the empty, size, top, push, and pop functions, all of which, except empty, appear in Program 31-19.

The std::queue Container Adaptor

A *queue* is a data structure that implements first-in, first-out operations on its elements. That is, elements in a queue are inserted at one end and removed from the other. STL implements queues with a container adaptor named std::queue. You can use the std::queue container adaptor to create a queue from an std::deque or std::list object.

Construct a std::queue object, as shown here:

```
std::queue<type, container> name;
```

The type parameter is the type of data the queue manipulates, and the container parameter is the type of container used in the queue implementation—either std::deque or std::list. For example, to create an std::queue object for integers based on a std::list object, you can write:

```
std::queue<int, std::list<int> > intQueue;
```

Program 31-20 shows how to create and manipulate an std::queue object.

Program 31-20: **Managing a queue**

```cpp
#include <iostream>
#include <list>
#include <queue>

int main()
{
    std::queue<int, std::list<int> > intQueue;
    std::cout << "Values pushed onto queue:" << std::endl;
    for (int x=1; x<11; ++x) {
        intQueue.push(x*100);
        std::cout << x*100 << std::endl;
    }
    std::cout << "Values removed from queue:" << std::endl;
    int size = intQueue.size();
    for (int x=0; x<size; ++x) {
        std::cout << intQueue.front() << std::endl;
        intQueue.pop();
    }
    return 0;
}
```

Program 31-20 produces the following output:

```
Values pushed onto queue:
100
200
300
400
500
600
700
800
900
1000
Values removed from queue:
100
200
300
400
500
600
700
800
900
1000
```

Because, like stacks, queues are such simple data structures, they require only basic operations. For this reason, the `std::queue` container adaptor defines only the `empty`, `size`, `front`, `back`, `push`, and `pop` functions, several of which appear in Program 31-20.

The std::priority_queue Container Adaptor

A *priority queue* is a data structure that pops elements from the sequence in order of priority; the priority is based on the supplied comparison function (called a predicate). For example, if you use the predefined `std::less<>` predicate each time you add or remove a value from the priority queue, the contents are arranged in descending order. This gives the value with the largest value the highest priority.

STL implements priority queues with a container adaptor named `std::priority_queue`. You can use the `std::priority_queue` container adaptor to create a priority queue from an `std::vector` or `std::deque` object.

Construct a `std::queue` object, as shown here:

```
std::queue<type, container, predicate> name;
```

The `type` parameter is the type of data the priority queue manipulates, and the `container` parameter is the type of container used in the priority queue implementation — either `std::deque` or `std::vector`. The `predicate` parameter is the predicate (comparison function) that is used to determine the priority of elements in the priority queue. The default predicate is `std::less<>`. For example, to create a `std::queue` object for integers based on an `std::vector` object and using the default predicate, you can write:

```
std::queue<int, std::vector<int> > intQueue;
```

Program 31-21 shows how to create and manipulate an std::priority_queue object.

Program 31-21: **Managing a priority_queue**

```
#include <iostream>
#include <list>
#include <queue>

int main()
{
    std::priority_queue<int, std::vector<int> > intPQueue;
    intPQueue.push(400);
    intPQueue.push(100);
    intPQueue.push(500);
    intPQueue.push(300);
    intPQueue.push(200);
    std::cout << "Values removed from priority queue:" << std::endl;
    int size = intPQueue.size();
    for (int x=0; x<size; ++x) {
        std::cout << intPQueue.top() << std::endl;
        intPQueue.pop();
    }
    return 0;
}
```

The program shown in Program 31-21 produces the following results:

```
Values removed from priority queue:
500
400
300
200
100
```

Because the program defines the priority queue using the default std::less<> predicate, values are removed from the sequence in order from largest to smallest. You can create a priority queue that organizes its contents based on other priorities. For example, if the program uses the predefined std::greater<> when it defines the priority queue, the highest priority value is the smallest because the values are arranged in the priority queue in ascending order. To see this in action, replace the line

```
std::priority_queue<int, std::vector<int> > intPQueue;
```

in Program 31-21 with this line:

```
std::priority_queue<int, std::vector<int>, std::greater<int> > intPQueue;
```

When you run the modified program, the output now looks like this:

```
Values removed from priority queue:
100
200
300
400
500
```

Summary

STL defines a set of common and useful sequence containers that easily enable you to add vectors, lists, queues, and other types of containers to your programs. The template classes that define these containers also provide the member functions needed to manipulate the container contents in useful ways. In the next chapter, you learn about another type of STL container, the associative container, which supports indexed retrieval of objects by value.

✦   ✦   ✦

Associative Containers

The STL associative containers are class templates that implement abstract data types for object containers that use key values to locate elements. In other words, think of an array that might take strings or dates as a subscript. Associative containers are different from sequences (Chapter 31) in that each element in an associative container has a key through which the element can be located.

Associative Containers

STL's associative containers include the following types:

- ✦ std::set: A type of random-access container in which the key and the data element are the same value. All elements of an std::set object must be unique values. That is, an std::set cannot contain duplicate elements.

- ✦ std::multiset: Another type of container in which the key and the data element are the same value. Unlike the std::set object, an std::multiset can contain duplicate elements.

- ✦ std::map: A type of container that contains pairs of values. One value is the actual data value and the other is the key used to locate the data value. Only one element can be associated with a specific key.

- ✦ std::multimap: Another type of container that contains pairs of values. Unlike a std::map object, however, an std::multimap's keys can be associated with multiple data elements.

- ✦ std::bitset: A type of container that contains a series of bit values. Each element in a bitset object can be the value 0 or 1.

In the following sections, you explore the various types of associative containers and how to use them in your programs.

The std::set Class Template

An std::set object enables a program to store a group of values in sorted order. In a set, the elements of the set act as both the stored data and the key to that data. Essentially, a set is much like an ordered list. You can construct an std::set object in several ways, as shown here:

```
std::set<type, predicate> name;
std::set<type, predicate> name(myset);
std::set<type, predicate> name(first, last);
```

The first example creates an empty std::set object named *name* that can hold data of the type *type*. The object uses the function specified by *predicate* for ordering the elements of the set. For example, to create an empty std::set object for integers, you can write:

```
std::set<int, std::less<int> > intSet;
```

The second example uses the copy constructor, which makes an std::set object from an existing set, *myset*. Finally, the third example creates a set from a range of elements that the iterators *first* and *last* specify. Note that the std::less<> predicate is the default so you do not need to include it in the declaration.

Program 32-1 shows how to create and display the contents of an std::set object.

Program 32-1: **Creating a simple set**

```
#include <iostream>
#include <set>

int main()
{
    // Create the set object.
    std::set<int> intSet;
    // Populate the set with values.
    intSet.insert(10);
    intSet.insert(5);
    intSet.insert(1);
    intSet.insert(3);
    intSet.insert(8);
    // Display the contents of the set.
    std::cout << "Contents of set: " << std::endl;
    std::set<int>::iterator iter;
    for (iter=intSet.begin(); iter!=intSet.end(); iter++)
        std::cout << *iter << std::endl;
    return 0;
}
```

Program 32-1 displays the following output:

```
Contents of set:
1
3
5
8
10
```

The first thing to notice about Program 32-1 is the #include <set> line, which includes the appropriate header file for the std::set class template. The program creates a five-element std::set object, containing the values 1, 3, 5, 8, and 10.

Inserting Set Elements

To insert new elements into the sequence stored in an std::set object, you use the insert member function. Program 32-2 creates an empty std::set object, populates the sequence with the characters "E" through "A," and displays the contents of the std::set object.

> Program 32-2: **Adding elements to a set**

```
#include <iostream>
#include <set>

int main()
{
    // Create the set object.
    std::set<char> charSet;
    // Populate the set with values.
    charSet.insert('E');
    charSet.insert('D');
    charSet.insert('C');
    charSet.insert('B');
    charSet.insert('A');
    // Display the contents of the set.
    std::cout << "Contents of set: " << std::endl;
    std::set<char>::iterator iter;
    for (iter = charSet.begin(); iter != charSet.end(); iter++)
        std::cout << *iter << std::endl;
    return 0;
}
```

Program 32-2 displays the following output:

```
Contents of set:
A
B
C
D
E
```

Removing Set Elements

To delete an element from the sequence stored in an std::set object, you call the erase member function. This function takes as arguments the position at which to start the deletion and the position of the element at which the deletion should stop (that is, this last element is not deleted). The second argument is not required. To delete a single element, simply supply an iterator for the element as the erase member function's single argument. Program 32-3 creates an empty std::set object and populates the sequence with the characters "A" through "E." The program then erases the character from the sequence's second position and displays the results.

Program 32-3: **Removing elements anywhere within a set**

```
#include <iostream>
#include <set>
int main()
{
    // Create the set object.
    std::set<char> charSet;
    // Populate the set with values.
    charSet.insert('E');
    charSet.insert('D');
    charSet.insert('C');
    charSet.insert('B');
    charSet.insert('A');
    // Display the contents of the set.
    std::cout << "Contents of set: " << std::endl;
    std::set<char>::iterator iter;
    for (iter = charSet.begin(); iter != charSet.end(); iter++)
        std::cout << *iter << std::endl;
    // Erase the set's second element.
    iter = charSet.begin();
    charSet.erase(++iter);
    // Display the new contents of the set.
    std::cout << "Contents of new set: " << std::endl;
    for (iter = charSet.begin(); iter != charSet.end(); iter++)
        std::cout << *iter << std::endl;
    return 0;
}
```

Program 32-3 displays the following output:

```
Contents of set:
A
B
C
D
E
Contents of new set:
A
C
D
E
```

Searching a Set

A program easily can locate an element in a set by calling the `find` member function, which takes as its single argument the value for which to search. The `find` function returns an iterator that points to the located element, or an iterator that points to the end of the set if it does not find the requested element. Program 32-4 demonstrates how to search a set.

Program 32-4: **Searching a set**

```
#include <iostream>
#include <set>
int main()
{
    // Create the set object.
    std::set<char> charSet;
    // Populate the set with values.
    charSet.insert('E');
    charSet.insert('D');
    charSet.insert('C');
    charSet.insert('B');
    charSet.insert('A');
    // Display the contents of the set.
    std::cout << "Contents of set: " << std::endl;
    std::set<char>::iterator iter;
    for (iter = charSet.begin(); iter != charSet.end(); iter++)
        std::cout << *iter << std::endl;
    std::cout << std::endl;
    // Find the D.
    iter = charSet.find('D');
    if (iter == charSet.end())
        std::cout << "Element not found.";
    else
        std::cout << "Element found: " << *iter;
    return 0;
}
```

Program 32-4 produces the following output:

```
Contents of set:
A
B
C
D
E

Element found: D
```

Comparing Sets

A program easily can determine whether sets are equal to each other or which set is less than or greater than another. Two std::set objects are equal when they have the same number of elements and each set contains elements identical to the other set. Program 32-5 demonstrates how to compare sets.

Program 32-5: Comparing sets

```cpp
#include <iostream>
#include <set>
int main()
{
    // Create the first set object.
    std::set<char> charSet1;
    // Populate the set with values.
    charSet1.insert('E');
    charSet1.insert('D');
    charSet1.insert('C');
    charSet1.insert('B');
    charSet1.insert('A');
    // Display the contents of the first set.
    std::cout << "Contents of first set: " << std::endl;
    std::set<char>::iterator iter;
    for (iter = charSet1.begin(); iter != charSet1.end(); iter++)
        std::cout << *iter << std::endl;
    std::cout << std::endl;
    // Create the second set object.
    std::set<char> charSet2;
    // Populate the set with values.
    charSet2.insert('J');
    charSet2.insert('I');
    charSet2.insert('H');
    charSet2.insert('G');
    charSet2.insert('F');
    // Display the contents of the second set.
    std::cout << "Contents of second set: " << std::endl;
    for (iter = charSet2.begin(); iter != charSet2.end(); iter++)
        std::cout << *iter << std::endl;
    std::cout << std::endl;
    // Compare the sets.
    if (charSet1 == charSet2)
        std::cout << "set1 == set2";
    else if (charSet1 < charSet2)
        std::cout << "set1 < set2";
    else if (charSet1 > charSet2)
        std::cout << "set1 > set2";
    return 0;
}
```

Program 32-5 produces the following output:

```
Contents of first set:
A
B
C
D
E

Contents of second set:
F
G
H
I
J

set1 < set2
```

Set Member Functions

The preceding examples show you how to perform the most needed operations with an std::set object. The std::set class template, however, defines more functions than we have shown you so far. Table 32-1 lists the std::set member functions along with their descriptions.

Table 32-1: Set Member Functions

Function	Description
begin	Returns an iterator that points to the first element in the set
clear	Erases all elements of a set
count(x)	Returns the number of instances of x in the set (either 0 or 1)
empty	Returns a true value if the set is empty
end	Returns an iterator that points to the last element in the set
equal_range(x)	Returns two iterators that represent x's lower and upper bounds
erase(i)	Erases the set element pointed to by the iterator i
erase(start, end)	Erases a range of set elements specified by the iterators start and end
erase(x)	Erases the set element x
find(x)	Returns an iterator that points to x. If x does not exist, the returned iterator is equal to end.
insert(i, x)	Inserts value x into the set. The search for x's correct position starts at the element specified by iterator i.

Continued

Table 32-1 *(continued)*

Function	Description
insert(start, end)	Inserts the range of values specified by the iterators start and end into the set
insert(x)	Inserts x into the set
lower_bound(x)	Returns an iterator to the element immediately preceding x
max_size	Returns the maximum size (the greatest number of elements that can fit) of the set
rbegin	Returns a reverse iterator that points beyond the last element in the set
rend	Returns a reverse iterator that points to the first element of the set
size	Returns the size (the number of elements) of the set
swap(set)	Swaps the contents of two sets
upper_bound(x)	Returns an iterator that points to x
value_comp	Returns the object of type value_compare that determines the order of elements in the set

The std::multiset Class Template

An std::multiset object enables a program to store a group of values in sorted order. Just as with a set, the elements of the multiset act as both the stored data and the key to that data. However, unlike a set, a multiset can contain duplicate values. You can construct an std::multiset object in several ways, as shown here:

```
std::multiset<type, predicate> name;
std::multiset<type, predicate> name(mymultiset);
std::multiset<type, predicate> name(first, last);
```

The first example creates an empty std::multiset object named *name* that can hold data of the type *type*. The object uses the function specified by *predicate* for ordering the elements of the set. (The C++ library defines these functions, or you can provide your own; see the "User Defined Predicates" section later in this chapter.) For example, to create an empty multiset object for integers, you can write:

```
std::multiset<int, std::less<int> > intSet;
```

The second example uses the copy constructor, which makes an std::multiset object from an existing multiset, *mymultiset*. Finally, the third example creates a set from a range of elements that the iterators *first* and *last* specify. Note that the std::less<> predicate is the default and you do not need to include it in the declaration. Program 32-6 shows how to create and display the contents of an std::multiset object.

Program 32-6: Creating a simple multiset

```
#include <iostream>
#include <set>

int main()
{
    // Create the multiset object.
    std::multiset<int> intMultiset;
    // Populate the multiset with values.
    intMultiset.insert(10);
    intMultiset.insert(5);
    intMultiset.insert(1);
    intMultiset.insert(3);
    intMultiset.insert(8);
    intMultiset.insert(5);
    intMultiset.insert(8);
    // Display the contents of the multiset.
    std::cout << "Contents of multiset: " << std::endl;
    std::multiset<int>::iterator iter;
    for (iter = intMultiset.begin(); iter != intMultiset.end(); iter++)
        std::cout << *iter << std::endl;
    return 0;
}
```

Program 32-6 displays the following output:

```
Contents of set:
1
3
5
5
8
8
10
```

Program 32-6 includes the ⟨set⟩ header, which includes the appropriate header file for the std::multiset class template. (Yes, it's the same header file used for the std::set class template.) The program creates a seven-element std::multiset object containing the values 1, 3, 5, 5, 8, 8, and 10.

Inserting std::multiset Elements

To insert new elements into the sequence stored in an std::multiset object, you use the insert member function. Because, like the std::set object, the elements of an std::multiset object are sorted, there are no push_front and push_back member functions. Program 32-7 creates an empty std::multiset object, populates the sequence with the characters "E" through "A" (including duplicates of "B" and "D"), and displays the contents of the std::multiset object.

Program 32-7: **Adding elements to a multiset**

```cpp
#include <iostream>
#include <set>

int main()
{
    // Create the multiset object.
    std::multiset<char> charMultiset;
    // Populate the multiset with values.
    charMultiset.insert('E');
    charMultiset.insert('D');
    charMultiset.insert('C');
    charMultiset.insert('B');
    charMultiset.insert('A');
    charMultiset.insert('B');
    charMultiset.insert('D');
    // Display the contents of the multiset.
    std::cout << "Contents of multiset: " << std::endl;
    std::multiset<char>::iterator iter;
    for (iter = charMultiset.begin(); iter != charMultiset.end(); iter++)
        std::cout << *iter << std::endl;
    return 0;
}
```

Program 32-7 displays the following output:

```
Contents of multiset:
A
B
B
C
D
D
E
```

Removing Multiset Elements

To delete an element from the sequence stored in an `std::multiset` object, call the `erase` member function. This function takes as arguments the position at which to start the deletion and the position of the element at which the deletion should stop (that is, this last element is not deleted). The second argument is not required. To delete a single element, simply supply an iterator for the element as the `erase` member function's single argument. Program 32-8 creates an empty `std::multiset` object and populates the sequence with the characters "A" through "E" (along with a duplicate "B" and "D"). The program then erases the character from the sequence's second position and displays the results.

Program 32-8: **Removing elements anywhere within a multiset**

```cpp
#include <iostream>
#include <set>

int main()
{
    // Create the set object.
    std::multiset<char> charMultiset;
    // Populate the multiset with values.
    charMultiset.insert('E');
    charMultiset.insert('D');
    charMultiset.insert('C');
    charMultiset.insert('B');
    charMultiset.insert('A');
    charMultiset.insert('B');
    charMultiset.insert('D');
    // Display the contents of the multiset.
    std::cout << "Contents of multiset: " << std::endl;
    std::multiset<char>::iterator iter;
    for (iter = charMultiset.begin(); iter != charMultiset.end(); iter++)
        std::cout << *iter << std::endl;
    // Erase the multiset's second element.
    iter = charMultiset.begin();
    charMultiset.erase(++iter);
    // Display the new contents of the multiset.
    std::cout << "Contents of new set: " << std::endl;
    for (iter = charMultiset.begin(); iter != charMultiset.end(); iter++)
        std::cout << *iter << std::endl;
    return 0;
}
```

Program 32-8 displays the following output:

```
Contents of multiset
A
B
B
C
D
D
E
Contents of new set:
A
B
C
D
D
E
```

Searching an std::multiset

A program easily can locate an element in an std::multiset by calling the find member function, which takes as its single argument the value for which to search. The find function returns an iterator that points to the located element, or an iterator that points to the end of the set if it does not find the requested element. Program 32-9 demonstrates how to search an std::multiset.

Program 32-9: **Searching a multiset**

```
#include <iostream>
#include <set>

int main()
{
    // Create the multiset object.
    std::multiset<char> charMultiset;
    // Populate the multiset with values.
    charMultiset.insert('E');
    charMultiset.insert('D');
    charMultiset.insert('C');
    charMultiset.insert('B');
    charMultiset.insert('A');
    charMultiset.insert('B');
    charMultiset.insert('D');
    // Display the contents of the multiset.
    std::cout << "Contents of multiset: " << std::endl;
    std::multiset<char>::iterator iter;
    for (iter = charMultiset.begin(); iter != charMultiset.end(); iter++)
        std::cout << *iter << std::endl;
    std::cout << std::endl;
    // Find the first D.
    iter = charMultiset.find('D');
    if (iter == charMultiset.end())
        std::cout << "Element not found.";
    else {
        std::cout << "Element found: "
        << *iter++ << std::endl;
        std::cout << "Next element: " << *iter;
    }
    return 0;
}
```

Program 32-9 produces the following output:

```
Contents of multiset:
A
B
B
C
D
```

```
D
E

Element found: D
Next element: D
```

Comparing std::multisets

A program easily can determine whether multisets are equal to each other or which multiset is less than or greater than another. Two std::multiset objects are equal when they have the same number of elements and all elements in the multisets have the same value. Program 32-10 demonstrates how to compare multisets.

Program 32-10: Comparing multisets

```cpp
#include <iostream>
#include <set>

int main()
{
    // Create the first set object.
    std::multiset<char> charMultiset1;
    // Populate the multiset with values.
    charMultiset1.insert('E');
    charMultiset1.insert('D');
    charMultiset1.insert('C');
    charMultiset1.insert('B');
    charMultiset1.insert('A');
    charMultiset1.insert('B');
    charMultiset1.insert('D');
    // Display the contents of the first multiset.
    std::cout << "Contents of first multiset: " << std::endl;
    std::multiset<char>::iterator iter;
    for (iter = charMultiset1.begin(); iter != charMultiset1.end(); iter++)
        std::cout << *iter << std::endl;
    std::cout << std::endl;
    // Create the second multiset object.
    std::multiset<char> charMultiset2;
    // Populate the multiset with values.
    charMultiset2.insert('J');
    charMultiset2.insert('I');
    charMultiset2.insert('H');
    charMultiset2.insert('G');
    charMultiset2.insert('F');
    charMultiset2.insert('G');
    charMultiset2.insert('I');
    // Display the contents of the second multiset.
    std::cout << "Contents of second multiset: " << std::endl;
    for (iter = charMultiset2.begin(); iter != charMultiset2.end(); iter++)
```

Continued

Program 32-10 *(continued)*

```
        std::cout << *iter << std::endl;
    std::cout << std::endl;
    // Compare the sets.
    if (charMultiset1 == charMultiset2)
        std::cout << "set1 == set2";
    else if (charMultiset1 < charMultiset2)
        std::cout << "set1 < set2";
    else if (charMultiset1 > charMultiset2)
        std::cout << "set1 > set2";
    return 0;
}
```

Program 32-10 produces the following output:

```
Contents of first multiset:
A
B
B
C
D
D
E

Contents of second multiset:
F
G
G
H
I
I
J

set1 < set2
```

Multiset Member Functions

The preceding examples show you how to perform the most needed operations with a std::multiset object. The std::multiset class template, however, defines more functions than we have shown you so far. Table 32-2 lists the std::multiset member functions along with their descriptions.

Table 32-2: Multiset Member Functions

Function	Description
begin	Returns an iterator that points to the first element in the multiset
clear	Erases all elements of a multiset
count(x)	Returns the number of instances of x in the multiset

Function	Description
empty	Returns a `true` value if the multiset is empty
end	Returns an iterator that points to the last element in the multiset
equal_range(x)	Returns two iterators that represent x's lower and upper bounds
erase(i)	Erases the multiset element pointed to by the iterator i
erase(start, end) start **and** end	Erases a range of multiset elements specified by the iterators
erase(x)	Erases all occurrences of the multiset element x
find(x)	Returns an iterator that points to the first occurrence of x in the multiset. If x does not exist, the returned iterator is equal to `end`.
insert(i, x)	Inserts value x into the multiset. The search for x's correct position starts at the element specified by iterator i.
insert(start, end)	Inserts the range of values specified by the iterators `start` and `end` into the multiset
insert(x)	Inserts x into the multiset
key_comp	Returns the object of type `key_compare` that determines the order of elements in the multiset
lower_bound(x)	Returns an iterator to the first occurrence of element x
max_size	Returns the maximum size (the greatest number of elements that can fit) of the multiset
rbegin	Returns a reverse iterator that points beyond the last element in the multiset
rend	Returns a reverse iterator that points to the first element of the multiset
size	Returns the size (the number of elements) of the multiset
swap(set)	Swaps the contents of two multisets
upper_bound(x)	Returns an iterator that points to the first element beyond x
value_comp	Returns the object of type `value_compare` that determines the order of elements in the multiset

The std::map Class Template

An `std::map` object enables a program to store a group of values in sorted order, with each element associated with a search key. This is unlike an `std::set` or `std::multiset`, in which the elements of the set act as both the stored data and the key to that data. You can construct an `std::map` object in several ways, as shown here:

```
std::map<key, type, predicate> name;
std::map<key, type, predicate> name(mymap);
std::map<key, type, predicate> name(first, last);
```

The first example creates an empty std::map object named *name* that can hold data of the type *type*. The *key* parameter is the type of key that is used in the map. The object uses the function specified by *predicate* for ordering the elements of the set. For example, to create an empty std::map object for integers, you can write:

```
std::map<int, int, std::less<int> > intMap;
```

The second example uses the copy constructor, which makes an std::map object from an existing std::map, *mymap*. Finally, the third example creates a map from a range of elements that the iterators *first* and *last* specify. Note that the std::less<> predicate is the default so you do not need to include it in the declaration.

Program 32-11 shows how to create and display the contents of an std::map object.

Program 32-11: **Creating a simple map**

```cpp
#include <iostream>
#include <map>

int main()
{
    // Create the map object.
    std::map<int, char> charMap;
    // Populate the map with values.
    charMap.insert(std::map<int, char>::value_type(1,'A'));
    charMap.insert(std::map<int, char>::value_type(3,'C'));
    charMap.insert(std::map<int, char>::value_type(2,'B'));
    charMap.insert(std::map<int, char>::value_type(5,'E'));
    charMap.insert(std::map<int, char>::value_type(4,'D'));
    // Display the contents of the map.
    std::cout << "Contents of map: " << std::endl;
    std::map<int, char>::iterator iter;
    for (iter = charMap.begin(); iter != charMap.end(); iter++) {
        std::cout << (*iter).first << " --> ";
        std::cout << (*iter).second << std::endl;
    }
    return 0;
}
```

Program 32-11 displays the following output:

```
Contents of map:
1 --> A
2 --> B
3 --> C
4 --> D
5 --> E
```

Program 32-11 includes the <map> header, the appropriate header file for the std::map class template. The program creates a five-element std::map object that associates the integer keys 1 through 5 with the characters A through E. At this point, Program 32-11 probably looks very confusing. Be assured that the following sections will explain everything in detail.

Inserting Map Elements

To insert new elements into the sequence stored in a `std::map` object, you use the `insert` member function. Because each map element consists of a key and a data item, however, new elements you insert must contain both the key and its associated data. To perform the insertion, then, you must use the class's `value_type` data type, which defines a data type for a pair of map values — a key and a data item. In Program 32-11, you saw how to create a `std::map` object and insert new elements. You probably thought — and rightly so — that the program was difficult to read, thanks to all the references to the `std::map` template definition. Program 32-12 shows the same program rewritten to use a `typedef` to replace all the `std::map` template references.

Program 32-12: **Adding elements to a map**

```
#include <iostream>
#include <map>

typedef std::map<int, char> mymap;

int main()
{
    // Create the map object.
    mymap charMap;
    // Populate the map with values.
    charMap.insert(mymap::value_type(1,'A'));
    charMap.insert(mymap::value_type(3,'C'));
    charMap.insert(mymap::value_type(2,'B'));
    charMap.insert(mymap::value_type(5,'E'));
    charMap.insert(mymap::value_type(4,'D'));
    // Display the contents of the map.
    std::cout << "Contents of map: " << std::endl;
    mymap::iterator iter;
    for (iter = charMap.begin(); iter != charMap.end(); iter++) {
        std::cout << (*iter).first << " --> ";
        std::cout << (*iter).second << std::endl;
    }
    return 0;
}
```

In Program 32-12, take special note of the `insert` member function's single parameter, which looks like this in the first call to `insert`:

```
mymap::value_type(1,'A')
```

The map object created by the `mymap` `typedef` defines a type definition for the data used in the object. In this case, the data type named `value_type` comprises an integer key and a character data item. You can access each part of the data pair by using `first` and `second`, as in the listing shown here:

```
std::cout << (*iter).first << " --> ";
std::cout << (*iter).second << std::endl;
```

Here, iter is an iterator that points to a map element. Just as with a pointer, to dereference an iterator—and so access the data it points to—you use the * operator. The * operator, however, is not enough. You also need to add first and second to specify which value in the pair you want to access. In the first line of the preceding code, the std::cout statement displays the current element's key. In the second line, the program displays the data item associated with the key, as well as increments the iterator so it points to the next map element.

The std::map class template defines the [] operator, enabling you to insert items without calling the insert member function. As you can see in Program 32-13, using the [] operator enables you to use a simpler syntax for inserting elements into an std::map object.

Program 32-13: Adding elements to a map using the [] operator

```
#include <iostream>
#include <map>

typedef std::map<int, char> mymap;

int main()
{
    // Create the map object.
    mymap charMap;
    // Populate the map with values.
    charMap[1] = 'A';
    charMap[4] = 'D';
    charMap[2] = 'B';
    charMap[5] = 'E';
    charMap[3] = 'C';
    // Display the contents of the map.
    std::cout << "Contents of map: " << std::endl;
    mymap::iterator iter;
    for (iter = charMap.begin();
            iter != charMap.end(); iter++) {
        std::cout << (*iter).first << " --> ";
        std::cout << (*iter).second << std::endl;
    }
    return 0;
}
```

Removing Map Elements

To delete an element from the sequence stored in a std::map object, call the erase member function. This function takes as arguments the position at which to start the deletion and the position of the element at which the deletion should stop (that is, this last element is not deleted). The second argument is not required. To delete a single element, simply supply an iterator for the element as the erase member function's single argument. Program 32-14 creates an empty std::map object and populates the map with the characters "A" through "E." The program then erases the character from the map's second position and displays the results.

Program 32-14: **Removing elements anywhere within a map**

```cpp
#include <iostream>
#include <map>

typedef std::map<int, char> mymap;

int main()
{
    // Create the map object.
    mymap charMap;
    // Populate the map with values.
    charMap[1] = 'A';
    charMap[4] = 'D';
    charMap[2] = 'B';
    charMap[5] = 'E';
    charMap[3] = 'C';
    // Display the contents of the map.
    std::cout << "Contents of map: " << std::endl;
    mymap::iterator iter;
    for (iter = charMap.begin(); iter != charMap.end(); iter++) {
        std::cout << (*iter).first << " --> ";
        std::cout << (*iter).second << std::endl;
    }
    // Erase the map's second element.
    iter = charMap.begin();
    charMap.erase(++iter);
    // Display the new contents of the map.
    std::cout << "Contents of new map: " << std::endl;
    for (iter = charMap.begin(); iter != charMap.end(); iter++) {
        std::cout << (*iter).first << " --> ";
        std::cout << (*iter).second << std::endl;
    }
    return 0;
}
```

Program 32-14 displays the following output:

```
Contents of map:
1 --> A
2 --> B
3 --> C
4 --> D
5 --> E
Contents of new map:
1 --> A
3 --> C
4 --> D
5 --> E
```

Searching a Map

A program locates an element in a map by calling the find member function, which takes as its single argument the key for which to search. The find function returns an iterator that points to the located element or an iterator that points to the end of the map if it cannot find the requested element. Program 32-15 demonstrates how to search a map.

Program 32-15: **Searching a map**

```
#include <iostream>
#include <map>

typedef std::map<int, char> mymap;

int main()
{
    // Create the map object.
    mymap charMap;
    // Populate the map with values.
    charMap[1] = 'A';
    charMap[4] = 'D';
    charMap[2] = 'B';
    charMap[5] = 'E';
    charMap[3] = 'C';
    // Display the contents of the map.
    std::cout << "Contents of map: " << std::endl;
    mymap::iterator iter;
    for (iter = charMap.begin(); iter != charMap.end(); iter++) {
        std::cout << (*iter).first << " --> ";
        std::cout << (*iter).second << std::endl;
    }
    // Find the D.
    mymap::iterator pos = charMap.find(4);
    if (pos == charMap.end())
        std::cout << "Element not found.";
    else
        std::cout << "Element found: " << (*pos).second;
    return 0;
}
```

Program 32-15 produces the following output:

```
Contents of map:
1 --> A
2 --> B
3 --> C
4 --> D
5 --> E
Element found: D
```

Comparing Maps

A program easily can determine whether maps are equal to each other or which map is less than or greater than another. Two std::map objects are equal when they have the same number of elements and all elements in the maps have the same value. Program 32-16 demonstrates how to compare maps.

Program 32-16: **Comparing maps**

```cpp
#include <iostream>
#include <map>

typedef std::map<int, char> mymap;

int main()
{
    // Create the first map object.
    mymap charMap1;
    // Populate the first map with values.
    charMap1[1] = 'A';
    charMap1[4] = 'D';
    charMap1[2] = 'B';
    charMap1[5] = 'E';
    charMap1[3] = 'C';
    // Display the contents of the first map.
    std::cout << "Contents of first map: " << std::endl;
    mymap::iterator iter;
    for (iter = charMap1.begin(); iter != charMap1.end(); iter++) {
        std::cout << (*iter).first << " --> ";
        std::cout << (*iter).second << std::endl;
    }
    std::cout << std::endl;
    // Create the second map object.
    mymap charMap2;
    // Populate the first map with values.
    charMap2[1] = 'F';
    charMap2[4] = 'I';
    charMap2[2] = 'G';
    charMap2[5] = 'J';
    charMap2[3] = 'H';
    // Display the contents of the second map.
    std::cout << "Contents of second map: " << std::endl;
    for (iter = charMap2.begin(); iter != charMap2.end(); iter++) {
        std::cout << (*iter).first << " --> ";
        std::cout << (*iter).second << std::endl;
    }
    std::cout << std::endl;
    // Compare the maps.
    if (charMap1 == charMap2)
        std::cout << "map1 == map2";
```

Continued

Program 32-16 *(continued)*

```
    else if (charMap1 < charMap2)
        std::cout << "map1 < map2";
    else if (charMap1 > charMap2)
        std::cout << "map1 > map2";
    return 0;
}
```

Program 32-16 produces the following output:

```
Contents of first map:
1 --> A
2 --> B
3 --> C
4 --> D
5 --> E

Contents of second map:
1 --> F
2 --> G
3 --> H
4 --> I
5 --> J

map1 < map2
```

Map Member Functions

The preceding examples show you how to perform the most needed operations with a std::map object. The std::map class template, however, defines more functions than we have shown you so far. Table 32-3 lists the std::map member functions along with their descriptions.

Table 32-3: Map Member Functions

Function	Description
begin	Returns an iterator that points to the first element in the map
clear	Erases all elements of a map
count(x)	Returns the number of instances of x in the map (either 0 or 1)
empty	Returns a true value if the map is empty
end	Returns an iterator that points to the last element in the map
equal_range(x)	Returns two iterators that represent x's lower and upper bounds
erase(i)	Erases the map element pointed to by the iterator i
erase(start, end)	Erases a range of map elements specified by the iterators start and end

Function	Description
erase(x)	Erases the map element with the key x
find(x)	Returns an iterator that points to x. If the key x does not exist, the returned iterator is equal to end.
insert(i, x)	Inserts value x into the map. The search for x's correct position starts at the element specified by iterator i.
insert(start, end)	Inserts the range of values, specified by the iterators start and end, into the map
insert(x)	Inserts x into the map
key_comp	Returns the object of type key_compare that determines the order of elements in the map
lower_bound(x)	Returns an iterator to the element immediately preceding the key x
max_size	Returns the maximum size (the greatest number of elements that can fit) of the map
rbegin	Returns a reverse iterator that points beyond the last element in the map
rend	Returns a reverse iterator that points to the first element of the map
size	Returns the size (the number of elements) of the map
swap(map)	Swaps the contents of two maps
upper_bound(x)	Returns an iterator that points to x
value_comp	Returns the object of type value_compare that determines the order of elements in the map

The std::multimap Class Template

A std::multimap object enables a program to store a group of values in sorted order. Just as with a map, the elements of the multimap contain a key and data item pair. However, unlike a map, a multimap can contain duplicate values. You can construct a std::multimap object in several ways, as shown here:

```
std::multimap<key, type, predicate> name;
std::multimap<key, type, predicate> name(mymultimap);
std::multimap<key, type, predicate> name(first, last);
```

The first example creates an empty std::multimap object named *name* that can hold data of the type *type* that is associated with *key*. The object uses the function specified by predicate for ordering the elements of the set. (The C++ Library defines these functions.) For example, to create an empty std::multimap object for integers, you can write:

```
std::multimap<int, int, std::less<int> > intSet;
```

The second example uses the copy constructor, which makes a std::multimap object from an existing multimap — *mymultimap*. Finally, the third example creates a set from a range of elements that the iterators *first* and *last* specify. Note that the std::less<> predicate is the default, so you do not need to include it in the declaration.

Program 32-17 shows how to create and display the contents of a std::multimap object.

Program 32-17: Creating and displaying a simple multimap

```
#include <iostream>
#include <map>

typedef std::multimap<int, char> mymap;

int main()
{
    // Create the multimap object.
    mymap charMultimap;
    // Populate the multimap with values.
    charMultimap.insert(mymap::value_type(1,'A'));
    charMultimap.insert(mymap::value_type(4,'C'));
    charMultimap.insert(mymap::value_type(2,'B'));
    charMultimap.insert(mymap::value_type(7,'E'));
    charMultimap.insert(mymap::value_type(5,'D'));
    charMultimap.insert(mymap::value_type(3,'B'));
    charMultimap.insert(mymap::value_type(6,'D'));
    // Display the contents of the multimap.
    std::cout << "Contents of multimap: " << std::endl;
    mymap::iterator iter;
    for (iter = charMultimap.begin(); iter != charMultimap.end(); iter++) {
        std::cout << (*iter).first << " --> ";
        std::cout << (*iter).second << std::endl;
    }
    return 0;
}
```

Program 32-17 displays the following output:

```
Contents of multimap:
1 --> A
2 --> B
3 --> B
4 --> C
5 --> D
6 --> D
7 --> E
```

Program 32-17 includes the <map> header, which includes the appropriate header file for the std::multimap class template. The program creates and displays a seven-element std::multimap object.

Inserting Multimap Elements

To insert new elements into the sequence stored in a std::multimap object, you use the insert member function shown in Program 32-17. You cannot use the [] operator to insert elements into a multimap.

Removing Multimap Elements

To delete an element from the sequence stored in an `std::multimap` object, call the `erase` member function. This function takes as arguments the position at which to start the deletion and the position of the element at which the deletion should stop (that is, this last element is not deleted). The second argument is not required. To delete a single element, simply supply an iterator for the element as the `erase` member function's single argument. Program 32-18 creates an empty `std::multimap` object and populates the sequence with the characters "A" through "E" (along with a duplicate "B" and "D"). The program then erases the character from the sequence's second position and displays the results.

Program 32-18: Removing elements anywhere within a multimap

```
#include <iostream>
#include <map>

typedef std::multimap<int, char> mymap;

int main()
{
    // Create the multimap object.
    mymap charMultimap;
    // Populate the multimap with values.
    charMultimap.insert(mymap::value_type(1,'A'));
    charMultimap.insert(mymap::value_type(4,'C'));
    charMultimap.insert(mymap::value_type(2,'B'));
    charMultimap.insert(mymap::value_type(7,'E'));
    charMultimap.insert(mymap::value_type(5,'D'));
    charMultimap.insert(mymap::value_type(3,'B'));
    charMultimap.insert(mymap::value_type(6,'D'));
    // Display the contents of the multimap.
    std::cout << "Contents of multimap: " << std::endl;
    mymap::iterator iter;
    for (iter = charMultimap.begin(); iter != charMultimap.end(); iter++) {
        std::cout << (*iter).first << " --> ";
        std::cout << (*iter).second << std::endl;
    }
    // Erase the multimap's second element.
    iter = charMultimap.begin();
    charMultimap.erase(++iter);
    // Display the new contents of the multimap.
    std::cout << "Contents of new multimap: " << std::endl;
    for (iter = charMultimap.begin(); iter != charMultimap.end(); iter++) {
        std::cout << (*iter).first << " --> ";
        std::cout << (*iter).second << std::endl;
    }
    return 0;
}
```

Program 32-18 displays the following output:

```
Contents of multimap:
1 --> A
2 --> B
3 --> B
4 --> C
5 --> D
6 --> D
7 --> E
Contents of new multimap:
1 --> A
3 --> B
4 --> C
5 --> D
6 --> D
7 --> E
```

Searching a Multimap

A program easily can locate an element in a multimap by calling the find member function. This function takes as its single argument the value for which to search. The find function returns an iterator that points to the first occurrence of the requested element or an iterator that points to the end of the set if it does not find the requested element. Program 32-19 demonstrates how to search a multimap.

Program 32-19: **Searching a multimap**

```
#include <iostream>
#include <map>

typedef std::multimap<int, char> mymap;

int main()
{
    // Create the multimap object.
    mymap charMultimap;
    // Populate the multimap with values.
    charMultimap.insert(mymap::value_type(1,'A'));
    charMultimap.insert(mymap::value_type(4,'C'));
    charMultimap.insert(mymap::value_type(2,'B'));
    charMultimap.insert(mymap::value_type(7,'E'));
    charMultimap.insert(mymap::value_type(5,'D'));
    charMultimap.insert(mymap::value_type(3,'B'));
    charMultimap.insert(mymap::value_type(6,'D'));
    // Display the contents of the multimap.
    std::cout << "Contents of multimap: " << std::endl;
    mymap::iterator iter;
    for (iter = charMultimap.begin(); iter != charMultimap.end(); iter++) {
        std::cout << (*iter).first << " --> ";
        std::cout << (*iter).second << std::endl;
    }
```

```
        std::cout << std::endl;
        // Find the first D.
        iter = charMultimap.find(5);
        if (iter == charMultimap.end())
            std::cout << "Element not found.";
        else {
            std::cout << "Element found: ";
            std::cout << (*iter).first << " --> ";
            std::cout << (*iter++).second << std::endl;
            std::cout << "Next element: ";
            std::cout << (*iter).first << " --> ";
            std::cout << (*iter).second << std::endl;
        }
        return 0;
}
```

Program 32-19 produces the following output:

```
Contents of multimap:
1 --> A
2 --> B
3 --> B
4 --> C
5 --> D
6 --> D
7 --> E

Element found: 5 --> D
Next element: 6 --> D
```

Comparing Multimaps

A program easily can determine whether multimaps are equal to each other or which multimap is less than or greater than another. Two std::multimap objects are equal when they have the same number of elements and all elements in the multimaps have the same value. Program 32-20 demonstrates how to compare multimaps.

Program 32-20: **Comparing multimaps**

```
#include <iostream>
#include <map>

typedef std::multimap<int, char> mymap;

int main()
{
    // Create the first multimap object.
    mymap charMultimap;
    // Populate the multimap with values.
```

Continued

Program 32-20 *(continued)*

```
charMultimap.insert(mymap::value_type(1,'A'));
charMultimap.insert(mymap::value_type(4,'C'));
charMultimap.insert(mymap::value_type(2,'B'));
charMultimap.insert(mymap::value_type(7,'E'));
charMultimap.insert(mymap::value_type(5,'D'));
charMultimap.insert(mymap::value_type(3,'B'));
charMultimap.insert(mymap::value_type(6,'D'));
// Display the contents of the first multimap.
std::cout << "Contents of first multimap: " << std::endl;
mymap::iterator iter;
for (iter = charMultimap.begin(); iter != charMultimap.end(); iter++) {
    std::cout << (*iter).first << " --> ";
    std::cout << (*iter).second << std::endl;
}
std::cout << std::endl;
// Create the second multimap object.
mymap charMultimap2;
// Populate the second multimap with values.
charMultimap2.insert(mymap::value_type(1,'C'));
charMultimap2.insert(mymap::value_type(4,'F'));
charMultimap2.insert(mymap::value_type(2,'D'));
charMultimap2.insert(mymap::value_type(7,'E'));
charMultimap2.insert(mymap::value_type(5,'F'));
charMultimap2.insert(mymap::value_type(3,'E'));
charMultimap2.insert(mymap::value_type(6,'G'));
// Display the contents of the second multimap.
std::cout << "Contents of second multimap: " << std::endl;
for (iter = charMultimap2.begin(); iter != charMultimap2.end(); iter++) {
    std::cout << (*iter).first << " --> ";
    std::cout << (*iter).second << std::endl;
}
std::cout << std::endl;
// Compare the multimaps.
if (charMultimap == charMultimap2)
    std::cout << "multimap1 == multimap2";
else if (charMultimap < charMultimap2)
    std::cout << "multimap1 < multimap2";
else if (charMultimap > charMultimap2)
    std::cout << "multimap1 > multimap2";
return 0;
}
```

Program 32-20 produces the following output:

```
Contents of first multimap:
1 --> A
2 --> B
3 --> B
4 --> C
5 --> D
```

```
6 --> D
7 --> E

Contents of second multimap:
1 --> C
2 --> D
3 --> E
4 --> F
5 --> F
6 --> G
7 --> E

multimap1 < multimap2
```

Multimap Member Functions

The preceding examples show you how to perform the most needed operations with an `std::multimap` object. The `std::multimap` class template, however, defines more functions than we have shown you so far. Table 32-4 lists the `std::multimap` member functions along with their descriptions.

Table 32-4: Multimap Member Functions

Function	Description
begin	Returns an iterator that points to the first element in the multimap
clear	Erases all elements of a multimap
count(x)	Returns the number of instances of x in the multimap
empty	Returns a `true` value if the multimap is empty
end	Returns an iterator that points to the last element in the multimap
equal_range(x)	Returns two iterators that represent x's lower and upper bounds
erase(i)	Erases the multimap element pointed to by the iterator i
erase(start, end)	Erases a range of multimap elements specified by the iterators `start` and `end`
erase(x)	Erases all occurrences of the multimap element x
find(x)	Returns an iterator that points to the first occurrence of x in the multimap. If x does not exist, the returned iterator is equal to `end`.
insert(i, x)	Inserts value x into the multimap. The search for x's correct position starts at the element specified by iterator i.
insert(start, end)	Inserts the range of values, specified by the iterators `start` and `end`, into the multimap
insert(x)	Inserts x into the multimap
key_comp	Returns the object of type `key_compare` that determines the order of elements in the multimap

Continued

Table 32-4 *(continued)*

Function	Description
lower_bound(x)	Returns an iterator to the first occurrence of element x
max_size	Returns the maximum size (the greatest number of elements that can fit) of the multimap
rbegin	Returns a reverse iterator that points beyond the last element in the multimap
rend	Returns a reverse iterator that points to the first element of the multimap
size	Returns the size (the number of elements) of the multimap
swap(set)	Swaps the contents of two multimaps
upper_bound(x)	Returns an iterator that points to the first element beyond x
value_comp	Returns the object of type value_compare that determines the order of elements in the multimap

The std::bitset Class Template

A std::bitset object enables a program to store a group of bit values (0s and 1s). You can construct a std::bitset object in several ways, as shown here:

```
std::bitset<size> name;
std::bitset<size> name(value);
std::bitset<size> name(str, pos, n);
```

The first example creates an empty std::bitset object named *name* that can hold *size* bits. For example, to create a bitset object with 8 bits, you can write:

```
std::bitset<8> bitSet;
```

The second example creates a bitset from the bits in an unsigned long value. Finally, the third example creates a bitset from the contents of a string; *pos* is the position within the bitset at which the values represented by *str* are placed. Both *pos* and *n* have default values, so you usually ignore them.

Manipulating Bits in a Bitset

Any element in a bitset can be the value 0 or 1, which represent an *unset* or *set bit*, respectively. The std::bitset class provides several member functions. Two of these functions are set, which sets a bit to 1, and reset, which returns the bit to the value 0. Table 32-5 describes all of these functions, and Program 32-21 demonstrates using the set and reset functions.

Program 32-21: **Manipulating bits in a bitset**

```
#include <iostream>
#include <bitset>

// Display a bitset.
```

```cpp
void display(std::bitset<8> bs)
{
    std::cout << "Bitset = ";
    for (int x=0; x<8; ++x)
        std::cout << bs[x];
    std::cout << std::endl;
}
int main()
{
    // Create and display the bitset object.
    std::bitset<8> bitSet;
    display(bitSet);
    std::cout << std::endl;
    // Set some bits.
    std::cout << "Setting bits 1, 2, 3, 5, and 7." << std::endl;
    bitSet.set(1);
    bitSet.set(2);
    bitSet.set(3);
    bitSet.set(5);
    bitSet.set(7);
    // Display the resultant bitset.
    display(bitSet);
    std::cout << std::endl;
    // Reset some bits.
    std::cout << "Resetting bits 2 and 3." << std::endl;
    bitSet.reset(2);
    bitSet.reset(3);
    // Display the resultant bitset.
    display(bitSet);
    std::cout << std::endl;
    return 0;
}
```

Program 32-21 produces the following output:

```
Bitset = 00000000

Setting bits 1, 2, 3, 5, and 7.
Bitset = 01110101

Resetting bits 2 and 3.
Bitset = 01000101
```

Testing Bits in a Bitset

A program easily can determine the status of a bit by calling the test member function. This function returns true if the specified bit is set, or false if the bit is not set. Program 32-22 demonstrates how to use the test member function.

Program 32-22: **Testing bits in a bitset**

```cpp
#include <iostream>
#include <bitset>

// Display a bitset.
void display(std::bitset<8> bs)
{
    std::cout << "Bitset = ";
    for (int x=0; x<8; ++x)
        std::cout << bs[x];
    std::cout << std::endl;
}
int main()
{
    // Create the bitset object.
    std::bitset<8> bitSet;
    // Set some bits.
    bitSet.set(1);
    bitSet.set(2);
    bitSet.set(3);
    bitSet.set(5);
    bitSet.set(7);
    // Display the resultant bitset.
    display(bitSet);
    std::cout << std::endl;
    // Test the bits.
    for (int x=0; x<8; ++x) {
        std::cout << "Bit " << x << " is ";
        if (bitSet.test(x))
            std::cout << "set";
        else
            std::cout << "unset";
        std::cout << std::endl;
    }
    return 0;
}
```

Program 32-22 produces the following output:

```
Bitset = 01110101

Bit 0 is unset
Bit 1 is set
Bit 2 is set
Bit 3 is set
Bit 4 is unset
Bit 5 is set
Bit 6 is unset
Bit 7 is set
```

Comparing Bitsets

A program easily can determine whether bitsets are equal to each other. Two bitset objects are equal when they have the same number of elements and the elements in the bitsets are equal. Program 32-23 demonstrates how to compare bitsets.

Program 32-23: **Comparing bitsets**

```cpp
#include <iostream>
#include <bitset>

// Display a bitset.
void display(std::bitset<8> bs)
{
    std::cout << "Bitset = ";
    for (int x=0; x<8; ++x)
        std::cout << bs[x];
    std::cout << std::endl;
}
int main()
{
    // Create and display the first bitset object.
    std::bitset<8> bitSet;
    bitSet.set(1);
    bitSet.set(3);
    bitSet.set(5);
    bitSet.set(7);
    display(bitSet);
    // Create and display the second bitset object.
    std::bitset<8> bitSet2;
    bitSet2.set(0);
    bitSet2.set(1);
    bitSet2.set(3);
    bitSet2.set(5);
    bitSet2.set(7);
    display(bitSet2);
    // Compare the bitsets.
    if (bitSet == bitSet2)
        std::cout << "bitset1 == bitset2";
    else
        std::cout << "bitset1 != bitset2";
    std::cout << std::endl;
    return 0;
}
```

Program 32-23 produces the following output:

```
Bitset = 10101010
Bitset = 10101011
bitset1 != bitset2
```

Bitset Member Functions

The preceding examples show you how to perform the most needed operations with a bitset object. The bitset class template, however, defines more functions than we have shown you so far. Table 32-5 lists the bitset member functions along with their descriptions.

Table 32-5: Bitset Member Functions

Function	Description
any	Returns true if any bit in the bitset is set
at(pos)	Returns the value of the bit at position pos
count(x)	Returns the number of bits in the bitset
flip	Toggles all the bits in the bitset
flip(pos)	Toggles the bit at the position pos
none	Returns true if none of the bits in the bitset are set
reset	Resets all the bits in the bitset
reset(pos)	Resets the bit at position pos
set	Sets all the bits in the bitset
set(pos)	Sets the bit at position pos
size	Returns the size (the number of bits) in the bitset
test(pos)	Returns TRUE if the bit at position pos is set

User-Defined Predicates

You've seen predicates mentioned in several places throughout the STL section of this book. A predicate is a function that returns bool and that STL uses to determine information about the elements of a container. The bool returned value from a predicate (true or false) determines the ordering of the elements in the container. Standard C++ defines many predicates for you, such as std::less<> and std::greater<>. You can, however, define and use your own predicates when you want to do something with the container that is not supported directly by the standard predicates. Program 32-24, for example, defines a predicate that not only determines which of two arguments is smaller but also displays the two arguments being compared. The display enables you to see the predicate in action as STL orders the contents of an std::map object.

Program 32-24: **User-defined predicates**

```
#include <iostream>
#include <map>

// User-defined predicate.
class compare
```

```
        {
        public:
            bool operator()(const int c1, const int c2) const
            {
                std::cout << "In Compare: "
                << c1 << " -- " << c2 << std::endl;
                return c1 < c2;
            }
        };
        int main()
        {
            // Create the map object.
            std::map<int, char, compare> charMap;
            // Populate the map with values.
            std::cout << "Adding elements to the map:" << std::endl;
            charMap.insert(std::map<int, char>::value_type(1,'A'));
            charMap.insert(std::map<int, char>::value_type(3,'C'));
            charMap.insert(std::map<int, char>::value_type(2,'B'));
            charMap.insert(std::map<int, char>::value_type(4,'D'));
            // Display the contents of the map.
            std::cout << std::endl << "Contents of map: " << std::endl;
            std::map<int, char>::iterator iter;
            for (iter = charMap.begin(); iter != charMap.end(); iter++) {
                std::cout << (*iter).first << " --> ";
                std::cout << (*iter).second << std::endl;
            }
            return 0;
        }
```

Program 32-24 produces the following output:

```
Adding elements to the map:
In Compare: 3 -- 1
In Compare: 1 -- 3
In Compare: 3 -- 1
In Compare: 2 -- 1
In Compare: 2 -- 3
In Compare: 1 -- 2
In Compare: 2 -- 3
In Compare: 4 -- 2
In Compare: 4 -- 3
In Compare: 3 -- 4
In Compare: 4 -- 3

Contents of map:
1 --> A
2 --> B
3 --> C
4 --> D
```

Now, examine the predicate more closely. The program defines the predicate like this:

```
class compare {
public:
```

```
bool operator()(const int c1, const int c2) const
{
    std::cout << "In Compare: " << c1 << " -- " << c2 << std::endl;
    return c1 < c2;
}
};
```

First, notice that the predicate is actually in the form of a small class. The class provides the predicate's name, compare, as well as overloads the () operator. It's the operator() function that does the predicate's work. STL calls this function each time the program's std::map object needs to perform a comparison in order to maintain the ordering of the std::map object's contents. Changing the predicate changes the way STL orders the map's contents. For example, you can reverse the order of the std::map object's elements simply by reversing the comparison in the predicate. To do this, you change the

```
return c1 < c2;
```

in the predicate function to

```
return c1 > c2;
```

Then, when you rerun the program, you get the following results:

```
Adding elements to the map:
In Compare: 3 -- 1
In Compare: 3 -- 1
In Compare: 2 -- 1
In Compare: 2 -- 3
In Compare: 3 -- 2
In Compare: 2 -- 3
In Compare: 4 -- 2
In Compare: 4 -- 3
In Compare: 4 -- 3

Contents of map:
4 --> D
3 --> C
2 --> B
1 --> A
```

Summary

STL includes a library of generic associative containers — the std::set, std::multiset, std::map, std::multimap, and std::bitset template classes. As with all STL containers, associative container classes define member functions that enable a program to manage the containers, adding elements to, removing elements from, and searching the container. In the next chapter, you learn about STL's generic algorithms that work with containers to support the generic programming model.

✦   ✦   ✦

Generic Algorithms

The Standard Template Library provides many types of containers for manipulating values of various types. To manage the contents of containers, STL includes *generic algorithms* that manipulate elements in common ways. This chapter explores these algorithms.

Introduction to Generic Algorithms

The generic algorithms fall into four categories, as listed here:

◆ *Non-modifying algorithms:* Do not modify the containers on which they work. Such algorithms include `std::adjacent_find`, `std::find`, `std::find_end`, `std::find_first`, `std::count`, `std::mismatch`, `std::equal`, `std::for_each`, and `std::search`.

◆ *Mutating algorithms:* Modify the containers on which they work. Such algorithms include `std::copy`, `std::copy_backward`, `std::fill`, `std::generate`, `std::partition`, `std::random_shuffle`, `std::remove`, `std::replace`, `std::rotate`, `std::reverse`, `std::swap`, `std::swap_ranges`, `std::transform`, and `std::unique`.

◆ *Sorting algorithms*: Sort the contents of containers in various ways. These algorithms include `std::sort`, `std::stable_sort`, `std::partial_sort`, and `std::partial_sort_copy`, as well as a number of related functions, including `std::nth_element`, `std::binary_search`, `std::lower_bound`, `std::upper_bound`, `std::equal_range`, `std::merge`, `std::includes`, `std::push_heap`, `std::pop_heap`, `std::make_heap`, `std::sort_heap`, `std::set_union`, `std::set_intersection`, `std::set_difference`, `std::set_symmetric_difference`, `std::min`, `std::min_element`, `std::max`, `std::max_element`, `std::lexicographical_compare`, `std::next_permutation`, and `std::prev_permutation`.

◆ *Numeric algorithms:* Perform numerical calculations on the contents of containers. This category includes `std::accumulate`, `std::inner_product`, `std::partial_sum`, and `std::adjacent_difference`.

In the following sections, you examine these different categories of generic algorithms and learn to use them in your own programs.

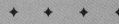

Non-Modifying Algorithms

Many functions do not modify the containers on which they work; for example, counting elements or finding an element. STL defines nine non-modifying algorithms, shown in Table 33-1.

Table 33-1: Non-Modifying Algorithms

Function	Description
adjacent_find(first, last)	Returns an iterator that points to the first element of an adjacent pair of equal values. The function searches the range of values specified by the iterators first and last. There is also a predicate version of this function that requires a comparison function as its third parameter.
count(first, last, val)	Returns the number of elements of a specified value, val, in a container. The function searches the range of values specified by the iterators first and last.
equal(first, last, first2)	Returns true if the range of values specified by the iterators first and last is equal to the range of the same length starting at first2. There is also a predicate version of this function that requires a comparison function as its fourth parameter.
find(first, last, val)	Returns an iterator that points to the first value in the range specified by the iterators first and last that equals val. There is also a predicate version of this function, named find_if, which requires a comparison function as its third parameter.
find_end(first, last, first2, last2)	Returns an iterator that points to the last element in the container within the range first, last that equals the container first2, last2. There is also a predicate version of this function that requires a comparison function as its fifth parameter.
find_first(first, last, first2, last2)	Returns an iterator to an element within the range specified by the iterators first, last that matches one of the elements in the range first2, last2. There is also a predicate version of this function that requires a comparison function as its fifth parameter.
for_each(first, last, func)	Performs the operation defined in a function, func, for each of the elements in the range first, last.
mismatch(first, last, first2)	Returns a pair of iterators that specify the positions of the first elements that are unequal in the range first, last and the range of equal length starting at first2. There is also a predicate version of this function that requires a comparison function as its fourth parameter.
search(first, last, first2, last2)	Returns an iterator that points to the first element within the range first, last that equals the sequence first2, last2. There is also a predicate version of this function that requires a comparison function as its fifth parameter.

Following are three programs that demonstrate several of the non-modifying algorithms. Program 33-1 uses the `std::adjacent_find` function to find two pairs of matching elements in an `std::multiset` object. Program 33-2 uses the `std::count` function to determine the number of 8s in a multiset. Program 33-3 uses the `std::for_each` function to display the contents of a multiset.

Program 33-1: **std::adjacent_find**

```cpp
#include <iostream>
#include <set>
#include <algorithm>

int main()
{
    // Create the set object.
    std::multiset<int, std::less<int> > intSet;
    // Populate the set with values.
    intSet.insert(10);
    intSet.insert(3);
    intSet.insert(1);
    intSet.insert(3);
    intSet.insert(8);
    intSet.insert(8);
    intSet.insert(5);
    // Display the contents of the set.
    std::cout << "Contents of set: ";
    std::multiset<int, std::less<int> >::iterator it = intSet.begin();
    for (int x=0; x<intSet.size(); ++x)
        std::cout << *it++ << ' ';
    std::cout << std::endl;
    // Find the first pair of equal values.
    std::cout << "First matching pair: ";
    it = adjacent_find(intSet.begin(), intSet.end());
    std::cout << *it++ << ' ';
    std::cout << *it << std::endl;
    // Find the second pair of equal values.
    std::cout << "Second matching pair: ";
    it = adjacent_find(it, intSet.end());
    std::cout << *it++ << ' ';
    std::cout << *it << std::endl;
    return 0;
}
```

Program 33-1 produces the following output:

```
Contents of set: 1 3 3 5 8 8 10
First matching pair: 3 3
Second matching pair: 8 8
```

Program 33-2: **std::count**

```cpp
#include <iostream>
#include <set>
#include <algorithm>

int main()
{
    // Create the set object.
    std::multiset<int, std::less<int> > intSet;
    // Populate the set with values.
    intSet.insert(10);
    intSet.insert(8);
    intSet.insert(1);
    intSet.insert(3);
    intSet.insert(8);
    intSet.insert(8);
    intSet.insert(5);
    // Display the contents of the set.
    std::cout << "Contents of set: ";
    std::multiset<int, std::less<int> >::iterator it = intSet.begin();
    for (int x=0; x<intSet.size(); ++x)
        std::cout << *it++ << ' ';
    std::cout << std::endl;
    // Count the number of 8s in the set.
    int cnt = count(intSet.begin(), intSet.end(), 8);
    std::cout << "Number of 8s = " << cnt;
    return 0;
}
```

Program 33-2 produces the following output:

```
Contents of set: 1 3 5 8 8 8 10
Number of 8s = 3
```

Program 33-3: **std::for_each**

```cpp
#include <iostream>
#include <set>
#include <algorithm>

// function to be called by for_each().
void show_val(int val)
{
    std::cout << val << ' ';
}
int main()
{
    // Create the set object.
    std::multiset<int, std::less<int> > intSet;
```

```
    // Populate the set with values.
    intSet.insert(10);
    intSet.insert(8);
    intSet.insert(1);
    intSet.insert(3);
    intSet.insert(8);
    intSet.insert(8);
    intSet.insert(5);
    // Display the contents of the set.
    std::cout << "Contents of set: ";
    std::for_each(intSet.begin(), intSet.end(), show_val);
    return 0;
}
```

Program 33-3 produces the following output:

```
Contents of set: 1 3 5 8 8 8 10
```

Mutating Algorithms

Some types of operations result in modifying the contents of a container. For example, you may want to copy part of a container into another part of the same container, or you may want to fill a container with a given value. STL's mutating algorithms provide for such operations, and Table 33-2 lists and describes them.

Table 33-2: Mutating Algorithms

Function	Description
copy(first, last, first2)	Copies the elements of the range specified by the iterators first and last to the range beginning at the element specified by the iterator first2
copy_backward(first, last, first2)	Copies the elements of the range specified by the iterators first and last to the range beginning at the element specified by the iterator first2. However, this function copies the elements starting with the last element and works backwards to the first.
fill(first, last, val)	Copies val into every element in the range specified by the iterators first and last
generate(first, last, func)	Calls the function func for each element, copying the result of func into the element
partition(first, last, pred)	Partitions a container into two sections, in which the first section contains the elements that return a true value from the predicate pred and the second section contains those elements that return false from pred. The function returns an iterator that points to the dividing point between the two partitions.

Continued

Table 33-2 *(continued)*

Function	Description
random_shuffle(first, last)	Randomly shuffles the elements in the range specified by the iterators first and last
remove(first, last, val)	Removes all values that match val from the range specified by the iterators first and last
replace(first, last, val1, val2)	Replaces val1 with val2 in the range specified by the iterators first and last
rotate(first, middle, last)	Left-rotates the elements from the range middle to last to the range starting at first
reverse(first, last)	Reverses the elements of the range specified by the bidirectional iterators first and last
swap(it1, it2)	Swaps the two elements specified by the iterators it1 and it2
swap_ranges(first, last, first2)	Swaps a range of values between the range first, last, and the range of the same length starting at first2
transform(first, last, first2, func)	Applies the function func to each element in the range specified by the iterators first and last and stores the results in the range beginning at first2
unique(first, last)	Removes all consecutive matching elements from the range specified by the iterators first and last

---

Following are four programs that demonstrate several of the mutating algorithms. Program 33-4 uses the std::fill function to fill a vector with zeroes. Program 33-5 uses the std::random_shuffle function to scramble the contents of a vector. Program 33-6 uses the std::partition function to place all occurrences of the number 5 at the beginning of a vector. Finally, Program 33-7 uses the std::rotate function to reorganize the characters in a vector.

Program 33-4: **std::fill**

```
#include <iostream>
#include <vector>
#include <algorithm>

// function to be called by for_each().
void show_val(int val)
{
    std::cout << val << ' ';
}
int main()
{
```

```
    // Create the vector object.
    std::vector<int> intVector;
    // Populate the vector with values.
    for (int x=0; x<10; ++x)
        intVector.push_back(x);
    // Display the contents of the vector.
    std::cout << "Contents of vector: ";
    std::for_each(intVector.begin(), intVector.end(), show_val);
    // Fill 1st 5 elements of vector with zeroes.
    std::fill(intVector.begin(), intVector.begin() + 5, 0);
    // Display the contents of the new vector.
    std::cout << std::endl << "Contents of vector: ";
    std::for_each(intVector.begin(), intVector.end(), show_val);
    return 0;
}
```

Program 33-4 produces the following output:

```
Contents of vector: 0 1 2 3 4 5 6 7 8 9
Contents of vector: 0 0 0 0 0 5 6 7 8 9
```

Program 33-5: **std::random_shuffle**

```
#include <iostream>
#include <vector>
#include <algorithm>

// function to be called by for_each().
void show_val(int val)
{
    std::cout << val << ' ';
}
int main()
{
    // Create the vector object.
    std::vector<int> intVector;
    // Populate the vector with values.
    for (int x = 0; x < 10; x++)
        intVector.push_back(x);
    // Display the contents of the vector.
    std::cout << "Contents of vector: ";
    std::for_each(intVector.begin(), intVector.end(), show_val);
    // Shuffle the vector.
    std::random_shuffle(intVector.begin(), intVector.end());
    // Display the contents of the new vector.
    std::cout << std::endl << "Contents of vector: ";
    std::for_each(intVector.begin(), intVector.end(), show_val);
    return 0;
}
```

Program 33-5 produces the following output:

```
Contents of vector: 0 1 2 3 4 5 6 7 8 9
Contents of vector: 8 1 9 2 0 5 7 3 4 6
```

Program 33-6: std::partition

```cpp
#include <iostream>
#include <vector>
#include <algorithm>

// function to be called by for_each().
void show_val(int val)
{
    std::cout << val << ' ';
}
// predicate for partition
bool equals5(int val)
{
    return val == 5;
}
int main()
{
    // Create the vector object.
    std::vector<int> intVector;
    // Populate the vector with values.
    intVector.push_back(8);
    intVector.push_back(5);
    intVector.push_back(7);
    intVector.push_back(5);
    intVector.push_back(2);
    intVector.push_back(5);
    // Display the contents of the vector.
    std::cout << "Contents of vector: ";
    std::for_each(intVector.begin(), intVector.end(), show_val);
    // Partition the vector.
    std::partition(intVector.begin(), intVector.end(), equals5);
    // Display the contents of the new vector.
    std::cout << std::endl << "Contents of vector: ";
    std::for_each(intVector.begin(), intVector.end(), show_val);
    return 0;
}
```

Program 33-6 produces the following output:

```
Contents of vector: 8 5 7 5 2 5
Contents of vector: 5 5 5 7 2 8
```

> ### Program 33-7: **std::rotate**

```cpp
#include <iostream>
#include <vector>
#include <algorithm>

// function to be called by for_each().
void show_val(char val)
{
    std::cout << val;
}
int main()
{
    // Create the vector object.
    std::vector<char> charVector;
    // Populate the vector with values.
    charVector.push_back('T');
    charVector.push_back('H');
    charVector.push_back('E');
    charVector.push_back('R');
    charVector.push_back('E');
    charVector.push_back(' ');
    charVector.push_back('H');
    charVector.push_back('I');
    charVector.push_back(' ');
    // Display the contents of the vector.
    std::cout << "Contents of vector: ";
    std::for_each(charVector.begin(), charVector.end(), show_val);
    // Rotate the vector.
    std::rotate(charVector.begin(), charVector.begin()+6, charVector.end());
    // Display the contents of the new vector.
    std::cout << std::endl << "Contents of vector: ";
    std::for_each(charVector.begin(), charVector.end(), show_val);
    return 0;
}
```

Program 33-7 produces the following output:

```
Contents of vector: THERE HI
Contents of vector: HI THERE
```

Sorting Algorithms

STL provides functions for sorting the contents of sequence containers with over 25 sorting and sorting-related functions. Table 33-3 lists the sorting-related functions and their descriptions.

Table 33-3: Sorting Algorithms

Function	Description
`binary_search(first, last, val)`	Searches for `val` in a range of sorted elements specified by the iterators `first` and `last`. Returns `true` if the element is found; it returns `false` otherwise. A second version of this function requires a predicate as its fourth argument.
`equal_range(first, last, val)`	Searches a range of sorted elements specified by the iterators `first` and `last` for the correct first and last position for `val` and returns the position as a pair of iterators. A second version of this function requires a predicate as its fourth argument.
`includes(first, last, first2, last2)`	Returns `true` if the range specified by the iterators `first` and `last` contains a sorted range equal to the range specified by `first2` and `last2`. A second version of this function requires a predicate as its fifth argument.
`lexicographical_compare(first, last, first2, last2)`	Performs a `lexicographical` (dictionary-like) comparison between the ranges specified by the iterators `first`, `last` and `first2`, `last2`. A second version of this function requires a predicate as its third argument.
`lower_bound(first, last, val)`	Searches a range of sorted elements specified by the iterators `first` and `last` for the correct first position for `val` and returns the position as an iterator. A second version of this function requires a predicate as its fourth argument.
`make_heap(first, last)`	Creates a heap from the contents of the sequence specified by the iterators `first` and `last`. A second version of this function requires a predicate as its third argument.
`max(val1, val2)`	Returns the greater of the specified arguments. A second version of this function requires a predicate as its third argument.
`max_element(first, last)`	Returns the greatest element in the range specified by the iterators `first` and `last`. A second version of this function requires a predicate as its third argument.
`merge(first, last, first2, last2, result)`	Sorts together two sorted ranges of values specified by the iterators `first`, `last`, `first2`, and `last2` into the range beginning at `result`. A second version of this function requires a predicate as its sixth argument.
`min(val1, val2)`	Returns the lesser of the specified arguments. A second version of this function requires a predicate as its third argument.

Function	Description
min_element(first, last)	Returns the smallest element in the range specified by the iterators `first` and `last`. A second version of this function requires a predicate as its third argument.
next_permutation(first, last)	Changes the range of elements specified by the iterators `first` and `last` into the next greater permutation (lexicographically). A second version of this function requires a predicate as its third argument.
nth_element(first, nth, last)	Sorts a range of values specified by the iterators `first` and `last` into two partitions, in which the `nth` element is filled with the value that would appear in that position if the sequence were sorted fully. All elements to the left of the `nth` element are less than or equal to all elements to the right of the `nth` element. A second version of this function requires a predicate as its fourth argument.
partial_sort_copy(first, last, first2, last2)	Sorts a range of values, specified by the `first` and `last` iterators, into partial order and places the smallest elements into the position specified by the iterator `first2`. No elements are copied beyond the position specified by the iterator `last2`. A second version of this function requires a predicate as its fifth argument.
partial_sort(first, middle, last)	Sorts a range of values, specified by the `first` and `last` iterators, into partial order. The sorted elements are placed into the first part of the sequence, with the remaining elements placed in the range specified by `middle` and `last`. A second version of this function requires a predicate as its fourth argument.
pop_heap(first, last)	Removes the largest element from the heap specified by the iterators `first` and `last`. A second version of this function requires a predicate as its third argument.
prev_permutation(first, last)	Changes the range of elements specified by the iterators `first` and `last` into the next smaller permutation (lexicographically). A second version of this function requires a predicate as its third argument.
push_heap(first, last)	Places an element on a heap specified by the iterators `first` and `last`. The element placed on the heap is located at `last-1`. A second version of this function requires a predicate as its third argument.
set_difference(first, last, first2, last2, result)	Creates a sorted range from the set difference of the sorted ranges specified by the iterators `first`, `last`, `first2`, and `last2` and returns an iterator that points to the end of the new range. The merged sequence will begin at the position specified by `result`. A second version of this function requires a predicate as its sixth argument.

Continued

Table 33-3 *(continued)*

Function	Description
set_intersection(first, last, first2, last2, result)	Creates a sorted range from the intersection of the sorted ranges specified by the iterators first, last, and first2, last2 and returns an iterator that points to the end of the new range. The new range will begin at the position specified by result. A second version of this function requires a predicate as its sixth argument.
set_symmetric_difference(first, last, first2, last2, result)	Creates a sorted range from the set symmetric difference of the sorted ranges specified by the iterators first, last, and first2, last2 and returns an iterator that points to the end of the new range. The new range will begin at the position specified by result. A second version of this function requires a predicate as its sixth argument.
set_union(first, last, first2, last2, result)	Creates a sorted range from the union of the sorted ranges specified by the iterators first, last, and first2, last2 and returns an iterator that points to the end of the new range. The new range will begin at the position specified by result. A second version of this function requires a predicate as its sixth argument.
sort(first, last)	Sorts a range of values specified by the first and last iterators. A second version of this function requires a predicate as its third argument.
sort_heap(first, last)	Transforms the heap specified by the iterators first and last into a sorted range. A second version of this function requires a predicate as its third argument.
stable_sort(first, last)	Sorts a range of values specified by the first and last iterators. This sort algorithm maintains the relative positions of equivalent elements. A second version of this function requires a predicate as its third argument.
upper_bound(first, last, val)	Searches a range of sorted elements specified by the iterators first and last for the correct last position for val and returns the position as an iterator. A second version of this function requires a predicate as its fourth argument.

Following are five programs that demonstrate some of the sorting algorithms. Program 33-8 uses the std::sort function to sort the contents of a vector. Program 33-9 uses the std::partial_sort function to sort the smallest five elements of a vector into the first half of a vector. Program 33-10 demonstrates the std::nth_element function, and Program 33-11 uses the std::merge function to merge two vectors. Finally, Program 33-12 uses the std::include function to locate a matching sorted range in two vectors.

Program 33-8: **std::sort**

```cpp
#include <iostream>
#include <vector>
#include <algorithm>

// function to be called by for_each()
void show_val(char val)
{
    std::cout << val << ' ';
}
int main()
{
    // Create the vector object.
    std::vector<char> charVector;
    // Populate the vector with values.
    charVector.push_back('Z');
    charVector.push_back('D');
    charVector.push_back('F');
    charVector.push_back('S');
    charVector.push_back('A');
    charVector.push_back('Q');
    charVector.push_back('C');
    charVector.push_back('G');
    charVector.push_back('M');
    charVector.push_back('Y');
    // Display the contents of the vector.
    std::cout << "Contents of vector: ";
    std::for_each(charVector.begin(), charVector.end(), show_val);
    // Sort the vector.
    std::sort(charVector.begin(), charVector.end());
    // Display the contents of the new vector.
    std::cout << std::endl << "Contents of vector: ";
    std::for_each(charVector.begin(), charVector.end(), show_val);
    return 0;
}
```

Program 33-8 produces the following output:

```
Contents of vector: Z D F S A Q C G M Y
Contents of vector: A C D F G M Q S Y Z
```

Program 33-9: **std::partial_sort**

```cpp
#include <iostream>
#include <vector>
#include <algorithm>
```

Continued

Program 33-9 *(continued)*

```
#include <string>

// function to be called by for_each()
void show_val(const std::string& val)
{
    std::cout << val << std::endl;
}
int main()
{
    // Create the vector object.
    std::vector<std::string> strVector;
    // Populate the vector with values.
    strVector.push_back("Zebra");
    strVector.push_back("Deer");
    strVector.push_back("Fish");
    strVector.push_back("Snake");
    strVector.push_back("Bat");
    strVector.push_back("Cat");
    strVector.push_back("Bird");
    strVector.push_back("Turtle");
    strVector.push_back("Horse");
    strVector.push_back("Cow");
    // Display the contents of the vector.
    std::cout << "Contents of vector: " << std::endl;
    std::for_each(strVector.begin(), strVector.end(), show_val);
    std::cout << std::endl;
    // Sort the vector.
    std::partial_sort(strVector.begin(),strVector.begin()+5, strVector.end());
    // Display the contents of the new vector.
    std::cout << "Contents of vector: " << std::endl;
    std::for_each(strVector.begin(), strVector.end(), show_val);
    return 0;
}
```

Program 33-9 produces the following output:

```
Contents of vector:
Zebra
Deer
Fish
Snake
Bat
Cat
Bird
Turtle
Horse
Cow

Contents of vector:
Bat
```

```
Bird
Cat
Cow
Deer
Zebra
Snake
Turtle
Horse
Fish
```

Program 33-10: **std::nth_element**

```cpp
#include <iostream>
#include <vector>
#include <algorithm>
#include <string>

// function to be called by for_each()
void show_val(const std::string& val)
{
    std::cout << val << std::endl;
}
int main()
{
    // Create the vector object.
    std::vector<std::string> strVector;
    // Populate the vector with values.
    strVector.push_back("Zebra");
    strVector.push_back("Deer");
    strVector.push_back("Fish");
    strVector.push_back("Snake");
    strVector.push_back("Bat");
    strVector.push_back("Cat");
    strVector.push_back("Bird");
    strVector.push_back("Turtle");
    strVector.push_back("Horse");
    strVector.push_back("Cow");
    // Display the contents of the vector.
    std::cout << "Contents of vector: " << std::endl;
    std::for_each(strVector.begin(), strVector.end(), show_val);
    std::cout << std::endl;
    // Sort the vector.
    std::nth_element(strVector.begin(),strVector.begin()+5, strVector.end());
    // Display the contents of the new vector.
    std::cout << "Contents of vector: " << std::endl;
    std::for_each(strVector.begin(), strVector.end(), show_val);
    return 0;
}
```

Program 33-10 produces the following output:

```
Contents of vector:
Zebra
Deer
Fish
Snake
Bat
Cat
Bird
Turtle
Horse
Cow

Contents of vector:
Cow
Bird
Cat
Bat
Deer
Fish
Horse
Snake
Turtle
Zebra
```

Program 33-11: **std::merge**

```cpp
#include <iostream>
#include <vector>
#include <algorithm>
#include <string>

// function to be called by for_each()
void show_val(const std::string& val)
{
    std::cout << val << std::endl;
}
int main()
{
    // Create the vector objects.
    std::vector<std::string> strVector1;
    std::vector<std::string> strVector2;
    // Populate two vectors with values.
    strVector1.push_back("Zebra");
    strVector1.push_back("Deer");
    strVector1.push_back("Fish");
    strVector1.push_back("Snake");
    strVector1.push_back("Bat");
    strVector2.push_back("Cat");
    strVector2.push_back("Bird");
    strVector2.push_back("Turtle");
    strVector2.push_back("Horse");
```

```
    strVector2.push_back("Cow");
    // Display the contents of the vectors.
    std::cout << "Contents of vector1: " << std::endl;
    std::for_each(strVector1.begin(), strVector1.end(), show_val);
    std::cout << std::endl;
    std::cout << "Contents of vector2: " << std::endl;
    std::for_each(strVector2.begin(), strVector2.end(), show_val);
    std::cout << std::endl;
    // Sort the vectors.
    std::sort(strVector1.begin(), strVector1.end());
    std::sort(strVector2.begin(), strVector2.end());
    // build a vector to merge the other 2
    int size = strVector1.size() + strVector2.size();
    std::vector<std::string> strVector3(size);
    // Merge the sorted vectors.
    std::merge(strVector1.begin(), strVector1.end(),
               strVector2.begin(), strVector2.end(),
               strVector3.begin());
    // Display the contents of the new vector.
    std::cout << "Contents of vector3: " << std::endl;
    std::for_each(strVector3.begin(), strVector3.end(), show_val);
    return 0;
}
```

Program 33-11 produces the following output:

```
Contents of vector1:
Zebra
Deer
Fish
Snake
Bat

Contents of vector2:
Cat
Bird
Turtle
Horse
Cow

Contents of vector3:
Bat
Bird
Cat
Cow
Deer
Fish
Horse
Snake
Turtle
Zebra
```

Program 33-12: **std::includes**

```cpp
#include <iostream>
#include <vector>
#include <algorithm>
#include <string>

// function to be called by for_each()
void show_val(const std::string& val)
{
    std::cout << val << std::endl;
}
int main()
{
    // Create the vector objects.
    std::vector<std::string> strVector1;
    std::vector<std::string> strVector2;
    // Populate two vectors with values.
    strVector1.push_back("Zebra");
    strVector1.push_back("Deer");
    strVector1.push_back("Fish");
    strVector1.push_back("Snake");
    strVector1.push_back("Bat");
    strVector2.push_back("Deer");
    strVector2.push_back("Antelope");
    strVector2.push_back("Turtle");
    strVector2.push_back("Snake");
    strVector2.push_back("Fish");
    // Sort the vectors.
    std::sort(strVector1.begin(), strVector1.end());
    std::sort(strVector2.begin(), strVector2.end());
    // Display the contents of the vectors.
    std::cout << "Contents of vector1: " << std::endl;
    std::for_each(strVector1.begin(), strVector1.end(), show_val);
    std::cout << std::endl;
    std::cout << "Contents of vector2: " << std::endl;
    std::for_each(strVector2.begin(), strVector2.end(), show_val);
    std::cout << std::endl;
    // Search for the sorted range Deer, Fish, Snake.
    bool result =
        std::includes(strVector1.begin(), strVector1.end(),
                    strVector2.begin()+1, strVector2.begin()+3);
    if (result)
        std::cout << "Found sorted range." << std::endl;
    else
        std::cout << "Did not find sorted range." << std::endl;
    return 0;
}
```

Program 33-12 produces the following output:

```
Contents of vector1:
Bat
Deer
Fish
Snake
Zebra

Contents of vector2:
Antelope
Deer
Fish
Snake
Turtle

Found sorted range.
```

Numeric Algorithms

STL's numeric algorithms implement four types of calculations that you can perform on a sequence of values. Table 33-4 lists these four functions along with their descriptions. Note that all of these algorithms are defined in the `std` namespace. However, for the sake of brevity, I left `std::` off their names in the table.

Table 33-4: Numeric Algorithms

Function	Description
`accumulate(first, last, init)`	Calculates the sum of `init` and each of the elements in the range specified by the `first` and `last` iterators. A second version of this function requires a predicate as its fourth argument.
`inner_product(first, last, first2, init)`	Returns the sum of `init` and the inner product of the ranges specified by the iterators `first`, `last`, and `first2`. An inner product is calculated by multiplying each element in the first range by the element in the same position of the second range and then summing all the results. A second version of the function requires two predicates as its fifth and sixth arguments.

Continued

Table 33-4 *(continued)*

Function	Description
partial_sum(first, last, result)	Calculates the partial sum of the elements specified by the iterators first and last, assigning the result to the range beginning at result. A partial sum is calculated as follows. First, the initial element in the source range is assigned to the first element of the result sequence. Then, the first two elements in the source range are summed, and the result is assigned to the second element of the result sequence. Next, the second and third elements of the source range are summed, and the result is assigned to the third element of the result sequence. This continues on up through the entire source range. A second version of the function requires a predicate as its fourth argument.
adjacent_difference(first, last, result)	Calculates the adjacent difference of the elements specified by the iterators first and last and assigns the result to the range beginning at result. An adjacent difference is calculated as follows. First, the initial element of the source range is assigned to the first element of the result sequence. Then, the first element of the source range is subtracted from the second element, and the result is assigned to the second element of the result sequence. Next, the second element of the source range is subtracted from the third element, and the result is assigned to the third element of the result sequence. This process continues through all the elements in the source range. A second version of the function requires a predicate as its fourth argument.

Programs 33-13, 33-14, 33-15, and 33-16, respectively, demonstrate the four numeric algorithms.

Program 33-13: **std::accumulate**

```
#include <iostream>
#include <vector>
#include <algorithm>
#include <numeric>

// function to be called by for_each()
void show_val(int val)
{
    std::cout << val << ' ';
}
int main()
{
    // Create the vector object.
    std::vector<int> intVector;
    // Populate the vector.
```

```
    for (int x = 0; x < 5; x++)
        intVector.push_back(x);
    // Display the contents of the vector.
    std::cout << "Contents of vector1: ";
    std::for_each(intVector.begin(), intVector.end(), show_val);
    // Calculate and display sum.
    int result = std::accumulate(intVector.begin(), intVector.end(), 5);
    std::cout << std::endl << "Result = " << result;
    return 0;
}
```

Program 33-13 produces the following output:

```
Contents of vector1: 0 1 2 3 4
Result = 15
```

Program 33-14: **std::inner_product**

```cpp
#include <iostream>
#include <vector>
#include <algorithm>
#include <numeric>

// function to be called by for_each()
void show_val(int val)
{
    std::cout << val << ' ';
}
int main()
{
    // Create the vector objects.
    std::vector<int> intVector1;
    std::vector<int> intVector2;
    // Populate the vectors.
    for (int x = 0; x < 5; x++)
        intVector1.push_back(x);
    for (int x = 2; x < 7; x++)
        intVector2.push_back(x);
    // Display the contents of the vectors.
    std::cout << "Contents of vector1: ";
    std::for_each(intVector1.begin(), intVector1.end(), show_val);
    std::cout << std::endl;
    std::cout << "Contents of vector2: ";
    std::for_each(intVector2.begin(), intVector2.end(), show_val);
    std::cout << std::endl;
    // Calculate the inner product.
    int result = std::inner_product(intVector1.begin(),
                    intVector1.end(), intVector2.begin(), 0);
    std::cout << "Result = " << result;
    return 0;
}
```

Program 33-14 produces the following output:

```
Contents of vector1: 0 1 2 3 4
Contents of vector2: 2 3 4 5 6
Result = 50
```

Program 33-15: **std::partial_sum**

```cpp
#include <iostream>
#include <vector>
#include <algorithm>
#include <numeric>

// function to be called by for_each()
void show_val(int val)
{
    std::cout << val << ' ';
}
int main()
{
    // Create the vector objects.
    std::vector<int> intVector1;
    std::vector<int> intVector2(5);
    // Populate the vector.
    for (int x = 2; x < 7; x++)
        intVector1.push_back(x);
    // Display the contents of the vector.
    std::cout << "Contents of vector1: ";
    std::for_each(intVector1.begin(), intVector1.end(), show_val);
    std::cout << std::endl;
    // Calculate the partial sum.
    std::partial_sum(intVector1.begin(),intVector1.end(), intVector2.begin());
    // Display the contents of the resultant vector.
    std::cout << "Contents of vector2: ";
    std::for_each(intVector2.begin(),
                  intVector2.end(), show_val);
    std::cout << std::endl;
    return 0;
}
```

Program 33-15 produces the following output:

```
Contents of vector1: 2 3 4 5 6
Contents of vector2: 2 5 9 14 20
```

Program 33-16: **std::adjacent_difference**

```cpp
#include <iostream>
#include <vector>
#include <algorithm>
```

```
#include <numeric>

// function to be called by for_each()
void show_val(int val)
{
    std::cout << val << ' ';
}
int main()
{
    // Create the vector objects.
    std::vector<int> intVector1;
    // Populate the vector.
    intVector1.push_back(3);
    intVector1.push_back(4);
    intVector1.push_back(12);
    intVector1.push_back(6);
    intVector1.push_back(10);
    // Display the contents of the vector.
    std::cout << "Contents of vector1: ";
    std::for_each(intVector1.begin(),
                  intVector1.end(), show_val);
    std::cout << std::endl;
    // build a vector to receive the result
    std::vector<int> intVector2(intVector1.size());
    // Calculate the adjacent difference
    std::adjacent_difference(intVector1.begin(), intVector1.end(),
                             intVector2.begin());
    // Display the contents of the resulting vector.
    std::cout << "Contents of vector2: ";
    std::for_each(intVector2.begin(), intVector2.end(), show_val);
    std::cout << std::endl;
    return 0;
}
```

Program 33-16 produces the following output:

```
Contents of vector1: 3 4 12 6 10
Contents of vector2: 3 1 8 -6 4
```

Summary

STL's generic algorithms provide various ways to manipulate and process the contents of containers including locating, sorting, copying, matching, and shuffling elements. The generic algorithms come in four types: non-modifying sequence algorithms, mutating sequence algorithms, sorting algorithms, and numeric algorithms. In the next and final chapter on STL, you learn more about iterators.

✦   ✦   ✦

Iterators

◆ ◆ ◆ ◆

In This Chapter

Input and output
iterators

Forward and
bidirectional iterators

Random-access iterators

Special-purpose
iterators

◆ ◆ ◆ ◆

For all intents and purposes, you can think of an *iterator* as a
pointer. You can think of an iterator as a specialized pointer that
allows your program to process the items within an STL container.
You typically use an iterator inside a loop to retrieve one or more elements from a container. The loop processes each element until it has
dealt with all elements in the container. STL defines five types of iterators, which are named according to the way you use them. In this
chapter, you explore iterators in detail.

Introduction to Iterators

Iterators behave like pointers. However, not all pointer operations are
legal for each type of iterator. Here's a summary of the iterator types
and the operations they permit:

   ◆ *Input iterators:* Used only to read from a sequence, this type of
      iterator can be incremented, dereferenced, and compared.

   ◆ *Output iterators:* Used only to write to a sequence, this type of
      iterator can be incremented and dereferenced.

   ◆ *Forward iterators:* Used for both reading and writing, this type
      of iterator combines the functionality of the input and output
      iterators with the ability to save its value in order to restart a
      traversal from the iterator's original position.

   ◆ *Bidirectional iterators:* Used for both reading and writing, this
      type of iterator is similar to the forward iterator, except that a
      bidirectional iterator can be incremented and decremented.

   ◆ *Random-access iterators:* The most powerful of the iterator
      types, random-access iterators have all the functionality of
      bidirectional iterators with the ability to use pointer arithmetic
      and all pointer comparisons.

Iterator types exist in a hierarchy as Figure 30-1 in Chapter 30 illustrates. The significance of this hierarchy is twofold. First, each iterator type has all the properties of those iterators above it in the
hierarchy, but an iterator type does not have the specialized behavior of those iterator types below it in the hierarchy; thus a random-
access iterator also works as a bidirectional iterator, a forward
iterator, and input and output iterators, whereas input and output
iterators have none of the properties of the other iterator types.
Second, the kind of iterator required to iterate a container depends
on the container.

Different STL algorithms require different types of iterators in order to function correctly. Because different STL containers support different kinds of iterators, you cannot use all algorithms with all containers. For example, a vector object uses random-access iterators, which makes sense because a vector requires random access to its elements. The sort algorithm also requires random-access iterators in order to function properly. This means that you can sort a vector object. In the following sections, you examine the different iterator types in more detail.

Input Iterators

Input iterators are (along with output iterators) the least powerful of all iterator types; as such, they are supported by all STL containers. A program can use an input iterator only to read the contents of a container. In order to traverse a sequence, an input iterator can be incremented (but not decremented) and compared for equality or inequality using the == and != operators. Program 34-1 demonstrates the use of input iterators.

Program 34-1: **Input iterators**

```
#include <iostream>
#include <vector>

int main()
{
    // Create a vector object.
    std::vector<int> intVector;
    // Populate the vector.
    for (int x = 0; x < 10; x++)
        intVector.push_back(x);
    // Display the contents of the vector.
    std::cout << "Contents of the vector: ";
    std::vector<int>::iterator it = intVector.begin();
    while (it != intVector.end())
        std::cout << *it++ << ' ';
    return 0;
}
```

Program 34-1 produces the following output:

```
Contents of the vector: 0 1 2 3 4 5 6 7 8 9
```

The program in Program 34-1 compares, dereferences, and increments an iterator used as an input iterator. Note that the std::vector member functions begin and end actually return random-access iterators. This means that the iterator it used in Program 34-1, as well as the iterators employed in many other listings in this chapter, actually are random-access iterators that the programs use to demonstrate the abilities of the other iterator types.

First, the program sets the it iterator to point to the first element of the intVector vector:

```
std::vector<int>::iterator it = intVector.begin();
```

Then, the program uses a `while` loop to iterate over the contents of the vector. The `while` loop's control statement compares the `it` iterator to an iterator (returned by the `end` member function) representing the end of the sequence:

```
while (it != intVector.end())
```

Within the body of the `while` loop, the program dereferences the iterator in order to access the contents of the currently referenced sequence element:

```
std::cout << *it << std::endl;
```

Finally, also in the loop, the program increments the iterator so that it points to the next element in the sequence:

```
++it;
```

Output Iterators

A program can use an output iterator only to write to the contents of a container. In order to traverse a sequence, an output iterator can be incremented (but not decremented). Program 34-2 demonstrates the use of output iterators.

Program 34-2: Output iterators

```cpp
#include <iostream>
#include <vector>

int main()
{
    // Create a vector object.
    std::vector<int> intVector(5);
    // Populate the vector.
    std::vector<int>::iterator out = intVector.begin();
    *out++ = 10;
    *out++ = 15;
    *out++ = 20;
    *out++ = 25;
    *out = 30;
    // Display the contents of the vector.
    std::cout << "Contents of the vector: ";
    std::vector<int>::iterator it = intVector.begin();
    while (it != intVector.end())
        std::cout << *it++ << ' ';
    return 0;
}
```

Program 34-2 produces the following output:

```
Contents of the vector: 10 15 20 25 30
```

The program in Program 34-2 dereferences and increments an iterator (actually a random-access iterator) used as an output iterator. First, the program sets the `out` iterator to point to the first element of the `intVector` vector:

```
std::vector<int>::iterator out = intVector.begin();
```

Then, the program uses dereferencing and incrementing to set the values of the vector's five elements:

```
*out++ = 10;
*out++ = 15;
*out++ = 20;
*out++ = 25;
*out = 30;
```

What exactly is the difference between the iterators in Programs 34-1 and 34-2? Internally they are the same. In use they are different. The `std::vector` container supports random-access iterators. What do we mean by that? When you declare an iterator for a vector container, as Programs 34-1 and 34-2 do, you are declaring a random-access iterator. Since a random-access iterator is also both an input and an output iterator — see again Figure 30-1 in Chapter 30 — you can use it where you can use those iterators. So what kinds of iterators are *only* input or output iterators? *Stream* iterators, discussed later in this chapter, are examples of iterators that can be used only as input or output iterators.

Forward Iterators

Forward iterators can iterate in a forward direction over the contents of a container, both reading and writing as required by the algorithm. In this way, a forward iterator combines the abilities of both the input and output iterators. However, a program can save the value of a forward iterator in order to start traversing a container from the same position. Program 34-3 demonstrates the use of forward iterators.

Program 34-3: **Using forward iterators**

```
#include <iostream>
#include <vector>

int main()
{
    // Create a vector object.
    std::vector<int> intVector(5);
    // Initialize iterators.
    std::vector<int>::iterator it = intVector.begin();
    std::vector<int>::iterator saveIt = it;
    // Populate the vector.
    *it++ = 10;
    *it++ = 15;
    *it++ = 20;
    *it++ = 25;
    *it = 30;
    // Display the contents of the vector.
    std::cout << "Contents of the vector: ";
    while (saveIt != intVector.end())
        std::cout << *saveIt++ << ' ';
    return 0;
}
```

Program 34-3 produces the following output:

```
Contents of the vector: 10 15 20 25 30
```

The program in Program 34-3 saves, dereferences, increments, and compares an iterator used as a forward iterator. First, the program sets the it iterator to point to the first element of the intVector vector:

```
std::vector<int>::iterator it = intVector.begin();
```

Then, the program saves a copy of the iterator:

```
std::vector<int>::iterator saveIt = it;
```

Next, the program uses dereferencing and incrementing to set the values of the vector's five elements:

```
*it++ = 10;
*it++ = 15;
*it++ = 20;
*it++ = 25;
*it = 30;
```

Finally, the program uses the saved iterator to iterate the vector and display its contents:

```
while (saveIt != intVector.end())
    std::cout << *saveIt++ << std::endl;
```

Bidirectional Iterators

Bidirectional iterators can iterate in a forward or reverse direction over the contents of a container, both reading and writing as required by the program. In this way, a bidirectional iterator combines the capabilities of a forward iterator with the capability to traverse a sequence in reverse. Program 34-4 demonstrates the use of bidirectional iterators.

Program 34-4: Using bidirectional iterators

```
#include <iostream>
#include <vector>

int main()
{
    // Create a vector object.
    std::vector<int> intVector(5);
    // Initialize iterators.
    std::vector<int>::iterator it = intVector.begin();
    std::vector<int>::iterator saveIt = it;
    // Populate the vector.
    *it++ = 10;
    *it++ = 15;
    *it++ = 20;
    *it++ = 25;
    *it = 30;
```

Continued

Program 34-4 *(continued)*

```
// Display the contents of the vector.
std::cout << "Contents of the vector: ";
while (saveIt != intVector.end())
      std::cout << *saveIt++ << ' ';
// Display the contents of the vector backwards.
std::cout << std::endl << "Contents of the vector backwards: ";
do
      std::cout << *--saveIt << ' ';
while (saveIt != intVector.begin());
return 0;
}
```

Program 34-4 produces the following output:

```
Contents of the vector: 10 15 20 25 30
Contents of the vector backwards: 30 25 20 15 10
```

The program in Program 34-4 saves, dereferences, increments, decrements, and compares an iterator used as a bidirectional iterator. First, the program sets the it iterator to point to the first element of the intVector vector:

```
std::vector<int>::iterator it = intVector.begin();
```

Then, the program saves a copy of the iterator:

```
std::vector<int>::iterator saveIt = it;
```

Next, the program uses dereferencing and incrementing to set the values of the vector's five elements:

```
*it++ = 10;
*it++ = 15;
*it++ = 20;
*it++ = 25;
*it = 30;
```

The program then uses the saved iterator to display the contents of the vector:

```
while (saveIt != intVector.end())
      std::cout << *saveIt++ << std::endl;
```

Finally, the program uses the same iterator to display the contents of the vector in reverse:

```
do
      std::cout << *--saveIt << std::endl;
while (saveIt != intVector.begin());
```

Random-Access Iterators

Random-access iterators are the most powerful of the lot. They can do anything any of the other iterators can do. In addition, you can manipulate — as well as compare — random-access iterators by using pointer arithmetic. That is, a program can:

✦ Add integers to and subtract integers from a random-access iterator (for example, it - 5 or it -= 10)

✦ Subtract one iterator from another, producing an integer offset (for example, it1 - it2)

✦ Compare iterators using the full set of comparison operators (for example, it < it2 or it1 >= it2)

Program 34-5 demonstrates the use of random-access iterators.

Program 34-5: **Using random-access iterators**

```
#include <iostream>
#include <vector>

int main()
{
    // Create a vector object.
    std::vector<int> intVector(5);
    // Initialize iterator.
    std::vector<int>::iterator it = intVector.begin();
    // Populate the vector.
    *it++ = 10;
    *it++ = 15;
    *it++ = 20;
    *it++ = 25;
    *it = 30;
    // Display the contents of the vector.
    std::cout << "Contents of the vector: ";
    for (it = intVector.begin(); it != intVector.end(); it++)
        std::cout << *it << ' ';
    it = intVector.begin();
    // Change the contents of the third element.
    *(it+2) = 100;
    // Display the contents of the vector.
    std::cout << std::endl << "Contents of the vector: ";
    for (it = intVector.begin(); it != intVector.end(); it++)
        std::cout << *it << ' ';
    return 0;
}
```

Program 34-5 produces the following output:

```
Contents of the vector: 10 15 20 25 30
Contents in reverse: 30 25 100 15 10
```

The program in Program 34-5 saves, dereferences, increments, decrements, and compares an iterator used as a random-access iterator. First, the program sets the it iterator to point to the first element of the intVector vector:

```
std::vector<int>::iterator it = intVector.begin();
```

Next, the program uses dereferencing and incrementing to set the values of the vector's five elements:

```
*it++ = 10;
*it++ = 15;
*it++ = 20;
*it++ = 25;
*it = 30;
```

Next, the program uses the iterator and the begin and end member functions of the vector class to iterate the vector and display its contents:

```
for (it = intVector.begin(); it != intVector.end(); it++)
    std::cout << *it << ' ';
```

The program then reassigns to the iterator the address of the first element in the vector and changes the value of the vector's third element by dereferencing the iterator offset by an addition operator in an assignment statement:

```
*(it+2) = 100;
```

Finally, the program uses the iterator to display the contents of the vector in reverse:

```
it = intVector.end();
while (it > intVector.begin())
    std::cout << *--it << ' ';
```

Special-Purpose Iterators

STL defines several special-purpose iterators. These include *stream iterators* — special types of input and output iterators that enable a program to manage data associated with I/O streams — and *insert* and *reverse* iterators, which are special-purpose iterators formed by iterator adaptors. In this section, you examine these types of iterators.

Stream Iterators

STL provides two stream-iterator classes. These classes are std::istream_iterator and std::ostream_iterator. The std::istream_iterator class defines an input iterator that you can use with input streams. That is, std::istream_iterator cannot handle output. Conversely, std::ostream_iterator is the stream output iterator, which cannot handle input.

Input Stream Iterators

To create an input stream iterator, you can write something like this:

```
std::istream_iterator<char>(strm)
```

This line creates an input stream iterator, for character data, which is attached to the stream object strm. Program 34-6 demonstrates how to use an input stream iterator.

Program 34-6: **Using input stream iterators**

```cpp
#include <iostream>
#include <vector>
#include <algorithm>
#include <iterator>

// function to be called by for_each().
void show_val(int val)
{
    std::cout << val << ' ';
}
int main()
{
    // Create a vector object.
    std::vector<int> intVector;
    // Populate the vector.
    std::cout << "Enter five integers separated by spaces: ";
    for (int x = 0; x < 5; x++)
        intVector.push_back(*std::istream_iterator<int>(std::cin));
    std::cout << "Contents of vector: ";
    std::for_each(intVector.begin(), intVector.end(), show_val);
    return 0;
}
```

Program 34-6 produces the following output (the numbers that appear depend upon the numbers you enter after the prompt):

```
Enter five integers separated by spaces: 34 75 29 92 15
Contents of vector: 34 75 29 92 15
```

Program 34-6 uses an input stream iterator to retrieve values from the standard input stream object std::cin and uses those values to populate the intVector vector object:

```cpp
for (int x = 0; x < 5; x++)
    intVector.push_back(*std::istream_iterator<int>(std::cin));
```

Because the push_back function requires as its argument a data value rather than an iterator, the program dereferences the std::istream_iterator object.

Output Stream Iterators

To create an output stream iterator, you can write something like this:

```cpp
std::ostream_iterator<char>(strm)
```

This line creates an output stream iterator, for character data, which is attached to the stream object strm. Program 34-7 demonstrates how to use an output stream iterator.

Program 34-7: Using output stream iterators

```cpp
#include <iostream>
#include <vector>
#include <algorithm>
#include <iterator>
#include <string>

// function to be called by for_each().
void show_val(const std::string& val)
{
    std::cout << val << std::endl;
}
int main()
{
    // Create the vector objects.
    std::vector<std::string> strVector1;
    std::vector<std::string> strVector2;
    // Populate two vectors with values.
    strVector1.push_back("Zebra ");
    strVector1.push_back("Deer ");
    strVector1.push_back("Fish ");
    strVector2.push_back("Cat ");
    strVector2.push_back("Bird ");
    strVector2.push_back("Turtle ");
    // Display the contents of the vectors.
    std::cout << "Contents of vector1: " << std::endl;
    std::for_each(strVector1.begin(), strVector1.end(), show_val);
    std::cout << std::endl << "Contents of vector2: " << std::endl;
    std::for_each(strVector2.begin(), strVector2.end(), show_val);
    std::cout << std::endl;
    // Sort the vectors.
    std::sort(strVector1.begin(), strVector1.end());
    std::sort(strVector2.begin(), strVector2.end());
    // Merge the sorted vectors to cout.
    std::merge(strVector1.begin(), strVector1.end(),
            strVector2.begin(), strVector2.end(),
            std::ostream_iterator<std::string>(std::cout));
    return 0;
}
```

Program 34-7 produces the following output:

```
Contents of vector1:
Zebra
Deer
Fish

Contents of vector2:
Cat
Bird
```

```
Turtle
```

```
Bird Cat Deer Fish Turtle Zebra
```

In Program 34-7, the program uses an output stream iterator to display values onscreen via
the std::cout object. The lines that accomplish the task look like this:

```
merge(strVector1.begin(), strVector1.end(),
      strVector2.begin(), strVector2.end(),
      std::ostream_iterator<std::string>(std::cout));
```

This call to the merge function merges the sorted vectors strVector1 and strVector2.
However, instead of the output iterator (the merge function's fifth argument) pointing to
another container, it directs the merged values to std::cout, causing the merged string values to appear onscreen.

Iterator Adaptors

Iterator adaptors modify one type of iterator into a special-purpose iterator. This is not unlike
the way container adaptors, discussed in Chapter 21, can change the capabilities of a container to suit another purpose, such as converting an std::list object into an std::stack.
STL defines two types of iterator adaptors that create reverse iterators and insert iterators.

Reverse Iterators

Reverse iterators traverse the contents of a container in the reverse direction. Because the
STL containers define reverse iterators, you don't need to define such iterators in your program. Instead, you can get a reverse iterator by calling a container's rbegin or rend member
function. Program 34-8 shows you how to use these functions, as well as compares their
usage with the begin and end functions with which you already are familiar.

Program 34-8: **Using reverse iterators**

```
#include <iostream>
#include <vector>
#include <algorithm>
#include <string>

// function to be called by for_each().
void show_val(const std::string& val)
{
    std::cout << val << std::endl;
}
int main()
{
    // Create the vector object.
    std::vector<std::string> strVector;
    // Populate the vector.
    strVector.push_back("Zebra");
    strVector.push_back("Deer");
    strVector.push_back("Fish");
```

Continued

Program 34-8 *(continued)*

```
    strVector.push_back("Snake");
    strVector.push_back("Bat");
    // Display the contents of the vector.
    std::cout << "Contents of the vector: " << std::endl;
    std::for_each(strVector.begin(), strVector.end(), show_val);
    std::cout << std::endl;
    // Display the contents of the vector in reverse.
    std::cout << "Reverse contents of the vector: " << std::endl;
    std::for_each(strVector.rbegin(), strVector.rend(), show_val);
    std::cout << std::endl;
    return 0;
}
```

Program 34-8 produces the following output:

```
Contents of the vector:
Zebra
Deer
Fish
Snake
Bat

Reverse contents of the vector:
Bat
Snake
Fish
Deer
Zebra
```

Notice in Program 34-8 how the loop that displays the vector in the forward direction looks identical to the loop that displays the vector in the reverse direction—with the exception of replacing the begin and end function calls with rbegin and rend function calls, which return reverse iterators. You also can initialize and use the reverse iterators as follows:

```
std::vector<std::string>::reverse_iterator begin =
    strVector.rbegin();
std::vector<std::string>::reverse_iterator end =
    strVector.rend();
std::for_each(begin, end, show_val);
```

Incrementing a reverse iterator actually points it to the preceding element in the container rather than the next.

Insert Iterators

An *insert iterator* enables a program to insert new values into a sequence using syntax that normally would overwrite the value at the specified location. STL defines three insert iterator adaptors: std::back_insert_iterator, std::front_insert_iterator, and std::insert_iterator. You can use the back_insert_iterator adaptor with any container that defines a push_back member function. You can use the front_insert_iterator adaptor with any container that defines a `push_front` member function. Finally, you can use the `insert_iterator` adaptor with any container that defines an `insert` member function.

To understand how an insert iterator works, first look at Program 34-9. This listing uses a conventional iterator to overwrite the zeroes that the five-element `intVector` object contains after it is constructed. The program's output follows the listing.

Program 34-9: **Overwriting values with an iterator**

```cpp
#include <iostream>
#include <vector>
#include <algorithm>

// function to be called by for_each().
void show_val(int val)
{
    std::cout << val << ' ';
}
int main()
{
    // Create the vector object.
    std::vector<int> intVector(5);
    std::vector<int>::iterator it = intVector.begin();
    // Populate the vector.
    *it++ = 23;
    *it++ = 34;
    *it++ = 45;
    *it++ = 56;
    *it = 67;
    // Display the contents of the vector.
    std::cout << "Contents of the vector: ";
    std::for_each(intVector.begin(), intVector.end(), show_val);
    return 0;
}
```

Program 34-9 produces the following output:

```
Contents of the vector: 23 34 45 56 67
```

The program in Program 34-9 defines a five-element vector. Because the size of the vector is given in the definition, each of the five elements is initialized with zeroes. That is, after the line

```
std::vector<int> intVector(5);
```

executes, you would see this if you displayed the contents of the vector:

```
Contents of the vector: 0 0 0 0 0
```

Next, the program defines an iterator that points to the first element in the vector:

```
std::vector<int>::iterator it = intVector.begin();
```

The program uses the iterator to overwrite the zeroes in the vector's five elements like this:

```
*it++ = 23;
*it++ = 34;
*it++ = 45;
*it++ = 56;
*it = 67;
```

Now, when you display the contents of the vector, you get the results shown above. In this example, it is a conventional iterator so the syntax used causes elements to be overwritten. You can change this behavior by using an insert iterator in place of the conventional iterator. Then, the same syntax causes the new values to be inserted into the vector — rather than overwriting existing values. This process causes the size of the vector to expand, as demonstrated in Program 34-10.

Program 34-10: **Inserting values with an iterator**

```cpp
#include <iostream>
#include <vector>
#include <algorithm>

// function to be called by for_each().
void show_val(int val)
{
    std::cout << val << ' ';
}
int main()
{
    // Create the vector object.
    std::vector<int> intVector(5);
    std::back_insert_iterator<std::vector<int> > it(intVector);
    // Populate the vector.
    *it++ = 23;
    *it++ = 34;
    *it++ = 45;
    *it++ = 56;
    *it = 67;
    // Display the contents of the vector.
    std::cout << "Contents of the vector: " << std::endl;
    std::for_each(intVector.begin(), intVector.end(), show_val);
    std::cout << std::endl;
    return 0;
}
```

Program 34-10 produces the following output:

```
Contents of the vector:
0 0 0 0 0 23 34 45 56 67
```

Because Program 34-10 uses an `std::back_insert_iterator`, the new values are inserted at the back of the sequence. An `std::front_insert_iterator` (which doesn't work with a vector because a vector doesn't define a `push_front` member function) enables values to be inserted at the front of a sequence. An `std::insert_iterator` (also not supported by a vector container) enables inserts at any location in the sequence.

Summary

Basically, an iterator is STL's version of a pointer — a special pointer that enables a program to iterate over the contents of an STL container. STL defines five types of iterators, which are named according to the way you use them. These different types of iterators consist of input iterators, output iterators, forward iterators, bidirectional iterators, and random-access iterators. In the next chapter, you start exploring exception handling, an advanced C++ topic that begins the final section of this book.

✦   ✦   ✦

Advanced Topics

Part V addresses the advanced features that Standard C++ supports. These are the chapters in Part V:

Exception Handling

Exception handling is a C++ feature that enables a program to intercept and process exceptional conditions — errors, usually — in an orderly, organized, and consistent manner. Exception handling allows one section of a program to sense and dispatch error conditions, and another section to handle them. Usually one category of code, perhaps the classes and functions in a library, can detect errors without knowing the appropriate handling strategy. It is just as common for other categories of code to be able to deal with errors without being able to detect them.

For example, a class library function may perform math by detecting overflow, underflow, divide-by-zero, and other exceptional conditions that are the result of user input. Selection of a strategy for handling the exception depends on the application. Some programs write error messages on the console; others display dialog boxes in a graphical user interface; still others request the user to enter better data; and others terminate the program. The error can result from a bug in the program or invalid (and invalidated) user input. A reusable library function should not presume to know the best exception-handling strategy for all applications. On the other hand, an application cannot be expected to detect all possible exceptions.

That a distant function can report an error to the using program has implications. Somehow, the detecting function must return control to the handling function through an orderly sequence of function returns. The detecting function can be many function calls deep. An orderly return to the higher level of the handler function requires, at the very least, a coordinated unwinding of the stack and destruction of objects as they go out of scope.

Exception Handling in C

Traditional C programs take two approaches to exception handling: They follow each function call with a test for errors; or they use setjmp and std::longjmp (refer to Chapter 26) to intercept error conditions. The first approach, which uses something like the global macro errno and zero or error function return values to report the nature of the error, is reliable but tedious. Programmers tend to avoid or overlook all the possibilities. The setjmp and std::longjmp approach is closer to what C++ exception handling strives for: an orderly and automatic way to unwind the stack to a state that was recorded at a specified place higher in the function-call hierarchy.

The setjmp and std::longjmp approach is intended to intercept and handle conditions that do not require immediate program termination. The syntax checker of a programming language translator, for example, can be in the depths of a recursive descent parser when it detects a syntax error. The program does not need to terminate. It simply should report the error and find its way back to where it can read the next statement and continue. The program uses setjmp to identify that place and std::longjmp to get back to it. Following is a code fragment that represents that process:

```
#include <setjmp.h>
std::jmp_buf jb;

void Validate()
{
    int err;

    err = setjmp(jb);
    if (err)
        /* An exception has occurred */
        ReportError(err);
    while (getInput())
        parse();
}

/* Parse a line of input. */
void parse()
{
    /* parse the input */
    /* ... */
    if (error)
        std::longjmp(jb, ErrorCode);
}
```

The std::longjmp call unwinds the stack to its state as recorded in the std::jmp_buf structure by the setjmp call. The initial setjmp call returns zero. The std::longjmp call jumps to a return from the setjmp call and causes setjmp to seemingly return the specified error code, which should be nonzero.

This scheme, however, contains anomalies. And, as you will soon learn, C++ exception handling does not solve all of them. Suppose that the parse function looked like this:

```
void parse()
{
    std::FILE *fp = std::fopen(fname, "rt");
    char *cp = std::malloc(1000);

    /* Parse the input */
    /* ... */
    if (error)
        std::longjmp(jb, ErrorCode);
    std::free(cp);
    std::fclose(fp);
}
```

Ignore for the moment that in a real program the function would test for exceptions to the std::fopen and std::malloc calls. The two calls represent resources that the program acquires before, and releases after, the std::longjmp call. The calls could be in interim functions that the program calls after the setjmp operation and that themselves call the parse function. The point is that the std::longjmp call occurs before those resources are released. Therefore, every exception in this program represents two system resources that are lost: a heap segment and a file handle. In the case of the std::FILE* resource, subsequent attempts to open the same file would fail. If each pass through the system opened a different file — for example, a temporary file with a system-generated file name — the program would fail when the operating system ran out of file handles.

Programmers traditionally solve this problem by structuring their programs to avoid it. Either they manage and clean up resources before calling std::longjmp, or they do not use std::longjmp where interim resources are at risk. In the preceding function, you can solve the problem by moving the std::longjmp call below the std::free and std::fclose calls. However, the solution is not always that simple.

Unwinding the stack in a C program involves resetting the stack pointer to where it pointed when the program called setjmp. The std::jmp_buf structure stores the information that the program needs to do that. This procedure works because the stack contains automatic variables and function return addresses. Resetting the stack pointer essentially discards the automatic variables and forgets about the function return addresses. All this is correct behavior, because the automatic variables are no longer needed and the interim functions are not to be resumed.

Exception Handling in C++

Using std::longjmp to unwind the stack in a C++ program does not work, because automatic variables on the stack include objects of classes, and those objects need to execute their destructor functions. Consider this modification to the parse function:

```
void parse()
{
    std::string str("Parsing now");
    // Parse the input.
    // ...
    if (error)
        std::longjmp(jb, ErrorCode);
}
```

Assume that the constructor for the string class allocates memory for the string value from the heap. Its destructor returns that memory to the heap. In this program, however, the std::string destructor does not execute, because std::longjmp unwinds the stack and jumps to the setjmp call before the str object goes out of scope. The memory used by the str object itself is returned to the stack, but the heap memory pointed to by a pointer in the string is not returned to the heap.

This problem is one that C++ exception handling solves. The unwinding of the stack in the exception-handling throw operation, the analog to std::longjmp, includes calls to the destructors of automatic objects. Furthermore, if the throw occurs from within the constructor of an automatic object, its destructor is not called; but the destructors of objects embedded in the throwing object are called.

The try Block

C++ functions that can detect and recover from errors execute from within a `try` block that looks like this:

```
try {
    // C++ statements
}
```

Code executing outside any `try` block cannot detect or handle exceptions even though code outside a `try` block can indeed throw exceptions. `try` blocks may be nested. The `try` block typically calls other functions that are able to detect and throw exceptions.

The catch Exception Handler

A `catch` exception handler with a parameter list follows a `try` block:

```
try {
    // C++ statements.
}
catch(int err) {
    // Error-handling code.
}
```

A catch handler "catches" exceptions thrown by a `throw` statement (discussed next) somewhere in the `try` block. There can be multiple `catch` handlers with different parameter lists:

```
try {
    // C++ statements.
}
catch(int err) {
    // Error-handling code.
}
catch(char *msg) {
    // Error-handling code with char *.
}
```

The type in the parameter list identifies the `catch` handler. The parameter in the `catch` parameter list does not have to be named. If the parameter is named, it declares an object with that name, and the exception-detection code can pass a value in the parameter. If the parameter is unnamed, the exception-detection code's argument to the `throw` statement is discarded.

The throw Statement

To detect an exception and jump to a `catch` handler, a C++ function issues the `throw` statement with a data type that matches the parameter list of the proper `catch` handler:

```
throw "An error has occurred";
```

This `throw` statement jumps to the `catch` exception handler function that has the `char*` parameter list.

The throw statement unwinds the stack, cleaning up all objects declared within the try block by calling their destructors. Next, throw calls the matching catch handler, passing the parameter object.

The try/throw/catch Sequence

Program 35-1 begins to bring the exception-handling steps together.

Program 35-1: **Throwing and catching an exception**

```
#include <iostream>

void foo();

// Exception class declaration.
class Bummer { };

int main()
{
    // The try block.
    try {
        std::cout << "calling foo" << std::endl;
        foo();
        std::cout << "return from foo << std::endl";
    }
    // Catch exception handler.
    catch(Bummer) {
        // Error-handling code.
        std::cout << "catching Bummer" << std::endl;
    }
    std::cout << "done" << std::endl;
    return 0;
}
void foo()
{
    int error = 1;
    // C++ statements to do stuff.
    if (error) {
        std::cout << "throwing Bummer" << std::endl;
        throw Bummer();
    }
}
```

Program 35-1 displays this output:

```
calling foo
throwing Bummer
catching Bummer
done
```

In Program 35-1, the program enters a `try` block; this means that functions called directly or indirectly from within the `try` block can throw exceptions. In other words, the `foo` function can throw exceptions and so can any function called by `foo`.

The `catch` exception handler function immediately following the `try` block is the only handler in this example. It catches exceptions that are thrown with a `Bummer` parameter. `Bummer` is a class set up specifically to identify the exception.

The `catch` handlers and their matching `throw` statements can have a parameter of any type. For example:

```
catch(ErrorCode ec) { ... }
// ...
throw ErrorCode(123);
```

This example assumes that there is a class named `ErrorCode` that can be constructed with an integer parameter list. The `throw` statement builds a temporary object of type `ErrorCode` and initializes the object with the value given in the `throw` statement. The parameter may be an automatic variable within the block that uses `throw` even if the `catch` uses a reference, as shown here:

```
void bar()
{
    try  {
        foo();
    }
    catch(ErrorCode& ec) {
        // ...
    }
}

// ...
void foo()
{
    // ...
    if (error)  {
        ErrorCode dt(234);
        throw dt;
    }
}
```

The `throw` statement builds a temporary `ErrorCode` object to pass to the `catch` handler. The automatic `ErrorCode` object in the `foo` function is allowed to go out of scope. The temporary `ErrorCode` object is not destroyed until the `catch` handler completes processing.

When a `try` block has more than one `catch` handler, a `throw` executes the one that matches the parameter list. That handler is the only one to execute, unless it throws an exception to execute a different `catch` handler. When the executing `catch` handler exits, the program proceeds with the code following the last `catch` handler. Program 35-2 demonstrates this behavior.

Program 35-2: **Multiple catch handlers**

```cpp
#include <iostream>

void foo();

// Exception class declarations.
class Bummer { };
class Dumber { };

int main()
{
    // The try block.
    try {
        std::cout << "calling foo" << std::endl;
        foo();
        std::cout << "return from foo" << std::endl;
    }
    // Catch exception handler.
    catch(Bummer) {
        // Error-handling code.
        std::cout << "catching Bummer" << std::endl;
    }
    catch(Dumber) {
        // Error-handling code.
        std::cout << "catching Dumber" << std::endl;
    }
    std::cout << "done" << std::endl;
    return 0;
}
void foo()
{
    int error = 1;
    // C++ statements to do stuff...
    if (error) {
        std::cout << "throwing Dumber" << std::endl;
        throw Dumber();
    }
}
```

Program 35-2 displays this output:

```
calling foo
throwing Dumber
catching Dumber
done
```

If there are multiple `catch` handlers with type parameters from a class hierarchy, the ones lower in the class hierarchy must be first. Otherwise `catch` handlers that specify the base class as a parameter will catch all the exceptions. For example:

```
#include <iostream>

class A { };
class B : public A { };

void foo()
{
    throw B();
}
int main()
{
    try     {
        foo();
    }
    catch(B)  {
        std::cout << "B";
    }
    catch(A)  {
        std::cout << "A";
    }
    return 0;
}
```

In the example just shown, if you moved the `catch` handler for objects of type A above the `catch` handler for objects of type B, the A handler would catch exceptions thrown with a B argument. Most compilers issue a warning when they see such a situation.

Catch-All Exception Handlers

A `catch` handler with ellipses for a parameter list, shown next, catches all uncaught exceptions:

```
catch(...)  {
    // error-handling code
}
```

In a group of `catch`es associated with a `try` block, the catch-all handler must appear last. Program 35-3 demonstrates the catch-all handler.

Program 35-3: **A catch-all handler**

```
#include <iostream>
// Function prototypes.
void foo();
// Exception class declarations.
class Bummer { };
```

```cpp
class Dumber { };
class Killer { };

int main()
{
    // The try block.
    try {
        std::cout << "calling foo" << std::endl;
        foo();
        std::cout << "return from foo" << std::endl;
    }
    // Catch exception handler.
    catch(Bummer) {
        // Error-handling code
        std::cout << "catching Bummer" << std::endl;
    } catch(Dumber) {
        // Error-handling code.
        std::cout << "catching Dumber" << std::endl;
    } catch(...) {
        // Catching leftovers.
        std::cout << "catching Killer" << std::endl;
    }
    std::cout << "done" << std::endl;
    return 0;
}
void foo()
{
    int error = 1;
    // C++ statements to do stuff...
    if (error) {
        std::cout << "throwing Killer" << std::endl;
        throw Killer();
    }
}
```

The catch-all handler in Program 35-3 catches the Killer exception, because none of the other catch handlers has a matching Killer parameter list. Program 35-3 displays this output:

```
calling foo
throwing Killer
catching Killer
done
```

Throwing an Exception from a Handler

You can code a throw with no operand in a catch handler or in a function called by a catch handler. The throw with no operand rethrows the original exception. Program 35-4 demonstrates this behavior.

Program 35-4: **Rethrowing exceptions**

```cpp
#include <iostream>
void foo();
// Exception class declaration.
class Bummer { };

int main()
{
    // The try block.
    try {
        // An inner try block.
        try {
            std::cout << "calling foo" << std::endl;
            foo();
        } catch(...) {
            std::cout << "rethrowing Bummer" << std::endl;
            throw;    // Rethrow the exception.
        }
    }
    // Catch exception handler.
    catch(Bummer) {
        // Error-handling code.
        std::cout << "catching Bummer" << std::endl;
    }
    std::cout << "done" << std::endl;
    return 0;
}
void foo()
{
    int error = 1;
    // C++ statements to do stuff...
    if (error) {
        std::cout << "throwing Bummer" << std::endl;
        throw Bummer();
    }
}
```

Program 35-4 displays this output:

```
calling foo
throwing Bummer
rethrowing Bummer
catching Bummer
done
```

Uncaught Exceptions

An uncaught exception is one for which there is no catch handler specified, or one thrown by a destructor that is executing as the result of another throw. Such an exception causes the std::terminate function to be called, which calls std::abort to terminate the program. Program 35-5 illustrates this behavior.

Program 35-5: **Uncaught exceptions**

```
#include <iostream>
void foo();
// Exception class declarations.
class Bummer { };
class Killer { };

int main()
{
    // The try block.
    try {
        std::cout << "calling foo" << std::endl;
        foo();
    }
    // Catch exception handler.
    catch(Bummer) {
        // Error-handling code.
        std::cout << "catching Bummer" << std::endl;
    }
    std::cout << "done" << std::endl;
    return 0;
}
void foo()
{
    int error = 1;
    // C++ statements to do stuff...
    if (error) {
        std::cout << "throwing Killer" << std::endl;
        throw Killer();
    }
}
```

Program 35-5 displays this output:

```
calling foo
throwing Killer

This application has requested the Runtime to terminate it in an unusual way.
Please contact the application's support team for more information.
```

The last part of the output depends on what the compiler's std::abort function displays before it terminates the program.

You can specify a function for std::terminate to call by calling the std::set_terminate() function, which returns its current value. Program 35-6 demonstrates this usage.

Program 35-6: **Catching uncaught exceptions**

```cpp
#include <iostream>
#include <cstdlib>
#include <exception>
// Exception class declarations.
class Bummer { };
class Killer { };

// Catch uncaught exceptions.
void terminator_2()
{
    std::cout << "catching the uncaught" << std::endl;
    exit(-1);
}
int main()
{
    std::set_terminate(&terminator_2);
    // The try block.
    try {
        std::cout << "throwing Killer" << std::endl;
        throw Killer();
    }
    // Catch exception handler.
    catch(Bummer) {
        // Error-handling code.
        std::cout << "catching Bummer" << std::endl;
    }
    std::cout << "done" << std::endl;
    return 0;
}
```

Program 35-6 displays this output:

```
throwing Killer
catching the uncaught
```

Selecting Among Thrown Exceptions

To review: One or more catch handlers, which are distinguished by their parameter lists, follow a try block. You must decide in your design how to differentiate the exceptions. You might code only one catch handler with an int parameter and enable the value of the parameter to determine the error type. This approach, illustrated next, makes the unlikely assumption that you have control of all the throws in all the functions in all the libraries that you use:

```
catch(int exception_code)  {
    switch (exception_code)
    {
        case 0:
            // Process code 0.
            break;
        case 1:
            // Process code 1.
            break;
        // ....
    }
}
```

Throwing intrinsic types is not the best approach. If all libraries threw integers, for example, the catch handlers would become a hodgepodge of collisions and conflicts. Most programmers use class definitions derived from the standard exception classes (discussed later in this chapter) to distinguish exceptions and categories of exceptions. A throw with a publicly derived class as its parameter is caught by a catch handler with the base class as its parameter. Consider this example:

```
class FileError  {
public:
    virtual void HandleException() = 0;
};

class Locked : public FileError  {
public:
    void HandleException();
};

class NotFound : public FileError  {
public:
    void HandleException();
};

void bar()
{
    try   {
        foo();
    }
    catch(FileError& fe)  {
        fe.HandleException();
    }
}

void foo()
{
    // ...
    if (file_locked)
        throw NotFound();
}
```

FileError is a public virtual base class. Its derived classes are NotFound and Locked. The only catch handler for this category of exception is the one with the FileError reference parameter. The handler does not know which of the exceptions was thrown, but it calls the HandleException pure virtual function, which automatically calls the proper function in the derived class. See the section "Standard Exceptions" later in this chapter for a discussion of the standard exception classes from which you can derive custom exception classes.

Exceptions and Unreleased Resources

Recall the discussion at the beginning of this chapter about the setjmp and std::longjmp anomaly of unreleased resources. C++ exception handling does not solve that problem. Consider this condition:

```
void foo()
{
    str::string *str = new std::string("Hello, Dolly");
    // ...
    if (file_locked)
        throw NotFound();
    delete str;
}
```

The new operator allocates the std::string object from the heap. If the program throws the exception, the delete operation is not performed. In this case, there are two complications. The memory allocated on the heap for the std::string object is not released, and its destructor is not called. This means that the memory that its constructor allocates for the string data also is lost.

The same problem exists with dangling open file handles, unclosed screen windows, and other such unresolved system resources. If the program just shown seems easy to fix, remember that the throw can occur from within a library function far into a stack of nested function calls.

Programming idioms have been suggested that address this problem, and programmers must consider them. Dr. Stroustrup suggests that all such resources can be managed from within automatic instances of resource-management classes. Their destructors release everything as the throw unwinds the stack. Another approach is to make all dynamic heap pointers and file and window handles global so that the catch handler can clean everything up. These methods sound cumbersome, however, and they work only if all the functions in all the libraries cooperate.

An Improved Calculator Program

Program 10-3 in Chapter 10 demonstrated recursion by implementing a simple four-function calculator. Program 26-3 in Chapter 26 improved the calculator by using the Standard C setjmp and std::longjmp functions to handle errors. Now, Program 35-7 further improves the program by encapsulating the calculator operations in a class and by using exception handling to manage data entry errors.

Program 35-7: **A calculator with exceptions**

```cpp
#include <iostream>
#include <cstdlib>
#include <cctype>
#include <string>

class Error { };

// Calculator class declaration.
class Calculator
{
    int pos;
    std::string expr;
    int addsubt();
    int multdiv();
    int number() throw(Error);
public:
    Calculator() { }
    int Compute(const std::string& str) throw(Error);
};

int Calculator::Compute(const std::string& str) throw(Error)
{
    int rtn = 0;
    try {
        pos = 0;
        expr = str;
        rtn = addsubt();
        if (pos < expr.length() && expr[pos] != '\0')
            throw Error();
    } catch(Error) {
        std::cout << '\r';
        while (pos--)              // position error pointer
            std::cout << ' ';
        std::cout << "^ syntax error" << std::endl << '\a';
        throw;
    }
    return rtn;
}
// Top of recursive descent: add/subtract.
int Calculator::addsubt()
{
    int rtn = multdiv();
    while (expr[pos] == '+' || expr[pos] == '-') {
        int op = expr[pos++];
        int opr2 = multdiv();
        if (op == '+')
            rtn += opr2;
        else
```

Continued

Program 35-7 *(continued)*

```cpp
                rtn -= opr2;
        }
        return rtn;
}
// Highest precedence: multiply/divide.
int Calculator::multdiv()
{
    int rtn = number();
    while (expr[pos] == '*' || expr[pos] == '/') {
        int op = expr[pos++];
        int opr2 = number();
        if (op == '*')
            rtn *= opr2;
        else
            rtn /= opr2;
    }
    return rtn;
}
// Extract a number.
int Calculator::number() throw(Error)
{
    int rtn;
    if (expr[pos] == '(') {
        // Parenthetical expression.
        pos++;
        rtn = addsubt();          // Back to top.
        if (expr[pos++] != ')')   // Must have ')'
            throw Error();
    } else {
        // Extract the number.
        if (!std::isdigit(expr[pos]))
            throw Error();
        char ans[80] = "0";
        int i = 0;
        while (std::isdigit(expr[pos]) && pos < expr.length())
            ans[i++] = expr[pos++];
        ans[i] = '\0';
        rtn = std::atoi(ans);
    }
    return rtn;
}
int main()
{
    int ans;
    do {
        // Read an expression.
        std::cout << "Enter expression (0 to quit):"
        << std::endl;
        std::string expr;
        std::cin >> expr;
```

```
        try {
            Calculator calc;
            ans = calc.Compute(expr);
            if (ans != 0)
                std::cout << ans << std::endl;
        } catch(Error) {
            std::cout << "Try again" << std::endl;
            ans = 1;
        }
    } while (ans != 0);
    return 0;
}
```

Program 35-7's first improvement over the earlier calculator programs is to implement the calculator in a class. The `main` function reads the arithmetic expression from the console, enters a `try` block, and instantiates a `Calculator` object. The program calls the `Calculator` object's `Compute` function, passing the expression string as an argument. If everything goes properly, the `Compute` function returns an integer value that is the result of the expression. If the value is zero, the program terminates. Otherwise, the program displays the value and asks for another expression to compute.

If an error occurs during the computation, the `Calculator` object throws an `Error` exception. The `main` function catches the exception, displays a "Try again" message, and asks for another expression.

Now, all the recursive-descent parsing algorithms are member functions in the `Calculator` class. The `Compute` member function initializes a subscript data member into the expression string, enters a `try` block, and calls the `addsubt` member function at the top of the recursive descent. If any part of that process encounters an error in the expression, the function throws an `Error` exception, which the `Compute` member function catches. When it catches an exception, the `Compute` function uses the current subscript data member to display where in the expression string the error was found. Then, the `Compute` function rethrows the exception so that the `main` function can catch it, too. If no exception is thrown, the `Compute` function returns the value returned by the `addsubt` member function. The rest of the program, which consists mainly of the recursive-descent parsing algorithm, works just as it does in the two earlier calculator programs.

Standard Exceptions

Standard C++ defines a standard mechanism for exceptions thrown by Standard C++ Library classes. Here is an overview of the standard exception mechanism:

✦ Exceptions thrown are objects of classes.

✦ Exception classes are derived from a common base.

✦ The base class supports polymorphic members that describe the exception to the run-time system.

As you learned earlier in this chapter, a `catch` handler with the base class as its parameter catches a `throw` with a publicly derived class as its parameter. Standard C++ defines a hierarchy of exception classes based on that behavior. Figure 35-1 illustrates its configuration.

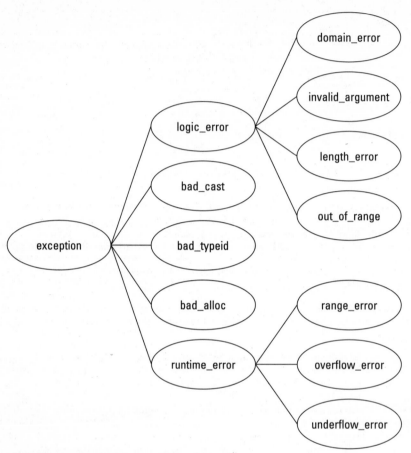

Figure 35-1: Standard C++ exception hierarchy

Programmers should follow the Standard C++ Library example and model their own exceptions after this hierarchy. Throw objects of these exceptions when appropriate, or throw objects derived from the most appropriate of these exceptions depending on the requirements of your application. Table 35-1 lists the standard exceptions and explains each purpose.

Table 35-1: Standard C++ Exception Classes

Exception Class	Purpose
std::exception	The top-level base class from which all exceptions are derived
std::logic_error	A base class representing programming errors that violate logical conditions, which should be detectable before the program runs
std::domain_error 1	A base class for exceptions that report violations of a precondition
std::invalid_argument	A base class for exceptions that report invalid argument values passed to a function

Exception Class	Purpose
std::length_error	A base class for exceptions that report attempts to create objects greater than the largest possible object
std::out_of_range	A base class for exceptions that report out-of-range argument values
std::bad_cast	Thrown by the dynamic_cast operator to report bad casts of reference objects
std::bad_typeid	Thrown for a null pointer argument to the typeid operator
std::runtime_error	A base class that represents errors detectable only after the program is running
std::range_error 2	A base class for exceptions that report violations of a postcondition
std::overflow_error	A base class for exceptions that report arithmetic overflow
std::underflow_error	A base class for exceptions that report arithmetic underflow
std::bad_alloc	A base class for exceptions that report failures to allocate memory

[1] A precondition is one that exists before an operation is carried out. For example, when an operation cannot proceed because something in the system related to the operation's domain is not in a state required to support the operation, the program throws an exception derived from domain_error.

[2] A postcondition is one that exists as the result of an operation. For example, when an operation causes an invalid data condition to occur, the program throws an exception derived from range_error.

Program 35-8 illustrates how a C++ program can derive exception classes from the Standard C++ Library exception class.

Program 35-8: **Deriving from the Standard C++ Library exception class**

```
#include <iostream>
#include <stdexcept>

// The Bummer exception class.
class Bummer : public std::runtime_error {
public:
    Bummer() : std::runtime_error("Bummer")
    { }
};

int main()
{
    try {
        throw Bummer();
    } catch(std::exception& ex) {
        std::cout << "Caught a standard exception";
    }
    return 0;
}
```

The std::exception::what Member Function

The std::exception class includes a member function named what that returns the address of the string value used to initialize the base class when the derived exception class object is instantiated. You can use the what function to display the specific exception that was caught, as Program 35-9 demonstrates.

Program 35-9: **The what member function**

```
#include <typeinfo>
#include <iostream>
#include <stdexcept>

// The Bummer exception class.
class Bummer : public std::runtime_error {
public:
    Bummer() : std::runtime_error("Bummer")
    { }
};
int main()
{
    try {
        throw Bummer();
    } catch(std::exception& ex) {
        std::cout << ex.what();
    }
    return 0;
}
```

Program 35-9 displays this information on standard output:

```
Bummer
```

Exception Specifications

You can specify the exceptions that a function may throw when you declare the function, as shown here:

```
void f() throw(Dumber, Killer)
{
    // C++ statements
    if (err1)
        throw Dumber();
    if (err2)
        throw(Killer());
}
```

The exception specification is part of the function's signature. You must include it in the prototype and in the function's definition header block. Otherwise, the compiler reports a type mismatch when it encounters the second declaration of the function.

Unexpected Exceptions

If a function includes an exception specification as shown previously, and if the function throws an exception not given in the specification, the exception is passed to a system function named `std::unexpected`. The `std::unexpected` function calls the latest function named as an argument in a call to the `std::set_unexpected` function, which returns its current setting. If no function address has been passed to `std::set_unexpected`, the `std::unexpected` function calls `std::terminate`, which usually calls `std::abort`, which aborts the program.

A function with no exception specification can throw any exception.

You must understand the implications of using exception specifications. If you declare a function with exception specifications, that function *and all the functions it calls directly or indirectly* may throw only those exceptions listed in the specifications except when the first function catches and does not rethrow any exceptions not listed in its exception specification. To properly use the feature, you must know about all the exceptions that might be thrown and either list or catch them all. Otherwise, a thrown exception will not be properly caught, even if another function higher in the call stack declares the exception in its exception specification.

Summary

Exception handling provides a structured technique for managing error and other exceptional conditions in a C++ programming. Chapter 36 discusses namespaces, the C++ feature that lets you put into a custom namespace what would normally be exposed in the global namespace.

✦   ✦   ✦

Namespaces

Namespaces have represented a problem in C and C++ since the language's inception in the early 1970s. In an interview in *Dr. Dobb's Journal* in 1989, Dr. Dennis Ritchie, the designer of C, addressed the namespace problem, saying that the ANSI/ISO X3J11 C standardization committee introduced " ... a convention that helps, but it certainly didn't solve the real problem."

The Namespace Problem

External, global identifiers are in scope throughout a program. They are visible to all object modules in the application program, in third-party class and function libraries, and in the compiler's system libraries. When two variables in global scope have the same identifier, the linker generates an error.

Programmers avoid such name collisions in their own code by assigning unique identifiers to each variable. Under Standard C (applying the convention mentioned by Dr. Ritchie), the compiler system prefixes its internal global identifiers with underscore characters, and programmers are told not to employ that usage to avoid conflicts. C programmers understand that some global identifiers were used by the standard library to identify functions, structures, and variables that the library provides, and programmers know that they must avoid using these identifiers for other things. Third-party library publishers addressed their part of the problem with mnemonic prefixes to global identifiers. This strategy attempts to avoid conflicts with other libraries, but it is unsuccessful when two publishers use the same prefix.

The problem is that the C language has no built-in mechanism with which a library publisher could stake out a so-called namespace of its own — one that would insulate its global identifiers from those of other libraries linked into the same program.

Programmers using multiple libraries with coincidental name collisions had three choices: Get the source code to the libraries and modify and recompile them; convince one of the publishers to rename identifiers and republish its library; or choose not to use one of the offending libraries. Often, none of the three choices was available.

The C++ committee approached this problem by introducing *namespaces*, a feature wherein identifiers declared within a defined block are associated with the block's namespace identifier. All references from outside the block to the global identifiers declared in the block must qualify, in one way or another, the global identifier reference with the namespace identifier. Publishers of libraries specify the namespace identifiers for the libraries' global identifiers. This feature is no more effective than using prefixes; two library publishers conceivably and unwittingly can use the same namespace identifier. Namespace identifiers, however, tend to be longer than the typical two- or three-character prefixes and stand a better chance of being unique. Many programmers make namespaces very long and then use namespace aliases (discussed later in this chapter) in their programs so the code is not too verbose.

Introducing Namespaces

As you just read, with hundreds of third-party libraries — not to mention C++'s considerable programming libraries — programmers sometimes find it a challenge to come up with variable or function names that are guaranteed not to conflict with other symbols. Standard C++'s solution to this growing problem is namespaces, an additional layer of identifier scope that enables a programmer to create meaningful symbol names without fear of stepping all over someone else's handiwork.

Simply put, a *namespace* is a named area of scope in which all identifiers created by the programmer are guaranteed to be unique — assuming that the programmer hasn't duplicated an identifier within the namespace and assuming that a previously defined namespace of the same name doesn't already exist. You define a simple namespace like this:

```
namespace MyNames  {
    int val1 = 10;
    int val2 = 20;
}
```

Here, two integer variables, val1 and val2, are defined to be part of the MyNames namespace. This is just an introductory example. Later in this chapter, you examine namespace definitions in greater detail.

Referring to Members of a Namespace

One example of a namespace is std, the namespace in which Standard C++ defines its library's identifiers. To use the cout stream object, you must tell the compiler that cout is found within the std namespace. You do this by prefixing the cout identifier with the name of the namespace and the scope resolution operator (::), as shown in Program 36-1.

Program 36-1: Using the std namespace

```
#include <iostream>

int main()
{
    std::cout << "Coming to you from cout.";
    return 0;
}
```

Program 36-1 displays a short message by using the cout object to stream text to the screen. Notice how the cout object's name is prefixed by the std namespace name with the :: scope resolution operator, a convention with which you should be familiar by now.

The using namespace Statement

Another way to gain access to the identifiers defined in a namespace is to include the using namespace statement in the source code file that references the namespace. For example, Program 36-2 is a version of Program 36-1 that includes the using namespace statement.

Program 36-2: **The using namespace statement**

```
#include <iostream>

using namespace std;

int main()
{
    cout << "Coming to you from cout.";
    return 0;
}
```

Program 36-2 works identically to Program 36-1. However, thanks to the using namespace statement, the program no longer requires that the std namespace name prefix the cout object's name. This may seem like a great timesaver, because not only does the cout identifier no longer require the std preface, but neither does any other identifier defined in the std namespace. Many programmers, however, avoid this practice, because the using namespace statement essentially places the specified namespace in the global namespace for this translation unit, which kind of defeats the purpose of having a namespace in the first place. Program 36-3 demonstrates the trouble you can get into by including the using namespace statement in a program.

Program 36-3: **Problems with the using namespace statement**

```
#include <iostream>

namespace MyNames {
  int val1 = 10;
  int val2 = 20;
}

namespace MyOtherNames {
  int val1 = 30;
  int val2 = 50;
}

using namespace std;
using namespace MyNames;
using namespace MyOtherNames;

int main()
```

Continued

Program 36-3 *(continued)*

```
{
    cout << "Coming to you from cout.";
    val1 = 100;
    return 0;
}
```

When you try to compile Program 36-3, Quincy's compiler provides the following error messages:

```
pr26003.cpp: In function `int main()':
pr26003.cpp:25: use of `val1' is ambiguous
pr26003.cpp:14:    first declared as `int MyOtherNames::val1' here
pr26003.cpp:8:    also declared as `int MyNames::val1' here
```

Here, the compiler tells you that, in the statement val1 = 100, the compiler doesn't know which version of val1 the program refers to. Is it the one defined in MyNames or the one defined in MyOtherNames? There's no way to tell. To avoid these types of problems, Program 36-4 eliminates the using namespace statements and unambiguously qualifies each reference with the appropriate namespace prefix.

Program 36-4: Avoiding the using namespace statement

```
#include <iostream>

namespace MyNames {
    int val1 = 10;
    int val2 = 20;
}

namespace MyOtherNames {
    int val1 = 30;
    int val2 = 50;
}

int main()
{
    std::cout << "Coming to you from cout.";
    MyNames::val1 = 100;
    return 0;
}
```

Defining a Namespace

A namespace can contain many types of identifiers, including those in the following list:

✦ Variable names

✦ Constant names

✦ Function names

✦ Structure names

✦ Class names

✦ Namespace names

A namespace can be defined in two places: at the global level of scope or within another namespace (which forms a *nested namespace*). Program 36-5 demonstrates a namespace definition that defines various types of variables and functions.

Program 36-5: **The namespace definition**

```
#include <iostream>

// Namespace definition.
namespace MyNames
{
    const int OFFSET = 15;
    int val1 = 10;
    int val2 = 20;
    char ch = 'A';
    int ReturnSum()
    {
        int total = val1 + val2 + OFFSET;
        return total;
    }
    char ReturnCharSum()
    {
        char result = ch + OFFSET;
        return result;
    }
}
int main()
{
    std::cout << "Namespace member values:" << std::endl;
    std::cout << MyNames::val1 << std::endl;
    std::cout << MyNames::val2 << std::endl;
    std::cout << MyNames::ch << std::endl << std::endl;
    std::cout << "Results of namespace functions:" << std::endl;
    std::cout << MyNames::ReturnSum() << std::endl;
    std::cout << MyNames::ReturnCharSum() << std::endl;
    return 0;
}
```

Program 36-5 produces the following output:

```
Namespace member values:
10
20
A

Results of namespace functions:
```

45
P

Nested Namespaces

Namespaces can be defined within other namespaces. In such a case, a program can reference identifiers defined in the outer namespace by using only the outer namespace name as a preface. Identifiers defined within the inner namespace, however, require as prefixes the names of both the outer and inner namespace. Program 36-6 demonstrates nested namespaces.

Program 36-6: **Nested namespaces**

```
#include <iostream>

// Namespace definition.
namespace MyNames   {
    int val1 = 10;
    int val2 = 20;
    namespace MyInnerNames  {
        int val3 = 30;
        int val4 = 40;
    }
}
int main()
{
    std::cout << "Namespace values:" << std::endl;
    std::cout << MyNames::val1 << std::endl;
    std::cout << MyNames::val2 << std::endl;
    std::cout << MyNames::MyInnerNames::val3 << std::endl;
    std::cout << MyNames::MyInnerNames::val4 << std::endl;
    return 0;
}
```

Program 36-6 produces the following output:

```
Namespace values:
10
20
30
40
```

Unnamed Namespaces

Although it's useful to give a namespace a name, you can declare unnamed namespaces simply by omitting the name in the definition. For example, the following example defines an unnamed namespace containing two integer variables:

```
namespace {
    int val1 = 10;
    int val2 = 20;
}
```

Identifiers defined in an unnamed namespace are placed, for all intents and purposes, in the global namespace, which pretty much defeats the purpose of a namespace. For this reason, unnamed namespaces are not particularly useful.

Namespace Aliases

Namespaces can be given aliases, which are alternative names for a defined namespace. Programmers use this feature to give namespaces long names to prevent external conflicts and shorter aliases to keep the code manageable. You can create a namespace alias simply by assigning the current namespace name to the alias, like this:

```
namespace MyNames  {
    int val1 = 10;
    int val2 = 20;
}

namespace MyAlias = MyNames;
```

Program 36-7 demonstrates the use of a namespace alias.

Program 36-7: **Namespace aliases**

```
#include <iostream>

namespace TeachYourselfCPPExampleCode {
    int val1 = 10;
    int val2 = 20;
}

// namespace alias
namespace tycpp = TeachYourselfCPPExampleCode;

int main()
{
    std::cout << "Namespace values:" << std::endl;
    std::cout << TeachYourselfCPPExampleCode::val1 << std::endl;
    std::cout << TeachYourselfCPPExampleCode::val2 << std::endl;
    std::cout << std::endl;
    std::cout << "Alias namespace values:" << std::endl;
    std::cout << tycpp::val1 << std::endl;
    std::cout << tycpp::val2 << std::endl;
    return 0;
}
```

Program 36-7 produces the following output, proving that both namespace names refer to the same identifiers:

```
Namespace values:
10
20

Alias namespace values:
10
20
```

Koenig Lookup

There is a special case where you do not need to provide the namespace prefix for an identifier declared in a namespace. When a function is declared in a namespace and one of its parameters is also declared in the namespace, a call to the function does not need to qualify the function name with the namespace as long as it properly qualifies the argument that matches the parameter. This behavior is named "Koenig lookup" after Andrew Koenig, the committee member who invented it. Consider the following program:

```
namespace personnel {
  class employee { };
  void paycheck(employee* emp)
  {
    // ...
  }
}

int main()
{
    personnel::employee empl;
    paycheck(&empl);
  // ...
    return 0;
}
```

Even though the paycheck function is declared inside the personnel namespace, the main function (which is, of course, outside the personnel namespace) can call the paycheck function without specifying the namespace — as long as the argument includes namespace information. The empl object is declared as being an object of type personnel::employee, which gives the compiler sufficient namespace information under the rules of Koenig lookup. However, suppose the main function looked like this:

```
int main()
{
    paycheck(0);
  // ...
    return 0;
}
```

In this case, the call to paycheck is invalid, because the argument, a zero value address, does not provide the compiler with any namespace information to use in selecting the function to call.

What is the purpose of Koenig lookup? Why is it necessary? What problem does it solve? Consider the following code:

```
std::cout << "hello";
```

The second line of code just shown is actually C++ shorthand for calling an overloaded operator function. In this case, the overloaded operator function is `std::operator<<` `(std::ostream&, const char*)`. Without Koenig lookup, the compiler would not know which `operator<<` function to call, and, as you've seen in examples in this book, there can be more than one such function, including ones you add to your own classes. Consider this code which overloads the << operator for displaying objects of type `employee` on `ostream` objects:

```
namespace personnel {
  class employee {
    // ...
  };
  std::ostream& operator<<(std::ostream& os, const employee& em);
}
```

The overloaded operator function is, in this case, in the `personnel` namespace. Now consider this program, which uses the `employee` class just shown:

```
int main()
{
    personnel::employee empl;
  // ...
  std::cout << "Employee: ";
  std::cout << empl;
    return 0;
}
```

The two calls to overloaded << operator functions call different functions in different namespaces, yet neither call explicitly tells the compiler which function to call. But both calls have arguments that reference objects of classes declared within those namespaces. Remember that the two statements are C++ shorthand for calling the overloaded operator functions. They could be coded like this, as well:

```
operator<<(std::cout, "Employee: ");
operator<<(std::cout, empl);
```

When the compiler looks for a function to match the first call, it looks in the `std` namespace because the first argument is in the `std` namespace. The compiler finds a function there with a parameter list that matches the two argument types, `std::ostream` and `const char*`. When the compiler looks for a function to match the second call, it does not find one in the `std` namespace because the Standard Library does not define an overloaded `operator<<` function with those two types; the Standard Library does not know about the user-defined `employee` class, which is the type of the second argument to the function call. So the compiler uses the `personnel` namespace from that second argument and looks for a matching overloaded `operator<<` function there, which, of course, it finds.

In short, without Koenig lookup, everything you learned in this book about using `std::cout` and overloading `operator<<` would not work. A side effect is that sometimes functions declared in namespaces behave as if they are in the global namespace because you can call them without specifying their namespaces.

Summary

Namespaces enable a program to isolate its global identifiers within a named space, thus avoiding conflicts with global identifiers of other parts of the program. In the next chapter, you learn about C++-style typecasting.

✦   ✦   ✦

C++ Typecasts

T ypecasting is a mechanism with which the programmer tells the compiler to ignore its notion of type safety and treat an expression as if it were some type other than what it is. You learned about traditional C-style typecasting in Chapter 7.

C-style typecasting has two problems. First, it is unsafe. You can use a C-style typecast to tell the compiler to do something that usually makes no sense, such as treating an integer value as a memory address. Second, C-style typecasts are difficult to find in large bodies of source code. Their syntax is similar to other code idioms, and searches with tools such as the grep utility for typecasts typically return many lines of code that are not typecasts at all. C++ supports C-style typecasts, but has an improved syntax, one that addresses these problems.

C++ Typecasts

In a perfect universe, programs would need no casts at all. Most programmers would like to eliminate them. However, research shows that many idioms require them, particularly in systems programming. The C-style cast is known to be unsafe, error-prone, difficult to spot in programs, and more difficult to ferret out in large bodies of source-code text. New-style casts improve the casting situation.

There are four new-style casting operators. Each one returns an object converted according to the rules of the operator. They use the following syntax:

```
cast_operator <type> (object)
```

The `cast_operator` is one of the following: `dynamic_cast`, `static_cast`, `reinterpret_cast`, and `const_cast`. The `type` argument is the type to which the object is cast. The `object` argument is the object being cast to something else.

dynamic_cast

The `dynamic_cast` operator casts a base class reference or pointer to a derived class reference or pointer, and vice versa. You can use `dynamic_cast` only when the base class has at least one virtual function.

The `dynamic_cast` operator permits a program to determine at run-time whether a base class reference or pointer refers to an object of a specific derived class, or to an object of a class derived from the specified class. This operation is called *downcasting*.

Downcasting Pointers

If a dynamic_cast operation on a pointer is not valid—if the type of the pointer being cast from is not a member of the class hierarchy being cast to—dynamic_cast returns a zero. Program 37-1 demonstrates downcasting pointers with the dynamic_cast operator.

Program 37-1: **Downcasting to pointers with dynamic_cast**

```
#include <iostream>

class shape {
public:
    virtual void foo() {}  // To enable dynamic_cast.
};

// classes derived from shape.
class circle    : public shape { };
class rectangle : public shape { };

// Process shape (circle and rectangle) objects.
void Process(shape* sp)
{
    // Downcast shape* to circle*.
    circle* cp = dynamic_cast<circle*>(sp);
    if (cp != 0)
        std::cout << "Processing a circle" << std::endl;
    else    {
        // Downcast shape* to rectangle*.
        rectangle* rp = dynamic_cast<rectangle*>(sp);
        if (rp != 0)
            std::cout << "Processing a rectangle" << std::endl;
        else
            std::cout << "Unknown shape, cannot process" << std::endl;
    }
}
int main()
{
    // Instantiate and process a circle.
    circle circle;
    Process(&circle);
    // Instantiate and process a rectangle.
    rectangle rect;
    Process(&rect);
    // Instantiate and process a generic shape.
    shape shape;
    Process(&shape);
    return 0;
}
```

The Process nonmember function in Program 37-1 knows about objects derived from the Shape base class. Process is a nonmember function rather than a member of Shape; the Shape class design does not need to know all the present and future specializations of itself. This approach is an alternative to having a pure virtual or empty Shape::Process function that is overridden by derived classes. Process represents some external generic process that does not implement any particular abstract data type's behavior, but it does need to use the interfaces of the object's classes.

If the object whose address is passed to Process is not a Circle, the dynamic_cast<Circle*> operation returns a zero value and Process knows not to call functions that are unique to Circles. Similarly, if the object is not a Rectangle, the dynamic_cast<Rectangle*> operation returns a zero value, and Process knows not to call functions that are unique to Rectangles.

A program that uses the dynamic_cast operator must include the <typeinfo> header and enable runtime type information as a compile option. The dynamic_cast operator uses internal runtime type information data structures to perform its checking and conversions. We cover runtime type information later in this chapter.

Downcasting References

If you use references rather than pointers, dynamic_cast throws a bad_cast exception when the target is not of the specified class. Program 37-2 demonstrates this behavior.

Program 37-2: **Downcasting to references with dynamic_cast**

```
#include <iostream>

class Control   {
public:
    virtual void foo() { }
};

class TextBox : public Control { };
class EditBox : public TextBox { };
class Button : public Control { };

void Paint(Control& cr)
{
    try {
        TextBox& ctl = dynamic_cast<TextBox&>(cr);
        std::cout << "Paint a TextBox" << std::endl;
    } catch(std::bad_cast) {
        std::cout << "nonTextBox, can't paint" << std::endl;
    }
}
int main()
{
    // Instantiate and paint Control.
    Control ct;
    Paint(ct);
```

Continued

Program 37-2 *(continued)*

```
    // Instantiate and paint Button.
    Button bt;
    Paint(bt);
    // Instantiate and paint TextBox.
    TextBox tb;
    Paint(tb);
    // Instantiate and paint EditBox.
    EditBox eb;
    Paint(eb);
    return 0;
}
```

Program 37-2 also demonstrates that a `dynamic_cast` works when the object is derived from the type from which it is cast. `TextBox` derives from `Control`. `EditBox` derives from `TextBox`. A reference to `Control`, the topmost base class in the hierarchy, can refer to an object of type `EditBox` — the bottommost derived class. The `Control` reference, which refers to an `EditBox` object, can be downcast to a reference to type `TextBox` — the inner class in this particular hierarchy.

Upcasting

Upcasting casts a reference, or pointer to a derived class, to a reference or pointer to one of the base classes in the same hierarchy. Most upcasting is done by implicit conversion. When the `main` function in Program 37-1 passes the address of a `Circle` object as an argument to the `Process` function's pointer-to-`Shape` parameter, an implicit conversion occurs. The compiler performs a static type-check to ensure that the conversion is permitted; if it is not permitted, the compiler issues a compile-time error message. You must fix the program's source code before you can compile it. The type-check in Program 37-1 passes because `Circle` is derived from `Shape` and because derived class objects can be referenced through pointers and references to their base class (or classes).

Inasmuch as implicit conversion involves static, compile-time type-checking, it follows that the actual contents of a pointer involved in an implicit cast do not enter into the process. A pointer may contain a null value or may never be initialized at all; the compiler still permits the conversion. You use `dynamic_cast` for upcasting when you need to determine at runtime whether a pointer to a derived class really contains the address of an object of that class. At the same time, you want to coerce the address into a pointer of one of the object's base classes.

static_cast

Unlike `dynamic_cast`, the `static_cast` operator makes no runtime check and is not restricted to base and derived classes in the same polymorphic class hierarchy. You can use `static_cast` to invoke implicit conversions between types that are not in the same hierarchy. Type-checking is static, wherein the compiler checks to ensure that the conversion is valid. This is opposed to the dynamic runtime type-checking that `dynamic_cast` performs. Assuming that you do not subvert the type system with a C-style cast to coerce an invalid address into a pointer or to initialize a pointer with zero, `static_cast` is a reasonably safe type-casting mechanism. Program 37-3 compares `static_cast` with C-style casts.

Program 37-3: **Comparing static_cast with C-style casts**

```cpp
#include <iostream>

class B {
    int i;
public:
    // Conversion constructor.
    B(int a) : i(a) { }
    void display()
    {
        std::cout << i;
    }
};
int main()
{
    // C-style cast int to B.
    B bobj1 = (B)123;
    bobj1.display();
    std::cout << '/';
    // Constructor notation.
    B bobj2 = B(456);
    bobj2.display();
    std::cout << '/';
    // static_cast.
    B bobj3 = static_cast<B>(789);
    bobj3.display();
    return 0;
}
```

If you are downcasting from a base to a derived type — a conversion that is not always safe — static_cast assumes that its argument is an object of (or pointer or reference to an object of) the base class within an object of the derived class. The cast can result in a different, possibly invalid address. Consider this code:

```cpp
class C : public A, public B { };
B *bp;

// bp is somehow initialized ...
C *cp = static_cast<C*>(bp);
```

If the bp pointer points to an object of type C, the cast works correctly. If it points to an object of type B, the cast makes the conversion, but the address is incorrect; it resides in a pointer to C but really points to an object of type B.

Similarly, if the pointer points to an object of the base class and you use the derived class pointer to dereference members of the nonexistent derived class object, then unpredictable behavior results.

If you are unsure about the safety of the cast, use dynamic_cast to downcast a reference or pointer and then check the result.

If you are casting from a derived to a base type—a safe practice—static_cast assumes that its argument is a valid object of the derived class or a pointer or reference to an object of the derived class.

reinterpret_cast

The reinterpret_cast operator replaces most other uses of the C-style cast, except those in which you cast away "constness" (discussed next). The reinterpret_cast operator converts pointers into other pointer types, numbers into pointers, and pointers into numbers. You should know what you are doing when you use reinterpret_cast, just as you should when you use C-style casts. That is not to say that you should never use reinterpret_cast. There are times when nothing else (except C-style casts) will do. Program 37-4 demonstrates a simple memory allocator that returns the address of a 100-character buffer as a void pointer. The main function assigns the return to a char pointer. Under the conversion rules of C++ (and unlike those of C), you cannot convert void* to char* implicitly, so you need a cast. Rather than employing a C-style cast, the listing uses reinterpret_cast.

Program 37-4: **Using reinterpret_cast**

```
#include <iostream>
#include <cstring>

void* getmem()
{
    static char buf[100];
    return buf;
}
int main()
{
    char* cp = reinterpret_cast<char*>(getmem());
    std::strcpy(cp, "Hello, Woody");
    std::cout << cp;
    return 0;
}
```

const_cast

The three cast operators just discussed respect "constness"—that is, you cannot use them to cast away the constness of an object. For that, use the const_cast operator. Its type argument must match the type of the object argument, except for the const and volatile keywords.

When would you want to cast away constness? Class designs should take into consideration users who declare a const object of the type. They do that by declaring as const any member functions that do not modify any of the object's data member values. Those functions are accessible through const objects. Other functions are not. Some classes, however, have data members that contribute to the management, rather than the purpose, of the objects. They manipulate hidden data that the user is unconcerned about, and they must do so for all objects regardless of `const`ness.

For example, consider a global counter that represents some number of actions taken against an object of the class, `const` or otherwise. Program 37-5 demonstrates such a program.

Program 37-5: **Using const_cast**

```
#include <iostream>

class AnObject {
    int val;
    int rptct;  // Number of times the object is reported.
public:
    AnObject(int v) : val(v), rptct(0) { }
    ~AnObject()
    {
        std::cout << val << " was reported " << rptct << " times.";
    }
    void report() const;
};
void AnObject::report() const
{
    const_cast<AnObject*>(this)->rptct++;
    std::cout << val << std::endl;
}

int main()
{
    const AnObject a(123);
    a.report();
    a.report();
    a.report();
    return 0;
}
```

If the declaration of the `A::report` member function were not `const`, the using program could not use the function for `const` objects of the class. The function itself needs to increment the `rptct` data member, something it normally could not do from a `const` member function because `const` functions cannot change data values. To cast away the `const`ness of the object for that one operation, the function uses the `const_cast` operator to cast the `this` pointer to a pointer to a non-`const` object of the class.

C++ provides the `mutable` keyword to specify class members that are never `const` — even when a `const` object of the class is instantiated. Chapter 18 discusses the `mutable` keyword.

Summary

This chapter showed how C++ typecasts respect the requirement to occasionally coerce the compiler into treating an expression as if it were something other than what it really is with respect to type. At the same time, C++ typecasts allow the programmer to use idioms that protect against careless and improper casting. Chapter 38 is about runtime type information, a programming idiom that allows the program to determine information about classes and objects at runtime.

✦   ✦   ✦

Runtime Type Information (RTTI)

◆ ◆ ◆ ◆

In This Chapter

The `typeid` operator

The `type_info` class

The `name` and `before` member functions

◆ ◆ ◆ ◆

C++ supports the ability to determine at runtime the type of an object, expression, or type. It might seem strange that a program would need to determine the type of one of these things given that the program itself is what declares these things. However, programs that make extensive use of polymorphism, may need to differentiate different types of objects at run time, not compile time. This chapter explains not only how RTTI works in the C++ language but also how you might use it.

The typeid Operator

The `typeid` operator supports the C++ runtime type information feature. Given an expression or a type as an argument, the operator returns a reference to a system-maintained object of type `std::type_info` that identifies the type of the argument. Here are examples:

```
typeid(int)
typeid(struct person)
typeid(Date)
typeid(*ObjPtr)
typeid(123)
```

Each of these expressions returns a reference to an object of the class `std::type_info`, which is defined in the `<typeinfo>` standard header.

If the argument is a pointer to a polymorphic class (one that has at least one virtual function), and the pointer contains a null value (zero), the `typeid` operator throws an exception of type `std::bad_typeid`.

You might see some similarities between what `typeid` does and what `dynamic_cast` (see Chapter 37) does. Both operators determine the type of an object given a pointer or reference to the object. The difference is that `dynamic_cast` requires an instantiated object whereas `typeid` does not. Furthermore, `typeid` always delivers the actual type of the object whereas `dynamic_cast` can be used in upcasting and downcasting operations. Also, `dynamic_cast` requires a pointer or reference to a polymorphic type as an argument, whereas `typeid` accepts expressions and types, including intrinsic types.

The type_info Class

The `type_info` class describes certain properties of types, and an object of this class describes the properties of a particular type. The only way to get a reference to an object of type `type_info` is with the `typeid` operator. The system maintains internally all the `type_info` objects for all the types a program uses. Given an argument, the `typeid` operator returns a reference to the appropriate system-maintained `type_info` object. You can use objects of type `type_info` to make runtime decisions about how to manage an object based on its type or to report to the user the name of an object's type. You should not assume that the system maintains only one such `type_info` object for each type in a program. There is no such guarantee.

There are only a few things that you can do with the `type_info` object reference returned by the `typeid` operator. You can compare it to another `type_info` object for equality or inequality. You can initialize a `type_info` pointer variable with the address of the `type_info` object. However, you cannot assign or copy a `type_info` object or pass it as a function argument. There are two `type_info` member functions.

const char* type_info::name()

The member function `type_info::name` returns a `const char*` pointer to the type's name. The conventions for this name are implementation dependent, which means different compiler implementations can generate different name formats for the same type. Standard C++ does not mandate a particular name format. The gcc compiler that Quincy hosts returns a single character string for intrinsic types. The string is prefixed by "P" if the object is a pointer, "PP" if it's the address of a pointer, and so on. For structures and classes and references to structures and classes, the `name` function returns the address of a string of characters displaying the character length of the class name followed by the class name. For example:

```
typeid(FooBar).name()
```

returns a `const char*` pointer to `"6FooBar"` (without the quote marks). See Program 38-1 in this chapter for other examples of what the `name` function returns.

bool type_info::before(const type_info& rhs)

The `type_info::before` member function returns a `true` or `false` value representing the order of the type in relation to the argument type. This order has nothing to do with the association of the type in a class hierarchy. Its purpose is so that objects of type `type_info` can be sorted by the compiler implementation. The function returns `true` if the object making the call precedes the argument object in the implementation's collation order.

Programming with RTTI

A program that uses the `typeid` operator must include the `<typeinfo>` header and must have the runtime type information compile option enabled. Program 38-1 demonstrates more of the behavior of the `typeid` operator and the `type_info` class.

Program 38-1: **Examining typeid behavior**

```cpp
#include <typeinfo>
#include <iostream>
#include <stdexcept>

class Control {
public:
    virtual ~Control() {};
};

int main()
{
    // Display name of type.
    Control ct;
    std::cout << "ct is a " << typeid(ct).name() << std::endl;
    // Compare typeids and display type of expression.
    double ctr = 1.23;
    const std::type_info& ti = typeid(ctr);
    if (ti != typeid(Control))
        std::cout << "ctr is not a " << typeid(Control).name() << std::endl;
    if (ti == typeid(1.23))
        std::cout << "ctr is a double" << std::endl;
    if (ti != typeid(int))
        std::cout << "ctr is not an int" << std::endl;
    std::cout << "ctr is a " << ti.name() << std::endl;
    std::cout << typeid(char).name() << std::endl;
    std::cout << typeid(unsigned char).name() << std::endl;
    std::cout << typeid(int).name() << std::endl;
    std::cout << typeid(long int).name() << std::endl;
    std::cout << typeid(float).name() << std::endl;
    std::cout << typeid(unsigned).name() << std::endl;
    void* p = &ct;
    std::cout << typeid(p).name() << std::endl;
    std::cout << typeid(&p).name() << std::endl;
    Control& rc = ct;
    std::cout << typeid(rc).name() << std::endl;
    try {

        Control* cp = 0;
        std::cout << typeid(cp).name() << std::endl;
        std::cout << typeid(*cp).name() << std::endl;
    }
    catch (...) {
        std::cout << "Caught that bad typeid" << std::endl;
    }
    return 0;
}
```

Program 38-1 displays the following output:

```
ct is a 7Control
ctr is not a 7Control
ctr is a double
ctr is not an int
ctr is a d
c
h
i
l
f
j
Pv
PPv
7Control
P7Control
Caught that bad typeid
```

Observe the output displayed from value returned by the name function for each argument. The Control class includes a virtual destructor so that the class is polymorphic. This property means that dereferencing the null pointer in a typeid argument throws the std::bad_typeid exception, which is the last thing the program does.

Uses for RTTI

How do you use runtime type information? What purpose is gained by determining the specific type of an object? The dynamic_cast operator is more flexible than the typeid operator in one way and less so in others. It tells you that an object is of a specified class or, in some cases, of a class in the same class hierarchy as the specified class. But for you to be able to use dynamic_cast, there must be an object of the class already instantiated. Furthermore, dynamic_cast works only with pointers and references to polymorphic class objects; at least one virtual function must exist somewhere in the class hierarchy. The typeid operator works with instantiated objects, pointers and references to objects, intrinsic type names, function names, class members, class names, and expressions.

RTTI in a Database Manager

Consider a persistent object database manager. It scans the database files and constructs memory objects from data values that it finds. How does it determine which constructors to call? RTTI can provide that information. If the first component of a persistent object record is the class name or an offset into an array of class names, the program can use RTTI to select the constructor. Examine the following example, in which the database scanner retrieves the class name of the next object and calls the DisplayObject function. In this example, the database records only three classes.

```
void DisplayObject(const std::string& cname)
{
    if (cname == typeid(Employee).name()) {
        Employee empl;
        empl.Display();
    }
    else if (cname == typeid(Department).name()) {
```

```
        Department dept;
        dept.Display();
    }
    else if (cname == typeid(Project).name()) {
        Project proj;
        proj.Display();
    }
}
```

This example is a contrived one that assumes that the database manager knows how to construct each object when the file pointer is positioned just past the type identifier in the record. This technique assumes that the scanner program knows about all the classes in the database and what conventions the compiler uses to name types. There would be much more to implementing this technique than the code fragment here suggests.

Summary

The RTTI feature of C++ has application in many ways. Some programmers never need it. Others use it all the time. It depends on what kind of programming you do. This chapter explained how it works and suggested how you might use it. Beyond that it's a matter of applying your knowledge of RTTI to the requirements of the programs you write to see if RTTI is the right tool for you. Chapter 39 completes your studies of the Standard C++ programming language by explaining how to write programs that can be adapted to the requirements of various international locales, and Chapter 40 concludes the book with an explanation of object-oriented programming as it relates to C++

✦   ✦   ✦

Locales

In general, as their names suggest, *locales* represent the various ways information is displayed in different areas of the world or for computer users of a specific culture. For example, the U.S.-style date 1/21/2000 is displayed as 21/1/2000 in Greece and as 21.1.2000 in Germany. Application developers who intend for their products to be distributed around the world need to be aware of these differences and know how to write their programs so that they are locale aware. In this chapter, you get a quick look at locales and how they are used in C++ programming. Even if you target only English speaking countries, there is a wide variation between, for example, the U.S. and the U.K. Locales don't just identify language, but can also refer to cultural groups, that may even be in the same country.

Elements of Internationalization

In the preceding paragraph, you learned that dates are one type of data you must consider when writing applications for an international market. In all, there are seven *elements of internationalization* that you must handle in such an application. Those elements are listed and described as follows:

✦ *Characters:* While you can represent a language—such as English—using the simple ASCII code, other languages require much larger character sets than a code set designed to represent a maximum of 256 characters. This problem gives rise to three types of character codes: single-byte ASCII characters, multibyte characters, and wide characters.

✦ *Character Ordering:* When sorting characters into order— a process called *collating*—different sorting rules apply for different languages. For example, in traditional Spanish, the double-symbol letter ll is considered to be a single character and so is not sorted in the same way a pair of l's is in English.

✦ *Character Classification:* Every language contains character codes for alphabetic, numeric, punctuation, and other types of symbols. The group that a character fits into is its classification.

✦ *Numbers:* Different countries represent numbers in different ways. For example, the U.S.-style number 34,785,000.75 is written as 34.785.000,75 in Germany.

✦ *Currency:* Different countries use different types of currency, and so they use different currency symbols. In the United States, the currency symbol is the dollar sign; in Germany, the currency symbol is DM. Also, the location of currency symbols in currency values varies from country to country. For example, the dollar sign is placed in front of the amount, as in $45.98. However, the DM symbol is placed after the amount, as in 12,45 DM.

✦ *Time and Date:* Times and dates are displayed differently throughout the world. You've seen examples of how dates differ. Time representations differ as well.

✦ *Case:* Various languages have different rules for the conversion between upper and lower case of text.

✦ *Language:* If English, Spanish, French, or any other language were the only language on Earth, writing international applications would be easier to say the least. As we all know, however, there are many different languages. Obviously, the text in an internationalized program should be displayed in the appropriate language, which usually means keeping text separate from the executable file in a resource that can be translated as needed.

The C++ Standard Library provides ways to manage most of the elements of internationalization. The exception is the native language of each locale, which, in most cases, must be translated manually, a procedure with its own set of problems, for example, the varying lengths of text messages, menu labels, and so on. In the rest of this chapter, you discover some tools that the C++ libraries provide for application internationalization.

The std::locale Class

In C++, an object of the `std::locale` class represents a locale. A `locale` object is a kind of container that holds objects called *facets*, which represent the elements of internationalization described in the preceding section. For example, a `locale` object contains facets that manage elements such as date and time formats, currency symbols, and number formats. Facets not only provide information about an element of a locale, but also provide an interface for internationalization services.

The Standard Facets

Although a programmer can create specialized facets, C++ defines seven standard facets, as listed here:

✦ *Code Conversion:* This type of facet converts between different character representations, such as converting from multibyte characters to wide characters.

✦ *Collate:* This type of facet manages character ordering for string collation.

✦ *Ctype:* This type of facet manages character classification, such as setting a character's case or determining whether a character is part of the language's punctuation group.

✦ *Numeric:* This type of facet manages number formatting.

✦ *Monetary:* This type of facet manages currency formatting.

✦ *Time and Date:* This type of facet manages time and date formatting.

✦ *Messages:* This type of facet manages message catalogs, which enable an application to translate simple responses such as "Yes" and "No."

Default and Global Locales

You probably don't realize it, but you've used locales already. In fact, you've used locales a lot. Every C++ program you write runs under the *default locale*, which is the United States ASCII locale. The C++ Library creates this locale object, called std::locale::classic, for you. Just like any locale, std::locale::classic determines the way many library functions display information.

There's also something called the *global locale*, which is the currently active locale. When you don't change the locale in your program, the default and global locales are the same. You can change the global locale, but you cannot change the default locale.

Creating a Locale Object

With the exception of the default locale, a locale object requires you to create the object first. The std::locale class provides four ways to create a locale object, as follows:

```
std::locale localeName();
std::locale localeName(localeCode);
std::locale localeName(locale1, locale2, cat);
std::locale localeName(locale1, localeCode, cat);
```

The first example creates a locale object from the global locale, whereas the second example creates the locale object from the locale code string specified by *localeCode*. (Table 39-1 shows locale codes you can use with the locale class's constructor.) The third constructor example creates a copy of the locale object *locale1*, replacing those facets in *locale1* with facets in *locale2* specified by *cat*. The fourth example is similar, except that a locale code string specifies the facet-source locale.

Table 39-1: Locale Codes

Language	Name
Chinese	"chinese"
Chinese (simplified)	"chinese-simplified" or "chs"
Chinese (traditional)	"chinese-traditional" or "cht"
Czech	"czech" or "csy"
Danish	"danish" or "dan"
Dutch	"dutch" or "nld"
Dutch (Belgian)	"belgian", "dutch-belgian", or "nlb"
English (default)	"english"
English (Australian)	"australian", "ena", or "english-aus"
English (Canadian)	"canadian", "enc", or "english-can"
English (New Zealand)	"english-nz" or "enz"

Continued

Table 39-1 *(continued)*

Language	Name
English (UK)	"english-uk", "eng", or "uk"
English (USA)	"american", "american english", "american-english", "english-american", "english-us", "english-usa", "enu", "us", or "usa"
Finnish	"finnish" or "fin"
French (default)	"french" or "fra"
French (Belgian)	"french-belgian" or "frb"
French (Canadian)	"french-canadian" or "frc"
French (Swiss)	"french-swiss" or "frs"
German (default)	"german" or "deu"
German (Austrian)	"german-austrian" or "dea"
German (Swiss)	"german-swiss", "des", or "swiss"
Greek	"greek" or "ell"
Hungarian	"hungarian" or "hun"
Icelandic	"icelandic" or "isl"
Italian (default)	"italian" or "ita"
Italian (Swiss)	"italian-swiss" or "its"
Japanese	"japanese" or "jpn"
Korean	"kor" or "korean"
Norwegian (default)	"norwegian"
Norwegian (Bokmal)	"norwegian-bokmal" or "nor"
Norwegian (Nynorsk)	"norwegian-nynorsk" or "non"
Polish	"polish" or "plk"
Portuguese (default)	"portuguese" or "ptg"
Portuguese (Brazilian)	"portuguese-brazilian" or "ptb"
Russian (default)	"russian" or "rus"
Slovak	"slovak" or "sky"
Spanish (default)	"spanish" or "esp"
Spanish (Mexican)	"spanish-mexican" or "esm"
Spanish (Modern)	"spanish-modern" or "esn"
Swedish	"swedish" or "sve"
Turkish	"turkish" or "trk"

Program 39-1 demonstrates creating and using locales by displaying the date format for English, French, and German.

Program 39-1: **Dates using different locales**

```cpp
#include <iostream>
#include <locale>
#include <time.h>

int main()
{
    char dateStr[81];
    time_t curTime;
    struct tm* tmTime;
    // Get the current time.
    time(&curTime);
    // Convert the time to a tm structure.
    tmTime = gmtime(&curTime);
    // Convert the time to a string.
    strftime(dateStr, 80, "%#x", tmTime);
    // Set the global locale to the native locale.
    std::locale native("");
    std::locale::global(native);
    // Output the date using the native locale.
    std::cout << "Native Date: " << std::endl;
    std::cout << dateStr << std::endl << std::endl;
    // Make the global locale French.
    std::locale french("french");
    std::locale::global(french);
    // Redisplay the date using the French locale.
    strftime(dateStr, 80, "%#x", tmTime);
    std::cout << "French Date: " << std::endl;
    std::cout << dateStr << std::endl << std::endl;
    // Make the global locale German.
    std::locale german("german");
    std::locale::global(german);
    // Redisplay the date using the German locale.
    strftime(dateStr, 80, "%#x", tmTime);
    std::cout << "German Date: " << std::endl;
    std::cout << dateStr << std::endl << std::endl;
    return 0;
}
```

Program 39-1 produces the following output on a system whose native locale is U.S. English:

```
Native Date:
Thursday, December 12, 2002

French Date:
```

```
jeudi 12 d_cembre 2002

German Date:
Donnerstag, 12. Dezember 2002
```

Program 39-1 is well documented by its comments. One line, however, deserves a closer look:

```
std::locale native("");
```

When the program calls the `locale` constructor with an empty string, the returned `locale` object is set to the native locale, which is based upon the system's user settings. Usually, users can set their native locales by setting system variables such as `LANG`.

Creating a Mixed Locale

You can create a mixed locale by changing the facet of one locale to the equivalent facet of another locale. For example, suppose you want all output done according to the French locale — except for dates, which you want displayed in the U.S. English format. Program 39-2 demonstrates how to solve this problem.

Program 39-2: Creating mixed locales

```cpp
#include <iostream>
#include <locale>
#include <clocale>
#include <ctime>

int main()
{
    char dateStr[81];
    time_t curTime;
    struct tm* tmTime;
    // Get the current time.
    time(&curTime);
    // Convert the time to a tm structure.
    tmTime = gmtime(&curTime);
    // Convert the time to a string.
    strftime(dateStr, 80, "%#x", tmTime);
    // Make the global locale French with USA dates.
    std::locale french(std::locale("french"),
                       std::locale("american"), LC_TIME);
    std::locale::global(french);
    // Redisplay the date using the mixed locale.
    strftime(dateStr, 80, "%#x", tmTime);
    std::cout << "French Date: " << std::endl;
    std::cout << dateStr << std::endl << std::endl;
    return 0;
}
```

Program 39-2 produces the following output:

```
French Date:
Thursday, December 12, 2002
```

As you can see, the locale object is French, but the call to the locale class's constructor replaces the time facet with the American version. This results in dates formatted for U.S. English, even though the rest of the locale supports French formatting. The LC_TIME constant comes from Table 39-2, which describes the constants for specifying facets.

Table 39-2: Locale Category Values

Value	Description
LC_ALL	Sets all categories
LC_COLLATE	Sets the locale category associated with collating functions
LC_CTYPE	Sets the locale category associated with character classification functions
LC_MONETARY	Sets the locale category that affects monetary formatting
LC_NUMERIC	Sets the locale category that affects numeric formatting
LC_TIME	Sets the locale category that affects time and date formatting

Streams and Locales

In many circumstances, using streams in an application can simplify the use of locales — especially when you want to support multiple locales concurrently. This is because you can *imbue* a stream with a locale, after which that stream will format data based on the facets of the locale. You can create and imbue streams for all the locales the program needs to support. To imbue a stream with a locale, call the stream object's imbue member function. Program 39-3 demonstrates how to use the imbue member function.

Program 39-3: **Using streams and the imbue() function**

```cpp
#include <iostream>
#include <locale>

int main()
{
    // Output a number using the native locale.
    std::locale native("");
    std::cout.imbue(native);
    std::cout << "Native Number: " << std::endl;
    std::cout << 10999.82 << std::endl << std::endl;
    // Redisplay the number using the Dutch locale.
    std::locale dutch("dutch");
```

Continued

Program 39-3 *(continued)*

```
std::cout.imbue(dutch);
std::cout << "Dutch Number: " << std::endl;
std::cout << 10999.82 << std::endl << std::endl;
// Redisplay the number using the French locale.
std::locale french("french");
std::cout.imbue(french);
std::cout << "French Number: " << std::endl;
std::cout << 10999.82 << std::endl << std::endl;
return 0;
}
```

Program 39-3 produces the following output:

```
Native Number:
10999.8

Dutch Number:
10999.8

French Number:
10999.8
```

Manipulating Facets

Because a `locale` object's facets provide services used to localize software, you need a way to access and use these services. Two template functions provide this important support: `std::has_facet` and `std::use_facet`. The `std::has_facet` template function returns `true` if a specified facet exists in a given locale. For example, to determine whether the German locale supports the `ctype` facet, you can write:

```
std::locale german("german");
bool OK = std::has_facet<std::ctype<char> >(german);
```

Each type of facet defines functions a program can call upon to manipulate data for a locale. You call `std::use_facet` to call a facet object's member functions. Although the many different facet functions are beyond the scope of this chapter, a simple example should get you on your way. Suppose that you want to call upon the `ctype` facet's `toupper` function to uppercase a string according to the rules of the German locale. You can write something like this:

```
std::string test = "abcdefghijklmnopqrstuvwxyz";
char* first = test.begin();
char* last = test.end();
std::use_facet< std::ctype<char> >
    (german).toupper(first, last);
```

Program 39-4 demonstrates how to call upon a facet's services.

> **Program 39-4: Accessing facets**

```
#include <iostream>
#include <locale>
#include <string>

int main()
{
    // Set the global locale to German.
    std::locale german("german");
    std::locale::global(german);
    // Check whether the facet is supported.
    bool OK = std::has_facet<std::ctype<char> >(german);
    if (!OK) {
        std::cout << "Can't perform the conversion.";
        return 1;
    }
    // Set up the string and string pointers.
    char test[] = "abcdefghijklmnopqrstuvwxyz";
    char* first = test;
    char* last = first + sizeof test;
    // Display the starting string.
    std::cout << "Original String:" << std::endl;
    std::cout << first << std::endl << std::endl;
    // Convert the string to uppercase.
    std::use_facet< std::ctype<char> >(german).toupper(first, last);
    // Display the converted string.
    std::cout << "Converted String:" << std::endl;
    std::cout << first << std::endl << std::endl;
    return 0;
}
```

Program 39-4 produces the following output:

```
Original String:
abcdefghijklmnopqrstuvwxyz

Converted String:
ABCDEFGHIJKLMNOPQRSTUVWXYZ
```

Summary

Locales enable a program to support the language conventions of a culture or geographical location. C++ provides the std::locale class for managing the elements of a locale. The real work in internationlization is the actual translation of strings, desiging forms that will fit the various languages, and font issues.

It is sometimes useful to put strings in a separate resource, something supported by many modern operating systems. This is important because a translator can just go through and work on the strings *en masse*.

✦   ✦   ✦

Object-Oriented Programming

Object-oriented programming is a programming model — an approach to the expression of a computer program that emphasizes data rather than procedures. C++ includes features that support object-oriented programming. This chapter explains the model so that you, the new C++ programmer, can associate what you have learned about the C++ language with the terms and concepts of object-oriented programming.

Objects and the C++ Programmer

As pervasive as object-oriented programming has become, many programmers still do not understand it. By using the exercises in this book, you have acquired a working knowledge of C++. That experience alone has exposed you to the object-oriented paradigm. Having built and used C++ classes in class hierarchies, you have written object-oriented programs. There are, however, many terms in the object-oriented lexicon that this book has intentionally postponed until this discussion. Simply writing a C++ program does not qualify a programmer as an expert on object-oriented technology. There are rules and procedures to follow, and there are benefits to be gained by understanding and following the disciplines.

The traditional procedure-oriented programmer does not intuitively understand object-oriented programming. The notations and approaches to design and code are different than what you learned and used in the past. Furthermore, explanations such as this one do not usually complete your understanding of object-oriented programming. You need reinforcement — both from experience and by a feeling that there is something to be gained from a new and different approach. Programmers might understand the concepts at the intellectual level and yet not accept them as a pragmatic approach to programming simply because they have been writing good programs all along and see no compelling reason to tamper with that success. For this reason, it is difficult to teach object-oriented programming, although it is not difficult to learn. Learning object-oriented programming is a process of discovery. Teaching it, therefore, becomes the management of that process.

Many of the current generation of programmers have learned and accepted object-oriented programming as a better way to express software algorithms. Most of them started from the procedural paradigm, having programmed in traditional procedural languages such as FORTRAN, COBOL, and C. Those who make the switch become object-oriented advocates. Enough of them have done so that the rest of us cannot deny that there is something to it. You can take a lesson from the observation that once a programmer takes the plunge, he or she almost always becomes a convert. Therefore, the best way to learn object-oriented programming is to try it.

The Basics

The first understanding of object-oriented programming is to be found in this design guideline:

> *The expression of an algorithm should model the application domain it supports.*

Or expressed at a higher level:

> *The solution to a problem should resemble the problem.*

A solution that follows these guidelines allows its observers to recognize its purpose without necessarily knowing in advance about the problem being solved. When you see a properly designed word processor, you intuitively understand that the problem being solved is one of capturing and manipulating textual data into an informational document. When you see a properly designed inventory management system, you recognize that its purpose is to maintain stock quantities, locations, and reorder points. You recognize those things because the designs resemble and therefore remind you of the problems that they solve.

Carrying this concept to a higher level of abstraction, you recognize that the purpose of a programming language is to express with algorithms the solution to a data processing problem. The techniques used in that expression determine how successfully the solution models its problem domain. Object-oriented programming is one of several different approaches to the expression of algorithms, and it is often misunderstood — primarily by those who do not use it.

Procedural Programming

In the classic approach to programming, a programmer designs functions and procedures to process the data. The requirements of the procedures dictate the data structure design needed to support the solution. This approach is called *procedural programming* because it starts with the procedures. We came to think of programming in this way because that is how programming was done for 40 years.

Procedural programming does not always deliver a solution that resembles the problem, however, because it emphasizes the functions rather than the data — the procedures rather than the objects. Furthermore, procedural programming does not encourage the programmer to separate and hide the procedures related to different data objects from one another. Programmers have long known that those are worthwhile practices, but most procedural programming languages do not encourage them.

Object-Oriented Programming

The world and its applications are not organized into values and procedures separate from one another. Problem solvers in other crafts do not perceive the world that way. They deal with their problem domains by concentrating on the objects and letting the characteristics of those objects determine the procedures to apply to them. To build a house, grow a tomato, or repair a carburetor, first you think about the object and its purpose and behavior. Then you select your tools and procedures. The solution fits the problem.

The world is, therefore, object-oriented, and object-oriented programming expresses computer programs in ways that model how people perceive the world. Since programmers are people, it is only natural that your approach to the work of the world reflects your view of the world itself. We have not, however, universally learned how to do that. The crafts of carpentry, farming, and mechanics are centuries old, beginning in cultures that lacked technology. The objects and objectives of those trades were understood long before the development of the technologies that support them. Computer programming is relatively new. We are still forming its disciplines, and the technologies are developing faster than we can adjust.

The Object-Oriented Program

An object-oriented program has four fundamental characteristics:

✦ *Abstraction* defines new data types.

✦ *Encapsulation* gathers a data type's representation and behavior into one encapsulated entity.

✦ *Inheritance* derives new data types from existing ones and forms them into hierarchies of classes.

✦ *Polymorphism* specializes the behavior of derived data types.

Object-oriented programming uses a vocabulary of such terms in ways unfamiliar to the procedural programmer. You hear these terms used frequently in discussions of object-oriented programming. Here is a more comprehensive list of object-oriented terms:

abstract base class

abstract data type

abstraction

base class

class

derived class

encapsulation

implementation and interface

inheritance

instance

instantiate

message

method

multiple inheritance

object

polymorphism

subclass

superclass

Now let's use some of those terms. The object-oriented programmer defines an *abstract data type* by *encapsulating* its *implementation* and *interface* into a *class*. *Inherited* abstract data types are *derived subclasses* of *base classes*. Within the program the programmer *instantiates objects* of classes as *instances* and sends *messages* to the objects by using the class's *methods*.

Confused? Don't be concerned; it all makes sense soon enough, and you have already done all of those things when you worked with the exercises in this book. The object-oriented programming community uses these terms universally. Therefore, when object-oriented programmers say "encapsulate," for example, you know that their meaning is consistent with the way others use it. When programmers acknowledge that a program is "object-oriented," you know that the program contains abstraction, encapsulation, inheritance, and polymorphism, and that it defines abstract data types, instantiates objects, and sends messages to the object's methods. The discussion that follows draws on your experience with C++ to explain these terms.

The Object

The first question that most procedural programmers ask is, "What are the objects in object-oriented programming?" The second question is, "What should be the objects in my design?" These questions reflect this more revealing one: What is it about object-oriented programming that sets it apart from and makes it better than traditional procedural programming? Early writings on the subject effectively explained object-oriented programming to those who already understood it, but their explanations were sometimes too abstruse for newcomers to fathom, and they did not always justify the paradigm as an improved way to express algorithms.

Simply stated, an *object* is an instance of a data type; in other words, what procedural programmers call a *variable*. The program in Figure 40-1 declares two objects. The first object is a simple integer; the second object is of an abstract data type.

```
void f()
{
    int ndays;   // an instance of an int
    Date cdt;    // an instance of an ADT
    // . . .
}
```

Figure 40-1: A program with two objects

Throughout this book you have been declaring objects — instances of the classes that you designed in the exercises. In your prior experience with other programming languages, you declared objects when you declared variables. So, what are the objects? They are the variables that you declare. What should be the objects in your object-oriented design? Anything that you build as a class is going to be the data type of an object. Objects are "smart data." They know how to do things to and for themselves. The programmer does not necessarily need to know how the objects do those things, only how to make it happen. In Figure 40-1, the statement cdt.addDays(ndays); does something, and you don't have to know, for example, how many days are in each month or about leap years for this to work.

Abstraction

Abstraction is the definition of an abstract data type, which includes the data type's representation and behavior. An abstract data type is a new type. It is not one of the *intrinsic* data types built into the programming language. The int, long, and float data types are intrinsic C++ data types. Their data representations and behavior are known to the compiler. For example, an integer data type's format — its representation — and response to arithmetic, assignment, and relational operators — its behavior — are defined as a part of the C++ language.

An abstract data type, however, is not known to the language; the C++ programmer defines the type's format and behavior in a class. For example, a calendar date class would be an abstract data type. The compiler and the computer do not know about calendar dates. Programmers have always had to define the behavior of dates by designing structures and functions or by using canned functions from published libraries. The Standard C library has several such date definitions, but they are defined with functions and structures, not with classes. When you define a C++ calendar date class like the one in Figure 40-2, you express its format and behavior in one design entity. It has month, day, and year data members. It might even support arithmetic and relational operations.

```
class Date  {
    int month, day, year;
public:
    Date (int mo, int da, int yr);
    int operator+(int n);
    // . . .
};
```

Figure 40-2: An abstract data type (ADT)

Having declared a Date class, you can declare an object that has the type of the Date class; you can add an integer value to the object, subtract from it, compare it with other objects, assign it to other date objects, and assign values to it, all depending on what methods have been provided and what operators have been overloaded. A C++ program declares instances of abstract data types the same way it declares instances of primitive data types. Refer again to Figure 40-1. The declaration of the cdt object is an instance of an abstract data type.

The term *instantiate* is used by object-oriented programmers for convenience. When an object-oriented program declares an instance of a data type, the program has instantiated an object, whether the data type is primitive or abstract. The program in Figure 40-1 instantiates the ndays and cdt objects.

Encapsulation

If abstraction defines a C++ class, encapsulation designs it. A programmer encapsulates the data representation and behavior of an abstract data type into a class, giving it its own implementation and interface. An encapsulated design hides its implementation from the class user and reveals its interface. Figure 40-3 is an example of an encapsulated class.

The *implementation* of a class, which consists of the private data members and private member functions, is essentially hidden from the using program. The month, day, and year data members in Figure 40-3 are the class's implementation. A user of the class does not care about the details of an implementation — only that it works. The class designer could totally change the implementation — perhaps changing the date representation to a long integer count of days — and the using programs, once recompiled and relinked with the new class implementation, would be unaffected.

```
class Date  {
// --- the class implementation
private:
    int month, day, year;
// --- the class interface
public:
    Date (int mo, int da, int yr);
    Date operator+(int n);
    // ...
};
```

Figure 40-3: Encapsulation

The *interface*, which is visible to the user of the class, consists of the public members, which are usually member functions. The class user reads and modifies values in the data representation by calling public member functions. The class interface in Figure 40-3 consists of the constructor, which contains initialization parameters, and an overloaded addition operator, which presumably allows the user of the class to compute and return a new Date object by adding an integral number of days to an existing Date object.

To use the abstract data type defined in Figure 40-3, a programmer makes assumptions about the interface based on its appearance and the programmer's understanding of C++ syntax. If the programmer is not the class's author, those assumptions could be invalid if the class interface design is not intuitive. In the case of Figure 40-3, most programmers would assume that the overloaded addition operator adds an integer to a Date object and returns another Date object with the result. Figure 40-4 illustrates how the class interface should work.

```
void f()
{
    Date dt (6,29,92);
    dt = dt + 30;   // should now be 7/29/92
}
```

Figure 40-4: An intuitive class interface

Designing an intuitive class interface is not automatic. The C++ language provides the tools for you to do a proper job, but nothing in the language enforces good design. The class author can use unnecessarily clever techniques that obscure the meaning of the interface. An object-oriented design is not a good design by default. Learning C++ does not turn a poor programmer into a good one.

Experienced C++ programmers generally agree on certain design standards for C++ classes. The data members are usually private and constitute most of the implementation. The interface consists mostly of member functions that hide the access to the data members. The interface is generic in that it is not bound to any particular implementation. The class author should be able to change the implementation without affecting the using programs. These apparent rules are only guidelines, however. Sometimes you need to step around them to achieve some purpose. The fewer times you do that, the stronger your design.

Methods and Messages

Method is another name for C++ public member functions. Methods may be constructors, destructors, regular member functions, conversion member functions, and overloaded operator functions. They define the class's interface. The constructor and overloaded plus operator in Figure 40-3 are methods.

A *message* is the invocation of a method, which, in C++, is the same thing as calling the member function. The program sends a message to an object, providing arguments for the method's parameters, if there are any.

Different kinds of methods are characterized by how they support the class definition. There are functional methods, data type methods, and implicit conversion methods. Note that this delineation and these terms are coined here for convenience and are not part of the official object-oriented lexicon. They define different levels of support that C++ provides for class design.

Functional Methods

Figure 40-5 shows three methods added to the Date class.

```
class Date  {
   // ...
public:
   // ...
   void Display();            // display the date
   void AdjustMonth (int m);  // +/- m months
   int DayOfWeek() const;     // return 0-6 = Sun-Sat
};
```

Figure 40-5: Functional methods

Figure 40-5 illustrates three typical kinds of methods. The first method tells the object to do something, in this case display itself. The class's implementation knows how to display the object's data representation. The programmer who uses the class is unconcerned about the details of the implementation.

The second method tells the object to change itself, in this case to adjust its month data value up or down by the integer argument in the method's parameter. Once again, the programmer who uses the class does not care how the object stores the month value or what algorithm adjusts the month, only that it works.

The third method is one that returns a value, in this case the day of the week represented by the object's current value.

The methods in Figure 40-5 define behavior related to the functional properties of the class. The class is a calendar date, and you want it to behave like a date.

Data Type Methods

Data type methods make a class act like a primitive data type by giving it the properties similar to those of a primitive data type. These properties are usually implemented as overloaded operators in the class interface. Figure 40-6 shows methods that compare dates, assign them to one another, and do some arithmetic on them.

```
class Date  {
   // ...
public:
   // ...
   // ---- arithmetic operators
   Date operator+(int n);
   Date operator-(int n);
   int operator-(Date &dt);
   // ---- assignment operators
   Date& operator=(Date &dt);
   // ---- relational operators
   int operator==(Date &dt);
   int operator!=(Date &dt);
   int operator<(Date &dt);
   int operator>(Date &dt);
};
```

Figure 40-6: Data type methods

Implicit Conversion Methods

The C++ language handles implicit conversion of intrinsic data types. If you write an expression with an *int* where the compiler expects a *long*, the compiler knows how to make the conversion and does so quietly. If, however, you write an expression where the compiler expects an abstract data type, and you provide a different data type, intrinsic or abstract, the compiler does not know how to deal with that. Similarly, if the expression expects an intrinsic data type, and you use an abstract data type, the compiler does not know what to do. In either case, unless you have provided implicit conversion methods, the compiler issues an error message and refuses to compile the program.

You can add implicit conversion methods to a class so that the compiler knows how to convert from one data type to another. The conversion constructor function constructs a data type to an abstract data type, and the member conversion function returns a data type converted from the type of the class in which the member conversion function is a member. When you code an expression where the compiler expects to see something other than what you provide as just described, the compiler executes one of your implicit conversion methods to convert the data type. This is an example of a method that you do not explicitly call (or send a message to) from within your program. It executes as the result of the implicit call inferred by the compiler by its interpretation of your expression. Your program implies a call to the method by the context in which it uses data types in an expression.

Figure 40-7 shows two implicit conversion methods added to the Date class. The first method converts an int data type to a Date object that is being constructed. Note that if the constructor function in Figure 40-7 were declared with the explicit qualifier, it would not function as an implicit conversion method. It could be used only as an explicit constructor to instantiate a Date object from an int argument.

The second method in Figure 40-7 converts a Date data type to an int object and returns that object to the sender of the message (invoker of the method, caller of the function, however you prefer to say it). The conversions are not restricted to converting between abstract data types and primitive data types. You can convert between different abstract data types in the same manner. For example, you might have a `Date` class and a `JulianDate` class, and the same principles apply.

```
class Date  {
   // ...
public:
   // ...
   Date (int n);   // conversion constructor
   operator int(); // member conversion function
};
```

Figure 40-7: Implicit conversion methods

Member Functions

Having just learned about methods and messages in this much detail, you soon find that the terms themselves are not used much in C++ circles. The terms come from the object-oriented lexicon and reflect the syntax of pure object-oriented programming languages such as SmallTalk and Eiffel. Most C++ programmers prefer to call member functions rather than send messages through methods, which are essentially the same thing. Nonetheless, you should understand the terminology, because you will encounter the object-oriented terms.

Inheritance

A class can inherit the characteristics of another class. The original class is called the *base class*, and the new class is called the *derived class*. You also hear these classes called the *superclass* and the *subclass*. The word *subclass* is sometimes used as a verb to mean the act of inheriting.

The derived class inherits the data representation and behavior of the base class except where the derived class modifies the behavior by overloading member functions. The derived class also may add behavior that is unique to its own purpose.

A program can instantiate objects of a base class as well as those of a derived class. If the base class is an *abstract base class* — one that exists only to be derived from — the program may not instantiate objects of the base class.

Inheritance is the foundation of most object-oriented designs, and it is often ill- or over-applied. Some programmers get carried away with the power of inheritance, and C++ can offer some surprises to the unwary designer. Many designs use inheritance to solve problems that would better be supported by a different approach, usually by embedding an object of the original class as a data member in the new class rather than deriving the new class from the original one. Despite this warning, inheritance is a powerful feature, which, when properly used, offers a rich design capability to the object-oriented programmer.

Single Inheritance

The C++ inheritance mechanism lets you build an orderly hierarchy of classes. When several of your abstract data types have characteristics in common, you can design their commonalities into a single base class and separate their unique characteristics into unique derived classes. That is the purpose of inheritance.

For example, a personnel system maintains information about employees. Employees are people, and people have common characteristics — name, address, date of birth, and so on — yet the system might record different kinds of employees. Managers, project workers, and support personnel might be recorded differently. Therefore, you could design a base class of employees that stores in each object of the base class the name, address, social security number, and date of birth of an employee. Then you could derive separate classes for managers, project workers, and support personnel. Each of the derived classes would inherit the characteristics of the employee class and would have additional characteristics common to themselves. For example, the manager class might include an annual incentive bonus data member that other employee classes do not have. The project worker class could have a list of project assignments. The support personnel class could record overtime hours worked.

Multiple Inheritance

A derived class can inherit the characteristics of more than one base class. This technique is called *multiple inheritance*. Not all object-oriented programming languages support multiple inheritance, and many experts assert that not only is it not a necessary design tool, but that it is also a dangerous one. Nonetheless, C++ supports multiple inheritance, and there are times when you might find it an effective way to express class relationships.

You recall that the effectiveness of a programming language can be measured in its ability to model the problem domains that it supports. The objects in the world reflect membership in multiple-inheritance hierarchies, and programmers are called upon to write programs to model those objects. A sofabed is a sofa and it is a bed, both of which are items of furniture. An amphibious airplane is a boat and an airplane, both of which are vehicles. A company car is an asset and a vehicle, but a leased car is a vehicle but not an asset, and cash is an asset, and on and on.

Class Relationships

Object-oriented designers strive to use inheritance to model relationships where the derived class *is a kind of* base class. A car *is a kind of* vehicle. An engineer *is a kind of* employee, which *is a kind of* person. This relationship is called, colloquially, the *ISA* relationship.

Inheritance is not appropriate for relationships where one class has an instance of another. An employee *has* a date of birth. A department *has* a manager. This relationship is called the *HASA* relationship. Instead of using inheritance, the class that has an object of another class embeds the object as a data member. The HASA relationship is appropriate when the embedded object is singular and belongs to the class that embeds it. An employee's date of birth belongs to that employee. Even when another employee has the same birthday, they each have a private copy of the data element.

A third relationship exists when a class uses the methods of another class. This relationship is called the *USESA* relationship and is usually implemented with an embedded pointer or reference in the using class to the used class. You would use this relationship when objects of the using class share the services of an object of the used class. The objects of the two classes exist in separate spaces, but those of one class depend on the presence of those of the other.

Polymorphism

Polymorphism exists when a derived class specializes the behavior of its base class to meet the requirements of the derived class. Polymorphism is the ability to treat multiple object instances with a common base class as though they were actually objects of the base class type. A C++ base class uses the *virtual* member function to specify that overriding member functions in derived classes have polymorphic behavior with respect to that method.

If a derived class overrides a base class method, and the base class method is not a virtual function, then the overriding behavior is effective only when the compiler is dereferencing a pointer, reference, or object of the derived class itself. If the object's pointer or reference refers to the base class, then the base class method has precedence. Such behavior is not polymorphic. However, if the base class method is virtual, then the compiler selects the overriding derived class method regardless of the type being dereferenced by the compiler.

Suppose, for example, that the support staff class in this discussion was further decomposed into derived classes that represented the various kinds of support personnel. You could have typists, corporate pilots, chauffeurs, maintenance personnel, instructors, and so on. The system measures skill levels differently for each of these disciplines, yet there is a requirement for a general-purpose skill index for the base support class. Each derived class exhibits different behavior for data entry and retrieval of the skill index, but some parts of the system invoke the skill method without knowing which kind of support personnel object is involved. The polymorphic skill method would modify the class's behavior at runtime based on the type of the derived class.

Summary

The object-oriented programming model is a rich medium for the expression of data formats and functions of an application. It is not necessary, however, for C++ programmers to immerse themselves totally in the object-oriented passion. The availability of improved design and programming methods does not automatically outdate all of the traditional approaches. C++ has the facility to support the basics of object-oriented programming while permitting the programmer to use traditional procedural programming where it seems appropriate. C++, in fact, encourages that approach. By supporting traditional C flow control of nested functions, C++ allows you to leverage your existing investment in mature and useful C function libraries. Furthermore, C++ does not force a pure object-oriented hierarchical data structure where every data type descends from one generic root base object. Instead, C++ allows you to build a number of class hierarchies representing the different problem domains that your application might deal with. There can be classes that define the data structures of the application's functional purpose; there can be classes that supply general-purpose container data structures such as strings, lists, queues, and so on; there can be framework classes that integrate your application with a particular user interface; there can be classes that encapsulate the processes of your particular problem domain. All these classes can coexist independently of one another in a system of hierarchies integrated by you into an object-oriented application.

✦   ✦   ✦

Library Listings

This appendix contains source code listings of program modules that are used in more than one example and more than one chapter of the book. Rather than repeat the listings or have you thumb through previous chapters looking for them, I organized them into this appendix for your convenience.

The source code modules are compiled and organized into object libraries for the example programs that use them. The header files are located in a common Include subdirectory typical of how many C++ projects are organized. This appendix groups the source code files according to the libraries that they support.

The DataTypes Class Library

Listing A-1: **Date.h**

```
#ifndef DATE_H
#define DATE_H

#include <iostream>

class Date  {
protected:
    static const int dys[];
    long int ndays; // days inclusive since
                    // Jan 1,1 (1/1/1 == 1)
public:
    // --- default and initializing constructor
    Date(int mo = 0, int da = 0, int yr = 0)
        { SetDate(mo, da, yr); }
    // --- copy constructor
    Date(const Date& dt)
        { *this = dt; }
    // --- destructor
    virtual ~Date() {}
    // --- overloaded assignment operator
    Date& operator=(const Date& dt)
        { ndays = dt.ndays; return *this; }
    // --- overloaded arithmetic operators
    Date  operator+(int n) const
        { Date dt(*this); dt += n; return dt; }
```

Continued

Listing A-1 *(continued)*

```
Date  operator-(int n) const
    { Date dt(*this); dt -= n; return dt; }
Date& operator+=(int n)
    { ndays += n; return *this; }
Date& operator-=(int n)
    { ndays -= n; return *this; }
Date& operator++()           // prefix
    { ++ndays; return *this; }
Date  operator++(int)  // postfix
    { Date dt(*this); dt.ndays++; return dt; }
Date& operator--()           // prefix
    { --ndays; return *this; }
Date  operator--(int)  // postfix
    { Date dt(*this); dt.ndays--; return dt; }
long int operator-(const Date& dt) const
    { return ndays-dt.ndays; }
// --- overloaded relational operators
bool operator==(const Date& dt) const
    { return ndays == dt.ndays; }
bool operator!=(const Date& dt) const
    { return ndays != dt.ndays; }
bool operator< (const Date& dt) const
    { return ndays <  dt.ndays; }
bool operator> (const Date& dt) const
    { return ndays >  dt.ndays; }
bool operator<=(const Date& dt) const
    { return ndays <= dt.ndays; }
bool operator>=(const Date& dt) const
    { return ndays >= dt.ndays; }
// --- getter and setter functions
void SetDate(int mo, int da, int yr);
void SetMonth(int mo)
    { *this = Date(mo, GetDay(), GetYear()); }
void SetDay(int da)
    { *this = Date(GetMonth(), da, GetYear()); }
void SetYear(int yr)
    { *this = Date(GetMonth(), GetDay(), yr); }
void GetDate(int& mo, int& da, int& yr) const;
int  GetMonth() const;
int  GetDay()   const;
int  GetYear()  const;
// --- test for leap year
bool IsLeapYear(int yr) const
    { return ((yr % 4)==0 && (yr % 1000)!=0); }
bool IsLeapYear() const
    { return IsLeapYear(GetYear()); }
  void Display(std::ostream& os);
};

std::ostream& operator<<(std::ostream& os, const Date& dt);
```

```
std::istream& operator>>(std::istream& is, Date& dt);

inline void Date::Display(std::ostream& os)
{
    os << "Date: "<< *this;
}

// ----- overloaded (int + Date)
inline Date operator+(int n, const Date& dt)
{
    return dt + n;
}

#endif
```

```
#include <iostream>

#include <Date.h>

const int Date::dys[]={31,28,31,30,31,30,31,31,30,31,30,31};

void Date::SetDate(int mo, int da, int yr)
{
    if (mo < 1 || mo > 12 || yr < 1) {
        ndays = 0;  // invalid month or year or null date
        return;
    }
    // compute days thru last year
    ndays = (yr-1) * 365 + (yr-1) / 4 - (yr-1) / 1000;
    for (int i = 0; i < mo; i++) {
        int dy = dys[i];
        if (i == 1 && IsLeapYear(yr))
            dy++;             // make Feb's days 29 if leap year
        if (i < mo-1)         // add in all but this month's days
            ndays += dy;
        else if (da > dy) {
            ndays = 0;        // invalid day
            return;
        }
    }
    ndays += da;  // add in this month's days
}

void Date::GetDate(int& mo, int& da, int& yr) const
{
    da = ndays;
    if (ndays == 0) {
        yr = mo = 0;
```

Continued

Listing A-2 *(continued)*

```cpp
            return;
        }
    for (yr = 1;; yr++)  {
        int daysthisyear = IsLeapYear(yr) ? 366 : 365;
        if (da <= daysthisyear)
            break;
        da -= daysthisyear;
    }
    for (mo = 1; mo < 13; mo++)        {
        int dy = dys[mo-1];
        if (mo == 2 && IsLeapYear(yr))
            dy++;    // make Feb's days 29 if leap year
        if (da <= dy)
            break;
        da -= dy;
    }
}
int Date::GetMonth() const
{
    int mo, da, yr;
    GetDate(mo, da, yr);
    return mo;
}
int Date::GetDay()   const
{
    int mo, da, yr;
    GetDate(mo, da, yr);
    return da;
}
int Date::GetYear()   const
{
    int mo, da, yr;
    GetDate(mo, da, yr);
    return yr;
}

std::ostream& operator<<(std::ostream& os, const Date& dt)
{
    os << dt.GetMonth() << '/'
        << dt.GetDay()   << '/'
        << dt.GetYear();
    return os;
}
std::istream& operator>>(std::istream& is, Date& dt)
{
    int mo, da, yr;
    is >> mo >> da >> yr;
    dt.SetDate(mo, da, yr);
    return is;
}
```

Listing A-3: **Money.h**

```
#ifndef MONEY_H
#define MONEY_H

#include <iostream>

class Money {
    double value;
public:
    Money(double val = 0);
    operator double() const
        { return value; }
     int operator<(const Money& m) const
            { return value < m.value; }
     int operator==(const Money& m) const
            { return value == m.value; }
     int operator!=(const Money& m) const
            { return value != m.value; }
     int operator>(const Money& m) const
            { return value > m.value; }
     int operator<=(const Money& m) const
            { return value <= m.value; }
     int operator>=(const Money& m) const
            { return value >= m.value; }
    friend std::ostream& operator<<(std::ostream&, const Money&);
};

#endif
```

Listing A-4: **Money.cpp**

```
#include <iomanip>
#include <Money.h>

Money::Money(double val)
{
    // ensure that the value is only 2 decimal places
    // and rounded up to the nearest penny
    long int nval = (long)((val + .005) * 100);
    float cents = nval % 100;
    cents /= 100;
    value = (nval / 100) + cents;
}

std::ostream& operator<<(std::ostream& os, const Money& cur)
{
    os << '$'
```

Continued

Listing A-4 *(continued)*

```
        << std::setw(10)
        << std::setprecision(2)
        << std::setiosflags(std::ios::fixed)
        << cur.value;
}
```

Listing A-5: **SSN.h**

```
#ifndef SSN_H
#define SSN_H

#include <iostream>

class SSN  {
    long unsigned int ssn;
public:
    explicit SSN(long unsigned int sn = 0);
    friend std::ostream& operator<<(std::ostream& os, const SSN& ssn);
};

#endif
```

Listing A-6: **SSN.cpp**

```
#include <ssn.h>

SSN::SSN(long unsigned int sn) : ssn(sn)
{
    if (ssn > 999999999L)
        ssn = 0;
}

std::ostream& operator<<(std::ostream& os, const SSN& sn)
{
    int lssn = sn.ssn / 1000000L;
    int mssn = (sn.ssn - (lssn * 1000000L)) / 10000;
    int rssn = sn.ssn - (lssn * 1000000L) - (mssn * 10000);
    os << lssn << '-' << mssn << '-' << rssn;
    return os;
}
```

The Personnel Class Library

```cpp
#ifndef PERSON_H
#define PERSON_H

#include <iostream>
#include <string>
#include <Date.h>
#include <Ssn.h>

class Person {
public:
    enum Sex {unknown, male, female};
    enum MaritalStatus {single, married, divorced, widowed};
protected:
    std::string name;
    std::string address;
    std::string phone;
    SSN ssn;
    Date dob;
    Sex sex;
    MaritalStatus mstatus;
public:
    Person(const std::string& nm = "")
            : name(nm), sex(unknown), mstatus(single)
        { }
    virtual ~Person() { }
    // --- setter functions
    void SetName(const std::string& nm)
        { name = nm; }
    void SetAddress(const std::string& addr)
        { address = addr; }
    void SetPhone(const std::string& phon)
        { phone = phon; }
    void SetSSN(SSN sn)
        { ssn = sn; }
    void SetDob(const Date& dtb)
        { dob = dtb; }
    void SetSex(Sex sx)
        { sex = sx; }
    void SetMaritalStatus(MaritalStatus st)
        { mstatus = st; }
    // --- getter functions
    const std::string& GetName() const
        { return name; }
```

Continued

Listing A-7 *(continued)*

```cpp
    const std::string& GetAddress() const
        { return address; }
    const std::string& GetPhone() const
        { return phone; }
    SSN GetSSN() const
        { return ssn; }
    const Date& GetDob() const
        { return dob; }
    Sex GetSex() const
        { return sex; }
    MaritalStatus GetMaritalStatus() const
        { return mstatus; }
    virtual void FormattedDisplay(std::ostream& os) = 0;
};

std::ostream& operator<<(std::ostream& os, const Person& person);

#endif
```

Listing A-8: **Person.cpp**

```cpp
#include <Person.h>

void Person::FormattedDisplay(std::ostream& os)
{
    os << "Name:           " << name    << '\n';
    os << "Address:        " << address << '\n';
    os << "Phone:          " << phone   << '\n';
    os << "SSN:            " << ssn     << '\n';
    os << "Date of birth:  " << dob     << '\n';
    os << "Sex:            ";
    switch (sex)  {
        case Person::male:
            os << "male" << '\n';
            break;
        case Person::female:
            os << "female" << '\n';
            break;
        default:
            os << "unknown" << '\n';
            break;
    }
    os << "Marital status: ";
    switch (GetMaritalStatus())  {
        case Person::single:
            os << "single" << '\n';
            break;
        case Person::married:
```

```cpp
                os << "married" << '\n';
                break;
            case Person::divorced:
                os << "divorced" << '\n';
                break;
            case Person::widowed:
                os << "widowed" << '\n';
                break;
            default:
                os << "unknown" << '\n';
                break;
        }
    }
}

std::ostream& operator<<(std::ostream& os, const Person& person)
{
    os << person.GetName() << '\n'
       << person.GetAddress() << '\n'
       << person.GetPhone() << '\n'
       << person.GetSSN() << '\n'
       << person.GetDob() << '\n'
       << person.GetSex() << '\n'
       << person.GetMaritalStatus() << '\n';
    return os;
}
```

Listing A-9: **Employee.h**

```cpp
#ifndef EMPLOYEE_H
#define EMPLOYEE_H

#include <person.h>

class Employee : public Person  {
protected:
    Date datehired;
public:
    Employee(const std::string& nm = "") : Person(nm)
        { }
    virtual ~Employee() { }
    Date GetDateHired() const
        { return datehired; }
    void SetDateHired(Date date)
        { datehired = date; }
    virtual void FormattedDisplay(std::ostream& os) = 0;
};

std::ostream& operator<<(std::ostream& os, Employee& empl);

#endif
```

Listing A-10: **Employee.cpp**

```cpp
#include <iostream>
#include <Employee.h>

void Employee::FormattedDisplay(std::ostream& os)
{
    Person::FormattedDisplay(os);
    os << "Date hired:     " << datehired << '\n';
}

std::ostream& operator<<(std::ostream& os, Employee& empl)
{
    os << ((Person&)empl) << '\n';
    os << empl.GetDateHired() << '\n';
    return os;
}
```

Listing A-11: **WagedEmployee.h**

```cpp
#ifndef WAGEDEMPLOYEE_H
#define WAGEDEMPLOYEE_H

#include <Employee.h>
#include <Money.h>

class WagedEmployee : public Employee  {
    Money hourlywage;
public:
    WagedEmployee(const std::string& nm = "") : Employee(nm)
        { }
    virtual ~WagedEmployee() { }
    Money GetHourlyWage() const
        { return hourlywage; }
    void SetHourlyWage(Money wage)
        { hourlywage = wage; }
    virtual void FormattedDisplay(std::ostream& os);
};

std::ostream& operator<<(std::ostream& os, WagedEmployee& cntr);

#endif
```

Listing A-12: **WagedEmployee.cpp**

```cpp
#include <WagedEmployee.h>

void WagedEmployee::FormattedDisplay(std::ostream& os)
{
    os << "----Waged Employee----\n";
    Employee::FormattedDisplay(os);
    os << "Hourly wage:    " << hourlywage << '\n';
}

std::ostream& operator<<(std::ostream& os, WagedEmployee& cntr)
{
    os << (static_cast<Employee&>(cntr)) << '\n'
        << cntr.GetHourlyWage() << '\n';
    return os;
}
```

Listing A-13: **SalariedEmployee.h**

```cpp
#ifndef SALARIEDEMPLOYEE_H
#define SALARIEDEMPLOYEE_H

#include <Employee.h>
#include <Money.h>

class SalariedEmployee : public Employee  {
    Money salary;
public:
    SalariedEmployee(const std::string& nm = "") : Employee(nm)
        { }
    virtual ~SalariedEmployee() { }
    Money GetSalary() const
        { return salary; }
    void SetSalary(Money sal)
        { salary = sal; }
    virtual void FormattedDisplay(std::ostream& os);
};

std::ostream& operator<<(std::ostream& os, SalariedEmployee& empl);

#endif
```

Listing A-14: **SalariedEmployee.cpp**

```cpp
#include <SalariedEmployee.h>

void SalariedEmployee::FormattedDisplay(std::ostream& os)
{
    os << "----Salaried Employee----\n";
    Employee::FormattedDisplay(os);
    os << "Salary:          " << salary << '\n';
}

std::ostream& operator<<(std::ostream& os, SalariedEmployee& empl)
{
    os << ((Employee&)empl) << '\n' << empl.GetSalary() << '\n';
    return os;
}
```

Listing A-15: **Contractor.h**

```cpp
#ifndef CONTRACTOR_H
#define CONTRACTOR_H

#include <Person.h>
#include <Money.h>
#include <Date.h>

class Contractor : public Person  {
    Date startdate;
    Date enddate;
    Money hourlyrate;
public:
    Contractor(const std::string& nm = "") : Person(nm)
        { }
    virtual ~Contractor() { }
    const Date& GetStartDate() const
        { return startdate; }
    const Date& GetEndDate() const
        { return enddate; }
    Money GetHourlyRate() const
        { return hourlyrate; }
    void SetStartDate(Date date)
        { startdate = date; }
    void SetEndDate(Date date)
        { enddate = date; }
    void SetHourlyRate(Money rate)
        { hourlyrate = rate; }
    virtual void Print1099(std::ostream& os, int AnnualHours);
```

```
    virtual void FormattedDisplay(std::ostream& os);
};

std::ostream& operator<<(std::ostream& os, Contractor& cntr);

#endif
```

Listing A-16: **Contractor.cpp**

```
#include <Contractor.h>
#include <Date.h>

void Contractor::Print1099(std::ostream& os, int AnnualHours)
{
    Money compensation(hourlyrate * AnnualHours);
    os << "--- IRS Form 1099 ---\n"
       << name << "   "  << ssn   << '\n'
       << compensation            << '\n';
}

void Contractor::FormattedDisplay(std::ostream& os)
{
    os << "----Contractor----\n";
    Person::FormattedDisplay(os);
    os << "Start date:   " << startdate  << '\n';
    os << "End date:     " << enddate    << '\n';
    os << "Hourly rate:  " << hourlyrate << '\n';
}

std::ostream& operator<<(std::ostream& os, const Contractor& cntr)
{
    os << ((Person&)cntr)       << '\n'
       << cntr.GetStartDate()  << '\n'
       << cntr.GetEndDate()    << '\n'
       << cntr.GetHourlyRate() << '\n';
    return os;
}
```

✦   ✦   ✦

What's on the CD-ROM?

The CD-ROM that accompanies this book contains all of the source code for the example programs, along with a complete C and C++ compiler system hosted by a Windows Integrated Development Environment (IDE) named Quincy 2002. Following is a description of each item on the CD-ROM listed by the subdirectories in which they are recorded.

In the CD-ROM's root directory, you'll find:

+ The Autorun.inf file automatically runs the Setup program whenever you load the CD-ROM.

+ The Setup.exe program installs Quincy, the compilers, and the example programs from the CD-ROM to your hard drive.

+ Quincy2002 contains everything you need to code, compile, debug, and execute C and C++ programs.

+ The Quincy2002.htm icon in \Quincy2002 opens the Quincy 2002 User's Guide in your browser.

+ Quincy2002\bin contains the executable binaries for Quincy 2002, the grep utility program, the astyle code beautifier tool, and Quincy's Uninstall program.

+ Quincy2002\lcc\bin contains executable binaries for a Windows resource editor program that is not covered in the book, but which Quincy integrates as a tool for developing Windows programs.

+ Quincy2002\mingw and subdirectories below it contain the executable binaries, libraries, and header files for the MinGW port of the gcc 3.2 compiler.

+ Quincy2002\programs contains the example programs. This sub-directory is organized by chapter; the subdirectories CHAP01 through CHAP39 contain the programs for the chapters.

+ The Source subdirectory is organized into subdirectories that contain the source code for Quincy 2002, a grep utility program integrated with the IDE, the CD-ROM's Setup program, Quincy's Uninstall program, and the astyle code beautifier tool. Source code for the C/C++ compilers and libraries is available online. The MinGW subdirectory contains a text file that tells where it can be downloaded.

✦ The HTML subdirectory contains HTML and GIF files, which combine to form the Quincy 2002 User's Guide. Double-click the Quincy2002.htm icon on the CD-ROM's Quincy2002 directory to read the document in your browser.

CD-ROM Installation Instructions

To use Quincy 2002 and the accompanying compiler, you must install them on your Windows computer.

Minimum Requirements

Quincy 2002 runs under Windows 95/98/ME/XP/NT/2000 and is compiled to run with a 486 processor, which means it works on anything from there up. You can install Quincy 2002 to run completely from the CD-ROM, in which case the hard disk requirements are negligible. A maximum installation requires about 52MB of hard disk. You should have at least 128K RAM. Quincy 2002 will run with less, but compiler performance is less than optimal.

Appendix C is a quick start user's guide for Quincy.

Installation

If your CD-ROM has AutoPlay enabled, the Setup program runs when you insert the CD-ROM into the drive. If not, you can run the Setup.exe program from the root directory of the CD-ROM. When run, the Setup program displays a dialog box where you can select the items you want to install. You do not have to install everything in order to use the compiler or the IDE. As you select and deselect items, the dialog box displays how much hard disk space is required. See Quincy2002.htm on the CD-ROM for details.

Type the drive and subdirectory where you want to install the files if c:\Quincy2002 is not what you want.

I did not test the example programs with commercial compilers. The gcc compiler suite is recognized as being reasonably compliant with the ISO standard definition of C++, which is why I chose to use it to develop the examples and included it on the CD-ROM. The programs should work properly with any compliant compiler, however.

In all cases, if you choose not to install something, you should reload the CD-ROM in the same drive from which you installed it whenever you restart Quincy 2002 so that Quincy can find the files that you left on the CD-ROM.

Upgrades, FAQs, and Support

You can find the latest version of Quincy at the following Web site:

http://www.alstevens.com/quincy.html

As I find and fix bugs and add features, and as the developers of the gcc compilers release newer versions, I will upgrade Quincy. The Web site is where you can learn about and download new releases of Quincy.

The site also includes a list of frequently asked questions (FAQs) and their answers.

You can send questions and comments about Quincy 2002 or anything else in the book to al@alstevens.com.

✦   ✦   ✦

Quincy 2002 User's Guide

This appendix provides a quick start guide for installing and using Quincy, the Windows-hosted integrated development environment with which you can compile and run the example programs in this book. You can also modify and test example programs and write and test completely new programs.

Quincy hosts the MinGW port of the GCC C and C++ compiler system and includes other tools to enhance your software development work. Quincy, the compiler and tools, and the complete source code for the examples in this book are included on the CD-ROM that accompanies this book.

For complete instructions in the use of Quincy, view the help documentation on the CD-ROM. The help documentation is installed when you install Quincy and is available from Quincy's Help menu. You can also read Quincy's help documentation without installing Quincy by double-clicking the quincy2002.htm icon in the CD-ROM's quincy2002 folder.

Installing Quincy

To install Quincy, follow these steps:

1. Put the CD-ROM in your CD-ROM drive.

   If you have Autorun enabled on your Windows PC, the Setup program launches automatically.

   If Autorun is not enabled:

2. Choose the Run command on the Windows Start menu.

3. Enter E:\setup in the Open text field. (Substitute your CD-ROM drive letter for E.)

4. Click OK.

Figure C-1 shows Quincy's Setup dialog.

Figure C-1: Quincy Setup dialog

5. Choose which of Quincy's optional components you wish to install by checking and unchecking the appropriate options. For explanations of the implications of each option, click the Help button and read the detailed installation procedures.

   By default, Quincy installs into the C:\Quincy2002 subdirectory. To choose a different location to install Quincy, enter the full path into the "Install into:" text field.

6. Click Install to install Quincy and the optional components.

7. Setup copies files from the CD-ROM to your hard disk and asks if you wish to add to a Quincy 2002 shortcut to your desktop. Click Yes or No to complete the installation procedure.

Running Quincy

When you first run Quincy, it opens with the IDE application window and the Example Programs dialog as Figure C-2 shows.

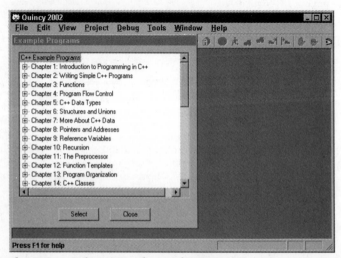

Figure C-2: Quincy IDE and example programs

1. Move the Example Programs IDE elsewhere to get a better look at the IDE.

2. Resize Quincy to a smaller size by clicking and dragging one of the window corners. The IDE does not need much screen space for the simpler programs.

Loading an Example Program

With Quincy open and running, you'll load one of the example programs from this book to see how to use Quincy to navigate through the lessons in the book and compile and run the example programs.

1. Click the + icon next to Chapter 1's entry to open the list of example programs in Chapter 1.

2. Double-click the entry for Program 1-1. This action loads the source code for the program into Quincy. The program doesn't do anything, so we won't bother with it. Program 1-2 does more, but we'll skip it, too.

3. Double-click the entry for Program 1-3 to load its source code into Quincy as shown in Figure C-3. That program does more than the ones before it, so we'll use it to learn how to use Quincy.

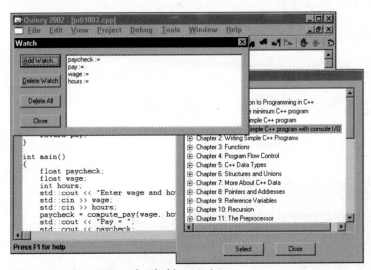

Figure C-3: Program 1-3 loaded into Quincy

You'll see that Program 1-3 opens with a Watch dialog. The Watch dialog displays the values of selected variables as you debug the program. The integrated tutorial includes programmed watch variables for many of the example programs. Quincy's help documentation explains how you can set your own Watch variables when you write your own programs.

4. Move the Watch dialog out of the way so you can read the source code.

Compiling the Program

Before you can run an example program, you have to compile and link it into an executable file. The CD-ROM does not include executable binaries for the example programs.

1. Load an example program as explained above.

2. Click the Build button on the toolbar. It's the little button with a hammer icon.

3. Follow the compiler's progress in the Build dialog, as shown in Figure C-4.

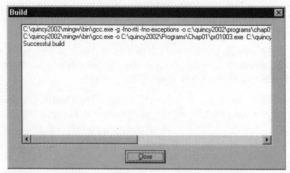

Figure C-4: The Build dialog

4. Click Close on the Build dialog to close its window.

Stepping Through the Program

You can run the program on its own or step through it one source code line at a time. You'll step through the program now.

1. Click the Step button on the toolbar. It's the leftmost little button with the shoe icon pointing to the left. When the program starts running, it opens a DOS console window as shown in Figure C-5.

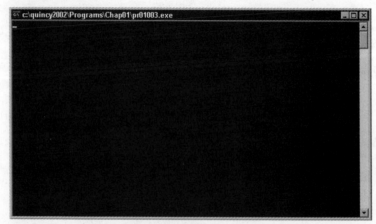

Figure C-5: Program's console window

2. Click on Quincy's IDE to see that the step cursor is pointed to the first executable line of source code in the main function as Figure C-6 shows.

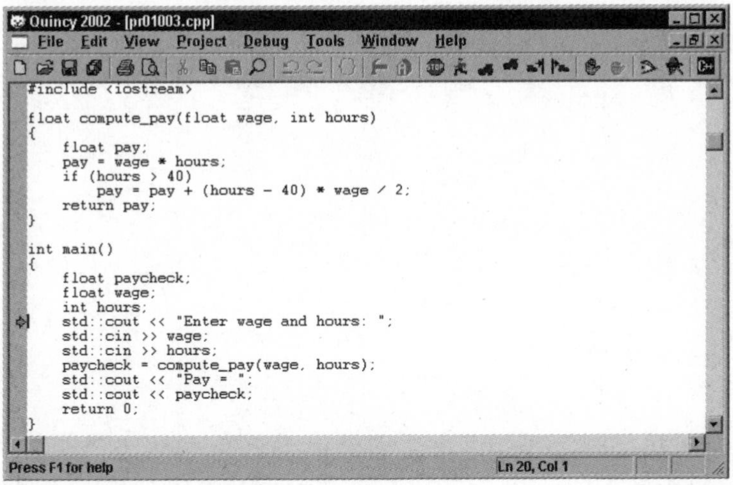

Figure C-6: Stepping through a program

3. Click on the Step button again. The message that the program writes to std::cout is written on the console window.

4. Click on the Step button again. Now the program is waiting for input from you at the console window.

5. Click somewhere in the DOS console window and type two numbers separated by a space character and follow it with the Enter key.

6. Return to Quincy's IDE and click the Step button again to get past the second input statement. Observe in the Watch dialog that the wage and hours variables now have the values you typed in Step 5.

7. Click Step once more to process the next statement, which steps into the compute_pay function.

8. Continue to click the Step button to observe the watched variables change and the standard output data written to the console window.

9. When you have clicked on the last statement in the main function, the program stops running, and the console window closes.

Exiting from Quincy

To exit from Quincy, choose Exit from the File menu. All Quincy's windows close. If there are unsaved source code files in the IDE, Quincy first prompts to see if you want to save them. The next time you run Quincy, the most recent program files and dialog windows open in the locations on the screen where you left them, thus preserving the continuity of your learning sessions.

Updating Quincy

You can upgrade Quincy to the latest version by downloading it from `http://www.alstevens.com/quincy2002/`. Follow the instructions in the INSTALL file found at the ftp site. You don't need to reinstall the compiler or tools unless there are newer versions that you want to get.

✦   ✦   ✦

C++ Reference Tables

This appendix contains reference Tables D-1 to D-12.

Table D-1: Standard C++ Keywords

asm	do	inline	short	typeid
auto	double	int	signed	typename
bool	dynamic_cast	long	sizeof	union
break	else	mutable	static	unsigned
case	enum	namespace	static_cast	using
catch	explicit	new	struct	virtual
char	extern	operator	switch	void
class	false	private	template	volatile
const	float	protected	this	wchar_t
const_cast	for	public	throw	while
continue	friend	register	true	
default	goto	reinterpret_cast	try	
delete	if	return	typedef	

Table D-2: International C++ Keywords

and	bitor	or	xor_e
and_eq	compl	or_eq	not_eq
bitand	not	xor	

Table D-3: Constant Escape Sequences

Escape Sequence	Description
\'	Single quote
\"	Double quote
\\	Backslash
\0	Null (zero) character
\0nnn	Octal number (nnn)
\a	Audible bell character
\b	Backspace
\f	Formfeed
\n	Newline

Escape Sequence	Description
\r	Carriage return
\t	Horizontal tab
\v	Vertical tab
\xnnn	Hexadecimal number (nnn)

Table D-4: Arithmetic Operators

Symbol	Description
+	Unary plus
-	Unary minus
*	Multiplication
/	Division
%	Modulus
+	Addition
-	Subtraction

Table D-5: Logical Operators

Symbol	Description
&&	Logical AND
||	Logical OR
!	Unary NOT

Table D-6: Bitwise Logical Operators

Symbol	Description
&	Bitwise AND
||	Bitwise OR
!	Bitwise exclusive OR (XOR)
~	1's complement

Table D-7: Bitwise Shift Operators

Symbol	Description
<<	Left shift
>>	Right shift

Table D-8: Relational Operators

Symbol	Description
>	Greater than
<	Less than
>=	Greater than or equal to
<=	Less than or equal to
==	Equal to
!=	Not equal to

Table D-9: Increment and Decrement Operators

Symbol	Description
++	Increment operator
--	Decrement operator

Table D-10: Assignment Operators

Symbol	Description
=	Assignment
+=	Addition assignment
-=	Subtraction assignment
*=	Multiplication assignment
/=	Division assignment
%=	Modulus assignment
<<=	Shift left assignment

Symbol	Description
>>=	Shift right assignment
&=	Bitwise AND assignment
|=	Bitwise OR assignment
^	Bitwise exclusive OR (XOR) assignment

Table D-11: Operator Precedence and Order of Evaluation

Precedence	Operators	Associativity
(Highest)	() []-> .	Left-right
	! ~ ++-- +- * & (type) sizeof	Right-left
	* / %	Left-right
	+ -	Left-right
	<< >>	Left-right
	< <= > >=	Left-right
	== !=	Left-right
	&	Left-right
	^	Left-right
	|	Left-right
	&&	Left-right
	||	Left-right
	?:	Right-left
	= += -= *= /= %= &= ^= |= <<= >>=	Right-left
(Lowest)	,	Left-right

Table D-12: Preprocessing Directives

Directive	Description
#	Null directive; no action
#include	Includes a source code file at the directive's position
#define	Defines a macro
#undef	Removes the definition of a macro

Continued

Table D-12 *(continued)*

Directive	Description
#if	Compiles code if the given condition is TRUE
#ifdef	Compiles code if macro is defined
#ifndef	Compiles code if macro is not defined
#elif	Compiles code if previous #if... condition is not TRUE and current condition is TRUE
#endif	Terminates #if...#else conditional block
#error	Stops compiling and displays an error message

Bibliography

Dattatri, Kayshav, *C++ Effective Object-Oriented Software Construction*. Prentice Hall PTR, 1997.

Koenig, Andrew and Moo, Barbara E., *Ruminations on C++*. Addison-Wesley, 1997.

Koenig, Andrew and Moo, Barbara E., *Accelerated C++*. Addison-Wesley, 2000.

Langer, Angelika and Kreft, Klaus, *Standard C++ IOStreams and Locales*. Addison Wesley Longman, 2000.

Lippman, Stanley B., *C++ Gems*. SIGS Books & Multimedia, 1996.

Meyers, Scott, *Effective C++*. Addison-Wesley, 1992.

Meyers, Scott, *More Effective C++*. Addison-Wesley, 1996.

Meyers, Scott, *Effective STL*. Addison-Wesley, 2001.

Musser, David R., Derge, Gillmer J., and Saini, Atul, *STL Tutorial and Reference Guide,* Second Edition. Addison-Wesley, 2001.

Pohl, Ira, *C++ for C Programmers*. Addison-Wesley, 1999.

Stroustrup, Bjarne, *The Design and Evolution of C++*. Addison-Wesley, 1994.

Stroustrup, Bjarne, *The C++ Programming Language*, Third Edition. Addison-Wesley, 1997.

✦ ✦ ✦

Glossary

This glossary defines C++ and object-oriented programming terms.

abstract base class A class definition that is always a base class from which to derive other classes. The program declares no specific objects of the base class. A C++ abstract base class has a pure virtual function, a protected constructor, or a protected destructor.

abstract data type Also called ADT. A user-defined data type built as a C++ class. The details of implementation are not necessarily a part of the ADT. See also *intrinsic data type* and *concrete data type*.

abstraction Defining an abstract data type by designing a class. Also called *data abstraction*.

address An expression that returns the memory address of a variable or function.

algorithm The formula or procedure by which a set of program instructions performs a defined task.

anonymous object An internal, temporary object created by the compiler.

application A program or group of programs that combine to support a defined, user-related function such as payroll, inventory, accounting, and so on.

applications program As opposed to *systems program*. A program developed for a specific purpose within an application.

argument The value passed to a function. Its type must match that of the function's corresponding parameter, as declared in the function's prototype. See also *parameter*.

array A group of variables of the same type organized into a table of one or more dimensions.

ASCII American Standard Code for Information Interchange. The 8-bit system for encoding digits, the alphabet, special characters, graphics characters, and certain control values.

assignment A statement that places the value of an expression into a memory variable.

associativity The order in which operands in an expression are evaluated: left-to-right or right-to-left. The operator determines associativity.

automatic variable A local variable that does not retain its value when it goes out of scope. Each recursive execution of functions has its own copy of automatic variables.

base class A class from which other classes derive characteristics. The derived class inherits all the characteristics of the base. Also called *superclass*.

binary operator An operator, such as +, that has two operands.

Boolean logic The system of logic that applies the AND, OR, and XOR operators to two bitwise operands.

breakpoint A debugging procedure in which the program's execution is stopped at a specified statement in the source code so that the programmer can examine the program's state.

byte An 8-bit quantity used to store a character value or an integer in the signed range (-128 to 127) or unsigned range (0 to 255).

cast A parenthesized expression with only a type. It tells the compiler to convert the expression that follows to the type in the parentheses. Also called a *typecast*.

character An 8-bit value that represents one of the units in the computer's character set.

class A user-defined data type that may consist of data members and member functions.

class hierarchy A system of base and derived classes.

code Computer instructions encoded in machine, assembly, or a high-level language.

comment An informational statement in a program. The comment provides program documentation for the reader of the code. It reserves no memory and has no effect on the program's execution. C language comments begin with /* characters and end with */ characters. They may span several lines, and they do not nest. C++ language comments begin with // and continue to the end of the line.

compiler A program that reads high-level language source code and generates object code.

concrete data type A user-defined or library data type, complete with interface and implementation. The CDT is meant to be instantiated as an object and is not intended for use solely as a base class.

condition An expression that returns a true or false value.

console The computer's keyboard and screen.

constant A memory object with a defined value that cannot be changed while the program is running.

constructor The function executed by the compiler when the program declares an instance of a class. See also *destructor*.

control structures The building blocks of structured programming: sequence, selection, and iteration. The sequence control structure is the sequential expression of imperative statements. The selection control structure is the if-then-else decision process. The iteration control structure is the while-until loop mechanism. Others are the for iteration and the switch-case selection control structures.

cursor A screen pointer that tells the user where the next keystroke will be echoed. When the system uses a mouse, an additional cursor points to the current mouse position.

data abstraction See *abstraction*.

data member A data component of a class. It may be any valid data type, including intrinsic data types, class objects, pointers, and references.

data type The definition of a datum; its implementation and behavior. See also *intrinsic data type* and *user-defined data type*.

database A collection of data files loosely integrated to support a common application.

debugger A systems program that helps a programmer debug an applications program. The debugger traces the program's source code and supports breakpoints, watchpoints, and the examination and modification of memory variables.

decision The process whereby a program alters the statement execution sequence by testing a condition.

declaration The program statement that associates an identifier with what it identifies. A declaration can declare a variable, specify the format of a structure, declare an external variable, or declare a function or subroutine's return value and parameter list. A declaration may or may not reserve memory.

definition The program statement that defines the existence of a variable or function. A definition reserves memory for the item. The definition sometimes doubles as the item's declaration.

derived class A class that inherits some of its characteristics from a base class. Also called a *subclass*.

destructor The function executed by the compiler when a declared instance of a class goes out of scope. See also *constructor*.

dimension The number of elements in an array. When the array is multidimensional, as in an array of arrays, the secondary dimension is the number of array elements in the array.

DOS The dominant disk operating system for older PCs. Also called PC-DOS and MS-DOS.

editor A utility program that a programmer uses to create and modify source code and other text files.

element One entry in an array of variables.

encapsulation The activity of defining a class with its data members and member functions encapsulated into the definition. Encapsulation implies an implementation that is hidden from the class user, as well as an interface that is visible to the class user.

error message A message that the program displays to tell the user that an error has occurred in the processing.

escape sequence Two-character combinations coded into string and character constants that begin with a backslash character and compile to a one-character value, which usually cannot be represented by a single character code in the context of the constant.

exception The signal that a program raises (throws) when it senses a condition that must interrupt the current procedure. Another part of the program, one that has run already and is higher in the call stack, can intercept (catch) and process the exception.

executable code The assembled (or compiled) and linked code that is loaded into the computer and executed. In a source program, executable code is distinguished from code that declares objects and function prototypes and defines object formats.

expression A grouping of one or more constant and variable references; function calls; and relational, logical, and arithmetic operators that return a numerical or pointer value.

external data Data objects that are declared external to any procedure. They are accessible to all procedures within their scope. See also *global data*.

extraction operator The overloaded >> operator that reads (extracts) values from an input stream. See also *insertion operator*.

field A single entity of data, usually one item of a data type. Collections of fields form files in a database. A field is also called a data element.

file A collection of records of a common format in a database.

file scope The scope of variables and functions that you may access only from within the translation unit. Macros, static functions, and static external variables have file scope.

firmware Software encoded into a read-only memory (ROM) integrated circuit.

floating-point number A number used to represent very large and very small numbers and nonintegral values.

free store The C++ heap. A dynamic memory pool that programs use to allocate and release temporary memory buffers.

friend A function that has access to the private members of a class but that is not a member function of that class. The class definition declares the function to be a friend.

function A program procedure that may return a value and may accept one or more arguments. A function consists of a function header and a function body.

function body The program statements that constitute the local declarations and executable code of a function definition.

function header The first statement in a function definition. It specifies the function's return type, identifier, and parameter list.

global data External data objects declared to be within the scope of the entire program.

global scope The scope of variables and functions that are accessible to all translation units in the program.

goto A statement that abruptly and unconditionally modifies the execution flow to proceed from a remote labeled statement. The goto statement specifies a source-code label that matches one attached to an executable source-code statement elsewhere in the function.

graphical user interface (GUI) A common user interface model that uses the graphics capabilities of the screen to support the "desktop" metaphor. A GUI provides generic menu and dialog box functions. Programs written to run under a GUI tend to have the same visual appearance to the user. Windows is the most popular GUI.

header source files Other source files that a program source file includes when it compiles. Header files typically contain things, such as global declarations, that independently compiled translation units need to see.

heap A large, system-controlled buffer of memory from which the program can allocate and deallocate smaller memory buffers dynamically. See also *free store*.

hexadecimal Base-16 numerical notation. The digits are 0-9, A-F.

hierarchy See *class hierarchy*.

identifier The name of a variable, macro, structure, or function.

implementation The private members of a class. The implementation defines the details of how the class implements the behavior of the abstract base type. See also *interface*.

information hiding An object-oriented and structured programming technique in which data representations and algorithms are not within the scope of those parts of the program that do not need to access them.

inheritance The ability of one class to inherit the characteristics of another class. The inherited class is derived from the base class. Also called *subclassing*.

initializer An expression specified as a variable's first assigned value when the variable comes into scope.

inline function A function that the compiler compiles as inline code every time the function is called.

input/output redirection A command-line option, when you run a program, which redirects standard input and output to disk files.

insertion operator The overloaded << operator that writes (inserts) values to an output stream. See also *extraction operator*.

instance A declared object.

instantiate To declare an object of a data type.

integer A whole number; a positive or negative value without decimal places.

Integrated Development Environment (IDE) A programming system that integrates a source-code editor, language translator (compiler or interpreter), linker, and debugger into one package.

interactive An operating mode in which the user communicates with the program using the keyboard and mouse during the program's execution.

interface The public members of a class that define the class user's interface to the class's data and its behavior. Usually implemented as member functions. See also *implementation*.

interpreter A programming language processor that executes the program by interpreting the source-code statements one statement at a time. Interpreters are contrasted with compilers, which compile the source code into linkable object code.

intrinsic data type A data type known to the compiler, as compared to a *user-defined data type*. Intrinsic data types in C++ are `bool`, `char`, `wchar_t`, `int`, `float`, and `double`. The integer types may be qualified further as `long`, `short`, `signed`, and `unsigned`. The `double` type may be qualified further as `long`. There are also pointer and reference variables, which refer to objects of specific types. Data aggregates may be organized as arrays of like types and as classes, structures, and unions of varying types. Also called *primitive data type*.

intrinsic operator An operator known to the compiler. That is, an operator that's an integral part of the programming language. For example, C++ includes intrinsic arithmetic operators such as +, -, *, and /.

iteration One of the three control structures of structured programming. (The other two are *sequence* and *selection*.) Iteration is the control structure wherein the program repeats a sequence zero or more times using some tested condition within the sequence or within a statement that controls the loop. This causes the program to cease repeating the sequence and, consequently, to exit from the loop. The `while`, `do...while`, and `for` statements support iteration in C++.

keyword A word that is reserved by the C++ programming language. Typical keywords are `if`, `else`, and `while`.

label An identifier followed by a colon that names a program statement. The `goto` statement specifies the label associated with the next statement that executes.

library A file of relocatable object programs. Applications reference external identifiers in the library and link their object code files with the library. The linker pulls the object files from the library that contains the referenced external identifiers.

linkage specification Notation that tells the C++ compiler that a function was or is to be compiled with the linkage conventions of another language.

linker A systems program that builds an executable program file from a specified group of relocatable object code files. The relocatable object code files can stand alone, or they can be selected from a library.

local scope The scope of automatic and static variables that are declared within a function body or as parameters in the function header.

local variable A variable that is defined in a statement block and is not in the scope of outer statement blocks or other functions.

loop A sequence of one or more program statements that iterates — executes repetitively — while, or until, a specified condition is `true`. See also *iteration*.

lvalue An expression that can be dereferenced to modify memory. It can exist on the left side of an assignment. See also *rvalue*.

macro A statement that assigns source-code meaning to an identifier. A macro may have arguments.

manipulator A value that a program sends to a stream to tell the stream to modify one of its modes.

member A component of a class — either a data member or a member function. Also a variable within a structure or union.

member function A function component of a class, also called a *method*. A member function may be virtual.

memory The internal storage medium of the computer. In a PC, semiconductor memory is divided into read-only memory (ROM) and random-access memory (RAM).

menu An interactive program's screen display of selections from which the user may choose. Each selection corresponds to an action that the program can take.

message A message is the invocation of a class's member function in the name of a declared object of the class. The message is sent to the object to tell it to perform its function. The message includes the function call and the arguments that accompany it.

method A method in C++ is a member function of a class. Programs send messages to objects by invoking methods.

multiple inheritance The ability of a derived class to inherit the characteristics of more than one base class.

multitasking An operating system model in which multiple programs run concurrently.

multiuser An operating system model in which multiple users share the processor. Each user runs independently of the other users. Users can run the same or different programs concurrently.

namespace The logical scope in which names are declared and are unique. Names in an inner namespace can override names in an outer namespace. Code in an inner namespace can reference overridden names by using the scope resolution operator. Two objects in the same namespace cannot have the same name.

object A declared instance of a data type, including standard C++ data types as well as objects of classes.

object code The machine language code that an assembler or compiler generates from source code. To produce executable code, the linker program must link object code with other object code files and with library object code files.

object database A collection of persistent objects. See *persistence*.

octal Base-8 number system. The digits are 0-7.

operand The variables and function calls that an expression uses with operators to produce its value.

operating system The master control program that operates the computer. It maintains the file system and provides a command interface for the user to execute utility and application programs. See also *DOS*.

operator The code token that represents how an expression uses its operands to produce a value.

overloaded function A function that has the same name as one or more other functions, but that has a different parameter list. The compiler selects the function to call based on the types and number of arguments in the call.

overloaded operator A function that executes when a C++ operator is seen in a defined context with respect to a class object.

overriding function A function in a derived class that has the same name, return type, and parameter list as a function in the base class. The compiler calls the overriding function when the program calls that function in the name of an object of the derived class. If the function in the base class is virtual, the compiler calls the derived class's function—even when the call is through a pointer or reference to the base class. See also *pure virtual function*.

parameter The declaration of a data item that a function uses to receive arguments passed to the function. This declaration includes the item's type and name and appears in the function's declaration block at the beginning of the function. When the parameter appears in the function's prototype, the parameter's name may be omitted. See *argument* and *prototype*.

parameter list The comma-separated, parenthetical list of parameter variable declarations in a function header or prototype. It specifies the types and identifiers of the function's parameters.

persistence The ability of an object to succeed its creator and subsequently to exist in space other than the space in which it is created.

persistent object An object that exhibits persistence.

platform A loosely applied term to mean the operating system or the programming environment. The computer itself, such as the "PC platform" or the "Macintosh platform." The operating environment, such as the "DOS platform" or the "Windows platform." The software development environment of a programming language, such as the "Visual C++ platform" or the "SmallTalk platform."

pointer A variable that can contain the address of functions or other variables. The item pointed to can be referenced through the pointer.

polymorphism The ability of methods in a class hierarchy to exhibit different behavior for the same message depending on the type of the object for which the method is invoked and without regard to the class type of the reference to the object.

precedence The property that determines the order in which different operators in an expression are evaluated.

preemptive multitasking A multitasking operating system model that does not require handshakes from the running programs. The operating system preempts the running program to enable others to run. Programs are given time slices within which they can run before they are preempted. Programs of higher priority can preempt programs of lower priority at any time.

preprocessor A program that reads source code and translates it into source code suitable for the compiler. The preprocessor defines and resolves macros, includes other source-code files, and causes specified lines of code to be included or deleted based on conditional expressions.

primitive data type See *intrinsic data type*.

private class members Members of a class to which access is granted only to the class's member functions and to friend functions of the class.

program A collection of computer instructions that executes in a logical sequence to perform a defined task. To write a program.

program flow control statement A statement that controls the flow of execution. The `if`, `do`, `while`, `for`, `else`, `break`, `continue`, and `goto` statements are program flow control statements.

proper programming A programming model in which procedures have one entry point at the top, one exit point at the bottom, and no endless loops.

protected class members Members of a class that are private, except to member functions of publicly derived classes.

prototype The definition of a function's name, return type, and parameter list.

public class members Members of a class to which access is granted to all functions within the scope of an object of the class.

pulldown menu A menu that drops down, usually from a menu bar, on top of the screen display. After the user makes a menu selection, the menu pops up out of sight to uncover the displays that it obscured.

pure virtual function A virtual function in a base class that must have a matching function in a derived class. A program may not declare an instance of a class that has a pure virtual function. A program may not declare an instance of a derived class if that derived class does not provide an overriding function for each pure virtual function in the base.

RAM Random-access memory. Volatile semiconductor memory. Most of the PC's internal memory is RAM.

random file A file with fixed-length records that you can access in random sequence by addressing the record number.

real number A number represented in a program with digits and a decimal point. See also *floating-point number.*

real-time A program's ability to respond to external events when they happen. The program's execution may not delay its reaction to those events. A spacecraft's guidance system uses real-time processing. Also refers to a program's ability to emulate events within time constraints that match the user's perception of the passage of time. A flight simulator is an example of such a real-time program.

recursion A function's ability to call itself directly or indirectly from functions that it calls.

reference A variable name that is an alias for another variable.

reference, pass by Pass a pointer to the actual argument. The called function acts upon the caller's copy of the argument. See also *value, pass by.*

relocatable object code Compiled or assembled object code with relative, unresolved memory address references. The linker program resolves the references when it builds an executable program from one or more relocatable object files.

reusable code Functions that perform utility and general-purpose operations that many unrelated programs use.

ROM Read-only memory. Nonvolatile semiconductor memory. The PC's BIOS is stored in ROM. A program may not change the values written in ROM, and the values persist when power is turned off.

rvalue An expression that cannot be on the left side of an assignment because it represents a value that may not be taken from a memory location. See also *lvalue.*

scope The range of source code that can access an identifier. An external identifier typically is in scope within the source-code file in which the object is declared. In C++, the scope extends from the position of the declaration to the end of the file. A global identifier's scope extends to all of the program's source-code files. A local identifier is in scope only within the statement block in which it is declared.

selection One of the three control structures of structured programming. (The other two are *sequence* and *iteration.*) Selection is the control structure wherein the program changes the sequential program flow based on the `true` or `false` value of a tested condition. The `if...else` and `else if` statements support selection in C++.

sequence One of the three control structures of structured programming. (The other two are *selection* and *iteration.*) Sequence is the control structure wherein program statements follow one another in top-down sequence.

sequential file A file of fixed- or variable-length records that are accessed in the sequence in which the records occur in the file.

shareware A technique for marketing software in which users try the programs first and pay for them only if they want to continue using them.

side effects The behavior of a macro that references an argument more than once. If multiple evaluations of an expression can change its meaning or imply unnecessary overhead, the expression is said to have side effects when used as an argument to such a macro.

source code Assembly or high-level programming language code statements.

stack A memory buffer from which the system allocates space for function arguments and automatic variables.

Standard C The C language as defined by the ANSI X3J11 Committee.

Standard C++ The C++ language as defined by the ANSI X3J16 Committee.

standard input/output devices The device files usually assigned to the keyboard and screen but that may be redirected to disk files.

statement A C++ language body of code that you terminate with a semicolon.

statement block A group of statements that starts with a left brace ({) and ends with a right brace (}).

storage class The manner in which a variable is stored in memory—as `auto`, `extern`, `static`, or `register`.

stream A category of character-oriented data files or devices in which the data characters exist in an input or output stream.

string constant A null-terminated, variable-length array of characters coded within an expression and surrounded by double quotation marks.

structure A record format consisting of one or more objects of multiple data types.

structured programming A programming model that uses the three control structures: sequence, selection, and iteration. Structured programming was extended to include the principles of modular programming.

subclass See *derived class*.

subclassing See *inheritance*.

subscript An integer value used in an expression to reference an element of an array.

superclass See *base class*.

systems program As opposed to *applications program*. A program, such as an operating system, which supports the computer system rather than the functional application.

test The application of a condition to alter the sequence of instruction execution. The `if` and `while` control structures are tests.

this A pointer that exists in all nonstatic member functions. The `this` pointer is a pointer to an object of the class. It points to the object for which the function is executed.

top-down design Designing a program beginning at the highest level of execution and proceeding downward. The programmer designs the program's entry point and the calls to lower procedures. Each design of a lower procedure decomposes the design into lower and more detailed levels of abstraction until the final design at the lowest level is an expression of the program's algorithms.

translation unit One independently compiled source-code unit consisting of the C or C++ source file and all included headers.

type The type of a program constant or variable, which can be of a primitive or abstract data type.

type conversion The conversion of one type to another. The compiler has built-in type conversions; a class may define its own conversions for converting from an object of the class to another type and from another type to an object of the class.

type qualifier A qualifying keyword in a variable declaration that specifies whether the variable is const or volatile.

type-safe linkage A technique ensuring that functions and function calls in separately compiled program modules use consistent parameter lists.

typecast See *cast*.

unary operator An operator, such as sizeof, that has only one operand.

user interface The interactive dialog between the program and the user. In the early days of the PC, user interfaces were invented or contrived by the programmer for each new program. That is why each spreadsheet, word processor, and so on had its own unique command structure. Users had to learn a different procedure for each program. Contemporary programs are written to run within operating environments, such as Windows, which support a common user interface.

user-defined data type A data type that the programmer builds by using struct, union, or typedef. See also *intrinsic data type*.

utility program A program that performs a utility function in support of the operating environment or the file system. The Scandisk program is a utility program that tests the integrity of the file system.

value, pass by Pass the value of argument. The called function acts upon its own copy of the argument, leaving the caller's copy intact. See also *reference, pass by*.

variable An object in memory in which the program can modify the value at any time.

virtual function A member function in a class from which other classes may be derived. If the derived class has a function with the same name and parameter list, the derived class's function is executed for objects of the derived class. See also *pure virtual function* and *overriding function*.

watchpoint A debugging procedure in which the debugger watches a memory variable for a specified value, or a specified expression for a true condition. When the watchpoint condition is satisfied, the debugger stops the program's execution at the point where the condition became true.

white space Spaces, newlines, and tab characters in a source-code text file.

Index

Continued